Group Psychotherapy of the Psychoses

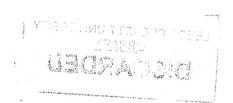

The International Library of Group Analysis
Edited by Malcolm Pines, Institute of Group Analysis, London

The aim of this series is to represent innovative work in group psychotherapy, particularly but not exclusively group analysis. Group analysis, taught and practised widely in Europe, has developed from the work of S.H. Foulkes.

Other titles in the series

Circular Reflections
Selected Papers on Group Analysis and Psychoanalysis
Malcolm Pines
International Library of Group Analysis 1
ISBN 1 85302 492 9 paperback
ISBN 1 85302 493 7 hardback

Attachment and Interaction
Mario Marrone with a contribution by Nicola Diamond
International Library of Group Analysis 3
ISBN 1 85302 586 0 paperback
ISBN 1 85302 587 9 hardback

Self Experiences in Group
Intersubjective and Self Psychological Pathways to Human Understanding
Edited by Irene Harwood and Malcolm Pines
International Library of Group Analysis 4
ISBN 1 85302 610 7 paperback
ISBN 1 85302 596 8 hardback

Taking the Group Seriously
Towards an Post-Foulkesian Group Analytic Theory
Farhad Dalal
International Library of Group Analysis 5
ISBN 1 85302 642 5 paperback

Active Analytic Group Therapy for Adolescents
John Evans
International Library of Group Analysis 6
ISBN 1 85302 616 6 paperback
ISBN 1 85302 617 4 hardback

The Group Context
Sheila Thompson
International Library of Group Analysis 7
ISBN 1 85302 657 3 paperback

Group
Claudio Neri
International Library of Group Analysis 8
ISBN 1 85302 418 X paperback

INTERNATIONAL LIBRARY GROUP ANALYSIS 2

Group Psychotherapy of the Psychoses

Concepts, Interventions and Contexts

Edited by Victor L. Schermer and Malcolm Pines

Foreword by Howard Kibel

Jessica Kingsley Publishers
London and Philadelphia

First published in the United Kingdom in 1999 by
Jessica Kingsley Publishers Ltd
116 Pentonville Road
London N1 9JB, England
and
325 Chestnut Street
Philadelphia, PA 19106, USA

www.jkp.com

Copyright © 1999 Jessica Kingsley Publishers

Library of Congress Cataloging in Publication Data
A CIP catalogue record for this book is available from the Library of Congress

British Library Cataloguing in Publication Data
Group psychotherapy of the psychoses : concepts, interventions and contexts. – International library of group analysis ; 2)
1. Psychosis – Treatment 2. Group psychotherapy
I. Schermer, Victor L. II. Pines, Malcolm
616.8'9152

ISBN 1 85302 584 4 paperback
ISBN 1 85302 583 6 hardback

Printed and Bound in Great Britain by
Athenaeum Press, Gateshead, Tyne and Wear

Contents

ACKNOWLEDGEMENTS   7

Foreword   9
Howard D. Kibel

PART 1: BACKGROUND AND THEORY

1   Introduction: Reality and Relationship in 'Psyche's Web'   13
Victor L. Schermer, psychologist
and Malcolm Pines, Group Analytic Practice

2   Psychosis from a Group Perspective   43
Marvin R. Skolnick, George Washington University Medical School

3   Splitting and Disavowal in Group Psychotherapy of Psychosis   83
Nicolas Caparrós, psychoanalyst and group analyst
(Translated by María Cañete and Arturo Ezquerro)

4   A Biography of Psychosis: Individuals, Groups, and Institutions   97
Salomon Resnik, psychoanalyst and consultant psychiatrist

PART 2: TECHNICAL ASPECTS OF GROUP PSYCHOTHERAPY

5   Group Therapy with Schizophrenic and Bipolar Patients:
Integrative Approaches   129
Nick Kanas, Department of Psychiatry, University of California

6   The Therapist's Role in the Group Treatment of Psychotic
Patients and Outpatients: A Foulkesian Perspective   148
Ivan Urlic, Psychiatric Clinic, University of Split Medical School

7   Resistance, Empathy, and Interpretation with Psychotic Patients   181
Stanley Schneider, Psychotherapy Program, Hebrew University, Jerusalem

8   The Group as Therapist for Psychotic
and Borderline Personalities   200
Rachael Chazan, Faculty of Psychotherapy, Tel Aviv Medical School

9 Supportive-Expressive Group Psychotherapy with Chronic
Mental Illness, including Psychosis   221

*Tetsuro Takahashi, psychoanalyst, Glenn Lipson, clinical and forensic
psychologist, and Lane Chazdon, Menninger Clinic, Topeka, Kansas*

10 Psychodynamic Group Psychotherapy with Chronically
Mentally Ill Women   251

*Lawrence L. Kennedy, Menninger Clinic, Topeka, Kansas,
Susan Bach, Community Psychiatric Clinic, Seattle, Shauna Corbin,
Southdown Institute, Ontario, Mary Ann Abbott, clinical psychologist,
and Bette Ferbrache, Menninger Clinic, Topeka, Kansas*

11 Clinical Interventions in Group Psychotherapy   280

*Raman Kapur, Threshold, Richmond Fellowship (NI),
and Queen's University, Belfast*

PART 3: TRAINING, SUPERVISION AND COUNTERTRANSFERENCE

12 Supervision of Group Psychotherapy with Chronic
Psychotic Patients   301

Eugene Della Badia, Horsham Clinic and Pennsylvania Hospital

13 Psychotherapy Training for Nurses as Part of a Group
Psychotherapy Project: The Pivotal Role of Countertransference   324

Dianne Campbell Lefevre, Basildon Hospital, Essex

PART 4: ADJUNCTIVE TREATMENT, SETTING AND CONTEXT

14 The Role of Assessment and Pharmacotherapy in
Group Psychotherapy for Psychosis   347

*Alan M. Gruenberg, Jefferson Medical College and Pennsylvania Hospital,
and Reed D. Goldstein, Pennsylvania Hospital, Philadelphia*

15 The Therapeutic Community and Schizophrenia   359

Geoffrey Pullen, Littlemore Hospital, Oxford

16 Confusions in a Therapeutic Milieu   388

Joseph H. Berke, Arbours Crisis Centre, London

17 Voluntary Work in the Area of Mental Health: The Voluntary
Worker's Role in a Therapeutic Centre in Florence   404

Gianni DiNorscia and Walter Romeo, Il Villino, Florence

THE CONTRIBUTORS   412
SUBJECT INDEX   417
AUTHOR INDEX   426

Acknowledgements

The network of those who contributed to this endeavor extends well beyond the editors and authors to the many who have variously inspired and assisted in the work, those who contributed to this volume as well as those who have made their mark in one way or another on the complex field of psychosis and groups. Thus, the editors will never be able to thank all who had an impact, but we sensed their influence in many ways and are ever grateful for it.

However, we would like, first and foremost, to thank specifically the chapter authors who contributed their precious time and effort to sharing their ideas and clinical knowledge for this work. At a time when professionalism and in-depth treatment are being challenged on many fronts, their dedication to the field, compassion for patients, erudition, and insight greatly inspired and heartened the editors as we hope they will the readers.

Gratitude is also to be expressed to those who have encouraged and educated the editors over the years and in the creation of this book. Encouragement from and conversations with such outstanding clinicians as Yvonne Agazarian, Christopher Bollas, Bert Cohen, Patrick DeMare, Ramon Ganzarain, James S. Grotstein, Sigmund Karterud, and others, supported us and at times challenged us to think through the concepts and goals of the work.

A special acknowledgement is due to Jay Fidler, who, for over twenty years, has been at the forefront of providing group psychotherapy for the most difficult-to-treat patients and has pioneered in advancing the cause of treatment of the psychoses in the International Association of Group Psychotherapy.

Thanks are due to Jessica Kingsley and Charles Catton of Jessica Kingsley Publishers and also to Barbara Phillips, secretary at the Group Analytic Practice, for their ongoing support, encouragement, and angelic patience as we coordinated material from around the globe in an age of computers, email, and other befuddling technology! We also are grateful to Mary Anne Clifft, of the *Menninger Bulletin*, for editing the chapter by Takahashi *et al.*, to Maria Canete and Arturo Ezquerro for translating Caparros' chapter and to Marisa Dillon-Weston for translating the chapter by diNorscia and Romeo. Sharing subtle ideas and expressions across diverse languages is a task fraught with difficulties, and we thank these editors and translators for doing such a fine job.

Above all, we know the chapter authors will concur with us that the greatest thanks of all are due to our patients, who enrich us and stimulate our thinking with their struggles and with their willingness to engage with us in the work of psychotherapy.

Foreword

The treatment of psychotic patients challenges every clinician. Psychosis has never been thoroughly understood and, therefore, has been the subject of much speculation. Over the years, the expectations of treatment have vacillated from hopeful to pessimistic. In the early nineteenth century, the age of moral treatment (in the United States and Great Britain) was one in which the treatment of hospital patients was infused with optimism. Discharge and even alleged cure rates were reported to be between 60 and 90 per cent. Subsequently, with the geographic upheavals during the industrial revolution and with massive immigration to the United States, hospitals were deluged with huge numbers of patients. Psychiatrists could not cope with the volume. Some have speculated that these sociological changes accounted for the decline of moral treatment. Rather than view patients in a humanistic way, clinicians began to think of psychotic illness in mechanistic terms. That was simpler, given the tasks faced by those who worked in the newly evolved, large hospitals of the late eighteen hundreds.

For more than a century, pessimism reigned. The burgeoning of psychoanalysis after World War II reactivated an attitude of hope. Shortly thereafter, the invention of the electron microscope created a new science of microbiology. Discovery of the effects of neuroleptics on synaptic transmission had minimal effect on practice until the mid 1980s. Since then, we have seen a converse effect on practice as occurred in the second half of the nineteenth century. Instead of patients flooding the system, now economic resources have dwindled. Once again, psychiatry has looked for a simpler explanation for the psychopathology of psychosis. Currently, the interest is in the synapses of the brain. Linear reasoning is fast replacing the richness of psychological understanding. However, a mechanistic view of the brain ignores how experience affects its patterns of functioning, that is, how psychic life shapes the form of thought and, thereby, the psychopathology of psychosis. Descartes' dualism of mind and body as separate, complex mechanisms is unwittingly being activated.

It is vital, for effective treatment to occur, that the clinician view the psychotic mind as a complex manifestation of yet unknown brain processes. The mind evolves in a social context, namely, the family. Treating psychosis with a social-like modality makes eminent clinical sense. That is the value of the treatment espoused in this book. Effective treatment allows for an appreciation of the complexities of the mind, particularly the psychotic mind, but in the only way we can study it, that is, inter-subjectively. This volume, a collection of diverse methods of group psychotherapy, sends a hopeful message to clinicians in a troubled time: these patients, although difficult to treat, can be helped.

Ultimately, Cartesian dualism will be replaced by a synthesized view of the mind-in-the-brain. For now, psychological understanding still has enormous explanatory power. Biology, while intriguing, should be appreciated as only one cornerstone of future theory. From a contemporary perspective, it is better to view psychology and biology as part of a 'bipolar' view of the mind/brain continuum. This viewpoint will allow hope to infuse treatment until more sophisticated, functional organic models of thinking are developed.

This book appropriately spans the breadth of the art and science of treatment, of clinical intuition and biology. The editors and chapter authors avoid the pitfall of over-simplification. As a whole, this book does an excellent job of presenting the reader with a plethora of psychological and descriptive methodologies. Thereby, one has the opportunity to take something from each to enrich one's work with these complex patients.

Once again, the editors, as in a previous volume, *Ring of Fire*, have brought together leading clinicians in the field who work with groups in diverse ways and in a variety of settings. This array of approaches gives the reader a wealth of opportunity to learn how others practise and think about this work. The reader should not attempt to synthesize these chapters nor to see which one is closer to his or her way of thinking. Rather, it is best to absorb the material of each and then, after finishing the book, to consider how the book as a whole informs the field.

Howard D. Kibel,
Valhalla, New York, 1998

PART 1

Background and Theory

Introduction

Reality and Relationship in 'Psyche's Web'

Victor L. Schermer and Malcolm Pines

> Much Madness is divinest Sense –
> To a discerning Eye –
> Much Sense – the starkest Madness –
> 'Tis the Majority
> In this, as All, prevail –
> Assent – and you are sane –
> Demur – you're straightway dangerous –
> And handled with a Chain –
>
> *(Emily Dickinson, #435)*

Psyche: n 1: that which is responsible for one's thoughts and feelings; the seat of the faculty of reason; "his mind wandered"; "I couldn't get his words out of my head" [syn: mind, head, brain, nous] 2: the immaterial part of a person; the actuating cause of an individual life [syn: soul] 3: a beautiful princess loved by Cupid in ancient mythology; became the personification of the soul.

Wordnet (R) 1.5 Database (Wn)

The dynamic of such a group [of psychotic patients] is full of pathological projections, projective identifications, splittings, disavowals, idealisations and other defences. The resulting group atmosphere is very fragmented, into multiple 'part-objects' and disparate particles of selves. Psychotic patients often see themselves as a 'self-sufficient group'. This can lead to the distortion of being a 'big group', made out of countless little fragments and part-object representations that are disconnected from exchangeable meaning – 'a huge, shattered and isolated self'.

Nicolas Caparros

hoses occupies a special place within the evolution of
therapy. Psychosis, by definition, connotes a profound
about and judging 'reality.' So the treatment of these
therapist knows what constitutes the real world (internal
thinking, in other words, that he is an oracular arbiter of
one, Lacan's *sujet suppose savoir* (Etchegoyan 1991,
rr.-..-/−140). Thus, as Emily Dickinson's poem suggests, the contact between
therapist and patient presages a clash of beliefs, of colliding worlds, especially
within the context of the group and society, and the task of the therapist then
becomes to establish rapport and a working alliance under this trying
circumstance. (See Berke, Chapter 16 , for cogent examples of this clash, leading
to states of confusion in patients and staff.) Furthermore, if the therapist, in the
process of examining his own assumptions, comes to the conclusion that he and
his colleagues are wrong and the patient right,[1] then he is faced with a difficult
dilemma: if he acknowledges the error, he runs the risk of joining the subgroup of
'insane patients' and if he conceals the new 'truth', he is forced to conduct his
work under false pretenses and to align himself with a specious 'socially
acceptable' or 'false self' reality.[2] Both extremes, the Scylla of overidentifying
with the patients' phantasies and the Charybdis of conformity to the
'establishment' mind set at the expense of authenticity, are genuine vulnerabilities
in this endeavor.[3] Thus, conducting group psychotherapy with psychotic patients
is a challenge not only to therapeutic technique, but to the 'reflective space'
(Hinshelwood 1994), the countertransference, and the very core of the therapist's
self. The chapters of this book take up these complex challenges, without which
this difficult work cannot go forward.

Another pervasive difficulty in conducting groups for psychotic patients is the
relational disturbance which results from the intense dispersal of projective
identifications in the group, such that the selves of the members, leaders, and
institution become refracted in a 'rainbow' effect like the breaking up of white

---

1   Such an experience of the therapist affirming the validity of apparent 'madness' occurs often, if not in
    terms of the patients' atavistic 'paleologic', then with respect to the patient's metaphorical expressions
    of what may be the core human condition. For, after all, we are all in some ways 'mad:' as S.R. Slavson
    once said, we all have our 'essential psychosis,' and madness, if not always 'divinest sense', often has
    creative potential.

2   The film, *Fanny*, about the ill-fated actress Fanny Farmer, who became the 'identified patient' in her
    family, was hospitalized, declared insane, and tragically lobotomized, epitomizes the extreme negative
    consequences of this 'countertransference' problem of the therapist (or the community of therapists)
    acting out a false self against the patient.

3   The popular book by Robert Lindner, *The Fifty Minute Hour* (1955), documents a case entitled 'The Jet
    Propelled Couch' in which the patient discloses delusions of traveling to other planets, and the
    therapist, in his effort to identify with the patient's dilemma, begins to believe the patient! The motion
    pictures *The Ruling Class* and *King of Hearts* and the play *Marat/Sade* all dramatize the fine line that can
    exist between reality and fantasy, between insight and folly.

light into component colors (Haugsgjerd 1983). This process, which occurs to some extent in groups of 'normals' as a result of the group regression, is quickened and heightened by psychotic level defenses and fragmentation processes, so that there is a sense of massive fusion of selves and confusion about which fragment or experience belongs to whom! The effect is like that of a huge spider web of dispersed mental content (hence the metaphor 'Psyche's Web,') described by Caparros (Chapter 3) in the above quotation.

In order to enter into the task of conducting group psychotherapy of the psychoses, it is necessary to consider the broad evolution of this field as well as the more recent rapid and massive changes in the understanding, diagnosis, and treatment of mental illness (changes fueled by cultural changes, shifts in the social and scientific *zeitgeist*, healthcare funding, and medico-biological science) which are taking place on a global scale at the very moment this book goes to press.

Changes in the understanding of psychotic disorders

Due to two major developments within the mental health field – increasing rights given to mental patients to choose their own life style, and the development of neuroleptic medications (which alleviate the so-called 'positive' symptoms such as hallucinations, delusions, affect dysregulation, agitation, and in some cases may reduce the 'negative symptoms,' such as apathy, blunted affect, and alogia), the scene, common even some thirty years ago, of large wards (immortalized in the novel and film *One Flew Over the Cuckoo's Nest*) of patients languishing for long periods of time in misery and episodically erupting in violence, is, if not yet a thing of the past, rapidly diminishing. The resultant changes have led to a spectrum of outcomes for psychotic patients, ranging from deterioration on the streets and in improperly managed boarding homes, to ameliorative therapy while living at home with a supportive family and the use of medication, to striking remissions, particularly with respect to bipolar disorder and psychotic depression but also, very recently, with some of the schizophrenias. This is a time of challenge and of opportunity for the treatment of psychoses.

Group therapy has come to play an important role in the treatment of psychotic disorders. Both psychoanalysis and intensive group therapy were initially used – in contrast to ameliorative measures – for 'higher level' disorders such as the neuroses, personality disorders, and traumatic stress. (As we know, group therapy received a strong impetus in both the USA and England via the treatment of traumatized soldiers at 'Veteran's Administration' and military hospitals during and after World War II.) As Frieda Fromm-Reichmann (1953) (cited by Urlic, Chapter 6, p.150) once observed, 'it took a decade to understand the patient, another decade to learn how to establish the contact with the patient, and a third decade to learn how to apply all this knowledge and experience.' And, we might add, another three to five decades to incorporate group therapy and therapeutic community into the armamentarium. Today, however, as Kanas (this volume, Chapter 5, p.145) concludes, there is much empirical data and clinical experience to 'support the value of these groups as being safe, useful, and relevant to the needs of psychotic patients.' The tested value of group psychotherapy for the psychoses is the 'selected fact' which inspired the present collection of new papers by highly qualified group therapists throughout the world.

Although each chapter takes up in detail a variety of issues regarding group therapy of the psychoses, it may be helpful to create here a view of the whole, in order to provide a framework for the reader to approach the specifics. The authors take up issues which fall primarily within the following areas: assessment and diagnosis; conceptual schema and models of the psychoses; variations of group therapy approaches and their effectiveness; interpretations and interventions; multimodal treatment; the importance of context; and training and supervision. We now take up each of these areas in turn, in order to provide a guide to orient the reader to the book as a whole.

Diagnostic schema and conceptualizations of the psychoses

As Urlic (Chapter 6) says, 'The psychotherapist who uses the group in his armamentarium for the treatment of psychotic patients, should ... first carefully define the concept of psychosis ... His attitude toward the application of the group medium will derive from this foundation.' Although the definition of psychosis as 'thought disorder' is generic, the particulars of which symptoms and personality trends belong to which category of psychosis, not to mention the problem of the etiology or causation of the disorders, has created controversy since the inception of psychiatry in the nineteenth century and up to the present day.

Diagnosis and assessment of the psychoses

Ever since the pioneering work of Kraepelin, Bleuler, and others, diagnostic schema for schizophrenia and other psychoses have been problematic and subject to periodic revisions as well as the influence of diverse schools of thought regarding the underlying nature of these diagnostic entities. Schizophrenia has been regarded as everything from a 'wastebasket category' and a way of mislabeling individuals for purposes of social control (Szasz 1984) to a biologically based disease with correlates in blood serum alterations and in brain activity distribution measured via PET-scans and other sophisticated brain-monitoring devices (cf. Kaplan and Sadock 1995). The co-editors, and we think, most of the chapter authors, take a moderate and synthesizing position, appropriate to the conduct of group therapy, that: (1) in accordance with the 'medical model,' the psychoses are major disorders, such that with careful clinical acumen, one can discern syndromes of ego regression and disturbance of mental functioning which constitute a 'disorder' or 'illness' *per se;* (importantly, these syndromes need to be distinguished from non-pathological eccentric personality traits, from personality disorders such as borderline, schizoid, and schizotypal, and from states of heightened creativity and awareness which may even be co-present in individuals who have a psychotic illness); (2) although we believe there is a significant biological component to psychotic conditions, the psychological, interpersonal, and social ramifications of the disorder make it necessary that the therapist consider a range of etiological factors and sequelae, not just the biochemical; and (3) group psychotherapy, as part of the broader treatment 'armamentarium,' can offer a significant opportunity to address any number of these complex and interweaving factors. Therapy groups deal with issues as relevant and diverse as medication, community resources, family dynamics, emotional support, interpersonal relations, defense mechanisms, and internalized object relations.

The DSM-IV (*Diagnostic and Statistical Manual of Mental Disorders,* fourth edition, Washington, DC: American Psychiatric Association, 1994), designed to be compatible with ICD-10 (the latest edition of the International Classification of Diseases), offers the following diagnostic schema for the psychoses (see Table 1.1).

As Skolnick (Chapter 2) states:

> In both DSM-IV (the American Psychiatric diagnostic manual) and the ICD (International Classification of Diseases), psychotic disorders are divided into those disorders which a) have a delineated pathophysiology that directly impair brain function such as drug and toxin ingestion, infectious, metabolic, endocrine, cardiovascular immune diseases and b) those 'functional' psychotic disorders such as schizophrenia, manic and depressive psychosis with organic etiology established but with the neuropathological yet to be fully delineated.

In the DSM-IV and ICD-10 the 'functional' psychoses have been further broken down into two broad categories: the schizophrenias, which essentially constitute disturbances in cognition and self-organization, and the affective psychoses, which are mood disturbances in which thought disorder nevertheless plays a significant role. Gruenberg and Goldstein (Chapter 14) emphasize further criteria for differential diagnosis of schizophrenia from the other psychotic states and disorders:

> Briefly, DSM-IV stipulates that for schizophrenia, at least two active symptoms (e.g., delusions, hallucinations, disorganized speech or behavior) must be present to a significant degree during a 1-month period, with ongoing signs of the disturbance present for at least 6 months. The presence of negative symptoms (e.g., flattening of affect; avolition; alogia), which is defined as a distinct criterion in DSM-IV, is now emphasized as well.

Table 1.1 DSM-IV diagnoses of psychotic disorders

Schizophrenia and Other Psychotic Disorders

295.xx	Schizophrenia
.30	Paranoid Type
.10	Disorganized Type
20	Catatonic Type
.90	Undifferentiated Type
.60	Residual Disorder
295.40	Schizophreniform Disorder
295.70	Schizoaffective Disorder
297.1	Delusional Disorder
298.8	Brief Psychotic Disorder
297.3	Shared Psychotic Disorder
293.xx	Psychotic Disorder Due to (General Medical Condition)
	.81 with Delusions
	.82 with Hallucinations

Substance-Induced Psychotic Disorder

298.9	Psychotic Disorder NOS

Mood Disorders [Selected here to include only psychoses]:

Depressive Disorders:

296.24	Major Depressive Disorder, Single Episode, Severe, with Psychotic Features
296.34	Major Depressive Disorder, Recurrent, Severe, with Psychotic Features

Bipolar Disorders:

296.xx	Bipolar I Disorder [manic and depressive phases]
296.89	Bipolar II Disorder [hypomanic and depressive phases, sometimes occurring together or in rapid alternation]

Source: Selected from pp.19–20 of the *DSM-IV Manual*

Interestingly, the 'schizo-affective disorder' forms a bridge between affective psychoses and schizophrenia, since it refers to a combination of schizophrenic symptoms and mood disturbances. It is also worth noting that the 'shared psychotic disorder' harks back to the so-called *'folie-à-deux'* (Laseque and Falret 1877/1964), which was the first psychiatric diagnosis of a 'group' or interpersonal nature.

The present work on group psychotherapy focuses on these disorders, which are by definition recurrent or chronic, with the exception of the single episode major depression with psychosis, and which, very importantly, are not attributable to substance abuse, dementia, or other extraneous physico-chemical changes as such, the treatment of which require special interventions and clinical experience of their own.

As Kanas emphasizes (Chapter 5), the particular distinction between schizophrenia and bipolar disorder is crucial in screening and selecting individuals for group. Patients with one of these two diagnostic entities require different types of group therapy structure, interventions, and levels of interpretations, and should ordinarily be in different groups, although there are some therapists (cf. chapters by Kapur, Chazan, Urlic) who are skilled at working with heterogeneous populations in groups and bridging the considerable gap between their differing needs and requirements.

A distinction also needs to be made between (1) the above diagnostic entities and (2) a more general and less rigorous term, 'chronically mentally ill,' which is a 'catch-all' phrase referring to patients with low level of functioning who are perennially recycled through the mental health system, with episodic hospitalizations and outpatient care. For practical purposes, as we will see from many of the actual groups described in this book, (see for example, Takahashi, *et al.*, Chapter 9 and Kennedy, *et al.*, Chapter 10) therapy groups are often convened for such patients without precise regard to more specific diagnoses. Included in such groups will be not only psychoses, but some borderline personality disorders, complex multiple diagnoses (e.g. post-traumatic stress disorder complicated by substance abuse history), and so on. (Such patients may have psychotic episodes but do not have the same fragility of ego structure or endogenous biochemical basis as the chronic or recurrent psychotic.) It is likely that the vast majority of groups which include psychotic patients are generic for the 'chronically mentally ill' and that only under specific circumstances are groups convened for a homogeneous diagnostic grouping. However, as diagnostic procedures and medications improve, we may see an increase in specialized diagnostic groups. One patient we know attends a self-help support group exclusively for bipolar disorder which keeps members updated on medications, political changes, and other developments which affect their treatment. We can expect an increasing consumer demand for homogeneous groups focused around a particular 'mental illness'.

The underlying nature of the psychoses

A most important controversy has persisted regarding the question: Do psychoses, 'borderline' conditions, and neuroses (the latter currently classified in the nomenclature of 'descriptive diagnoses' among anxiety disorders, dysthymia, some personality disorders, etc.) represent a continuum of disorders, with psychoses being the most severe? Or are they 'discontinuous,' i.e. sufficiently different in nature and causation to represent inherently different kinds of pathology? The prevailing 'psychodynamic' view, as well as within other theoretical formulations such as learning theory and family dynamics, has been to consider these variations in 'level of severity' as continuous, with psychosis being distinguished only by the degree to which reality perception and affect regulation is altered. Thus, for example, Karl Abraham (1927) regarded psychosis as psychogenic pathology having its origins in developmental disturbances of the oral and anal stages of development. Abraham, and later Melanie Klein (1977a, b), Bion (1959a, 1962, 1977), Rosenfeld (1965, 1987), Searles (1965), and others treated psychotic patients psychoanalytically, extending Abraham's viewpoint through contemporary object relations theory. Kohut's 'self-psychology' has also been extended for use with psychotic patients via the notion of the selfobject having 'self-soothing' affect-regulating functions (Druck, 1989 pp.13–29) which are notably lacking in psychotic patients. Modern ego psychology, deriving as it does from Hartmann's (1958) theory of adaptation, has provided a more complex picture, holding that psychoses imply an ego deficit (cf. Blanck and Blanck 1974, pp.72–73; Druck 1989, pp.29–39), but nevertheless expressing optimism about the potential for emotional growth.

On the other hand, it is felt by some, especially within the biological perspective, that psychosis is a distinctly different species of 'illness' from higher level disorders. In this view, psychosis is held to be the result of a brain disease and as such is not responsive to traditional 'talk' therapies. (The functions of group therapy, in this view, are to provide amelioration, support and education, not to facilitate internal changes.) From the 1970s a research base involving PET-scans, blood serum levels, hereditary concordance ratios, and so on has accumulated suggesting strong biological and hereditary components of mental illness, and particularly the chronic psychoses (cf. Kaplan and Sadock 1995). However, the enthusiasm in some circles for this point of view has all but ignored the fact that even in the most rigorous genetic studies, a considerable portion of the variance is attributable to environmental and psychological factors. Further, it has been shown (Skolnick, Chapter 2) that brain changes themselves can be induced by developmental and environmental factors, not to mention the pharmaceutical effects of prolonged use of medications.

In the present volume, the majority of the authors do not appear to take a strong stand on this biological versus psycho-social controversy, but they do appear to have varied implicit biases. Those who work intensively with the object relations and interpersonal relations of the patients in group, for example Della Badia in Chapter 12, Chazan, Chapter 8 or Schneider in Chapter 7, appear to go along with Harry Stack Sullivan's view that 'We are all more simply human than not,' that is, continuum theory. Resnik (Chapter 4) shows how Freud's and others' thinking about the psychoses evolved in tandem with the understanding of the neuroses and the mechanisms of defense. Freud did not draw a sharp distinction between neuroses and psychoses other than to cite the element of defective reality-testing in the latter.

Resnik, in keeping with the 'Back to Freud' movement fostered by Lacan and others, adopts a controversial position that psychotic mechanisms can be best understood in terms of Freud's early formulations of trauma and hysteria. Looking closely at the psychotic mechanisms present in Freud and Breuer's pioneer case of 'Anna O,' Resnik argues that the psychotic individual attempts to avoid psychic suffering through splitting and dissociative defenses which ultimately lead to fragmentation of the personality. This early view of Freud lost favor with the emergence of object relations theory, which suggested that psychotic functioning is established developmentally at a much earlier period than hysteria. However, as we understand the more primitive layers of hysteria and trauma, we are seeing a return to this viewpoint in which psychosis, hysteria, borderline personality, and post-traumatic disorders are interlinking affect/ defense patterns of coping with psychic pain.

By contrast, those, such as Kanas, Chapter 5, and Gruenberg and Goldstein, Chapter 14 who emphasize the importance of medication management along with structure, education, and modifications of treatment, seem to lean towards a 'discontinuity' theory which holds that these patients have special functional inadequacies which cannot be compared with the less severe pathologies of what one acerbic commentator termed 'the worried well.' However, most of our authors' views on this subject are complex and will not be easily 'pigeon-holed.' Unlike those who feel that psychoses are purely medical diseases which will eventually yield to biological research, our authors believe that psychoses are complex biological, psychological, interpersonal, and social/contextual syndromes which mirror multiple aspects of the human condition. This is not a popular view in an era of bio-genetic enthusiasm, but it seems to speak to a deeper truth and allows for a greater variety treatment options than a monistic, reductionistic model.

The deficit or dilemma in interpersonal relations (object relations)
of the psychotic patient

A universally agreed-upon notion, rare in this difficult and complex field, is that the psychotic suffers from a defect in interpersonal relations which limits his capacity for communication, intimacy, and participation in the social matrix. Among the psychoses, chronic schizophrenics are the most debilitated interpersonally: even in the premorbid personality, well before the disease process sets in, or during periods of remission, they have few if any relationships outside the family and tend to appear superficial, detached, and avoidant interpersonally. (Skolnick, Chapter 2, cites a poignant study in which such a deficiency can be observed in 'home movies' made by family members well before the onset of psychosis.) By contrast, bipolar patients, when not in a severe manic or depressive phase, may be capable of sustaining friendships, marriages, and a range of interpersonal emotions, but give an impression of superficiality and grandiosity. Group psychotherapy may provide an optimal opportunity to enhance the quality of interpersonal relatedness for psychotic patients, although the extent to which they are capable of improvement is subject to controversy.

A view of schizophrenic detachment which held sway in the past and is still maintained in some quarters is that it is due to a fundamental lack of 'libido', what we would now consider a biochemical brain deficiency which presages a lack of interest or ability to engage in relationships with others. Following that line of reasoning would suggest that group therapists provide considerable support, structure, and education for schizophrenics but minimize the relational aspect of group treatment, other than to facilitate a degree of compassion and companionship for the sick individual.

In recent decades, however, a view has emerged which says that the schizophrenic profoundly wants and needs to engage in relations with others, but that the process of engagement is ominously fraught with intense conflict and ambivalence. Fromm-Reichmann (1950, 1959), Rosenfeld, Searles, and others showed that schizophrenics do form intense transferences and in some cases may be capable of the rigors of psychoanalytic treatment. Interpersonal theorists point to what they call the 'need/fear dilemma' (Burnham, Gibson, and Gladstone 1969) in which the schizophrenic manifests intense dependency states fraught with fears of regression, self-annihilation, harm to others, loss of boundaries, mistrust, and abandonment, all of which can be understood in Kleinian terms as a fear of the resurfacing of a split-off and 'encapsulated' or externalized bad object.

Caparros (Chapter 3) insightfully states this dilemma in terms of the earliest psychic development:

> Psychotic patients are autoerotic, narcissistic and frightened of external reality; although they disavow the environment, they later may even idealise it! But, can they achieve inter-subjectivity proper? I do not think so, because they have

a marked tendency to avoid meaningful contact with others. It is possible to observe attempts at 'fusion', which are usually followed by 'confusion', or acute reactions of 'panic' and subsequent 'running away'.

The schizophrenic's inner world is narcissistically 'fused' with his interpersonal, group world. He has not achieved differentiated object relationships, a prospect which is fraught with annihilation anxiety, the fear of a psychic catastrophe, the loss of self.

Group therapists who believe that schizophrenics are capable of relationships but experience a catastrophic dilemma with regard to them are more optimistic about their ability to engage in interaction with other group members, and to achieve higher levels of object relations such as intersubjectivity and empathy. One way to help achieve these goals is to understand the cryptic or symbolic ('internal object') communications of the psychotic as allusions to real relationships in the past or the here-and-now. A Kleinian analyst, for example, once interpreted a schizophrenic's complaint that the left side of his body was warring against the right side as an encapsulated expression of his parents' intercourse. Herbert Rosenfeld, in a case seminar, emphasized how virtually all the tangential and obscure fantasy expressions of the patient were expressions to the therapist of what she wanted or needed from him and also about the therapist's countertransference. In the present volume, Schneider (Chapter 7), Chazan (Chapter 8), Urlic (Chapter 6), and Della Badia (Chapter 12) all give theoretical rationales for and clinical examples of relating empathically to such patients and encouraging group interactions. Resnik (Chapter 4) suggests how Freud's early understanding of psychoses presaged an affect/defense rather than a deficiency-based view of psychosis. Lefevre (Chapter 13) proposes that difficulties engaging with psychotic patients may be due more to institutional conflicts and problems, as well as therapist countertransference, mis-education, and lack of education, than to a deficiency in the patients themselves. Ample clinical evidence is provided in this volume to suggest that schizophrenics are capable of intersubjectivity, relatedness, and group interaction, although with great difficulties. Bipolar (manic-depressive) patients can engage rather readily, although their narcissistic interactive 'style' triggers countertransference problems in the therapist and threatens the stability and cohesion of the group.

The emergence of newer 'atypical' antipsychotic medications (see Gruenberg and Goldstein, Chapter 14) is believed in some circles to promise a significant improvement in the capacity of schizophrenics to engage in interpersonal relations. This development may have important implications for the way in which group therapy is conducted (see discussion, below).

Variations of group therapy approaches and a consideration of their effectiveness

As mentioned earlier, the way in which group therapy is conducted with the psychotic population is largely dependent on the therapist's theoretical orientation. The therapist who believes in a psychodynamic model of the mind and sees the psychoses on a continuum with other disorders is likely to conduct the group in a relatively unstructured way (with special modifications) to allow for the partial emergence of primitive regressive and transferential experiences which can then ideally be resolved through interpersonal interactions and interpretations. The therapist who holds to a biological deficit model is more likely to provide a structure which will minimize anxiety and regression and foster coping skills. Many therapists today believe in a 'systems' model which allows for complex interactions between biological, psychological, and social factors, and, like Kanas (Chapter 5), they try to incorporate the merits of both points of view in group treatment which includes both structured and unstructured features.

Several approaches to group therapy are formulated and exemplified in this book. They include: (1) supportive/problem-solving/educative; (2) interpersonal/interactive/relational; (3) psychoanalytic/psychodynamic; (4) group analytic and group-as-a-whole approaches; and (5) Kanas' 'integrative' model. We now take up each of these in turn.

The supportive/problem-solving/educative emphasis

The most pressing need of the psychotic patient at any point in time is to 'contain' the illness so that it does not become overwhelming and cause serious disruption in a number of sectors. For example, one of the co-editors recently worked with a manic-depressive patient who suffered a severe episode of mania despite the proper use of antipsychotic medications. The primary purpose of outpatient therapy during that time was to keep the patient out of harm's way and to help him function as effectively as possible within the community despite his hallucinations and other mental status problems. When the manic episode subsided, the patient was extremely grateful for the support he received and had a feeling of mastery that he was able to function successfully outside the hospital despite his symptoms. The technique utilized was to align with and strengthen the patient's healthy ego, that is the non-psychotic part of his personality.

Psychoses have periods of stability but may slowly or rapidly move into severe states where patients are at risk for suicide, homicide (which occurs very rarely but needs to be evaluated), lack of self-care, accidents (one patient, for example, left a session and walked into the path of an oncoming automobile), altercations, and disorientation. Medication is the first line of containment for the psychoses because in many cases it quickly and markedly stems the tide of ego-regression.

Group therapy, particularly in an inpatient or partial hospital setting, is frequently evoked for support and containment as well. A 'holding environment' (Winnicott) can sometimes be established in a group by keeping the focus on patients' strengths and coping skills; offering education and information relevant to the disease and resources for problem-solving; and setting appropriate limits, boundaries, and behavior guidelines. While such groups are often felt to be ameliorative rather than growth-producing, they do reduce the risk of psychotic regression and help patients to manage better their illness. All therapy groups, even the most intensive, may take on such ego-supportive functions. This is amply illustrated in Kennedy *et al.* in a discussion of their work with a psychodynamic women's group (Chapter 10) where sharing of information about women's issues, medication, and so forth played a significant role even though the primary focus was upon transference relationships in the group.

Blanck and Blanck (1974, pp.314–337) pointed out the value of ego-supportive interpretations which access and reinforce the individual's strengths and healthy defense mechanisms, in contradistinction to 'uncovering' interpretations which seek to overcome defenses and increase depth of insight and 'mutative' inner change. In the present volume, Takahashi, Chazdon, and Lipson (Chapter 9) provide examples of sensitively attuned and compassionate therapist interventions which convey to the patients an appreciation of uncommon strengths in even their very regressed behaviors such as avoidance and withdrawal. (Avoidance, for example, can be a way of postponing gratification; withdrawal protects the group members from the patient's aggression, etc.) They call these interventions 'positive interpretations' because they focus on strengths and – very likely – mitigate the profound sense of shame and failure which haunt these patients, thus alleviating narcissistic injury. Takahashi, *et al.*, give evidence of very specific benefits of such interventions to both patients and the group atmosphere.

Kennedy *et al.* (Chapter 10) point out that even in psychodynamic groups, the educative function is important for the chronically mentally ill. Useful information about medication and community resources is often shared. The women in their long-term group acquired valuable skills for living by using the therapists and group members as role models. They learned to recognize and respond more maturely to biological and sociocultural issues particular to women and which may have been neglected or used against them in other treatment experiences. Sorting out what is psychotic illness from problems stemming from medical conditions, culture, and family is a very important function of group support. Skolnick (Chapter 2) emphasizes the importance of sorting out the psychotic and non-psychotic parts of the patients' personalities.

Interpersonal / interactive / relational group psychotherapy

Harry Stack Sullivan (1953) advanced the notion that psychopathology is the outcome of difficulties in interpersonal relations (socialization, communication, etc.). Bateson, *et al.* (Bateson *et al.* 1956), as well as Laing (1967) suggested that communications difficulties such as the 'double bind' (conflicted messages transmitted along two different channels, e.g. verbal and non-verbal) lead to severe emotional conflict and behavioral regression. Bowlby (1969) emphasized attachment, bonding, loss, and abandonment factors especially with respect to depression. More recently, object relations theory and self-psychology have evolved an 'intersubjective perspective' (Stolorow, Atwood, and Brandchaft, 1994) and 'relational model' (Mitchell, 1988) which forthrightly places interpersonal interactions at the center of etiology, diagnosis, and treatment. In the group therapy context, these approaches suggest that the therapist emphasize the 'horizontal dimension,' that is interactions within the group in the here-and-now, rather than the 'vertical dimension' of past object relations. (Interestingly, with psychotics, primitive phantasies can often be best understood as archaic metaphors for current interactions, a process sometimes referred to as 'interpreting upward' developmentally rather than reconstructing past experience.) With psychotic and chronically mentally ill patients, interpersonal factors which can to some extent be taken for granted with 'higher functioning' patients become crucial to both the survival of the group itself and treatment effectiveness (cf. Kapur, Chapter 11). For the psychotic patient, rapport and engagement, trust, safety, boundaries, nurturing, and emotional availability are under constant internal and external threat of what is experienced catastroph- ically as 'annihilation anxiety' or what Grotstein (1990) describes as a 'black hole' experience in which mental contents and the sense of self are engulfed and then fragmented by the gravity of intense regressive pressures, and are crucial factors in treatment outcomes. Under such severe anxiety, the interpersonal world becomes both increasingly important and increasingly fragile. Models of group psychotherapy which emphasize the quality of interactions within the group may be called 'interpersonal,' or if one prefers, 'interactive' (cf. Durkin 1964) or 'relational' models.

Della Badia, (Chapter 12) emphasizes the importance of the therapeutic alliance in groups of schizophrenics. He holds that specific interpretations and insights are secondary to establishing a significant relationship. A similar view, from a self-psychology perspective, was expressed by Wolf (1988), a position which differs from the 'classical' Freudian stance which maintains the converse, that the working relationship and positive transference drive the patient towards uncovering and insight. Della Badia's sentiments are on the side of the therapist being an active force and an involved participant-observer rather than a passive, 'neutral' 'screen'.

This emphasis on the importance of relatedness as a potent therapeutic ingredient is echoed, with variations, throughout this book. Kapur (Chapter 11) cites research suggesting that group cohesion is a major curative factor with this population. Kanas (Chapter 5) emphasizes the importance of 'interpersonal learning.' Schneider (Chapter 7) holds that empathy and interpretation are not detached processes but result from intense interactions and co-resistances between therapist and patients. Urlic (Chapter 6) repeatedly emphasizes that the primary task of the group therapist with psychotic patients is actively to engage in establishing and maintaining a working group, since the group members are not easily able to take over this function.

The equivalent here of the real estate salesman's dictum that the three most crucial factors are 'location, location, location' would be that the most important factors in treating psychoses in groups are 'connection, connection, connection.' The psychotic process disrupts mentation and interaction by 'attacks on linking' (Bion 1959a; Gordon 1994) and the therapist must engage the patient in efforts to build links and connections in order to reduce splitting, to facilitate bonds among the group members, to make connections between disparate, fragmented, and scattered thoughts, and to integrate feelings and the thoughts behind them. It is axiomatic in this work that the engagement between patient and therapist, the cohesion of the group-as-a-whole, and the felicitous integration of the personality are intercalated processes.

The psychoanalytic/psychodynamic reconstructive approach

Virtually all the contributors to this book have a psychoanalytic background but are also aware that factors other than uncovering repressed or split off material are important in the treatment process. The question is whether, when, and how a psychodynamic or psychoanalytic approach can be adapted for use with psychotic patients.

Psychodynamic group psychotherapy strives to uncover and re-work pathological traumata, object relations, defenses, and primitive phantasies – in contrast to treatment modalities which provide sufficient structure to facilitate repression and to support the healthy ego. Few therapists today would aim to foster the extreme 'regression to dependence' which Winnicott, for example (cf. Little 1990), advocated in the 1960s and 1970s. Too often, psychotic patients merely become sicker from such experiences, and even when it could prove helpful, the cost of such intensive, extended treatment is often prohibitive. However, it does appear useful to promote a moderate degree of regression and its attendant anxiety in order to influence, if not the psychotic core itself, then the psychotic defenses and distortions reflective of primitivized object relations. In this way, the patient is gradually 'brought up' to a higher level of development.

The present volume is strewn with excellent examples of psychodynamic work with groups of psychotics. Kennedy, *et al.* (Chapter 10), show how selective analysis of the transference to the therapist and the interactions between female 'chronic' patients led to more assertive and mature interactions for a group of women whose pathology and place in society held them down for many years. Takahashi, *et al.* (Chapter 9) suggest how the use of metaphors, music, and projective techniques can facilitate group communication and exploration of object relations in patients who ordinarily avoid such communication and self-expression. Chazan (Chapter 8), Urlic (Chapter 6), and Schneider (Chapter 7) all provide examples of group interactions where the members productively explore emotionally laden issues involving defense mechanisms, object relations, the need/fear dilemma, and movement from the paranoid-schizoid into the depressive position.

The ingredients crucial to successful psychodynamic group psychotherapy with psychotics include (1) as mentioned above, the engagement of the group by the therapist, (2) a focus on the here-and-now (horizontal) interactions rather than the 'there-and-then' (vertical, historical) dimension, (3) frequent detoxification of countertransference reactions (cf. especially Della Badia, Chapter 12 and Lefevre Chapter 13) which could contaminate the treatment process, and (4) a supportive institutional context (cf. Lefevre's chapter for examples of problems and conflicts in institutions and their working through via a training process; Berke, Chapter 16 for examples of the productive use of the treatment team to resolve confusional states of patients and groups.)

Psychodynamic treatment of psychotics can rarely, if ever, be done without effective 'parameters' (Eissler 1958), that is, clearly defined limits on acting-out and acting-in, and 'modifications' (Kernberg 1975), that is, strategies such as deflecting or minimizing transference, setting limits to free association (e.g. 'no monopolizing or cross-talk'), or the use of 'upward interpretation' (interpreting primitive processes in terms of more mature ones, as when the patient says 'I'll have you for dinner!' and the therapist interprets 'You aren't sure if it's safe to absorb my knowledge and support.') which are the opposite of classical technique.

Group analytic and group-as-a-whole frameworks

'Group analysis' refers to the school of thought developed by S.H. Foulkes and expanded by his students and followers into a comprehensive framework for group psychotherapy. The fundamental emphasis of group analysis is on the 'group matrix,' which is the network of evolving communications among the members, thus making the social process and context the most fundamental aspect of group treatment while utilizing a variety of psychodynamic formulations as well (cf. DeMare 1972).

Group analysis places great emphasis on the potential evolution of the group into a democratic process in which treatment is 'of, by, and for the group' (Foulkes 1964). Optimally, the therapist role evolves from being a 'leader' and authority figure to becoming a 'conductor,' one who leads, follows, and consults for an ongoing process. Foulkes identified a number of processes such as mutual mirroring, whereby the group itself becomes the curative agent.

A key question, taken up at several points in this volume (cf. Urlic, Chapter 6; Chazan, Chapter 8) is to what extent groups of psychotic patients can evolve a democratic group culture. Because of their fragile ego structures, tendency towards regression, and unstable symptoms and lifestyle, psychotics have great difficulty with rudimentary socialization processes. Therefore, an active, directive therapist, a supportive setting, and liberal provisions of structure and limits appear to be necessary. On the whole, it would appear that the safest and most helpful strategy is to lean towards such active leadership and structure. Therapist engagement (Della Badia, Chapter 12) and empathy (Schneider, Chapter 7) along with selected topical themes (Takahashi *et al.*; Kapur, Kennedy *et al.*), structured tasks (Takahashi *et al.*), and cognitive emphases (Kanas) are important in maintaining cohesion and a work group climate.

To some extent 'here-and-now' interpretations can fulfill a quasi-structuring role by acting as containers (cf. Berke, Chapter 16; Caparros, Chapter 3) for primitive projective identifications which are otherwise disruptive forces. Effective management of powerful countertransference dynamics (Della Badia, Chapter 12; Lefevre, Chapter 13; Berke, Chapter 16) is necessary for the therapist to serve such a containing function. Self-psychology would also emphasize that the therapist must accept and work with his inevitable *failures* to contain, which with this population, can sometimes be overwhelming.

With these caveats, Urlic (Chapter 6), Chazan (Chapter 8), and Schneider (Chapter 7) express a cautious optimism that group therapy with psychotics can evolve partially into a democratic situation where therapy is 'of, by, and for' the group. This process is more gradual than for higher functioning patients, and it is perhaps never complete. In terms discussed elsewhere (Ashbach and Schermer 1987, pp.188ff.), the group revolt (Slater 1966) or 'barometric event' (Bennis and Shepard 1956) (which is essentially an Oedipal manifestation in which the group metaphorically overthrows the therapist and adopts his leadership functions) is too laden with intrapsychic and interpersonal pressures for psychotics to manage. However, a skilled and empathic group therapist can facilitate significant intermember communication and help the members to support each other and to reflect on their own and each others' behavior. To that extent, the members can introject some of the leadership functions and the group itself can become a curative agent.

An interesting question is whether psychotic patients can make use of specifically group-as-a-whole interpretations such as are employed in Tavistock and A.K. Rice groups and to some extent in contemporary systems-centered therapy (Agazarian 1994). Della Badia (personal communication 1998) and Agazarian (personal communication 1998) echo a majority of therapists who feel that, with psychotic patients, group-as-a-whole interpretations are alienating to psychotic individuals because (1) they interfere with the crucial and fragile one-to-one connection to the therapist as a benign parental figure (Della Badia, Chapter 12); and (2) the group interpretation may be concretized by the patients into a psychotically 'real' bad and threatening persecutory object which Bion (1959b) saw as a 'bad breast' and to which Harold Bridger once referred light-heartedly as the 'group animal'. One of the most awesome experiences in psychotherapy is to see the group become a delusionally persecutory object for its members! This regression and example of the so-called 'condenser phenomenon' (DeMare 1972, p.174) can and does happen briefly in groups of normals and neurotics, but they are able to reconstitute adequately, whereas psychotic patients can be seriously traumatized by such an occurrence, and the group may disintegrate.

On the other hand, some therapists do work with group-as-a-whole issues and interpretations with psychotic patients. Resnik (1994), Skolnick (1994), and others who have extensive psychoanalytic and group-as-a-whole training, appear to be able to create a 'holding environment' in which it is possible for psychotic patients to address such difficult-to-process ideas and experiences. In addition, those with a background in therapeutic community (Pullen, Chapter 15; Berke, Chapter 16) have a 'faith' that even the most regressed patients are attuned to and can address group-as-a-whole issues. One of the co-editors (Pines) has felt that some psychotic patients actually 'thrive' in large group situations, perhaps because they can maintain psychological distance and may be able to access considerable supports within such groups. Speck (cf. Speck and Attneave 1973) has worked with extended families and even whole communities to mobilize group energy to help the schizophrenic 'identified patient'. Cohen (B. Cohen, personal communication), conducted an open-ended therapy group which consisted of both staff and chronically mentally ill patients in which the group-as-a-whole processing was containable for several years possibly because of the unusual heterogeneous mix and the respect implied to the patients by including them as equals with staff. A group therapist who wishes to use a 'group-*qua*-group' approach for psychotics is, however, urged to proceed with caution and to consult with a highly skilled and experienced supervisor or treatment team.

In the next decades, it will be of great interest to see whether the newer 'atypical' antipsychotic medications (cf. Gruenberg and Goldstein, Chapter 14) will sufficiently stem the tide of regressive manifestations while facilitating enhanced ego capacities such that these patients will be able to utilize and benefit from more 'intensive' and probing group therapy experiences with group developmental processes and group-as-a-whole interpretation becoming regular parts of the treatment process. This could become an exciting area where group therapists and psychopharmacologists would work hand in hand in both research and treatment efforts. The potential gain for the patients in a group-as-a-whole or group-as-system type of treatment would be the vital and elusive enhancement of members' group identity and sense of self-in-relation which are often untreated even when the psychotic symptoms are alleviated. Pharmacologists will have an opportunity to define ever more sharply just how their medications affect complex functions such as emotional range, self-cohesion, and interpersonal relations.

Kanas' 'integrative' model

Kanas (Chapter 5) has evolved a model for group psychotherapy with psychotic patients which selectively combines advantages of each of the approaches described above and circumvents some of the potential disadvantages of each. His model seems well-adapted for use with homogeneous groups for short-term inpatient and time-effective outpatient groups, since it rapidly facilitates cohesiveness, enables therapeutic focusing of specific clinical techniques, and avoids interventions potentially harmful for that population. (Kanas points out, however, that the integrative model can be applied to longer-term and to heterogeneous groups with some significant modifications.) Kanas' approach is based on sound reasoning, extensive clinical experience, and careful research, and, since brief, empirically based psychotherapy is highly compatible with the cost consciousness of today's health care environment, we can expect that his model will become increasingly utilized.

Kanas succinctly states the basics of the integrative model as follows:

> In its evolution over time, it has taken on a biopsychosocial perspective that allows it to correct some of the disadvantages of other models without sacrificing the advantages. Like the educative approach, it helps patients learn to cope with psychotic symptoms, discuss topics related to their specific needs in a safe environment, and interact in a group environment where regression-preventing structure is provided through the interventions of the therapists. Like the psychodynamic approach, integrative groups use open discussions where members develop the topics and are not bound by lectures and formal exercises, where long-term problems and maladaptive behaviors may be examined without dwelling on the past, and where ego functions like reality testing and reality sense are strengthened. Like the interpersonal approach, a major goal of the integrative model is to help the members become less isolative and enhance their relationships through the discussions, through the experiences the patients

have in interacting with each other during the sessions, and through immediate feedback from the therapists in the here-and-now on ways in which they can relate more appropriately.

There are two major goals of the integrative group approach. The first is to help psychotic patients learn ways to cope with their symptoms. For most of the patients, this means learning to test reality and deal with hallucinations and delusions. The second treatment goal is to help the patients learn ways to improve their interpersonal relationships. This is accomplished through the discussions as well as through the experience of interacting with others during the sessions.

While Kanas' integrative model has the potential difficulty of 'eclecticism' as such – namely that the combining of strategies may obviate some of the gains were each approach to be exclusively applied – its careful attention to 'outcomes' is a good way to offset this problem, and its practicality is of great advantage in settings which require safe and efficient attention to the immediate needs of psychotics, rather than those increasingly rare situations which promote and offer the supports to conduct a deeper, reconstructive type of treatment.

Coping with countertransference, counter-identification and counter-resistance

The best strategies and techniques of psychotherapy, when applied without attention to the therapist's own needs, feelings, and conflicts as they are aroused in the treatment situation, are likely to founder. With the psychotic population, attention to the therapist's countertransference is indispensable on account of the intense emotions which are routinely produced.

The most potent model for understanding countertransference with psychotic patients is that of projective identification. As Resnik (Chapter 4) points out, the underlying defect of psychosis is an intolerance of psychic anguish (or *angst*). When frustrated, misunderstood, or experiencing loss, the psychotic individual splits off, disavows, and projects into others significant aspects of the self and object world in order to rid himself of psychic suffering for which he has not yet learned to make a sufficient container or thought apparatus. The therapist and group members then are the recipients of these massively projected fragments which are dispersed throughout the group (cf. Caparros, Chapter 3) Until worked through, these projections escalate into further confusional states, fragmentation, and mutual hostility within the group and institution (Berke, Chapter 16) The therapist may 'counter-identify' with the projection, and re-project it into the patient as a bad object (Etchegoyan 1991, pp.281–285) rather than help the patient or group contain and metabolize the projection so that it becomes a tolerable, comprehensible part of the mental life. Or, as Racker (1968) suggested, he may develop 'counter-resistance,' or even a 'countertransference psychosis,' avoiding the pain which the patient also evades, thereby reinforcing the 'code of silence' which is so common in groups of psychotic patients, and at possible serious cost to the therapist himself. Ultimately, therapist and patient alike are fending off anxieties having to do with either contact (the need/fear dilemma) or self (awareness of need, boundaries, separateness, existential unknown) and also the intense struggle with aggression, sadism, and rage, whether self-destructive or other-directed.

Schneider (Chapter 7) provides a 'micro-analysis' of how the empathy process can become disrupted. It is inevitable, he says, that the group will use resistances and acting-out to avoid emotional issues as well as to sabotage progress which is paradoxically undone with a 'negative therapeutic reaction.' These responses, of course, serve as 'grist for the mill,' allowing the therapist to clarify and interpret the patients' difficulties and to point in the direction of recovery. However, as Schneider astutely points out, the therapist's narcissism may be undermined by the intense resistances which arise in psychotic groups, since the patients often convey a message that the therapist has 'failed' in some way. (A wise and wizened psychoanalyst, the late Harold Feldman of Philadelphia, would often ask borderline and psychotic patients quite directly and compassionately: 'How have I failed you?') Faced with such 'narcissistic injury,' the therapist's 'reflective space' (Hinshelwood 1994) becomes vulnerable as does his ability to hold and contain the patients' projections, symptomatic expressions, and failures to communicate. In other words, patients sabotage the empathy they so much require. Schneider suggests that hallucinations and delusions, traditionally regarded as stemming from poor reality testing, may themselves represent forms of resistance. This hypothesis suggests that such distortions can be clarified and interpreted like all resistances, but any therapist who has tried to confront a delusional patient can tell you that this needs to be done with great care, tact, and timing! The extent to which psychotic states are responsive to reality testing can vary considerably.

To sum up, psychotic individuals, especially in group situations, evoke powerful and disturbing feelings in therapists which interfere with the empathic stance. By carefully attending to the countertransference, the therapist can address his counter-resistances and restore empathy and engagement. In work with higher level patients, such a process occurs on an occasional basis, but with groups of psychotics, most of the 'work' the therapist does may be in managing his own intense affects and restoring his ability to empathize.

Multimodal treatment and the importance of context

Group psychotherapy does not occur in a vacuum. Traumatic events, for example, impinge upon groups (Klein and Schermer in press). In one group, (cf. Schermer and Klein 1995) bereavement surrounding the departure of the therapist became a total focus, especially since virtually all the members had major dependency, loss, and separation-individuation issues. Hopper (personal communication 1995) described a group in which a bomb blast occurred not far from the therapy site, evoking 'annihilation anxiety'. Urlic (this volume, Chapter 6) describes groups conducted in the midst of the war in former Yugoslavia. The 'adaptive context' (Langs 1976, p.19) – whether personal, societal, familial, or institutional – forms a significant component of what takes place in the group and is all too often ignored because the patient's 'ailment' (Main 1957) and the treatment process have been summarily bracketed off from daily life in a manifestation of Sartre's existentially based statement that 'The worst crime is to make abstract that which is concrete.'

A key contextual element is the process of training and supervision, which involves dynamics which both impinge upon and parallel the therapy group. Two additional contextual features are treatment modalities which have evolved a crucial ongoing significance for the psychoses: antipsychotic medication and therapeutic community. The first addresses the biochemical underpinning of psychoses (although it also has profound psychosocial implications). The second forms a large-scale institutional umbrella, somewhat artificially interpolated into a hospital-based or residential system, within which pharmacological, individual, group, and family therapy all take place. The therapeutic community manifests and is a way of self-regulating, large group dynamics of the institution, and it affects all the activities which occur within it.

Training and supervision

Training and supervision in group psychotherapy are subjects which have received insufficient attention in the literature, and the question of supervision in work with the chronically mentally ill patient has been subjected to active avoidance! (Della Badia, Chapter 12, Lefevre, Chapter 13) In addition to its important didactic value, the supervisory experience is of vital emotional support to therapists who work with psychotics and subjected to intense 'role strain,' which may lead to activation of past conflicts, discouragement, 'burnout,' and even psychosomatic disorders (see Lefevre, Chapter 13).

Both Della Badia and Lefevre point out several important factors involved in supervision and training for therapy work with this population: (1) the necessity of the supervisor to be skilled in group therapy specifically with psychotic patients; (2) the importance of motivational and supportive factors within the supervision process; (3) an emphasis on the humanness, authenticity, and the personal/experiential element in both the treatment process and therapist-supervisor interactions; and (4) ongoing work with mutual projective identifications and other countertransference issues *in all the relevant systems* – therapy group, supervision, and administration – which impact on treatment.

Treatment of psychoses unfortunately has been left to its own devices in many settings. To put it bluntly, treatment providers, mirroring attitudes in the society-at-large, all too often discriminate against psychotic patients, who are very vulnerable individuals to begin with. Therefore, this most challenging and important work is often left up to the least qualified personnel, however heroic their efforts may be. Della Badia (Chapter 12) recalls how, during his psychiatric residency, he could not locate a single supervisor familiar with group psychotherapy for psychoses. If the present volume encourages the development of 'train-the-trainer' programs for supervisors of this difficult endeavor, it will have served an important purpose.

Della Badia and Lefevre (Chapter 13) are in agreement that an essential 'qualification' of both supervisors and therapists working with psychotic patients is access to their own humanness, which also includes perhaps the ability to 'metabolize' and process their own psychotic-like experiences or 'essential psychosis'. Loewald (1981) puts this in terms of the therapist's ability to symbiotically fuse with the patient while maintaining 'one foot in the door of reality.' Many supervisors and therapists become intimidated when they experience the powerful 'fusion' experience of mutual projective identification which is an everyday aspect of work with this population. The power of these projections is so intense that one highly experienced therapist fainted in response to the virtually trance-inducing behavior of a patient in a psychotic state. Consider what working with a *group* of such patients can be! The supervisor must be prepared by training and self-analysis to assist therapists-in-training to cope with such disconcerting experiences and use them effectively in the treatment process.

Della Badia, Lefevre, Berke (Chapter 16) and Kennedy *et al.* (Chapter 10) provide cogent examples of how supervision is a mutual learning process involving the humanity and subjectivity of supervisors and therapists which hopefully will lead towards the humanization and rehabilitation of patients. As Searles (1965) has pointed out, many psychotic patients retreat to inanimate objects to cope with the severe anxiety they experience in human interactions. The therapist must restore his own humanity in order to help patients enter fully into the human condition. The 'emotional charge' for the therapist's side of the 'working alliance' must at first be instilled by the supervisor, unlike work with higher level patients who are capable of generating great interest and empathy in fledgeling therapists. As Berke so well illustrates, psychotic patients have a knack for generating 'negative attention,' and sometimes 'rescue fantasies' in others, but they have difficulty inducing nurturing responses with appropriate boundaries in those around them. The work of Stern (1984), Brazelton (Brazelton and Cramer, 1989), and others suggests that these vital 'executive' and relationship-defining interpersonal functions are established in the earliest weeks of the mother–infant interaction, where some of the groundwork for schizophrenic psychopathology may be established. Early dehumanizing experiences may get repeated in both the therapy and supervision processes.

Della Badia (Chapter 12) stresses the importance of instilling curiosity and the search for meaning in therapists who might otherwise have difficulty forming a working relationship with the psychotic population. He also considers that the supervisor must be emotionally available to his supervisees, especially at crisis points in treatment, prepared to work through countertransference problems and even forthrightly to recommend personal therapy to the therapist if indicated. He argues that the border between supervision and psychotherapy becomes inevitably blurred: supervision itself may have therapeutic implications for supervisees since psychotic patients demand that therapists look inwardly at themselves and often stay symptomatic or have a 'negative therapeutic reaction' (Schneider, Chapter 7) if the therapist does not engage in his own personal growth (cf. Searles 1975). Impersonal detachment is no more helpful for supervision than it is for the therapy process itself. Della Badia's views are consistent with those of the intersubjective (Stolorow, Atwood and Brandchaft 1994) and relational (Mitchell 1988) perspectives within psychoanalysis. Through intragroup dialogue (cf. the work of Bakhtin, explicated in Emerson 1997), there occurs a sorting out of phenomenological worlds, which has the potential to reintegrate the severely distorted and fragmented inner lives of these patients. This process is radically different from the 'experience distant' objectivity of the traditional supervisory and therapy roles. The supervisor needs to be a 'subject' or 'subjective object' (Winnicott cf. Ogden, 1990, pp.94–95, 105–105) for the therapist-in-training, thus role modeling the personhood, engagement, and empathy, and symbol-making capacity the therapist needs to manifest with psychotic patients.

Lefevre (Chapter 13) empathizes with the plight of therapists and patients in these situations, specifically the notable lack of support they may experience in the institutional and the 'managed care' (USA) or 'evidence based' (Britain) contexts which stress control rather than encounter. She and her colleagues developed an educational and training program which empowered therapists to integrate intensive therapy techniques and group process principles into daily practice on the psychiatry ward. Like Della Badia, she remarks upon the motivating and energizing value of training and also the detailed attention which must be given to the countertransference in order to reduce serious disruption of the group therapy process.

Antipsychotic medications

The clinical intervention which is now considered almost mandatory with psychotic patients is medication. In the USA, for example, one rarely treats psychosis without medicine. Somerville (personal communication, 1990) expressed the view that there are a significant number of what she called 'ambulatory psychotic' patients, often misdiagnosed as character disorders or borderlines, who don't get medicated. But, by and large, virtually every patient in a group of psychotic patients will be on medicine. In the present volume, Gruenberg and Goldstein (Chapter 14) give a clear and concise depiction of current neuroleptic medications and medication issues relevant to the group practitioner.

Medication impacts on the body's 'internal environment,' affecting the central nervous system, the aim of which is to alleviate symptoms but which also may cause side effects and emotional states secondary to the desired impact. The newer, 'atypical' antipsychotic medications such as risperdal, clozaril, and zyprexa have the potential to alleviate 'positive' symptoms such as hallucinations, delusions, confusion, etc. with less of the 'doped up' apathy previously associated with 'typical' antipsychotic medications such as thorazine and haldol. In this respect, when medications work effectively, they simply allow the therapist to do a much better job.

In addition, the positive life changes and experiential changes which occur in the patients as a result of 'atypical' medications can lead to the ability to face hitherto overwhelming issues which are well addressed in group therapy: problems such as personal autonomy and life goals, how to function in a workplace, and how to live with the awareness of lost years. Foster (1997, unpublished lecture) compared the impact of some 'atypicals' to the 'Awakenings' which Oliver Sacks (1974) observed in patients who 'slept' for years as a result of neurological disease and were suddenly revived via medication. From this vantage point, if it is supported by subsequent clinical experience and research, therapy groups will help patients learn how to live with their improved biological equipment, and to work through the re-birth experience.

Medication, however, is not administered in a vacuum. Psychosocially, medication has profound implications for both the practitioner and the user. For example, it gives the practitioner radical power over the patient and may also reinforce his counter-resistance to dealing with the patient's emotions by providing both parties with a quick chemical escape hatch. For the psychotic patient, ingesting medicine can become a ritualized eucharistic act of oral incorporation representing the radical taking into the self of 'goodness' or 'badness' and leading to specious improvement or conversely an actual worsening of symptoms. It can also mean giving up symptoms which have, often for years, served important equilibrating purposes: the hallucination which is more available than the absent parent, the manic high which temporarily fills the dysphoric emptiness of the core self. The treatment team should have enough access to their own issues (cf. Lefevre, Chapter 13) to be able to work through such problems in themselves and in the patient population, rather than merely doling out prescriptions and leaving patients to their own devices, which is all too often the case. The group psychotherapist can serve a vital function of aiding the members to sort out their feelings and thoughts about their medications in a way which gives them maximum autonomy, individuation, and self-esteem and suggests avenues for growth which go beyond the medications, so that life does not become fixated or stagnant. Group psychotherapy can also assist the patients to have a better working relationship with the medicating doctor, a process which can markedly improve medication compliance.

The therapeutic community

Institutions and organizations have a profound effect on all aspects of treatment. On a 'macro' level, economics, social trends, ideals (or the absence thereof), and beliefs are significant determinants of what occurs in day-to-day care of patients (cf. Lefevre). On a 'micro' level, events in the clinic or psychiatric ward impact on the therapy group. An example of the latter occurred when a group member protested to the director about the noise and cigarette smoking in the clinic waiting room. This triggered a (fortunately containable) dispute between administrators and some patients, fueled by mutual projections, which caused a temporary splitting of one of the therapy groups into two 'warring' subgroups. Containing the splitting in the group helped resolve the institutional dispute.

The therapeutic community movement evolved as a self-conscious effort to bring such institutional issues into focus and to allow for patient participation in the process of resolving problems and differences as well as in setting institutional goals, objectives, and procedures. Its impact has been felt worldwide, leading to major changes in the way in which treatment programs are run, although full democratization and empowerment of patients remains only a hoped-for ideal.

Pullen (Chapter 15) provides a broad and detailed history of the therapeutic community movement, especially in Great Britain, which in many respects has served as the hub of this powerful development with its therapeutic and large-scale social and humanitarian implications. Maxwell Jones played a key role in formulating and developing a rationale for the therapeutic community. Pullen also recalls its early origins in social experimentation and its gradual elaboration as a systematic approach to treatment, whether with the use of therapeutic community models to improve the hospital milieu and the effectiveness of treatment or the experimentation with regressive, abreactive therapies in the 1960s such as the work of Ronald Laing and others at Kingsley Hall, an experience of which is reported in the well-known book about the Kingsley Hall patient, Mary Barnes (Berke and Barnes 1991), stating from the viewpoints of both patient and therapist the impact (mostly positive in her instance) of such a radical approach on her own psychosis and personal growth. (The therapist, Dr.

Joseph Berke is a contributor to the present volume, Chapter 16 on 'Confusions in a Therapeutic Milieu.')

In Britain and elsewhere, the therapeutic community movement was facilitated by its conjunction with an interest in large group dynamics (cf. Kreeger 1975). The Northfield Military Hospital, where Bion, Rickman, Foulkes, Bridger, and others initiated major modifications of treatment involving more active use of groups and communities, and 'felt their oats,' so to speak as innovators in the field (Pines 1985); The Group Analytic Institute of London, with pioneers in large group interactions such as Lionel Kreeger and Patrick DeMare developing median and large group training and therapy; and the Tavistock Institute, where the 'Tavistock conference' model evolved under the aegis of Bion and others, emerged as 'hotbeds' of interest in large group interactions. These developments paralleled and interacted with developments in the family network treatment of psychoses (cf. Speck and Attneave 1973), the understanding of primitive object relations, and the study of social interactions and cultures (applying the work of social theorists like George Herbert Mead and cultural anthropologists like Margaret Mead and Claude Levi-Strauss) to provide an exciting observational and theoretical knowledge base for the development of therapeutic communities.

Berke provides a glimpse into the functioning of a small therapeutic community, actually a residential treatment program, showing how live-in and external staff members work together as a team to contain stormy projective identifications and 'confusional states' in the individual, group, and social system. Many of the critical situations that arise are triggered by separations, losses, and terminations, which are regular events in such a community, disturbing an already fragile sense of a 'place,' a 'home,' or in primitive object relational terms, a 'good nurturing breast.' It is clear that for the therapeutic community to be an effective part of treatment, and not merely a formality, treatment teams must work together, must become themselves a cohesive group, to contain projective identifications. Such coordinated functioning forms an important backdrop to the group therapy sessions conducted within the institution, and without it, the best of clinicians will be minimally effective in conducting group treatment.

The Arbours Program discussed by Berke represents a uniquely felicitous collaboration and dedication of staff, administrators, funding sources and the community. Today, with the 'downsizing' of psychiatric hospitals and substance abuse rehabilitation centers, there are, unfortunately, fewer opportunities to pursue therapeutic community work as such, but its impact will be felt for years to come in the empowerment of the mentally ill and the systems understandings which are a direct result of this important component of the treatment process. The group therapist who wishes to work with the psychotic population should be thoroughly familiar with the therapeutic community model.

Finally, to round out the exploration of context, it is important to note that both within and outside of facilities, many individuals other than psycho-therapists serve important roles in the care of psychotic patients. Whether it is a storekeeper or employer who shows unusual compassion to a schizophrenic individual, a residential counselor, a student doing a field placement, or a volunteer in a clinic or mental hospital, such persons may have a positive and lasting impact on patients who otherwise feel severely misunderstood and rejected by society-at-large. In Italy, volunteers play a major role in the mental health system. DiNorscia and Romeo (Chapter) provide a discussion of the role relationships, systems impact, and quasi-therapeutic aspects of the volunteer working with psychotic patients.

Conclusion

In thus providing an 'aerial view' of the substantial ground covered in this volume, it is clear that there is no 'single thread' which runs through and unifies group psychotherapy for the psychoses. Instead, there is a 'spider web' of ideas which, hopefully does have a center (the patient) and an epicenter (the group) which will keep the dialogue from becoming the legendary Tower of Babel. The seeker of absolute 'truth' will find little here of solace. But the searcher after multiple perspectives and vertices – diverse ways of grasping complex phenomena, hopefully combined with compassion and a tolerance for the unknown (negative capability) – will find much to excite him and test his mettle as a therapist, a thinker, and a person. By thus flying into 'psyche's web,' he hopefully will not get caught there, but will find much to learn from and much to give to a population of patients who are among the most genuinely suffering human beings to come the way of the psychotherapy 'establishment.'

References

Abraham, K. (1927) *Selected Papers on Psycho-Analysis*. London: Hogarth.
Agazarian, Y. (1994) 'The phases of development and the systems-centred group.' In V.L. Schermer and M. Pines, M. (eds) *Ring of Fire*. London: Routledge, 36–85.
American Psychiatric Association (1994) *Diagnostic and Statistical Manual of Mental Disorders*, 4th Edition. Washington, DC: American Psychiatric Association Press.
Ashbach, C. and Schermer, V.L. (1987) *Object Relations, the Self, and the Group*. London: Routledge and Kegan Paul.
Bateson, G., Jackson, D., Haley, J., and Weakland, J. (1956) 'Towards a theory of schizophrenia.' *Behavior Science 1*, 251–264.
Bennis, W.G. and Shepard, H.A. (1956) 'A theory of group development.' *Human Relations 9*, 415–437.
Berke, J. and Barnes, M. (1971) *Mary Barnes: Two Accounts of a Journey through Madness*. London. MacGibbon & Kee. Republished 1991. London: Free Association Books.
Bion, W.R. (1959a) 'Attacks on linking.' *International Journal of Psycho-Analysis 40*, 308–315. Republished in Bion, W.R. (1967) *Second Thoughts*, London: William Heinemann.
Bion, W.R. (1959b) *Experiences in Groups*. New York: Ballantine Books.
Bion, W.R. (1962) 'A theory of thinking.' *International Journal of Psycho-Analysis 43*, 306–310. Republished in Bion, W.R. (1967) *Second Thoughts*, London: William Heinemann.

Bion, W.R. (1977) *Seven Servants: Four Works by W.R. Bion*. New York: Jason Aronson.

Blanck, G. and Blanck, R. (1974) *Ego Psychology: Theory and Practice*. New York: Columbia University Press.

Bowlby, J. (1969) *Attachment and Loss*. 2 vols. New York: Basic Books.

Brazelton, T.B. and Cramer, B.G. (1989) *The Earliest Relationship: Parents, Infants, and the Drama of Early Attachment*. Reading: Addison-Wesley.

Burnham, D., Gibson, R., and A. Gladstone (1969) *Schizophrenia and the Need-Fear Dilemma*. New York: International Universities Press.

DeMare, P.B. (1972) *Perspectives in Group Psychotherapy: A Theoretical Background*. New York: Science House.

Druck, A. (1989) *Four Therapeutic Approaches to the Borderline Patient*. Northvale: Jason Aronson.

Durkin, H. (1964) *The Group in Depth*. New York: International Universities Press.

Eissler, K. (1958) 'Remarks on some variations in psychoanalytical technique.' *International Journal of Psycho-Analysis 39*, 222–229.

Emerson, C. (1997) *The First Hundred Years of Mikhail Bakhtin*. Princeton: Princeton University Press.

Etchegoyen, R.H. (1991) *The Fundamentals of Psychoanalytic Technique*. London: Karnac.

Foster, J. (1997) Unpublished lecture on psychotropic medications. Sponsored by Greenspring of Eastern Pennsylvania. Workshop location: King of Prussia, PA.

Foulkes, S.H. (1964) *Therapeutic Group Analysis*. New York: International Universities Press.

Fromm-Reichmann, F. (1950) *Principles of Intensive Psychotherapy*. Chicago: University of Chicago Press.

Fromm-Reichmann, F. (1959) *Psychoanalysis and Psychotherapy: Selected Papers*. Chicago: University of Chicago Press.

Gordon, J. (1994) 'Bion's post-Experiences in Groups thinking on groups: a clinical example of -K.' In V.L. Schermer and M. Pines (eds) *Ring of Fire*. London: Routledge, 107–127.

Grotstein, J.S. (1990) 'The "black hole" as the basic psychotic experience: some newer psychoanalytic and neuroscience perspectives on psychosis.' *Journal of the American Academy of Psychoanalysis 18*, 1, 29–46.

Hartmann, H. (1958) *Ego Psychology and the Problem of Adaptation*. New York: International Universities Press.

Haugsgjerd, S. (1983) 'Toward a theory for milieu treatment of hospitalized and borderline patients.' Unpublished paper.

Hinshelwood, R. (1994) 'Attacks on the reflective space: containing primitive emotional states.' In V.L. Schermer and M. Pines (eds) *Ring of Fire*. London: Routledge, 86–106.

Kaplan, H. and Sadock, B. (eds) (1995) *Comprehensive Text Book of Psychiatry*. Baltimore: Williams and Wilkins.

Kernberg, O. (1975) *Borderline Conditions and Pathological Narcissism*. New York: Jason Aronson.

Klein, M. (1977a) *Love, Guilt, and Reparation and Other Works: 1921–1945*. New York: Delta.

Klein, M. (1977b) *Envy and Gratitude and Other Works: 1946–1963*. New York: Delta.

Klein, R.H. and Schermer, V.L. (eds) (in press) *The Healing Circle: Group Psychotherapy for Psychological Trauma*. New York: Guilford.

Kreeger, L. (1975) *The Large Group: Dynamics and Therapy*. London: Constable.

Laing, R.D. (1967) *The Politics of Experience*. New York: Ballantine Books.

Langs, R.L. (1976) *The Bipersonal Field*. New York: Aronson.

Laseque, C., and Falret, J. La Folie À Deux (ou folie communiquée) (1877) *Annals of Medical Psychology 18*, 321–335, 1877; English tr. Michaus, R. (1964) *American Journal of Psychiatry, 121* (supplement), 1–23, October.

Lindner, R. (1955) *The Fifty-Minute Hour: A Collection of True Psychoanalytic Tales*. New York: Rinehart.

Little, M.I. (1990) *Psychotic Anxieties and Containment: A Personal Record of an Analysis with Winnicott*. Northvale: Aronson.

Loewald, H. (1981) 'Regression: some general considerations.' *Psychoanalytic Quarterly 50*, 22–43.

Main, T. (1957) 'The Ailment.' *British Journal of Medical Psychology 30*, 3, 129–145.

Mitchell, S.A. (1988) *Relational Concepts in Psychoanalysis: An Integration.* Cambridge: Harvard University Press.

Ogden, T. (1990) 'On potential space.' *Tactics and Techniques in Psychoanalytic Therapy.* Vol. 3: *The Implications of Winnicott's Contributions.* Northvale: Jason Aronson, pp.90–112.

Pines, M. (ed) (1985) *Bion and Group Psychotherapy.* London: Routledge & Kegan Paul.

Racker, H. (1968) *Transference and Countertransference.* New York: International Universities Press.

Resnik, S. (1994) 'Glacial times in psychotic regression.' In V.L. Schermer and M. Pines (eds) *Ring of Fire.* London: Routledge, pp.275–307.

Rosenfeld, H. (1965) *Psychotic States: A Psychoanalytical Approach.* London: The Hogarth Press.

Rosenfeld, H. (1987) *Impasse and Interpretation.* London: Routledge.

Sacks, O. (1974) *Awakenings.* New York: Doubleday.

Schermer, V.L. and Klein, R.H. (1995) 'Termination in group psychotherapy from the perspectives of contemporary object relations theory and self psychology.' *International Journal of Group Psychotherapy 46,* 1, 99–116.

Searles, H. (1965) *Collected Papers on Schizophrenia and Other Subjects.* New York: International Universities Press.

Searles, H. (1975) 'The patient as therapist to his analyst.' In P.L. Giovacchini (ed) *Tactics and Techniques in Psychoanalytic Therapy:* Vol. 2. *Countertransference.* New York: Aronson, 95–151.

Skolnick, M. (1994) 'Intensive group and social systems treatment of psychotic and borderline patients.' In V.L. Schermer and M. Pines (eds) *Ring of Fire.* London: Routledge, 240–274.

Slater, P. (1966) *Microcosm: Structural, Psychological, and Religious Evolution in Groups.* New York: Wiley.

Speck, R.V. and Attneave, C.L. (1973) *Family Networks.* 1st edn. New York: Pantheon Books.

Stern, D. (1984) *The Interpersonal World of the Infant.* New York: Basic Books.

Stolorow, R.D., Atwood, G.E. and Brandchaft, B. (eds) (1994) *The Intersubjective Perspective.* Northvale: Aronson.

Szasz, T.S. (1984) *The Myth of Mental Illness* (revised paperback edition). New York: HarperCollins.

Sullivan, H. (1953) *The Interpersonal Theory of Psychiatry.* New York: Norton.

Wolf, E.S. (1988) *Treating the Self: Elements of Clinical Self Psychology.* New York: Guilford.

CHAPTER 2

Psychosis from a Group Perspective

Marvin R. Skolnick

Unaccommodated man is no more but such a poor, bare, forked animal.

(Shakespeare, King Lear)

To live in an inner and outer world that is alienated from the world of others is to be an unaccommodated man, a poor forked animal. Shakespeare poetically captures Lear's banishment from the group and his descent into madness. King Lear, stripped of his authority, role, and family; deprived of his retinue; and exposed to the storming elements raves madly about his estranged condition. Today there are many individuals stripped of their societal roles, family membership, exposed to the elements, raving on street corners, as living reminders of failure, despite the advent of modern psychiatry to accommodate many we call schizophrenic or psychotic.

How can group psychotherapy be used in the treatment of psychotic disorders – to restore the 'unaccommodated' to membership in the human group? In order to approach this question meaningfully, I believe it is necessary first to explore what it means to link 'psychotic' to the name of an emotional or mental disturbance. Modern institutional psychiatry has attempted to cleanse the term madness of its superstitious and non-scientific attributions by replacing it with the clinical term 'psychosis.' Today's diagnostic nomenclatures are presumably based on reliable and precise criteria to distinguish between the psychotic and the normal through systematic objective observations of persons and brains.

Since ancient times madness has taken protean forms. It has been variously understood as disorder of the bodily humors, Dionysian excess, demonic possession, spiritual or moral degeneracy, and psychological regression. Madness, what ever its cause, has been understood to exist outside of the boundaries of rational meaningful human discourse. Shakespeare captures Lear's transformation into madness as his raging internal storm merges with the environmental storm on the desolate heath at the margins of the kingdom.

The portrait of mad Lear on the heath is not so dissimilar from the growing numbers of the 'persistently severely mentally ill' who roam our urban streets often raving but unheard on the margins of our society. However, Shakespeare with his genius for multiple perspectives also captures the irony and paradox that Lear's madness is not only a descent into chaos but also can be seen as an ascent into clarity. In his madness Lear has perhaps never been more sane and penetrating in his insights about the inequities and cruelties of his kingdom. That madness is a disorder of individuals which not only menaces the individual but also the group is a common thread in most social narratives about madness throughout history justifying extreme and sometimes violent 'treatments' such as trephining, immolation, exorcisms, spinning chairs, immersion in ice water, lobotomy, castration, induction of coma with electric shock, and insulin. Failure to respond to treatment has often been followed by long term confinement in socially impoverished isolated environments or abandonment to status of barely visible wandering pariahs.

Since the Enlightenment the values and methodology of science have supplanted theology and the supernatural as ways of understanding madness. However, theories about madness have oscillated between organic medical perspectives that focus on disease of the brain and moral, psychological perspectives that focus on psychopathology of the mind. This oscillation mirrors the ambivalence and tension inherent in the Cartesian mind–body split that has dominated the western conception of the self for the past three centuries. Both the organic and psychological camps tend to agree that there are sharply drawn boundaries between the mad and the sane. 'I think therefore I am,' the Cartesian hallmark of the proof of the existence of the individual, also links sanity with rationality. The rational person has the capacity to know what is real and moral and appreciates the separateness of his mind from the mind of others.

The psychotic, on the other hand, is assumed to be dominated by irrational passions, an inability to perceive reality, moral irresponsibility, and a confusion between his mind and the mind of others. Since the late 1970s there has been an apparent resolution of the mind–body split in regard to psychosis. A dramatic paradigm shift has been led by a burgeoning neuroscience with new technologies that purport to prove that psychosis is a disease of the brain. The legacy of Cartesian dualism with its split of the human being into a domain of body with its hard physics, genetics and chemistry and the mind with its soft psyche, psycho-social dynamics or soul, has largely been resolved in the turn to hard science and a reductive biological materialism. Focus on the brain has gained dominance while the mind has been relegated to an epiphenomenon. Causation is understood to flow unidirectionally from the most elemental levels of the human organism such as molecules, genes, neuronal cells, to more macro levels of the organism manifest in distorted perceptual beliefs, and bizarre behavior (Mender

1994). Following the lead of nineteenth century physics, human psycho-pathology like the movement of bodies subject to the forces of gravity is increasingly believed to be determined by biology and chemistry. It is not uncommon to relate to affected individuals as though they are inexorably impelled by virtue of inheritance of the wrong genes through abnormal development of the brain and 'chemical imbalances' toward a schizophrenic illness as a life sentence.

Psychiatry increasingly asserts that major psychiatric disorders are diseases of individual brains and that objective observation and classification is not only possible but imperative if psychiatry is to attain a credible place in the scientific medical pantheon. This perspective – which philosophically could be characterized as a logical positivism medical model – has also been largely adopted by the media and the public at large. Despite frequent mention of a bio-psycho-social model, psychiatry has eliminated the hyphens and sharply reduced its interest in the psyche and the social as manifest in the overwhelming number of articles on neurochemistry, pharmacology and classification of diseases that fill journals of psychiatry compared to those that explore the psychosocial domain of emotional disturbance (Mender 1994, p.16).

In both DSM-IV (the American Psychiatric diagnostic manual) and the ICD (International Classification of Diseases), psychotic disorders are divided into those disorders which (1) have a delineated pathophysiology that directly impairs brain function such as drug and toxin ingestion, infectious, metabolic, endocrine, cardiovascular immune diseases and (2) those 'functional' psychotic disorders such as schizophrenia, manic and depressive psychosis with organic etiology established but with the neuropathological yet to be fully delineated. Positive symptoms such as delusion and hallucination are considered symptoms of a subtle pathology of the brain involving imbalance of neurotransmitter systems such as dopamine. Negative symptoms such as apathy or lack of motivation that are prominent in the more severe cases of schizophrenia are also considered to be intrinsic to a disease or genetic determined pathology of brain development or disease process (Thomas 1997, p.22).

The vast majority of neuropsychiatrists today are satisfied that schizophrenia, the flagship of the functional psychoses, is a biological disease (Carpenter and Buchanan 1995, p.889). They argue that twin and adoptive studies have established a dominant role for genetics. The discovery of the spirochete in the brains of psychotic demented patients, and the creation of psychotic symptoms in subjects given LSD and dexedrine has given credibility and hope to those invested in finding etiology in toxic or infectious agents. MRI and CAT scans showing enlarged ventricles and PET scans revealing deviations of patterns of blood flow and metabolism in the brains of some schizophrenics as compared to normals are cited to establish the role of structural brain pathology. Double blind studies that purport to show that the use of neuroleptics reduces acute psychotic symptoms and rehospitalization rates are cited to fortify the conclusion that functional psychosis like schizophrenia psychosis is a disease of the brain that requires biological treatments for its amelioration (May 1968).

Although psychoanalysis has made significant forays into rich exploration of the mind, it also has been encumbered by the mind–body dichotomy with a surprising bias toward reductive materialism. Freud although known as the father of psychoanalysis and psychodynamic psychology was first a neuroscientist in the tradition of the materialistic science of his time. He set his sights on a medical psychology that ultimately would move beyond the softness of psychology to the hardness of physics and chemistry to provide the definitive answers to questions about human behavior (Mender 1994). In regard to psychosis, Freud (1973 p.190) wrote 'The second limitation upon analytic success is given by the nature of the illness … psychotic conditions are unsuitable to a greater or lesser extent. It would be entirely legitimate to guard against failures by carefully excluding such cases.' So while a few psychoanalysts like Sullivan (1962), Fromm-Reichman (1952), Karon and Vandenbas (1981), Bion (1992), Rosenfeld (1965), Resnik (1994), and Searles (1965) have recognized the psychotic as more than anything else a social being amenable to psychodynamic understanding, the preponderance of psychoanalysts without the benefit of intimate contact with psychotics has implicitly or explicitly tended to embrace a reductive biology when it comes to psychotic disorders. For example Grotstein (1990), known for the richness of his thought on the depths of the human psyche has joined those that suggest that the schizophrenic is schizophrenic because he has fallen into a psychological black hole that is born out of a biological disaster and defect that puts his plight beyond analytic understanding. Even Jaspers, who introduced into psychiatry Husserl's existential phenomenological psychology that stressed understanding of disturbed individuals with a minimum of preconceptions or assumptions about causation, concluded from his inability to experience empathic understanding of schizophrenic patients that they must suffer from organic disease that locates them beyond the boundaries of existential psychiatry (Thomas 1997, p.176).

In this frame of reference, psychotic manifestations like delusions and hallucinations are considered primarily signs of brain dysfunction like froth on the waves without significant personal, interpersonal, intrafamilial or intragroup communicative meaning.

The almost complete shift in focus toward the biological origins of functional psychosis and away from the psychological and social dimensions has led to comparable shifts toward biological treatment approaches and away from psychological and social treatments. In what can also be characterized as a sophisticated return to Hippocrates' humoral beliefs about mental illness, neuroleptics and mood stabilizers such as lithium and tegretol, believed to correct neurochemical imbalances have become the mainstays of treatment of psychotic illnesses. Psychosocial interventions are either absent or relegated to an ancillary role of support. They are employed primarily to promote compliance with drug regimens and to educate the patient and family about disabilities imposed by this disease which like diabetes is believed to be a lifetime affair. Patients are also taught through behavioral approaches to suppress or ignore the psychotic aspects of their experience in favor of learning how to adapt and conform with social norms. 'Treatment resistant' has come to mean in psychiatry that the patient did not respond to psychotropic medications (Liberman 1994).

To what extent has modern psychiatry with its 'scientific method,' double blind studies, computers and technologies that open the brain and the genes to analysis at micro levels heretofore inconceivable, transcended the often superstitious, frightened, irrational, inhuman and destructive relationship of society to its mad? I would like to explore in this chapter the notion that modern psychiatry in its neglect of the psychosocial domain of psychosis has failed to notice that madness and sanity constitute each other and that non-psychotics or 'normals' whose conscious mental life restricts itself to the boundaries defined by the normative culture tend to recoil from the psychotic in a way that mirrors the psychotics' tendency to recoil from them. In the neglect of the domains of the psychological and the social, the treatment may be part of the disease rather than its cure. Rather than liberate, it may further lock vulnerable individuals into the role of estranged unaccommodated man.

I will attempt to make the case that there are compelling reasons to question the increasingly accepted beliefs: that psychosis is the result of primarily a disease of the brain; that psychosis is a disorder of contained individual selves ; that psychosis can be understood without regard to the historical social-political-economic-family context in which it occurs; and that the madness of the psychotic has nothing to do with reality. Evidence from multiple perspectives strongly suggests that consideration of group process should be central to both the exploration of the etiology and treatment of psychosis.

The lack of evidence for an exclusively biological framework

While the data base supporting biological factors in psychosis cannot be dismissed, there exists a growing body of studies, meta-analyses and sophisticated critiques about functional psychoses like schizophrenia that have largely remained outside of mainstream psychiatry and the public eye. These studies seriously challenge many fundamental assumptions of biological psychiatry and the treatments that it has spawned.

1. Schizophrenia is a chronic deteriorating disease of the brain

There have been a number of long-term longitudinal outcome studies that show that as many as 50 per cent of patients diagnosed with schizophrenia show considerable improvement with and without treatment (Bleuler 1978; Ciompi 1980). The claim that the brains of schizophrenics show pathological changes is put into question by failure to demonstrate brain pathology in autopsies and that findings of enlarged ventricles by non-invasive technologies like MRI and CAT scan can be explained in many studies on the basis of brain damage due to long-term use of neuroleptic and debilitating lifestyle factors such as poor nutrition (Breggin 1997, Cohen 1997, Robbins 1993). Statistical analysis of the number of schizophrenics with enlarged ventricles compared with normals suggests that while there may be a small subset of schizophrenics with compromising neurological factors that make them more likely to adopt a schizophrenic way of being, enlarged ventricles occur in normals suggesting that it is a non-specific factor not pathognomonic for schizophrenia (Breggin 1991, pp.61–65). PET scan studies that purport to show abnormal patterns of metabolism in the frontal lobe of schizophrenics can also be explained on the basis of states of mind like apathy and lack of motivation rather than indicative of traits of the brain. What is cause and what is effect is seldom taken into sufficient consideration in many of these studies (Thomas 1997).

2. Schizophrenia is a genetically determined neurodevelopmental disorder of the brain

Meta-analysis of twin and adoption studies suggest that the genetic factor in schizophrenia has been overrated and the environmental factors underrated (Lidz and Blatt 1983). For example, Tienari (1992) has shown that children loaded with biological relatives with schizophrenia who are adopted into healthy families show much lower incidence of schizophrenic spectrum disorders than those children adopted into disturbed families. Brain development is increasingly being shown by neurophysiologists to be much more plastic and responsive to experience than heretofore thought (Mender 1994). The possibility that enriched experience can lead to proliferation of neural connections not only during early phases of development, but throughout life, suggests that assumptions that schizophrenics are sentenced to a constricted emotional life because of brain pathology may well create unwarranted therapeutic pessimism and act as a self-fulfilling prophecy. The significant correlation between schizophrenia and social environmental factors like poverty, unemployment, and social class cannot be explained away by invoking the notion of a social downward drift caused by the disease (Hollingshead and Redlich 1958; Thomas 1997).

3. Schizophrenia is caused by a chemical imbalance and should be treated psychopharmacologically

None of the numerous reports of abnormal factors in the blood, urine, and spinal fluid have stood the test of time or attempts at replication. The 'chemical imbalance' associated now with the mythos of psychiatric disorders may well be more created than corrected by psychotropic drugs (Breggin 1997). A great deal of contradictory evidence is casting very serious doubts about the validity of the dopamine hypothesis (Cohen 1997, p.175). Studies (May 1968) that purport to establish the superiority of dopamine-blocking neuroleptics to psychosocial treatments in resolving acute psychosis and reducing relapse rates are questionable on a number of grounds. Double blind drug placebo trials have been shown in fact not to be double blind to patients because of the absence of 'side-effects' with placebo (Fisher and Greenberg 1997, p.372). The exacerbation of positive symptoms associated with stopping neuroleptics, rather than proving their efficacy, may be at least partially caused by withdrawal syndromes related to the unmasking of neuroleptic induction of supersensitivity at dopamine receptors.

The most alarming possibility is that neuroleptics reduce overt evidence of positive symptoms like delusions, hallucinations and agitation through interdicting connections between the limbic system and the frontal lobes – a chemical lobotomy – that only covers over positive symptoms by inducing states of apathy, blunting of affect, and loss of motivation (Breggin 1997). The apparent improvement and decrease of relapse into hospital could be explained by the fact that individuals in this state are less disturbing to others and themselves but at the cost of vitality and emotional aliveness. Carpenter, Bartko and Strauss (1978) has shown in the collaborative WHO studies that the only reliable predictor of poor prognosis in schizophrenia is the extent of negative symptoms such as apathy, lack of motivation, and blunted affect which are centrally implicated in the impoverishment of social relations in schizophrenics – the most treatment resistant and disabling dimension of the chronic form of the 'illness.' The WHO studies have also shown that the outcome of schizophrenia is better in traditional cultures than in the industrialized west even though most patients in traditional cultures receive considerably less neuroleptic treatment (Cohen 1997). Negative symptoms are remarkably similar to the neuroleptic-induced deficit syndrome in animals and humans (drowsiness, lack of energy, indifference, dysphoria, and reduced initiative) that has been inextricably linked to neuroleptic antipsychotic potency in laboratory testing of animals and clinical use with patients (Thomas 1997, p.112). The initial expectation that atypical antipsychotics like resperidol and clozaril – 'cleansed' of debilitating side-effects such as tardive dyskinesia, parkinsonian syndrome, and neuroleptic deficit syndrome – will provide the definitive treatment for schizophrenia should be called into question. More extensive clinical experience suggests that they are not so 'atypical' in their side-effect profile nor do they cure negative symptoms (Breggin 1997, p.71).

Regardless of the evidence gleaned from scientific studies, considerations of common sense alone cast serious doubt on biologically reductive explanations of psychosis. It seems beyond dispute that all human behavior, thought, and imagination would not exist outside of a body, with a physical-chemically active brain, but on the other hand can the mental life and behavior of any human being, including individuals considered psychotic, be understood by biological processes alone as devoid of meaning, purpose, and desire?

Not only is it reductive to try to understand and treat psychosis as primarily a disease of individual brains, it is also a mistake to consider psychosis as solely a matter of isolated diseased minds. The conception of psychosis as a matter of deranged isolated minds grew out of the western Enlightenment construct of the individuated self that rests on a foundation of splitting and a valorization of self-sufficiency and rationality that was heavily influenced by the Cartesian perspective.

Challenge to the belief in the discontinuous self of the psychotic and the non-psychotic

In the comprehension of a material domain perceived by the senses that abides by the laws of cause and effect physics (such as that bodies fall down instead of up) the boundary between what is real and what is delusion seems rather clearly drawn; however, in the immaterial domain of the mind in which values, morals, reasons, social organization and control, purpose and meaning are the currency, the boundary becomes blurred and may exist only through the more arbitrary process of social construction.

Foucault (1965), a giant of postmodernism, asserts that the isolated mind and the western Enlightenment conceptions of the sane *vs.* insane self are more normative delusion than fact. Different conceptions of selves and relationships of selves emerge as supporting rationales in the complex interdependent system of social control that come and go in historical time. The Enlightenment perspective is no more fact than the conception of the subordinated merged self that grew out of the Middle Ages' system of hierarchical social relationships that relied on the notion of the 'Great Chain of Being' extending from God on the top to the serf on the bottom. Foucault defines madness as radical challenge to the prevailing social order. 'It is that constantly changing region of human experience which defies any regulating intentionality; which speaks in the language of the fantastic and the passionate; which dwells not merely in historical time but also in a violent, timeless stream of subversion, flooding the secure banks of all that is positively known about the order of the self and world.' (Bernauer 1987, p.349). Madness according to Foucault is met with an elaborate system of rewards, discipline, and punishment designed to defeat whatever threat it might pose to the prevailing social order.

From a Foucaultian point of view it seems fitting that modern psychiatry, one of the subsystems of control, should define mental illness as a laundry list of disorders with its primary 'therapeutic' task mental hygiene and the restoration of order. Even an eminent biologically oriented psychiatrist like Gary Tucker in an editorial in the biologically oriented *American Journal of Psychiatry* (1998) challenged the misleading and destructive tendencies inherent in reifying psychiatric diagnosis that diverts attention from the uniqueness of the person and threatens the vitality of psychiatry as a profession at risk of becoming no more than a pale imitation of neurology. 'All the apparent precision [in the DSM] overlooks the fact that as yet we have no identified etiological agents for psychiatric disorders ... In psychiatry no matter how scientifically and how rigidly we use scales to estimate the patient's pathological symptoms, we are still doing pattern recognition. We are still making an empirical diagnosis and not an etiological diagnosis based on disruptions of either structure or function.' It follows from Foucault that psychosis cannot be meaningfully explored without consideration of the social, political, economic, and familial systems that it challenges.

Peter Barham (1984), in his groundbreaking book, *Schizophrenia and Human Value*, develops a well documented and plausible narrative history of the creation of schizophrenia from a historical/economic/social perspective. He contends that schizophrenia in its chronic form arose out of the medicalization of the casualties created by the traumatic changes in societal relationships that occurred in the wake of the emergence of capitalism, industrialization, and urbanization and displaced millions of vulnerable people from stable smaller communities in which their identities were sustained by well established role relationships and holding environments to chaotic impoverished environments in which a sense of identity had to be created. Many were forced to swim in entirely new ways, or sink. In eighteenth-century London, as an alternative to the sinking hordes roaming the streets, pauper and work houses were established in order to contain the social problem that threatened revolutionary contagion. People who failed to adapt at first tended to be considered lazy and morally derelict. Without resources and skills to survive some of these displaced persons fell into deviant defensive states of mind as a means to cope with catastrophe, estrangement, and unbearable emotional suffering. Pauper and work houses were gradually replaced by large hospitals that often were no more than warehouses for the impoverished. The inmates of these institutions received a reprieve from designations as moral derelicts by being transformed into patients with incurable mental diseases like schizophrenia.

This shift did not signal a real turn in a humanitarian direction but rather became another way to dispose of or at least marginalize a group of people who did not fit. A metaphorical reading of their 'delusional' narratives of suffering could be interpreted as indictment of the family and social system that failed them. Now with the authoritativeness of a scientific psychiatric diagnosis their complaints could be discounted as meaningless aberrations of sick minds or brains. Medicalization of the disorderly and those that fell between the cracks did not improve treatment for most but in many respects led to a cruel and inhuman step backward from small moral treatment facilities which could more rightfully claim a dignified approach and a much better rehabilitation rate. Over-medicalization can also be seen as providing society with an effective diversion from facing the damaging impact of political, economic, and social change on the most vulnerable and those not predisposed to fit the system. This analysis raises the disturbing question about how much psychiatry in the west is used in a more subtle way to silence dissidents as it has been used in more blatant ways in cold war Communist countries.

Sociologists and anthropologists like Goffman (1961), Caudil (1958), Stanton and Schwartz (1954), who studied the mental institution as a social system found much in modern psychiatric hospitals that resembled nineteenth-century abuses in more subtle form. They noted that even in mental hospitals with the best reputations like St Elizabeths, Chestnut Lodge, and the Yale Psychiatric Institute, these institutions were subject to political, social, and economic pressures that tended to put patients on the bottom rung of a social hierarchy that was antithetical to meaningful treatment and their development as autonomous persons. Goffman noted how a totalistic system fostered regression and abject dependency and what came to be considered the iatrogenic effects of institutionalization. Menzies (1975), Main (1975) and Miller and Gyne (1972) in consultations with institutions designed to treat 'incurables' noted the social psychological barriers constructed between patients and staff to insulate the staff from experiencing the anxieties about death and madness inherent in the human condition that are stirred by involvement with the very sick. They concluded that while impersonal distancing procedures like objectifying patients as things or diseases protected staff from anxiety, it also obstructed development of I–Thou relationships, a necessary ingredient in humane effective treatment. Seen from this perspective psychiatric hospitals are organized as social systems so as to reify a dichotomized split between the sane self and the insane. Patients become like a different species which has a monopoly on madness. The 'reform' movement that gained momentum in the 1970s ostensibly designed to respect the civil rights of mental patients and reduce iatrogenic effects of institutionalization by unpacking state mental hospitals seems to have been more motivated by the desire to spend less on care in light of the failure to establish suitable treatment facilities in the community. This has resulted in even worse fates for the chronically psychotic, forcing many to roam the streets.

In an experiential group for psychiatric residents designed to learn about group process through exploring the here-and-now, the members had been struggling for weeks with growing despair about the compromises imposed on their learning and capacity to meaningfully treat the very sick patients that were coming and going at an accelerating revolving door process driven more by limitations of insurance coverage and financial problems of the sponsoring university than clinical criteria. Residents complained that it was difficult to do much more than render a DSM diagnosis, medicate and then discharge. The difficulty in treating a patient who was a physician suffering from schizophrenia was also discussed until one of the residents suggested that this was 'too close to home' and that 'maybe we are all a bit crazy.'

The next session followed a Grand Rounds appearance by an internationally eminent neuropsychiatrist replete with intricate colorful map-like PET scans purporting to show physical evidence of thought disorder in schizophrenics compared to normals. This meeting was uncharacteristically animated and full of optimism about the potential of modern psychiatry, contrasting with the somberness and anxieties of previous meetings. The consultant wondered aloud about why this discussion seem to go on and on and what it meant about how they were coping with the anxieties that emerged in the previous session and their concern about being overwhelmed and identified with the madness of the their patients.

This was followed by the development of a shared group fantasy about how fascinating it would be to be able to project onto a screen an ongoing monitoring of the PET scan of all the members of the group. The consultant then raised a question about how this kind of data base could help them understand the current group process and their struggles with their patients, other staff, and painful complexities involved in the process of becoming psychiatrists. Following a mood of deflation, the group began a serious and moving exploration about a shared tendency to withdraw from emotional contact with patients, each other and faculty as a way to cope with feelings of impotence, fears about their own emotional problems and concerns that expressing their opinions might invite retaliation from faculty who already are experienced as under too much stress themselves.

This vignette about students entering the field may well illustrate ways in which leaps into technology, while undeniably rich scientific probes into the universe of the brain, may also serve to distract from appreciation and exploration of how underlying sociopolitical and economic forces are forging mind sets that disconnect treaters from the treated and are having major impacts on quality of treatment and of care.

Linking the psychotic and the non-psychotic

A Lacanian perspective on the relationship between psychosis and reality, in which no human being has access to what is actually reality, suggests that psychotics are disorganized and disturbed not because of loss of contact with reality, but because they are overwhelmed by too much contact with reality (the Real) which is inherently chaotic and menacing (Lacan 1977; Muller 1996). It is the failure of individuals prone to psychosis adequately to internalize the symbolic register of the culture (the Other) with its comforting, organizing myths, and social defenses that protect 'normals' but leave the psychotic with more reality than can be tolerated. From this point of view the notion of the bounded unitary self is a normative delusion. The experience of individual self emerges from an underlying dialogical process of the subject who desires a register of the imaginary (realization in fantasy of wish about self and other), the internalized Other (culture) embedded in the unconscious and the Real. A gap between the registers looms like an abyss that the underdeveloped self can plummet through into annihilation or psychotic anxiety. Neurotics avert the catastrophic experience of the gap, except in dreams or tolerable brushes with it in a Lacanian or Kleinian psychoanalysis. The psychotic who experiences porous boundaries between himself, the intrusions of others in the form of voices or the TV controlling his mind has his capacity to negotiate consensual social reality severely compromised. Having fallen into the gap too often, he exists on the edge, anticipating nameless dread, reluctant to risk the experience of emotional aliveness. However, a case can be made that despite his lodging in a solipsistic world as a desperate way to keep the terror of the chaos of the Real at bay, he is more familiar with the pressures to conform to the dictates of the culture and significant others than the non-psychotic who has more thoroughly digested or has been digested by the Other. Freud (Thomas 1997) is reputed to have reflected in a rare moment of modesty that perhaps Schreiber may have been more in contact with what is real than himself.

The work of Bakhtin (Thomas 1997, p.197) like that of Lacan emphasizes the internalization of languages as a vital element in creating the core of the psyche. Like Lacan he believed that the unconscious is structured like a language. However, Bakhtin introduced another level of complexity by suggesting that rather than one symbolic register, there exist multiple, sometimes conflicting, symbolic registers or many fathers in the unconscious and that the unconscious is not static. Like Heraclitus's river the 'Other' in the unconscious changes with the flow of cultural, social, political, and economic change that provides the context or background of the experienced self. The individual internalizes the language genres that have been spoken in the subject's intimate and family contexts, those that have been spoken in the variety of group contexts in which the subject participates, such as neighborhood, political party, church, and work; and the language genres that have been spoken in history that are passed on through the generations in media such as art and myth. In this sense the individual person is made of multiple selves derived from group experiences which shape the experience of the subject in what Bakhtin refers to as the multiple voices of dialogical internal speech of the psyche. In his analysis of the novels of Dostoevesky, for example, each of the brothers in Karamazov can be understood as different selves of the author which grew out of his social and personal history and the culture in which he was embedded. Is the psychotic who hears voices just mad or is he experiencing in an overt disruptive way the voices unconsciously influencing everyone?

From a Jungian perspective every differentiated ego of the individual is floating on a collective sea of archetypal reality (Jung 1961). Psychotic symptoms are seen as the disruptive emergence of mythological and fantastic themes into consciousness which are manifestations of disturbing aspects of collective unconscious but which overwhelm individuals whose inadequately formed egos are overwhelmed. With adequate support of the compromised ego, psychotic experience can lead toward a more differentiated self.

A Kohutian universe in which narcissism is an unending developmental process suggests that an ongoing experience of a cohesive self differentiated from others is contingent on the experience of others as selfobjects that affirm the experienced self which is inherently unstable and vulnerable to fragmentation throughout life (Kohut 1971). In this view it is a matter of to what extent good enough mirroring, twinning and idealizing self–other experiences have historically strengthened the experienced self as well as the quality of the current environmental and intersubjective matrix in which the individual is embedded that determines what point an individual resides on a continuum of cohesive vitality versus fragmentation and psychosis.

Melanie Klein (1952) through analytic play therapy discovered a phantasmagoric inner world of very young children that grew out of defensive reactions to destructive aggression and envy of the breast and the couple unleashed by the inevitable failures of the breast to gratify and to comfort. Through the use of splitting and projective identification, the child's developing psyche and internal representations of a good enough breast and a good enough self are preserved. However, if this process is excessive, an inner world of phantasies of bad menacing objects like cavernous devouring breasts, poisonous penises, and fecal babies may dominate the psyche. While Klein considered this paranoid-schizoid organization of the psyche as developmentally normative for the young child, the failure to achieve a stable depressive position – in which emerges the capacity to experience guilt, ambivalence, concern for others and the use of symbols necessary for thinking as an alternative to projection – was also considered a major factor in the development of psychosis in later life.

Hanna Segal (1957) identified a problem in language and thinking inherent in the paranoid-schizoid mode of organization which is also a characteristic of the psychotic process and which she termed 'symbolic equation.' The inability to transform the frustration of absence of the desired 'breast' into symbols that can be used for thinking leads to the inchoate use of symbols as equivalent to the 'thing-in-itself.' For example, Segal describes a patient whose career as a violinist was destroyed by his inability to distinguish between the violin as a phallic symbol that could enrich his playing with erotic energy and the thing in itself – a penis. His imprisonment in a paranoid-schizoid mode of experience made playing his violin in public equal to masturbating in public, subjecting him to terrifying castration anxiety and shame.

While Klein emphasized that constitutionally determined envy and aggression in the child contributed heavily to malignant use of projective identification and vulnerability to psychosis, others of the Kleinian school particularly Bion (1967, 1977) underscored the importance of the mother's reverie and containing function as a vital intersubjective factor that determined whether babies learned to manage nameless dread and move into depressive development or whether excessive projective mechanisms and the psychotic part of the personality emerged as dominant in their personalities. Bion and later Odgden (1989) noted the dialectical nature of the relationship between the paranoid-schizoid and depressive states as oscillating positions essential to processing experience throughout life rather than as achieved developmental steps. Eigen (1986), citing the work of Klein and Bion, has emphasized the ubiquity of psychotic process in everyday life, suggesting that the boundary between the psychotic and the non-psychotic is much less discontinuous than we like to believe. It is failures to negotiate the dialectic between the paranoid-schizoid and the depressive positions with resultant inflexible but fragile pathological organizations that limit the vitality and perspective of experience that leaves the individual under stress at risk of falling into overt clinical psychosis (Steiner 1982; Jacques 1974).

Matte-Blanco's theory of bilogic postulates the existence of a logic of the unconscious based on symmetrization and infinite sets in which the differentiated world of self and other dissolves into a sameness not limited by space and time (Matte-Blanco 1975; Rayner and Wooster 1997; Reyes, Reyes and Skelton 1997). This logic exists in a dialogical relationship with the more conscious Aristotelian logic of desymmetrization which allows for the experience of differentiation of self and others and a differentiated world in which space and time are crucial factors in experience. As with the dialectic relationship between the paranoid-schizoid and depressive positions, the dialectic between the logic of the conscious and the unconscious enables individuals to experience sameness (a factor in empathy, cohesiveness, and religious states of transcendence), and also a capacity to negotiate the practical physical universe of difference and linear causation. It is uncontained intense painful frightening affect that drives the individual toward an imbalance in the dialectic in which an inflexible idiosyncratic blend of dysemmetrization and symmetrization and psychosis are likely to prevail. As with Bion's notion of the other as container and Winnicott's (Winnicott 1965; James 1984) notion of the environmental mother and holding, Matte-Blanco's formulations point to the essential role of the environment and receptive others in managing intense affects as an alternative to falling into psychotic states.

From a postmodern perspective, Sass (1992) suggests that chronic schizophrenia rather than arising from an unleashing of primitive passions that overwhelm rationality, arises from an exaggeration of the postmodern cultural tide to valorize thinking and introspection at the expense of emotional connections with others. It is the vertiginous spin of the hypertrophied intellect of the subject unheld by emotional relatedness that precipitates the fall into the black hole of psychosis.

All of these analytic perspectives on the development of and ongoing emotional life of the person, while reflecting important differences of perspective imply a common denominator that involves an inherent incompleteness of the self and much less of a clear distinction between the normal mind of the individuated rational self and the pathological irrational mind of the psychotic. Like Winnicott's assertion that 'there is no such thing as a baby,' they all seem to converge on the principle that psychosis cannot be understood as an affair of an individual standing alone. Bion (1992) has suggested that each individual no matter how ostensibly bizarre or sane has both a psychotic and non-psychotic personality.

The relationship between the group nature of being and psychosis

In his seminal work, *Experiences in Groups* (1961), Bion joined Aristotle by asserting that man is essentially a political group animal. The development of humanness arises from emotional involvement in group life. The relationship with the group begins with the relationship with the maternal other or breast. Mother not only provides food and other biological imperatives necessary for physical survival but it is through her socialized self and her maternal capacity for reverie, holding, containing, and emotional responsiveness that she imparts the non-verbal and verbal language of her group culture which becomes the foundation for becoming a person. The mother–infant dyad is not a closed system but is permeated by the group culture in which it is embedded. From this perspective social group psychology precedes individual psychology. The organism becomes a person through an ongoing dialectic between the individual's uniqueness and the group. Foulkes (1975) advanced the perspective that the mind of the individual is social and in contrast to the brain does not exist as a separate entity encased in a skull. It exists rather as a nodal point in a matrix of interconnected minds.

The individual mind and the group mind mutably constitute each other. Like the moebius strip, the notion that there is a distinct boundary between the inside and the outside of the mind turns out to be an illusion that emerges and recedes as one moves along its contours. From a Foulkesian perspective (Pines 1978), when sufficient tension arises between the individual and the group, the individual becomes a focal point of disturbance in the field. Bion has identified the dilemmas and precariousness that arise from our nature as group animals. According to Bion, while group membership is imperative, man is also at the same time at war with his groupishness. While the group provides the nutrient waters from which the self emerges and is sustained, it also continually threatens to drown the self in its sea of basic assumptions. In his review section of *Experiences in Groups* in which he integrates his insights about group process with Kleinian dynamics, Bion provides a link between group process and psychosis. As the symbiotic mother of infancy recedes into the background, it is the group which increasingly becomes the container that protects its members from nameless dread and annihilation. However, it is the inevitable frustrations and gaps inherent in group life that stir the most threatening and painful emotions.

Bion (1961) has noted 'The adult must establish emotional contact with the group in which he lives. This task appears as formidable to the adult as the relationship with the breast is to the infant and the demands of the task are revealed in his regression' (p 141). In Bion's bifocal theory of groups, group basic assumptions exist like currents under the surface of the work group, endlessly forming and shifting in all groups regardless of size or reason for being – from the small family group to the macro groups like institutions or organizations or nations. From his use of the Kleinian vertex Bion describes the Basic Assumption Groups as instinctive defensive reactions to psychotic anxiety. They cohere out of a sea of projective and introjective identifications from its members. Bion suggests that at an unconscious level the group is experienced by its members as the contents of the mother's body with its coveted prizes and medusa-like terrors. They continually pose sphinx-like riddles to the work group which must be answered well enough, consciously or unconsciously, so as to allow a viable working marriage between the rational and irrational process. Just as in the mind of the Kleinian infant, the group must preserve the group as breast against destructive greed, envy, and hatred through primitive mechanisms of paranoid-schizoid defenses that also allow space for a functioning work group. Under sufficiently stressful circumstances the basic assumption group can so dominate the work group that the group devolves into the 'terrible mother' which is ready to devour or dehumanize any or all of its children in order to preserve itself and its cultural illusions that are extreme variations on the basic assumptions of dependency, pairing, fight/flight and oneness. Lawrence *et al.* (1996) have identified a fifth basic assumption, Me(ness), which paradoxically is a shared group illusion that persons and their psychology can exist as separate self-sufficient islands. This fifth basic assumption seems to be on the rise in tandem with increase in a sense of failed dependency of the family and other institutions which makes schizoid forms of relating more the rule than the exception – fertile ground for chronic psychosis (Miller 1993). In its most malignant and destructive form, the fifth basic assumption is captured in the sentiment, 'I'd rather starve than feed those lazy no good bastards next to me.'

Group basic assumptions are double edged. They can exert destructive influence by reducing complexities to banal simplicities, and distort reality in ways that can rival the most florid delusion of the psychotic individual. On the other hand they can provide energy for the creative aspects of high culture that impart meaning and structure to the nihilistic chaos latent in the experience of being human. In their most malignant forms, basic assumptions can envelope whole nations in belief systems in which scapegoats are experienced as bizarre objects – such as disgusting body parts, body functions or non human things. Through the most primitive psychotic process groups can engage in wholesale torture and murder of dehumanized others while as individuals all the trappings of sanity are retained including the absence of criteria for a DSM diagnoses. High culture and highly developed rationality is no insurance against the breakthrough of psychotic process in groups whose record of mayhem and destructiveness has dwarfed the destructiveness of individuals who qualify as clinically psychotic. In the middle of the twentieth century, Germany, recognized as aesthetically and scientifically advanced as any culture in the west, perpetrated the holocaust. Scholars have argued that this horror was not just the work of a few psychopathic madmen, but enthusiastically and widely participated in by the population (Goldhagen 1996; Glass 1997). Although it has been customary to focus on the pathology of Germans and aberrant German culture, the history of the twentieth century with its material scientific achievements has been replete with other holocausts and ethnic cleansing fueled by very similar mad black holes in the group mind that can be considered as tantamount to group psychosis. Institutional psychiatry has not been immune from being handmaidens of group madness: witness the documented role of 'reputable' psychiatrists in Germany, Russia, and Serbia/Croatia. In Germany, psychiatrists and other physicians embraced the eugenics that found the mentally ill, homosexuals, Jews and Gypsies genetically unworthy of life: but whose bodies and brains were worthy of study post-mortem. In the United States during slavery runaway slaves were given a psychiatric diagnosis ('drapetomania') that pathologized their desire for freedom (Pope and Johnson 1987, p.387). The tendency to confuse the madness of the individual with the madness of the group is explored in the novel *The White Hotel* by D.M.

Thomas, as a fictional Freud analyzes apocalyptic dreams of a patient as evidence of her psychotic oedipal psychopathology rather than as early warnings coming from the unconscious life of the unfolding social catastrophe.

The nonrational, and in its most extreme form, psychosis is the not exclusive property of the individual or the group. From a Winnicottian perspective the differentiating developing individual as the infant with the mother must in phantasy be able continually to murder the group but must have it continually reappear 'to say hello.' However, the group, too intent on its survival, poses a phantasied and real threat to murder the troublesome individual. The rational and the nonrational aspects of the individual and group exist in a dialectical relationship in which they both support and threaten each other. The nonrational mind grapples with raw experience closest to what Lacan termed the real or what Bion described as 'unalphabetized beta elements.'

The rational part of the mind by contrast metabolizes and symbolizes raw experience into tamer and more differentiated forms that can be spoken in the language of reason. What determines which is foreground and which is background? Just as dreams can either provide peaceful guardians of sleep, timely wake-up calls to realities not noticed by the conscious rational mind, or devolve into pathological nightmares, the eruption of the irrational in the individual or the group can exert both constructive and destructive influence. What determines whether the nonrational aspects of the group process serves as building blocks and inspiration for high culture and a necessary ordering of what otherwise be an overwhelming chaos or spawns scapegoating and pathologizing of individuals? What determines whether the emergence of the irrationality identified in individuals catalyzes creativity or alerts the group to unnoticed menace or traps the individual into a stagnating and destructive clinical psychosis? When is the dance between the irrationality of the individual and the group a creative affair and when does it become a dance of death?

Bion (1977) offers some interesting responses to these questions. He formulated three types of relationship between individuals (mystics) who introduce inspirational and creative but disruptive ideas (the uncontained) and the establishment (container) which is devoted to the familiar ways of being and thinking. The relationship can be *symbiotic* in which the individual and the group mutually enhance each other. The uncontained is contained. The group endures revolutionary catastrophic change and is positively transformed while the mystic is appreciated and supported. A *commensal* relationship is a second possibility in which the mystic and the group coexist but neither benefit from each other. A third possibility is a *parasitic* relationship in which the individual and the group are mutually destructive. Freud as a genius was able to form a predominantly symbiotic relationship with a group (a psychoanalytic establishment) in which insights about the unconscious irrational aspects of the mind were contained and metabolized leading to transformations in western culture. Christ as a mystic was betrayed and crucified by the group but later his revolutionary ideas were incorporated into the group through an established church. Dostoevesky reflecting on the instability of these relationships imagined in his tale 'The Grand Inquisitor' that on Christ's return during the Spanish Inquisition, he was thrown into jail, again establishing a parasitic relationship.

The acutely psychotic individual can be understood as a vulnerable mystic in a desperate search for a container to deal with bombardments from the Real which have not been contained within themselves or the family. If he can form symbiotic links with others, both the psychotic and the group can be enhanced. On the other hand, if the psychotic in the throes of catastrophic change is not afforded symbiotic connections, emotional petrification results. Emotional links within the self of the psychotic and between the psychotic and the group are attacked and either deadened or frozen in destructive hate characteristic of commensal and parasitic forms of relationship. The unaccommodated agitated mystic is in danger of becoming chronically psychotic. The boundaries of his mind become fixed around a deviant solipsistic inner world of bizarre objects that is estranged from the world of others. He attempts to resolve the war with his groupishness by murdering the group permanently with the tragic loss of the holding, containing, love, and work possibilities inherent in the group nature of being. The family and the larger group are at risk of denying what perils the collective by splitting if off into the psychotic. Rather than using the psychotic member as a mystic to help incorporate new realities by suffering catastrophic change together, the family or the larger collective resorts to damage control through a reciprocal denial, splitting, projective identification that results in sacrificing the emotional life of one or more of its members.

Although clinical psychosis can seem to occur abruptly like Athena springing from the head of Zeus, there is compelling evidence that it more often develops insidiously as a complex systemic group process involving the psychotic individual, the mother, the family, and the society. Walker and Levine (1990) have shown that adults diagnosed as schizophrenics in adulthood can be identified blindly from childhood home movies suggesting that the path toward a psychotic way of life begins much earlier than the eruption of the first clinical psychotic episode which usually occurs in late adolescence or early adulthood. In a sophisticated attempt to overcome the legacy of the Cartesian mind-body split, Michael Robbins (1993) has delineated a hierarchical systems model to explain the development of schizophrenia in terms of a complex interaction between biologically determined predispositions and mutually constituting relationships with the primary caretaker, the family and the culture.

The primary parental caretaker might either confront and ameliorate her infant's constitutionally determined tendencies to elaborate vulnerabilities into schizophrenic character traits and teach him more mature ways of coping, or she might unconsciously stimulate the efflorescence of these traits and help to create a state which is pathologically symbiotic for her and vegetative or parasitic for her child in which they are simultaneously exploited and compensated for. (Robbins 1993, p.189)

Robbins goes on to make the case that at the next higher level of organization in the natural history of schizophrenia, the future schizophrenic and his family adapt to pathological elements in each other that establish a pathological symbiotic family group which becomes the matrix for the flowering of clinical schizophrenia.

The vulnerable child's involvement in the group relations of the nuclear and extended family can serve to rectify this skew, or propel the child further down a path toward schizophrenia. In this respect the family group can be seen as a primary training ground for both healthy group relations and schizophrenia. The move from the symbiotic mother–infant relationship to the more complex psychology of the multiperson field of the family is crucial to become a feeling, thinking member of peer, school, family, community and work groups of adult life. Failure to take this step leaves the child excessively dependent on the primary caretaker, without role flexibility and capacity to contend with competition, jealousy, envy, and other complex emotions inherent in group life.

Many investigators and pioneering family therapists have considered the family a powerful influential agent in the creation of a schizophrenic. Sullivan (1962) traced delusional and hallucinatory behavior in schizophrenics to severe disapproval for expression of feelings, impulses or traits that were considered 'Not Me' in the family belief system. Lidz, Fleck and Cornelius (1965) identified patterns of relationships in the family (*skew* and *schism*) that maneuvered children into pathological roles designed to hold failed marriages together. Bateson (1956) and his colleagues formulated the double bind hypothesis in which coded psychotic communication was the only vehicle for expression of negative feeling in a family in which fundamental contradictions and conflicts could not be directly addressed (without the threat of expulsion). They also hypothesized that families could be understood as systems in which the imperative to maintain a familiar equilibrium could force vulnerable family members into pathological roles. Wynne *et al.* (1958) identified a *rubber fence* phenomena that isolates schizophrenogenic families from meaningful communication with outsiders and a pseudo-mutuality that alienates family members from each other on the inside. Bowen identified pathological relational patterns that in three generations produced a schizophrenic member. Further analysis of studies of adopted children genetically predisposed for schizophrenia revealed that in most instances a pathological family environment was a necessary ingredient to bring the schizophrenic syndrome into being. Searles (1965) suggested that schizophrenics sacrifice themselves by introjecting the pathology of their parents out of love and their need to preserve their parents as sane. Shapiro (1985) and colleagues applied Bion's group model to the analysis of families with borderline and schizophrenic members. He shows how group projective and introjective identification, driven by the need to defend against denied emotional pain stirred by loss and individuation, led families to install vulnerable children into pathological roles. Greenspan (1989) has demonstrated that early detection and intervention with at-risk mother–infant pairs and families can help to form developmentally effective bonds that may well head off the emergence in later life of a schizophrenic disorder.

While the above studies reflect a diversity of theoretical orientations including psychoanalysis, systems theory, infant research, and cybernetics, they share important common denominators. They focus on the social psychological domains, and imply that schizophrenia is not a single-body biological phenomenon but exists in an interactive disturbed social field molded by collaborative unconscious group dynamic processes. For a multitude of reasons such as constitutional vulnerability, birth order, 'bad fit' and characteristics that draw projections of parental introject, the preschizophrenic becomes stuck in roles that serve vital purposes within family dynamics but are maladaptive in other social contexts and block psychosocial development.

Furthermore, according to Robbins, society is not objective about its criteria for defining who is psychotic and who is not. At the highest societal level of organization, mental health institutions may align with the family's attempt to maintain equilibrium at the expense of developmental opportunities for their schizophrenic member, or align with the schizophrenic's needs for autonomy at the expense of family and social order. From this perspective it seems fitting that modern psychiatry has defined emotional disturbance as disorder.

The group as treatment

To the extent to which the treatment of psychosis is approached not as the treatment of a disease within a medical model, but a disordering dis-ease with disruptive uncontained emotions and thoughts, two divergent ways to use the group as therapy emerge. The group can be used as a powerful medium to help restore order in the system which defines the patient as a disruptive focal disturbance in groups in which the patient is significantly involved; or the psychotherapy group can be used to promote the patient's growth and development which is likely to have further disruptive disordering effects described by Bion as catastrophic change for not only the patient, but the family, and the treatment system itself. This dichotomy seldom if ever occurs in pure culture in real treatment systems. The restoration of order usually involves some growth; and, conversely, some restoration of order is often essential to a growth process. However, whether growth or order is embraced as the primary value has profound implications for how the therapy group is conducted.

Group as a training ground to promote adaptation

Group therapists who assume that psychosis emanates from an intrapsychic dynamic or pathophysiology in isolated diseased minds or brains incline group treatments toward the restoration of order, and the reduction of symptoms experienced as disruptive. From the perspective of an objective observer of a determinist universe, investigation tends to be limited to exploring linear causes rather than recursivity, reasons or meaning. Hallucinations, delusions, and other positive psychotic symptoms are treated as essentially symptoms of a disease to be suppressed or eradicated rather than as understood as communication. Group norms which limit spontaneous emotional expression and medication tend to discourage the kind of emotional links of love, hate, and knowing (L, H, K) described by Bion (1988) within and between members. Behavioral modification and educative interventions can help members build more adaptive false selves that conform to the established culture's consensual reality. Groups that work successfully from this paradigm enable increased (even if emotionally shallow) connection with family and work groups. A reduction in manifest deviancy also increases the individual's group connection at unconscious levels in culturally sanctioned basic assumption life as an alternative to the role of mad pariah or container of what cannot be contained within the normative culture.

Ironically, this increased joining in normative basic assumptions decreases empathy for other deviants and sometimes encourages patients to scapegoat other patients. Kanas (1986) has shown in his meta-analysis of treatment of schizophrenia that group psychotherapy contributes significantly to positive treatment outcome. However, most clinical studies use criteria for success, such as reduction of relapse rate and positive symptoms, which favor adaptation over development of the self of the patient and quality of life considerations. Most psychotherapy groups that treat chronic psychotics are not designed to withstand or contain the intense emotional turbulence involved in the transformation of psychotic experience. They are either short term, infrequent, or are conducted by therapists in training who turnover frequently. Medication compliance is often a central focus of the group work. The development and exploration of the role of family except as assistants in the treatment who are innocent with regard to perpetuating psychopathology manifest in the designated patient is minimal (Kuipers 1979). This results in what Robbins (1993) calls iterative rather than mutative treatment. The psychotic intrapsychic and interpersonal attacks on linking are iterated in a treatment in which both patients and treaters avoid and undermine emotional engagement with each other. The result is an impersonal mirroring rather than transformations. Robbins stresses that iterative treatment is not necessarily inhumane. It may diminish emotional suffering and restore stability in families which in his view are generally aligned with conservative forces in society that oppose the chaos that ensues when attempts are made to integrate too much deviancy into the social order. The patient in effective treatment of this type, by encapsulating the disruptive aspects of his personality, is often able to establish a more stable relationship to his family and other social groups. At least in the short term less labor intensive therapies reduce financial and social costs exacted. The non-integration of madness from a sociological perspective serves a vital boundary function by defining what is not considered sane within the establishment. It diminishes the suffering of pain. However, is this approach less costly in financial and human terms in the long run?

The psychotherapy group as an arena for transformation of the psychotic and uncontained: the mutative psychotherapy group

While in many respects principles of group psychotherapy that are derived from intrapsychic, interpersonal, existential, object relations, self-psychology and group as a social system perspectives with neurotic patients also obtain with the treatment of psychotic patients in the mutative psychotherapy group the psychotic patient who is carrying what could not be contained or metabolized both threatens the equanimity of naturally occurring groups and also suffers on its behalf. In order to serve as an arena for transformation of what has been dismissed as too threatening or bizarre, the mutative psychotherapy group must be able to survive the unleashing of intense primitive emotions and discover or create human meaning out of what at first encounter seems meaningless or non-human.

Because many schizophrenics have their first psychotic break precipitated by a disruption of the tie to the symbiotic mother, they are unconsciously in a desperate search for another. The impetus to find the mother in the group can be a powerful antidote to despair and incentive toward a healthier adult life that involves acquiring the capacity to assume part of the mothering responsibility for the self and other members. However, since the preoedipal symbiotic mother is also associated with the bad breast or terrible destructive mother, joining with 'her' feels highly dangerous. Any therapeutic group culture that aspires to grapple with madness must provide space for the experience and transformation of primal rage. Semrad, famous for his intuitive work with schizophrenics and residents at Harvard made the observation that the schizophrenic chooses psychosis and estrangement as an alternative to homicide or suicide (Robbins 1993, p.125). The failure to integrate primal rage into the personality contributes to the arrest of emotional development and the sense that one cannot be real in the world without inviting catastrophe. During acute psychotic upheavals rage is channeled into phantasmagoric struggles with bizarre persecuting demonic figures and cataclysmic scenarios of world destruction. In more overtly quiet periods, rage is directed inward to subvert the agencies of the mind necessary to experience emotion, process experience and maintain links with internal and external objects – an insidious murder of the experiencing socially connected self. For example, a patient who sat for months like a statue of Buddha with her eyes closed later reported a dream in which eyes, ears, and mouths were dissolving in a vat of acid. She associated this dream with her belief that if she could rid herself of the organs of language she might be able to find a safe place in the world. For many patients rage is omnipresent, threatening to destroy whatever is good inside them or in others on whom they depend for survival. For the patient to be able to experience this rage directed not at the self or delusional objects but at others in the group, and then to discover that the self and the group are still present to 'say hello' is a crucial step into the world of group relations with real others, a developmental milestone that perhaps never occurred adequately with primary caretakers.

The lifeless emptiness that tends to pervade groups of chronically psychotic patients often results from unaddressed paranoid and depressive anxieties that overwhelm defenses and collapse the space for experience. As members begin to trust that the emergence of their hate and love will not destroy themselves or others, the group can be used increasingly as a stage for improvisational theater in which patients begin to take on characteristics of borderline patients. With the sense that the group as container is good enough, rigid psychotic defenses loosen. Many of the most damaging traumas of childhood cannot be remembered or worked with until they are experienced in action. Group members can now enlist each other as characters in their respective inner world, tragic paranoid and depressive inner world dramas as an alternative to schizoid slumber or entanglement with bizarre objects outside the room.

Through a flow of introjective and projective identifications in the basic assumption dramas, whatever is problematic for the group members such as aggression, dependency sexuality, envy, and jealousy can be externalized and personified in unconsciously chosen others with the valence to comply – a less impersonal and impenetrable defense than fixed delusions. Group members locate in each other, the therapist or the group-as-a-whole, parts of themselves that resist integration because of the prohibitions of harsh and exacting superegos. The fact that the unintegrated bits of the psyche are being experienced in the room rather than in psychologically inaccessible outer space presents new opportunities but also new pitfalls. It is here that the dynamics of the families of origin are recreated. Unconscious maneuvering places group members into familiar strait-jacketed roles of scapegoat, identified crazy, sadistic bully, sacrificing masochist, pervert, and the greedy monopolist, playing out primal versions of group basic assumptions. The flow between the group dynamics and the unintegrated part of the personalities of the members fills a transitional group space. If the basic assumption dramas can be contained within the group and worked interpretatively, it becomes possible for members to develop empathic understanding for the scapegoat in their midst and an appreciation of how they maneuver each other into pathological roles that condemn individuals for what should be a shared responsibility. This understanding and empathy facilitates the reintrojection of what has been projected in less toxic form with movement toward an integrative depressive capacity to experience oneself and others as whole objects.

The therapist's skill in negotiating the basic assumption world of projective and introjective identification in which he is also often an unwitting player can make the difference between a group that is therapeutic and one that traps its members in pathological roles and deepens despair (Hinshelwood 1987). The therapist needs to strike an artful balance between a permissiveness that allows the dramas to unfold and a willingness to intervene to protect members at risk of becoming casualties (Resnik 1994). Groups which are conducted on strict rules prohibiting disruptive behavior or hostility, or impede the emergence of psychotic material by reactive reality checks may foster normative behavior at the cost of leaving the disturbed affect-laden inner worlds of members relatively untouched. In the course of treatment it often becomes apparent that most schizophrenic patients have lived in their psychotic capsules in part to avoid overwhelming shame and guilt – hence their tendency to react to any intervention as criticism or condemnation. For patients to use interpretations about the self or the group, interpretations must be framed in a way that conveys empathic acceptance rather than criticism or cold neutrality. This requires a more personal warmth than is commonly associated with the picture of the 'detached Bion' process consultant.

Like the developmentally creative transitional world of mother and infant described by Winnicott, the effective psychotherapy group for psychotics should not be deadened by a solemnity and over-concern with propriety but allowed to become a transitional space for creative play in which fixed delusions can become the stuff of creative illusion. This allows for a play between the inner and outer worlds in which it need not be so clear what is inner and what is outer. The opportunity for play in the good enough container is not just play with mother group but the opportunity to play with peers.

The psychotherapy group that assumes that psychotic phenomena are not meaningless epiphenomena and that clinical psychosis cannot be adequately treated as a disorder of isolated minds or brains, shifts its perspective toward a view that the individual psychotic patient is not an isolate with meaningless suffering but a radically disturbed part of an intersubjective field. However, at the same time that the group-as-a-whole phenomena are embraced as an antidote to the solipsism of chronic psychosis, the group must also afford a secure place for the psychotic patient as an autonomous thinking feeling person who has the right to direct his own life. In the zeal to eradicate disease, a constructive dialectic tension between the individual and the group inherent in group life can readily be lost. The uncontained aspects of the patient are at risk of becoming the enemy which must be annihilated or fled from rather than understood. To apprehend more fully the person of the psychotic, it is necessary to appreciate that he is more than anything else a human being with multiple and often contradictory characteristics. As Bion (1992) has underscored, there are both psychotic and a non-psychotic dimensions of the personality. Without adequate response and containment of his emotional pain and anxiety by significant persons in his environment, the patient relies heavily on the defensive mechanisms of the psychotic part of the personality with its massive projection and splitting and reversal of sense perceptions from intake to output creating non-human bizarre objects and what to others is experienced as delusional versions of what is real. The attack on the feeling thinking part of the personality resulting in a deadened state of being which also undermines emotional links with others is another disabling mechanism to reduce unbearable suffering. Particularly when the opossum-like defenses predominate, it becomes easier to assume that the patient is devoid of common sense. 'The schizophrenic patient has common sense but makes uncommon use of it' (Bion 1992, p.103). The patient does stop at red lights on the street. The psychotic seemingly hopelessly out of contact with reality can respond with alacrity and competence to emergency situations.

When groups have developed a feeling of being safe enough to endure the turbulence inherent in emotional links, other parts of patients' personalities emerge. Psychotic patients are able to contribute movingly deep empathic reflections about other patients and the therapist that often surpass the capacities of normals. What is most likely to be lost in the haze of pathologizing the person of the psychotic are their capacities as mystics in which they offer the group insights in the form of strange unfamiliar metaphors. Packed into the bizarre and the delusional are inchoate apprehensions from the real that have been censored or barred from consideration of the reality of the family or the normative culture. Family tragedies that have been well known secrets that may have plagued the family for generations are alluded to elliptically within the apparently delusional rambling that are easily dismissed as crazy. That these metaphors are often presented in forms that are concrete and confuse the symbol with the thing in itself makes it easy to dismiss them as meaningless rather than important work in progress. Identified psychotics do not have a monopoly on madness, but the normative group whether family, workplace, religion, nation, or world can be pervaded by covert madness that catches vulnerable individuals in its web. Exploration of the perceived madness outside the psychotherapy group is not just treated as defense for psychotics who have been marginalized but as grist for the psychotherapy group mill and a potential contribution to the larger social discourse. Hallucinated voices can be understood as unmetabolized residues of interpersonal and intergroup traumatic hostile and destructive experience both from in the immediate family, the work place and the larger societal stage that are inaccessible to most normals having been more encapsulated in the social unconscious. Rather than suppress or eradicate these often frightening or violent voices, conversations with them in the group can promote digestion and putting them into a perspective that makes them less dominant in the personality. In my experience, even mega-doses of antipyschotic medications do not eliminate voices but only make them more inaccessible where they can damage the personality more insidiously.

The shift in perspective moves the group toward the development of a culture that is distinctly different and to some degree counter to the prevailing one and the culture of groups that emphasize adaptation and conformity.

Coleridge, Keats, Shakespeare, and Bion have spoken to what I regard as essential beliefs and capacities of group culture that are crucial for effective work with psychotic patients. It is essential to be able to suspend disbelief in order to learn from texts that are on the frontier of the normative culture – what has been responded to as meaningless and bizarre. Shakespeare in his genius was able to imagine almost an infinite number of passion-filled perspectives moving beyond the frontiers of establishment truth. Kafka (1989) revisited Bateson's formulation of the double bind hypothesis. As a modification he suggested that the closure of a transitional space in families to allow for validation of multiple realities becomes a fertile ground for psychosis. The use of psychotic defenses and obscure metaphors serves as a way to express difference within an intolerant culture.

Bion (1977) took inspiration from the poet Keats who stressed the importance of negative capability. The therapist who has faith that enduring the anxiety and mystery of experience without irritable reaching after fact or reason affords group members a rare opportunity and a model for growth. Particularly with psychotic patients it is essential for the therapist to be able to live in the unfamiliar world of the patients – like a visitor on a alien planet, to enable the patient to also join the therapist and other group members in the more conventional world of planet earth. Often what is being communicated is not translatable into the mode of the symbolic (what Bion calls K) but can only be apprehended (what Bion called O). A responsive face and eyes might be at times more meaningful than a verbal response. Too quickly putting shared experience into words may convey to the patient that the therapist fears living in the realm of experience before words, a domain where much went wrong for the patient in the beginning. Psychotic patients as they leave their isolation can be uncannily empathic with each other at levels that may not be possible for the therapist. Bion recommends that the therapist develop the negative capacity, or a reverie without intention or desire approaching a negative hallucinosis, particularly when working with psychotic patients. This state of consciousness in the therapist allows for the reception of the patients' constructive use of projective identification, a process that probably misfired in infancy. From this perspective, delusional or hallucinatory experience, weird dress, and strange nonverbal behaviors are considered not just as pathology or regression requiring additional medication but as trial balloons sent from besieged, semipetrified selves testing the responsivity of the group to news about catastrophes past, current, or impending.

The transition from the apprehended experience to the domain of symbolic and metaphoric communication is a next step. It falls on the therapist to catch seemingly disconnected threads floating randomly around the room and weave them into connected tapestries that reveal shared meaning. Flirting with reclaiming split-off parts of self to establish links with each other is slow work. Group members in their ambivalence, like Ulysses' wife Penelope, weave and unweave the metaphorical tapestries that bind them to each other. The poignant question often at this juncture is: is there an afterlife? That is, can there be an emotional life in the human group after catastrophic loss of the symbiotic other? Can relationships be based on interdependence rather than on abject dependency?

For the therapist to help transform a group culture initially dominated by schizophrenic despair about the efficacy of human relationships into one of hope and connection, he must be able to serve as a container into which patients projectively identify overwhelming feeling states that played a major role in driving them into psychotic fortresses in their early life. These feeling states are often amplified by the group process and stir disturbing archaic feelings in the therapist. Ordinarily under repression, these feeling states are very difficult to bear alone no matter how well analyzed one may be. Headaches, backache, tightness in the abdomen, boredom, sleepiness, irritability, insomnia, shame, or guilt and the fear of being driven crazy are indications that the therapist is receptive to the unmetabolized pain of the group members mixed with his own. When these symptoms persist, it is a warning that the therapist needs focused self-analysis or the help of others to transform the inarticulate pain into understanding or be at risk of joining a culture of despair. Often this is the juncture where the therapist detaches from the emotional interchange and moves toward resignation or distancing behavioral techniques as a method of self-cure.

The group therapist must be Janus faced. The task of transforming emotional isolates into cohesive group members inside the boundaries of the group is formidable work, but often maintaining the integrity of the boundary between the group and its environment can be the greatest challenge of all. Pressures from families, institutions, and society threaten to collapse the space required for developmental work either through withholding necessary support or direct opposition.

Often the schizophrenic mutes his radical dissent from the family and the social order and embraces a discrediting pathological role in return for receiving sustenance. A developmentally sound therapeutic group or program challenges this collusion by offering the patient an opportunity to suffer his pain, learn from his experience, take on responsibility for his own being and speak with a more credible voice. However, shedding his role as his family and society's deranged madman stirs conflict between the patients' developmental interests and the vested interests in the status quo of the patient's and therapist's benefactors.

Enmeshed in the grip of a need/fear dilemma (Burnham, Gibson and Gladstone 1969), the schizophrenic radically renounces bonds with others, yet at the same time relies on others for the basics of existence. It seems eminently understandable that despite conscious intentions to treat, institutions mandated to minimize and control social disturbance and burdened with inadequate resources have little time or energy to contend creatively or therapeutically with this paradox. The critical element in addressing it is to provide an environment that is containing and holding which also allows space for autonomy and learning through experience. However, often the pressures of the primary task of social control leads mental health institutions to bypass interaction with the patient's autonomous self to settle for false self-compliance and imposition of order. Group programs based on the principle that some chaos and turbulence is inherent in developmental process is likely to be experienced as unruly and subversive by the larger system. Tensions and conflicts at the boundaries of such programs and their institutional and social environment must be managed so that necessary connections are not severed while the integrity of the therapeutic culture is maintained (Singer *et al.* 1979; Miller and Rice 1967). Just as technically competent surgery performed in a field of pathogenic bacteria may be doomed no matter how skilled the operating team, so group therapy in a social institutional context dominated by antidevelopmental dynamics is also unlikely to do more than create non-productive dissonance.

Conversely, group therapies composed of predominantly neurotic patients can be deeply enriched by a patient with a psychotic disorder when the unusual experience of the psychotic member is not dismissed as crazy but as a potential catalyst to explore encapsulated psychotic parts of the neurotic members. In my experience there have been many neurotic patients who harbor a fear of madness linked to the shadowy presence of a mad relative that tends to constrict areas of their personalities. For example, a schizophrenic member of a group of neurotics slipped into a psychotic state repeatedly when new members were introduced into the group. As the oldest of eight children, she experienced traumatic abandonment each time a sibling was born and she was thrust into the role of caretaker which overwhelmed her. In later life she developed a delusional belief that there was a family conspiracy to kill or abort children in her extended family.

The working through of her psychotic experience in the group precipitated by the 'birth' of new members helped her metabolize her delusional belief and enabled other members to discover encapsulated traumas of their own related to envy and murderous impulses toward their family members that had been exerting a constricting effect on their personalities.

Clinical illustration

The following group vignettes are taken from a twice a week outpatient psychotherapy group with patients who are phasing out of a long-term intensive day therapeutic community, a less restrictive alternative to long-term hospitalization that utilizes multimodal group therapies including psychodrama, art, music, family dynamic group psychotherapy, patient government and community meetings (Skolnick 1994). Varying in age from late twenties to early fifties, all since early adulthood had frequent or prolonged psychiatric hospitalizations where they received diagnoses of schizophrenia, schizoaffective, or borderline disorder. These patients on admission to day treatment were all taking moderate to large doses of neuroleptic, mood stabilizers, and antidepressant drugs. They were unmarried, unemployed and while some were living with family they were all essentially estranged and socially isolated. While each of the patients on admission appeared calm to the point of apathy, some probing revealed that all were actively hallucinating and clung to beliefs that most would consider delusional. Ms R experienced herself surrounded by raging black evil things that swarmed around her like a cloud of hornets, Mr A only seldom spoke or made eye contact burying himself in his Bible that was always close at hand. Ms M alluded to voices commanding her to murder or cut off penises of men who got too close. Ms L claimed that nothing was wrong in a barely audible voice despite months of aimlessly wandering on the streets. Ms B insisted that her brain was constantly being assaulted by forces that were implanting bad and destructive thoughts. Ms J acknowledged that her quietness was a precaution against the cult that was everywhere trying to entrap and discredit her by spreading malicious gossip. Ms N experienced herself chosen by God to perform a mission for humanity but constantly diverted by assaults from secular authorities, all of whom seemed to resemble her autocratic father. After an average of two to five years in the day treatment program the patients were either not taking or taking considerably less psychotropic drugs, were living independently, were working part time or enrolled in a rehabilitation program, were less socially isolated, more emotionally responsive, but all continued to wrestle with what would likely be diagnosed as persistence of a psychotic disorder. With the exception of two patients who had brief crisis hospitalizations, each had broken the patten of revolving door hospitalizations since entering the day program.

At the time of the vignettes members had been attending the group regularly for about two years. The therapist conducting the group has consistently encouraged members to express feelings, thoughts, dreams, fantasies, and hallucinatory experience. He has stressed the usefulness of keeping a dialogue going while also emphasizing that it is up to each member to decide what to say or not say. All experience of all members including the therapist is assumed to be meaningful until proven otherwise. The only stipulated ground rules are maintaining confidentiality and a prohibition on violence or standing threats of violence.

[The group begins in tense silence. Ms J is lying on the floor behind a desk. The other members are shifting uneasily in their chairs. Ms N breaks the silence in a barely audible voice.]

Ms N: I want to change chairs or close the blinds. There's too much light and it hurts my eyes.

Mr A: If you do that I won't be able to see the expression on your face.

Ms B: [peering up from notes that she was intently writing]: I don't want my expression seen. It's dangerous to be seen. Those tricky forces lurking around might get some nasty ideas if they knew more about what I'm thinking. I believe that the forces have already taken over Dr S because he said some hurtful things last meeting that he would never say. Does anybody mind if I turn on the AC [air conditioning]?

Ms M: I'm cold already. Why don't you take off your coat and sweater?

Ms B: I want more ventilation.

Ms L: I can't hear with the AC on.

Ms J: I don't think I want to be heard. It is safer to keep your thoughts to yourself anyway.

Ms N: This is the one time I agree with J. When I'm heard I just get attacked.

Ms B: J get off the floor. Don't you know that is rude. My father would never let me do that!

Ms J: Fuck you!

Ms B: Fuck you too!

Dr S: I think that J might be telling us without words that she has been floored. Sometimes words just don't seem to work. J was telling us last time how despairing and suicidal she felt [turning to J] but maybe J you felt you didn't get enough response from us. It seems that in a way everyone feels floored today and uneasy about being in the group. The light, temperature, ventilation, the sound, doesn't all seem wrong and maybe goodwill seems to be in short supply. Last time almost everybody was getting help with things that they felt guilt or shame about.

Ms N: I have trouble responding to J. She keeps accusing me of blabbing about what she tells us. I would never do that.

Ms J: Prove it. People on the street know my business. How do they find out? Then the heresy spreads all over town ruining my reputation. This group is vital to me but I can't use it if I can't trust.

[J interrogates several members about what they have said to others assuming that they are guilty of breaking confidentiality until they have proved otherwise. Dr S is reminded of her descriptions of interrogations she experienced from her lawyer father in her home. Other members, after spirited angry protests, begin to withdraw as if to say here we go again. Ms J has frequently taken on the role of prosecuting attorney when the group seems to be warming up too fast for comfort.]

Ms J: If I find out that anyone has talked out of the group I will feel like becoming a sniper!

[She emphasizes 'feel' in what seems like an attempt to intimidate without breaking the group ground rules.]

Dr S: [concerned that murderous feelings are getting out of hand, tries to reinforce ground rules against violence and detoxify through play]: I object your honor! Out of order. I want the court to consider just how many noses J has to spare before we proceed with this trial.

Group: [laughter followed by looks of puzzlement]: What do you mean?

Dr S: J deeply wants to trust so she can get help with feelings that have been plaguing her all her life, but J you seem to be antagonizing everyone going on the kind of heresy evidence that you hate when others do it to you. I think that we go along with the courtroom thing with J leading the way when everybody is scared to go further with things that bring us close, but stir up fear of being attacked or humiliated, or called crazy. M was telling us about voices telling her to cut off my penis and we were helping her understand instead of withdrawing and attacking herself. I thought in the beginning we were trying to get the group to feel right and safe enough to go further, but it hasn't seemed to work yet. Perhaps we might keep trying.

Ms M: I really like you – it's your penis that I hate [M had years of incest with her older brother and the penis is to her a body part filled with destructive projections that interfere with any intimate relations with men].

Ms J: Dr S you are the only one in mental health who tells me to have conversations with my voices and talk about them in the group instead of taking more medication. Are you crazy too? It feels terrible to be dogged by the cult but it's easier than feeling my guilt about the abortion and that my father died the day that I screamed at him.

[A freer discussion follows in which most of the members reflect on how good it feels to be able to talk to others and to have someone to listen to things that they have felt to be nameless, too awful or frightening for speech.]

Ms L: There were so many secrets in my family, but saying them meant all hell would break loose. I was always afraid that my father would have a stroke. When I tried to say it the way I saw it everyone said I shouldn't feel that or that's crazy or worse. It was as if I were invisible and hadn't said anything.

Ms M: I set the curtains on fire to tell my mother about the incest with my brother but she never got it.

Ms B: I always seem to be saying things that my father says are stupid because I fried my brain. Usually I think he's right. I have a chemical imbalance in my brain. Uh oh! I forgot to take my pills. I'll be back in a little while. [B walks out as she often does when negative feelings come up about he father who takes care of her but treats her as if she is retarded. She is actually very thoughtful and articulate when she is not frightened. Others ask her to stay but she leaves.]

Mr A: When they put me in the hospital I refused drugs. When this aid kept pushing me around and I complained they shot me up with thorazine and put me in seclusion. Hey, it doesn't pay to talk about what other people think is crazy unless you want to be carted off.

Ms L: That happened to be too so many times I learned to stop complaining. Just take my medicine and shut up. Sometimes I feel so terrible that being carted off and put to sleep seems like the only thing between me and suicide.

[Ms B returns swallowing some pills.]

Ms J: I think sometimes that we are more normal than the normal. We can talk more about things here than other people can. When I was at the job today, I felt everyone was looking down their noses at me because I don't want to work but I hate my job. You can't ever talk about feelings there unless you want to be fired.

[A warm close feeling seems to envelope the group. However, Mr A does not look up from his bible and shows no sign of involvement. Now it seems to the therapist that he is serving as a brake to the worries about too much intimacy.]

Ms J: Hey the building is closed on Monday because of the holiday. Why don't we meet in that restaurant around the corner?

Ms N: J isn't that setting yourself up? Think about all the cult members that might overhear you.

Ms J: Don't believe all that shit about the cult. It's just my paranoia. [Addressing A, still peering at his Bible.] Just doesn't feel safe until A says something. Damn it, nobody encourages A to talk. People talk for him. [J has had a close friendship with A that for a short time involved sexual intimacy, but sees him now as also an embodiment of her most attacking judgements about herself and her sexuality.]

Ms L: A always thinks he is right and we are wrong. That damn Bible. When he stands up he scares me. He is a big penis. I am late to work because of all those damn men lurking on the street. [L also had incest with her brother. She has acknowledged that she is often desperately trying to live up to her father's standards of purity but doesn't know what to do with her murderous impulses and intense sexual desires. She often prays to be relieved of the her 'sins' – that now seem to her to reside in A and sometimes in Dr S.]

Ms L: Why does J care so much about what A feels? He is just a man!

Dr S: [without thinking about transference and countertransference to him under the surface says spontaneously]: I think we're struggling with some of the worries and dangers that come along with loving.

Ms R: I now remember that my father sodomizing me when I was one – that creep. No wonder I hate men.

Dr. S: [feeling that he may have sodomized the group and feeling defensive]: Sometimes it is hard to tell what goes on in our mind and what actually happens with others.

Subgroup of women: [to the therapist it feels like a band of furies attacking]: You are just a man protecting those bastards – you can't understand!

Ms R: Dr S you are turning into a vampire. You are disgusting.

Dr. S: [feeling knots in his stomach and chest and trying to contain the experience of shame and being treated like a bizarre object without withdrawing or retaliating]: I feel that I may have scarred people by mentioning love without appreciating how dangerous it feels because of past hurts and shame.

Ms R: Dr S you are now turning into a weasel.

[Ms J walks out of the room.]

Ms R: I can tell what is going on in people's genitals and what they look like by looking at faces. Damn it, N, stop flashing your old disgusting vagina! Sometimes you flash your disgusting breast. [R's mother was psychotic and often attacked her for being stupid and ugly. R has recognized that she feels that to keep her mother's love she must conform to her mother's reality even though it means a dead end for herself.] The group is a disgusting vagina that is just trying to suck me in.

[Everyone in the group begins to withdraw. The time for the end of session is approaching and the therapist wrestles with trying to recoup the good group feeling but decides that it is best to end the group on time.]

Dr S: I think we have really made some headway into some very tough stuff today but again it raises fears that we are at risk of getting sucked into the past with its hurts – painful memories with fathers, mothers, brothers, psychiatrists and penises that are hateful or vaginas that suffocate. We have our ways of putting the brakes on when it feels too dangerous in here. See you Friday.

[Everyone returns on Friday, the next scheduled session, with members seeming glad to see each other. The group was killed on Monday but is there to say hello on Friday.]

Like Penelope this group of psychotics weaves and unweaves links of hate, love, and pursuit of knowing about their painful existential realities with each other and the group as a whole. Slipping into delusional capsules, deadened states, or pummelling each other with malignant projections keeps what feels like the hostile world of others and the group at bay either out of despair, dread, or an endless waiting for a Ulysses-like savior. However, the group and its members including the therapist continually revive and weave again. Over the long haul the patients who at first seems unreachable and living in bizarre worlds of their own increasingly become more than anything else human to themselves and each other. Often abruptly leaving their psychotic fortresses they offer each other and themselves penetrating insights and sometimes love that is extremely moving and an antidote to despair.

It can be argued that the rough and tumble described in the group vignettes with its overt expressions of hate, envy and unleashing of primitive projections is the last thing that chronically psychotic patients handicapped by dysfunctional brains need. However, it has been my experience that when many of these patients discover that encapsulated trauma can be experienced and metabolized in the group, and that emotional involvement rather than ending in destruction of themselves or others can lead to deep kindred feelings with fellow human beings, many of the apparent impairments in brain function begin to disappear, and the missing common sense reappears. The psychotherapy group that develops a culture that has faith that all experience can be food for emotional and mental growth and that nameless dread can be named, played with and transformed into meaning is not a panacea but can go a long way toward restoring the unaccommodated to a respectful place as a thinking feeling social being that is not so readily accomplished in individual treatment alone.

The large group

Participation in a large group committed to explore and contain the full spectrum of human experience and suffering rather than promoting pathological regression can be a powerful restorative medium for the estranged psychotic. All of the patients described in the vignette participate in social systems designed to help them survive and live in the community. However, the patients' perspective when it is in conflict with that of the 'providers' is more often than not dismissed as resistance or manifestations of illness rather than deserving a hearing in a social discourse. The large group as microcosm has the potential to be a social space that allows for the voicing of points of view that are ordinarily silenced, marginalized or dismissed as shameful or insane in the society at large. By opening a discourse across what are ordinarily socially constructed barriers between the sick and the well, issues such as economics, class, gender, race and power emerge as important factors in the social dynamics that lock vulnerable individuals into pathological roles. The large group can be thought of as comparable to the classic Greek theater which was an important community process that allowed for the enactment of not just interpersonal conflicts but also an exploration of the predicament of individuals caught in the maelstrom of conflictual social religious and political forces.

The belief that non-directed expressive large group meetings are dis-organizing for psychotic patients and that personal involvement of staff frightens, disillusions, traumatizes and interferes with transference has discouraged their use in psychiatric facilities in recent years. Klein (1993) however, in a review of the literature on large group psychotherapy has noted that in addition to improving the quality of hospital milieux, the benefits of large group psychotherapy with competent leadership may well equal that of small group psychotherapy. Lofgren (1976) has reported that a psychiatric hospital ward organized as group treatment and committed to include all patients regardless of severity of psychotic symptoms in treatment as responsible agents expected to help themselves and others, led to faster recovery from psychosis and more successful post-hospital treatment than traditionally run wards in the same hospital. In my experience benefits strongly outweigh risks. Instead of regressing, psychotic patients often seem to come more alive. Patients do not project or transfer into thin air but target real parts of others and are deeply motivated to heal their therapists as they were with their families (Searles 1965). Patients seldom learn much about therapists that they don't already know, but because of their allegiance to symbiotic politics, they seldom address these issues unless they are encouraged and have a receptive forum that protects them from retaliation. The large group gives the community an opportunity to discover and work through the extent to which patient pathology is an adaptation to the pathology of the staff and the institution, repeating the familiar family dynamic (Skolnick 1994). The community meetings also allow the opening of space to grapple creatively with the dilemmas inherent in the systemic tangles between sickness and dependency that can result in powerful incentives to remain 'sick' in order to make a living. Main (1975) has noted how the use of large group patient–staff meetings are effective in reducing the pathogenic effects of splitting which locates the health in the staff and illness in the patients. Turquet (1974) has observed that psychotic processes are inherent in large groups, organizations and institutions even when the participants are mentally healthy. Without a commitment to identify, recognize, and process scapegoating, the most vulnerable members often become isolates or are maneuvered into caricatured bizarre roles that express and hold psychotic elements of the group. Large group meetings conducted with the aim of enabling all participants to reown projections can help free patients from inflexible roles which have not only been used for their defense but also for the defense of those around them.

Conclusion

Like all other perspectives and modalities of treatment, the group perspective and group therapies are no panacea for psychosis. All groups experience failures. Some patients will not join, drop out prematurely, don't change, or commit suicide. The integration of biological psychological and social perspectives in the same treatment program is desirable if a real bio-psycho-social-developmental model is to be realized. This integration of psychotherapeutic approaches and medication without neutralizing both is too complex to address in the space afforded in this paper but remains more of a challenge than is currently recognized. I have tried to make the case that an understanding of group dynamics, enabling the psychotic to rejoin the group as an emotionally alive contributing person rather than an objectified thing to be repaired, is essential to all meaningful treatment. It may be that chronic psychosis as a modern form of madness will always defy cure since madness and sanity constitute each other. However, when treatment consists too much of a clash of the dogmatism of sanity versus the dogmatism of insanity everyone loses and the tragedy for vulnerable individuals is exacerbated rather than ameliorated.

References

Barham, P.(1984), *Schizophrenia and Human Value*. New York: Basil Blackwell.

Bateson, G., Jackson, D., Haley, J., and Weakland, J. (1956) 'Towards a theory of schizophrenia.' *Behavior Science 1*, 251–264.

Bernauer, J. (1987) 'Oedipus, Freud, Foucault: fragments of an archaeology of psychoanalysis.' In D.M. Levin (ed) *Pathologies of the Modern Self*. New York: New York University Press, 350–84.

Bion, W.R. (1961) *Experience In Groups*. London: Tavistock.

Bion, W.R. (1967) *Second Thoughts*. London: Heinemann.

Bion, W.R. (1977) *Seven Servants*. New York: Jason Aronson, Inc.

Bion, W.R. (1991) *Memoir of the Future*. London: Karnac Books.

Bion, W.R (1988) 'Attacks on Linking.' In E.B. Spillius (ed) *Melanie Klein Today*. London: Routledge.

Bion, W.R. (1992) *Cogitations*. London: Karnac Books.

Bleuler, M. (1978) *Schizophrenic Disorders: long-term patient and family studies* (tr. S.M. Clemens). New Haven and London: Yale University Press.

Bowen, M. (1978) *Family Therapy in Clinical Practice*. New York: Jason Aronson.

Breggin, P. (1991) *Toxic Psychiatry*. New York: Saint Martin's Press.

Breggin, P. (1997) *Brain Disabling Treatments in Psychiatry*. New York: Springer Publishing Company.

Burnham, D. Gibson, R., and Gladstone, A. (1969) *Schizophrenia and the Need–Fear Dilemma*. New York: International Universities Press.

Burrow, T. (1984) *Toward Social Sanity and Human Survival*. New York: Horizon Press.

Carpenter, W.T., Bartko, L.J. and Strauss, J.S. (1978) 'Signs and symptoms as predictors of outcome: a report from the International Pilot Study of Schizophrenia.' *American Journal of Psychiatry 35*, 940–945.

Carpenter, W.T., Buchanan, R. (1995) 'Schizophrenia: introduction and overview.' In H. Kaplan, H. Sadock and B, Baltimore (eds) *Comprehensive Text Book of Psychiatry.* Baltimore: Williams & Wilkins.

Caudil, W. (1958) *The Psychiatric Hospital as a Small Society.* Cambridge: Harvard University Press.

Ciompi, L. (1980) 'The natural history of schizophrenia in the long term.' *British Journal of Psychiatry 1,* 36, 413–420.

Cohen, David (1997) 'A critique of the use of neuroleptic drugs in psychiatry.' In S. Fisher and R. Greenberg (eds) *From Placebo to Panacea.* New York: John Wiley & Sons Inc.

de Girolamo, G. (1996) 'WHO studies on schizophrenia.' *The Psychotherapy Patient 9,* 213–231.

Eigen, M. (1986) *The Psychotic Core.* London: Jason Aronson Inc.

Fisher, S. and Greenberg, R.(1997) 'What are we to conclude about psychoactive drugs? Scanning the major findings.' In S. Fisher and R. Greenberg (eds) *From Placebo to Panacea.* New York: John Wiley & Sons.

Foucault, M. (1965) *Madness and Civilization.* New York: Pantheon.

Foulkes, S.H. (1975) *Group-Analytic Psychotherapy, Method and Principles.* New York: Gordon and Breach.

Freud, S. (1973) *New Introductory Lectures on Psychoanalysis* (trans. J.Strachey). London: Pelican.

Fromm-Reichman, F. (1950) *Principles of Intensive Psychotherapy.* Chicago: University of Chicago Press.

Fromm-Reichmann, F. (1952) 'Some aspects of psychoanalytic psychotherapy with schizophrenics.' In E. Brody and F. Redlich (eds) *Psychotherapy with Schizophrenia.* New York: International University Press.

Glass, J.M. (1997) *Life Unworthy of Life.* New York: Basic Books.

Goldhagen, D. (1996) *Hitler's Willing Executioners: Ordinary Germans and the Holocaust.* New York: Knopf.

Goffman, I. (1961) *Asylums.* New York: Anchor Books.

Greenspan, S. (1989) *The Development of the Ego: Implications for Personality Theory, Psychopathology, and the Psychotherapeutic Process.* Madison, CT: International University Press.

Grotstein J. (1990) 'The "Black Hole" as the basic psychotic experience: some newer psychoanalytic and neuroscience perspective on psychosis.' *Journal of the American Academy of Psychoanalysis 18,* 29–46.

Hinshelwood, R.D. (1987) *What Happens in Groups.* London: Free Association Books.

Hollingshead, A. and Redlich, F. (1958) *Social Class and Mental Illness.* New York: John Wiley & Sons.

Jabiensky, A. (1987) 'Multi-cultural studies and the nature of schizophrenia: a review.' *Journal of the Royal Society of Medicine 80,* 162–167.

Jacques, E. (1974) 'Social systems as a defense against persecutory and depressive anxiety.' In G.S. Gibbard, J.J. Hartmann and R.D. Mann (eds) *Analysis of Groups.* San Francisco: Jossey-Bass.

James, D.C. (1984) 'Bion's "containing" and Winnicott's "holding" in the context of the group matrix.' *International Journal of Group Psychotherapy 34,* 201–213.

Jung, C.G.(1961) *Memories Dreams and Reflections* (ed. A. Jaffe). New York: Random House.

Kafka, J.S. (1989) *Multiple Realities In Clinical Practice.* New Haven: Yale University Press.

Kanas, N. (1986) 'Group therapy with schizophrenics: controlled studies.' *International Journal of Group Psychotherapy 36,* 339–351.

Karon, B. and Vandenbas, G. (1981) *Psychotherapy of Schizophrenia.* New York: Jason Aronson Inc.

Karon, B. and Whitaker, L. (1996) 'Psychotherapy and the fear of understanding schizophrenia.' In P. Breggin and M. Stern (eds) *Psychosocial Approaches to Deeply Disturbed Persons.* New York: The Haworth Press.

Kernberg, O. (1973) 'Psychoanalytic object-relations theory, group processes, and administration: toward an integrative theory of hospital treatment.' *Annual of Psychoanalysis 1,* 363–388.

Klein, M. (1946) 'Notes on some schizoid mechanisms.' In Klein *et al.* (eds) *Developments in Psychoanalysis.* London: Hogarth Press, 1952.

Klein, M. (1959), 'Our adult world and its roots in infancy.' *Human Relations 12,* 291–303.

Klein, E. (1993) 'Large groups in treatment and training settings.' *Group 17,* 4,198–210.

Kohut, H. (1971). *The Analysis of the Self.* New York: International University Press.

Kovel, J.(1987) 'Schizophrenic being and technocratic society.' In D.M. Levin (ed) *Pathologies of the Modern Self.* New York: New York University Press.

Kuipers, L. (1979) 'Expressed emotions: a review.' *British Journal of Social and Clinical Psychology 18*, 237–243.

Lacan, J. (1977) *Escrits: A Selection* (tr. A. Sheridan). New York: Norton.

Lawrence, W.G., Bain, A. and Gould, L. (1996) 'The fifth basic assumption.' *Free Association 6*, 28–25.

Liberman, R. (1994), 'Psychosocial treatments of schizophrenia.' *Psychiatry 57*, 104–115.

Levin, D.M. (1987) 'Clinical stories: a modern self in the fury of being.' In D.M. Levin (ed) *Pathologies of the Modern Self.* New York: New York University Press.

Lidz, T. and Blatt, S. (1983) 'Critiques of Danish–American studies of biological and adoptive relatives of adoptees who became schizophrenic.; *American Journal of Psychiatry 41*, 11, 1252–1260.

Lidz, T., Fleck, S. and Cornelius, A. (1965) *Schizophrenia and the Family*, New York: International University Press.

Lofgren, L. (1976) 'A process oriented group approach to schizophrenia.' In L.J. West and D.E. Finn (eds) *Treatment of Schizophrenia.* New York: Grune & Stratton.

Main, T.F. (1975) 'Some psychodynamics of large groups.' In L. Kreeger (ed) *The Large Group, Dynamics and Therapy.* London: Constable.

May, P.R.A. (1968) *Treatment of Schizophrenia: A Comparative Study of Five Treatment Methods.* New York: Science House.

Matte-Blanco, T. (1975) *The Unconscious as Infinite Sets.* London: Duckworth.

Mender, D. (1994) *The Myth of Neuropsychiatry.* London: Plenum Press.

Menzies, E. (1975) 'A case study in the functioning of social systems as a defense against anxiety.' In A.D. Coleman and W. Bexton (eds) *Group Relations Reader 1.* Washington DC: A.K. Rice Institute.

Miller, E.J. (1993) *From Dependency to Autonomy.* London: Free Association Books.

Miller, E.J. and Gyne, G.V. (1972) *A Life Apart.* London: Tavistock Social Science (paperback edition 1974).

Miller, E.J. and Rice, A.K. (1967) *Systems of Organization: Control of Task and Sentient Boundaries.* London: Tavistock Publications.

Muller, J. (1996) *Beyond the Psychoanalytic Dyad.* New York: Routledge.

Ogden, T. (1982) *Projective Identification and Pyschotherapeutic Technique.* New York: Jason Aronson.

(1989) *The Primitive Edge of Experience.* London: Jason Aronson.

Pines, M. (1978) 'The contribution of S.H. Foulkes to group analytic psychotherapy.' In L.R. Wolberg, M.L. Aronson and A.R. Wolberg (eds) *Group Therapy an Overview.* New York: Stratton Intercontinental.

Pope, K. Johnson, P. (1987) 'Psychological and psychiatric diagnosis: theoretical foundations, empirical research, and clinical practice.' In M. Levin (ed) *Pathologies of the Modern.* New York: New York University Press.

Rayner, E. and Wooster, (1997) 'An introduction to bi-logic.' *Melanie Klein Journal 15*, 553–561.

Resnik, S. (1994) 'Glacial times in psychotic regression.' In M. Pines and V.L. Schermer (eds) *Ring of Fire.* London: Routledge.

Reyes, A., Reyes, P. and Skelton, R. (1997) 'Traumatized logic: the containing function of unconscious classifications in the aftermath of extreme trauma.' *Melanie Klein Journal 15*, 665–683.

Robbins, M. (1993) *Experiences of Schizophrenia.* London: The Guilford Press.

Rosenfeld, H. (1965) *Psychotic States.* London: Karnac.

Sass, L. (1992) *Madness and Modernism.* New York: Basic Books.

Searles, H. (1965) *Collected Papers on Schizophrenia and Related Subjects.* London: Hogarth Press.

Segal, H. (1957) 'Notes on symbol formation.' *International Journal of Psycho-Analysis 38*, 391–397.

Shapiro, R. (1985) 'An analytic group-interpretative approach to family therapy.' In A. Coleman and M. Geller (eds) *Group Relations Reader 2.* Washington DC: A.K. Rice Institute Series.

Singer, D.L., Astrachan, B.M., Gould, L.J. and Klein, E.B. (1979) 'Boundary management in psychological work with groups.' In W.G. Lawrence (ed) *Exploring Individual and Organizational Boundaries.* New York: Wiley.

Skolnick, M.R. (1985) 'A group approach to psychopharmacology with schizophrenics.' *Yale Journal of Biology and Medicine 58*, 317–326.

Skolnick, M.R. (1994) 'Intensive group and social systems treatment of borderline and psychotic patients.' In M. Pines and V.L. Schermer *Ring of Fire*. London: Routledge.

Stanton, A. and Schwartz, M. (1954) *The Mental Hospital*. New York: Basic Books.

Steiner, J. (1982) 'Perverse relationship between parts of the self: a clinical illustration.' *International Journal of Psycho-Analysis 63*, 241–252.

Sullivan, H.S. (1962) *Schizophrenia as Human Process*. New York: Norton.

Thomas, Phillip (1997) *The Dialectics of Schizophrenia*. London: Free Association Books.

Tienari, P. (1992) 'Implications of adoption studies on schizophrenia.' *British Journal of Psychiatry 161* (supplement 18), 52–58.

Tucker, T. (1998) 'Putting DSM-IV in perspective.' *American Journal of Psychiatry 155* 2, 159–62.

Turquet, P. (1974) 'Threats to identity in the large group.' In L. Kreeger (ed) *The Large Group*. London: Karnac.

Walker, E. and Levine, R.J. (1990) 'Prediction of adult-onset schizophrenia from childhood home movies of the patients.' *American Journal of Psychiatry 147*, 1052–1056.

Winnicott, D.W. (1965) *The Maturational Process and the Facilitating Environment*. New York: International Universities Press.

Winnicott, D.W.(1969) 'The use of an object and relating through identifications.' *International Journal of Psychoanalysis 50*, 711–716.

Wynne, L., Ryckoff, M.I., Day, J. and Hirsh, S. (1958) 'Pseudo-mutuality in the family relations of schizophrenics.' *Psychiatry 21*, 205–220.

CHAPTER 3

Splitting and Disavowal in Group Psychotherapy of Psychosis[1]

Nicolas Caparrós

Ultimately, he died of his pathological self love

(Freud to Martha Bernays, 16 November 1883)

Introduction

The group, external and internal, is both a real and imaginary space where either the healthy or pathological elements of 'splitting' and 'disavowal' can operate. Both mechanisms become increasingly important as a greater number of psychic structures are being explored. I believe that splitting and disavowal are involved in a larger quantity of mental processes than I had originally thought. Therefore, I will first try to formulate a revised theoretical framework, which partly departs from classical psychoanalytic theory; I will then focus on the group.

Who is afraid of 'contradictions'? Although psychoanalysis is naturally familiar with them, in some circles there has been a tendency to defuse one of the foremost psychoanalytic principles: mastering complex intersubjective relationships and deep intrapsychic conflicts. The relative comfort of educational adaptation is foreign to the 'instability' of psychoanalysis. From the Sophists to Hegel, the history of philosophy shows that contradictions are uneasy. It seems that only in the twentieth century have we been able to accept that psychic life is paradoxical, unpredictable and does not follow a linear (cause-effect) pattern. Modern mathematics and chaos theory, as well as recent developments in non-Aristotelian logic and in linguistics itself, contribute to our understanding of the 'polysemic' nature of psychoanalysis; this escapes the praxis of positivism. Contradictions are present at birth, or even earlier; I will outline some.

---

1   Translated by María Cañete and Arturo Ezquerro.

First dilemma: 'to be *or* to be-with' – from 'wholeness' to 'separation' (amputation?)

The subjectivity and the capacity to form interpersonal relationships ('to be and to be-with') are complementary achievements that a healthy adult has needed to acquire; they are not innate genetic traits. Sooner or later, each person must 'jump' from the 'non(pre)-human biology' to the 'human psyche', from an organic existence to the ontological one. 'Being' cannot be taken for granted: it is an acquisition, not a gift.

In order to disentangle the complex relationship between the 'internal' and the 'external', we need to think about concepts such as link, bind, bond and vinculum ('attachment'). In my opinion, they are not exactly the same; while the first three refer primarily to an external connection, vinculum ('attachment') connotes a more internal tie. This is why I prefer to use it. The gnosis of the relationship between 'object' and 'subject' is a starting point for many philosophers; object and subject are seen as clearly defined external entities from the beginning. In contrast to this, psychoanalysis tries first to investigate the process through which object and subject become two separate entities; it then tries to define the relationship that is built 'between' and 'within' the two different 'selves'. The true psychoanalyst cannot possibly avoid our basic human contradictions. For example, love and hate, life and death, 'being one self' and 'being the other'; above all, 'to be out of not to be'. Education often aims to conciliate opposites and achieve a stable adaptation. Usually, maladjustment is seen as an illness, but it is also an enigmatic side of our human condition.

Freud seemed to enjoy paradoxes. He conceived the child as the father of man, culture as a symbolic and sublimated expression of the instincts, repression as a *sine qua non* for human development, and so on. But it is even more striking to think that we, literally, need an 'amputation' in order to be born. The foetus is restricted to a limited existence. It can only come to exist when the 'paradise' is lost. 'Being' means separating from wholeness. 'Amputation' is the uncanny (Umheimlich) door to existence. In this context, my interpretation of the Latin axiom *inter urinam et foeces nascimur* would be as follows: 'we come to be through restrictions'.

Towards the end of his life, Freud (1938) wrote in *An Outline of Psychoanalysis*: 'A child's first erotic object is the mother's breast that nourishes it; love has its origin in attachment to the satisfied need for nourishment. There is no doubt that, to begin with, the child does not distinguish between the breast and its own body; when the breast has to be separated from the body and shifted to the 'outside', because the child so often finds it absent, it carries with it as an 'object' a part of the original narcissistic libidinal cathexis. This first object is later completed into the person of the child's mother, who not only nourishes it but also looks after it and thus arouses in it a number of other physical sensations, pleasurable and unpleasurable. By her care of the child's body she becomes its first seducer' (p.188).

As Ilse Grubich Simitis and others have pointed out, the late Freud gave more importance to the maternal function. I believe that Freud also drew a new hypothesis on 'splitting' and 'narcissism', in which he enhanced the status of the 'object'. This revised object became an active agent in the process of forming the 'structural' perspective of the psyche, which complemented the 'economic' concepts. In my view, Freud implicitly postulated that 'splitting' was performing a new function within the 'ontogenetic' or developmental perspective. This was different from the old concept of *Ichspaltung* that he had related to fetishism in 1927, and which he was now, in 1938, elaborating in respect of the psychoses. I can now, in 1997, see more clearly what I had suspected for a long time: 'splitting' plays an essential role in normal development, that of being responsible for the initial breeze of subjectivity. In other words, 'splitting' is the first step towards subjectivity. My own formulation of this paradox would be as follows: 'We come to exist because we have been split off'.[2] But, how can this happen? What is it that needs to be divided up?

'Wholeness', or to be more precise, 'the absolute' described by the Greek philosophers exists by itself. Through an unknown process, it demands an 'amputation' to allow for the psychological birth of the individual self. Wholeness can be regained through 'attachment', which requires having previously experienced separation and loss. Inside, outside, and all possible vicissitudes derived from their relationship, are initially governed by a 'narcissistic model', both at conscious and unconscious levels. 'Primary splitting' is mysterious and powerful. Following the ideas of Matte-Blanco (1988) and Caparrós (1994), the most primitive form of splitting can only be comprehended with the aid of a discipline called 'bi-logic'.[3] In the beginning there is only pleasurable, non-differentiated and non-human wholeness. Within it, there is an ominous (bad) breast that, with its hazardous activities and absences, is going to precipitate the splitting. Wholeness seems to ignore everything else, including the nourishing (good) breast. Schematically, the evolution of splitting can be conceptualized as follows:

---

2   In my view, normal development and psychosis follow different paths.

3   The 'bi-logic' in concerned with the integration of conscious and unconscious paths.

Inside   Outside
'Self-Breast' <> 'Breast-Self'
(First step: pseudo separation based on 'narcissistic symmetry')
Self <> Breast
(Second step: separation based on 'part-object' differences)
Self <> Other
(Third step: separation based on 'otherness' or 'whole object')

Still within the borders, or to be more pointed, on the borders of wholeness, the 'primitive splitting' based on 'symmetric mirroring' creates a type of relationship that is imaginary and nearly delusional: 'there is an outside that is myself'. The 'ontogenetic splitting' occurring in normal development symbolically resembles the process through which a clone is formed; it is different from the 'pathological splitting' that occurs in psychosis. As we discussed earlier, Freud eventually related human existence to the process of being split off. The first step of subjectivity consists in separation from wholeness, the loss of the most symbiotic form of narcissism, to become a 'split unit'.

This is not quite a dyad yet but, according to Pichon-Rivière, a 'dual unit' having two parts ('self-breast'). In fact, the breast is not generic but unique; it is my breast ('breast-self'). The metaphor of the 'big bang theory' could be used to describe the emergence of subjectivity: following the 'explosion' of an undifferentiated mass everything began to be and to acquire increasingly more distinct characteristics. Sigmund Freud and Melanie Klein differ in the emphasis they put on the 'original loss'. While he refers to it as the 'ending of wholeness', she concentrates on the intermittent 'absence of the external object'. Freud starts with a nostalgic narcissistic perspective, which is close to the Platonic metaphor of the Androgynous; Klein starts with the missed, absent object. I would put it this way: Narcissism versus Melancholy, Monism versus Dualism. The Freudian 'narcissistic wound' reminds me of Adam's lost rib, an 'amputation' which turns into another person. In contrast to this, the Kleinian 'womb' becomes the utopian symbol of full existence.

In my opinion, primitive or biological attachment is initially triggered off by the injury of primary narcissism; it later becomes a more psychologically differentiated subject–object relationship, with specific psychoanalytic qualities. Pichon-Rivière thought that attachment (*vínculo*) was 'bi-corporal', but before this separation is achieved there is some overlapping. The baby gradually changes the perception of his own body. At one point, the baby still perceives the breast within the boundaries of his own corporeality but, at the same time, begins to perceive it outside. Inside and outside are two different psychic spaces that are born out of the same 'pregnancy'. In a way, attachment is a result of the 'negative' aspects of becoming a subject, which means to be separate, different and 'smaller' than wholeness. In order to achieve this, it is necessary to go through a process of healthy 'splitting' of the primitive narcissistic libidinal cathexis. The infant faces a daunting task: to progress from the original state of 'non-human' existence[4] to the recognition of 'the other', who is inside and outside at the same time. This demands the intervention of complex processes.

Matte-Blanco thought about this paradox and concluded that our topographical mental representations possess more than three dimensions. This multidimensional reality of our psychic life allows for the simultaneous presence of the object inside and outside.[5] In the initial stage, the object is cathected only with narcissistic libidinal energy; in later stages it is cathected and re-cathected with the libidinal energy of the object itself, which requires the maturation of the narcissistic libido. In the beginning, inside is both 'with' and 'against' outside; they symbolically behave like neighbours with different levels of psychic energy. Healthy 'splitting' is needed in the construction and development of a balanced psychic structure: external world, internal world (the place for mental representations) and self.

The external object plays a crucial part in this process, with the quality and timing of its presence and absence. The vicissitudes of the object influence the type of internal working models and the patterns of attachment that the infant will evolve. The more and better the 'absences' and 'presences' of the object are, the greater the number of opportunities the infant will have for healthy growth. The process commences with a tension and negotiation between the 'here' and the 'not-here'. The absence of the object ('not-here') will enable the primitive self ('self-breast') to become separate and recognize the object as 'the other' and, later, accept it as 'an-other' person. Before this is accomplished, the infant is in an intermediate position between 'oneness' and 'otherness'. The harmonious repetition of the sequence 'in-sight' and 'out-sight' develops the awareness of borders, boundaries and limits: the seed of social life and morality.

Second dilemma: the object as recipient of instincts or the object as trauma

The same object that builds the 'humanizing bridge' is also a violent happening. The object is a source of pleasure and, at the same time, is a limit to infantile omnipotence. The absence of the object is a basic trauma in the beginning of psychic life, without which the birth of subjectivity is not possible. Subjectivity is

---

4   A state of fundamentally biological existence.

5   I have also explored this theme regarding the mechanism of 'projection'.

intimately close to the concept of boundaries.[6]

Freud and Klein also differ in their formulation of the first 'duality': the advent of boundaries. On the one hand, Freud talks of the binomial 'pleasure–unpleasure'; boundaries are discovered through unpleasure which, only at a later stage, becomes a 'persecutory' experience. Sulloway classified him as a 'biologist of the mind', and the link biology–pleasure is a good starting point where increasingly more complex structures can gradually be introduced. On the other hand, Klein starts with the binomial 'pleasure–persecution', which already belongs to a psychological category since it establishes a difference between persecuted and persecutor. For Klein, the first developmental stage in human life is the 'paranoid-schizoid' position. Such a position implies the original presence of a self-object duality in the infant's psychic space. This assumption overlooks the obvious connections with and the 'anaclitic' (*Anlehnungs*) leaning on biology.

In this early period, the external object or maternal function plays an essential role in terms of survival. This mother or 'first seducer', as Freud put it, unfolds with her actions and fantasies the path for the infant towards 'oneness' and 'otherness'. Boundaries, aggressiveness and sexuality all come from the same 'womb'. The process is not linear but complex and unpredictable. Some maternal fantasies can be pathological. For example, the colloquial and innocent expression 'my child' can have different meanings: it may mean a young, little person growing as a separate individual in his own right, and becoming able to form new attachments. This would be consistent with what Freud called 'secondary process'. But, maybe, 'my child' means in a subtle way 'my property', a tautology on the surface but with profound consequences: the mother 'disavows' the separateness of the infant, who is condemned 'to be for her'. The maternal fantasy could go even further, to the point of denying the child all his rights, so 'my child is myself'. Here, the child is treated as a limb or extension of the mother's body. Only illness could give him the right to be cared for as a separate entity, which Matte-Blanco called an 'epistemological see-saw'. Otherwise, the child is engulfed by the mother and is nothing but a physiological reality.

Any drive for independence or relatedness in the infant is perceived, by such a mother, as a threatened 'amputation'. In the circumstances, the processes of 'separation-individuation' and the formation of boundaries become impossible. The fantasies repeat themselves in a vicious circle of 'narcissistic mirroring': 'myself-infant' <> 'infant-myself'. Something similar may happen when the child plays with a toy: it can be perceived as a part of himself. However, when the

---

6   Hinshelwood (1997) states: 'She [Melanie Klein] did not explain how such an extremely fragile ego could introject and project. These processes require a firm idea of inside and outside, and a boundary between'. Hinshelwood also quotes Bick (1968): 'The stage of primal splitting ... can now be seen to rest on this earlier process of containment of self and object by their respective skins' (p.309). My own hypothesis is that the 'skin' works in an 'anaclitic' way to permit 'primal splitting' to operate.

transitional function is fulfilled, the child leaves the toy 'abandoned' or 'decathected' on the floor and it becomes a 'no-thing'.

Primitive 'splitting' is a necessary but insufficient condition for the psychological birth of the human infant; it needs to be complemented by 'disavowal' (*Verleugnung*). Both mechanisms are inextricably linked. The primitive breast represents a 'disavowed-thing'. We, the adults, are supposed to know that disavowal modifies the reality of things, with the aim of establishing a more pleasurable relationship with them. The infant cannot yet tolerate reality as it is; he would feel overwhelmed by it. Disavowal provides a transitional and legitimate 'black spot' that serves psychological survival. It protects the developing infant from an anxiety that is much deeper than the oedipal fear of castration. While in fetishism only the penis is in danger, the threat here is 'to be without wholeness' or 'to be non-wholeness'; in other words, 'annihilation anxiety'.

After the first disavowal, the infant can be in a 'delusional' state believing that he is still wholeness or, at least, nearly wholeness. The breast is seen as an object that is not outside, at a time when 'internalization' is not possible yet. Infantile dependency needs are disavowed: 'I am the breast' rather than 'the breast is mine'. So, the object is not the object: a most radical 'disavowal' that will influence the quality of future 'disavowals'. At the same time, it represents the beginning of our psychic structure. At this point, I propose summing up with the following hypothesis:

Attachment is produced in the infant's psychic life with the help of an 'anaclitic' leaning on the 'social breast' and the 'biological world'. It requires three steps to become fully operational. The first step is an imaginary one: 'narcissistic splitting'. The second step is imaginary as well and concludes with an 'object relation'. The third step is a symbolic 'inter-subjective relation', which represents the most advanced structure of psychic development. Attachment is 'socially imposed' too but, in the early stages of subjectivity, the infant is unaware of this 'social initiation'. Psychological birth is a social reality in which 'splitting' and 'disavowal' unconsciously play a crucial role. Maratos (1996) refers to this theme with singular clarity: 'That our psychological and our bodily Self constitute our being is far from contentious, but the idea that our being is also made up of our attachments is probably less widely accepted. Attachment is often seen not as a part of the individual but as a function of it; it is thought that an individual can form attachments or not; can be helped to develop them or influenced in forming distorted ones.' Like Maratos, I also think that 'attachment' is a primary component and a condition of our psychic structure; it is not a mere adjunct or function.

Third dilemma: the group

The group is one of the natural consequences of splitting, disavowal and attachment. It is the humanizing space *par excellence* – an expression of real human life, which includes internal and interpersonal conflicts. The group also is a therapeutic space. From the beginning of life we carry the raw material for our 'groupishness'; groups are at the core of human existence. The individual self is not only a part of a group but 'it is a group': the old antagonism individual versus group is epistemologically redundant. We are a group even without knowing it; in a subsequent tour de force we acquire the insight of 'being in a group', for which we need to give up the 'illusion' of existing in an isolated 'autoerotic omnipotence'. After this discovery we face the conflict of achieving a personal identity in the group.

Splitting and disavowal manifest themselves with an ever greater complexity. This implies the presence of threatening, real dangers that can activate various deviations from the healthy developmental path of our emerging psychic structure. Psychosis is one of these deviations. A special sort of pathological splitting, in conjunction with other defensive mechanisms, induces psychosis; while benign splitting promotes healthy psychological development. In a favourable upbringing, narcissistic splitting is a transitional first step towards more mature forms of splitting. However, if there is an abnormal narcissistic fixation,[7] narcissism itself becomes the ultimate goal in the infant's life: the return to the 'still wholeness' of the womb. The more primitive the psychosis is, the more necessary for the patient that his therapist provides a space where boundaries and psychic separation can occur.

The group, whether or not primarily concerned with therapy, is a paradox. On the one hand it is a space where relationships can develop; on the other hand it can play the 'regressive' role of becoming a symbolic womb. The group is a locus where separation and fusion, intrapsychic and interpersonal phenomena, growth and catastrophe take place; 'everything' human can happen in the group. Before 'primary envy' (as conceived by Klein) starts to show, the narcissistic wound performs a decisive function. If 'the other' is not perceived as separate, or at least as 'partly separate', not even primary envy can manifest itself. The first fantasies of separateness bear a fear of a catastrophe. In normal development, but not in psychotic development, the relation with the 'object' mitigates the violence of this process.

From a psychoanalytic viewpoint, I find it helpful to differentiate between two main categories of 'psychotic deviations', as follows:

---

7   This abnormal fixation is related to specific styles of mothering.

1. A more primitive type of psychosis where there are no boundaries and separation is never achieved, which means that attachment becomes an impossible notion.

2. A psychotic development that is secondary to abandonment. In other words, a damaging disruption that leads to a failure in the construction of consistent 'good internal objects'; these are replaced by 'persecutory objects'.

Understandably, a 'persecuting object' awakes an overwhelming anxiety, which interferes with the process of forming stable and secure attachments. Such an object is 'mobile': it moves freely from inside to outside, and the other way round, in massive defensive manoeuvres of externalization (projection and projective identification) and internalization (introjection and introjective identification). The psychic structure becomes fragmented into multiple parts.

In groups of psychotic patients, we can meet with these two types of psychopathology. It is possible to observe different degrees of pathological non-attachment, attachment and detachment. The group is invaded by very powerful and primitive fantasies. These are governed by 'primary process', and the reality principle cannot operate: 'the others are myself'. Interpersonal and intrapsychic conflicts are usually the main themes in groups of neurotic patients. With the psychotic, they are supplanted by the expectation of an impending catastrophe, in the face of separation, and by the narcissistic wound that would inevitably follow. The object fades away and cannot be restored. The psychotic mental structure is clearly manifested in the psychotic way of being in the group: other people can be 'mirrored selves' or 'amputated selves', but they do not become a real other that is similar and different, familiar and strange – as it is true of neurotic patients who have had the singular experience of 'object relations'. 'Mirroring' is the only way for some psychotic patients to communicate, which is an even more primitive form of relating than the 'persecutory' one described earlier.

We now need to formulate a more specific question: what kind of relationships can psychotic patients establish between themselves and with the group? The answer can only be yet another paradox. Psychotic patients are autoerotic, narcissistic and frightened of external reality; although they disavow the environment, they later may even idealize it! But, can they achieve inter-subjectivity proper? I do not think so, because they have a marked tendency to avoid meaningful contact with others. It is possible to observe attempts at 'fusion', which are usually followed by 'confusion', or acute reactions of 'panic' and subsequent 'running away'. These phenomena can be explained by the fact that the other is either perceived as dangerously persecuting or it is not recognized at all as a separate object. The dynamic of such a group is full of pathological projections, projective identifications, splittings, disavowals, idealizations and other defences. The resulting group atmosphere is very fragmented, into multiple 'part-objects' and disparate particles of selves. Psychotic patients often see themselves as a 'self-sufficient group'. This can lead to the distortion of being a 'big group', made out of countless little fragments and part-object representations that are disconnected from exchangeable meaning – 'a huge, shattered and isolated self'.

Pines (1996, p.183) writes:

> The notion of 'the group as a Self' is challenging. Is there any point in linking an individualistic notion such as the Self with the plurality of a group? The rationale for doing so becomes more evident when we consider in the first place 'the Self as a group'. For if there is an essential element of 'group' in the constitution of the individual, as indeed group analysis affirms, then it becomes more possible to consider that there is value in regarding 'the group as a Self'.

In a peculiar way, this is particularly 'true' in a group of psychotic patients: a distorted self, a distorted group.

Psychotic people have been unable to work through the processes of non-attachment, attachment and detachment. In the most extreme form of psychosis, there is a state of 'fusion' with the maternal breast that is only invested with narcissistic cathexis: the perception of the other as a whole object is not achieved. Less damaged patients have achieved 'part-object relations', as described by Melanie Klein. They are only 'partly attached', but quite able to obtain pleasure from and feel persecuted by a 'part-object' that is outside. This is possible because something that was 'myself' gradually becomes something that is 'strange' to me and is 'not-me'. However, there is no real separateness of the object yet; boundaries are not clear and the incipient psychic structure can easily be smashed to pieces. The psychotic patient loves and fears his own shadow. This shady world of 'as if' relationships reminds me of the Platonic myth of the cave.

Disavowal and mirroring often act together to try to develop the primitive self, while keeping wholeness and omnipotently controlling it. Attachment is still inside as a potential for a relationship with the other. The mechanisms that Karl Abraham called 'metabolic' (projection, projective identification and internalisation) need the involvement of splitting and disavowal to become operational. The more primitive the psychosis is, the more important the working-out of therapeutic separation becomes. Envy, before it can show, demands the acknowledgement of a separate other who has got 'something I have not got'. This recognition of differences makes it possible for the original imaginary space, based on 'symmetry', to be gradually taken over by 'asymmetric' attachments: the loss of wholeness begins to be accepted.

In the more primitive type of psychosis, the narcissistic self can be violently invasive, in order to keep alive the fantasy of fusion and wholeness; separation and differences are avoided largely through mirroring. However, in the more benign type it is possible to discover a part of the other or a 'part-object' that is outside, but isolated from the wider external realities.[8] These specific qualities that part-objects own, together with the feelings of loss and rage that the 'part-subject' experiences, contribute to the sensation of living in a persecuting universe. This is represented by the 'paranoid-schizoid' position that is inhabited by multiple and unconnected 'part-objects'. In structural terms, however, this formation is more advanced and complex than the original state of undifferentiated wholeness.

In the less severe form of psychosis, the self is split off into two basic components. The first one sustains an unstable equilibrium between narcissistic mirroring and persecution. The second one tries to establish the beginning of an 'object-relation'. This sort of mirroring can be interpreted as a pseudo attachment or an 'as if' attachment. I think it is important to bear in mind these two categories of psychosis; one that is based on a 'no-object', the other one on 'part-object relations'. They deserve different styles of group therapeutic interventions.

Fourth dilemma: the clinical material

Before the infant is ready to commence a more adventurous enterprise, the maternal function has to be 'good enough'. The mother must be emotionally available, but 'absent' as well to promote the setting up of boundaries and limits required for growth. The psychoanalytic psychotherapist needs to understand the primitive fantasies of fusion, narcissistic mirroring and persecution, that are present in the minds of psychotic patients. These fantasies play a part in the maintenance of precarious inter-subjective relations; they also have a powerful influence on the transference. Traditional psychoanalytic interpretations based on symbolic meaning often have to be surrendered to a more literal and concrete type of 'translation' (e.g. '… it seems that you wish this …, … maybe you are afraid of that …, or … this thing appears to resemble that one …'; followed by '… it seems that they also wish this …', etc.).

Good interpretations normally bring about a new insight, both at cognitive and emotional levels. In a group, this promotes connectedness and the formation of a common therapeutic 'matrix', where it is possible to make links between past and present, the concrete and the symbolic. Psychotic patients can only go from the concrete to the concrete; any intervention that tries to envelope more than one

---

8   I have also referred to this elsewhere, and have insisted that a reality made of part-objects lacks any sense of process.

level will generate confusion, and will put the group at risk of becoming a 'Tower of Babel'.[9]

I also think that the balance 'neither too close nor too distant' is crucial in group psychotherapy with psychotic patients. Well, saying it is easier than doing it! As Heimann (1950) pointed out, puzzling clinical material has to be illuminated by the findings of the countertransference. Psychotic patients tend to compulsively repeat their earliest experiences; the countertransference can give important clues regarding some of the old fantasies that their mothers may have had about them ('my child').

Sometimes, these patients establish an 'as if' type of attachment and relate to others as if they were 'another myself'; the inter-subjectivity is disavowed. The group psychotherapist is sometimes treated as a 'no-thing' or as something that is alienated; other times, as an absolute 'nothing'. The countertransference is characterized by a mixture of numbness and anger that diminishes the capacity to think. Before the therapist can provide a sympathetic understanding, it is critical to be aware of the 'dual unit' device (as opposed to a proper dyad) that is a by-product of primitive splitting. In some situations, the therapist is not even the 'mirrored self' of the patient, but little more than his shadow. Therapeutic containment, which often means having to put feelings and fears into words on the patients' behalf, is the best way to eventually enable them to sense the group conductor as a separate other.

If the psychotic patient has established 'part-object relations', the psychotherapist will become the recipient of envy and aggression through projective identification. This mechanism, through which a disavowed part of the self is inserted in the self of the other, is reminiscent of primary narcissistic splitting. Two distinctive factors are implicit:

1. The recognition of some separateness in the other, which leads to envy, as well as fears of abandonment and persecution.

2. The survival of an archaic infantile world where the self can be enfolded, unfolded and mirrored.

From this perspective, projective identification fails to achieve a proper separation, although it may be the only way to gain an incipient autonomy, while still holding on to a primitive narcissistic fantasy of fusion. Projective identification, both normal and pathological, is complex; it encompasses several mechanisms, such as splitting and disavowal, that may have narcissistic or

---

9   Symbol (Greek, *Sumbolon*) etymologically means to relate something with something else with the aim of achieving a whole. The two parts of the *Sumbolon* enable their owners to recognize one another and set up mutual complicity. This reciprocity is a key note in symbolism. The neuroses are a 'symbolic kingdom' of symbols.

persecutory elements, and even the manic grandiosity of later stages. Projective identification breaks the traditional philosophical discourse that sees subject and object as two clearly defined external entities. Behind the binomial 'self-other' there is a primitive claim that resists moving on: the pseudo binomial 'self-self'.

But, what about the transference? How does the patient bring old experiences of partial subjectivity to the 'here and now' in the therapy group? I will try to answer these questions with some clinical vignettes.

Patient A addressed to the group conductor: 'Last time you did not care for me'. As the group conductor was attempting to respond, patient B interrupted: 'I am bored'. The two complaints appear to be unrelated.

In a group of neurotic patients, the first complaint would have been expressed within a context; either a possible carelessness of the therapist, or a past experience of real neglect that is manifested in the transference. In a psychotic patient, however, the complaints seem to lack any context or process.

On the surface, patient B's comment could be interpreted as an 'envious' one; in fact, through mirroring, he is expressing his 'emptiness'. The whole group is 'mirrored' and its potential diversity melts away; patient B cannot cope with the difference between external and internal realities, and tries to seek refuge in a state of 'fusion'. In contrast to him, patient A tries to relate to a frustrating and persecutory 'breast' from a 'paranoid-schizoid' position.

In a peculiar way, patient A and patient B 'manufacture' two different therapists in the same room: one is boring, the other persecuting. As a result, a group interpretation becomes impossible. However, both, the imaginary and the real group are there, witnessing a confrontation between the two levels of narcissistic development. I would like to speculate that carelessness equals boredom. The psychic structures of these two patients are different, but both share a catastrophic fear of separation and try to hold on to a narcissistic object. They differ in the way their anxieties are manifested. A group of this kind requires a significant therapeutic dose of reparative mothering.

The next vignette refers to the serious suicide attempt that another patient made. He was pulled back to safety at the last minute; I will call him Jim. At the session that followed the suicide attempt, he said: 'That hurts.' John, a fellow patient, replied: 'Yes, it was impressive.' But Jim persisted: 'No, that hurts, it is hurting me; I am hurt!' Literally, there seemed to be 'symmetry' between the suicide attempt and the pain that Jim was experiencing. The more frequently the symmetric mirroring is used, the more deeply ingrained and unconscious the narcissistic role becomes.

Klein (1946) described a primitive form of anxiety in which the self feels threatened by its own aggressive drives and the violence of the object; both are seen inside. Then, the mechanism of projective identification starts to operate.

This represents an important step forward, which helps the developing self discriminate between inside and outside.

In the group psychotherapy of psychosis the paramount task is to foster the good use of splitting and disavowal. This will help projective identification ameliorate psychotic deviations and encourage healthy development.

References

Caparrós, N. (1992) *Psicopatología Analítico Vincular*. Madrid: Quipú Ed.

Caparrós, N. (1992) 'El narcisismo y el autoerotismo en la vorrespondencia de Freud.' In O. Alvarez (ed) *El Narcisismo*. Madrid: Quipú Ed.

Caparrós, N. (1994) *Tiempo, Temporalidad y Psicoanálisis*. Madrid: Quipú Ed.

Freud, S. (1938) *An Outline of Psycho-Analysis*. Standard Edition, Vol. 23. London: Hogarth Press (1964).

Heimann, P. (1950) 'On countertransference.' *International Journal of Psycho-Analysis 31*, 81–4.

Hinshelwood, R.D. (1997) 'Catastrophe, objects and representations: three levels of interpretation.' *British Journal of Psychotherapy 13*, 3, 307–17.

Klein, M. (1946) 'Notes on some schizoid mechanisms.' In *The Writings of Melanie Klein*, Vol. 3, 1–24. London: Hogarth Press (1975).

Maratos, J. (1996) 'Self through attachment and attachment through self in group therapy.' *Group Analysis 29*, 2, 191–98.

Matte-Blanco, I. (1988) *Thinking, Feeling and Being*. London: New Library of Psychoanalysis.

Pines, M. (1996) 'The self as a group: the group as a self.' *Group Analysis 29*, 2, 183–90.

CHAPTER 4

A Biography of Psychosis
Individuals, Groups, and Institutions

Salomon Resnik

Individual analysis: the origins of Freud's psychoanalytical approach

An interest in psychosis was present in Freud's work from his early years as a student of medicine. In addition to his spontaneous humanistic approach to mental illness and to mental suffering as an integral part of life, his concern for human suffering and physical and mental pain was already evidenced in his research into the uses of cocaine, where his avowed intention was to discover a remedy for pain and anxiety.

The cocaine episode between 1884 and 1887 was essential. Freud's own account runs as follows: 'In 1884 I obtained from Merck some of what was then the little-known alkaloid cocaine … to study its physiological action.' In the middle of this work he made a journey to visit his fiancée from whom he had been separated for three years. He suggested to his friend Königstein, the ophthalmologist, that he investigate the anaesthetizing properties of the drug applicable to diseases of the eye. When Freud returned, he found that another of his friends, Carl Koller, had performed the decisive experiments on animals' eyes. Koller is therefore rightly regarded as the discoverer of the properties of cocaine as a local anaesthetic. Freud regretted that his work had been interrupted by his journey. When he began himself to suffer from illness, he used cocaine to relieve the pain he felt. We can therefore say that Freud experienced pain and suffering in his own body, as well as relief.

Another close friend of Freud's was Ernst von Fleischl-Marxow (1846–1891), who suffered from neuromas which required repeated operations. As a result, his life became an unending torture of pain and slowly approaching death. Freud attempted to cure Fleischl's addiction to morphine by suggesting that he replace it with cocaine.

Freud's approach to mental pain was very much related in his mind to physical pain. In November 1882, Freud began his relationship with J. Breuer, and through him came to know the interesting case of Fraulein Anna O. Freud was very concerned with the mental suffering of Anna O and with her need to split her personality. At that time, people were fascinated with the problem of double personality in literature, in theatre and also in the field of psychiatry through the research and writings of the American psychiatrist Morton Prince. Prince was well-known in America for his research into the case of Sally Beauchamp, whose case had similar features to those Breuer and Freud found in Anna O, in particular the split personality. These cases fascinated Freud, and led him to a deeper understanding of the phenomena of splitting (*Spaltung*) and of the delusional and hallucinatory aspects of mental afflictions.

When he started working with Th. Meynert during his training in neurology in 1883, Freud was very interested in the latter's ideas but his personality was so very difficult that it was almost impossible to establish a dialogue with him. Freud thought him obsessive and paranoid, and even almost delusional. Meynert could be very hard on Freud, and in fact opposed Freud when he began to put forward some of his ideas on hysteria and was obviously breaking new ground – founding what was later to become psychoanalysis.

In the preliminary communication of 1893, Breuer and Freud employ the term 'psychosis', in reference to the apparently hereditary aspects of the illness (a point of view typical of the time). Freud was intrigued by the family background, working either through a specific hereditary influence or because of the pathological models of family life. It seems to me that here Freud had some intuition of the importance of the family as a group or cultural background influencing the life of each of its members.

Freud's main interest was in the suffering of the psychotic patient; he attempted also to gain an understanding of the psychopathology of psychosis, and of delusional and hallucinatory phenomena. (Breuer, of course, was reporting the theatrically delusional and hallucinatory experiences of Anna O and her pathological sensory perceptions of the transformation of her world – for example, she saw people, who had apparently no connexion whatever with her, turn into wax figures.) This upsetting and tragic experience gave her a picture of a paralysed, petrified, frozen world, a world in which everybody looked as if they had just stepped out of a wax museum.

Nowadays, we would tend to consider Anna O as non-schizophrenic. She was hysterical with powerful splitting mechanisms and delusional experiences, including hallucinations, recalling what the classic French psychiatrists at the end of the eighteenth century called a *'folie hystérique'*. I myself treated several patients like Anna O in the 1950s and 1960s; I found them in some ways much more difficult than clear-cut schizophrenics. The reason for this is that they produce a delusional transference with a capacity to control the environmental situation, including their analyst, since they manage to preserve a neurotic ego which is able to maneouvre reality. Edward Glover, some years ago now, used to say that the classic nosographic semiology of psychiatry would have to be reviewed in the light of psychoanalytical discoveries – for instance, he would speak of 'neurotic schizophrenia' and 'obsessional psychosis'. When I was in supervision with Bion with analyses of real schizophrenics, he was very keen to show me the times – sometimes within the same session – when the (psychotic) patient would behave in the transference as a neurotic or as a psychotic.

Breuer was very interested – and very upset – by Anna O, not only because she was attempting to seduce him but also, as far as I can see, because of her psychotic anxieties and her splitting (*Spaltung*) mechanisms, with which of course at that time he was quite unable to deal. Freud himself did not then have enough experience to deal with cases of deep regression like Anna O. Though Freud himself never met her – at least in a clinical situation – he was very interested in Breuer's experience. It cannot be denied that the early papers of Freud and Breuer should be considered as the fundamental starting points in any psychoanalytical biography of psychosis and psychotic phenomena.

When Anna O theatrically dramatized a dissociated and uncoordinated world, Breuer and Freud understood that she was expressing a splitting disturbance of her thinking and her difficulty in establishing *links* between her thoughts. Thus, her troubled free associations were typical of the psychotic patient. As my aim here is to comment both on the historical facts and on my present outlook, I would say that the difficulties in associating experienced by psychotics should be called, in schizophrenic patients particularly, *free disassociations*. By this neologism, I mean that we should be able to enquire where and when the patient's split ego has gone, in order to follow its mental itinerary.[1]

The phenomena of hallucination in Anna O, the building of a perceptual world peopled by characters recreated in her mind and sense organs (positive hallucination) contrasts with the mental confusion that appears when she complains of the 'smoke' and 'clouds', which prevent her from perceiving clearly what was happening all around her in her visual world. This phenomenon upset her very much because she could no longer find or make any space for herself in life. Sometimes also she was unable to perceive things which were 'there', that is to say she was experiencing negative hallucinations. Negative hallucination is a very important subject which developed in Freud's thinking (and in my own) since he wrote his paper *On Negation* (1925). I myself wrote a paper on Cotard's syndrome in 1952, in which I tried to make my own clinical contribution to the subject.

1   See on this point chapter 7 of my *Personne et Psychose* (1973) 'L'expérience de l'espace dans la situation analytique' (in French). An updated English edition of this book is in preparation.

Concerning the clinical aspects of Anna O's case, one has the impression that for Breuer and Freud, the difference between neurosis and psychosis is not only qualitative but also quantitative, a question of degree of psychotic anxiety and psychotic mechanisms. Curiously enough, Freud never knew Anna O directly, but he was so much involved with this case through Breuer that it is in fact difficult to believe that he never met her. Indeed, he did meet her 'mentally' through Breuer, and it is possible that, as a friend of Freud's wife, he met her socially at one point in Vienna.

In October 1885, Freud travelled to Paris to meet Charcot, whom he admired very much and with whom he was to collaborate in his teaching and research until February 1886. The Salpétrière hospital was at that time the 'Mecca' of neuro-psychiatry, and Freud was fascinated by Charcot's lectures and by the way in which he could show, in public, his way of relating to the patient. Charcot's lectures became in a theatrical way the '*spectacle de l'hystérie*', the theatre of madness in which patients, though mainly hysterical had a psychotic background, which enabled Freud to develop a *comprehensive approach to psychosis*.

At that time, there was a great deal of interest about the phenomena of *Spaltung* (splitting) and double personality, which culturally speaking played an important role in the literature and theatre of the time (and later in cinema). Pierre Janet was very interested in the subject. Freud mentions him several times in his Preliminary Communication (1893), speaking about 'splitting of consciousness' and 'double conscience', saying that he agreed with Pierre and Jules Janet, and also Alfred Binet, in their description of these phenomena (note p.12). Later in the same paper, Freud showed concern about the fact that on the one hand hysteria is a psychosis yet on the other the same symptoms can be found in people who are almost normal. The splitting phenomena appear also in hypnoid states and in dreams. Freud had already the intuition that the psychotic state corresponds to the *intrusion* of hypnoid phenomena and dream thoughts into daily life.

In 1888, five years before his preliminary communication, Freud began to treat in psychotherapy several interesting cases which were destined to play a very important part in his new conception of psychiatry – psychoanalysis – and the development of a technique which was to become in time the psychoanalytic method. His cases, at that time, were Frau Emmy, Fraulein Elisabeth, Miss Lucy and Katharina, with all of whom Freud related to in a very direct and involved spirit. From the beginning he was concerned with the feelings and fantasies transferred from the patient to the analyst; he realized also that the term 'transference' had already been employed by Charcot. For the latter, transference refers to a phenomenon of 'translation' or 'transport' of symptoms from one part of the body to another part of the body of the hysterical patient. For me, this idea of Charcot's goes back to the primitive conception of Greek and Oriental mythology, in which 'hysteria' was a uterus moving about inside the body. In reality, the discovery of the transference phenomena is due to Burq in 1876, who asked Charcot to authorize him to apply certain metals to the hysterical patient's body (with conversion symptoms), particularly in order to transmit from a 'living' part of the body to certain anaesthetized zones some energy or force which would then re-awaken a lost sensitivity. This was considered a major discovery in the field of physiology, and in 1877 the Council of the Paris Biological Society accepted the term *'transfer'* to describe it. The example that Charcot gives (in Charcot 1890, p.237) concerns a colleague of his, Gellé, who was treating a patient by 'metallotherapy' for a hearing deficit. Gellé noted that the healthy ear in fact lost about as much acuity as the 'anaesthetized' one gained, under the action of the metal. 'In other words,' says Charcot, 'there was no actual benefit gained, but a simple *'transfer'* (...) from one side to the other'. Charcot wanted to give a scientific basis to Burq's research, who was on his side attempting to discover which metals (copper, gold, lead, etc.) would be most effective in transmitting this kind of energy. Burq, thanks to Charcot, was able to demonstrate that waves of energy could re-awaken certain sensitivities in the anaesthetized or contracted zones, and this new state could last for several hours – or even several days. To my mind, this experience, part of the *biography of transference*, enables us to understand metaphorically the fact that transference is not only an *inter-personal* experience but is also related to *intra-corporeal* phenomena going on inside the patient. Perhaps nowadays we would say, in Kleinian terms, that internal objects can transfer feelings and meanings from one object to another, 'from one side to the other' of the psychic apparatus, or from the mind into the body – this is what I call *internal projections* in cases of conversion hysteria and hypochondriasis – and thereby influence other internal objects or the bodily zones these inhabit. We can conceive here of a dramatization of inter-personal and intra-personal phenomena, in terms of energy or drives or internal and external object relationships (Resnik 1994).

In his anatomo-clinical approach, Freud was very concerned, as I suggested before, with the differentiation between neurosis and psychosis. Following this tradition, his initial preoccupation was with inherited predisposition to illness and with the concepts of causation and aetiology. Frau Emmy interested him in that certain members of her family also suffered from chronic psychosis or paranoia; on the other hand, in the case of Fräulein Elisabeth there was no family history of mental illness. Freud developed these points in his papers 'A reply to criticisms of my paper on anxiety neurosis' (1895) and 'Heredity and the aetiology of the neuroses' (1896). In the former, he writes of the role played by sexual factors in the aetiology of the neuroses *per excessum et defectum* (for example, sexual abstinence) and discusses the traumatic aspects of the neuroses (traumatic neurosis) present according to him in hysteria. The traumatic experience is not necessarily present or clear-cut in anxiety neurosis; though it may be denied, it will re-appear in the form of a somatic sexual tension which has been deflected from the mind into the body. This concept of Freud's is very interesting: it gives us some understanding not only of conversion hysteria, but also and above all of hypochondriasis. At that time, Löwenfeld insisted on the fact that a number of cases of states of anxiety appear immediately or shortly after a psychic shock, accident or state of panic. The role of trauma in one case presented by Freud, in provoking an attack of gout in the injured limb is probably no different, he tells us, from the role it plays in the aetiology of tabes and general paralysis of the insane. These ideas are an intuitive anticipation of the concept of psychosomatics and somaticization, which were developed much later in psychoanalytical theory. Ferenczi's concept of pathoneurosis (Ferenczi 1919) was to be influenced by these ideas of Freud's in this early paper of his. Ferenczi's conception of pathoneurosis was an attempt to integrate somatic illness, for instance the way in which a syphilitic patient regresses psychologically to a particular dispositional point in the development of the ego when the specific neurosis was repressed during childhood.

In his 1895 paper 'On the grounds for detaching a particular syndrome from neurasthenia under the description "Anxiety Neurosis"', Freud draws a distinction between the quality of anxiety in neurotic and psychotic patients, between *Angstneurose* and *Angstpsychose*, a distinction which, according to Löwenfeld, had already been established by Karl Wernicke in 1894. According to Freud, the term *Angst* has many shades of meaning expressed by its cognates *Furcht* and *Schreck*. He stresses the anticipatory element and absence of the object – and therefore the depressive element in Freud's and Klein's theories. The term appears as a psychiatric term either as *Angstneurose* or *Angstanfall* and in cardiology, *Angst* is related to *angor pectoris*, since the word *Angst* derives from the Latin *angere*, to throttle or squeeze, referring to the sensations of constriction in the patient's thorax. Freud considered that there are situations in which a certain amount of *Angst* can be normal.

The difference, which is not only qualitative but also quantitative, between anxiety, anguish and *Angst* is a very useful one from a semiological point of view. As to the phenomena of transference in the psychoanalytic session, I was able to experience the transmission or the invasion of *Angst*, in particular psychotic anxiety, from a patient into and around me as almost a material presence that tends to get into the other person or float around him. Relatives of such patients will also refer to this kind of phenomenon. The same is true of some recovered psychotic patients (psychotic hysteria – *folie hystérique*), who tend to impose their power and control over their entourage through *Angst* of this type, an 'expansive' anguish which is not simply a projected one. I consider this phenomenon from a phenomenological point of view to be a founding element of the 'climate' or 'nature' of the anxiety that may be floating around … The concept of *Stimmung* corresponds to the particular climate and modality of the psychiatric or the psychoanalytic encounter. In fact, *Stimmung* is derived from *Stimme* (voice) which leads to the idea of the tone of the session; of course, this does not depend solely on the patient, but also from a transference point of view, on the psychoanalyst's countertransference and physical (body) presence.

A case of chronic paranoia

Freud analysed a case of chronic paranoia which I consider to be crucial to our understanding of Freud's personal development, particularly concerning his feelings about the transference 'psychosis'. For a considerable time, he thought that paranoia was a psychosis of defence; that is to say, that like hysteria and obsessions, it proceeds from the repression of distressing unbearable memories. According to Freud, paranoia must have a special method or mechanism of repression, but one could say that the persecutory feelings of the patient require him to build up a mask, a wall, a defensive element against a dangerous and threatening world. Freud's paper is fundamental also in that he there defines, for the first time, the term 'projection', as we will see later. He speaks of the case of Frau P, a woman of 32, married and with a child of 2. In her middle twenties she became confused and depressed. A few months after the birth of her child, she showed the first signs of paranoia: she became uncommunicative and distrustful, showed aversion to her husband, brothers and sisters, and complained about her neighbours. According to her, the neighbours were beginning to be rude and inconsiderate towards her. She thought people had something against her, though she had no clear idea what. Then she added that people in general began to show no respect for her and to do things against her. We know from the classic descriptions of paranoid schizophrenia and from the psychoanalytic approach to psychosis that ideas of reference which lead to delusions of reference, described first by Karl Wernicke then by Bleuler, as *Eigenbeziehungen* usually begin in the 'neighbourhood' of the psychotic patient; it would seem that the inner persecutory feelings are being thrown into the nearest available surrounding space, then, later, if the degree of persecution increases the projection becomes more 'athletic', to paraphrase a term used by Bion – and so the projections become 'cosmic' as it were, up into other planets. For the moment, I shall return to Frau P walking in the street.

She complained that she was being watched by people in the street, who were able to read her thoughts and so knew everything about her. One evening she thought that she was being watched while undressing, thereby adding an erotic element to the picture of her unwilling exhibitionism. She was describing a transformation in her world, which from our point of view could be seen as a distortion of the world-picture.

In addition, she experienced strange symptoms in her body. One day, when she was alone with her housemaid, she had a sensation in her lower abdomen, and thought that the girl had at that moment an improper (i.e. sexual) idea. These erotic sensations increased, and she felt her genitals 'as one feels a heavy hand' (*dixit* Freud). Then she began to develop horrifying sexual hallucinations of naked women showing the lower part of the body – the pubic region, and pubic hair, sometimes with male genitals. All this delusional somatic distortion added to her distorted transformation of the world. Here we have through Freud's description an excellent picture of the beginning of a delusional universe.

She went to Freud for treatment in the winter of 1895. Freud notes that her intelligence was undiminished in spite of all her delusions and hallucinations. Influenced as he was at that time by Breuer's technique, Freud was aiming at removal of the hallucinations and treatment of her persecutory feelings in a case which he diagnosed as paranoia.

Freud was still placing his hand on his patients' forehead (he was following the Mesmer tradition of magnetism) in order to help them to remember and to associate, and in this way make contact with their unconscious fantasies and fears. He suggests that some of Frau P's delusions and hallucinations were to some extent based on actual facts – for instance, the first hallucinated images of a woman's abdomen appeared in a hydropathic establishment, a few hours after she had in fact seen a number of naked women at the baths. Freud showed interest in her memories about the past; the patient responded by mentioning scenes from her adolescence, at age 17 or 18, when she had felt *ashamed* of being naked in her bath in front of her mother, her sister and her doctor. Then she was able to associate her brother with a scene at the age of 6, when she was undressing in the nursery before going to bed; in that situation she had felt no shame. Freud suggests that she had omitted to feel shame as a child, and therefore that she repressed her sexual play with her brother (voyeurist and exhibitionist experiences). The repressed feelings returned as shame in her delusional, hallucinated, erotic compulsion.

The patient spoke also about her depression (here is the *Angstanfall* of which Freud speaks in his earlier paper). In fact, she 'fell' into depression after witnessing a quarrel between her husband and her brother. She regretted that after the quarrel her brother, of whom she was fond, would no longer come to their house, for she missed him very much. Frau P thought at one point that her sister-in-law reproached her with managing things in such a way as to make it impossible for her brother to come back. However, the patient was later able to meet her brother again, but could not talk to him clearly, and she thought that he would understand her suffering since he knew the cause. My impression from Freud's account is that the patient was certain that there remained between her brother and herself some image related to their infantile sexuality which should be kept secret between them. Freud says that he was able after a time to help his patient talk about the various sexual scenes with her brother; these were related to the physical sensations in her abdomen. According to Freud, after this abreaction, the hallucinatory sensations and images disappeared; this enabled him to formulate the idea that the hallucinations were no more than parts of the content of repressed sexual experiences in childhood.

Frau P spoke constantly about her 'inner' voices and 'inner' hallucinations – one of them used to say 'Here comes Frau P'. At other moments the voices would repeat what she was reading in a book (this recalls Echo and Narcissus).

Freud thought that these voices had their origin in the repression of thoughts related to self-reproaches about her traumatic childhood sexual experiences: the voices were symptoms of the return of the repressed, and also a compromise between the resistance of the ego and the strength of the returning wishes. Freud writes at this point of 'distortions'[2] following Frau P's experiences with her hallucinated voices – distortions of her feelings and perceptions. The patient felt criticized by her inner hallucinated persecutory world, or, we could say, her inner 'neighbours'. Her only relief lay in her mental space, once the inner persecutors moved from the internal to the external world. But then she felt that people 'outside' were making mocking and critical remarks about her: 'There goes Frau P', was felt to mean that everybody in her environment was pointing at her in full knowledge of her infantile sexual fantasies and experiences. This atmosphere of criticism and mockery became unbearable, but it was the price she had to pay for her projections. It is in fact in this paper and thanks to this clinical case that Freud describes publicly for the first time the concept of 'projection',[3] the birth of which I shall now go on to discuss.

According to the Strachey translation, 'in paranoia, the self-reproach is repressed in a manner which may be described as *projection*'. This 'repression' is a particular one in that it consists of the erecting of a defensive symptom of distrust of other people. Freud uses the term projection as a *pro-ject* – a way of ejecting (*Verwerfung*[4]) the persecuting voices (the self- reproach) outside onto/into the world; the movement is much clearer in the original German text, where this kind

---

2   Freud uses the term 'distortion' to suggest the idea of a mistaken perception or a wrong interpretation of reality. This has to do with what Money-Kyrle was later to call 'misperception' and 'misunderstanding'.

3   In an earlier draft of the paper, sent to Fliess, he goes into it more fully (Freud 1950a, Draft H, Standard Edition, 1, 206).

4   The French psychoanalyst Jacques Lacan uses the term *Verwerfung* (repudiation or foreclosure) as a specific projective or 'rejective' mechanism which he terms *forclusion*. According to Lacan, this mechanism lies at the root of the psychotic experience, and consists in the primary ejection of a fundamental 'signifier' (for example, the 'name of the father' – an internal object? – as a rejected phallus) which is thrown outside, into the external world – i.e. out of the subject's symbolic and imaginary world.

of repression (*Verdrangung*) is a moving or *transfer* from inner space to the outer world, or 'inside the neighbours' – Frau P's persecuting inner voices were repressed (*verdrangt*) *into the Other*,[5] into persons in the outer world. It is clear to my mind that Freud's original formulation, whereby in paranoia projection takes place *into* other people, *into* objects is a precursor of Melanie Klein's notion of projective identification.

I must draw the reader's attention also to the fact that in the German text of his paper, Freud uses the expression *Wiederkehr des Verdrangten* (*Gesammelte Werke*, 1, p.401), translated as the 'return of the repressed'. Freud says that Frau P is 'deprived of a protection against the self-reproaches which return in (her) delusional ideas'; this today could be understood as a psychotic re-introjection, the re-introjection of a psychotic or deluded objet.

What I am really attempting to transmit here are my feelings and experience with psychotic patients and in particular with the phenomena of projection. My way of putting it is to use the term 'stereoscopic projection'. By this I mean a three-dimensional projection into other people or other objects or elements of reality. It is important to differentiate between normal and pathological projective identification, as some of the kleinian authors have attempted to do (e.g. Herbert Rosenfeld, in a personal communication). What can be misleading, in my opinion, is the fact that one does not acquire a real identity simply by projection, since, as Ferenczi put it (quoted by Freud in his 'Group Psychology' (1921)), it is nomal introjection which leads to the acquisition of an identity. Sandor Ferenczi introduced the term introjection as symmetrical to projection (*Introjektion und Ubertragung*, 1909); he pointed out that the paranoid patient expels unpleasant or persecutory tendencies from his ego, whereas the neurotic solution is to take into the ego as much as he possibly can from the external world and transform it into unconscious fantasy (which remains 'bearable' to his ego as Bion (1992) would put it).

I would now like to add something concerning projection of hallucinated objects, which was the case of Frau P when she 'transferred' or 'moved' her inner persecuting hallucinations into external 'houses' or living containers (her neighbours).

Leonardo, a 26-year-old Italian patient of mine, suffered from serious schizophrenia. After about two years' analysis with me, he said in one session:

> I am in a state in which I feel sleepy almost all of the time, and I must make a tremendous effort to wake up. A dream is pulling me back inside myself, and it won't allow me to come out from a disturbing experience in which various

5   Bei Paranoia wird der Vorwurf auf einem Wege, den man als Projektion bezeichnen kann, verdrängt, indem das Abwehrsymptom des Misstrauens gegen andere errichtet wird; dabei wird dem Vorwufe die Anerkennung Entzogen, und wie zur Vergeltung fehlt es dann an einem Shutze gegen die in den Wahnideen wiederdehrenden Vorwürfe. G.W. I, p.401.

voices are struggling among themselves in my head and sometimes in my stomach. One of them is the voice of Jesus Christ, another of a feminine version of Buddha (sometimes it is a masculine one, which I call 'Buddho'), another is the voice of Krishnamurti, the famous philosopher, or sometimes there is an Italian actor whom I admire very much, Carmello Bene. Then again, there is a black priest, an exorcist, Father Milingo. All these voices are in complete disagreement, with each wanting to convince the others. That's what's driving me crazy. Some days ago I had a wonderful idea. I put in front of myself an image of Jesus Christ, one of Buddha, a photo of Carmello Bene, one of Krishnamurti and another of Father Milingo – and I felt a great sense of relief.'

I asked him why. 'Because the voices disappeared from inside me, and appeared outside – you see, it was as though those pictures were talking to me, each in its own voice, sometimes separately.'

Like Frau P, Leonardo was able to transfer and to 'repress' (*verdrängen*) projectively his internal hallucinated voices into the others (the external representations). And so, like Frau P, he felt relieved inside because apparently he was able to control them better once they were 'framed' either as photos or graphic images. Sometimes, before his sessions in Paris, 20 rue Bonaparte in Saint-Germain-des-Prés, he would go to the romanic-style abbey church there and talk to the statue of Jesus Christ. In his dialogue with the sacred image, he could recognize in his own internal voice – so that, when he began the actual session, for Leonardo his session had already started some moments previously, since he had been talking to the holy analyst he had been able to create, by projective identification (repression into the object), in the space of the church, which was already equated with the analytical space of his session, with the idealized but deluded superego object located in the analyst.

The example of Leonardo enables me today to experience in my daily work with schizophrenic patients the same feelings that Freud wrote of in his work with Frau P. For me, 'A case of chronic paranoia' remains an essential example for understanding Freud's train of thought concerning his intuition of the experience of normal and pathological projective phenomena.

Griesinger (1817–1868), one of the pioneers of modern psychiatry, was already aware of the projective and depressive aspects of psychotic phenomena. Freud was keen on his work, since Griesinger was intuitively aware of the relationship between delusions and dreams, as well as the importance of wish-fulfilment. Delusions of grandeur, in psychosis, was, for Griesinger an expression of the wish to dominate and control a persecuting world around the individual.

I would like now to say a few words about Schreber's case, then I shall add a few comments about the 'Wolf-man', in order to highlight Freud's three main clinical examples, representing three important steps in the development of Freud's approach to the world of the psychoses.

The case of Daniel Paul Schreber

In his *Memoirs*, Daniel Paul Schreber wrote an open letter to his psychiatrist, Professor Fleschig in March 1903, when he had just finished writing the biography of his illness. To my mind, this letter is a vivid example of transference, in particular the delusional transference, which concerns the intensity of his emotional involvement with the paternal and maternal aspects of the transference situation – and this before the concept of transference was developed by Freud (1912).

In this letter, Schreber was trying to express aspects of his affection and concern with respect to his psychiatrist, in terms of regard and care for Professor Fleschig's feelings and sensitivity (so as not to hurt his feelings and to preserve a good object relationship). Schreber wrote: 'What I will say to you may well be painful for you. The hallucinatory voices come back from time to time and cry out your name. Sometimes they will do this several times a day. Apparently there is no conscious reason for your presence inside me, but you are nevertheless there, mainly when we do not see each other, that is when we are physically separated.'

This extract is an expression of Schreber's capacity to develop a positive and negative transference situation, and shows also the intensity of the link between him and Fleschig and the infantile transference that developed when he called for the presence of 'his' doctor, when they were separated. His desire for his doctor is a nostalgic infantile emotional need of a relationship with a warm 'maternal' father as against the image of a very cold and dominating figure. The word *desiderare* in Latin comes from *de* (away) + *sidus* (star), hence to desire an object implies the awareness of its absence and separate existence. In other words, a depressive experience underlies every feeling of desire; we should not therefore confuse desire with impulse or drive. In this sense, Griesinger suggested that depressive anxiety and melancholia appear at the onset of every psychotic breakdown as the expression of the loss of an object, a part of the body (surgical operation), or other similar situations. He called this 'the basic anxiety', from which different clinical psychopathological symptomatology develops, for example deep melancholia or, reactively, mania, obsessions, depersonalization, personality splitting, etc.

In his paper on President Schreber, Freud (1911) was concerned about the dichotomy between what was reported in Schreber's autobiography and the *raison d'être* of the complexities of his breakdown. In other words, Freud was interested in the real facts or events in his life which might have precipitated the psychotic regression and mental distortions.

We know from Ida Macalpine's study that Daniel Paul Schreber was the son of a distinguished family, and that his father Daniel Gottlob Moriz Schreber, of Leipzig, the son of an advocate, was a famous physician and lecturer at Leipzig University, where he founded an Institute of Gymnastics and Orthopaedics. The father was an educationalist and social reformer, with a quasi-apostolic mission 'to bring health, happiness and bliss to the masses through physical culture'. He published a number of books, in which he attempted to convince 'the world' that his medical ideology of bringing health through concrete physical activity was sufficient, even though it left no room whatever for any emotions or romantic conception of life. It would appear that the young Daniel Paul Schreber had – from his early childhood on – to deal with a persuasively mechanical and rigidly moralistic and 'inhuman' concept of life. I would think that his inner world of childhood fantasy and playful tendencies was very stifled; the only way to develop his personality was probably in terms of a concrete and rigid truth which no doubt played some role in his identification with his grandfather, the advocate – hence his study of law and his later becoming a judge, so identifying himself partly at least with a rigid paternal superego. This may well have implied for him a continuation of his father's system of values, that of a moralistic (ethical?) mission – to save mankind. The father's mechanistic ideology of life left no space for emotional or personal social life. In Freudian terms, his concrete body ego made no allowance for a living place for his mental or psychic ego: in this conception the human being could be no more than a physical being, and so it was only from his body that Daniel Schreber could find a solution to the mental and social vicissitudes of his life. This charismatic father-conception of life with no room for mental space made Daniel's life very restricted, as though his body was confined in some kind of strait-jacket. For the young Schreber, the father's inflexible law became a part of his professional attitude towards daily life, with no room for fantasy in everyday reality – only in his inner, personal, eccentric reality. One could suggest that his delusion was a way of solving the problem of how to identify with a rigid, obsessional and paranoid father – it was only through his delusion that he was able to have creative fantasies. I would suppose that he found it impossible to introject a good and flexible image of a paternal superego or inner father, which would allow him to take responsibility for the paternity of his own life and his own system of ideas. This may be the reason why he did not himself have children – other than in his delusion, as a woman identified with his maternal inner object or maternal superego.

For Schreber, the only way to be alive and creative was on the one hand to identify with his mother – a delusional identification which enabled him to be *pregnant* during his major breakdown, when his body was transformed into that of a woman able to procreate – and therefore *to be creative*; and on the other hand, the only possible alternative father figure that he could introject as different from his own father was Professor Fleschig, during an intense transference situation, in which the idea of infantile, delusional and erotic aspects is already present. Daniel Schreber 'introjected' an idealized delusional and megalomaniac (persecutory) father figure, thus allowing him to change his very nature and become pregnant by the idealized good father. One could see his autobiography not only as a self-analysis and an attempt at self-healing, but also a rich delusional world which, together with his depth of culture and his scholarly knowledge allowed him to produce an interesting book: in other words, to give birth to his *Memoirs*.

One could interpret his book as an expression of his spiritual and cultivated world in his attempt to find his way, his mental space, as against only a bodily, concrete space that his father emphasized. Indeed, the only way the paternal superego would allow him to live was though his physical body – and this is precisely what he is struggling against through his delusional world and delusional transformation in becoming a woman. To be a woman, indeed a pregnant woman, was also a metaphorical, delusional way of being creative. Becoming pregnant by his analyst in the delusional transference was Schreber's way of becoming a fertile couple, in contrast to the sterile couple that was Schreber and his wife.

One could hypothesize, as we follow Schreber's life through the different versions extant – his own, that of Freud, and the other major studies – that, just as in any delusion or other psychotic illness, there was something concrete and real in his family and social life which stimulated his own psychotic tendencies.

During his first crisis, in 1884, Schreber suffered in his body in a delusional hypochondriac way from what could not be mentalized. He was admitted to the Leipzig psychiatric clinic, where he remained for over a year, until the end of 1885, treated by Professor Paul Emile Fleschig. He responded in a positive way, and this enabled him to take up his post again as a judge in the Supreme Court, where he remained for several years.

Until he fell ill a second time, he was able to continue working as a judge; in other words, he accepted the role and the responsibility of an *official* paternal function. This, however, was in itself insufficient in that he was unable to father children or to have a wife able to give him children. In October 1893, after taking up office as *Senatspräsident*, he was again admitted to Fleschig's clinic. In June 1894, he was then sent to Lindenhof, a private asylum in Coswig near Dresden. A fortnight later, he was transferred to Sonnenstein asylum, close to Dresden, where he remained for almost nine years; this was where he wrote his *Memoirs*. In the preface to this book, dated 1902, he stated his intention to leave the asylum early in 1903. He had succeeded in having his tutelage rescinded in September 1902 and from then on was free to discharge himself. The 'open letter' to Professor Fleschig, which also prefaces the *Memoirs*, was written in Dresden in March 1903, which implies that he had left the asylum by then. There are no subsequent reliable data about him.

Perhaps 'producing' his Memoirs, as I mentioned above, was, for Schreber, equated with fathering the child he was also able to procreate as a woman. In this sense, we could see his complex delusional world as a pathological realization of an ideal ego through which he would also be able to recreate the idealized image of a divine androgyne, as in Plato's *Symposium*. Schreber's delusional construction was in some ways a wish-fulfillment that had its own (delusional) logic in his metaphysical and philosophical conception of the universe.

According to Baumeyer (1951), Schreber had a third relapse after the death of his wife in 1907. This painful experience in reality woke him from his self-centred delusional world and plunged him into reality, thus enabling him to experience the loss of a woman, his wife, who was not at that time equated with any successful realization of his own androgynous fantasy. As I said above, the importance of the mourning process after the loss of an object is a starting point in what Griesinger calls the 'basic depression', which precedes every psychotic breakdown. In the case of Schreber, the fantasy of becoming a pregnant woman and thereafter a grandiose mother dramatizes in a fetishistic manner his own body with feminine ornaments and cheap jewellery which, I am sure, he felt was very valuable. This means for me that his depressive breakdowns were related to disillusion concerning his ego ideal when the reality principle drove him back to feelings of impotence and sterility. Thus, there is a disillusion not only concerning the object but also about his own narcissistic illusions and wishes. I call this phenomenon 'narcissistic depression', a concept based on the loss of an important part of the ego, the idealized delusional ego ideal that is sometimes treated as an object but usually takes the place *of* the object, that is, of *otherness*.

In his study of Schreber (1911), *Psychoanalytische Bemerkungen Uber Einen Autobiographishch Beschiebenen Fall von Paranoia* (dementia paranoides), Freud attempts to understand the world view or *Weltanschaaung* (Jasper's term) of such an interesting delusional person, as well as the divorce, in psychosis, between inner and outer reality. Freud realized that the delusional person is able to transform everyday reality into a personal reality which has its *own* principles, in contrast to the normal reality principle.

The concept of psychotic transference, already present in Schreber's memoirs, enables us to understand the effect and implications of his early childhood and adolescent experience in a pathological family climate, with a rigidly obsessive father figure whom he was unable to face up to in reality and perhaps also a mother who was of little help in his wish to develop his own personality in a non-delusional way, which reinforced the psychotic part of his personality. One can imagine also that many of the normal questions of a child and of an adolescent found no adequate answer, and many misunderstandings on his part, about his daily life, could not be corrected through adequate responses from his environment. We could say, following Money-Kyrle's ideas on cognitive development, that delusional ideas of a persecutory kind have their roots in real events that have been misunderstood by the child and perhaps also by his parents, with no opportunity or space for clarification. It is difficult to imagine Schreber's father, with his strongly dogmatic conceptions on the role of an absolute bodily ideology, with no space for ambiguity or discussion, helping him to understand the doubts that must have been present in his mind.

Thanks to his delusional realization, Schreber was able to find a place for himself. In his delusional world, according to his 'logical' formulation, he speaks of his 'father Fleschig', his ideal ego, as being 'God'. In this mythical and religious system of ideas, he speaks of two categories of 'rays'. One, inferior, came from Ariman and changed him into a woman, and the other, superior, from Ormuzd, allowed his masculinity to be restored. This was his way of installing a sort of delusional reparation or reversibility of his transformations, related always to his delusional transference towards the God-Fleschig.

As in every delusion built on a basic misunderstanding, there was a grain of truth: he wished to create or re-create through his father-Fleschig a father figure enabling him to internalize or re-introject his need to be a productive and helpful mate for his wife.

In his self-centred conviction, he spoke of 'little souls' dispersed throughout the universe being attracted to him. This spatial phenomenon introduces Karl Wernicke's conception of *Eigenbeziehungen* (see above). In the verb *ziehen* there is the idea of pulling or being attracted by. This implies a transformation of the picture of the psychotic world, in which the patient becomes the centre of a planetary system where his illuminating delusional ideas change him into an infantile God-child and his environment into a devoting universe of admirers. This reminds me of one of my own cases, Leonard, who phoned me a few days ago to ask whether God and Christ were the same thing. In his delusional transference, he transformed me into the God of the Old Testament, while he as Christ tried to outshine me. I answered that he should not confuse me with himself in our respective roles – something we would attempt to clarify in the next session. In my account of Freud's view on Schreber's *Memoirs*, I cannot avoid associating with my present experience as a psychoanalyst working with psychotic patients. It is also one way of establishing a sort of imaginary dialogue with Freud – or with Schreber.

Schreber's delusional construction is an expression of an ideological conception of his existence which also liberates him from his father's prison. In this sense, the onset of his psychotic crisis is a moment of liberation – except that, in order to find his way in this newly transformed world, he needs to use delusional ideas as a triumphal flag which no one else can take from him or cast down. For French classical psychiatry, a strong delusional system of ideas is equated with unshakeable conviction (*conviction inébranlable*). Another function of Schreber's expansive delusional system is to fill an immense emptiness in his life: the limits imposed by a castrating judge-father. I can understand that it must have been a difficulty for the real judge that was Daniel Schreber to struggle for his freedom with the unshakeable judge that was his father.

The case of Daniel Paul Schreber, in Freud's reading of it, is very present in my work as a psychoanalyst. This is particularly so when I read of Schreber's feeling of being changed into a woman and being fertilized by powerful divine rays – these, the centre of his universe, acquire the character of a sidereal ejaculation – since one of my own cases, Henri, a young schizophrenic, told me with great emotion in one session that the previous evening he saw a comet in the shape of a giant spermatozoid. For Henri, this had the meaning of an eroticized transference in a sidereal relationship with me, in which he needed me to be transformed into a powerful ideal ego that would change him and help him to emerge from his obscure and sterile life. (It is interesting to note that the Stoic philosophers used to speak of *logos spermatikos*, the creative principle which helped to organize and coordinate the life of micro-cosmos and macro-cosmos.) In terms of present-day psychoanalytical concepts, in particular of Melanie Klein's writings on the maternal ideal ego as the embodied universe containing the original primitive father, and also Herbert Rosenfeld's ideas on the neurotic transference of psychotic patients (which requires a very delicate approach), one could say that excessive idealization or eroticization is the corollary of a depressive or persecutory experience in which death impulses dominate the life-instincts.

The 'Wolf-man'

Freud's paper on the 'Wolf-man' (1918 [1914]) completes my outlook on what I regard as the three fundamental clinical texts by Freud which describe his approach to psychosis. In the case of the Wolf-man, Freud was very involved in his countertransference; this demonstrated his great interest in understanding the complexities of his patient's life. Apparently, in his transference relationship, Freud showed a certain freedom and he needed to discover a new outlook on the technique of psychoanalysis as applied to psychosis.

He saw this young Russian patient for the first time in 1910, describing him as a young man whose health had broken down in his eighteenth year after a gonorrheal infection. The boy tried to continue his studies, but his neurotic disturbances and his obsessional symptoms did not allow him to succeed, develop his personality and make his way in life. A recurrent element in his analysis consisted of his memories and fantasies of having being seduced as a child of three by his governess, as well as having felt threatened with castration when for educational reasons (or perhaps in a playful way) she would tell him that she was about to bite his 'widdler'.

Apparently, his games with his elder sister were highly erotic in nature; in addition, he felt very persecuted by his new English governess and by his father. The basic material which Freud explores is the 'dream of the primal scene', which the patient could remember very clearly – this was in fact more a nightmare than a dream. 'I dreamt it was night; I was lying in my bed. In front of the window stood a row of old walnut trees. I know it was winter. Suddenly the window opened of its own accord and I was terrified to see several wolves, all white, sitting on the branches of the big walnut tree. The wolves looked more like foxes or sheep-dogs, for they had big tails like foxes and their ears pricked like dogs when they pay attention to something.' The little boy was in great terror of being eaten by the wolves: 'I screamed and woke up.' How did the wolves come to be on the tree? This reminded him of a story he had heard his grandfather tell. The story runs as follows: a tailor was sitting at work in his room, when the window opened and a wolf leapt in. The patient said at first that the tailor hit out at the wolf with his yard-stick, then corrected himself and said that the tailor caught the wolf by the tail and pulled it off. Later, in the forest, the tailor is attacked by a pack of wolves, including the one whose tail he had pulled off. He climbs a tree, the wolves make as though to follow him, but he shouts out 'Catch the tail of that one', and they all tumble down as the tail-less wolf, terrified by his recollection of the earlier incident, runs off.

Freud was concerned by his patient's cannibalistic tendencies and castration complex. For Freud, the wolf stood for the patient's father in a persecutory role and it seems that this threatening image was related to punishment for his voyeuristic experiences or fantasies concerning the primal scene. It is not exactly clear at what age the patient had this nightmarish dream, but in the tree there are five branches and five wolves, one of which, near the middle of the drawing, looks like a lion. It seems to me that the tree must stand for his 'chronological' life – in other words that the five branches stand for five years, which would be therefore his age approximately. As to the 'wolf-lion', the patient was told, when he was about seven or eight, that the next day a new tutor was coming for him. That night, he dreamt of his tutor in the shape of a lion that approached his bed, roaring loudly, and in the posture of the wolf in the drawing of the dream. The patient remembered the master at secondary school who taught him Latin – the name of this teacher was Wolf.

In his 'Seminar' (1955–1956), the French psychoanalyst, Jacques Lacan, considered the Wolf-man's dream as a key to understanding psychosis. This patient, according to Lacan (1981), manifested strong paranoid tendencies at the end of his analysis with Freud. Lacan thought that the patient needed to reject any approach to the idea of castration and, through his dream-nightmare, managed to 'throw' this threat out of the window (*Verwerfung*) in order to protect himself from complete madness.

I mentioned above the German version of the first use Freud makes of the term 'projection', understood in Frau P's case as getting rid (*verwerfen*) of her inner persecuting voices by throwing them into her neighbours. This, as I have said, could indicate that the concept of projective identification was already present – perhaps unconsciously – in Freud's way of thinking at that time.

For Lacan, the word 'wolf' related to the Latin teacher and 'lion' related to the tutor, acquired the meaning of 'signifiers'. This is one of the major concepts in Lacan's theory, which I have found very useful to further my understanding: words, names or facts of life remain unconsciously strongly meaningful throughout the individual's whole life. A 'signifier' (*signifiant*) is an important vehicle for containing – and for transporting – meanings (*signifié*). Lacan introduced the concept of 'forclosure' or 'repudiation' (*forclusion* in French, corresponding to *Verwerfung* in German as used by Freud). According to my reading of Lacan, the tree can stand for the 'phallus' as a signifier of the Oedipal complex, thrown out of the window (*verweft*) together with all the meaningful wolves (and goats, lions, dogs ...) as upsetting and maddening '*signifiés*' the patient was trying to get rid of. The repudiated signifier, projected outside into open nature, becomes merged with the landscape in such a way that it cannot come back and be re-introjected in order to become part of the patient's inner reality. In the case of Wolf-man, the terms '*verwerfen*' and '*verwerfung*' are very often present in Freud's account. Lacan uses Freud's text on 'Negation' (*Die Verneinung*, 1925) in order to define the relationship between forclosure and the primary process, defined as two complementary processes – *Einbeziehung ins Ich* (introduction into the individual) and *Ausstossung aus dem Ich* (expulsion from the individual). As in the phenomenon of hallucination, what is being repudiated out of the 'imaginary' and 'symbolic' networks emerges in the real world in a concrete manner like the Wolf-man's oneiric or deluded hallucination.

For Lacan, in the Wolf-man case, the principal signifier is what he calls 'the name-of-the-father', what the father represents in our unconscious. As to the concept of forclosure or repudiation, Lacan uses the expression 'ejaculating words' (*paroles jaculatoires*) in his chapter entitled 'The Phallus and the Meteor' (1981, p.349); this idea recalls what I said above on the subject of Henri and his ejaculatory hallucination of seeing a comet (or a meteor) in the sky. Bion speaks of long-distance projections into other planets, where the projected or rejected object is too upsetting or persecutory. I have in earlier papers pointed out that psychotic or severely borderline patients are very much afraid of establishing an intimate object relationship; in such a case, the transference has to find long-distance mediation, a communication 'via satellite'; Henri seemed to need to use the meteor/comet as a kind of satellite mediator in order to transform hallucination into a psychoanalytical logos (*logos spermaitkos*) (Resnik 1952).

I do not for the moment wish to elaborate further on these topics. I shall simply point out the fact that some of Freud's clinical cases enable me and other writers to project ourselves into Freud's mind in order to understand how he felt in the transference and countertransference situation whenever he was faced with psychotic *phenomena*.

Further developments, other authors …

In 1919, Victor Tausk published his *Ueber die Entstehung des 'Beeinflussungsapparates'
in der Schizophrenia* – to my mind a highly original work which furthers my
understanding of the delusional aspects of the psychotic transference. In this
clinical case, Tausk studies the delusion of patients who feel themselves
persecuted by a hallucinated 'magic mystical machine' or who experience in their
body – for instance, in the bowels – the fact that their gastro-intestinal system is
being directed in its 'movements' (peristaltic) by specific demons who live there
and direct the patient's life. Tausk calls this phenomenon 'paranoia somatica',
term which I find interesting in that it indicates that outer persecutors are being
introjected or re-introjected into parts of the body, becoming the subject of a
delusional hypochondriasis. Tausk puts the accent on the eroticization of the
influencing machine and of parts of the body, in terms of projections of the
patient's unconscious erotic fantasies. In the case of Fraulein Natalia A, the
influencing machine took on the shape of a human body, as a projection –
according to Tausk – of the patient's own body.

I recall the case of a chronically deluded patient who said to me: 'I should be
awarded a Nobel Prize, because I have invented a machine which makes other
people deluded.' This made me think that it is necessary to differentiate the
deluded object projected into others or into the patient's own body from the
'delusional' object, which can transform reality in a way similar to my patient,
who was able to make *reality* deluded. This difference is important from the point
of view of the psychotic transference, inasmuch as the analyst's countertransference depends on his capacity for reverie (Bion) – the ability to introject a
deluded object without becoming deluded, as the psychotic patient sometimes
tries to make us in order to demonstrate his alchemical powers that enable him to
change the nature and meaning of matter.

Paul Federn, a pupil of Freud who was interested in the treatment of psychotic
patients, developed (1953) the concept of the affective contact or relationship
with the psychotic patient, someone who has lost his ego feelings. Federn speaks
also of the analyst's ego feelings and of the possibility of establishing an
emotional transference relationship. According to this author, the psychotic
patient is afraid to establish contact with the analyst because of the vulnerability
of his ego, hence the importance of the positive transference and the difficulty for
such patients to tolerate the negative transference.

In 1920, Herman Nunberg presented the case of a catatonic patient to the
Vienna Psychoanalytic Society. He was able to communicate with the patient,
even though in one session he was constrained in a strait-jacket. The patient,
unsurprisingly, felt 'crucified'. Nunberg established a relationship with him, and
the negative transference was expressed through the fact that he had been
imprisoned in the strait-jacket by the authorities of the institution – at the same
time, he was therefore able to protect his analyst from his destructive tendencies,

an expression of his positive transference. In 1928, Ruth Mack Brunswick speaks explicitly for the first time on the concept of psychotic transference.

In the United States, Paul Federn and Harry Stack Sullivan (a pupil of Adolf Meyer) developed in the 1930s – and, later, with the collaboration of Freda Fromm-Reichmann at Chestnut Lodge, near Washington – a major research and application centre for the psychoanalysis of psychotic patients, including schizophrenics.

In England, a very important contribution to the understanding of infantile autism and adult psychosis was developed around the work of Melanie Klein, whose seminars and supervisions I was personally able to attend until her death in 1960. Klein's work on the *Importance of Symbol Formation in the Development of the Ego* (1930) was a major contribution to the understanding of the transference psychosis in patients almost incapable of play and self-revelation. The paper furthers our comprehension not only of autistic phenomena but also of negativism and the inability to relate to others. Klein was able to make contact with the inner world of deeply regressed patients; this requires an intuitive understanding of archaic models of communication. She was able to establish contact with Dick, a four-year-old boy who had no language; little by little he was able to develop a playful capacity to relate to his therapist, thanks to which she could further her ideas on proto-symbolic phenomena (such as the symbolic equation and the origins of symbol formation).

After Klein's death, at a time when I was in analysis with Herbert Rosenfeld, I was able to follow the contributions to psychosis made by Rosenfeld himself, Bion and Hanna Segal. Already a psychoanalyst in Argentina, where I had been a pupil of Enrique Pichon-Rivière, a major figure in the psychoanalytical field in that country, I was introduced to the kleinian school of thought by him and by Angel Garma (who trained in Europe while Freud was still alive). Pichon-Rivière wrote a paper on the psychoanalysis of schizophrenia (1947) in which he shows that he was already aware of the dynamic changes in psychotic patients in psychoanalytic psychotherapy, when the transference develops either in an individual context or in an institutional setting. Some of his patients were chronic because they had no opportunity to relate to someone both intuitively sensitive to primitive modes of functioning and capable of withstanding mental pain and psychotic anxiety. He believed, following Greisinger, that the psychotic process – as well, probably, as the neurotic one – starts in general with a painful mourning experience (separation anxiety) related not only to the loss of another significant person in the patient's life, but also to that of 'internal' object relationships and parts of the body (after, for example, a surgical operation). This phenomenon was described by Greisinger many years ago as characteristic of the basic depressive situation, leading to 'castration anxiety' and feelings of mental mutilation. Following Freud's and Abraham's ideas on regression to primitive erogenous zones, and through his understanding of regressive models of relationships,

Pichon-Rivière attempted to clarify the various clinical mental 'organizations' (obsessional, manic, hypochondriac, melancholic and schizophrenic) and modes of reaction to the feeling of loss. The basic post-traumatic depression gives a *unified* conception of the different ways in which regression to pre-genital stages is stimulated, contributing thus to the construction or organization of those psychiatric clinical categories which for other schools of thought are so diversified (Kraepelin, etc).

Pichon-Rivière thought that Bleuler's contribution to ideas on the splitting of the ego and the phenomenon of dispersion and disorganization of the world (inner and outer) was very important. I have discussed above the birth of delusional phenomena in the case of Frau P, Schreber and the Wolf-man in Freud's research. Pichon-Rivière explored the way in which such phenomena appear in the (delusional) transference. He considered that schizophrenia is the most complex psychotic organization in which almost all the regressive mechanisms he described appear once the transference is mobilized. He spoke of three periods of evolution: the period of loss and delusional recovery of the object, the period of expulsion or evacuation of the persecutory or anxiety-generating object, and the period of psychotic restitution or psychotic organization in order to recover lost relationships within an 'imposing' delusional model of the world (what H. Rosenfeld was later to call the political and mafia organization).

In Buenos-Aires, David Liberman and I, under the supervision of Pichon-Rivière, began analysing psychotic patients in the late 1940s. We were at that point very interested in what Knight was doing at the Menninger Clinic in Topeka (California), in Frieda Fromm-Reichmann's work at Chestnut Lodge, and in Rosen's paper on *direct analysis* (1947). We considered Rosen's contribution both fascinating and dangerous, because of the possibility of 'acting' in the transference: his aim was to identify with the persecutory object which he transformed 'seductively' into a good object, thus avoiding the negative transference and stimulating erotomanic behaviour. In those days, Sechehaye's book (1951) also had a great influence on French and English-speaking psychoanalysts.

Later still, Harold Searles' papers on transference and countertransference in psychosis developed Margaret Mahler's views on the symbiotic transference and were a very useful contribution to thinking in this field. Bion's explorations of the maternal reverie in the transference were of course illuminating, though they have to be completed by the concept of 'paternal' reverie.[6] These two types of reverie are based not only on object relationships but also on the paternal and maternal functions in all human beings. I recall Bion's saying that inasmuch as each of us has a father and a mother, we internalize two different and complementary

---

6   The term is due to Flavio Nose of Verona, with whom I developed the idea.

models of being. Thus, the containing 'function' of the mother in the transference (Winnicott and Bion) needs to be completed by the organizing and structuring 'function' of the paternal ego. I prefer therefore to speak in terms of 'functions' (maternal and paternal) rather than simply in terms of 'objects'. Thus, a male or female psychoanalyst should be able to make contact with his own capacity to experience maternal and paternal transference and countertransference.

Donald Winnicott's approach to young children and early maternal relationships, with their deep and intimate primitive feelings, helped me to understand severe regressions in the transference of psychotic patients. His concept of transitional phenomena, transitional space and transitional objects enabled me to develop my views on the psychopathology of space in the transference situation with such severely regressed patients. Symbiotic, fusional or adhesive (Meltzer) aspects of the transference sometimes appear as an unavoidable step towards understanding of the 'construction' of a space for transference, though at the same time they seem, to my mind, to be a defensive mechanism against the actual – real – space between patient and analyst. Sometimes this 'space-between' mother and child or patient and analyst is experienced as an upsetting, bottomless, chaotic space in which the infantile self of one or other of the protagonists can collapse and fall to pieces. This gives rise to an unconscious collusion between the partners in order to annul the now panic-laden and agoraphobic experience of space.

Money-Kyrle's papers, such as *On Cognitive Development* (1968) and *The Fear of Insanity* (1969) are quite remarkable; they further our understanding of the genesis or construction of a delusional conception of the world. He speaks of early (unconscious) misunderstandings between child and parents – and also, he suggests, between patient and analyst – which lead to misperceptions and misconceptions, for instance of the primal scene and the oedipus complex. Money-Kyrle believed that psychotic patients suffer from unconscious misunderstandings which, in not being questioned or properly understood, engender through time rigid delusional conceptions. The classical French psychiatrists used to speak of 'delusional convictions' which appear to be 'unshakeable and unmovable'.

Dr Pietro Bria, from the Catholic University of Rome, and I followed Money-Kyrle's idea that the basic unconscious misunderstandings in life can lead to delusional thinking; however, according to us, the misunderstandings in this case were probably shared by both child and parents. These basic mis-understandings were originally ambiguous or equivocal situations leadi͏ strong 'disagreements' which turned into rigidly held beliefs concer͏ bringing-up of children or reality-testing. These phenomena are repe͏ in the transference of psychotic patients, particularly schizophr͏ can usually be present as witnesses or co-actors in the dramati͏ ambiguous or contradictory experience in the mind of the patient (intra-psychic phenomenon) or between him and his family and societal environment (inter-psychic or inter-personal phenomenon). Both situations have to do with inner and outer transference phenomena.

In England, I was in contact with R.D. Laing, when, in 1958, he was correcting the proofs of his famous book *The Divided Self.* Reading it I found myself very enthusiastic over his subtle phenomenological descriptions and deep understanding of psychotic phenomena (mainly splitting of the personality and delusional conceptions of the world in schizophrenic patients). We were able to exchange views on the psychoanalytic approach of such patients. We met through Dr Jock Sutherland, who was at that time the director of the Tavistock Clinic, who became interested in my experience with psychotics in groups and in individual treatment, as well as in the fact that I came from Paris, where during one year, I had been a student of Merleau-Ponty's at the Collège de France in phenomenology (on the child's relationship to its mother and the way it experiences its living environment and daily landscapes). Sutherland thought that it would be interesting for me to meet Laing through the Tavistock – and so, in 1958 and 1959, Laing, Esterson, Cooper and I, together with a small group of other colleagues, met every week in one house or another to read our own draft papers on psychotic patients, their families and various institutions. We would discuss papers by Ludwig Binswanger, E. Minkowski and others who were working on a phenomenological approach to such questions. Later, I became a friend of Joseph Berke, who followed in Laing's footsteps; his book on Mary Barnes,[7] written in collaboration with his patient, from the point of view of old misunderstandings and the construction of a delusional world, is really quite important – and here both patient and analyst could express what they felt throughout a delusional transference experience.

My aim in this paper is to address my English-speaking colleagues, with some of whom I was in touch during my London years. As to the French school, I was inspired by some of the outstanding psychiatrists of the 1960s such as Daumezon and Henri Ey as well as the psychoanalyst Pierre Mâle, who at that time was working with Daumezon. I had the opportunity of following the seminars of Jacques Lacan, and I knew Piera Aulagnier, who made a significant contribution to the psychoanalytical approach to psychotic patients; I was aware, too, of the on-going work of Racamier, R. Diatkine, the Kestembergs, Green and others. I do not, however, consider myself sufficiently in touch with these writers to deal adequately with their various contributions to this field, some of which are extremely significant and valuable.

Berke, J. and Barnes, M.(1871) *Mary Barnes: Two Accounts of a Journey through Madness.* London: MacGibbon & Kee.

On the other hand, I owe it to E. Pichon-Rivière and to G. Daumezon for enabling me to have further training in clinical psychiatry and for putting me in contact with the major clinical and theoretical papers of Séglas, Cotard, Chaslin, Charcot, Pierre Janet and de Clérambault which helped me to make a review or 'biography' of the concept of psychosis and the psychoanalytical approach to this disturbance, the main matter of this chapter. When I worked with Daumezon, I began to participate in the work of a group dealing with the understanding of the psychotic patient, particularly chronic schizophrenics, in institutional settings. In France, this group is known as '*psychothérapie institutionnelle*', represented mainly by François Tosquelles, Jean Oury and others.

The psychoanalytic approach to groups of psychotic patients

In the *Preliminary communication* with Breuer (1893), which I still consider to be a very important paper from a historical point of view, Freud uses the expression '*group of ideas*' to refer to the capacity – or incapacity – to associate ideas. He speaks of 'dissociation' or splitting of ideas, and of ideas being split off into the body (in the case of hysteria), corresponding to a concept he was soon to develop of conversive hysteria. In the case of Frau Emmy von N (whom he began treating in May 1889) Freud speaks of the inaccessibility of certain ideas or *groups of ideas* that can become disconnected from the mind. He uses also the expression 'feelings of the mind' or '*group of feelings*'. On this occasion (1893, p.89) Freud uses the term *Besetzung*, translated as 'cathexis' but which corresponds more to the idea of 'sites' of the mind or of the body, to which some quantity of psychic energy or feeling is unconsciously attached or invested. Already by then Freud was thinking in terms of the group-mind, as a way of thinking about ideas and about the vicissitudes of the 'life' of the unconscious. He speaks also of mental forces, a concept related to that used by Kurt Lewin with respect to the idea of 'field'.

In 1921, Freud suggested that there is no contradiction between an individual and a group outlook when it comes to human phenomena. In this text, he describes social phenomena in contrast to the narcissistic tendencies, or autistic ones (Bleuler 1912). He anticipates Bion's metaphors when the latter speaks of narcissism and social-ism. Freud's preoccupation with groups and the psychoses are potentially present in his comments on Le Bon and MacDougall's concepts of masses and *group minds* as a collective phenomenon in which the individual can lose control of himself. As with borderline patients and psychotics, Freud suggests that the group or mass in a state of regression tends to act instead of thinking. In disturbed groups, contradictory ideas can exist side by side, with apparently no logical contradiction – just as in the psychotic's split personality. The group or mass under such conditions becomes mentally weak and falls under the sway of the dictator-leader. This concept will later be developed by Bion in his writings on the mystic and the group (Bion, 1970) and the significance of the charismatic leader. In such a case, the group becomes 'blind' – there is a 'blind spot' – on which the charismatic leader projects his illuminations.

In his 1921 text, Freud speaks of two artificial groups, the church and the army, organized in such a way that they avoid disintegration and achieve their ideological aims. The important factor in this paper is the fact that Freud developed the concept of identification in both normal and pathological dimensions. The latter refers to massive identification with the idealized father (the ideal of the ego); in this part of his paper, Freud, following his 1914 text on narcissism, sees this as a further confrontation between the individual ego ideal and that of the group.

Since my aim in this chapter concerns the applications of Freud's concepts to the field of groups of psychotic patients (and in particular schizophrenics) – he himself had no direct experience of this kind of work – my thread of thought takes me to something familiar to my own practice. I began working with groups of psychotics in 1950, when very few papers describing a genuine psychoanalytical approach existed – that is, working within the psychotic and neurotic transference situations. I knew of some experimental work being done by Paul Schilder, J.W. Powell, A. Stone, J.D. Frank, F. Powdermaker and others. (I shall comment on the work done by these practitioners in another publication.) Harry Stack Sullivan was by then becoming well known, as well as Freida Fromm-Reichmann, concerned as they were by the social aspects of the daily life of institutional patients. I began working with groups of chronic schizophrenics in the mental hospital of Buenos Aires on the initiative of Dr Raul J. Usandivaras, at a time when we were both trainee psychoanalysts. As soon as we started a group of ten patients (mainly chronic schizophrenics) we were fortunate that Dr John Morgan was returning from the Tavistock Clinic after a six-month stint during which he attended Bion's experiments with groups. Thanks to Morgan, we were able to make indirect contact with the way in which Bion managed the psychotic and neurotic transference in groups. The most outstanding aspect of our once-weekly group was its climate or atmosphere of emptiness and desolation. In one session, after a long upsetting silence, during which Dr Usandivaras, Dr Morgan and I felt very lonely and abandoned, one of the patients raised an empty metallic cup; another patient began mumbling something indistinctly, saying that as he was unable to speak clearly, perhaps he could communicate his feelings through singing. He sang an impressive but monotonous and nostalgic litany, expressing the same emptiness as the raised cup; this was a symbolic expression of a transference phenomenon which acted upon our countertransference. Another patient, very regressed and autistic, had mannerisms which we were unable fully to comprehend. Still another pronounced the words 'brother' and 'doctor'. We understood that the group was trying to experience some degree of brotherhood between the members, unable as they were to communicate properly in their search for boundaries and for a place able to contain the full extent of their confusion and distressing emptiness. We interpreted this to the common denominator of the group (Ezriel 1950). At the same time as we were attempting to discover the common element of the group – this was also Bion's way of proceeding – we were concerned by the different levels and means of communication within the group: gestures, stereotypes, mannerisms and pre-verbal expression became material for our research in the field. Three years later, I published a paper on the subject (Resnik 1953).

When I arrived in France in 1957, I was able to organize a group – for diagnostic purposes – of psychotic patients in the admissions ward of the Sainte-Anne psychiatric hospital, Paris, under the direction of Dr Daumezon. This was a comparative study of psychiatric semiotics, comparing the same patients in an initial individual interview and in a group or social interactive interview; this was, obviously, an 'open' group. In 1958, I went to London, where I remained for 14 years, during which I worked with groups of psychotic patients in various places, such as Netherne Hospital (Coulsdon, Croydon) where I was in charge of the therapeutic community of young psychotic patients. I was then able to exchange views with Maxwell-Jones, who was responsible for a unit of psychopathic patients in Belmont. In 1959, and for the following few years, I worked, thanks to Malcolm Pines, at the Cassel Hospital in Richmond; there I followed some psychotic patients on an individual basis as well as in groups. I was permitted to work with psychotics because my research interest and some of my published papers were becoming known.

At that point, I contacted S.H. Foulkes, who – gently – allowed me to take a group of schizophrenic patients (originally from the Netherne Hospital – they followed me to London after their discharge from hospital) and treat them in his private practice. I discussed with Foulkes and his assistants (mainly Malcolm Pines and Patrick DeMare) different aspects of the neurotic and psychotic transference as manifested in group work. At that time, I had supervision with Bion for schizophrenic patients in individual analysis. Bion himself was then focusing on psychotic patients in analysis, though, since 1952, he was no longer working in a group setting with such patients. Nevertheless, like Freud at the outset, he was still using concepts such as 'group of ideas' in all their pathogenic (and normal) adventures in the thinking process (again, both normal and delusional). *His Experiences in Groups* (1961) begins with his experiences at the Northfield Military Hospital, in a paper written in collaboration with John Rickmann on 'intra-group tensions in therapy'. Bion worked with therapeutic groups at the Tavistock until 1952, dealing mainly with patients suffering from neuroses or character disorders. Since I arrived in London in 1958, I never actually saw Bion practise with groups, but, on the other side of a two-way mirror, I was able to see how Drs Sutherland, Turckey, R.H. Gosling and other followers of Bion worked in this field.

When I returned to Paris in the 1970s, I continued my practice of working with groups of schizophrenics, in different settings, including the University Hospital and Sainte-Anne; this work formed the basis for my 'Space of madness' (Resnik 1985). My 'Glacial times in psychotic regression' (Resnik 1997) is based on a teaching experiment in a mental hospital in Italy, where for three years I treated a group of young severely schizophrenic patients. Since then, I have been treating another group of schizophrenics from the same hospital on a regular basis; the director and another doctor assist me as observers. I will call this period an adventurous one, in which I can work with the hospital staff with psychotic patients whom I treat on a group basis, and who are also treated individually by other doctors; some of these have also seen the patients' families on a regular basis. The resultant discussions on the 'whole picture' are very fruitful.

Though I have worked continuously for more than forty years in different contexts and in different countries with psychotic patients, including the 'folie hystérique' of which I spoke about earlier, the main part of my work, however, is with schizophrenics. I must say that I find each new adventure even more interesting. I confess that I am still learning a great deal from the patients themselves, and helping them through the transference (psychotic and neurotic); this implies a difficult and sometimes strenuous working through (*Durcharbeitung*) in which the counter-tansference of the analyst is put to the task. All this work is an attempt at research into and understanding of unconscious psychic phenomena expressed on a number of levels, as well as through the particular meaningful atmosphere of the group sessions, themselves part of a confrontation of languages which might one day become a shared discourse. I find that in a group, patients are able to gain much understanding as long as the analyst refrains from intruding too much with the language of a particular psychoanalytical school; above all, he has to listen and learn, sharing with them unexpected intuitive discoveries which lead to interpretation. Interpretation means an exchange or negotiation in which the material found or discovered has to be formulated in a helpful and productive way. I will show how a group of patients make interpretations for one another – I recall one schizophrenic girl saying to a young schizophrenic patient who always felt cold in spite of the many pullovers he wore, that it was not going to help him if he kept on covering himself up like that – 'because the cold wind is coming from inside you'. This young man was in identification with a corpse, where he felt that parts of his cheeks were rotting and falling off as he walked along the street. In the session, one patient said to him that his upsetting experience of being a dismantling corpse corresponded to his inner feeling of falling to pieces without any opportunity of holding his dead body together. This story reminds me of a patient of Florence Powdermaker (1952) who said to the therapist: 'to bring together pieces of myself means being a kind of a person, and means "able to understand" '.

I shall close this chapter by mentioning Marvin Skolnick's 1994 paper read to the Panel on group Psychotherapy with Schizophrenics, which begins with a quotation from R.D. Laing: 'Madness need not be all breakdown. It may also be breakthrough... a potential liberation.' Skolnick discusses Bion, Freida Fromm-Reichmann, Searles, Levine, Stone, myself and others. Skolnick is very experienced in working with schizophrenics in groups, and I agree with him that the personality of the therapist is a very important factor in the treatment of schizophrenics in a group setting. I would add that positive and negative transference can be looked at not only from the classic psychoanalytical view, but as something which alternates constantly in the here and now. We should be able to understand that sometimes what we call 'negative' transference is, in psychotics, an affirmation of his delusional ideology. The patient – or the group – can sometimes feel that losing or surrendering the construction of a delusional world is equivalent to a catastrophic and apocalyptic experience, as I have demonstrated in my earlier papers. When the delusion diminishes and falls to pieces like the rotten body of the young patient I mentioned above, the patient experiences a dreadful depressing catastrophic feeling which I have elsewhere called 'narcissistic depression'. The patient feels that losing his delusional beliefs implies a total deflation of his omnipotent, expansive, megalomanic construction or re-construction of the world. It is as if the whole capital (intelligence and culture, as in Schreber's case) of the mind placed in the ego ideal, will be lost and nothing else at all will be left for him. If, during a narcissistic depression leading to deflation or disillusionment, a chronic patient is not well contained in the transference, in the family or in the institutional context and sufficiently well understood, this is the moment when he may become suicidal. I find that, in a group of psychotics, there always appears the need to transform the group network into a small mental hospital enabling the patients to be protected and at the same time giving them enough secure space in which a kind of breakdown can take place. As Joseph Berke puts it, there is a need for a 'breakdown centre'. This is one of the reasons for the fact that most of my experiences with groups of psychotics have taken place within a hospital setting or at any rate somewhere hospital staff can be relied upon to be present.

References

Baumeyer, F. (1951) 'New insights into the life and psychosis of Schreber.' *International Journal of Psychoanalysis* 33, 262.

Berke, J. and Barnes, M. (1971) *Mary Barnes. Two Accounts of a Journey through Madness.* London: MacGibbon and Kee.

Bion, W.R. (1961) *Experiences in Groups.* London: Tavistock.

Bion, W.R. (1970) *Attention and Interpretation.* London: Tavistock Publications.

Bion, W.R. (1992) *Cogitations.* London: Karnac Books.

Bleuler, E. (1912) *Dementia Praecox oder die Gruppe der Schizophrenien.* Translated by J. Zinkin (1950) as *Dementia Praecox or the Group of Schizophrenias.* New York: International Universities Press.

Brunswick, R. Mack (1928) 'A supplement to Freud's "History of an infantile neurosis".' *International Journal of Psychoanalysis 9*, 439–476.

Charcot, J.M. (1890) *Oeuvres Complètes*. Vol. 9. Paris: Lecrosnier et Babé.

Ezriel, H. (1950) 'A psychoanalytical approach to group therapy.' *British Journal of Medical Psychology 23*, 59–74.

Federn, P. (1953) *Ego Psychology and the Psychoses*. London: Imago.

Ferenczi, S. (1919) *Hysterie und Pathoneurosen*. Leipzig: Barth.

Foulkes, S.H. (1948) *Introduction to Group-Analytic Psychotherapy*. London: Heinemann. Reprinted Karnac (1983).

Foulkes, S.H. (1964) *Therapeutic Group Analysis*. London: Allen and Unwin. Reprinted Karnac (1984).

Freud, S. (1893) *Preliminary communication*. Standard Edition 2. London: Hogarth Press.

Freud, S. (1895) *On the Grounds for Detaching a Particular Syndrome from Neurasthenia under the Description 'Anxiety Neurosis'*. Standard Edition 3,85. London: Hogarth Press.

Freud, S. (1896) *Further Remarks on the Neuro-psychoses of Defence*. Standard Edition 3, 157–185. London: Hogarth Press.

Freus, S. (1911) *Psycho-Analytic Notes on an Autobiographical Account of a Case of Paranoia (Dementia Paranoides)*. Standard Edition 12, 3–82. London: Hogarth Press.

Freud, S. (1912) *The Dynamics of Transference*. Standard Edition 12, 97–107. London: Hogarth Press.

Freud, S. (1918 [1914]) *From the History of an Infantile Neurosis*. Standard Edition 17, 3–123. London: Hogarth Press.

Freud, S. (1921) *Group Psychology and the Analysis of the Ego*. Standard Edition 18, 69. London: Hogarth Press.

Freud, S. (1925) *Negation*. Standard Edition 19, 235–239. London: Hogarth Press.

Freud, S. and Breuer, J. (1893) *On the Psychical Mechanism of Hysterical Phenomena: A Preliminary Communication*. Standard Edition 2, 1–7. London: Hogarth Press.

Fromm-Reichmann, F. (1950) *Principles of Intensive Psychotherapy*. Chicago: University of Chicago Press.

Griesinger, W. (1845) *Pathologie und Therapie der psychischen Krankheiten*. Stuttgart: Krabbe.

Klein, M. (1930) 'The importance of symbol-formation in the development of the ego.' In *Love, Guilt and Reparation and Other Works*. London: Hogarth Press.

Knight, R.P. (1953) 'Borderline States.' *Bulletin of the Menninger Clinic 17*, 1–12.

Lacan, J. (1981) *Le Séminaire – III: Les psychoses*. Paris: Le Seuil.

Money-Kyrle, R. (1968) 'Cognitive development.' In D. Meltzer (ed) (1978) *The Collected Papers of Royer Money-Kyrle*. Strath Tay: Clunie Press.

Money-Kyrle, R. (1969) 'On the fear of insanity.' In D. Meltzer (ed) (1978) *The Collected Papers of Royer Money-Kyrle*. Strath Tay: Clunie Press.

Nunberg, H. (1948) *Practice and Theory of Psychoanalysis*. New York: International Universities Press.

Pichon-Rivière, E. (1947) 'Psicoanalisis de la esquizofrenia.' *Revista de Psicoanalisis 5*, 2 (Buenos Aires, Argentina).

Powdermaker, F. (1952) 'Concepts found useful in treatment of schizoid and ambulmatory schizophrenic patients.' *Psychiatry 15*, 1.

Resnik, S. (1953) 'Formas de expresion en un Grupoo terapeutico.' *Revista de psicoanalisis, 12*, 4.

Resnik, S. (1973) *Personne et Psychose*. Paris: Payot.

Resnik, S. (1985) 'The space of madness.' In M. Pines (ed) *Bion and Group Psychotherapy*. London: Institute of Group Analysis and the Tavistock Clinic.

Resnik, S. (1994) *La Visibilità dell'Inconscio*. Castrovillari: Teda Edizioni.

Resnik, S. (1997). 'Glacial times in psychotic regression.' In M. Pines and V.L. Schermer (eds) *Ring of Fire*. London: Routledge.

Rosen, John N., (1947) 'The treatment of schizophrenic psychosis by direct analytic therapy.' *Psychiatric Quarterly 21*, 3–37, 117–119.

Sechehaye, M.A. (1951) *Symbolic Realization*. New York: International Universities Press.

Tausk, V. (1919) *Ueber die Entstehung des 'Beeinflus-sungsapparates' in der Schizophrenia*. Vienna: Zeitschrift für Psychoanalyse.

PART 2

Technical Aspects of Group Psychotherapy

Group Therapy with Schizophrenic and Bipolar Patients

Integrative Approaches

Nick Kanas

Psychotic individuals have difficulty distinguishing reality from fantasy. There are several types of psychotic conditions. Functional psychoses are due to genetic and developmental factors; they are present in a latent, acute, or chronic form throughout much of adulthood; and they negatively affect a person's ability to work, care for him or herself, and relate with other people. When the predominant deficiency is in the area of thinking, we speak of a thought disorder, such as schizophrenia or delusional disorder. When the predominant deficiency is in the area of emotion, we speak of a mood disorder, such as bipolar disorder (e.g. manic attacks with or without depression). With the functional psychoses, patients have sequelae of their disease, even during those times when their illness is less acute or in relative remission.

There are other types of psychotic conditions. People who abuse drugs (such as alcohol, stimulants, or hallucinogens) may experience psychotic states when they are inebriated or are withdrawing from the drug. Similarly, patients on toxic levels of medication and those with severe medical problems (e.g. thyroid disease, brain tumor, HIV or neurosyphilis, dementia) may be psychotic. Finally, borderline patients undergoing moderate stress or normal people undergoing extreme stress may experience transient psychotic conditions.

Group therapy has been shown to be an effective modality of treatment for patients suffering from neurotic and other non-psychotic conditions. But how useful is it for patients suffering from the psychoses? At first glance, it would seem that a talk therapy would not be terribly helpful with these severe conditions and that one should focus the treatment enterprise on antipsychotic medications and mood stabilizers such as lithium. However, recent evidence suggests that specialized forms of group therapy may be useful adjuncts to medications in helping psychotic patients deals with the symptomatic and interpersonal sequelae of their disorder.

The purpose of this chapter will be to review this evidence and to describe important clinical issues related to the use of group therapy in treating patients with functional psychotic conditions. These include patients with schizophrenia, schizophreniform, and schizoaffective disorder; patients with delusional disorder; and patients suffering from bipolar disorder (or manic-depression). Excluded will be people suffering transient psychotic states due to drugs, medications, or medical conditions, since they usually become non-psychotic after a few days of proper medical management. Also excluded will be demented patients with severe cognitive and memory deficits, since they have difficulty working in a group environment due to impaired insight and inability to remember issues that are discussed from session to session. Finally, people responding to stress with transient psychosis will clear after a few days once the stressor is removed, and borderlines usually are not psychotic and may be treated with specialized group and individual approaches that are beyond the scope of this chapter.

Homogeneous *versus* heterogeneous groups

The cohesiveness of a group is affected by how homogeneous, or how similar, the members are to one another. However, the degree of similarity is relative, since homogeneity is a concept that can be expressed on a continuum in terms of many different parameters. For example, Erickson (1986) classifies patients in terms of cognitive functioning, whereas Leopold (1976) constructs groups in terms of the members' ability to relate interpersonally. Using criteria such as these, similarities or differences among patients are determined by psychological tests or by clinical judgment.

I have found diagnosis to be a useful construct in setting up groups with psychotic patients, using standard criteria systems such as the American Psychiatric Association Diagnostic and Statistical Manual of Mental Disorders (1994), or DSM-IV, and the World Health Organization ICD-10 Classification of Mental and Behavioural Disorders (1992). At least in principle, a patient is included or excluded on the basis of meeting a set of clinical criteria that are objective and well known to mental health professionals and students. This results in a fair degree of homogeneity, since most of the group members have the same cluster of symptoms.

In short-term inpatient groups composed of acutely psychotic patients or in brief time-limited outpatient groups, this homogeneous focus offers several advantages. First, since patients have much in common, they are able to relate quickly to one another. This rapid development of cohesiveness is useful in settings where the patients can only attend a limited number of sessions. Second, specific clinical techniques can be employed which are particularly useful for these patients. For example, an approach that focuses on coping strategies for psychotic symptoms would be quite relevant, whereas it might be inappropriate and boring for group members who had never experienced a break in reality. Finally, techniques can be avoided which might be harmful for psychotic patients. For example, clinical strategies that try to stimulate the emergence of unconscious material (e.g. long silences, emphasis on past conflicts) may be useful for neurotics, but they may produce anxiety and regression in schizophrenic patients which may increase psychotic symptoms (Drake and Sederer 1986; Geczy and Sultenfuss 1995; Kanas *et al.* 1980; MacDonald, Blochberger and Maynard 1964; Pattison, Brissenden and Wohl 1967; Strassberg *et al.* 1975; Weiner 1984).

Despite the clinical advantages, there may be a practical problem in establishing a homogeneous psychotic group in some inpatient and outpatient settings: not having enough patients who have this or a related diagnosis. Thus, one must consider forming a group with patients from two (or possibly more) wards or clinics, which is workable provided that the staff from these different settings communicate with one another and ensure that all of the patients attend. It also helps if they communicate special problems to the therapist or, in groups using a co-therapy approach, if each of the leaders is from one of the units.

Where homogeneous groups are not possible, heterogeneous mixtures of psychotic and non-psychotic patients may be tried. In inpatient settings, such groups sometimes consist of the patients and therapists from the same treatment team (Yalom 1983). In outpatient settings, the heterogeneous approach works best when all of the patients are clinically stable and are able to tolerate some degree of anxiety and regression. This usually results in a format that is supportive and focuses on current problems. The non-psychotic patients in these groups generally are low-functioning and suffer from severe personality disorders or other chronic conditions. These individuals sometimes are very helpful to thinking or mood disordered patients by providing reality-based advice and relatively undistorted feedback concerning hallucinations, delusions, and maladaptive relationships. Such groups generally are found in clinics dealing with the chronically mentally ill or in day treatment settings.

Groups of patients with schizophrenia and other related conditions

Due to similarities in symptomatology, interpersonal deficits, and chronicity of impairment, patients suffering from schizophrenia and a number of related conditions described in the DSM-IV (American Psychiatric Association 1994), such as schizophreniform, schizoaffective, and delusional disorders, all may be treated together in groups. Schizophrenia is a severe mental illness that affects the process and content of thought. These patients experience hallucinations and delusions to the point of being psychotic, and their thinking becomes disorganized in a variety of ways (e.g. loose, circumstantial, tangential). Additional difficulties include problems with interpersonal relationships, affect, employment, self-care, and general quality of life. Schizophreniform disorder is similar to schizophrenia, but the duration of the disturbance may only last from one to six months. In addition, there is no requirement that severe social or occupational dysfunction be present. In schizoaffective disorder, there needs to be a long period of time where symptoms of schizophrenia and a mood disorder (either manic or depressed) coexist. However, this period needs to be preceded or followed by at least two weeks of delusions or hallucinations without evidence of mood symptoms. Finally, in a delusional disorder, non- bizarre delusions have to be present for at least one month in the absence of prominent symptoms related to schizophrenia or a mood disorder. In addition, functioning is not markedly impaired, and behavior is not obviously strange or bizarre.

Although antipsychotic medications are a major treatment intervention for these patients, not all of them respond optimally to these drugs, even when taken as prescribed. Some do not take these medications on a regular basis due to serious side effects. Therefore, it is important to develop adjunctive forms of treatment that help these patients deal with their psychotic condition. Group therapy has been found to be one such valuable treatment modality.

Background

To evaluate the usefulness of group therapy for schizophrenic patients, a literature review was made of controlled studies that dated back to the time that antipsychotic medications began to be used in the clinical setting, spanning over 40 years from 1950 to 1991 (Kanas 1986; Kanas 1996). All studies compared at least one group therapy experimental condition that involved schizophrenics with a no group therapy control condition. A total of 46 studies involving 57 therapy groups were evaluated. Overall, 70 per cent of the studies concluded that on the various measures of outcome that were used, schizophrenic patients in the therapy groups did significantly better than their counterparts in the no group therapy control conditions. Furthermore, group therapy was as effective or more effective than individual therapy for schizophrenics in those outpatient studies that made this comparison. There was a trend for long-term inpatient groups to be more effective than short- or intermediate-term groups. Insight-oriented approaches emphasizing uncovering and psychodynamic issues were significantly less effective than interaction-oriented approaches emphasizing interpersonal problems and relationship issues, especially in the inpatient setting.

Schizophrenics have been treated in therapy groups since the early 1920s, when Lazell (1921) described a model that utilized a lecture format and group discussion. This led to other group educative approaches that emphasized the biological and phenomenological aspects of schizophrenia and helped the members learn to cope with the symptoms of the illness and the real problems that these symptoms caused. Techniques included lectures, advice-giving, question and answer periods, problem-solving, role-playing, and homework assignments between the sessions. In the 1930s, psychoanalytic methods began to be used. These emphasized the psychological aspects of schizophrenia and related conditions by helping the members understand how long-term psychological problems and maladaptive behaviors interfered with their lives. The hope was to lessen the impact of these difficulties and improve ego functions. Techniques included discussions where topics were generated by the patients, the uncovering of important unconscious issues, and interpretations of transference. The 1950s saw the development of interpersonal models that focused on the social aspects of the disease. The goals of these groups were to help the patients become less isolated and improve their ability to interact with other people. Techniques included facilitating discussions of interpersonal problems, encouraging group members to relate with each other during the sessions in the 'here-and-now' using a variety of techniques (e.g., structured exercises, reinforcing patient-to-patient eye contact), and interpreting maladaptive interactions that were observed in the group.

The educative, psychodynamic, and interpersonal approaches have continued to be used but in their pure forms have some disadvantages. The educative approach does not pay enough attention to the interpersonal needs of these isolated patients, and the lecture format may not allow enough time for corrections to be made in maladaptive interactions observed in the here-and-now of the sessions. Also, the presence of a lecture sequence does not allow enough flexibility to deal with crises and topic areas that may be of special interest to the patients in the group that day. The psychodynamic approach can deal with such issues, but its emphasis on insight, transference, and regression may uncover unpleasant memories and affects that produce anxiety. As indicated earlier, too much anxiety and regression has been found to exacerbate psychotic symptoms in schizophrenic patients (Drake and Sederer 1986; Geczy and Sultenfuss 1995; Kanas *et al.* 1980; MacDonald, Blochberger, and Maynard 1964; Pattison, Brissenden, and Wohl 1967; Strassberg *et al.* 1975; Weiner 1984). In addition, transference-oriented interpretations have not been terribly useful with severely mentally ill patients (Kapur 1993), and this model does not emphasize the here-and-now as much as events that occurred in the past. The interpersonal approach does, but at the risk of short- changing issues related to coping with symptoms, strengthening ego functions, and discussing psychological problems concerning non-relational issues. Also, like too much uncovering, the here-and-now focus can at times be too intensive, particularly around affect expression, and it can lead to anxiety and regression.

Clinical issues

As a result of our series of clinical research projects aimed at developing a strategy for safely treating patients with schizophrenia and related conditions in therapy groups, a model has been developed which I call the integrative approach. In its evolution over time, it has taken on a biopsychosocial perspective that allows it to correct some of the disadvantages of other models without sacrificing the advantages. Like the educative approach, it helps patients learn to cope with psychotic symptoms, discuss topics related to their specific needs in a safe environment, and interact in a group environment where regression-preventing structure is provided through the interventions of the therapists. Like the psychodynamic approach, integrative groups use open discussions where members develop the topics and are not bound by lectures and formal exercises, where long-term problems and maladaptive behaviors may be examined without dwelling on the past, and where ego functions like reality testing and reality sense are strengthened. Like the interpersonal approach, a major goal of the integrative model is to help the members become less isolative and enhance their relationships through the discussions, through the experiences the patients have in interacting with each other during the sessions, and through immediate feedback from the therapists in the here-and-now on ways in which they can relate more appropriately.

There are two major goals of the integrative group approach. The first is to help psychotic patients learn ways to cope with their symptoms. For most of the patients, this means learning to test reality and deal with hallucinations and delusions. The second treatment goal is to help the patients learn ways to improve their interpersonal relationships. This is accomplished through the discussions as well as through the experience of interacting with others during the sessions.

In groups on short-term, acute-care inpatient units, the main focus is to help the patients deal with psychotic symptoms, and interpersonal problems usually are discussed in terms of being by-products of the psychotic state. In outpatient groups that are newly formed or are short-term, discussions include both symptoms and interpersonal issues. After a group has met for a while and the patients have learned to cope with their psychotic symptoms, issues concerning relationships gain in importance, and long-standing interpersonal problems and maladaptive behaviors may be discussed with reference to their impact on current functioning.

Inpatient groups tend to be open and usually meet for 45 minutes three times a week. Daily groups are beneficial if staff availability allows. Sessions are not conducted with fewer than three patients, and more than eight make the group difficult to manage. The ideal range of patients is five to seven. In the outpatient setting, the groups tend to be closed and meet for 60 minutes once a week. This frequency can be increased in day hospitals and day treatment programs. The groups usually begin with eight to ten patients, and an average attendance of six to eight is optimal.

Although most of the patients receive antipsychotic medications, using group time to discuss dosages and side effects is discouraged, since this can be done better individually with their physicians outside of the group. However, sharing feelings about having to take medications and the use of these drugs in coping with psychotic experiences are appropriate discussion topics. Patient-to-patient feedback is encouraged rather than advice-giving from the therapists.

A co-therapy approach is preferred, since groups of psychotic patients can be chaotic and unpredictable at times, and it may take two therapists to maintain control and deal with unsafe situations. Two leaders also can model non-psychotic interactions and provide feedback in reality testing situations. Male–female co-therapy teams are useful but not essential in groups of psychotic patients. The professional backgrounds of the therapists are not important, so long as both are equally involved and trained to do the group.

The therapists should be active and directive in keeping the members focused on the topic. Interventions should be clear, consistent and concrete. It never hurts to repeat important statements in groups consisting of psychotic patients. Comments should be made in a supportive and diplomatic manner, and the therapists need to be open and willing to give their opinions about important issues. Therapists should encourage the patients to interact with each other in the group, since this allows them to share common experiences and to practice relating with other people in a safe, controlled setting. Discussions that focus on the here-and-now are more productive than those that focus on the past.

When the members are interacting productively around topics that are related to the needs of psychotic patients, then the therapists should remain quiet and let the discussion evolve. However, when the group members are disorganized and cannot remain on a topic, or when the members are quiet or discussing irrelevant issues, then the therapists can intervene to provide structure or to help the patients focus on an issue. When the environment is tense or unsafe, the therapists should change the subject or comment on the potential for danger and suggest a change in the topic.

Discussions should meet the needs of psychotic patients. Examples of useful topics are: auditory hallucinations; persecutory, referential and grandiose delusions; thought insertion and thought broadcasting; disorganized thinking; relations with others; and emotional themes that typically are well tolerated by psychotic patients, such as loneliness, depression and despair. Since topics that produce anxiety may cause regression and an intensification of symptoms in these patients, caution needs to be exercised around themes related to anger, aggression, and sexual orientation or identity. Issues that expose unconscious conflicts and flood the patients with painful insights also should be avoided in groups of psychotic individuals.

A typical session begins by identifying an appropriate topic for discussion, then generalizing it to all the members, and finally asking the patients to share coping strategies. These strategies usually cluster into one of two major areas: lowering the amount of stress in the members' lives, or providing more stimulation when their environment is impoverished.

New patients being evaluated for admission to an ongoing open group should be oriented to the goals and ground rules before they start. At the beginning of their first session, they are told the kinds of topics that are discussed by the continuing members, and they are asked to share which of these issues are problematic for them. In this way, new members realize that they are not alone with their problems, and they are encouraged to talk about them as early as possible. Time also is provided in the sessions to say goodbye to members who are being discharged.

Clinical illustration

At the beginning of the sixth session of a 12-session time-limited therapy group for outpatient schizophrenics, patient A announced that he had recently been diagnosed as having emphysema. Although there was some concern expressed about this by other group members, A didn't seem especially worried since it was a mild case. The discussion drifted into a variety of issues, including food costs, housing prices, and other chronic medical conditions. Aware that the group was having problems settling on a relevant topic area, Dr X asked the patients about concerns they may be having about mental disease. Patient A responded by saying he sometimes has weird thoughts and that his mind wandered. Other patients shared similar experiences related to loose associations and delusional thinking. After giving all the members a chance to participate in this discussion, Dr X asked the members how they coped with these experiences. Patient B said that she was able to discipline her thinking so that her mind didn't wander so much. Other coping strategies were offered by the group members, such as taking more antipsychotic medications, watching television or reading a book to take one's mind off of irrational thoughts, and talking to oneself in order to deal with the voices.

Dr X then asked the group members to consider what made their symptoms worse. B alluded to difficulties relating to her daughter, A acknowledged having problems with his sister, and C described general family stresses. D countered by saying that he received support from his wife and that she helped him deal with day to day problems. This led to a discussion about the difficulties some of the patients had in trusting other people. The other group leader, Dr Y, offered her opinion that it helps to talk with people you trust. E related feeling controlled by his mother, with whom he lived. As a show of independence, he said he recently went out and had a milkshake on his own, an idea he got from C during a previous session. Dr X praised C for giving E some helpful advice and commented that the group members seemed to trust each other.

After a discussion on ways the members could reward themselves with food or hobbies, C said that he never has company and that the only friends he ever had were people he met in Italy during World War II. Several other group members also stated that they had no close friends at the present time. A, C, and E acknowledged feeling controlled and vulnerable when around other people. Dr X concluded the session by suggesting that the patients consider doing activities together outside of the group and taking the risk that friendships would develop.

Effectiveness

This integrative group therapy model has been empirically developed and supported by a number of studies dating back to 1975. These studies have taken place in a variety of inpatient and outpatient settings in the United States and abroad, including city and government hospitals, veterans hospitals and clinics, and university outpatient programs (Kanas 1996).

In terms of outcome, psychotic inpatients in these groups have rated their experience as being helpful at the time of discharge, especially younger and non-paranoid patients (Kanas and Barr 1982). Some outpatients have experienced symptom reduction and a lowering of social anxiety, with improvements in relating with others and coping with psychotic experiences lasting up to four months after the group has ended (Kanas et al. 1989b; Kanas, Stewart, and Haney 1988). The majority of outpatients who have completed a short-term, 12-session group choose to participate in a similar group within two years (Kanas and Smith 1990). Attendance rates typically are in the 80–90 per cent range, and drop-out rates are under 20 per cent (Kanas et al. 1989a; Kanas, DiLella and Jones 1984; Kanas and Smith 1990; Kanas et al. 1989b; Kanas et al. 1988).

Studies of the group process suggest that in both inpatient and outpatient settings, the members engage in high quality work, show low levels of avoidance and conflict, and confront significant aspects of their problems with minimal resistance and anxiety (Kanas and Barr 1986; Kanas, Barr and Dossick 1985; Kanas et al. 1989a; Kanas and Smith 1990). In one study at a hospital in England (Kanas 1996), an inpatient group based on my model scored significantly higher than an inpatient group in America on a measure of cohesion and significantly lower on measures of avoidance and anxiety, possibly reflecting a number of gender and cultural differences in the two groups. The outpatient integrative groups show a pattern of increased cohesion and decreased avoidance and conflict as time goes on (Kanas *et al.* 1989a; Kanas *et al.* 1984). The patients value the groups more as a place to learn strategies of interacting with others, of testing reality and coping with psychotic symptoms, and of expressing emotions than as a place to develop insight and to receive advice concerning their illness, medications or economic situation (Kanas and Barr 1982; Kanas *et al.* 1988). The therapists are active and successful in defining the unique parameters of the groups, and new therapists can reliably be taught the group model (Kanas *et al.* 1985; Kanas and Smith 1990). Time-limited groups lasting 12 sessions have been found to be helpful and practical for schizophrenic outpatients (Kanas 1991; Kanas 1996). For patients who feel that one course of treatment is enough, the experience of successfully terminating a therapeutic activity increases their confidence and prevents unnecessary treatment dependency. For those who need additional therapy, regularly attending sequential short- term 'repeater's' groups or a long-term closed group presents the patients with viable treatment options.

The managed care revolution has encouraged the development of treatment modalities that are both useful and cost-effective, and the integrative group model meets these criteria. Patients receive help for their psychotic symptoms and for their interpersonal problems, and attendance rates are high. Inpatients value their experience and become interested in participating in similar groups as outpatients, which improves their clinical course. In co-therapy groups, the staff to patient ratio is still a respectable 1:3 or 1:4. For many patients, participation in the groups obviates the need for more staff-intensive individual therapy, and group therapy for patients with schizophrenia and related conditions has been found to be as or more effective than individual therapy in controlled studies. Finally, short-term groups that are based on the integrative model have been found to be safe and beneficial, and especially in the outpatient setting these represent a less expensive alternative to long-term group therapy.

Groups of patients with bipolar (manic-depressive) disorder

Bipolar disorder (previously called manic-depressive disease) is an episodic psychotic condition characterized by disturbances in mood. Two forms are recognized: bipolar I and bipolar II (American Psychiatric Association 1994). The essential feature of bipolar I disorder is a history of at least one manic or mixed manic and depressive episode. Often, patients with this condition have had periods of depression as well. Men and women are equally likely to have this disorder, and the prevalence in the population ranges from 0.4 to 1.6 per cent. In bipolar II disorder, the clinical course is characterized by one or more depressive episodes and at least one period of hypomania. This condition is more likely to affect women than men, and the prevalence is 0.5 per cent. Both forms of bipolar disorder are recurrent, with a strong genetic predisposition affecting first degree biological relatives at a higher rate than normally expected (American Psychiatric Association 1994).

Traditionally, patients with bipolar disorder have been viewed as difficult to treat in group therapy, especially when in a manic phase (Yalom 1975). During these times, they are intrusive, hyperactive, irritable, impatient, and disruptive. Their thoughts are speeded up and tangential, and they often have grandiose delusions. The stimulation of being in a room with other people makes their symptoms worse. Although more manageable when depressed or euthymic, the tendency of bipolar individuals to deny problems and their poor interpersonal skills still make them challenging patients for group therapists. These therapeutic difficulties, the success realized in treating these patients with lithium and other mood stabilizing medications, and the evidence supporting a strong genetic/constitutional basis to this mental disease (Kaplan and Sadock 1989) have contributed to focus attention on psychopharmacological treatments rather than on psychotherapeutic approaches. However, there is evidence to support the notion that bipolar patients may benefit from psychotherapy, especially if it is used in conjunction with mood stabilizing and antipsychotic medications. Most therapeutic approaches address psychodynamic and interpersonal issues that are problematic for these patients. These now will be reviewed, with particular reference to group therapy.

Background

In intensive psychoanalytic case studies of bipolar patients, these individuals often have been found to experience conflicts during the late oral stage of development, resulting in heightened dependency needs and poor self-concept. Their strong dependence on others and their increased separation anxiety make these patients cautious in their expression of aggression, superficial in their relationships, and socially conventional (Winther 1994). Furthermore, their families frequently are different demographically from others in their surroundings, causing additional pressures to conform and to adhere to conventional standards (Cohen *et al.* 1954; Gibson, Cohen and Cohen 1959). These factors produce a situation where dependency needs and familial insecurities are denied, where values are oriented in terms of social convention, and where the developing individual is engaged in envious and competitive interactions with others. Depressive episodes have been seen as intensifications of dependency needs, and manic episodes have been seen as periods of denial of these needs.

These concepts were tested in a study involving 39 manic-depressive patients and 17 schizophrenic patients (Gibson 1958; Gibson *et al.* 1959). The bipolar patients scored significantly higher on scales measuring envy, competitiveness, and social conformity. In addition, they were more likely to come from families who were trying to rise socioeconomically and who used them to further this familial goal. Thus, there is some empirical support for the classical psychodynamic formulation characterizing these individuals, and this gives credence to the notion that dynamically oriented therapeutic approaches may be of value for bipolar patients. Important interpersonal issues also have been evaluated in case studies involving bipolar patients. Janowsky, Leff and Epstein (1970) have described a number of these: manipulation of others' self-esteem for personal gain; ability to recognize vulnerability and internal conflicts in others; denial and projection of responsibility, which arouses guilt in other people; frequent testing of limits; and alienation from family and friends.

Some of these interpersonal ideas were supported in a study involving 29 inpatients suffering from a number of psychotic disorders (Janowsky, El-Yousef, and Davis 1974). The bipolar subjects scored significantly higher than the others on measures evaluating limit-testing, projection of responsibility, sensitivity to others' vulnerabilities, splitting of staff, flattery, and ability to provoke anger. Interestingly, the scores diminished as the patients were treated and became more euthymic.

Many of the above psychodynamic and interpersonal issues have been described in therapy groups involving bipolar patients. Ablon *et al.* (1975) reported that some of their patients lost fathers as children to death and frequent business separations. Volkmar *et al.* (1981) noted that bipolar patients in group therapy described problems with dependency, anger, and impulsivity, and they used denial as a typical defense mechanism. Since most of their patients were euthymic, these characteristics were viewed as personality traits rather than as part of an extreme mood swing. Interpersonally, the group members were externally conventional and sociable in a way that seemed to defend against becoming intimate with each other. Finally, Cerbone *et al.* (1992) reported that their bipolar group patients exhibited declines in work and interpersonal performance. This was felt to result from developmental disruptions in identity and capacity for intimacy during late adolescence and early adulthood, which was a time that many of their patients began to exhibit symptoms of their disorder.

Clinical issues

Based on the above studies and a review of clinical work involving therapy groups with bipolar patients (Kanas 1993), a number of treatment issues can be outlined. In general, group therapy is not indicated for patients who are in an acute manic phase since the stimulation of receiving multiple interpersonal inputs may escalate their symptoms and lead to further decompensation. Hypomanic and depressed patients usually can tolerate the group experience, however. Many so-called 'euthymic' outpatients demonstrate some degree of emotional fragility in the group, such as mild euphoria and high energy or excessive cynicism and proneness to despondency. Some patients have difficulty telling whether an emotional high or low represents a transient mood variation or signals the beginning of a prolonged manic or depressive episode. Other patients experience fear and despair over the destructive impact that a future mood swing may cause in their vocational and interpersonal life. Thus, emotional themes are paramount in bipolar groups, and these issues go beyond simple discussions of psychotic mood swings.

The literature suggests three useful treatment goals for patients in bipolar groups, and these have been incorporated in the treatment model discussed below. The first goal involves learning more about their illness, either from the group leaders or from other patients. Individuals with bipolar disorder tend to be cognitively aware, non-psychotic, and reasonably well informed during their baseline periods, and they are curious to learn more about their illness and ways to avoid factors that may precipitate manic or depressive episodes. It is important that they understand the value of taking medications and avoiding stress (Swendsen et al. 1995), and good use is made of group time that is spent discussing such issues. A second goal involves learning to cope with the vicissitudes and sequelae of their illness. Residual mood swings, family problems, work difficulties, low socioeconomic status despite high intelligence – these are byproducts of this disorder. It is useful for the patients to share feelings and gain support from others who are in the same situation, and in the process ways of coping with these issues can be discussed. A final goal relates to gaining insight and improving relationships through group discussions of important psychodynamic and interpersonal issues related to bipolar disorder. Therapy groups are excellent vehicles for exposing dependency needs, confronting denial, and examining maladaptive patterns of relating with others that can be observed by all in the here-and-now of the sessions.

As may be inferred from these goals, my outpatient treatment model (Kanas 1993; Kanas and Cox 1998) uses an integrative approach that borrows from educative, psychodynamic, and interpersonal theories and techniques, much as is the case for the schizophrenic group method discussed earlier. However, important differences exist. Unlike the schizophrenic group model, education concerning the course of the illness over time and specific issues regarding medications (e.g. dosages and side effects of mood stablilizers) are incorporated into the bipolar group discussions. In addition, since gaining insight into important psychodynamic themes related to bipolar disorder is a major therapeutic goal, transference interpretations and regressions are more likely to occur during the sessions. The expression of emotions in the here-and-now is encouraged, and anxiety is much better tolerated. Finally, bipolar patients are able to interact with each other spontaneously (sometimes with great energy!), and the therapists can be less active, directive, and structuring than in groups with schizophrenic members.

In reviewing the literature (Hallensleben 1994; Kanas 1993), outpatient bipolar groups have tended to use a closed or 'slow open' format, whereas one study involving an inpatient group (Pollack 1990) described it as being open in order to accommodate the rapid patient turnover of the acute care setting. Most groups (including our integrative groups) met weekly for 60 to 90 minutes. They were homogeneously composed of from 4 to 14 bipolar patients, with a median number of 7 to 8 per session. The outpatient groups were fairly stable once the members committed themselves to attend, and many patients participated for several months to several years. In four of six outpatient groups, mood stabilizing medications were prescribed by the therapists; in the other two groups, prescriptions were written by other physicians. In our outpatient integrative groups, most patients receive their medications in a separate clinic, but some have prescriptions filled by one of the group leaders after the session (Kanas and Cox 1998).

Medication effects and side effects frequently are discussed in integrative bipolar groups. As in other therapy group settings, medication-related discourse can reveal information about the members' attitudes concerning their illness and treatment, conflicts they may have with authority figures and control, and problems they experience with intimacy and interpersonal relationships (Zaslav and Kalb 1989). But with bipolar patients, compliance with medications takes on special meaning since it may mean the difference between a relatively normal life and extreme mood swings of psychotic and suicidal proportions. However, when medication discussions dominate the group session after session, this may indicate a denial of the psychological aspects of the disease by the patients.

Bipolar patients may be difficult to work with in psychotherapy. Cohen *et al.* (1954) have pointed out two important transference issues in dealing with these individuals: their clinging dependency and their stereotyped approach to others. At times they appear to use people for their own needs in an exploitative manner. These traits arouse strong countertransference feelings in some therapists, who may view demanding and extroverted bipolar patients as superficial and uninteresting (Winther 1994). In dealing with these patients, therapists need to set firm limits, engage them at an emotional level rather than being seduced by outward attempts at friendship, focus on rational issues, and be aware of their own feelings of anger and frustration.

In bipolar groups, a co-therapy model is the norm. This allows leaders to support one another during group sessions, model appropriate interpersonal interactions, cope with chaotic group process, cover for each other during absences, and help each other deal with strong countertransference feelings. In keeping with the goals of integrative bipolar groups, co-therapists play a number of roles that range from being educative, accepting, and supportive to facilitating group discussions of important psychodynamic and interpersonal issues.

A number of discussion topics are appropriate for integrative groups. Examples include: effects and side effects of mood stabilizing medications, frustration at having future manic or depressive episodes, inability to control one's own emotional state, potential for suicide, use of denial, dependency and counter-dependency, interpersonal sequelae of the disease, marital and occupational problems, and despair over having a chronic mental illness. Ideally, patients will spontaneously raise such issues and share emotions, insights, and coping strategies. At times, therapists will have to intervene by challenging denial systems, interpreting resistance, and encouraging member interactions in the here-and-now of the sessions.

Cerbone *et al.* (1992) and Hallensleben (1994) have found that early in the life of closed outpatient bipolar groups, issues involving using medications, learning about the disease, supporting one another, and establishing cohesion and camaraderie dominate the sessions. Later, attention shifts towards intrapsychic and interpersonal issues. I have found the same progression in our integrative groups. When new people are added, there seems to be a regression toward earlier themes until the new members are brought up (very quickly) to the same level of understanding as the members who have been in the group longer. This 'new' group then moves forward in terms of intimacy and mutuality. A number of therapeutic factors (Yalom 1975) operate in bipolar groups, including instillation of hope, imparting of information, interpersonal learning, universality, group cohesiveness, insight, catharsis, and mutual support.

Clinical illustration

In an outpatient bipolar group consisting of seven patients and two psychiatrist therapists, one of the sessions began with several members discussing medication side effects and the need to take mood stabilizers to deal with their illness. Patient F said that despite taking medications, he felt depressed during most of the two years following his last manic episode, and this seemed to be a baseline state for him. Dr Z asked if others had similar experiences, and G and H said they felt either high or low much of the time, whereas the other patients recognized feeling more euthymic.

G then went on to describe feeling depressed and hopeless over the past several months. His manner was complaining and cynical. When J tried to console G by suggesting that volunteer work might help him gain some purpose in life and raise his spirits, G lashed back by saying that this wouldn't work since he couldn't keep a job and that he had even been 'fired' from a previous volunteer job. When other group members tried to console him, he repeatedly and angrily rejected their input in a manner that seemed intent on convincing the others of his worthlessness, while at the same time putting them down and dominating the group discussion. Dr Z commented on G's rejecting behavior and wondered if this were more of a personal characteristic than a manifestation of his bipolar illness, and if perhaps it contributed toward his job-related problems. This led to a general discussion of character traits versus symptoms of mania and depression and how difficult it was at times to tell the difference.

Effectiveness

A number of studies support the value of specialized homogeneous therapy groups for bipolar patients when used in conjunction with mood stabilizing medications. In one study (Ablon et al. 1975; Davenport et al. 1977), 12 patients who received both medications and couples group therapy did much better than 53 patients who received medication management alone in terms of rehospitalizations, marital failures, overall functioning, and family interactions. In a study of 20 bipolar patients receiving outpatient group therapy (Shakir et al. 1979; Volkmar et al. 1981), the number of weeks of hospitalization was lower and the number of patients employed was higher in the two years following entry into the group versus the two years preceding this event. In over ten years working with a bipolar therapy group, Kripke and Robinson (1985) reported that 8 of the original 14 members still remained, that the rate of hospitalization decreased after entering the group, and that the socioeconomic functioning of 5 patients improved. Wulsin, Bachop and Hoffman (1988) reported that the bipolar patients who participated in their 4½ year long therapy group benefited from the experience and related to one another in a cohesive manner, despite a relatively high dropout rate of 55 per cent. Cerbone et al. (1992) found that patients who participated in a bipolar group for one year experienced significant pre-post improvements in ratings of severity and duration of affective episodes, school/work productivity, interpersonal functioning, and number and days of hospitalization, and there was no significant change in medication usage. Hallensleben (1994) found that in her ten years' experience in leading a bipolar group, patients became more self-supporting and autonomous, and rehospitalization rate was reduced. In two separate evaluations in 1988 and 1991, over 80 per cent of the patients responding said that they had benefited from their group experience. In the only inpatient report found, Pollack (1990) concluded that her bipolar group patients were able to interact and discuss issues and coping strategies related to their illness, as well as ways of improving their interpersonal relationships.

Experiences with the integrative bipolar group approach generally have echoed the above comments (Kanas 1993; Kanas and Cox 1998). The patients have been able to interact productively, to examine a number of intrapsychic and interpersonal issues related to their bipolar disorder, and to support one another during hypomanic and depressive episodes. The goals of sharing information about the disease, talking about ways of coping with its symptoms and sequelae, and gaining insight and improving relationships through discussions of psychodynamic and interpersonal issues generally have been attained. For example, in a process study of the first 31 weekly sessions of an outpatient bipolar group, 81 per cent of the discussion topics were related to one of these goals (Kanas and Cox 1998). Compared with a normative sample of general psychotherapy groups for patients with neurotic and characterological problems, the bipolar group scored significantly higher on a measure of cohesion and significantly lower on measures of avoidance and conflict. Although 4 of the 12 patients enrolled in the group dropped out, the overall attendance rate was a respectable 72 per cent.

Conclusions

Therapy groups have been found to be useful as an adjunct to psychotropic medications for a variety of psychotic conditions. Patients with both thinking and bipolar disorders benefit from an integrative approach that utilizes educational, psychodynamic, and interpersonal theories and techniques. The therapists should be supportive and should encourage the patients to discuss topics that are relevant to the group goals. Short-term, time-limited groups are possible in managed care settings so long as an opportunity exists for needy patients to enroll in a 'repeaters' group later on. Although more controlled studies evaluating group outcome and process should be done, clinical trials to date support these groups as being safe, useful, and relevant to the needs of psychotic patients.

References

Ablon, S.L., Davenport, Y.B., Gershon, E.S. and Adland, M.L. (1975) 'The married manic.' *American Journal of Orthopsychiatry 45*, 854–844.

American Psychiatric Association (1994) 'Schizophrenia and other psychotic disorders.' In *Diagnostic and Statistical Manual of Mental Disorders*, 4th edition (DSM-IV). Washington, DC: American Psychiatric Association.

Cerbone, M.J.A., Mayo, J.A., Cuthbertson, B.A. and O'Connell, R.A. (1992) 'Group therapy as an adjunct to medication in the management of bipolar affective disorder.' *Group 16*, 3, 174–187.

Cohen, M.B., Baker, G., Cohen, R.A., Fromm-Reichmann, F. and Weigert, E.V. (1954) 'An intensive study of twelve cases of manic-depressive psychosis.' *Psychiatry 17*, 103–137.

Davenport, Y.B., Ebert, M.H., Adland, M.L. and Goodwin, F.K. (1977) 'Couples group therapy as an adjunct to lithium management of the manic patient.' *American Journal of Orthopsychiatry 47*, 495–502.

Drake, R.E. and Sederer, L.I. (1986) 'The adverse effects of intensive treatment of chronic schizophrenia.' *Comprehensive Psychiatry 27*, 4, 313–326.

Erickson, R.C. (1986) 'Heterogeneous groups: a legitimate alternative.' *Group 10*, 1, 21–26.

Geczy, B. and Sultenfuss, J. (1995) 'Group psychotherapy on state hospital admission wards.' *International Journal of Group Psychotherapy 45*, 1–15.

Gibson, R.W. (1958) 'The family background and early life experience of the manic-depressive patient.' *Psychiatry 21*, 71–90.

Gibson, R.W., Cohen, M.B. and Cohen, R.A. (1959) 'On the dynamics of the manic-depressive personality.' *American Journal of Psychiatry 115*, 1101–1107.

Hallensleben, A. (1994) 'Group psychotherapy with manic-depressive patients on lithium: ten years' experience.' *Group Analysis 27*, 475–482.

Janowsky, D.S., El-Yousef, M.K. and Davis, J.M. (1974) 'Interpersonal maneuvers of manic patients.' *American Journal of Psychiatry 131*, 250–255.

Janowsky, D.S., Leff, M. and Epstein, R.S. (1970) 'Playing the manic game: interpersonal maneuvers of the acutely manic patient.' *Archives of General Psychiatry 22*, 252–261.

Kanas, N. (1986) 'Group therapy with schizophrenics: a review of controlled studies.' *International Journal of Group Psychotherapy 36*, 339–351.

Kanas, N. (1991) 'Group therapy with schizophrenic patients: a short-term, homogeneous approach.' *International Journal of Group Psychotherapy 41*, 33–48.

Kanas, N. (1993) 'Group psychotherapy with bipolar patients: a review and synthesis.' *International Journal of Group Psychotherapy 43*, 321–333.

Kanas, N. (1996) *Group Therapy for Schizophrenic Patients.* Washington DC: American Psychiatric Press.

Kanas, N. and Barr, M.A. (1982) 'Short-term homogeneous group therapy for schizophrenic inpatients: a questionnaire evaluation.' *Group 6*, 4, 32–38.

Kanas, N. and Barr, M.A. (1986) 'Process and content in a short-term inpatient schizophrenic group.' *Small Group Behavior 17*, 355–363.

Kanas, N., Barr, M.A. and Dossick, S. (1985) 'The homogeneous schizophrenic inpatient group: an evaluation using the Hill Interaction Matrix.' *Small Group Behavior, 16*, 397–409.

Kanas, N. and Cox, P. (1998) 'Process and content in a therapy group for bipolar outpatients.' *Group, 22*, 1, 37–42.

Kanas, N., Deri, J., Ketter, T. and Fein, G. (1989a) 'Short-term outpatient therapy groups for schizophrenics.' *International Journal of Group Psychotherapy 39*, 517–522.

Kanas, N., DiLella, V.J. and Jones, J. (1984) 'Process and content in an outpatient schizophrenic group.' *Group 8*, 2, 13–20.

Kanas, N,, Rogers, M,, Kreth, E,, Patterson, L. and Campbell, R. (1980) 'The effectiveness of group psychotherapy during the first three weeks of hospitalization: a controlled study.' *Journal of Nervous and Mental Disease 168*, 487–492.

Kanas, N. and Smith, A.J. (1990) 'Schizophrenic group process: a comparison and replication using the HIM-G.' *Group 14*, 4, 246–252.

Kanas, N., Stewart, P., Deri, J., Ketter, T and Haney, K. (1989b) 'Group process in short-term outpatient therapy groups for schizophrenics.' *Group 13*, 2, 67–73.

Kanas, N., Stewart, P. and Haney, K. (1988) 'Content and outcome in a short-term therapy group for schizophrenic outpatients.' *Hospital and Community Psychiatry 39*, 437–439.

Kaplan, H.I. and Sadock, B.J. (1989) *Comprehensive Textbook of Psychiatry*, 5th edn. Baltimore, MD: Williams & Wilkins.

Kapur, R. (1993) 'Measuring the effects of group interpretations with the severely mentally ill.' *Group Analysis 26*, 411–432.

Kripke, D.F. and Robinson, D. (1985) 'Ten years with a lithium group.' *McLean Hospital Journal 10*, 1–11.

Lazell, E.W. (1921) 'The group treatment of dementia praecox.' *Psychoanalytic Review 8*, 168–179.

Leopold, H.S. (1976) 'Selective group approaches with psychotic patients in hospital settings.' *American Journal of Psychiatry 30*, 95–102.

MacDonald, W.S., Blochberger, C.W. and Maynard, H.M. (1964) 'Group therapy: a comparison of patient-led and staff-led groups on an open hospital ward.' *Psychiatric Quarterly 38* (suppl.), 290–303.

Pattison, E.M., Brissenden, E. and Wohl, T. (1967) 'Assessing special effects of inpatient group psychotherapy.' *International Journal of Group Psychotherapy 17*, 283–297.

Pollack, L. (1990) 'Improving relationships: groups for inpatients with bipolar disorder.' *Journal of Psychosocial Nursing 28*, 5, 17–22.

Shakir, S.A., Volkmar, F.R., Bacon, S. and Pfefferbaum, A. (1979) 'Group psychotherapy as an adjunct to lithium maintenance.' *American Journal of Psychiatry 136*, 455–456.

Strassberg, D.S., Roback, H.B., Anchor, K.N. and Abramowitz, S.I. (1975) 'Self-disclosure in group therapy with schizophrenics.' *Archives of General Psychiatry 32*, 1259–1261.

Swendsen, J., Hammen, C., Heller, T. and Gitlin, M. (1995) 'Correlates of stress reactivity in patients with bipolar disorder.' *American Journal of Psychiatry 152*, 795–797.

Volkmar, F.R., Bacon, S., Shakir, S.A. and Pfefferbaum, A. (1981) 'Group therapy in the management of manic-depressive illness.' *American Journal of Psychiatry 35* 226–234.

Weiner, M.F. (1984) 'Outcome of psychoanalytically-oriented group psychotherapy.' *Group 8*, 2, 3–12.

Winther, G. (1994) 'Psychotherapy with manic-depressives: problems in interaction between patient and therapist.' *Group Analysis 27*, 467–474.

World Health Organization (1992) *The ICD-10 Classification of Mental and Behavioural Disorders.* Geneva: World Health Organization.

Wulsin, L., Bachop, M. and Hoffman, D. (1988) 'Group therapy in manic-depressive illness.' *American Journal of Psychotherapy 42*, 263–271.

Yalom, I.D. (1975) *The Theory and Practice of Group Psychotherapy*, 2nd edn. New York: Basic Books.

Yalom, I.D. (1983) *Inpatient Group Psychotherapy.* New York: Basic Books.

Zaslav, M.R. and Kalb, R.D. (1989) 'Medicine as metaphor and medium in group psychotherapy with psychiatric patients.' *International Journal of Group Psychotherapy 39*, 457–468.

CHAPTER 6

The Therapist's Role in the Group Treatment of Psychotic Patients and Outpatients

A Foulkesian Perspective

Ivan Urlic

Introduction

The psychotherapist who uses the group in his armamentarium for the treatment of psychotic patients, should, in my opinion, first carefully define the concept of psychosis, and in particular, that of schizophrenia. His attitude toward the application of the group medium will derive from this foundation, particularly if the therapeutic goals include personal growth and transcend the restitution of the patients' psyche at the level preceding psychotic decompensation. Further, how one understands psychoses and group experiences will determine the therapist's several roles.

The psychotic frame of reference

> How shall your houseless heads and unfed sides,
> Your loop'd and widow'd raggedness, defend you
> From seasons such as these?

> *(Shakespeare,* King Lear, *III, iv.30)*

In terms of schizophrenic 'seasons,' the schizophrenic process can be viewed as a disease, disorder, or state which to a greater or lesser extent disturbs and damages a number of psychological functions. Although the notion of schizophrenia developed early in the twentieth century from Kraepelin's description of 'dementia praecox,' its meaning remains controversial even now. For almost a century, attempts have been made to explain this group of symptoms through classification into syndromes, but the essence of the notion remains unclear. It is certain, however, that schizophrenia includes hereditary, biochemical, immunological, and psychosocial factors, but even these etiological forces remain somewhat vague despite a massive quantity of research, analyses, and syntheses (Urlic and Caktas 1987).

Substantial research data have been collected which clarify the high risk factors for the onset of psychosis, including predisposing, facilitating and precipitating factors (e.g. Cannon and Mednick 1993; Howells and Guirguis 1985; Rose 1994), but they do not as yet provide a clear etiological picture. Consequently, Boyle (1990) even wonders if schizophrenia is just a scientific delusion. Many authors, accepting the biological and cognitive theories, give priority to the disturbance of the thinking process and its content, followed by concomitant difficulties in affectivity, interpersonal relationships, the feeling of the self, will, and psychomotor activity (Kanas 1996). Additional defects include social disturbances, insufficient self-care, and disruption of the quality of life.

On the other hand, it is also possible to consider that affect preceded cognition developmentally. For instance, it appears that during intrauterine life, before the development of thinking, recognizing, and naming capacities, some early experiences become impressed which show a clear relationship between the stimulus and the affective reaction of a psychomotor type, which can now be followed during the earliest development by means of modern technology and scientific research. Since it is also known that emotional states affect the direction of the thought process, I would advocate the view that *affective states can have a basic effect on the modelling of later thinking processes and their vicissitudes.* In my opinion, the clarification and basic comprehension of what occurs in a psychotic state or personality has more than academic value, since it can considerably affect the choice of therapeutic approaches to the schizophrenic patient and the definition of the roles that the therapist will be able to utilize in the relationship with the patient.

I have expressed my views on several occasions (Urlic, 1989, 1994) that the development of man as an individual is inseparable from the group he comes from. The individual receives his basic communication and interaction model from his primary family group. Within the continuum between biological and psychological birth on one side and biosocial functional unity on the other, the first dyadic relationship (to the caregiver or mother-figure) represents the cornerstone of further development. During that development, the interactions with the environment are multiplied and transformed until a certain level of maturity is reached. In this way, the experience of oneself and one's environment is gradually established. Intrapsychic and interpersonal dynamics become progressively filled with both cognitive and affective elements.

Outlining the framework for the analysis of theoretical and therapeutic approaches to psychoses, Adler, Astrachan and Levinson (1981) write about the problematic states which must be controlled or eliminated, such as disease, defect, deviation or arrested development. These problematic states can be observed in psychotically structured persons. In reconstructing a pathological state, or development, we can follow two directions. The first is to focus upon the individual, and here we try to reach and experience the patient and his primary group as well as the constructive and destructive situations in which he is involved. The other direction concerns the here-and-now group setting *per se*, where the focus is the ongoing social communication. Both approaches offer diagnostic and therapeutic possibilities.

The history of the development of psychology and psychiatry shows that the dyadic form has always been the preferred approach to both the study of psychological phenomena and therapy. Regarding the evolution of psycho-therapeutic approach to psychosis, Frieda Fromm-Reichmann (1953) mentions that it took a decade to understand the patient, another decade to learn how to establish the contact with the patient, and a third decade to learn how to apply all this knowledge and experience.

The therapeutic use of the group medium in the treatment of psychotic patients began as early as the 1930s, but it was only in 1950s that the awareness of the advantages of the group setting increased in terms of helping schizophrenic patients to express their feelings and thoughts, and to structure their inner lives and relationships in a protected but supportive environment. This approach was considerably facilitated and aided by the development of psychopharmaco-therapy. Skolnick (1994, p.241) points out that:

> There are a multiplicity of meanings embedded in processes that culminate in breakdown, whether the breakdown is categorized as major depression, bipolar disorder, addiction, borderline disorder or schizophrenia. Meaning, relevant for the self of the patient, the family and the larger social system is buried when the field of inquiry and action is reduced to the study and treatment of the patient's diseased or 'chemically imbalanced brain'. When individuals identified as mental patients don't respond to treatment and remain in states considered diseased or socially disruptive, they tend to become dismissed as mad and are stripped of a meaningful voice in the human community.

Therefore, it is imperative to apply the group setting in the treatment of psychoses, whether within the hospital, transitional therapeutic institutions (e.g. residential programs and partial hospitals), or outpatient care. The consideration of the value of group psychotherapy is primarily based on the view of the man as *zoon politikon* (a socially determined and intertwined being). The therapeutic group may re-activate the problem but also bring it back where it originally belongs and where it started, to the family environment (Murray Cox, personal communication) which exerts the crucial genetic and environmental influence. As stated by Kanas (1996, p.141):

> Both biomedical and psychosocial treatment approaches are necessary. Although antipsychotic medications are a major treatment intervention, not all schizophrenic patients respond optimally to these drugs, and others do not take them on a regular basis due to serious side effects. Therefore, counseling, individual, group and family therapy, and social services are important components of a complete biopsychosocial treatment plan. Given the characteristics of schizophrenia, group therapy would seem to be an especially valuable treatment modality, because its interpersonal nature presents a forum for these patients to share ways of coping with their symptoms, to gain support and test reality in the here-and-now of the sessions, and to improve their ability to relate with other people.

However, despite the large amount of professional literature on both psychotherapeutic and psychopharmacological approaches to schizophrenic patients, Levine (1990, p.100) mentions that:

> Most of the papers ... considered the outcome of schizophrenic patients treated with one medication regimen or another or one form of psychotherapy or another. What did not seem to be addressed was the particular effect that antipsychotic and other medications have on the various dimensions of the psychotherapy of schizophrenia, such as transference and countertransference, quality of relatedness and engagement, the therapeutic alliance, freedom of expression of affects, ability to process interpretative interventions and the development and depth of insight.

Medications are used in order to decrease anxiety, control the level of regression, facilitate cognitive organization, and to support the interpersonal contact between the patient and his environment. Here, one is reminded of Michael Balint's favourite expression, 'drug doctor,' which can be broadened in the case of the treatment of schizophrenic patients to 'drug therapist' or 'drug therapeutic team' in order to underline the emotional needs of such patients.

Within such a framework the activity of the therapist represents a highly complex task, the integration of a number of roles within a presupposed stable feeling of personal integrity.

The group analytic approach to group psychotherapy of the psychoses

The contemporary psychiatric ward is conceived of as a sociotherapeutic community. Today it is impossible to imagine a psychiatric ward where different forms of group therapy are not used as basic methods of treatment (Hummelen 1994a, b; Milders 1994; Plante, Pinder and Howe 1988; Sandison 1994; Schlachet 1989; Scheidlinger 1997).

When group psychotherapy is applied in hospital conditions, it includes patients with various psychic disorders. The indications for this kind of treatment are much greater in hospital than in outpatient conditions. Group therapy in hospital conditions can be appropriate if it is adjusted to the reality of the setting in which it is conducted. What seems to dominate current theoretical conceptualizations and therapeutic approaches is a tendency to positive eclecticism due to the increasing 'emphasis on diversity and on the integration of diverse perspectives into one's own personal "style" and perceptual gestalt' (Schermer 1994, p.11).

With regard to analytically oriented therapy, Muacevic (1975) states that only 'targeted or focal' therapy is predominantly applied in hospital conditions. This therapy is aimed at eliminating the manifest picture of the disorder and establishing 'meaningful and supportive interpersonal exchange and repair' (Yalom 1983, p.31). It is more directed at current conflicts and less at the interpretations which relate the present state to past, particularly infantile experiences. However, the same can be generally said about the group psychotherapeutic approach to psychotic patients in both transitional and outpatient conditions.

In spite of lengthy experience in the application of group psychotherapy for the treatment of psychotic disorders, the literature on the subject appears to be comparatively poor. According to Hummelen (1994), this is more due to the vagueness of the concept of psychosis than to clinical practice. This conceptual vagueness gives rise to differences in diagnostic criteria and therapeutic approaches, which in their turn make difficult the comparison between particular group psychotherapeutic approaches in terms of their efficiency in treatment of psychotic patients.

Kanas (1996) (see Chapter 5) mentions three fundamental treatment approaches: educative, psychodynamic and interpersonal. In agreement with the tendency toward positive eclecticism he advocates the integrative approach which would include all constructive elements from all types of approaches in group psychotherapy of psychotics. The strengthening of ego functions via group therapy, and especially 'reality testing,' still remains the basic aim of this approach. In other words, it is coping with symptoms and improving interpersonal relationships that should be constantly addressed and that represent the basic aims of the treatment. In achieving these objectives, psychopharmacotherapy and psychotherapy represent two parts of a whole.

Since there is yet no satisfactory conceptualization of psychosis and its etiology is most probably multifactorial, multidimensional thinking about the psychotic patient is preferred in clinical practice. Within this context the psychoanalytic approach cannot represent the basic theoretical approach as with neurotic patients. From the clinician's standpoint, multidimensionality of the therapeutic approach to the psychotic patient in both hospital and outpatient conditions means the use of antipsychotic medication, family therapy, and a variety of social and rehabilitative interventions. The integrative therapeutic approach to psychotic patients demands selectivity, continuity and a long, often 'endless' time perspective.

The selection and screening of patients for group should emphasize the level of regression and the depth and intensity of psychotic symptoms, regardless of the domination of productive or unproductive, positive or negative symptoms. Acute or exacerbated chronic psychotic states indicate the need for hospitalization, i.e., a 'privileged regressive setting', as it has been called by Haynal and Pasini (1984). The structured, but partially regressive, hospital environment represents the framework for the symbiotic experience, which on its corrective, constructive pole includes:

1. A structured, personal and dyadic relationship to the doctor and to medical personnel.

2. Medication, which along with its pharmacological effects also represents a transitional object which is often ambivalently invested and incorporated, and consequently, experienced independently of its pharmacological properties.

3. The group experience as a place of exposure as well as of possible 'practicing' of the triadic situation, and which aids in the assessment of the patient's capacity for social readjustment, and of the diffusion level of part-objects and the degree of their integrity and constancy, i.e. in psychoanalytic developmental terms, the entry into the depressive position and the oedipal phase.

Most frequently, hospital treatment further represents a screening and selection process for the continuation of group psychotherapy in outpatient treatment. The characteristics of the outpatient group of psychotic patients can be described as follows:

1. It includes patients who are already sensibilized and motivated (many ambivalently) for group psychotherapy of psychoses.

2. The transference relationship to the therapist, though regressive and ambivalent, represents the essential factor for the establishment and continuation of treatment (in this respect the initial contact with the doctor can play a decisive role through the perception of introjected 'good' or 'bad' characteristics).

3. The opportunity for constancy and spatial-temporal continuity with either limited or open perspective (with the 'oceanic-like' element of 'infinity' which is important for the experience of acceptance and containing).

A small or extended therapy group is a forum for encounters and confrontations as well as a transitional space which stimulates projections and introjections, and in which reality and fantasy (in the Winnicottian sense) exist in parallel.

Reality is mainly observed in the function of experiencing and distinguishing the quality of internal or external, past or present, pleasant or unpleasant, protective or threatening, regressive or progressive elements. This differentiation is encouraged:

1. In the encounter with the structured setting, new people and different ways that stimulate meaningful interpersonal communications.

2, In the encounter with diseased experiences in the world of others and in one's own world, which stimulates the development of a more adequate relationship toward the disorder and facilitates insight into the necessity of treatment.

3. With the possibility of modifying autistic barriers (cf. the work of Frances Tustin and of Thomas Ogden on infantile autism) which enables the establishment of more integral relationships to others and to outer reality.

4. With the possibility of focusing certain relationship issues in the 'here-and-now' situation, which are of particular importance for one or more patients, or the group-as-a-whole.

Here, the value and the importance of the 'here-and-now' strategy should be pointed out. Yalom (1983) says that 'more accurate, alive data will result from the patient's observation of direct interpersonal behaviour in the 'here-and-now' situation.' He adds that 'the patients who correct unadjusted interpersonal behaviour and take the risk of new behaviour in the here-and-now group situation, will be able later to transfer the acquired knowledge to life situations outside the group'. According to Yalom, two components are needed for a therapeutic process to develop in this direction: experience acquired in the group and the understanding of this experience via self-reflection.

For the most part, primitive *fantasies* relate to the patient's own world of diseased ideas, experiences and corresponding feelings. In other words, according to Kernberg, they are derivatives of impulses and the corresponding affect disposition in the situation of deep regression and fragmentation, and which form pathological strata. Thus, what is seen as the current 'picture' of the disorder paradoxically represents pathological reparatory processes with respect to 'problematic states' of very early formed obstructions and distortions of the separation-individuation process (Urlic 1989). (In M. Mahler's conceptualization, such states occur, at the latest, in the differentiation subphase, or between this subphase and the practising subphase of the rapprochement phase.)

The role and the goals of group psychotherapeutic approach to psychotic patients in hospital and outpatient conditions are viewed in the following way:

Hospital group psychotherapy of psychoses serves the functions of:

1. The establishment and regulation of temporal, spatial and interpersonal limits (ego limits).

2. The occurrence of the corrective symbiotic experience.

3. The confrontation and establishment of more adequate relatedness towards outer and inner reality.

4. The stimulation of interpersonal exchange.

5. The support of healthy ego.

Outpatient group psychotherapy of psychoses can be directed at the development of the following elements of the therapeutic relationship:

1. Improved structuralization of ego functions (in these terms, Winnicott maintains that introjected representations of the therapeutic situation can function similarly to transitional objects in childhood) (Sugarman and Jaffe 1987).

2. The attenuation and dissolution of the transference to the therapist, i.e., redirecting the corrective symbiotic experience towards more adequate reality testing.

3. The enhancement of insight within the basic frame of the therapy relationship, which includes also the duration of treatment;

4. The transmission and application of what is learned in the group to other social and interpersonal situations.

5. The support of healthy ego.

Generally, the following three conditions must be met in group psychotherapy:

1. The group primarily relies on verbal communication.

2. The individual group member is the object of the treatment.

3. The group itself is the main therapeutic factor.

If the therapist wants to make the shift from ego-supportive group psychotherapy towards analytic group therapy (group analysis) modified, of course, for psychotic patients, another three conditions should be met:

1. Verbal communications are encouraged to develop into 'group associations' by means of 'free floating discussion', the group analytic equivalent of free associations in psychoanalysis. Everything manifested in the group is analyzed, including behaviors and interactions between members. It is not only the dynamic processes of the group, but also the analysis of these processes within the whole group, that produces the

therapeutic effect. Group psychoanalytic therapy uses the manifest content to reach the latent level through the process of interpretation.

2. The group analyst directs group processes and his own behaviour in agreement with the above assumptions.

3. The analytic group is basically a transference group. However, all relationships in the therapeutic situation should not be called transference, and it would be better to consider the total situation with its specific features as the therapeutic situation. Foulkes conceptualizes the group situation as a whole representing the matrix of all individual processes (Brown and Pedder 1991). The communication of the individual patient is observed through the response of the group as a whole, just as if it comes from the group through the mouth of the individual person. In the analytic group, the patient's disorder is expressed here-and-now in the current group situation, not genetically, in terms of its historical origins.

Foulkes described two types of contents that appear in the group from the very beginning: 'the foundation matrix' and 'the dynamic matrix'. The foundation matrix is based on biological values, as well as on conscious and unconscious cultural, ethnic, linguistic values, properties and reactions. They are transmitted and developed in the primary group, then extended to the social network and maintained by the group with which one lives. Pines (1996) writes that:

The matrix is the shared common history of the group, the conscious and unconscious repository of all events. The group analyst's faith, belief in the matrix concept, enables him or her to offer this to the group members from the moment of conception of the group in the mind of the therapist.

By the phrase dynamic matrix, Foulkes means the group activity of socialization and reflection that allows the individual to find and redefine himself or herself. Cividini-Stranic (1996a) mentions:

The matrix can be understood as an imaginary place which enables and allows manifold, mutual communications and dialogue. It is the basis of all manifest group behaviours, all individual behaviours and activities which cannot be separated from the group as long as it is physically bound.

According to Foulkes, the individual in the network of communications represents a nodal point, not as a closed, but as an open system.

There are several levels of communication in the group (Foulkes 1964). The *transference level* is the one that stimulates the most and offers the most as a ground for clarification, interpretation and insight. At the *autistic level*, the group as a whole or its individual members can represent the projections of inner images. In this way, the group can represent the mother, i.e., the body as the first recipient of someone's speech. At this level, the image of the body extends to the group, which can furthermore assume the role of a transitional object, forming in this way the basis for further development of both the individuals and the whole group.

The next level is *realistic*, that is, the level of current reality which includes the therapist, the group members, a particular person, etc. At this level, relationships can be completely submerged into the common reality, conventionality, anxiety, etc., depending on the personality structure of the particular person. Within such a range, all the complexity of the meanings of relationships and communications faced by group analysis comes into expression.

Analysis through the group is also one of Foulkes' basic concepts. As Pines (1994) says, 'the concept of 'group-as-a-whole' is intrinsic to group analysis; it was there from the start.'

The understanding of and distinction between manifest and latent processes seems more appropriate for neurotically structured personalities than for acute hospitalized patients, who lack sufficient structure to warrant this distinction. Within this context, the principles of group analysis seem to be more appropriate for the understanding of processes reflected in the matrix, which reflect the personal and interpersonal dynamics of the 'here-and-now' situation, than the application of principles preferred in group analysis for neurotically structured personalities. The structure of both the individual personalities and of the group itself is insufficient in the case of hospitalized psychotics. But, if the therapist integrates the psychodynamic approach incorporating group analytic principles into his professional culture and practice (Cividini-Stranic 1996b; Klain 1996; Moro 1996), he will be able to introduce them into the methodology of work whenever they appear to be appropriate, and this process will assist in raising the group work above the usual routine to achieve goals of transformation and growth.

The roles of the therapist and their potential evolution in the group: Foulkes' concepts

Some basic elements of the psychotic patient–therapist relationship

The following are of fundamental importance in group psychotherapy with psychotic patients: (1) the assessment of the patient's capacity to establish a relationship with the therapist, and, through him, with others, and (2) the personality traits and education of the therapist.

1. The capacity of the psychotic to establish the relationship with another person primarily refers to the capacity for introjection. The integrity of the patient's intrapsychic experience is interwoven with his capacity to perceive outer reality and to introject the therapist from this reality as a separate external object. Another dimension of the relationship to outer reality is projection, which is interwoven with introjection. The constant

exchange of introjection and projection determines the experience of the self and the definition of the external objects and environment.

In the assessment of the patient's capacity to establish the relationship with the therapist, along with the mechanisms of projection and introjection, the 'successful' use of the mechanism of splitting, which protects the personality from the threat of further regression, also plays a decisive role. The depth of the personality split will also determine the possibility and the level of the transference experience, i.e., the therapeutic level.

The capacity to establish relationships with others is related to the possibility of establishing transference in psychotics. By definition, transference is the repetition of relationships to primary objects. The transference of the psychotic patient is a projection from very early, psychotic-like phases of development (i.e., M. Mahler's phases of so-called 'normal autism' – a concept now questioned by recent infant research- and 'normal symbiosis'). Because of its regressed level, such a transference stands out strikingly within the situation in which it occurs. In the case of a favourable development of the psychotic patient's relationship with the therapist, the therapist will become a new primary object for the patient, and by the repetition of the relationship, the new introject will develop into a constant object, while the transference of the psychotic patient will represent the repetition of the relationship to the therapist from their first encounter. This enables the patient to reduce the depth of regression and to improve his relationship to reality via the therapist. The therapist intervenes between the patient and reality in the achievement of the therapeutic goals, which are based on an objective assessment of the patient's capacities for more adequate structure and functioning, with a possible establishment of a corrective symbiotic relationship. It is assumed that the therapist feels the need to develop this relationship toward higher levels, or more autonomous functioning of the patient.

2. To complement what the patient brings to the therapy relationship, the therapist must supply the following therapeutic features:

   a) unpossessive warmth (a primary, undirectional, non-verbal capacity for relatedness)

   b) empathy (the therapist's capacity to introject the patient as an object and to structure the image of the patient with as much data as possible from all developmental phases. The image of the patient in the therapist is shaped through the arrangement of non-verbal and verbal data perceived unconsciously and consciously)

   c) genuineness (which enables the therapist to spontaneously direct and measure his behaviour toward the patient).

Also essential are the educative experience and orientation of the therapist, as well as the integrated theoretical framework within which the group phenomena are defined. Although on the one hand such experience and orientation are a necessary aid in structuring and comprehension of intrapsychic and interpersonal relationships, on the other hand, they can also create certain limitations.

The need and meaning of the leadership role

The role of the leader logically results from the group context and situation. In the initial group phase, or when a new member joins the group, this situation is usually one in which the therapist dominates the group. In such situations, the group usually establishes a regressive, dependent relationship to the therapist, expecting from him gratification of infantile needs. Realizing the needs of the group, the psychotherapist has two possibilities: to submit or to resist their wish. In fact, the only things the group members have in common at the beginning are their therapist and their difficulties (Foulkes and Anthony 1965). At first, the group shows the tendency to put its leader into the center and to expect instructions from him.

The therapist and the group can represent objects, such as husbands, wives, friends, while individual members can mutually react within transference in a narrower sense, as to sisters, brothers, mothers, spouses and so forth. Their feelings for these persons or their inner images of them can be projected in the group. At times, the therapist may be seen almost as an idolized godlike parent, while sometimes he can be experienced as bad parent whom they dread and reject, as if he is an angry 'God', sitting by himself, having everything and giving nothing. The therapist can be also perceived as a powerful individual who treats the group as weak and helpless people.

The therapist can be further seen as a potent healer in comparison to the patients, as normal in relation to them as disturbed, as parent in relation to them as children, as strong in relation to them as weak and helpless, and so on. He can be also be experienced as immune to emotional provocations, capable of maintaining stability and cheerfulness while faced with volcanic eruptions of emotions. On the other hand in the 'mature,' healthy transference or treatment alliance, the therapist is generally regarded as the embodiment of the progress directed to maturity, who meaningfully and professionally improves healthy patterns of life.

On account of the immature need of the group for the leader, the therapist's activity may eventuate in an authoritarian 'fixation' of the group. In order to prevent this occurrence, and after creating an appropriate and dynamic situation for the therapy, the group therapist should leave the patient to face his or her problem, treating him with the least possible interference. The therapist plays an important role in encouraging the group members to expose their thoughts, feelings and experiences, and in stimulating the interactions within the group.

For Foulkes, the differentiation between the roles of therapist and patient is a polarity which must be sustained in group treatment. In his early considerations on group psychology, Freud refers to two psychologies present in every group: the psychology of the leader and the psychology of the led (the group members.) Therefore, it is not sufficient to view the therapist's contribution as one among others. It is the interaction of the therapist's psychology with that of other participants that give each group its specificity. Even in a more advanced stage, the two psychologies remain present, and patients often put pressure on the therapist to become a patient like them, but at the same time they are afraid that he might really succeed and make them 'a leaderless group', left to their own resources under the burden of all the regressive, destructive forces present in them. The therapist's attitude basically involves the rejection of the authoritative role and the inclination to accomplish the work through and with the group with as little interference as possible. The aim of the therapist is to wean the group from its orientation to the leader, that is, to transform the leader gradually into the 'conductor' or facilitator of the group. During this process, Slavson (1973) warns about the permissive behaviour of the group therapist at the very beginning of the therapy which might result in a very disturbing atmosphere.

From the psychotherapist, as the group leader, the group demands different roles according to its needs. On the other hand, the psychotherapist has his own ideas about his role in the group context, as well as his own needs. Here, the therapist's personality with all its countertransference moments, education, and training come into expression. Wolf and Schwartz (1962) write about authoritative therapists dominated by either id or superego: 'In the id dominated group every expression is intense. In the superego dominated group any intense affect is either disapproved or regarded as acting out. Too permissive or too repressive therapy negates the meaning of group experience.'

Within this context Yalom (1970) points out that some therapists prefer to be seen as 'almighty,' while others can act as discouraged and helpless. Some therapists feel so threatened when patients search for their autonomy that they unintentionally 'do not allow them to grow up', and they can sometimes be so provocative and sarcastic that patients in the group form a permanent alliance against them. Yalom further says that the most difficult thing to define about the therapist–patient relationship is not what the therapist does or really is, but what he evokes in the fantasies of each patient. The transference distortions evoke parental authority, dependency, power, revolt and autonomy, which are all frequently personified in the therapist's person. The clarification and working out of transference distortions in the patient–therapist relationship bring about significant changes in the therapeutic process. However, such development of the group process is not characteristic for the regressive group of psychotic patients, and, furthermore, a comparatively short hospital treatment is also unfavourable to such a development. It is, however, important that the therapist does not lose sight of this potential perspective in his own experience and conduct of the group.

One of the central problems in the group is thus the conflict over authority. Cividini-Stranic (1980) mentions that due to the ambivalences in the life of every group, conflicts and crises of authority are unavoidable.

The solving of the authority crisis contributes to the process of separation and differentiation of the self from the therapist's self, which further offers the possibility of differentiation among the members. The central crisis is the wish for individual and group autonomy, and the conflict between the fear and the wish to remove the leader. The problem is how to deal with, make understandable, and work out the authoritative and powerful role of the therapist, which is at times needed by the group, and at times by the therapist, when during the entire group process it is both rejected and asked for. It is a long journey, full of challenges and obstacles, for the therapist to give up the authoritative role and to transfer it to the group. The therapist is authoritative and powerful because of his or her profession and knowledge, which enable him to conduct the group and lead it to the goal. The group demands that from the therapist. The members of the group expect the therapist to give them all his knowledge, they hope that they can be easily cured by him, while they themselves do not have to make contributions. They frequently see him as an expert and openly or indirectly request solutions from him. The psychotherapist is aware that many members of the group need the function of the therapist's strength and power to feel safe. The group often expects the therapist to be 'the one' who gives orders and makes decisions, which means that the therapist represents authority.

Analytically oriented group psychotherapy in hospital conditions is mostly applied in the form of 'focal' therapy. Focal therapy prevents excessive regression, transference neurosis or potential development of psychotic transference. It is limited in time and depth, while its aim is less ambitious than in classical psychoanalysis. According to Muacevic (1975) the following ingredients are important in focal therapy: (1) the capacity to perceive and solve the actual conflict; (2) attaining insight into defense mechanisms; and (3) learning how to find the way out of the unfavourable life situation.

Psychopharmacological treatment is as a rule applied only in necessary quantities, and as little as possible, because its excessive usage prevents interactions within and outside the group.

The therapist in the hospital group situation is seen by Muacevic (1975) mostly as the representative of reality. Popovic (1975) states that within the hospital setting, group therapy serves the important function of helping the patient population to reduce the amount of irrational conduct in the hospital 'society'. The individual should achieve changes through cooperation with others, and not by overdependent asking for 'help'. In this function, the therapist plays a crucial role. For this reason, the personality traits of the group therapist are as important as his or her professional function or education.

Much more has been written on the roles and meaning of the group therapist than on his or her personality. The fact that the therapist is the cause of the existence of the group and its organizer, who for many reasons is assigned a special place within the group, does not mean that he must be 'special'. The personal and professional qualities which are required of the therapist belong to the sphere of basic humanity. He should be the person who accepts risks in life situations as a member of the community to which he belongs, whose rules he either accepts, or is able calmly to disapprove of in a way which enables further dialogue (Moro 1996). This means that the therapist should from the beginning enable each member of the group to feel safe and welcome in the group, and to trust the therapist knowing that he will not hurt him intentionally. This level of professional and personal integrity is difficult to achieve and maintain. On one hand, 'the regressive impact is unlikely not to touch the conductor, while on the other hand, the leadership function emanates from the deeper recesses of internalized models of authority' (Nitsun 1996). The achievement and maintenance of this level of professional and personal integrity requires continuous learning from interpersonal relations, consultations and supervisions.

The following examples are intended to show the roles of the therapist in the context of actual group situations.

Clinical illustration 1: a hospital-based group of psychotic patients

The practical implications of the above discussion are best understood through clinical examples. The first will be taken from a hospital group consisting mostly of psychotic patients (with some borderlines as well) with an average of 10 to 14 members. The large number of members represented a concession to the situation in which approximately the same number of acute patients with psychotic, borderline or neurotic disorders judged as suitable for group psychotherapy is usually found. The group met twice a week for 60 to 70 minutes per session. All patients were younger or middle aged males. Some of them had a history of alcohol abuse, but it never dominated the clinical picture. They all received medication therapy and had individual sessions with the doctors of the ward. The length of hospitalization rarely exceeded three weeks and tended to be shorter. Notes with brief commentary were kept for each session, and excerpts from these notes are reported here. The names used are pseudonyms.

The sequence of group therapy work which occurred after a short interruption of the group will be presented.

A brief commentary for the first session of the group included the following: 'The therapist constantly prodded the individuals to participate in the work of the group. The interactions between group members are superficial and short. The members of the group often refer to the therapist when talking about themselves.'

During the following session, the communications within the group are reported to be 'somewhat better structured.' Here, the example of the patient Davor will be presented. Can he tell us how he feels? Davor says that he is tired of this long stay in hospital. The drugs helped him only the first day, and he would agree with Damir that drugs are of no use and that he does not care to talk to others. Davor suffers from paranoid psychosis and the above was his response to the statement of Marko who said that he had undergone hospital treatment several times and considered it necessary at these times. He said that one feels safer in the hospital.

The therapist asks Davor whether he thinks that this group will not understand him. Davor: 'Yes ... It seems to me that I should like best to be alone in my own world, without anyone to give me drugs, to be left alone to do what I want. I think that the doctor understood well what I wanted to say.' The therapist then asks him if there is some other group that would understand him better. Davor: 'No. My people at home say all the time that I am crazy and have unrealistic ideas, but my ideas are hundred times better than theirs.' The therapist then suggests that maybe his environment cannot understand him and therefore has difficulty accepting him. Davor: 'Why must the majority exert pressure on the minority? Maybe nobody has such ideas as I have, or almost nobody. So what? Who says that the majority is always right?'

The therapist's confrontation of Davor's request for discharge from the clinic with empathic clarifications and interpretations helped the group members to gain insight into their own behaviour and resistance. Addressing the whole group, whenever it is possible, shifts the communication of individuals from the initial strong attachment to the therapist, and by this, facilitates therapy by the group rather than just the therapist.

During the third session, the discussion is continued about whether treatment plans and length of stay should be left to the doctor. Patient Luka does not want to make this decision by himself and 'leaves it to the doctor.' The group is asked about whether Luka is ready to be discharged. Some give no reply, while others say that he might be discharged soon. Luka becomes angry at the lack of support: 'Why don't you say something, why do you keep silent? Why am I the only one to speak? Of course, I am well, so that perhaps I am in a better position to speak up, but others have to say something too.'

Josip leans forward, with his face blushing: 'Why do you have to yell so much? Don't presume to be the doctor! It seems that nothing bothers you anymore. I think that you are still not ready to take responsibility for yourself.' Both Luka and Josip are psychotic patients with paranoid features.

The dialogue continues:

Luka: 'Don't get angry. I didn't want to make trouble, I just wanted to invite the others to join the conversation and to animate them.'

Ante: 'But you are not a hostess.' (Everyone laughs.)

Therapist: ' Josip, I have the impression that Luka made you angry by taking the initiative.'

Josip: 'No, it does not make me angry. I get angry only when someone talks like a big shot.'

Therapist: 'Let's see, if we left the initiative to you, would that frighten you –?'

Josip: 'I think it still would. I still don't feel free enough to speak in front of this group. I know what you mean … Maybe I envy Luka. He always makes noise and thinks he is the best. I like him, but he seems to me a little childish …'

Luka: 'Maybe you are right. I know that myself … I suppose I will also grow up some day. I only wanted to help you and the others.' (Luka then talks about his post-discharge plans.)

The further development of this session reveals the ambivalence about the dilemma of dependency/autonomy, but at the same time, an improvement in communication between the group members is observed. Patients with major psychotic disorders have great difficulty fitting into the group milieu. The session notes mention that 'such a group requires continuous verbal activity of the therapist to stimulate the group members with deeper regression to participate verbally. With longer work in the group, both the possibility of accurate diagnostic assessment and the overall therapeutic effect are also improved'.

During the fourth session of this sequence, two patients say goodbye to the group. They have had the longest time in the group, which gives them a special position among the members. Other patients also associate this situation with the possibility of their own discharge in the near future, particularly those who show stronger resistance to further treatment. The resistance in the group grew to a high degree, but the verbalization was so abundant that it was difficult to intrude and bring up the issue of resistance. The members were rather oblivious to the idea of mutual listening! Complaints and aggression were often directed at the therapist. The acceptance of such feelings and behaviours without reprisal made the group atmosphere much warmer toward the end of the session, when resentments were projected outside the group onto the clinic, food, hygiene and similar targets, a tactic quite familiar to every therapist who works with psychotic patients.

During the fifth session new members join the group, and thus the group becomes divided into old and new members. A rich exchange between the group members is observed. By the end of the session, Josip says that it is important for him to know if the others can hear him. The others say that they can hear him quite well, but they think that only the doctor can really help him. Dinko puts his hand on Josip's shoulder and says: 'I have children like you – boys. When you spoke, some sadness and helplessness came over me. I thought that none can understand me, that I am a hopeless case. I thought I suffered from the worst possible disease. To you and to all the others I can say that I have started to feel better since I came to this group and heard how the others are doing. You see, it's not hard only for you. This made me think.' He says that today his treatment at the hospital is ending and he wants to thank them all. Josip says that maybe soon they will also see such a day.

Therapist: 'Renato and Dinko get along well. How do the others feel when they listen to this conversation?' Marko says that he now feels safer, as among friends. At the beginning, he was passing through the hospital hallway as if it were a street full of strangers. Now, he is among good friends, which makes his life at the ward and in the group much easier. Davor says that he was displeased when the doctor told him to join the group, but he is now glad that he did. 'Here I can see best what I can do and how much I still need to be able to go back home and to my friends. It seems to me that Marko is much better, but Renato needs longer treatment.'

Renato says that he is not happy to hear that but he will not oppose it. 'It will be as the doctor says, but I suppose he will ask me too.'

During the sixth session, the last one in this sequence, almost half of the group consists of new members. They introduce themselves, and the older members sometimes encourage them to say more about themselves and their current feelings. They usually cast a glance toward the therapist looking for a sign of approval of their activity. Sometimes, though rarely, they also verbalize their wish for approval.

By the end of this session a new member of the group, Milan, says that he can see that patients who have completed treatment leave the hospital, and that he hopes that the others will also get better. He promises to show his drawings. The commentary from the notes for this session indicates that the more senior members of the group can help the therapist in conducting the group since they are familiar with the style and method of work. Frequent silences are understood as an appeal to the therapist to stimulate group communication.

Clinical illustration 2: an outpatient group of psychotic patients

For the sake of comparison with the above inpatient group, I will now put forward an example from an outpatient group of psychotics. It meets once a week for about 80 minutes. As with the inpatient group, after each session, pharmacotherapy is reviewed and revised if indicated. The group was co-conducted by an older male therapist and a younger female colleague. In terms of continuity, this group experienced frustrations caused by the temporary absence of the older, male therapist during a three week holiday season. The majority of the group members had participated previously in the hospital group.

During the first sessions following the departure of the male therapist, lamentations about him were frequently expressed. This was particularly seen in frequent reminiscences on earlier therapeutic episodes from individual and group sessions. Here, the recollection of patient S is presented. He remembered how he often felt the need to physically attack the (previously absent) therapist, so that on one occasion he really made an attempt to hit him during the individual session. As he said, he gave up because of the attitude of the therapist who was willing to accept the assault and did not respond with aggression to his own aggression. 'At that moment I realized that I have him,' he said, 'that he understands me and really loves me.' He recalled almost wistfully how the therapist helped him in mitigating his high anxiety with long silent walks on the hospital balcony when it seemed to him that 'they think and feel the same'.

The two therapists were frequently compared by the group. The female therapist was experienced as protective, and as a person who tries to explain things and bring everything closer to home in a simple way. The male therapist was remembered as more rigid and demanding, particularly with respect to reality factors (treatment, sick leave, family situations, etc.). On the one hand, the group frequently emphasized that 'they can be more themselves' with the female therapist, while on the other they constantly enquired about the return of the male therapist.

The following are the excerpts from the two sessions conducted by the female therapist at the end of the period of absence of the male therapist (Urlic and Krstulovic 1990).

Session 1

When the conductor entered the room, the already gathered group sat speechless. On a small table, she noticed a piece of paper on which was written 'There is no way out.' Nobody looked at the therapist; rather, they were all staring at that piece of paper, when patient Slavko asked female patient Anka to analyse the handwriting. She took the note and said that 'there is no' is written as if really there is no, while 'way out' is written as if some possibility of a way out is still left. Slavko then began to emphasize that there is no way out and he should know that. The others remained silent as if they did not understand what he said. The conductor intervened by asking him to explain to her what did he mean by that, and he said that for days he has felt that his situation is hopeless: 'It is more and more clear to me that there is no way out … everything is meaningless. Everything should be stopped. We don't exist anyway, and these fools (gesturing to other group members) do not see it. I cannot find myself in anything.' He was very excited, speaking quickly in an elevated tone. He addressed the group in a commanding way, demanding that they accept the 'fact' that there is no way out. He insulted them and shouted at them that they were stupid if they could not see that he was finished, etc. (a phrase which the conductor, becoming quite alarmed, experienced as an expression of manifest suicidality).

However, patient Jakov reacted and started to shout at Slavko to 'stop talking nonsense', since he cannot listen to these speculations anymore, while Slavko responded to him similarly. Then Jakov stood up with the intention of hitting Slavko, but was stopped by two patients (Dinko and Milan). The remaining members of the group appeared to watch attentively what was going on. Then Jakov said: 'I don't want to listen to you anymore! Why do you force your ideas on me? If there is no way out for you, it is your problem. I can find my way out. Do you want me to prove it? (Jakov made a sudden move toward a door – made of glass, that was always locked and out of use – as if he were going to break the glass.) At that moment, the therapist stood up and showed the patient the door that was always used, saying that it was the exit. At that point, Jakov suddenly turned around and quickly sat in his place. It seemed to the therapist that the whole group was in a state of fear and she told them so. After that, patients Dinko and Milan suggested changing the topic, and the group chose the theme of 'family and work situations'. The therapist suggested that conflict situations in family, at work, or elsewhere can lead to feelings of anger and helplessness, an interpretation which was accepted by some members and created a more relaxed atmosphere. She asked to what extent the group situation might be affecting the agitation and strong feelings in the group: after all, the older therapist was temporarily absent ... The group responded with silence. The therapist then told them about her experience of the feeling of sadness within the group, as if they were in a situation of separation and loss. One member of the group said: 'Well, we are "veterans",' a familiar phrase that had been used by the absent therapist.

Session 2

The next session was attended by the same members, and again, the group began in silence. The therapist thought that the group was still affected by the previous meeting and initiated a conversation about that: 'Have you thought about your possible way out?' Upon which, Slavko began: 'After the last session, I had a stupid dream.' He laughed and looked cheerful. 'I dreamed that I was in my village, V, where both Serbs and Croats live ... We are waiting for a bus heading to town. The village is hopeless and we have to get on the bus, but there are too many people there ... My brother manages to get on the bus, which sets out and goes away from me ... I reach the door of the bus, but it is shut in my face, and the people on the bus explain to me that I am not allowed to go on board because I am "S", which in my dream should mean that I am Serb.' Slavko begins to laugh and sets the whole group in a roar. The therapist reminds him that in his dream his brother managed to go on board. Slavko says: 'For me, there is no way out from this village, he has always been ahead of me, the son of a bitch, and I am "S –

schizophrenic," upon which everyone again burst out laughing. During the remainder of the session, the therapist helped the group to see that village V can denote the experience of a therapeutic, family, or some other group, in which 'those who manage to go on board', that is, are healthy, or healthier, and 'those to whom the door is shut in their face' can be recognized. Many members brought up associations to their own life situations, particularly those reflecting their recognition that it is the disorder that separates them from their environment. In the process, the most regressive idolized the therapist. Upon that, Slavko said to the therapist: 'You understand us best ... and you are healthy, but don't think that you have all the advantages. You don't know what it means to be psychotic. You are deprived of this extraordinary experience.'

Soon after the above mentioned sessions, the older, male therapist returned, and the younger, female left the group for some time. Here is a brief account of what then happened:

The older therapist was welcomed with joy, handshakes and smiles. When the group started working, patient Slavko spoke first, after a short silence: 'I would like to talk about death today.' He then became quiet. Patient Boris, again after a short silence, said that he went to a disco club, where he met some girls and had a nice time. The group preferred this more cheerful subject, but one of the members referred to the suggestion given by Slavko, and the group became confused, anxious and silent. The therapist's interpretation then indicated that the conversation about death, joys of life and friendships might reflect the sequence of events in the group, in which one therapist leaves and the other comes back, and when sudden changes occur in 'our small community' they potentially evoke feelings of uncertainty and fear. This interpretation was at first followed by aggressive associations implying that the therapist abandoned them and did not care for them. Subsequently, the therapist was praised as the father and mother, even like God. Through the confrontation of such extreme feelings and experiences in a very regressive situation, a whole spectrum of transference experiences and reactions to the therapist gradually came out, while the possibility of their manifestations gradually re-established a certain cohesiveness within the group, familiar from the previously settled framework. This framework enabled the psychotic members of the group to expose their emotions and experiences, intermixing past and present events, first of all to the members of the therapeutic team, and then to a certain extent also to other group members. Such a process, involving a better integration of personality and a more adequate relationship to reality, is proportional to the group constancy and the ability of the therapist to use both the members' transference and his or her own countertransference.

Analyses and syntheses

Experiences from the small group of psychotic inpatients

After all is said and done, every group, like every therapist, has its own specific quality. First, I will give an account of the above dynamics of the extended small group in hospital conditions, which, as I have already mentioned, represents diagnostically a heterogenous combination of male psychiatric patients. They have in common serious pathology and deep regression, manifested clinically by serious disturbances of ego functions. The beginning work in every group has some common characteristics. One of them is that all communications tend to be directed toward the therapist who frequently stimulates communications and interactions. In a group of psychotics, this stimulation is aimed at individuals within the group.

As early as the beginning of the second session, as shown by the presented sequence, the splitting mechanism is manifested at the group level. Some of the patients are stimulated toward greater verbalization, while others withdraw, or protect themselves from exposure. A paranoid patient becomes a representative of such an atmosphere, revealing his aggressive feelings from earlier bad experiences, actualized in the here-and-now in relation to the treatment, hospital environment, medications and the therapist.

The stimulation of individuals may be accompanied by confrontations, particularly those related to resistances to treatment. In this sense, managing and reducing aggression becomes a prerequisite for the enforcement of libidinal investments aimed at establishing clearer ego boundaries and object relations. The therapist must be constantly verbally active, and at the same time empathically very involved.

The patient's dilemma of whether to accept the treatment or to reject it and demand discharge frequently occurs in hospital conditions. This ambivalence is very clearly highlighted in a group situation if it is enforced by a paranoid patient. It is questionable to what extent paranoiacs are able to participate in group activity, and how much they can help the group in clarifying the confronted content or emotions. After all, Bleuler early included deep ambivalence and autistic encapsulation among the basic traits of the psychotic personality structure, which is particularly pronounced in paranoiacs. Clinical experience suggests that such individual and group situations can sometimes be resolved by introducing a humorous note into interactions, but tactfully and cautiously, so that it is not experienced as mockery or rejection, which would close the communication channel.

The initial dilemma of this group involved the members' acceptance of treatment, reflected by aggressive manifestations in interpersonal relations, and enabling the evolution of the dependency–autonomy dilemma. The latter dilemma contains elements of both reality and transference. The therapist is able to clarify paranoid fears and their origins, and to relieve them. At the same time, new diagnostic impressions and therapeutic assessments are made in the here-and-now situation of the group interaction.

During the course of the group psychotherapy of psychotics, aggression that is increasingly released can sabotage the work of the group. Perhaps 'stop' is not the most adequate term, since work on aggression is one of the fundamental elements of psychotherapy. In such situations, the principle of the therapist's unpunishing acceptance, along with a clear structuring of the group climate, enables the group to direct aggression, expressed verbally, as acting-out, or as autistic encapsulation, toward the therapist first, and then to 'dilute' and divert it in relation to the elements of the institution and the society which he represents.

The arrival of new members and the departure of the old ones is constantly repeated in the group. New members introduce themselves, while old members are able to say more about their experiences in the group. The division into old and new members allows those with experience to reveal the importance of both confiding and being heard, and to oscillate between their orientations toward the therapist and other group members. It is possible, in this situation, to interpolate didactic, educational elements into the group work. Older members can help the therapist conduct the group and contribute to the development of positive transference toward him. If the new primary object is perceived as 'good,' a corrective symbiotic experience is initiated through him or her.

Experiences from the small group of psychotic outpatients

As previously noted, the hospital group experience frequently represents the basis for the continuation of outpatient group treatment. The importance of continuity with 'infinite perspective,' that is, the need for treatment throughout the life cycle, is particularly emphasized. A situation – the absence of one of the therapists – in which a sudden change caused insecurity and fear, occurred in the group, resulting in difficulties in adjustment. The result was the fragmentation of the 'mother' object, the group, which was verbally expressed as the dilemma: death or discoclub (life)!

The sequence of these examples from therapy reveals, first of all, the deficiency of ego functions in psychotically structured personalities with deep regression. The archaic common language of human beings is the language of emotions. It is particularly revealed in transference situations of psychotics. The archaic levels of functioning of psychotic patients prevent their using more mature defense mechanisms, which in a situation of impending further fragmentation leads to fear of destruction ('There is no way out,' says patient Slavko. 'I am trying to find my way out,' says patient Jakov.)

In such situations, there is a massive use of archaic defense mechanisms (splitting, negation, projection and projective identification, omnipotence and primitive idealization). During the presented sessions, these mechanisms were constantly manifested, in either individuals or the group, with varied intensity. The interaction between patient Jakov and patient Slavko revealed projections and projective identifications with 'bad' part-objects, the reintrojection of which in patient Jakov led to a state of an overwhelming, 'unthinkable' anxiety which he agitated in the group. In terms of the drives, their defusion led to clear predominance of aggressive drives over libidinal ones.

The continuous oscillation between aggressive and libidinal themes, expressed in ambivalent transference situations, are most intensely manifested in both psychotic transference and briefer transference psychoses. In the outpatient group, this ambivalence manifested in the transference onto the therapist as alternately 'good and protective', versus 'severe and demanding', while in states of deep regression or fragmentation, it was expressed through projections of omnipotent fantasies and primitive idealization, or total underestimation, accusations and rejections. The latter was manifested as a result of the fear of separation, insecurity and shaken trust in the constancy of the already established therapeutic framework. The earlier work on corrective symbiotic experience and gradual establishment of more stable object relations was shaken, which was reflected in the transference by reactivation of earlier traumatic experiences ('We don't exist anyway!', patient Slavko.)

The release of archaic strata in patient Jakov in the form of acting-out contained, in addition to the fear of further destruction, the message for help. In other words, the regression to deep pregenital levels of functioning has both pathological and defensive meaning in terms of the return to infantile or archaic integration levels. In such situations, the therapist's function of 'holding' (in the Winnicottian sense) is indeed put to the test. When the patient experiences his situation as hopeless (the group in the village separates, the bus door is shut to his face, he remains alone and abandoned), the emphasis is on basic trust in the therapist's capacity to hold and contain the projections of the patient's part-objects from early experiences. In terms of affective expression, this need for containment is reflected in extreme libidinal and aggressive imagery ('At that moment I realized that I have him (i.e., the therapist), says patient Slavko, 'Both Serbs and Croats live … in the village.')

At this point, the therapist's primary function consists of helping the patient to establish a better inner balance between aggressive and libidinal drives. In the situation of a transference psychosis, this means the establishment of control over unrelated, deneutralizing aggression, which can be then utilized by both observing and experiencing ego (e.g. Jakov to therapist: 'I don't want your way out! I want my way out!', expressing aggression which is subsequently neutralized, thus enabling Jakov to find his place in the group and the session after the return of the older therapist).

The reparatory idealization of the parental figure through the re-established trust and earlier, familiar way, enabled the reconstruction of the cohesive feeling in the group, led to increased trust in the therapist and members of the therapeutic team, and facilitated better communication among the group members, all of which favoured improved personality integration of individual members and the establishment of a more adequate relationship to reality. In this respect, the group can represent an important container for both aggressive and libidinal drives, and it can strengthen the boundaries, becoming in this way a vital structuring factor in psychotics. Coping styles and relationships to reality can be constructively supported and improved. However, the limitations determined by the disorder should always be kept in mind, and such patients should not be exposed to unnecessary stresses.

I would like to cite briefly another clinical episode involving an outpatient group of psychotics during the time of the war in Croatia, in autumn, 1991. It was rumoured at the hospital that in the center of the town snipers were shooting at civilians getting out of the local buses, and that people looked for the shelters. The patients did not show up at group time. The therapist's fear and feeling of responsibility for the patients greatly increased, and the only way to cope was to postpone the start the session in order to prevent the general insecurity and anxiety that might ensue. After a short time, however, the members did show up, excusing themselves for being late on account of the snipers and the need to stay in the shelter. The therapist reacted countertransferentially in an inconsiderate way, inflicting his earlier fears on the group, saying angrily: 'Why did you come to group in such dangerous circumstances?' They looked calm, and one of them said: 'How can we allow ourselves not to come, when you are here?' (The constancy of the work in this group was maintained throughout the whole war period, often in threatening conditions. From time to time, for a variety of reasons, the number of the members was reduced, but the group work was never interrupted. On the one hand, good group cohesiveness with all its meanings could be observed, while on the other, a certain autism, or insufficiently adequate relationship towards outer reality was present.)

The manifestly less exposed leadership role of the therapist can open more space for the position of a democratic, facilitative 'conductor' in Foulkes' sense. However, the therapist of the psychotic group should never lose sight of the fact that he deals with patients in 'problematic states which should be either put under control or eliminated, such as disease, defect, deviation or stunted growth' (Foulkes 1964). This potential risk is always latently present, regardless of external manifestations at the level of the symptoms. As Gaetano Benedetti (1991, p.xvii) wrote, 'Over a half century of psychodynamic research has proved that schizophrenia is not only a medical disorder, but a biographical facet of the human being – it is a challenge to the whole of society to understand, accept and reintegrate the psychotic patient amongst us.'

The dilemma of the group therapist: leader *versus* conductor

In Foulkes' group analysis, the dilemma of the group therapist is the possible transformation of the leadership role into a 'conducting' role. Foulkes (1964) states that 'while the therapist does not assume active leadership of the group, he conducts it continuously ... He follows the lead of the group and makes himself an instrument of the group'. This role, frequently utilized with groups of neurotics, is much more difficult to achieve in groups of psychotics. However, if the therapist is not a rigid and conformist person, but one who accepts the analytic approach to the group as a continuous challenge, the above-mentioned evolution of the therapist's work in the group is likely to occur sooner or later, although sporadically. This shift of course applies more to outpatient groups, where psychic functioning generally is less regressive.

The group therapist must balance two functions or processes: supportive and analytic. With respect to the group's need for leadership, the therapist recognizes the regressive quality and accepts it as a model of the relationships transferred from different sociocultural groups to the therapeutic group. While confronting the group members with this regressive need in the situation of 'here-and-now' and relating it to the experiences of 'there-and-then', the therapist should not directly teach or impose ideas on the group, but assist the members in their own spontaneous learning process. Self-understanding is achieved slowly and painfully. Foulkes (1964) says that, at the beginning of group life, everything depends on good guidance, which will develop forces within the group that will enable it to take this function upon itself, while at the same time providing the therapist with the opportunity to work at a higher level.

The members' expression of feelings and experiences toward other members of the group is facilitated by the therapist's attitudes. The therapist accepts and encourages a freedom from censorship which could not occur in ordinary social situations. The group analytic atmosphere, as designed by the conductor, is characterized by tolerance and encouragement of such free disclosures.

According to Foulkes, the group analyst is not just a 'blank screen' for transference but represents a part of the actual problem and is faced with the whirlpool of conflicts in the group as a real person. While in a group of neurotics, the therapist remains passive and detached in order to stimulate the group interaction, in a group of psychotics such levels of functioning of the therapist as the group 'leader' is rarely achieved, and the therapist must be considerably more active and engaged.

In groups of psychotic patients, the therapist is available and ready to get involved when the group members require it, and the members learn how to engage him or her when they are unable to reach a satisfactory resolution of their issues. (In the group of psychotic patients such dynamics dominate the group process, while with neurotic patients the therapist's interventions are dictated by the needs of the group rather than of individuals, or a particular situation. Ordinarily, in the group analytic approach, it is the task of the therapist to shift the group process toward a new stage of development while avoiding interference with autonomous development, and without paying much attention to individual demands and situations, except in cases of psychotic patients or of decompensation.)

In a permissively conducted group, the type of communication is directly related to the technique of the therapist's minimal interference. In an authoritatively conducted group with an active conductor, this dramatic way of communication rarely comes into expression.

The therapist should pay the greatest attention to the interpretative recognition of the group movement, either progressive or regressive, and of the group dynamics that initiated it. In groups of psychotics, such focus on the group-as-a-whole will primarily assume a shape of the care for the relationship to reality and coping styles.

The question of identity becomes increasingly important during therapy in terms of personal identities and possibly the group identity ('collective image'), as well as the increasing consciousness of the identity of the therapist and his capacity to stimulate the group ideals. In this context, the therapist is perceived as a person who successfully mastered the process of maturity and as such, is an object worthy of respect and a representative of the reality.

On other occasions, however, the therapist is perceived as a regressive seducer who draws them back to childhood with all its parentally oriented attractions and dependencies. He is no longer a new figure with whom they would like to identify, but one from whom they wish to escape. For psychotic patients, the 'need–fear dilemma' is constantly present, either manifestly or latently, within persistent symbiotic patterns. It reflects the permanent dilemma of dependency versus autonomy. As the group oscillates between the two positions, the therapist is also pushed into one or another direction, which may make it appear that he is following the respective needs of the group.

Ultimately, the members may begin to see the group through the group analyst's eyes. They come to perceive group as a vital and serious event in their everyday life, an important support and stable framework for a more adequate acceptance of their own human condition. The ancient Greeks formulated this purpose by the saying: 'Tell me where to stand and I will move the Earth' ('Dos pe sto kai ten gen kineso'). For psychotic patients, the therapeutic group and especially its therapist may represent this 'foot on the Earth', from which an individual world can be moved.

Taking the above attitudes as basic therapeutic concepts for group work aimed at transforming the leadership role into the position of the 'conductor', I would like to add to these considerations some additional views on the group therapist's role.

Wolf and Schwartz (1962) point out that the development of the locus of control is directed from the outside toward the inside, moving in therapy from the authoritative figure through the members of the group to the individual. In his or her perception of the group, the group analyst tends toward one-sidedness. He observes the patients and their behaviour from above. Consequently, the therapist's impression of what is going on is limited by his paternalistic, comparatively non-participating position. When he gets involved in the group activity, the quality of his participation is different, which modifies his perception of events. The group, on the other hand, judges the interpersonal forces in action from another standpoint. Their consciousness of what happens is limited by their position in the group. To achieve a harmony that will lead toward integrated group activity, the roles of the analyst and the patients must become interlaced. The conduction that attains that goal is therapeutic.

The concept of 'partial deegoization' of the individual as a prerequisite for group membership was developed by Slavson (1973). According to this view, an individual, joining a group, gives over to the group, and particularly to the leader as its representative, a part of his or her ego. In other words, the individual must submit to the group to become a part of it, and groups originate and survive on account of this partial deegoization of its members. Out of all individual-delivered ego parts the 'group ego' emerges. The superego weakens each member's judgement because of group rules, its sanctions and permissions. The id released in this way is invested into the leader who becomes the representative of the 'group superego'.

Yalom (1970), referring to the position of group therapist, says that the therapist never becomes a full member of the group, regardless of the extent in which he establishes models or participates in the group. His concern for the survival of the group and his special feeling of responsibility for the group never decrease. He is often the only member who views the process in the perspective of the whole development, movements and obstacles. He has better perception of the group history than others, and he influences the ways or particular sequences which have evolved in the group throughout time. In spite of that, interpretation is not reserved only for the therapist. If the group is conducted informally, the patients with time become capable of reaching as accurate and useful interpretative conclusions as the therapist. The author mentions Foulkes' view that the interpretations given by other patients are often more efficient and acceptable, provided that the one who interprets accepts the role of the patient and does not try to gain prestige, influence or a privileged relationship with the therapist.

I will conclude these considerations on the leader-conductor dilemma of the group therapist with Foulkes' suggestion that 'a mature group therapist is a genuinely modest person, who can say sincerely to his group: "We are here to consider together realities and basic problems of human existence. I am just one among you, nothing more or less".' Though this attitude may look like idealization, it can represent a model to which the psychotherapist working with a group of psychotics can be directed to maintain his flexible, but consistently reliable role.

Conclusions

Different theoretical schools view the functions of the therapist in relation to the hypotheses and focus to which they are directed. Revising and summing up earlier experiences, Scheidlinger (1997) holds that the majority of group therapists would agree that their activity in therapeutic groups consists of the following: (1) structuring the group's composition, time, meeting place, and remuneration procedures; (2) structuring the conduct of the sessions with reference to confidentiality, agenda, physical contact, therapeutic techniques; (3) emphatically accepting and caring for each patient, coupled with a belief in the latter's potentiality for change and growth; (4) encouraging the open expression of feelings and concerns; (5) fostering a climate of tolerance and acceptance of variance in feelings and behaviours and on peer helping; (6) controlling within acceptable limits the drive expression, tension, and anxiety levels in individual patients; (7) controlling group-level manifestations; (8) using verbal interventions ranging from simple observations through confrontations to interpretations, aimed at reality testing and at eliciting meaning and genetic connections. With respect to the principles of group analysis, the above mentioned would be a wider framework, in which the creation and understanding of the group matrix concept, the conduct of the group as a whole, as well as the evolution concept of the therapist's role from leader to conductor would represent some of the fundamental assumptions. According to them, the therapist should organize the group, understand group phenomena and make his interventions in the here-and-now situation.

Conducting a group of schizophrenics, or of other psychotic patients, the therapist acts differently than in a group of persons able to function at a higher level. The aims of group work are related to the needs of the patients. Because of the difficulties of psychotic patients in experiencing and interpreting both inner and outer realities, Kanas (1996) describes the functions of the therapist in such groups in the following way: The therapist is (1) active and directive in keeping group members focused on the topic; (2) clear, consistent, and concrete with interventions; (3) supportive and diplomatic with comments; (4) open and willing to give opinions and advice that are appropriate to the discussion; (5) here-and-now (rather than there-and-then) focused; (6) encouraging of patient-to-patient (rather than patient-to-therapist) interactions.

Within the context of the therapist's role in the group of psychotics, the consideration of Yalom and Lieberman (1971) is interesting. They write about the dilemma between the two basic types of conductor: 'energizer' or 'provider'. In terms of measured action, it seems that the patience of the 'provider' is more acceptable for the psychotic population, as it appears that the therapist's role as a 'new primary object' is more adequately realized in this way, although it requires a fuller and longer engagement from the therapist.

The question can be raised as to the specific group-analytic psychotherapy of psychotic patients in particular hospital conditions, where patients may stay for a short time, and when even a short interruption of the work creates a situation of a new beginning. Group psychotherapy represents a therapeutic and diagnostic method which should take into account both the time factor and the number of patients. Some patients are admitted to hospital when others are discharged, and for each of them there is a possibility of revealing his social communication potentials through the interaction with other members of the group. They are a reflection of the personality and its current possibilities. The group appears to be a good medium for the stimulation of healthy ego potentials. Since the time span is narrowed, the group remains focused around its therapist, who has the function of the leader. Most often, this structuring role cannot be modified without a high risk for the members with a very weak and fragmented ego.

In addition to therapeutic and diagnostic purposes in hospital conditions, group work prepares the patients for the continuation of group treatment (along with psychopharmacological therapy) in outpatient conditions. In the outpatient group, the expected extent of reality-testing is higher and more constant than in hospital groups.

The question can be also raised about the roles and their range of flexibility that the group therapist can assume in the group of psychotic patients in hospital and outpatient settings. In this respect, and particularly on the therapist's role, it could be said that:

1. The therapist conducts the individual in the group. From experience, this situation does not change considerably from the beginning to the end of group treatment in hospital conditions, due to patients' deep regression and fragmentation, while in the case of outpatients, a more flexible approach is possible.

2. In hospital groups, due to time limitations in terms of the ward treatment and heterogeneity in the regression depth, the therapeutic aims are necessarily limited.

3. The outpatient group, on the contrary, needs constancy, or spatial and temporal continuity, with an open and adjustable perspective at the level of the ego functions and stability of the patient's object relations.

4. In the outpatient group of psychotics, the possibility of the evolution of the therapist's role from leader to conductor is more realistic and often more adequate than in hospital conditions. This means that the distinctions between these two ways of conduct become more permeable for a wide range of influences and, therefore, considerably more flexible in their exchange.

5. The therapeutic work in the group setting can be aimed at corrective symbiotic experience, as well as at dilution of the dyadic transference relationship in terms of the development directed at the triadic, socially better adjusted, one.

6. Group psychotherapy of psychotic patients represents in both hospital and outpatient conditions, together with psychopharmacological therapy, an essential complementary part of the treatment of psychotic patients (with the possible exception of manic patients, or those inclined to acting-out, and with a questionable benefit for acute paranoiacs).

7. Group psychotherapy of psychotics represents an important part of both therapeutic and diagnostic approaches to the patient. It can represent a part of the usual routine within the therapy spectrum, or it can reach high levels of creativity and represent a challenge for further scientific research.

References

Adler, D.B., Astrachan, B. M. and Levinson, D.J. (1981) 'Framework for the Analysis of Theoretical and Therapeutic Approaches to Schizophrenia.' *Psychiatry 44*, 1–12.

Benedetti, G. (1991) 'Foreword'. In G. Benedetti and P.M.Furlan (eds) *The Psychotherapy of Schizophrenia*. Seattle, Toronto, Bern, Gottingen: Hogrefe & Huber Publishers.

Boyle, M. (1990) *Schizophrenia. A Scientific Delusion?* London and New York: Routledge.

Brown, D. and Pedder, J. (1991) *Introduction to Psychotherapy*, 2nd edn. London and New York: Tavistock/Routledge.

Cannon, T.D. and Mednick, S.A. (1993) 'The schizophrenia high-risk project in Copenhagen: three decades of progress.' *Acta Psychiatrica Scandinavica* (suppl. 370), 33–47.

Cividini-Stranic, E. (1980) *Psihoterapeut u grupnoj psihoterapiji*. Beograd: Zbornik radova III kongresa psihoterapeuta Jugoslavije.

Cividini-Stranic, E. (1996a) 'Matriks grupe.' In E. Klain (ed) *Grupna analiza*. Zagreb: Medicinska Naklada.

Cividini-Staranic, E. (1996b) 'Primjena grupne analize.' In E. Klain (ed) *Grupna analiza*. Zagreb: Medicinska Naklada.

Foulkes, S.H. (1964) *Therapeutic Group Analysis*. London: George Allen & Unwin Ltd.

Foulkes, S.H. and Anthony, E.J. (1965) *Group Psychotherapy. The Psychoanalytic Approach*. London: Penguin Books.

Fromm Reichmann, F. (1953) *Principles of Intensive Psychotherapy*. Chicago and London: University of Chicago Press.

Haynal, A. and Pasini, M. (1984) *Medicine Psychosomatique*. Paris: Masson.

Howells, J.G. and Guirguis, W.R. (1985) *The Family and Schizophrenia.* New York: International Universities Press.

Hummelen, J.W. (1994a) 'Group analysis and the psychoses.' *Group Analysis 27*, 389–391.

Hummelen, J.W. (1994b) 'Psychotic decompensation during group psychotherapy: early recognition and treatment.' *Group Analysis 27*, 4, 433–440.

Kanas, N. (1996) *Group Therapy for Schizophrenic Patients.* Washington, DC and London: American Psychiatric Press, Inc.

Klain, E. (1996) 'Grupa kao cjelina.' In E. Klain (ed) *Grupna Analiza.* Zagreb: Medicinska Naklada.

Levine, M.S. (1990) 'An integrated approach to the treatment of schizophrenia with medications and psychotherapy: the Chestnut Lodge experience.' In P. Borri and R. Quartesan (eds) *USA–Europe Joint Meeting on Therapies and Psychotherapy of Schizophrenia.* Perugia: Associazione per la ricerca in psichiatria.

Milders, C.F.A. (1994) 'Kernberg's objects-relations theory and the group psychotherapy of psychosis.' *Group Analysis 27*, 4, 419–432.

Moro, L. (1996) 'Voditelj grupe.' In E. Klain (ed) *Grupna Analiza.* Zagreb: Medicinska Naklada.

Muacevic, V. (1975) *Grupna psihoterapija u uvjetima bolnickog lijecenja.* Beograd: Publikacije Zavoda za mentalno zdravlje.

Nitsun, M. (1996) *The Anti-Group.* London and New York: Routledge.

Pines, M. (1994) 'The group-as-a-whole.' In D. Brown and L. Zinkin (eds) *The Psyche and the Social World.* London and New York: Routledge.

Pines, M. (1996) 'The self as a group: the group as a self.' *Group Analysis 29*, 2, 183–190.

Plante, T.G., Pinder, S.L. and Howe, D.M.S.W. (1988) 'Introducing the living with illness group: A specialized treatment for patients with chronic schizophrenic conditions.' *Group 12*, 4, 198–204.

Popovic, M. (1975) *Grupna Terapija.* Beograd: Publikacije Zavoda za mentalno zdravlje.

Rose N.D.B. (1994) *Essential Psychiatry*, 2nd edn. Oxford: Blackwell Science Ltd.

Sandison, R. (1994) 'Working with schizophrenics individually and in groups: understanding the psychotic process.' *Group Analysis 27*, 4, 393–406.

Scheidlinger, S. (1997) 'Group dynamics and group psychotherapy revisited: four decades later.' *International Journal of Group Psychotherapy 47*, 2, 141–159.

Schermer, V.L. (1994) 'Between theory and practice, light and heat.' In V.L. Schermer and M. Pines (eds) *Ring of Fire.* London and New York: Routledge.

Schlachet, P.J. (1989) 'The metabolization of primary process in groups.' *Group 13*, 3 and 4, 217–224.

Skolnick, M.R. (1994) 'Intensive group and social systems treatment of psychotic and borderline patients.' In V. L. Schermer and M. Pines (eds) *Ring of Fire.* London and New York: Routledge.

Slavson, S.R. (1973) *An Introduction to Group Psychotherapy.* New York: International Universities Press.

Sugarman, A. and Jaffe, L.S. (1987) 'Transitional phenomena and psychological separateness in schizophrenic, borderline and bulimic patients.' In J. Bloom-Feshbach and S. Bloom-Feshbach (eds) *The Psychology of Separation and Loss.* San Francisco and London: Jossey-Bass Publishers.

Urlic, I. (1989) *Utjecaj simbiotskog iskustva i faktora pojedinih zivotnih razdoblja na pojavu i razvoj shizofrene bolesti.* Zagreb: Medicinski fakultet Sveucilista u Zagrebu.

Urlic, I. (1994) 'Caratteristiche delle dinamiche psichiche nei gruppi di pazienti psicotici interni ed esterni all'Ospedale Psichiatrico.' In N. Benedetto (ed) *Pensare l'Apprendere.* La Formazione in Gruppoanalisi. Torino: UPSEL Editore.

Urlic, I. and Caktas, J. (1987) 'Ciklotimno i shizotimno u meduodnosu.' *Medicinski anali* (supl. 1) 13, 45–50.

Urlic, I. and Krstulovic M. (1990) 'Agresivnost u transferu shizofrenih osoba.' *Medicinski anali 16*, 2, 135–144.

Yalom, I.D. (1970) *The Theory and Practice of Group Psychotherapy.* New York: Basic Books.

Yalom, I.D. (1983) *Inpatient Group Psychotherapy.* New York: Basic Books.

Yalom, I.D. and Lieberman, M. (1971) 'A study of encounter group casualties.' *Archives of General Psychiatry 25*, 1, 16–30.

Wolf, A. and Schwartz, E.K. (1962) *Psychoanalysis in Groups.* New York and London: Grune & Stratton.

Suggested further reading

Aaltonen, J. and Rakkolainen, V. (1993) 'Integrating systemic and psychoanalytic approaches to schizophrenia in a psychiatric ward.' In G. Benedetti and P.M.Furlan (eds) *The Psychotherapy of Schizophrenia.* Seattle, Toronto, Bern, Gottingen: Hogrefe & Huber Publishers.

Agazarian, Y.M. (1994) 'The phases of group development and the systems- centred group.' In V. L. Schermer and M. Pines (eds) *Ring of Fire.* London and New York: Routledge.

Ashbach, C. and Schermer, V.L. (1994) *Object Relations, the Self, and the Group.* London: Routledge.

Bacal, H.A. (1990) 'Heinz Kohut.' In H.A. Bacal and K. M. Newman. *Theories of Object Relations: Bridges to Self Psychology.* New York and Oxford: Columbia University Press.

Bion, W.R. (1990) *Second Thoughts.* London: H. Karnac (Books) Ltd.

Cox, M. (1995) *Structuring the Therapeutic Process: Compromise with Chaos.* London: Jessica Kingsley Publishers.

Dittmann, J. and Schüttler, R. (1990) 'Disease consciousness and coping strategies of patients with schizophrenic psychosis.' *Acta Psychiatrica Scandinavica 82,* 4, 318–322.

Foulkes, S.H. (1975) *Group-Analytic Psychotherapy: Method and Principles.* London: Gordon and Breach.

Fromm Reichmann, F. (1959) *Psychoanalysis and Psychotherapy.* Chicago and London: University of Chicago Press.

Haugsgjerd, S., Sandin, B., Pylkkanen, K., *et al.* (1993) *Crossing the Borders. Psychotherapy of Schizophrenia.* Ludvika: Dualis Forlag AB.

Mare, P.B. de (1972) *Perspectives in Group Psychotherapy.* New York: Science House, Inc.

Nitsun, M. (1996) *The Anti-Group.* London and New York: Routledge.

Ondarza Linares, J. (1993) 'On the guiding principles of group-analytic psychotherapy in schizophrenic subjects.' In G. Benedetti and P.M.Furlan (eds) *The Psychotherapy of Schizophrenia.* Seattle, Toronto, Bern, Göttingen: Hogrefe & Huber Publishers.

Peris, C. (1993) 'Psychotherapeutic approaches to schizophrenic patients.' *Triangle 32,* 1, 45–51.

Urlic, I. (1996) 'Procesi u grupi.' In E. Klain (ed) *Grupna Analiza.* Zagreb: Medicinska naklada.

Note

Editor's note: Some of the therapy groups on which this chapter is based were conducted during the tragic, prolonged war in ex-Yugoslavia. The courage of both the therapists and the patients in maintaining democratically run groups during such traumatic historical circumstances is, in the editors' opinion, remarkable and praiseworthy.

CHAPTER 7

Resistance, Empathy, and Interpretation with Psychotic Patients

Stanley Schneider

Introduction

Psychotic patients present many difficulties in the therapeutic situation. In group therapeutic interactions this difficulty is compounded because of the interface within the group matrix and the impact upon the other group members as well as the conductor. This paper will address the psychotic patient in a group psychotherapy context, and how the patient's difficulties impinge upon the conductor's empathic and interpretive stance.

In order for us to pursue this line of thinking, we first need to focus upon the concepts of resistance, acting-out and the negative therapeutic reaction and how patients manifest these in the group psychotherapy situation. Then we will explore how the empathic and interpretive stance of the conductor can be affected by the patient's resistance both via the conductor's countertransference as well as by the patient's projective identification.

Resistance

When a patient doesn't permit our therapeutic work to continue, in the manner we would like it to, we become unnerved for the moment and sometimes wonder how to respond – or possibly, how not to respond. We may not be sure if we are assessing the situation correctly. Or, to put it more succinctly, we need to be clear as to whether the patient's obstruction of the therapeutic process is in fact a resistance. Freud was very clear on this: 'Psychoanalysis is justly suspicious. One of its rules is that *whatever interrupts the progress of analytic work is a resistance*' (Freud 1900, p.517). Freud taught us that while resistance may impede our therapeutic work, it is also the key to understanding the reason for the obstruction. Here Freud was able to tie together the concepts of resistance and repression (1897, p.266). The same forces of psychic energy are at work here, both in the 'desire' to repress and in the manifestation known as resistance.

Laplanche and Pontalis sum it up thus: 'In psycho-analytic treatment the name "resistance" is given to everything in the words and actions of the analysand that obstructs his gaining access to his unconscious' (1980, p.394).

In a group psychotherapy situation, the resistance of a patient may connect to the latent unconscious of other group members rendering a 'blocked' group. Interestingly, the way to deal with the resistance of the individual and also of the group, is by utilizing the resistance (the 'block') to treat the resistance. This fits in well with Freud's idea that a person may try to divest himself of personal responsibility by abdicating his own ego to a collective or group ego (Freud 1921a). The individual has removed himself from assuming responsibility and instead thrusts the burden upon the group.

Thus, we need to deal with the resistance in a group both through the individual patient as well as with the other group members. The way to deal with this is by observing and trying to understand the transference reaction. The conductor needs to ascertain whether he has a responsibility for this particular resistance; he will need to look at himself. 'It might be to the therapist's advantage to explore whether or not feelings, fantasies and/or expectations of a countertransference nature exist towards the group members' (Kadis *et al.* 1974, p.143).

In order for the conductor to deal with the resistance, he 'needs to articulate the resistance for the group and comment on its *usefulness* to the group system' (Cohn 1988, p.325). By defining the resistance we enable group members to better define their own sense of self and how they interact with other members of the group, including the conductor. This is a form of making group members aware of their own boundaries *vis-à-vis* the others in the group (Durkin, 1981). This awareness needs to be brought about in a very direct manner; the group members need to be very clear about the existence of the resistance, the conductor's being in- control of the situation and how the group members need to extricate themselves from the current 'blocked' situation. As Foulkes has stated: ' It is important in dealing with all these resistances to be always as concrete as possible' (1975, p.168).

How the conductor uses himself will, in effect, determine how the group members will respond. Judicious use of empathy will be helpful here. However, if the conductor is feeling overwhelmed or attacked, his capacity for an empathic stance may be severely limited. Thus, the interactional dyad of conductor and group members needs to be at a meta-communicative level that allows the conductor the ability to be flexible and aware of his own self. With schizophrenics, 'when the negative transference is established, and inhibits *verbal* communication, the analyst proceeds to resolve this resistance' (Spotnitz 1969, p.40).

Acting-out

When a patient acts out, it means that he is responding to unconscious wishes and fantasies that he feels impelled to act upon. This sense of urgency and immediacy is exacerbated by the compulsion to repeat in actions what cannot yet be expressed in words. As Freud stated: ' He acts it before us, as it were, instead of reporting it to us' (1940, p.176). In the Dora case (1905), Freud now used the term: acting-out. 'Thus she *acted out* an essential part of her recollections and phantasies instead of reproducing it in the treatment' (1905, p.119). In other words, Dora took out her revenge on the man who she felt had deceived and deserted her.

We recognize in this acting-out the gratification of a hostile, retaliatory wish. The operative mechanism of defense, displacement, fueled the acting-out of Dora which led her to prematurely terminate the treatment. Since Dora was an adolescent young woman, we can better understand her action as an adolescent's propensity for action as opposed to verbalization.

For our purposes, in the group situation, it is very important for the conductor to be aware of the acting-out. The transference is the key to recognizing and understanding the acting-out. The conductor needs to look at what function the acting-out is serving in the group at that particular point in time. Awareness needs to take into account how the group members are affected by the acting-out, if the conductor feels certain/uncertain that it can be contained, and a plan of action on the part of the conductor – which can mean responding with an interpretation or not responding. 'There is a general consensus that acting-out should be interpreted in groups, as in any psychotherapy. There is some disagreement, however, regarding the setting of limits to appropriate behavior' (Ganzarain 1989, p.137).

Another aspect to contend with is the possibility that the acting-out is not by one particular group member but by the entire group or a major portion of the group. The impulsivity and repetitiveness, with conscious or unconscious collusion, is the tip-off here. Acting-out can be played out in various ways; some subtle and some more manifest. 'Acting-out – somebody over-punctual, somebody always late, protest against the physician's tyranny, autocratic privileges. This is paralleled by behaviour in life itself' (Foulkes and Anthony 1957, pp.92-93).

With psychotic patients the concept of acting-out is somewhat more difficult to define. Much will depend on whether the patient is capable of functioning without a well-defined delusional or hallucinatory system. For if the thought processes and actions are articulated through delusions and hallucinations, one could make the case that the patient is not able to differentiate reality from non-reality. In a recent paper (Schneider 1997), I attempted to show that we need to understand delusions (and hallucinations) as a way for the patient to express feelings and thoughts, not necessarily always from a non-reality aspect. This point of view would allow for the psychotic to act out just like any other person. On the other hand, if we view delusions and hallucinations as manifestations of a patient who is incapable of functioning in any realistic way, then we may have difficulty in defining that patient's aberrant, impulsive behavior as acting-out.

Negative therapeutic reaction

An interesting type of resistance is the negative therapeutic reaction. Just as the therapist feels that the patient is getting better and doing well, the patient resists the interpretation of the therapist and begins to deteriorate. It is almost as if the patient is so upset with the positive comment, that he needs to negate this by verbal and acting-out expressions. In 1923, Freud elaborated on this theme: 'such people cannot endure any praise or appreciation ... they react inversely to the progress of the treatment. Every partial solution that ought to result, and in other people does result, in an improvement or a temporary suspension of symptoms produces in them for the time being an exacerbation of their illness; they get worse during the treatment instead of getting better. They exhibit what is known as a "negative therapeutic reaction" ' (p.49).

Freud connects the negative therapeutic reaction with an unconscious '..."moral" factor, a sense of guilt, which is finding its satisfaction in the illness and refuses to give up the punishment of suffering ... this sense of guilt is dumb; it does not tell him he is guilty; he does not feel guilty, he feels ill' (1923, pp.49–50). The paradoxical character of this reaction points to a masochistic core, as it is the suffering itself that matters. Freud felt that this 'moral masochism ... originates from the death instinct and corresponds to that part of that instinct which has escaped being turned outwards as an instinct of destruction' (Freud 1924, p.170).

Loewald (1972) makes the point that the negative therapeutic reaction is

> not primarily a by-product of reactions against the therapist and his efforts but stem from a deeply rooted intrapsychic imbalance between libidinal and aggressive drives (or the life and death instincts) ... In its more intractable forms the negative therapeutic reaction is rooted in pre- oedipal, primitive distortions of instinctual and ego development and is thus hardly amenable to interpretations in terms of guilt, conscience and the need for punishment ... (The) prevalence of self-destructive forces has something to do with particular interactions with the primitive environment (pp.323–324).

Loewald's statement raises several interesting points. First, while the negative therapeutic reaction can be viewed as a type of resistance, it has to be seen in the context of unconscious processes that are fueling its emergence. Not all negativisms are a negative therapeutic reaction (Maldonado, 1989). Reactions against the therapist, in the transference, what we had earlier placed under the category of acting-out, may not be part of the negative therapeutic reaction. Also, the aggressive drive, is seen as being rooted in the death instinct. This causes problems for Freud who later modified the idea of a death instinct. Finally, the primitiveness of the underlying dynamics of the negative therapeutic reaction, point to a need to understand that primitive mechanisms are at work here.

In order better to understand the infantile, primitive underlying elements, we need to revert to Kleinian theoretical formulations. Melanie Klein(1957) believed that 'envy, and the defences against it, play an important part in the negative therapeutic reaction' (p.185). She felt that the patient's need to devalue the analytic work, the destructive criticism and sadistic pleasure are all connected with envy. In addition, she felt that the inability to move forward in the treatment process was also part of envy, which she said 'is an oral-sadistic and anal-sadistic expression of destructive impulses, operative from the beginning of life' (p.176).

Lane (1985), reviewing the literature on the negative therapeutic reaction states that: 'Klein listed among the defenses against envy ...: omnipotence, denial, splitting, idealization and devaluation of the object and the self, confusion, flight from the original object leading to dispersal of feelings (flight from mother and her breast to others), awakening envy in others by means of success (reversal of the envious situation), and possessiveness' (p.86). The important factor here is that the patient has a need to on one hand disavow, and on the other hand the urge/impulse to discredit and devalue. The emptiness and helplessness that the patient feels within is so strong that projective and introjective mechanisms are needed in order to 'not feel' the very strong guilt and envious feelings.

We can readily see how envy and the primitive defenses against it are, according to Klein, part and parcel of the negative therapeutic reaction mechanism. This all fits in with Klein's conceptualization of the death instinct. 'Envy is ambivalent since it rests on the recognition of need and satisfaction and represents a fusion of the death instinct with the life instincts, but one in which the death instinct is in the ascendant' (Hinshelwood 1991, p.268).

Since the intensity of destructive impulses is so prevalent in all of us, there is a 'natural' tendency to negate and destroy objects; even an 'object that is intent on keeping the subject alive ... This (was) called "envy", an attack on anything that is the source, or support, of life' (Hinshelwood 1994, p.136).

In the group situation, a negative therapeutic reaction on the part of one group member can easily mushroom and explode into an entire group effect. This is especially true with psychotic patients who are fearful of expressions of praise by their therapists. Positive expressions are often extremely anxiety provoking to the psychotic as they interfere with the patient's view of himself, as any type of change is a threat to his identity (Searles 1961). The conductor needs to confront the negativity before a generalization effect takes place. Interpretations in the here-and-now, without focusing on genetic interpretations, offer the best opportunity for identifying the underlying guilt and envy. In addition, recognition of primitive defenses such as splitting and projective identification, can help the conductor make the group more aware of the underlying processes.

The conductor needs to be aware that the psychotic patient's 'anxiety-concerning-change, is an *unconscious* anxiety' (Searles 1961, p.456). This will reduce the possible effects of the schizophrenic's projective identification into the conductor, as well as the conductor's potential countertransference. As therapists, we often 'try too hard,' and this raises our anxiety level in our drive to make our patients better. This, in turn, increases the probability of our patient's experiencing a negative therapeutic reaction. Needless to say, psychotic patients, since their anxiety level is a mirroring of the external environment, tend to pick up the anxious cues 'in-the-air' and relate accordingly.

Before leaving this section, it is important to recall the important contribution of Simmel (1929) in relation to the schizophrenic's family. As we know from modern family therapy studies, families utilize a 'key' member of the family as the identifactory component of the family's pathology. This identified patient is the scapegoat of the family group. Upon him/her are projected the family's problems and issues. Simmel (1929) noted that many times the family, in order not to get in tune with the family's pathology, doesn't allow the identified patient to recover. Simmel (1929) called this a negative therapeutic reaction. If we broaden Simmel's concept to the group situation, we can see a wider potential for interplay whereby group members, in order to avoid group issues, may make the scapegoat look even better than s/he is in order not to allow the group to delve too deeply into issues that may affect them.

Resistance, in its general sense, as conceived of by Freud (1900), and its derivatives such as acting-out and the negative therapeutic reaction, cannot only impede the therapeutic work on the part of the patient but can also cause a reaction in the therapist. The therapist is influenced by the patient's thoughts, feelings and actions, and this can manifest itself in the empathic and interpretive stance of the therapist. What follows is an in-depth analysis of empathy and interpretation and how they can be affected and interfered with in the therapeutic interaction.

Empathy

Empathy is composed of two Greek words: *empatheia* (em), meaning affection, and *paschein* (path), meaning to suffer. In the interactive relationship between therapist and patient, the two are expected to develop strong emotional feelings for one another. This will enable the therapist to 'understand' the suffering and pain of the patient. In German, this is referred to as: *einfuhlung*, to feel into.

One of the major questions that theoreticians are faced with in dealing with the concept of empathy, is whether empathy can be learned or acquired. Or, is it an inborn natural characteristic that not every one of us possesses? The 'standard' comment that one is empathic if he can put himself in the shoes of the other, is not a realistic one. If I, as a physician, am treating a cancer patient, I *do not* want to be in the patient's shoes! Rather, I think that empathy means that I am trying to understand (both cognitively and emotionally). As I try to understand, I can help my patient to understand. When he feels that I am trying to understand him, that, I think, is empathy. I am placing the emphasis on the emotional and cognitive interface in the relationship.

Greenson alluded to that when he said that empathy is 'emotional knowing, the experiencing of another's feelings ... a very special method of perceiving' (1960, p.418). The issue here, is whether everyone can be trained to perceive in this way. Freud noted (1912) that the analyst 'must turn his own unconscious like a receptive organ towards the transmitting unconscious of the patient' (p.115). It seems that some underlying, unconscious mechanism is operating whereby the patient and analyst become attuned with/to one another. Then, somehow, the patient *feels* that the therapist is emotionally with him. Kohut (1977) felt that the therapist also *feels* something. He stated that empathy is 'our ability to know via vicarious introspection ... the persevering empathic-introspective immersion of the observer into the inner life of man' (p.306).

This *feeling* according to Kohut (1984) needs to be conveyed verbally to the patient by the therapist, in order for the therapeutic effects of empathy to be felt: 'the analyst verbalizes to the patient that he has grasped what the patient feels; he describes the patient's inner state to the patient, thus demonstrating to him that he has been 'understood', that is, that another person has been able to experience, at least in approximation, what he himself experienced' (pp.176–177). Thus, the patient feels enriched because he has been understood, his position has been validated and he has been able to 'actively' engage another into 'seeing' his point of view. While the therapist may not agree with the patient's position, the patient feels that the therapist has, in effect, taken the client's point of view (in feeling, thought or action). The facts are less important here. What really counts is the underlying feeling and confirmation. This fits in well with Winnicott's position: 'Gradually, the ego-supportive environment is introjected and built into the individual's personality' (Winnicott 1958, p.36).

We need to look at how empathy is transmitted. The therapist needs to put himself into the same feeling mode as the patient. Since empathy has a 'sharing' quality, the therapist must become involved in the emotional experiences of the patient. This emotional involvement creates a 'neutrality' conflict on the part of the therapist, who needs to oscillate between being detached and becoming involved. Since empathy involves a close, emotional relationship, 'one's capacity for empathy can be influenced by the other person's resistance or readiness for empathic understanding. There are patients who consciously and unconsciously want to remain ununderstood; they dread being understood' (Greenson 1960, p.422). We are now entering into another area – the willingness of the patient to engage rather than resist. Can a therapist be empathic when he feels resistance on the part of the patient or perceives a negative therapeutic reaction? What will the therapist feel if the patient is acting-out – can he feel empathic when devalued or subjected to acting-out phenomena?

An interesting anecdotal piece of history may illuminate this potential narcissistic injury on the part of the therapist. Kohut (1977) notes that when Freud learned that his close friends (and family) were thinking of keeping from him the truth of his malignancy, he responded with anger. According to Kohut, not anger (displaced) at his impending death, as many analytically trained persons might think. But rather, Kohut states: 'I believe the core of Freud's self was related more to the function of perceiving and thinking and knowing than to physical survival and that his nuclear self was threatened more by the danger that knowledge was withheld from him than by the danger of physical destruction' (p.65). Here Freud was unable to see the desire on the part of his close friends and family to spare him psychological hurt and pain.

The same holds true for the therapist who is being devalued. It is hard to separate oneself from the psychological badgering and not be affected emotionally by the patient's onslaught. This must surely have an effect on the empathic stance of the therapist.

Azima (1989) attempts to offer us a way of viewing empathy in the group situation. Empathy, she says is

> a process in which the therapist puts himself into the same experiential mode as the individual evoking the response. Next, he compares these responses with his own thoughts and feelings, and finally he assesses the degree of empathy toward other members in the group. The variation in the degree of empathy within the group allows the therapist to be aware of the feelings and thoughts of any member, the reciprocal responses of others, and his own self-reflection. These constant empathic shifts monitor and broaden the therapist's appreciation, but may also realistically dilute the empathy to any one member. Because of the primitive, directly incorporative nature of empathy, the therapist is put in jeopardy for unconscious countertransference reactions. (p.8)

From the above statement, we can see several aspects to the issue of empathy. The group situation, rather than a dyadic one, provides a bouncing-off board whereby empathy is assessed not only by the two-involved partners in the dyadic therapeutic relationship, but rather by the feeling tones and responses of the other group members. This can provide the conductor with a varied and rich input that can clarify as well as complicate the situation. But, what is clear is that the conductor has extra players in the constellation that broadens the therapeutic stage. Azima feels that there is a potential problem here in that the other group members may dilute the available empathy. I don't think that that is the problem.

What I think may occur is that the conductor, being so involved with so many group members, may not have the emotional energy available to be able to offer his best efforts. In addition, and here I agree with Azima, there is a strong potential for countertransferential feelings and reactions. I would also add the potential projective identification of the group members, which would also have an effect on the empathic feeling and response.

Countertransference does present us with a problem. The conductor cannot be involved in the group process without having the ideas and feelings generated in the group resonating within his own self thoughts, feelings and perceptions. Where is the fine line that separates understanding, feeling and identification from countertransference? To complicate matters we have the following statement from Helene Deutsch: 'Countertransference includes not only pathological responses but also the process of unconscious identification with a patient through revival of memory traces from the analyst's own developmental experiences that are similar to those of the patient. It is this identificatory process that forms the basis of "intuitive empathy" ' (1926).

We have here countertransference, identification and 'intuitive empathy.' It is important for us to have these countertransference feelings. They enable us to identify with the group members and to feel what they are saying (and not saying). Annie Reich (1966) offers us an interesting way of cognitively separating-out the normal from the pathological. She says that 'there is an essential difference between the empathic use of one's unconscious and acting-out in countertransference. Empathic understanding represents an ego activity, while countertransference is based on the break-through of id impulses which have to be warded-off with more or less neurotic defenses' (p.360).

Foulkes (1948) saw no conflict between the analyst participating 'with full empathy in his patient's mental life, while at the same time maintaining that degree of aloofness and detachment which is indispensable for his function' (p.36). Foulkes saw no difficulty in maintaining both the neutrality necessary on the part of the analyst as well as the empathic aspect: 'we can retain a certain necessary detachment, despite all empathy; these do not need to be in opposition to each other' (1974, p.280). Sometimes 'it is at times indicated for the conductor to analyse his countertransference openly within the group process. This can be extremely important and useful, but must not be made a routine' (Foulkes 1975, p.114). Searles (1958) notes that since the psychotic patient's ego is weak and not able to always successfully negotiate the space between what the therapist thinks, feels and says, it may be important for the therapist to share with the patient the patient's perceptions in order to concretize the feeling and thought of the schizophrenic.

What seems clear, is that on the feeling level there is much similarity and overlap with the concepts of empathy and countertransference. The resistant and difficult patient may arouse in the conductor many feelings that can lead to potential countertransferential feelings and potential 'acting-out' on the part of the conductor. There is also the potential of projective identification feelings projected into the conductor, that can affect the conductor's feelings and responses. It will clearly have an impact on the empathic quality that can be engendered, for the conductor will be absorbed in maintaining his neutrality, in trying to understand what the individual group members are saying and feeling, in trying to avoid being devalued and having this affect him and so on. If the conductor can be aware of these competing feelings and thoughts, then his empathic stance can be conveyed even if his energy level is being worn down. What is important is that the realness of the situation has to come through, and the conductor is seen as a real person with feelings. As Ogden states: 'the therapist and members of the group must be able to contain the projections without immediately rejecting, defending against or responding to them' (1979, p.365).

Because the schizophrenic patient may fear 'attack' from the outside world (i.e. reality), the therapist needs to be very careful that the patient feel secure and not threatened. Bion masterfully described the experience of the schizophrenic as being 'preoccupied with the conflict, never fully resolved, between destructiveness on the one hand and sadism on the other' (1956, p.344). One way to help the therapeutic process is by utilizing empathic comments (Albert 1983). 'The words therapists use, their tone of voice and manner of presentation are all components of their attitude toward the patient' (Berger 1987, p.226). In schizophrenic patients there is a loss of the capacity for sublimation (Abraham 1908, p.12), and they have to rely heavily on their intuitive understanding since they are not always capable of being part of a verbal interchange, so they may have to infer what others are feeling, thinking and saying and be able to somehow convey that via verbal or non-verbal communication. If the schizophrenic feels an 'empathic network … (s/he) may drop his or her schizophrenese and talk plainly with us' (Pao 1984, p. 329). Jacobson (1967) even went so far as to say: 'I let him 'borrow' my superego and ego' (p.57).

Since the schizophrenic is attuned to 'para-psychological' phenomenon (Freud 1921b; Freud 1922; Freud 1933) – meaning that there is an unconscious ultra-sensitivity to feelings and thoughts of the 'other' – 'empathic feedback loops … are not established easily, although they break down easily' (Pao 1979, p.351). The schizophrenic is highly sensitive to the thoughts (Searles 1958), feelings and statements of the therapist. Federn (1953) called this 'preconscious falsification' (p.235). In the group situation, this sensitivity is compounded by the interactive matrix (Foulkes 1948) of the other group members as well as the therapist (i.e. the conductor). Rogers, Gendlin, Kiesler, and Traux (1967) in their study of psychotherapy with schizophrenics found that those schizophrenic patients who perceived a high degree of empathy and congruence in the therapist (i.e. the therapist appeared as genuine and responded as a 'real' person) showed better outcomes than other patients.

Not only the patient is highly sensitive. The therapist also senses in a supra-emotional manner, the emotional feeling state of the patient. Rosenfeld wrote that we need to be sensitive to whatever projections the patient projects into us by non-verbal and verbal means (1954, p.127). As Pao (1979) states: 'the therapist will, from time to time, experience very strong emotion in reverberation with the patient's. Such strong emotions (usually rage and hate) can diminish the therapist's capacity to use his empathy' (p.351). Since empathy is (at least) a dyadic response, any hyper-sensitivity (either on the part of the patient or therapist) will be felt. Empathy, therefore, is affected by the strong emotional state of one or both of the dyadic parties. Freud (1921b) referred to this unconscious reverberation as 'thought transference' (p.193). It seems clear, then, that the therapist is, of necessity, affected by the patient's feelings and actions. If the therapist's self-esteem feels attacked or threatened, this will have an effect on the empathic stance that is conveyed. This is not necessarily a conscious response – but, it is a response, nonetheless.

Interpretation

Just as empathy is affected by the resistances and fears of psychotic patients, so too is interpretation influenced by the impingements upon the therapist/conductor. We need to look at exactly what constitutes an interpretation, as opposed to a reflection or clarification, in order to see if all of these equally are affected by the patient's resistances and/or acting-out.

Freud (1900) was very pragmatic in his discussion of interpretations, as this was the path the analyst traveled in his understanding, from latent ideas to manifest content. However, this wasn't a sufficient enough definition for *all* types of interpretations; not just dream interpretations. Greenson (1967), tried to clarify the cloudiness. He felt that before one made an interpretation, there needed to be some ordering of the material to analyze it. Following upon Gill's (1954) suggestion that the essence of analytic procedures is to make an interpretation, Greenson set out to clarify the term 'analyzing'. 'The term "analyzing" is a short-hand expression which refers to those insight-furthering techniques. It usually includes four distinct procedures: *confrontation, clarification, interpretation,* and *working-through*' (Greenson 1967, p.37). For Greenson, interpretation is making '... an unconscious phenomenon conscious ... The analyst uses his own unconscious, his empathy and intuition, as well as his theoretical knowledge, for arriving at an interpretation. By interpreting we go beyond what is readily observable and we assign meaning and causality to a psychological phenomenon. We need the patient's responses to determine the validity of our interpretation' (p.39).

We can see that interpretation is a more genetic analysis, trying to get at the underlying psychodynamics. By contrast, reflection refers to the analyst's statement that mirrors back to the patient what the analyst thinks is going on. It is based in the here-and- now, rather than being a reconstructive statement that connects present behavior/feelings with the past.

In order to make an interpretation that will be heard/felt by the patient, there are two essential aspects. Firstly, the analyst must find the correct interpretation. This means that the interpretation feels right to the patient. Secondly, the analyst must time the interpretation so that it is interpreted at the right moment. This means that the patient is receptive and there is a good chance that the interpretation will be accepted because the patient is 'ripe' for the interpretation. This fits-in well with Greenson's statement that the patient's response is necessary in order for us to validate the correctness of our interpretation.

On the surface, this seems to be quite straightforward. Yet, there are other elements that can compound the process. Didier Anzieu (1969) feels that since the analyst is not a robot, there are rational as well as irrational aspects of his self that are revealed in the interpretation. In other words, as much as the analyst tries to use the patient's words and material as the basis of the interpretation, how and what the analyst chooses to interpret reveals something about the analyst. As Etchegoyen (1991), explaining Anzieu says: 'interpretation expresses the analyst's secondary process infiltrated by the primary process, since, he says, interpretation could not reach the unconscious if it were radically extraneous to it' (p.337). We can see how the interpretation is affected by the spiral movement back-and-forth from primary to secondary process of the analyst. Needless to say, there has to be an effect on the analyst by the patient's resistance. This will inevitably impinge upon the analyst's feelings and the interpretation of the analyst will be affected by his primary and/or secondary processes.

Interestingly, Etchegoyen (1991), quotes Pichon Rivière in showing that the analyst need not be afraid of any misunderstandings or countertransference feelings, as the interpretation will put the analyst back on-course: 'interpretation not only corrects the misunderstanding, but also "cures" the analyst of his countertransference conflict of the moment, because each time one makes an interpretation one recovers himself as an analyst, to the extent that one returns to the analysand what really belongs to him' (p.439).

A correct interpretation has to not only be related to the understanding and correct timing by the conductor, but also to 'the readiness of the other group members' (Scheidlinger 1987, p.349). If the conductor feels threatened, hurt, angry, confused etc. by what is going on in the group, this will affect how he will interpret (or, not interpret). It is, therefore, very important to gauge what the group atmosphere is; both for the group as well as in relation to any particular group member.

Countertransference feelings, which may lead to possible actions/reactions on the part of the therapist, as well as projective identification feelings which may be projected into the conductor, have a definite impact upon the interpretation that may (or, may not) be made. As Tansey and Burke (1989) state: ' In the ... empathic process, the therapist conveys through verbal and non-verbal channels, in both implicit and explicit ways, the extent to which the projective identification from the patient has been processed' (p.100). Both empathy as well as the interpretative stance of the therapist is affected by the activities of the individual group members as well as by the group-as-a-whole. What is important is that the conductor needs to be aware that this is occurring and that will help him to decide how to respond, for 'the interpretation offered will, in the main, be related to the theoretical framework of the therapist' (Debanne, de Carufel, Bienvenu and Piper 1986, p.519).

In an interesting paper, Hamburg (1991) tries to advance our knowledge of empathy and interpretation by reading 'Lacan's exploration of the unconscious through the prism of Kohut's emphasis upon empathy as the basis for psychoanalytic interpretation ... For Kohut, interpretation depends on the prior establishment of a stable, sustaining transference ... Lacan's more structural approach to the inner world provides an important counterweight to Kohut's narrow preoccupation with the two-person field' (p.360). For our purposes in the group realm this means that the relationship, both real as well as through the transference, is an important ingredient in the process, and this will determine and be determined by empathy as well as interpretation. Lacan's emphasis on the inner world would mean for the group conductor that he needs to be aware of the inner worlds of *all* the group members. Thus, we need to contend with multiple impingements upon the conductor, which will, in effect, determine the empathic stance as well as the interpretation.

The conductor needs to know (cognitively as well as emotionally) that observation will help him determine what is going on in the group. Time will be needed in order to note the process and then be able to see where the group is moving. This will help to understand the individual in the group as well as the entire group. If we experience pressure by the actions of group members, we will not be free to feel what is going on. We need the free-floating atmosphere. 'Insight most richly attained occurs when it is most simply attained' (Schwaber 1990, p.239).

Kanas (1986), in a review of 43 controlled studies, found that therapy groups with schizophrenics are useful if they are more long-term and interaction oriented rather than insight oriented. Schizophrenics need the time and space in order to grow and not feel anxious and pressurized. Once the schizophrenic feels threatened, primitive defensive, projective and introjective mechanisms become released. In a group of psychotics, this can potentially unleash a group psychotic transference and it will be difficult for the conductor to run a therapeutic group.

Interpreting with psychotic patients in a group needs to be done judiciously. As Fromm-Reichmann wrote: 'successful treatment (depends) … on the basic attitude of the individual therapist towards psychotic persons' (1939, p.126). Sandison (1994) feels that conductors need to find 'a common ground between their own inner life and that of the patients' (p.401). Searles (1958) feels that there is an introjective process that occurs within the therapist who takes in the patient's pathological conflicts, re-works them within his own strong ego, and then allows the patient the benefit of this re-worked material. Any interpretation made after this introjective process is 'tainted' with the therapist/conductor's own psychological processes. One can readily see how the patient can affect the therapist in his choice of interpretation. Day and Semrad (1978) feel that a therapist's own experience of 'being a little crazy' is seen as helpful; this allows an unconscious identification.

Harry Stack Sullivan (1974) makes the important point that any interpretation by the therapist needs to take into account the psychosocial history of the patient, otherwise the interpretations that will be made will be devoid of any connection to the total reality of the patient's life and history. While it is possible to err in making interpretations, Sullivan puts a strong case for interpreting cautiously with schizophrenics because 'in dealing with people … whose margin of adjustive safety is greatly reduced … misinterpretations – interpretations of low probability – imposes an additional burden that may have very serious consequences' (p.311). Fromm-Reichmann (1939) was fearful that mis-interpretations obstructed communication. I would go further and, following Sullivan's analysis of the schizophrenic as having unbearable anxiety which can lead to misunderstandings and strong feelings of intrusion, say that the schizophrenic is so in tune with the surrounding outside world that this supersensitivity impinges upon the therapist and often creates a feeling of threat in the mind of the therapist, thus forcing an incorrect interpretation that further exacerbates the situation and makes the schizophrenic even more hypervigilant.

Clinical examples

In the following examples we will try to show how empathy and interpretation are affected by what the conductor is feeling. Our explanations will only be directed towards empathy and interpretation.

Group 1

(This is a group of nine emotionally disturbed adolescent males who are on an inpatient service. The analytically oriented group meets twice a week with two male conductors, Ed and Fred.)

The group was very quiet today. They seem to be reacting to Ed's comment last week about the importance of parental involvement in the treatment process of their children. Bob broke the silence by angrily attacking Ed for 'not allowing the group members freedom of choice.' The other group members were wary of getting involved, and were silent. Bob continued with his tirade and started to get more upset with Ed and said that Ed 'wouldn't want his wife to be involved with the group.' Fred tried to defuse the situation by reflecting to the group the difficulty with having family involved since the group members were all adolescent and wanted to be independent. The other group members began to relate to Fred's comment.

Ed's comment the week before, while appropriate in content and affect, was somewhat difficult for many of the group members. They felt that Ed had gone 'too far' in 'suggesting' that parents become more involved in the treatment of the group members. An interpretation could have been made stating that the group members may be fearful of parental involvement. Fred sensed from the group response of silence that this type of comment would have been too strong for the group members – it would have further exacerbated the atmosphere of tension and anxiety. Instead, Fred chose to address the group-as-a-whole feeling-tone and related, albeit indirectly, to the underlying tension. This was an empathic response that allowed the group members not to feel intruded upon. On the contrary, they felt a warm response that empathically related to their fears without having to state so explicitly.

Group 2

(This analytic group consists of ten co-ed residents of a half-way house. There are two conductors, a male and a female.)

The group was talking a lot about aggression: towards the government for raising their fees (the half-way house is partially funded by government fees, the rest comes from the monthly disability payments each patient receives), and towards the conductors for not voicing opposition to the government move. The outpouring of angry emotional feelings at the government also allowed the group to get angry at just about everything and everybody. Some group members even got angry at each other. The group noticed that Sally was silent. At the last group meeting Sally was also silent, but, with the conductor's encouragement, she was able to talk about her feelings of depression and her fears that she may hurt herself. The group members were not able, in their expression of anger and aggression, to talk with Sally. The conductors interpreted that the group was expressing anger and frustration at everything but were afraid to express anything to Sally. The group members were silent. The male conductor, at this point, turned to Sally and asked: 'How can the group help you?'

The group members were afraid to talk with Sally because they were afraid that she might hurt herself. Their silence was their way of expressing their fear. It was interesting that the aggression that they were expressing was probably also partially directed towards Sally – as it was towards all the other group members. But they were afraid to say anything to her for fear that anything they said might be interpreted as anger and might set her off to do something to herself. The conductors were also unsure how to respond as they were also the objects of the group's anger and didn't want their comments to Sally to be interpreted as a way for them to avoid the anger of the group. The conductors decided first to try for a group interpretation in order to voice for Sally her fears of what was really going on. When the group couldn't respond to this, the conductors felt encouraged that they were on the right track. They now made an empathic statement to Sally. It is important to note that the group's anger and aggression had the potential for silencing the conductors' interpretations. However, in this case, the neediness of one of the group members enabled the conductors to make both a group interpretation as well as an empathic statement. Because of the aggressive atmosphere, it would have been 'easy' for the conductors to assume a less empathic response in their interpretations. However, they were able to 'rise above the occasion' and make an empathic interpretation while not being affected by the tense and angry group feelings.

Group 3

(This is a group of eight severely disturbed young adults, four males and four females. This analytically-oriented group meets four times a week on an inpatient service. There are two conductors, a male and a female.)

Fran, one of the group members, announced to the group that she was probably going to leave since her mother had told her how well she was doing. She said that she wasn't convinced that her mother was right, but she wanted to leave. The two conductors wanted to reflect to Fran the need to stay in the hospital longer, but were not able to articulate this. The other group members were fearful to say anything to Fran for fear that she might get upset with them. Joe ventured forth with a comment to Fran and said that he felt that the entire group had improved but they had a long way to go. Fran became tearful.

The group leaders were not sure how to handle Fran's negative therapeutic reaction. This vignette illustrates both the classic Freudian interpretation as well as Simmel's interpretation of the family's need to accentuate the positive and ignore the reality, in order to avoid getting into the family psychopathology. Her dramatic statement caught the conductors unaware how to respond. Their lack of empathy at this point and their inability to make an interpretation left the group in their fearful posture, feeling anxious because there wasn't any support from the conductors nor from one another.

Conclusion

We have attempted to show how difficult, psychotic patients impact upon the conductor's empathic and interpretive stance. In discussing resistance, acting-out, the negative therapeutic reaction, countertransference and projective identification, we have tried to show how interpretations and empathy cannot be 'technically neutral.' Several vignettes illustrated these issues. Often the angry expressions of patients projected onto (and sometimes into) the conductor can affect the level of empathy and the type of interpretation. In the first vignette, since there were two conductors and only one was being attacked, the other conductor was 'free' and able to respond unhampered by the angry barrage of the patient. In the second vignette, both conductors were being verbally attacked, but the neediness of one of the patients forced them to respond supportively and empathically irrespective of the angry outbursts of the patients. In the third vignette, the conductors felt impotent because of the negative therapeutic reaction on the part of the patient. Another patient made the comment that needed to be said, saving the situation because of the conductors' inability to respond appropriately.

As conductors in group situations with difficult patients we need to be cognizant of how patients affect us by their emotionality. This can have direct and indirect effects upon our empathic feelings and interpretive stance.

References

Abraham, K. (1908) 'The psychosexual differences between hysteria and dementia praecox.' In *Selected Papers of Karl Abraham*. New York: Basic Books (1968).

Albert, H.D. (1983) 'Psychotherapy of schizophrenia: the early phase of treatment .' In M.H. Stone, H.D. Albert, D.V. Forrest, and S. Arieti, *Treating Schizophrenic Patients*. New York: McGraw Hill.

Anzieu, D.(1969) 'Dificulté d'une étude psychanalytique de l'interprétation.' *Bulletin de l'Association Psychanalytique de France 5*, 12–33.

Azima, F.J. Cramer (1989) 'Confrontation, empathy and interpretation issues in adolescent group psychotherapy.' In F.J. Cramer Azima and L.H. Richmond (eds) *Adolescent Group Psychotherapy*. Madison, CT: IUP.

Berger, D.M. (1987) *Clinical Empathy*. Northvale, NJ: Jason Aronson.

Bion, W.R. (1956) 'Development of schizophrenic thought.' *International Journal of Psycho-Analysis 37*, 344–346.

Cohn, B.R. (1988) 'Keeping the group alive: dealing with resistance in a long-term group of psychotic patients.' *International Journal of Group Psychotherapy 38*, 319–335.

Day, M. and Semrad, E.V. (1978) 'Schizophrenic reactions.' In A. Nicholi (ed) *The Harvard Guide to Modern Psychiatry*. Cambridge, MA: Belknap Press.

Debanne, E.G., de Carufel, F.L., Bienvenu, J.P. and Piper, W.E. (1986) 'Structures in interpretations: a group psychoanalytic perspective.' *International Journal of Group Psychotherapy 36*, 517–532.

Deutsch, H. (1926) 'Occult processes occurring during psychoanalysis.' In G. Devereux (ed) *Psychoanalysis and the Occult*. New York: IUP (1953).

Durkin, J.D. (1981) *Living Groups: Group Psychotherapy and General Systems Theory*. New York: Brunner/Mazel.

Etchegoyen, R.H. (1991) *The Fundamentals of Psychoanalytic Technique*. London: Karnac.

Federn, P. (1953) *Ego Psychology and the Psychoses*. London: Maresfield (1977).

Foulkes, S.H. (1948) *Introduction to Group-Analytic Psychotherapy*. London: Maresfield (1984).

Foulkes, S.H. (1974) 'My philosophy in psychotherapy.' In *Selected Papers*. London: Karnac (1990).

Foulkes, S.H. (1975) *Group Analytic Psychotherapy*. London: Maresfield (1986).

Foulkes, S.H. and Anthony, E.J. (1957) *Group Psychotherapy: The Psychoanalytical Approach*. London: Maresfield (1984).

Freud, S. (1897) 'Letter to Fliess. October 27, 1897. Letter 72.' *Standard Edition*, Vol. 1. London: Hogarth Press (1981).

Freud, S. (1900) 'The interpretation of dreams.' *Standard Edition*, Vol. 5. London: Hogarth Press (1981).

Freud, S. (1905) 'Fragment of an analysis of a case of hysteria.' *Standard Edition*, Vol.7. London: Hogarth Press (1981).

Freud, S. (1912) 'Recommendations to physicians practising psycho-analysis.' *Standard Edition*, Vol. 12. London: Hogarth Press (1981).

Freud, S. (1921a) 'Group psychology and the analysis of the ego.' *Standard Edition*, Vol. 18. London: Hogarth Press (1981).

Freud, S. (1921b) 'Psycho-analysis and telepathy.' *Standard Edition*, Vol. 18. London: Hogarth Press (1981).

Freud, S. (1922) ' Dreams and telepathy.' *Standard Edition*, Vol. 18. London: Hogarth Press (1981).

Freud, S. (1923) 'The ego and the id.' *Standard Edition*, Vol. 19. London: Hogarth Press (1981).

Freud, S. (1924) 'The economic problem of masochism.' *Standard Edition*, Vol. 19. London: Hogarth Press (1981).

Freud, S. (1933) 'Dreams and occultism.' (Lecture 30). *Standard Edition*, Vol. 22. London: Hogarth Press (1981).

Freud, S. (1940) 'An outline of psycho-analysis.' *Standard Edition* Vol. 23. London: Hogarth Press (1981).

Fromm-Reichmann, F. (1939) *Psychoanalysis and Psychotherapy*. Chicago: University of Chicago Press (1975).

Ganzarain, R. (1989) *Object Relations Group Psychotherapy*. Madison: IUP.

Gill, M.M. (1954) 'Psychoanalysis and exploratory psychotherapy.' *Journal of the American Psychoanalytic Association 2*, 771–797.

Greenson, R.R. (1960) 'Empathy and its vicissitudes.' *International Journal of Psycho-Analysis 41*, 418–424.

Greenson, R.R. (1967) *The Technique and Practice of Psychoanalysis*. New York: IUP.

Hamburg, P. (1991) 'Interpretation and empathy: reading Lacan with Kohut.' *International Journal of Psycho-Analysis 72*, 347–361.

Hinshelwood, R.D. (1991) *A Dictionary of Kleinian Thought*. London: Free Association Books.

Hinshelwood, R.D. (1994) *Clinical Klein*. London: Free Association Books.

Jacobson, E. (1967) *Psychotic Conflict and Reality*. New York: International Universities Press.

Kadis, A.L., Krasner, J.D., Weiner, M.F., Winick, C., and Foulkes, S.H. (1974) *Practicum of Group Psychotherapy*. New York: Harper and Row.

Kanas, N. (1986) 'Group therapy with schizophrenics: a review of controlled studies.' *International Journal of Group Psychotherapy 36*, 339–351.

Klein, M. (1957) 'Envy and gratitude.' In *Envy and Gratitude and Other Works*. New York: Delta (1975).

Kohut, H. (1977) *The Restoration of the Self*. New York: IUP.

Kohut, H. (1984) *How Does Analysis Cure?* Chicago: University of Chicago Press.

Lane, R.C. (1985) 'The difficult patient, resistance and the negative therapeutic reaction: a review of the literature.' *Current Issues in Psychoanalytic Practice 1*, 83–106.

Laplanche, J. And Pontalis, J.-B. (1980) *The Language of Psycho-Analysis*. London: Hogarth Press.

Loewald, H.W. (1972) 'Freud's conception of the negative therapeutic reaction, with comments on instinct theory.' *Papers on Psychoanalysis*. New Haven: Yale University Press (1980).

Maldonado, J.L. (1989) 'On negative and positive therapeutic reaction.' *International Journal of Psycho-Analysis 70*, 327–339.

Ogden, T.H. (1979) 'On projective identification.' *International Journal of Psycho-Analysis 60*, 357–373.

Pao, P.-N. (1979) *Schizophrenic Disorders*. New York: International Universities Press.

Pao, P.-N. (1984) 'Therapeutic empathy and the treatment of schizophrenics.' In J.Lichtenberg, M. Bornstein and D. Silver (eds) *Empathy*. Hillsdale, NJ: Analytic Press.

Reich, A.(1966) 'Empathy and countertransference.' In *Annie Reich: Psychoanalytic Contributions*. New York: IUP (1973).

Rogers, C.W., Gendlin, E.G., Kiesler, D.J., and Truax, C.B.(1967) *The Therapeutic Relationship and Its Impact: Study of Psychotherapy with Schizophrenics*. Madison, WI: University of Wisconsin Press.

Rosenfeld, H.A. (1954) 'Considerations regarding the psycho-analytic approach to acute and chronic schizophrenia.' In *Psychotic States: A Psychoanalytical Approach*. London: Maresfield (1982).

Sandison, R. (1994) 'Working with schizophrenics individually and in groups: understanding the psychotic process.' *Group Analysis 27*, 393–406.

Scheidlinger, S. (1987) 'On interpretation in group psychotherapy: the need for refinement.' *International Journal of Group Psychotherapy 37*, 339–352.

Schneider, S. (1997) 'Jerusalem, religious awakenings and schizophrenia.' *Group Analysis 30*, 379–393.

Schwaber, E.A. (1990) 'Interpretation and the therapeutic action of psychoanalysis.' *International Journal of Psycho-Analysis 71*, 229–240.

Searles, H.F. (1958) 'The schizophrenic's vulnerability to the therapist's unconscious processes.' In *Collected Papers on Schizophrenia and Related Subjects*. New York: International Universities Press (1965).

Searles, H.F. (1961) 'Anxiety concerning change, as seen in the psychotherapy of schizophrenic patients – with particular reference to the sense of personal identity.' In *Collected Papers on Schizophrenia and Related Subjects*. New York: International Universities Press (1965).

Simmel, E. (1929) 'Psychoanalytic treatment in a sanatorium.' *International Journal of Psycho-Analysis 10*, 70–89.

Spotnitz, H. (1969) *Modern Psychoanalysis of the Schizophrenic Patient*. New York: Grune & Stratton.

Sullivan, H.S. (1974) *Schizophrenia as a Human Process*. New York: W.W. Norton.

Tansey, M.J. and Burke, W.F. (1989) *Understanding Counter-Transference*. New Jersey: Analytic Press.

Winnicott, D.W. (1958) 'The capacity to be alone.' *The Maturational Processes and the Facilitating Environment*. London: Hogarth Press (1985).

CHAPTER 8

The Group as Therapist for Psychotic and Borderline Personalities

Rachael Chazan

In this chapter I describe a group analytic model for work with severely disturbed outpatients, including schizophrenic, bipolar and borderline personalities. The group is empowered to be therapist; there is facilitation of the translation of symptoms into interpersonal problems. It arrives at basic human feelings such as loneliness and the difficulty of relating, the need for love and the fear of abandonment, doubts about freedom and self-determination.

Specific difficulties in different settings

Group work with inpatients and outpatients poses different problems, and no doubt each of us has their own style of dealing with these. It is useful, too, to work with the families of patients. In this context, I shall discuss:

- Inpatient groups – acute chronic populations
- The multiple family group.

Inpatient work

When I worked in Talbieh Hospital, Israel, in 1967, I began to work with daily ward groups, which became my main therapeutic tool. This was considered revolutionary and was probably dropped after my year of work there. I began a more permanent project in the acute admission unit of Kfar Shaul Hospital (1968–1978). All the patients were invited to take part in the thrice weekly group, together with nursing staff and occupational therapists. I aimed to make administration as transparent as possible. There was a book for patients to request weekend or longer leave. Staff members were asked to make all observations about patients in the group meeting in their presence.

The group dialogue was usually lively. Therapeutic change could be quite dramatic. One newcomer told the group that he thought everyone was pretending; the patients were pretending to be patients, the nurses pretending to be nurses. Group members replied that this was not the case: they were certainly patients and the nurses really were nurses. The newcomer quickly came out of his psychotic state.

My aim was to turn the ward into a therapeutic community as far as was possible, within the limits of the structure of the hospital hierarchies. I did not attempt to give up pharmacotherapy, nor did I entirely waive individual therapy, but I was aware that favouring some patients in this way created inequality.

Family members visited the patients, and made their requests (or demands) to me and the rest of the staff. I had a glimpse of the pathological nature of their relationship to the identified patient. I decided to start a multiple family therapy group which would include patients and their families. As motive I used whatever impulse they had to communicate with the system (usually in the person of myself): I instructed nursing staff to refer any relative requesting to see me to the group. This worked very well. When, in some cases, I saw a family separately as well, I noticed that this brought no advance. I decided to channel all family therapy into the group. We did have to urge both parents to attend the groups, as often only one would come, or they would alternate. This might have been an unconscious attempt to avoid exposing family pathology. Another defence was non-verbal or esoteric communication between family members, countered by requiring families not to sit together. The group was run as a slow-open group, and continued for over eight years. I have written about it elsewhere (Chazan 1974).

In some cases it was the family group that was crucial in bringing about change in the patient.

Case examples

Joseph, 16, was the son of Holocaust survivors. His father had lost his own mother when aged 7, and at 15 had been interned in a concentration camp, where he witnessed the death of his father and sister. As an infant, Joseph was pampered by mother and grandmother. If necessary, he got his way through breath-holding attacks. The mother aborted one pregnancy because of Joseph's jealousy. The next time she took care to tell Joseph early on in the pregnancy. Soon after the birth of his brother, Joseph's grandmother died. Some time later, he attempted to jump from a balcony, was hospitalized and diagnosed as schizophrenic. There were several admissions before he came to us. Joseph's mother continued to give him all he wanted; he behaved wildly when frustrated.

In our hospital, it was difficult to communicate with Joseph; he did little in occupational therapy. In the family group, his mother often asked Joseph if he loved her, and whether he loved her more than his father.

The father at first failed to come. When he did (following my message), he said he regarded fear as a weakness. Family relations were a battle in which giving in meant weakness. He shocked the group by stating his belief that all mentally ill people should be killed. On being questioned he replied that this would include his son, if there were no hope.

Hearing this outright seemed not to harm Joseph: perhaps the unspoken death wish had done more harm than the explicit words. Joseph improved and went home, continuing as a day patient. Soon, mother complained that Joseph was 'getting nervous.' He complained that his shirts were stained; he had never complained before. Two women in the group remarked that this was natural, all boys were like that. The mother continued: 'He gets up in the morning all by himself; I used to have to get him up. He really *is* getting nervous.'

After 16 months of group family therapy, Joseph held down a job for the first time in his life. We were pleased to hear his father declare his affection for him.

Clarification, interpretation and demystification can be very effective in acute psychosis (as I had been taught by Dr R.D. Scott, who had done much work with schizophrenics at Napsbury Hospital, St Albans, England). This is vividly illustrated by the following case: Erez, aged 18, about to be recruited to the Israel Defence Forces, was admitted in acute psychosis. He told me that his elder brother had died of influenza several years ago, or so his mother told him. However, he believed that he was still alive and working somewhere as a secret agent. Now he wanted to kill himself. On telling his mother of his intention, she was appalled. 'You too? Your brother committed suicide.' She had kept this secret, telling a tale of death from influenza. After some sessions with mother in the family group, the mystification was resolved. Erez quickly recovered. He returned to school and served successfully in the Israel Defence Forces.

In chronic wards, group work is much more difficult. This may be because nothing happens in these patients' world and they are not given responsibility for their day to day lives. I administered such a ward in Eitanim at a later stage, and found that the patients had little to talk about. I noticed that the very 'motherly' ward sister made the patients far more dependent on her than was at first evident. They had to ask for soap for their shower, and for every single cigarette. These were often given as rewards for services rendered, thus becoming a means of wielding power. The sister paid lip service to my idea of meetings with all the nurses, but none materialized.

One of these patients, Alex, had nothing to say in individual interview, any more than in the group. He had no wishes, no hopes and no aspirations. Some time later, I became psychiatrist to the Internal Rehabilitation Unit. (This was a unit of 24 patients, run as a therapeutic community by social workers, psychologists and occupational therapists. There was no nurse in the team, which was probably fortunate; the nurses were trained to institutionalize patients, and could do this very subtly and powerfully.)

I then met Alex in a new role: he and a woman patient were now in charge of the unit catering. (This involved ordering meals and raw materials from the main kitchen, serving and in some cases cooking the meals; the medical staff merely provided backing.) I thought he would make a good chairman for the monthly residents' meeting, and indeed he did. We allowed him to take charge, with the staff taking a back seat.

I reorganized the daily morning meeting, which had been a half-hour formality, which only a handful of patients attended. The group soon realized, as I did, that current problems could not be discussed unless all were present, and agreed to make attendance obligatory for everyone except those who worked in town. One resident volunteered to keep an attendance register. The meeting was extended to an hour, so that it became a therapeutic group. I did not think that small group therapy was enough; the life of the unit was, after all, reflected in the large group, as this example illustrates.

Case example

One morning, on my arrival, Esther asked me for a sleeping pill. I asked her to bring this up in the meeting. In the large group, she related that she had been unable to sleep. We asked her why. She told us that Naama had gone to visit Zeev last night. The latter had a regular girlfriend. This encouraged a discussion of the issue by all concerned, including the rather shy and quiet Zeev himself. It was clear that Esther had *wanted* the issue to be discussed in the group. The sleeping pill was merely an admission ticket.

To sum up, it can be difficult to run meaningful groups with chronic psychotic patients. One way of making them viable is to run the ward as a therapeutic community.

Outpatient groups with patients who have been psychotic
History
When I began to work in a community mental health clinic in 1978, I brought with me a small 'rehabilitation' group from Kfar Shaul: patients who had left, and some who were almost ready to leave, hospital. I noticed that some of the outpatients of the clinic assigned to me for weekly individual therapy did not do at all well. One man, Yochanan, believed that 'the doctors' were arranging girls for him. He continually implored me to tell 'them' to stop it. Surely I ought to be able to do that; was I not one of the powerful doctors? One young woman, Helen, had fallen ill during her final class at grammar school. She lived with her parents and

did not work. What she wanted from me was advice as to whether it would help her to repeat certain sentences. Perhaps she saw in me another mother who would keep her safe, while what she needed was to be with siblings. I invited both these patients to join the group.

Although both Helen and Yochanan had some initial difficulty in communicating with the group, I found that quite soon an interesting and lively group had developed. I endeavoured to interest Dr S. Littman, then director of the clinic, in organizing similar groups.

After a period of initial misgivings, he decided to apply the model to the psychotic outpatient population and did much for its continuation and its spread to other clinics. We ran various kinds of groups, some bi-weekly and some weekly, each conducted by two therapists from different disciplines. An absorption group was developed, for initial treatment and assessment of patients discharged from the hospital. I myself did stints of running two other groups, but my original one is still going strong – with changes of population. My own model, with special reference to this group, is the main subject of this paper.

The new patients had to learn something; their communications now had to be such that they were intelligible to the group. An early task of mine was to insist that they address the whole group, and be understood by the group. While the dyadic relationship was like a mother–infant one, with the therapist having to decode inarticulate 'cries', the group situation forced the members to speak in adult language. The group member who felt 'sick' or 'depressed' was asked what was troubling him in the interpersonal sphere. Yochanan, not unexpectedly, found it difficult to reveal his predicament to the group. Yet when he eventually did, he met with acceptance. Helen at first literally turned her back on the group. She claimed that one group member, Dan, was her enemy. When he addressed her, she rudely shut him up. In time, she learnt to listen to the group dialogue, and made perceptive comments.

During the years, new patients were referred for inclusion in the group, some by other staff members – mainly patients recently discharged from hospital. Others were patients brought in by me, who had been referred to me for first interview, or for individual treatment. One of the latter was Daniel, a religious young man who thought people were slandering him. He had never been treated in hospital. In the group, he was given the role of guru and adviser. After about two years, he discussed marriage with the group and was indeed married. I decided to invite his wife to join the group too, so that problems between them could be discussed in the group. A daughter was born to them: the baby of the group.

Another example was Bernie, a borderline personality, ex-drug addict and ex-alcoholic, who referred himself to the clinic because he wanted a letter recommending that, as a disabled person, he be given a kiosk to run. In individual therapy he had been more often absent than not. The question of joining the group was brought up: I told him that he must attend the group regularly for three months before anything would be done for him. He became a regular attender and an involved group member. The group had become an end in itself.

Bernie, in spite of having been addicted to drugs and alcohol, had the makings of a conscience. Though he might at times be demanding, he was interested in the other group members and endeavoured to help them. After some years, he joined a social club and was elected to its committee. When Reuma Weizmann, wife of the President of Israel, visited the club, it was he who was chosen to read the welcoming address. When a journalist visited his district, he drew his attention to the houses of those worse off than he was. In short, he became interested in others, in society, rather than himself alone.

The group analytic model and the psychotic

The group analytic model is the one developed by S.H. Foulkes. It is characterized by the use of the group as the agent of therapy, rather than as a background for individual therapy. Foulkes (1948) described the need for the conductor to develop and perfect this instrument, rather than use his own person. The leader, therefore, should not be a dominant figure. The striving should be for a 'group-centred' (Figure 8.1) rather than 'leader-centred' group (Figure 8.2). In the latter, bonds are primarily between conductor and individual members, rather than between group members.

Foulkes advised the group conductor to allow group members to comment on one another's problems and believed they were capable of making interpretations. The conductor was 'leader by default', intervening only when the group was stuck: when it was unable to do the work of analyzing by itself, or when processes were destructive.

Foulkes held that the group can take the occasional psychotic member. This has been done in the group analytic practice in London, and described by Kreeger (1991). Foulkes did not run a group all of whose members had been psychotic, nor is much written on it by others of his school.

Difficulties

The difficulties that may tempt a conductor to engage in individual therapy in the group are threefold:

1. The patient's dependency needs.

2. The conductor's countertransference.

3. The prevalence of the medical model.

The three are interconnected.

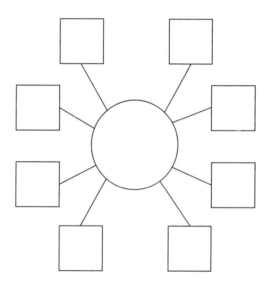

Figure 8.1 Types of group (after Foulkes (1948)): Leader-centred – bonds are between each member and the conductor

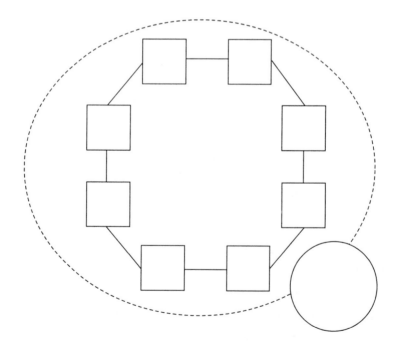

Figure 8.2 Types of group (after Foulkes (1948)): Group-centred – bonds are between group members. The conductor is outisde the group and yet in touch with the whole group

Dependency needs

The patients referred to these groups are mostly of immature personality. They tend to demand a direct relationship with the therapist. They perceive her as a mother who can soothe and heal all ills, as the omnipotent father/healer who has all the answers. They want the therapist all to themselves and see other group members as rivals.

Transference and countertransference

In the transference, the conductor is an all-powerful father, or a comforting mother, whose soothing touch can make all ills go away. (The group, too, becomes a mother in the transference, or is perceived as one's family. This, however, happens only in the course of time.) Concordant countertransference may occur (Racker, 1968): the conductor feels impelled to respond to the group members' crying need to relate to them individually. If she does, the group will become leader-centred. Her time and attention will become divided between the members. Rivalry will become a real issue; group members will have to compete for her attention. There will never be enough to go round. This is what happened when a co-therapist of mine was drawn to make interpretations directed at one or two individuals. His first observation in the after-group discussion was: 'There is not enough of us to go round. The blanket is too short.'

The medical model

This has been internalized both by patients and therapists (even non-medical therapists). For the patient, it means that the doctor is accepted as a powerful figure. One tells him one's symptoms, he gives advice and dispenses drugs. From the doctor's point of view, the patient is a 'good' patient if he 'complies'.

The group conductor brought up on the medical model may perceive the patient as suffering from symptoms which must in the first instance be treated by drugs. Even if he is a social worker or psychologist he may refer the patient for change in drug treatment.

The conductor's work with countertransference involves giving up the omnipotent position conferred by the medical model and empowering the group to do its own work. Symptoms have to be tolerated and not regarded as a sign of medical failure. They have to be perceived as signs of emotional and interpersonal distress.

Dealing with the difficulties

To deal with these problems, the conductor has to be, in some ways, more active – not in addressing individual members, but in training the group to be therapist. Communications addressed to the therapist have to be redirected to the whole group. This conveys to the group that the conductor is not the only therapist and that, in fact, it is expected to do most of the work. The conductor may draw attention to a group member's clarification, to make sure that it is heard. She may explain it or expand on it. On the other hand, each time she responds to an individual member directly, or makes an immediate interpretation, she creates a precedent which perpetuates her role as the only therapist.

In principle this is similar to the conductor's work in any group analytic group, but there is more of it in a group with post-psychotic patients. Foulkes did not choose the term 'conductor' by accident; it is reminiscent of the conductor of an orchestra or choir. The latter does not only direct but also trains his musical group. The post-psychotic group undergoes a longer period of training than a group of neurotic patients.

The administration of the group

The group is a slow-open one, meeting once weekly for an hour. The general rule is co-therapy, with the co-therapist often being in a more junior and temporary position.

There has to be selection. Although the groups may be an efficient way of using human resources, they must not be perceived as a wastepaper basket, or as second best to individual treatment. It has to be a privilege to be accepted by a group.

New candidates are invited for an interview with the co-therapists. It is best to ask the candidate to attend the group for a month's trial. This means selection through the group process, which is the best way of assessing suitability.

Mixing diagnostic categories enriches the group. Kanas (1993) advocates homogenous groups for acutely psychotic patients, as mixed groups bring the danger of psychotic regression. He also structures the group; for example, groups of schizophrenics are told in advance that they should discuss one of four topics: hearing voices, feeling confused, being suspicious and relating poorly to other people (p.413). Such groups, it seems to me, are more didactic than analytic or interpersonal. (As to psychotic regression, I have never found it to occur in my groups.)

In the mixed group, one group member will show strength where another is weak, and mutual help will be facilitated. Bernie became a valuable group member partly because he was not schizophrenic and had social know-how.

However, not everyone with personality disorder is suitable for group analysis. Another addict, who was on a treatment order, was initially accepted but did not make it in the group. He attended irregularly, was persistently aggressive, and was not accepted by the group. He eventually had to leave. Treatment by order turns out, not surprisingly, to be incompatible with the motivation needed to become part of the group.

In general, the group itself gives signs that a new member is unsuitable because of aggressiveness, lying, or similar reasons; the unwritten rules of the group have become part of the group culture.

Pharmacotherapy is used, but my policy is to play it down. I do not allow a problem to be solved by change of medication. When a patient talks about his drugs, this is usually interpreted as a way of gaining individual attention (as insistence on physical symptoms may be).

It is generally unnecessary to see patients individually, either after or between group sessions. There is the rare exception: Avram's sister asked to see the therapists urgently after one meeting. We heard her: he had lost his temper in her home, trodden on a bottle, splintering his foot as well as the glass. She demanded his hospitalization.

We decided to ask Avram to sign a declaration that he would not act violently towards himself or others, on pain of being admitted to hospital. He agreed and the contract turned out to be very effective. He told the group, on various occasions, that the declaration in his pocket had made him control himself, angry as he was.

Family members sometimes ask to see us, or to tell us about the group member on the telephone. We insist that this be in the presence of the group member, and whenever possible in the presence of the group. We ask the group member concerned, as well as the group's, permission to use group time in this way. They are naturally jealous of their time. The ideal would be to have an additional session once monthly for family problems.

Why groups for psychotic patients?

There are several benefits in group psychotherapy for patients who have been psychotic. I have written about this elsewhere (Chazan 1993). The most important ones are these:

1. Learning to communicate.

This has two components: finding a common language, and learning to take part in the group dialogue.

2. Finding one is not alone in being troubled as one is.

3. Being accepted as an equal and being expected to take responsibility.

4. Finding that one can make a difference to others.

5. Becoming flexible in perception of self and others.

Learning to translate symptoms into interpersonal language

Foulkes (1948) argues that it is mistaken to consider the person as an isolated unit: 'Each individual – itself an artificial, though plausible abstraction – is basically and centrally determined, inevitably, by the world in which he lives. By the community, the group of which he forms a part' (p.10). He quotes Erikson who holds that a child who has just learned to walk is not driven only by libidinal pleasure in Freud's sense, but is aware of being perceived as 'he who can walk' (p.11). When Foulkes was exploring the roots of a patient's impotence – in individual therapy – he found the key in the patients' mental relationship to his sister-in-law. He concluded that 'the patient's problems represent only one aspect of an intricate group problem' (p.21–22). 'This type of observation ... made me become a Group Analyst.'

Further, he holds that neurotic symptoms are expressions of interpersonal problems, arguing that 'neurotic peculiarities, symptoms are relieved ... as they can be retransformed, by Analysis, from incommunicable experience to communicable experience' (p.30).

The patient describing symptoms behaves as if others were inside his skin. As Ruesch and Bateson (1951) point out, 'the immature patient may communicate by the means used in early childhood, transmitting messages involving pain or touch, conveyed by short distance receivers, rather than sight or hearing which operate at longer distance.'

The symptoms of the post-psychotic are similarly incommunicable: they may manifest themselves in somatic sensations such as feeling strangled, in being depressed, unable to function, having compulsive thoughts. The group can do nothing with these symptoms and refers them to the conductor. We have found that the group member can translate these symptoms into interpersonal problems. After some modeling by the conductor, the group learns to facilitate this kind of translating.

Case example

Shira is a patient with bipolar disorder, divorced with two grown-up children, living with a long-time partner (a schizophrenic who rehabilitated himself and works as a bookkeeper). She likes to be the centre of attention, and succeeds when she is hypomanic. At one time she persuaded a family doctor who was observing the group to see her every day (as we discovered *post facto*). She talks in a whining voice when depressed, complaining she just feels bad, can do nothing. The group has learnt to ask her to translate this into interpersonal problems. Has she quarreled with her boyfriend? Is there a problem with her son or her daughter? She proceeds to reveal the issue and this is discussed, fruitfully, in the group.

Another instance of such translation occurred in the case of Dan.

Case example

Dan was undecided whether to go out on an excursion with the social club; he had an earache. Avram asked why he was talking about earache. Dan admitted that the problem was his father who did not want him to go. He revealed the extent of his symbiotic relationship with his father, discussed it with the group and found this helpful.

In individual treatment of chronic post-psychotic patients, one often does not get beyond symptoms. The patients appear uninteresting, there is little to talk about. It is only in the group that they discuss the human issues which preoccupy them. If the individual therapist does translate symptoms into interpersonal problems, he or she is like the mother of a small infant who understands its inarticulate cries and grunts. In the group, the patient is expected to effect this himself; this is one of the reasons why the group relationship is a less dependent one than that of the patient in individual therapy.

The benefits are many: not only has the symptom become a problem discussable in the group, the group member has learnt to verbalize his feelings about himself and others. This in itself is beneficial; it may even, as Foulkes said of neurotic symptoms, make it disappear.

Learning to take part in the group dialogue

Learning to participate in the group dialogue is another aspect of learning to communicate; process as well as content is important. To know how to take part in the group dialogue is an aspect of maturity. The small child will interrupt adult conversation and address his mother or father. Later, he learns to wait until someone has finished talking, though his communication is by no means part of the general flow of conversation.

The immature group member attempts to address the group conductor. He does not respond to what others are bringing to the group and cannot integrate his own communication into the dialogue: He keeps it wrapped in isolation until he can bring it to the attention of the conductor. It is up to the conductor to redirect such a communication to the group: the questioner is invited to address the whole group, to make sure he is understood by them. The group is invited to respond, though only the conductor is addressed. The group learns that it is expected to act as therapist and is empowered to do so.

Case example

Helen is a 45-year-old woman who became psychotic in her last class in High School. When she joined the group, she would often sit with her back turned to the others. When Dan, her neighbour, addressed her, she told him to shut up. It seemed that she had delusions about him. She was living with her teacher parents and doing nothing. After two years in the group, she went to live with her sister in Ramat Gan to help with her children. She continued to come to Jerusalem to attend the group. She began to work in a sheltered workshop. The next step was a flat of her own, near that of her parents, who had moved to Ramat Gan. In 1996 she was introduced to a graduate librarian, with a slight physical disability. They married; she keeps house for her husband and continues working. She finds this requires a lot of adjustment and has become even more involved in the group. For all that, she still has difficulty, at times, in joining in the group dialogue.

In a recent meeting, she complained that she was ignored at work. People would not talk to her. The group asked if she talked to them. She said she had nothing to talk about. Did she greet them on arriving in the morning, the group asked. 'You know, you come here and sit in the group room while we all sit in the waiting room, chatting. You do not even greet us.' She replied that she liked her own company. 'But you complain that people at work do not talk to you.' 'I have nothing to say to them.' 'Greet them, ask them how they are; this will start a conversation,' said Bernie. Earlier in the meeting, Avram had complained that she came up with her own problem, addressing the conductor, rather than relating to what he had said.

This kind of interaction with Helen occurred more than once. She reminds one of a high-grad autistic who lacks 'theory of mind'; she has little sense of what is expected of her in social interaction. Often, the group works hard to help her hold a conversation: not only talking, but listening to the answers, listening to others. When she talks fast and unintelligibly, the conductor assures her that what she has to say is worth hearing and she ought therefore to talk distinctly. The group have a good deal of patience with her.

The value of finding 'friends in suffering'

Yalom (1985) described this therapeutic factor and called it 'universality'. The patient who has been psychotic is even more likely than the neurotic to believe that his problems are unique. He may suffer a good deal of anxiety and loss of self-esteem on this account. It takes some courage to take the plunge and reveal one's problems to the group; some do not venture until another group member has done so. On the other hand, to hear that others suffer in a similar way is a great relief. It makes one feel 'normal'.

Case example

Dan believed that thoughts were put into his head by means of an EEG machine. He had been reluctant to reveal this; when he did, Yochanan confided that he too had suffered from this kind of thing. Yochanan had never talked about this before; it was difficult enough for him to reveal to the group that 'the doctors' were 'arranging girls for him'. Dan was very glad to hear that he was not alone in his predicament. Interestingly, Yochanan's problems changed in the course of time to the belief that there was interference with his television broadcasts. It may be that this is a less embarrassing symptom to discuss. It may also be that it stood for problems in communication with others (which was an interpretation offered to him).

Case example

Avram often complained that he feared someone was hiding in his flat, wanting to kill him. This particularly troubled him at night. On one occasion he dreamt that he was to be taken out and shot by a firing squad. The group and I offered interpretations; we concluded that the judge and firing squad were his own conscience, as he had (understandably) murderous thoughts towards the family that had been rejecting him. Yet the night fears recurred. In one session, Deborah confessed that she sometimes had thoughts of killing someone. Avram was very interested and clearly relieved that he was not alone in this, particularly as Deborah was one of the more healthy group members, married and bringing up a small child. Deborah, too, had not talked about this aspect of herself; it belonged to the time of her breakdown. I pointed out that 'wanting to kill' and fear of being killed were two sides of the same coin.

Being treated as an equal and being allotted responsibility

Most of us have responsibilities not only for ourselves, but for others: responsibilities for our children and other family members, responsibilities in connection with our work. It is an essential part of our lives, a function of being needed. Patients who have been psychotic are almost always relieved of responsibility (which is suitable for the actue, but not the chronic phase of the illness). Their families, however caring, usually relieve them of responsibilities towards others. In hospital settings, however enlightened, we too often hear: 'Let him be responsible for himself, then he can be responsible for others.' The key to the success of the therapeutic community is, surely, that patients *are* given responsibility.

In our outpatient groups, the schizophrenic or manic-depressive is treated as a responsible person. He comes to understand that he is expected to take responsibility for his life, and for the way he relates to members of his family. It is understood that group members have responsibility in the group; they are not only 'patients' but also agents of therapy. It is understood that the conductor has no magical solutions; the expectation is that problems be discussed in the group and that everyone take part in this to the best of their ability.

The group thus becomes the setting par excellence, perhaps the only setting, in which the post-psychotic is treated neither like a backward child nor a fragile favourite to be wrapped in cotton wool. He is a responsible adult, an equal to others in the community who all have their strengths and weaknesses.

Learning that one can make a difference to others

Laing (1961, pp.66–72) writes of the importance of complementarity. A mother cannot be a mother without a child. A child needs not only to receive from his mother, he needs to be allowed to give. 'The good breast is a breast that can receive as well as give.' Emptiness is not only physical, it can be due to lack of meaning in life. 'Emptiness and futility can arise when a person has put himself into his acts, even when these acts seem to have some point to him, if he is accorded no recognition by the other, and if he feels he is not able to make any difference to anyone.'

When the psychotic first comes to the group, he is surprised that he is expected to help others. ('I am sick myself.') The conductor makes it clear that this is exactly what is expected. After a time, the group member listens to others, is sympathetic or critical. Group members can make valid clarifications and interpretations.

The knowledge that they can make a difference to others, be needed by others, be effective – even if they can scarcely help themselves – is very important to these patients and evidently plays a part in their progress to health.

Perception of self and others

Bateson (1972) has a theory of learning at different levels. 'Learning One' concerns the adaptive response; 'Learning Two' is the identification of context, since each context requires a different response. Non-adaptive 'Learning Two' is neurosis (or psychosis). Learning Two is acquired unconsciously and mainly in early infancy. It is self-validating; no event in reality can disprove it. Moreover, the person who believes everyone hates him will behave in a way that provokes that response.

Psychotherapy aims to alter Learning Two, not merely making it more adaptive, but facilitating the process of change, promoting flexibility. We may apply his model to group psychotherapy. Since the group member is presented with a variety of different perceptions, it is likely to help him see that his own perception is only one of many possible ones. Instead of the black–white confrontation of patient–therapist, patient–authority figure, there is the multi-coloured palette of the group.

This is particularly important in the case of schizophrenic patients, who may become locked into their own perceptions of the world. The problem with the paranoid is not so much that his perceptions are mistaken, as the rigidity with which they are held.

The group as instrument of therapy: interpretation by the group

Foulkes held that the conductor should forge the group as his instrument of therapy, rather than directly treat the group or its members. He believed that the group itself could treat the individual, that it was capable of making interpretations. He gives a series of examples of unconscious understanding and interpretation by the group (1948 pp.119–123).

It may be difficult to believe that a group of post-psychotic patients can make interpretations and other positive interventions, yet they do have this ability. Such interventions are usually more acceptable coming from the group than from the therapist. Here are some examples.

Case example

In one meeting, Deborah had once more brought a problem concerning her little girl, now aged five. 'You know,' said Bernie, 'you always talk about Hannah's problems, never about the problems between you and Daniel.' Deborah retorted by apparently bringing a marital problem: They were planning to go out to dinner the other evening, and Daniel had told his parents. She did not think that parents ought to know what went on between husband and wife. This was a rule of theirs. 'Who makes the rules?' I asked. 'Deborah does,' said Daniel. The group discussed the issue of a couple keeping things to themselves.

I observed that Deborah was also telling the group that problems between husband and wife were confidential and not for the ears of the group. On the other hand, we had been wondering why she was taking all the childcare problems upon herself, rather than involving Daniel who was willing and able to play the paternal role.

She ignored my interpretation, but did take up the matter of involving her husband. Daniel was taking stronger drugs than she was, she argued. Daniel said he did play with Hannah each day, and made her a sandwich in the morning. The group continued to discuss the issue.

Comment

Bernie's interpretation was correct and very much to the point. Deborah almost always discussed problems of mothering. She saw herself as the principal parent, leaving a merely supportive role to Daniel. It was she who called the shots, made the rules in the family. She was reluctant to bring the marital relationship to the group and Daniel was fearful of doing so. (Deborah married David while he was in the group, and had become a group member herself.)

The use of metaphor

The unconscious understanding mentioned by Foulkes (1948, pp.119–123) can lead to the use of metaphor by group members, which may serve as an appropriate comment or interpretation. Groups of psychotic or post-psychotic patients readily show such unconscious understanding.

Case example

In a multiple family group on an admission ward, Miriam (a schizophrenic woman) complained that her mother was always doing things for her, while she could quite well do them for herself. Yaffa, a woman who had become psychotic after childbirth, retorted: 'More than the calf wants to suck, the cow wants to suckle.' This is a well-known proverb, but it made an apt interpretation which the mother seemed to understand.

Sometimes this unconscious understanding leads a group member to talk in parables or metaphors which may require interpretation.

Case example

In a group of psychotic outpatients, members were complaining of going unheard by others; each brought a problem which seemed to fall on deaf ears. They felt quite frustrated. Peter told a Talmudic tale: 'One day Kamza was out riding on a horse, when a poor man asked for food. Kamza said he was hungry himself and would not get off his horse until he had eaten. His hands withered; this was his punishment.'

'What does that have to do with what we are talking about?' a group member asked angrily. 'He does not relate to me at all,' said Avram.

'He does not relate to his own son; what do you expect,' said Dvorah.

'Maybe his story *is* relevant,' I said. 'Everyone in the group is so hungry and needy that he cannot spare a thought for others.'

What appears, at first sight, an irrelevancy of schizophrenic thinking, may in fact be a metaphoric contribution to the group dialogue.

Sometimes I use metaphor and parable by way of interpretation.

Case example

The meeting was just before the Jewish New Year, which is associated with repentance and reviewing one's actions. It also meant that a meeting would be missed.

Avram wanted to wish his neighbour a Happy New Year, but thought he might be rejecting his good will. Helen expressed doubts about people liking her, wanting her.

Peter had been worried how he would be received at his nephew's Bar Mitzva celebration; it went off all right.

There was much talk about help from heaven, even about the Messiah, though Daniel (the most religious group member) emphasized the need to help oneself. There were isolated appeals for help and little comment on one another's problems.

I told a story from S.Y. Agnon's 'Days of Awe'. A man was lost in the forest and wandered about for three days. When he met another man he was overjoyed: now he would find the way out. However, the other man told him that he too had erred for days, 'Together, maybe we can take a different route and find our way out of the wood.'

I added that I thought the group today was like the men lost in the forest.

'Yes,' said Simon, 'maybe the group is like a wood.'

Change brought about by the group

Some call groups with post-psychotic patients 'follow-up groups', because they are drawn from the population of 'follow-ups' after admission. It is rather like patients coming to see a surgeon (no matter which one) after an operation to ensure that there are no complications and there is no recurrence. The implication is that no further improvement or development is expected.

I find, however, that the group is therapeutic and change does occur, although it may take several years. The kind of change expected is growth in autonomy, individuation, taking responsibility and initiative, learning to understand the other's point of view and being able to put oneself in his place.

The group is a particularly good place to learn the latter. Like siblings, who are at first jealous and compete for attention, group members learn to empathize and identify with one another. Shira, who was totally self-centred, would slowly learn how her children felt when she complained in their presence, using emotional blackmail, implying by her behaviour that their neglect would make her more sick.

Sometimes the change is quite marked.

Case example

Avram used to monopolize the group when he first joined. He had to be the centre of attention. The group might devote half an hour to him, yet he would become very angry when the group moved on to the problems of others. 'You don't care a damn about me. I am going to set myself on fire.'

We were often quite worried and my co-therapist and I wondered whether to hospitalize him.

Over the years, Avram changed. He began to be interested in others in the group. He would listen carefully and discuss their problems. He became the champion of mutual aid.

In a recent meeting, Deborah was talking about her four-year-old daughter Hanna. Her husband would come home from work feeling very tired, and the little one wanted to play with him. On one occasion he had told her he was too tired and went to bed; Hanna had given him a slap to wake him. This was very wrong of her, should Deborah slap her?

Avram had a suggestion: Daniel should rest with a cup of coffee for ten minutes on returning from work, then play with his daughter for half an hour. The couple accepted this.

We thought this was a good piece of lateral thinking on Avram's part, particularly as he had never had children and had always been irritated by the presence of small nephews and nieces.

Incidentally, group members would spontaneously call one another when there was sickness or distress. In the case of post-psychotics, we did not discourage such out-of-group contact – in any case, it was usually fed back to the group.

There are group members who recover completely.

Case example

Gideon had been hospitalised for the fourth time with acute paranoid psychosis, developed when doing his service in the Israel Defence Forces. He was in the 'rehabilitation group' at Kfar Shaul and remained in it after discharge. Recovering from his psychosis, he became depressed and was quite unwilling to do anything about his life. The group was encouraging but did not push him. His depression lasted for two years. One day he decided to take a Ministry of Labour course for office work and passed the examination. Some time later, he brought his girl friend to see me. She wanted to know his prospects of leading a normal life.

Gideon began to work and married his girl friend. He moved with the group when I began to work at the West Jerusalem Mental Health Clinic. After recovering he continued for a time, mainly because he enjoyed encouraging others through his own success.

Gideon has a steady job as clerk at the Law Courts. He is happily married and has two children.

The content of the group dialogue

Having transmuted symptoms into the language of emotion and relationships, the group dialogue tends to centre around interpersonal problems. Beyond that, the themes are existential ones: loneliness and the difficulty of relating to others; self-esteem and sense of inferiority; the wish to be loved and doubt whether one is lovable; anger and what to do with it; whether one can control one's anger and can generally be in control of one's life.

Thus, Deborah wonders whether other mothers in the kindergarten regard her as 'different'. Was sending a New Year card eccentric? Will her daughter be treated differently from others?

Helen marvels, again and again, that someone loved her enough to marry her. However, she asks, repeatedly, how often she should go and see her aged parents. It sounds like a conflict of roles, but turns out to be more than that. It transpires that she visits them excessively. She finds it difficult to be alone. Daniel responds: 'In the Gulf War, there was a song: "I want to go home." The question is: which is home? With one's partner or with one's parents? My father told me: home is with your wife.'

Avram says he is lonely, yet he has no patience for people, even for the weekly visit from his social work student which is so important to him. Ron recalls an incident when he lost his temper with his little nephew and hit him. Peter says he too loses his temper. He tries to hitch a lift to work, and he goes berserk when drivers do not stop for him.

Before festivals, everyone in the group talks about loneliness: the unmarried and divorced members in particular. Everyone in the street greets neighbours happily; people are going to their families, to a festive meal. They alone are going home to an empty house. Their concerns are essentially human, like those of the rest of us – only more so.

Conclusion

A group of psychotic patients can be run on group analytic principles; it can competently act as therapist. The conductor, however, has to work harder than usual to make the group into a therapeutic tool. Group members have to learn to communicate, to understand and to be understood, which means translating symptom language into the language of interpersonal problems. Such a group encourages a sense of responsibility and an ability to put oneself in the other's place. It gives the group member a sense of competence and the knowledge that, in spite of his defects. he can make a difference to the other. In the long run, this expresses itself in the way group members run their lives.

References

Bateson, G. (1972) 'The logical categories of learning and communication.' In *Steps to an Ecology of Mind*. London: Chandler.

Chazan, R. (1974) 'A group family therapy approach to schizophrenia.' *Israel Annals of Psychiatry and Related Disciplines 12*, 3, 177–193.

Chazan, R. (1993) 'Group analytic therapy with schizophrenic outpatients.' *Group 17*, 3, 164–178.

Foulkes, S.H. (1948) *Introduction to Group-analytic Psychotherapy*. Studies in the Social Integration of Individuals and Groups. London: Heinemann.

Kanas, N. (1993) 'Group psychotherapy with schizophrenia.' In H.I. Kaplan and B. Sadock (eds) *Comprehensive Group Psychotherapy* (3rd edn). Baltimore: Williams and Wilkins.

Kreeger, L. (1991) 'The psychotic patient.' In J. Roberts and M. Pines (eds) *The Practice of Group Analysis*. London: Routledge.

Laing, R.D. (1961) *The Self and Others*. London: Tavistock.

Racker, H. (1968) *Transference and Countertransference*. London: Hogarth.

Ruesch, J. and Bateson, G. (1951) *Communication: the Social Matrix of Psychiatry*. New York: Norton.

Springman, R. (1974) 'Psychotherapy in the large group.' In L. Kreeger (ed) *The Large Group*. London: Constable.

Yalom, I. (1985) *The Theory and Practice of Group Psychotherapy*, 3rd edition. New York: Basic Books.

CHAPTER 9

Supportive–Expressive Group Psychotherapy with Chronic Mental Illness, including Psychosis

Tetsuro Takahashi, Glenn Lipson, and Lane Chazdon

Structured and evocative techniques as well as supportively framed interpretations can enhance the effectiveness of group psychotherapy for psychotic and chronically mentally ill patients. In this chapter, we describe a coordinated psychotherapy and research project which examined the value of such interventions within a contemporary object relations perspective.

In the extended-care unit of a mental hospital in the midwestern United States, the unit team developed a supportive-expressive group psychotherapy structure to treat inpatients with chronic illness, including schizophrenic, affective, and borderline disorders. Our efforts to develop an effective approach to treatment with this population spanned a period of ten years. During this time, traditional long-term treatment modalities were drastically modified in response to the national trend of decreasing the length of hospital stays. As changes in insurance coverage and treatment programs took place, the variation in length of hospital stay ranged from two weeks to a few years. Within the context of milieu treatment advocated by Gunderson *et al.* (1983), all patients received comprehensive treatment that consisted of pharmacotherapy; individual and group psycho-therapy; and activity therapy, psychoeducation and psychosocial group treatment.

The group psychotherapy structure consisted of three component substructures: clinical, training, and research. The study group met once a week for group supervision. Chaired by the section chief, the group focused on integrating these three components through supervision, reading relevant articles, and discussing the clinical project. This small *ad hoc* research team began to develop efficacy assessment scales that had to be put on hold because of the changes noted earlier. As for training, each group alternately received supervision from the study group.

This chapter focuses on our experience within the clinical substructure, where we conducted three kinds of groups: a music interaction group (group M), and two talk groups (groups A and B). Each group contained no more than eight patients. All newly admitted patients started in a music interaction group right away and were first treated in the entry group (group A). Group A, an introductory or holding group, was for assessment and support. When patients were deemed ready, they advanced to a more conversational, interactive, and expressive group (group B).

In the music interaction group (group M), patients were helped to interact with one another through music. These patients could be categorized as typically having limited ability to interact emotionally with others. Patients assigned to group A were less verbal than those in group B. When patients were able to interact and communicate more effectively, they might be moved to group B. Many patients in groups A and B continued to work concomitantly with the music group.

In all three groups, the evolving process was understood utilizing an object relations perspective. In the M group, music served as the 'transformational object' (Bollas 1987), meaning it could transform discomfort or displeasure to its opposite – comfort or pleasure. Within this 'environmental' place of safety and healing, patients could gradually develop their capacity for effective verbal communication.

On the other hand, in group A, projective techniques in psychological testing were found helpful in inducing patients to talk about themselves. With this technique, the objects of patients' projections served as the transitional space (i.e. the location of cultural experience (Winnicott 1966)). In this space, they could express themselves with less fear of exposure, and they could create something for themselves. In group B, more traditional object relations approaches were employed, with patients being helped to work through psychotic-like anxieties, fantasies, and primitive defenses.

These groups were conducted in an inpatient setting during a time of great change in the health care delivery system. Nevertheless, it is our belief that the same types of groups and group structures could be applied to outpatient or daycare treatment, beyond the limitations imposed by the current medico-economic situation.

Group M: music interaction group

The music interaction group served as a transformational group, in that it facilitated a feeling of being in an environmentally safe place.

The musical function

As a therapeutic medium, music should be understood as a symbolic function, a process rather than a product. People in general tend to identify music with specific creators (composers, recording artists), with products (pieces, songs, recordings), or with the specific activity of listening. However, within the present perspective, the creators and products are epiphenomena of a deeper function. Whether or not a musical expression is 'art,' or whether or not one has 'talent,' is quite beside the point. Although Segal (1952) was deeply concerned with the nature of both art and artist, her emphasis on Klein's depressive position anxieties seems applicable to anyone involved in self-expression through an artistic medium. The narcissistic challenges aroused by the artistic task tend to stimulate depressive anxieties. In an appropriately managed therapeutic group, such challenges become opportunities for self-expression, interaction, and increased self-esteem.

From this perspective, the aesthetic experience around the transformational object (Bollas 1987; John 1995) involves an interlocking system of expressive and receptive functions. The musical product, the composer, and the listener are constituent parts of a Gestalt, which is deeper and greater than the sum of its parts. The cultural matrix, the biological and psychological parameters, and the environmental/existential givens all contribute to the context of the musical function (Benenzon 1997).

The musical function is symbolic in every sense of the word (McGlashan 1987). Music's special ability to effect reparation rests on its capacity to symbolically represent and work through depressive position anxieties (Segal 1952). Symbols carry affective meaning insofar as they originate in the linking together of different internal objects, each associated with the same affect, such as rage, pleasure, or satisfaction (Segal 1964). Langer (1957) has suggested that there are conscious and unconscious links between the emotional responses stirred by music and the psychoacoustic phenomena of pitch, loudness, consonance and dissonance, timbre, and formal structure.

Klein held that sublimation, a key concept in activity therapy fields, is born of the attempt to save the good object from aggression by redirecting and modifying the destructive energy to other, more constructive and socially acceptable, ends. Thus we believe that reparation through spontaneous musical expression holds much potential for the healthy channeling of rage experienced by persons with schizophrenia (Bion 1957; John 1995; Symington 1986).

The re-owning of projected part objects, feelings, and related mental capacities that apprehend these is a tortuous process for persons with schizophrenia (Bion 1957, 1962). The non-referential nature of meaning in music (McGlashan 1987) may facilitate this process in a more benign manner (Stewart 1997).

In addition to protecting the good object, Klein also observed that symbolization protects the infant from its own terror of having, in fantasy, penetrated and devoured the contents of the mother's body. Without such a buffer, the infant would never feel safe enough to explore the world. We believe that this buffer capacity makes music quite useful to the individual living in the often terrifying world of psychosis. Furthermore, the interplay among individuals engaged in musical interaction operates as a more benign concretization of projective identification, the defense by which patients renounce reality (Bion 1957, 1962; Stewart 1997).

Creativity and primary process

To grasp fully the nature of group musical improvisation, we must pay attention to the creative process within the individual. Creative self-expression seems to require some degree of liberation of primary process operations in conjunction with well-chosen secondary process expressive mechanisms (Arieti 1967). Matte-Blanco's (1988) concept of 'bi-logic,' the mixing of symmetric and asymmetric modes of thought, as a fundamental feature of the unconscious, is helpful in understanding the confluence of primary and secondary processes. The ideas that cannot be put into words, which are the kernels of works of art, develop from primary process 'amorphous cognitions,' or 'endocepts' (Arieti 1967). Endoceptual awareness is essential to one's sense of being truly alive; however, an excess of this attunement is characteristic of psychotic regression, particularly schizophrenia. Since the endocept corresponds to nonverbal, unconscious or preconscious cognition, Arieti (1976) identified music and abstract art as the creative forms that most closely reflect the endoceptual cognitive stage. Thus, the predominance of this level of cognition in schizophrenic disorders helps explain music's effectiveness in assisting persons with schizophrenia to communicate their feelings. The benefits derived from improvisational musical interaction by patients with affective psychoses are due to its facilitation of primitive cognitive experience from which the psychotically depressed individual is pathologically cut off. It also supports interpersonal contact and, particularly important to those in manic states, a sense of responsibility to the group. More will be said about this in the course of discussing Ogden's (1989) three object relations positions.

The improvisation dialectic

The musical improvisation process must be considered in terms of the relationship between the self and the environment. The act of musical improvisation is a kind of psychological dance or dialectic involving a shifting of attention between inner and outer phenomena. It is a dynamic process involving a balance of internal and external realities. In schematic and simplified form, the improviser plans the musical events internally to some degree, executes the motor tasks of playing a musical statement, and monitors the acoustical events that result from playing. To complete the loop, the player responds affectively to what he or she has played. This cyclic process drives and structures the unfolding improvisation (Figure 9.1).

The inner reality component deals with the intrapsychic processes of the improvisational situation. This component includes affects and value judgments, as well as plans on the motor and conceptual levels. It is represented by the following questions:

- What do I wish to express? (including endoceptual awareness)
- What will it sound like if I do 'this'?
- How do I make 'this' [imaged] sound or feeling?
- Do I like these sounds?
- How does it feel?
- How will I respond to what I am hearing?
- Am I playing well?

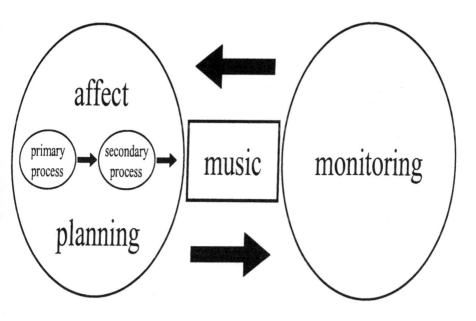

Figure 9.1 The improvisation dialectic

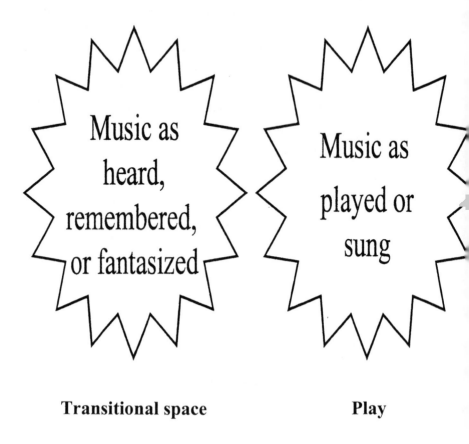

Transitional space   **Play**

Figure 9.2 Music in transitional space and in play

The outer reality of the process is involved with taking in objective data as input to the inner process. This level of the process is represented by the following questions:

- What am I hearing others playing?
- What am I hearing myself play?
- Is this the sound I meant?
- Is this the feeling I meant to express?
- How are others responding?
- Am I making any contact with others?

Let us now consider the structural similarity between the dynamic interplay in musical improvisation and Winnicott's (1971) transitional space. Here we suggest a correspondence between transitional experience and music as a purely auditory experience, and between play and music making (Figure 9.2). Both player and listener, however, experience music as an auditory message existing simultaneously in both inner and outer worlds. When awareness of music transcends the physical accoutrements of instruments, notation, or speakers, the experience resides within Winnicott's 'realm of illusion' – mental experience without tangible substance. These aspects of musical improvisation are part of its power as a medium operating within the transitional space between individuals.

Ogden's three positions

Ogden's (1989) formulation of object relations added a third mode of experience (the autistic-contiguous [A–C]) to Klein's two object relations positions (the P–S and the D positions). The A–C phase is sensory-dominated and involves a self made of accrued skin-level experience. Stressful conditions in adulthood often leave one prone to reassure oneself of one's physical integrity in a somewhat autistic mode.

An important emphasis in Ogden's object relations theory is the dialectic between the three modes of experience. One cannot live a healthy existence solely in the D mode. Although it offers integration, it can become stagnant and too certain. For the condition of good health, one needs the stimuli of the other two positions (A–C and P–S) operating in a dialectical manner. Each position holds a vital ingredient missing in the others.

This dialectic is the basis of the thinking behind our music interaction group: that the group can be influenced in healthier directions through engagement in exercises that bring to the fore the characteristic aspects of the three positions through the form of the activity at hand (Figure 9.3). One recognizes, of course, that a person's predominant position is an enduring personality trait. In no way can lasting change in object relations be brought about through short-term participation in the group, or through the use of the group as the only therapeutic intervention. But, through regular experiences in the group, the person is exposed to alternative experiences provided by the three positions. Such experiences might not be accessible to the person otherwise, and thus seem to encourage working toward a healthier balance of positions.

As is well documented in the group psychotherapy literature (Wells 1985), it is common for the constellation of individual anxieties to congeal into group themes that can be understood in object relations terms. Session planning aims to emphasize aspects of the position that the group needs to experience most. Through attunement to the group, the leader can identify group-as-a-whole themes and positional trends that assist the leader in slanting the experience

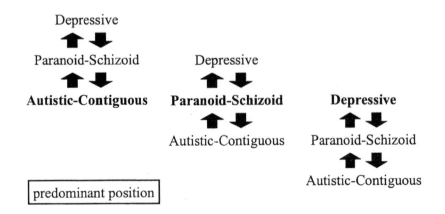

Figure 9.3

toward the position most needed by the group. Under certain conditions, these trends may convince the leader to choose unplanned exercises that might better address group needs. A particular verbal approach is constructed to heighten the experiential mode needed most by the group.

Music interaction group

The music interaction group is one of several groups that form part of an extended care unit in a mental hospital in the midwestern United States. It meets for thirty-five minutes, three times a week. The group is designed for patients with chronic mental illnesses, including schizophrenia. The typical group size is six patients. This clinical musical improvisation group, which is led by a music therapist, operates on the principle that simple, spontaneous musical expression can serve as a nonverbal means of interaction. Through musical interaction, the group serves a transformational function by taking the members from 'disintegration to integration,' in the words of Bollas (1987, p.14), where such movement echoes the satisfactions of the early developmental stage in a facilitating environment (Winnicott 1971). The group's equipment includes a selection of hand percussion instruments, paddle drums, and three tonal Orff instruments (xylophone, metalophone, and glockenspiel). The guitar is often used by the music therapist as an accompaniment instrument.

Each session moves through a sequence of five phases. The sequence is organized according to a principle of moving from simplicity to increasing complexity, with consideration also being given to the predictable needs of a group of people with schizophrenia. These needs include a gradual engagement in interaction, an opportunity to withdraw or participate passively, and an opportunity to organize and understand the experience. The phases are as follows: rhythmic warm-up involving little interaction, rhythmic interaction, passive participation or withdrawal, tonal interaction, and a closure activity.

Rhythmic functions are more primary neuropsychologically than tonal functions, and self-contained or autistic expressions are less demanding than those involving others. The middle passive phase allows participants to withdraw from interactive efforts, if they so wish. Closure of the session is achieved either through verbal or nonverbal processing, such as through the singing of a simple song. Group singing encourages a final simultaneous release of affect, which can be shaped through the dynamics of the music; beginning softly, becoming louder, then tapering off. Verbal processing usually takes the form of asking individuals how they felt at selected points in the session.

This approach differs from a traditional group psychotherapeutic technique in that the leader provides a great deal of structure. Stewart (1997) reported on a long-term outpatient psychodynamic improvisational music therapy group that follows a verbal psychotherapy model more closely. In contrast, this music group is an interactive activity therapy process, because chronically psychotic inpatients have a greater need for structure and leader involvement (Kibel 1993).

Musical metaphors of the three positions

Musical metaphors of the three positions (A–C, P–S, and D) are structured therapeutic musical improvisation experiences that invite a type of relatedness to sound, to other individuals, and to the group, which leans toward and can be focused on experience in one of the three positions. Yet the actual experiences of the participants are colored by their own typical modes of relating. The musical metaphors for the three positions (described below) pull for a certain mode of experience that can be enhanced through careful verbal intervention.

Autistic-contiguous metaphors

In autistic-contiguous experience, the sense of self is generated at the surface of the skin. Temporal contiguity, represented by regular rhythm, is another aspect of the autistic-contiguous position. Experience in this mode is encouraged through exercises that feature sensory awareness, steady rhythm, and inner rather than outer focus. A sense of primitive, self-involved rhythmicity prevails. Pruyser (1983) referred to 'autistic' impulses in music as impulses to make sounds – a type of raw emotional discharge that can take the form of 'a shriek, a moan, a sigh, a wail, or a grunt' (p. 195). Thus he believed that vocal expression was more prone than instrumental expression to autistic expression.

In fact, Benenzon (1997) has noted that the human body is really the most primary instrument. Body sounds offer a wide range of primitive sound experiences. In Ogden's formulation, rhythmic and skin-to-skin contact might serve to bring one into the realm of this position. Thus, hand drumming offers an experience of both physical and temporal contiguity, contributing to a sense of soothing for A–C anxiety. This representation might extend to any instrument that is struck, scraped, or shaken rhythmically. Playing within the A–C position is focused on the purely sensual level of physical contact with the instruments and the continuity of the rhythmic pulse. If the group is involved, it is secondary to the individual taking a turn as the leader.

Paranoid-schizoid metaphors

Ogden notes that the unreflective 'self-as-an-object' attitude of the P–S position can provide revitalizing stimulation to the stagnation and dull certainty of the depressive position. This beneficial effect can be achieved through the use of musically interactive exercise formats that resemble the mental processes of the P–S position yet offer a sense of safety, security, and possible satisfaction. As patients express themselves musically and receive others' musical expressions and respond to them, group musical improvisation can serve as a metaphor and perhaps as a concrete reification of projection and projective identification. The metaphor is assisted by musical techniques such as imitation, variation, and call-and-response. Further elements of P–S experience can be drawn forth through exercise formats possessing some of the following characteristics:

1. Continual present (de-emphasis on form or past experience, arrhythmic playing).

2. Spontaneity through the lack of true subjectivity or reflectivity, experiencing rather than evaluating.

3. Mild sense of anxiety from impending threats, as in responding to an unpredictable stimulus.

4. Splitting, discontinuity of experience, aspect of separation of the endangered from the endangering, as in stark musical contrasts.

5. Sense of omnipotence, lack of responsibility or guilt, as in conducting the group's playing.

Depressive position metaphors

As noted earlier, Segal (1952) believed that investment in esthetic values originates from efforts at reparation for one's past destructiveness and at rebuilding one's lost inner world. Ogden (1989) noted that once a truly subjective space develops, resting on a defined, unshifting past, it makes possible the conscious use of symbolism. In addition to explicit symbolization, depressive position expression also involves more elaborate artistic form, resulting from artistically motivated repetitions of rhythmic, melodic, harmonic, and timbral themes.

In Ogden's (1989) formulation, the D position features 'historicity' generated through acceptance of the immutability of time, renunciation of omnipotent defenses, and an associated acceptance of self and others as whole objects. The integration of one's own expressions with those of others occurs concomitantly with identification and investment in the group. Drawing specific attention to the group's sound often brings about a maturation effect. Encouraging participant awareness of individual parts in the group sound fosters a sense of responsibility to the group.

The developmentally necessary experiences for managing a dialectic between object relations positions can be augmented and reinforced through the symbolic medium of musical interaction. Anxieties associated with each position can, to some extent, be experienced and resolved within the context of structured exercises designed and focused verbally to present symbolic expressions of such anxieties.

Group A: holding group

The first 'talk' group that patients participated in was an introductory or holding group that provided assessment and support through the use of projective tasks.

Projective techniques

When attempting to treat severely mentally ill patients in an inpatient therapy group, we were faced with a number of challenges: first, how to structure the group to actively engage the members and, second, how to create group cohesion and a sense of safety with individuals with different disorders and needs. When patients were put on the spot and asked to share something in prior groups, they soon fell into a litany of typical complaints and observations. Their statements often described a list of side effects stemming from their medications or how well they had slept. Vacant and detached, these complaints repeated themselves like an endless digital recording. From a dynamic perspective, the patients' reports needed to be empathetically listened to and closely attended. Every member of the group struggled with the issue of being seen, appreciated, and heard. However, the patients' responses to the group therapists' questions did not reveal the complex meanings, individuality, and depth of their individual experiences of severe mental illness. Rather than promulgate a group culture in which a forum was provided for patients to provide individual reports on their biological functions, a new approach to conducting these groups was sought.

We conceived our challenges as the following: first, to get the patients involved in the treatment process; and second, to make their participation valuable. The difficulties for such patients in understanding and making sense out of their experience often leaves them isolated within the community (Takahashi and Washington 1991). Without the bedrock of consistency in their knowledge of themselves, their interpersonal skills are on shaky ground. Bringing self-confused and preoccupied patients together into a functioning group is a challenge.

Primitive fears, anxieties, hallucinations, and affective swings buttress the patients in their own isolation. Borrowing from the fields of clinical psychology and art therapy, we used projective tasks to assist the patients in revealing more of who they are. This approach also has applications in other settings, such as outpatient work with less severely disturbed individuals. In particular, projective techniques are identified as a way to enlist patient involvement, to help patients reveal their internal experience, and, finally, as a way to create a shared context of experience that provides the sense of belonging and relatedness to others that is so vital for restoration of mental health.

Theoretical background

The use of projective techniques as an approach borrows heavily from techniques and understandings derived from psychological testing. Group psychotherapy has many similarities to psychological testing. Similar to psychological testing, meetings take place within a set structure of time. Typically, in psychological testing, there are more ambiguous and unstructured tasks – the projective tests.

The inpatient group is highly structured in terms of its starting and concluding rituals (Yalom 1983). In a 45-minute meeting, announcements are made, then followed by asking individuals what their agenda is for the session. The group concludes with a five-minute rehash, at which time the patients are encouraged to discuss their experience of the group. Here a projective task facilitates a response. For example, the therapist could ask the group members to describe the group as a type of 'ride.' There are many types of rides, including roller coasters, sailboats, and buses, each connoting a different experience that can be briefly explored. The co-therapists encourage group members to find universal aspects in their shared experience.

Most of these patients have experienced numerous hospitalizations, which provides them with some expertise pertaining to their treatment and the treatment of others. In addition, living within the same therapeutic community provides a context of similarity of ongoing experience.

During the administration of the psychological testing, the tester assumes a non-judgemental stance, not responding to the very primitive material the patient might present. For example, if a patient sees sexual, violent, revolting images in the Rorschach, the examiner treats that percept during inquiry like any other response. In the group, we try to create the same open atmosphere toward accepting modulated primary process. We approach our exploration of patient behavior here with the following assumption: behavior has a meaning and people can discover the unconscious dynamics that influence their behavior. An aptly worded question will invite whatever self-observing capacity members possess. One female member of the group responded to this type of question about her self-mutilation by revealing that she did it 'to rid her body of evil.' Her response facilitated a lively group discussion where other members discussed how they felt about 'cutting' and why in the past they had injured themselves. The co-therapists' role in such situations is to help the group titrate the discussion so as to be able to keep some distance from the topic.

A degree of acceptance of primary process is communicated by vocalizing an appreciation of what the patients have shared. For instance, to use a more collective perspective in the 'cutting' example, the therapists could indicate to the group that drawing blood makes psychic sense, although in reality it does not accomplish what the patient wished. The therapist might relate that for thousands of years people have believed in 'bad blood' and considered bloodletting a cure. By first accepting, then exploring in the group as whole, and finally challenging and interpreting beliefs, the therapist helps group members process the more primitive material.

The group's main emphasis in working with lower-functioning patients is to foster communication between individual members. Finding a conversational common ground breaks down isolation. Music, education, and historical and current events are all experiences that group members usually have in common. We encourage what appear to be banal non-issue-related conversations. However, from a projective orientation, the group members' choices of topics can be very revealing of their sense of themselves and the world. Sharing seemingly unimportant information, which can be talked about more benignly and safely, enhances group cohesion and culture. Individual members are often better at talking about what has happened in their past than about what is evolving in their current relationships.

With these patients, we progressed in our discussions from the 'there-and-then' to the 'here-and-now.' With higher-functioning patients, it is possible to emphasize consciously the here-and-now of group experience. The adage, 'strike while the iron is hot' has been used to emphasize the immediate interactive exploration of group dynamics and conflicts. With lower-functioning inpatients, 'striking while the iron is cold' (Pine 1985) provides them with the opportunity to develop the confrontational skills that are so difficult for them to muster. Hence, with lower-functioning patients, we often progress from the there-and-then to the here-and-now. First, emphasizing past experiences reinforces individual boundaries, especially the patient's sense of time. Lower-functioning patients are prone to have a distorted sense of time, in part because they so easily become swept up in the timeless primary process of the unconscious (Hartocollis 1972) Helping patients demarcate limits assists them in eventually addressing more here-and-now conflicts. There are, of course, times when immediacy is important to addressing group interactions, especially when the therapists need to modify the holding environment or to provide more containment in structure.

Another unique aspect of working with lower-functioning inpatients is the need for a greater degree of tolerance of resistance, flight, and the other defense mechanisms they find necessary in order to feel safe. When a patient does not want to attend the group, he or she is asked to come and inform other patients of the inability to stay. If a patient needs to leave a group during a session, this is respected as well and the patient is assisted in articulating the reason for the departure.

From a coping perspective, group members frequently use manic defenses (Ganzarain 1989). Co-therapists may join in this form of resistance with the goal of communicating that it is acceptable at times to avoid more troubling material. For example, the patients may ask to go on a walk together rather than to spend the session talking. They converse during the walk, however, often providing and sharing valuable information that the group is able to contain later. The therapist benignly underscores the initial avoidance, demonstrating that it is all right to avoid feelings if, in due time, they can be explored/ With the lower-functioning patients' lack of malleability and adaptability, a structured but flexible approach is essential. With higher-functioning patients, the therapist is more likely to remain neutral and to interpret resistance and avoidance sooner in the process.

The apparent balance between work and play is different for lower-functioning inpatients. They are encouraged to enjoy themselves and to work toward having a positive experience while in the group. However, just like play therapy with a small child, this group work involves an earnest effort by the patients to reveal to the therapist their internal world. Work with adults is very different from work with children in that talking replaces physical activity and the means of exploration of a topic is thus verbal. Although toys are not appropriate with adults, patients do appear to benefit from involvement in playful activities.

The therapist's function as a semipermeable boundary

The therapists use themselves as tools, physically or psychologically, to function as a 'dynamic semipermeable membrane.' The concept of a semipermeable membrane is a theoretical metaphor that explains how a living organism can selectively facilitate the exchange of information. The patients utilize a [...] boundaries to help them understand what is part of them and what is sep[...] Feelings of guilt, responsibility, belonging, and/or confusion produce[...] appreciation of boundaries. Likewise, individuals in the group maintain their ow[...] boundaries with regard to others, the group as a whole, and the environmen[...] within which the group interacts (Takahashi 1988). A patient may have a fluid ego boundary, which may make both the individual and the group feel threatened.

In order for the patient and the group to do therapeutic work, the therapist may serve as an auxiliary ego boundary that sets limits on the time spent, the extent of the content to be shared, and the amplitude of the affect to be expressed. One patient may have a rigid ego boundary, immobilizing both the patient and the group. In that case, the therapist may serve as the auxiliary ego boundary that moves the patient to disclose more personal information. Another patient may feel that the group is not helpful and wants to stop coming. The therapist may respond by assisting both that patient and other members of the group to examine what is and what is not helpful in group psychotherapy.

One effective use of group therapy related to boundaries is to help patients separate their own conflicts from other issues having an impact on the milieu. Group therapy for all patients helps them determine what they are responsible for and how others react to them. For lower-functioning patients, in particular, the group helps them observe their fantasies pertaining to fears of rejection and their over-developed sense of responsibility that arises out of their own omnipotent fantasies and fear of destructiveness (Klein, Heiman and Riviere 1952). Group members often fear that they will lose their sense of boundaries: this fear may produce an impasse where patients resist experiencing themselves as part of the group. Among the primitive fears related to the loss of boundaries is that of contagion; that accessing another patient's experiences makes one vulnerable to that patient's illnesses, fantasies, or 'evilness.' The fear of losing one's self can be handled through the use of activities such as listening to music. Activities like this reaffirm separateness yet foster relatedness. If the group is distracted by music in another room, the therapist may serve as the auxiliary ego boundary, observing the patients' investment in this music and inviting them to associate to it. Thus, what would otherwise be a violation of the group boundary can now be accommodated into the newly created group boundary. Through projective methods employed by the therapist, the group cathects this creative boundary.

Whether the individual's ego boundary or the group boundary is modified, the therapist's intervention is crucial. A patient's direct experience of the repetition of his or her pathological behavior, of the therapist's intervention that produces changes in the patient's interaction with others, and of the group as a whole results in the enrichment of the group process. It appears as if the therapist out of the various kinds and levels of boundaries in the ... a dynamic boundary to provide the group with ...its, tension, flexibility, and creativity. ...ieve that, with adulthood, one becomes more serious. ...s often suffer from being too serious and overly critical. ...tes an attachment to experience. By facilitating humor and , the therapist can help group members to step back and gain new ...pectives. The patients in the group can be seen as progressing developmentally from parallel play to being able to engage with others. For patients in group A, to experience dependency is progress. It means they have moved beyond a perception of their frightened separateness into group membership.

Therapeutic activities and projective tasks

The activity therapists who are part of the multidisciplinary team are clearly aware that these patients reveal themselves through their activities. Some group activities resemble activity therapy. For example, group members have cut out pictures from magazines and pasted them on a poster board to make a group collage. In this exercise, group members discussed why they selected a particular picture and what its meaning was for them. The collage ultimately represents the integration of different group members' contributions.

The difference between activity therapy and an activity used by the group is akin to the difference between an art therapy activity and a diagnostic projective task, such as drawing a person. When psychologists ask patients to draw a person, they are using that exercise expressly to see how much the patients will reveal about themselves. An activity therapist also concentrates on helping persons use that medium for self-expression and for increasing skills through tasks that facilitate work on issues or impasses.

The mastery that patients obtain in activity therapy has both psychological and practical value. Within the group context, when an activity is undertaken, the product or object the member brings into the group is explored not only from the individual's psychological perspective but also from others' perspectives as to what is revealed about the person and his or her values. Tasks are used infrequently so as to maintain the novelty necessary for less defended and more revealing responses. The emphasis is not on the task – after all, an exercise is only a vehicle – but rather on helping the patients arrive at enhanced self- and other-awareness.

Another use of group exercises is to help patients with assertiveness. Patients are encouraged to respond honestly regarding their reactions to what other members discuss or bring into the group. One of the first experiences of safe confrontation can be when a group member tells another patient, for example, that he or she could not understand the lyrics in a piece of music which that patient has elected to share with the group. In one particular group where assertiveness was a problem, we asked the members to pretend they were panelists on the television show 'American Bandstand,' so that they could rate the pieces of music that group members selected to share.

Working in metaphor is very important with inpatient groups (Katz 1983). The use of metaphoric displacement (Alexandrowicz 1962) provides a way for patients safely to communicate feelings in a contained fashion, incorporating split-off parts of their experience or themselves (Segal 1964). Music, books, and television shows can all serve as retrieval stimuli for important memories. Almost every patient will have a keepsake that represents a wish or an idealized object or time. Items of an aggressive or repulsive nature can represent the patients' attempts to integrate or neutralize those aspects of themselves. The capacity of objects such as photographs (Colson 1979) to contain memories and affective experience is easy to illustrate. A photo album containing pictures of ourselves can change our conscious state; a song from an important occurrence can bring to the fore a flood of memories. These objects, when shared with the group, can provide access to memories of soothing pleasant times or of repressed hurt. The capacity for a common object metaphorically to become a talisman, like a container of experience, was apparent in a survey conducted on our hospital unit in which more than 80 per cent of the adult patients indicated that music, at times, can better communicate what they are feeling than they themselves can. The very titles of the songs the patients selected as describing their treatment were diagnostically revealing (Lipson 1988): 'I'm All Out of Love,' 'Suicidal Failure,' and 'Go On and Cry,' among others. Working metaphorically with these containers provides a safe 'potential space' for exploration (Ogden 1986).

Finding the shared metaphorical ground where all patients can relate to each other is difficult. Clues for how to proceed to any given topic are often supplied by patients in the comments they make just as the group is starting, in the clothes they are wearing, such as sweatshirts with slogans, or in the food or other items they bring to group. On occasion, we have had group members bring important photographs to share. We help them discuss what is important to them about the photograph and then draw others into the conversation. Other members may not connect to the affect but, instead, to the location in the photograph. In one group I was struck by the fact that a young man named Bill could find no photographs to bring. He told the group that his family never took photographs of him and never bought any of his school pictures. Everyone was able to sense how detached his family felt to him. Without a photograph to share, he came to group with the baseball cap he always wore. He explained to the group that the cap literally held his head together; that it reminded him that, despite his voices, he was here on earth and that the color green represented land and so was a source of comfort.

Until then, the group's impression of his cap had been simply that Bill was a fan of a particular baseball team.

The therapist's own ability to use free association can also be helpful in finding a tack to bring all group members into a discussion. For example, one group member wore a T-shirt of a rock star whose name sounded like a popular toy. Other group members who observed the sweatshirt agreed that the name sounded like a toy. The topic then progressed to the group members' memories of important toys they had owned in childhood. This seemingly innocuous topic provided the platform from which patients could eventually describe fundamental, often traumatic, experiences. For example, one patient commented on how whatever toys she owned or cherished ended up being destroyed.

In the Menninger Self-Administered Test Packet, patients are asked to indicate what three wishes they would make if these could be granted. Furthermore, they are asked to describe what they would like to be if they were not human. Experienced psychologists interpret patients' responses to these questions. Similar projective techniques have been used as tasks for the group. For example, group members have been asked to describe their childhood heroes. The task is left ambiguous so that each individual must determine his or her own answers, such as whether to talk about a fictitious character or someone in real life. Akin to the level of defensive operation in this group, which often relies on projection and splitting, the previously described assignment was followed by one in which members were asked to describe villains and monsters. One patient poignantly indicated that she was afraid of werewolves. She mentioned that, even when she walked on the hospital grounds, although she knew werewolves did not exist, at times she would run between the buildings, afraid of being attacked by one. This patient was able to tell the group that what frightened her about werewolves was that they looked like normal people, so no one was aware of the monster inside. The therapist then helped the patient connect this fear to her concerns about her alcoholic family.

The overall level of functioning of the group as a whole and of its individual members forms metaphorical topics that the group might discuss. More tactile and sensory-based exercises are used with the lowest functioning members. For example, in one group where three of the women were talking about perfume before the group started, group members were asked to bring in their favorite fragrances. The olfactory experience of the group was connected to historical life events, such as the various fragrances purchased for parents and other intimates on special occasions. One group member was able to discuss the guilt she felt after she bought her abusing father his favorite cologne.

Similar to the work accomplished in adolescent groups (Scheidlinger 1989), group members are supported in their expression of what they need from the group. Group members are not deterred from bringing food into the group, if they feel they need that type of fortification. This behavior is subject to interpretation, depending on the patient's diagnostic issues, and everyday events such as whether or not lunch was missed. Group members have at times drawn pictures to place on the wall of the group room. On one occasion, three of the six group members collaborated on a drawing of a fireplace to tape on the wall. This facilitated a discussion, stirred by the winter holidays, that pertained to the patients' wishes for the group.

Contemporary events that happen on the unit very often can be used to foster discussion. For example, whenever a patient attempts suicide, the therapist may ask the group to discuss, from their own experience, why people attempt suicide as well as how they have handled their own suicidal impulses. More commonly, if someone goes to the dentist, everyone in the group can discuss individual experiences with dentists. Discussion on this level also progresses from the more general to the more specific, which is in line with a group-centered approach (Takahashi and Washington 1991). It should be added, however, that we start by reaffirming individual boundaries by clarifying what the patients want to say, then progress to group statements during the course of the session.

The function of media

Winnicott (1966) proposed that the transitional object that the baby simultaneously recognizes as 'me' and 'not me' is a substitute for the breast. He later postulated that the third potential area is a transitional phenomenon from, and in which, an infant can draw and create something while introjecting from or identifying with it and sharing and enjoying it together with others. The area later becomes the place where play, art, and other cultural activities develop (Winnicott 1966). In the third potential area, where the infant simultaneously finds 'me' and 'not me,' the self and object illusory unity is being created in the infant's mind. This is not the same as a security blanket used as a transitional object, which serves more as a buffer for separateness from the breast. A two-year-old baby smiles when mother kisses the stuffed animal he cherishes. The stuffed animal serves more as a 'substitute self' than does the security blanket.

Objects used in projective techniques often serve as patients' substitute selves. Hence, there are two fundamental types of transitional objects: those that represent nurturance and succor, and those that represent the self. These traditional self-objects assist the patient in examining the 'me' and the 'not me.' Group therapists must be aware of the type of object a patient brings into the group because it has significance in terms of how the patient will structure the group interaction. A therapist does not want to allow other group members to attack or devalue any patient's self-transitional object. Furthermore, an awareness of the distinction between these two types of transitional objects helps patients examine which aspects belong to the individual group member and which are paired with the desires of others. Ultimately, a transitional object allows other group members to discuss developmentally sensitive topics without a direct threat to the patient's or others' sense of self. Moreover, it allows others in the group to provide input, thus helping group members to modify their own sense of identity. Transitional objects are important parts of the patients' selves, yet they retain the qualities of 'me' and 'not me.'

A female patient had a very small plastic pig called Arnold that she frequently placed on her leg. She informed fellow group members that Arnold helped her cope with the voices she heard. To get a better sense of the difficulties she was experiencing, group members would ask her directly how Arnold was doing. Another patient collected a few stuffed animals and spoke with them in a baby-like voice. Her longing for emotional nurturance was expressed through obtaining objects that oscillated between being maternal transitional objects and self-objects. Similar to the way that children work with such objects, this patient was able to use the voice of the stuffed animal to express in the group what she was unable to state more directly. Ultimately, she learned more adaptive ways of dealing with her needs in relating to others through the substitute practice self.

Move toward inter-relatedness

The uses of props and projective techniques has its role in group therapy. With patients with deficits in interpersonal skills, the responsive nature of the group to contemporaneous metaphor teaches members how to converse and make connections with others. Most healthy individuals will think of a similar experience to one related by a speaker, and thus participate in a social exchange. In lower-functioning individuals with mental illness, this is not always the case. Mental illness tends to isolate people. One of the goals of a group is to break that isolation and promote inter-relatedness. A projective group task can facilitate this accomplishment.

This move toward inter-relatedness is particularly important with inpatient or outpatient groups composed of more severely ill individuals. In these groups, the boundary-affirming function of a task can assist patients in addressing issues related to their identity and their relationships with others. Tasks that evoke memories of forgotten objects particularly can provide access to past experiences that played formative roles in the patient's psychological maturation, allowing the expression of emotion in a more modulated way.

With a higher-functioning group, an occasional projective task can break through resistance. A projective task can help the group move more rapidly to a greater sense of commonality. When a clinician interprets a patient's answer, a theoretical frame helps assign meaning. To recognize projection requires a theoretical grounding in models of self- and other-representations. An understanding of the condensation of drives, of the impact of systems, and how psyche uses metaphor is also a necessity. When these tools are in hand, the group therapist can allow metaphors to bubble to the surface, harnessing the energy in this material to provide fuel to move the group toward its destination of greater self-knowledge and intimacy.

When we have presented these considerations in workshops, there have always been attendees who are looking for a certain projective task to take home and implement. Specific tasks can be helpful. However, the timing for using a particular task should be decided by the group therapist. As with the Rorschach, what is just as important as the actual cards, techniques, and procedures is how to interpret and recognize the findings. What is more significant than a group exercise or task is the way of thinking about the meaning of what emerges in the group setting and how to capitalize on it. The noise of the group, what clothes its members wear, and the patients' comments on arriving for a session can all be used to establish an appropriate timing for an intervention or project. Ultimately, the appreciation of the need for play and the possible layers of communication within the group provide for a richer, more enjoyable, and more productive group experience.

Group B: working through group

As patients became better able to verbalize their emotions, they moved to Group B, where the focus was on helping them work through their concerns in a more expressive environment.

Expressive psychodynamic approach

The use of group structure for treatment of chronic mental patients (including psychotic patients) has been documented since the beginning of the era of moral treatment (Butler 1887; Marsh 1931). In recent years, various modalities, especially psychoeducational and psychosocial approaches, have been utilized more and more. Psychodynamic approaches to group psychotherapy with this population of patients have been underutilized; hence few articles exist (Steiner 1979; Stone 1996; Takahashi and Washington 1991).

Whether psychodynamic approaches are effective with severely disturbed patients, including schizophrenic and borderline patients, has long been disputed largely because of the technical difficulties inherent in such work and the difficulty of conducting scientific research on it. In addition to the accumulated experiences of those interested in treating severely disturbed patients (Buckley 1988), of note are recent publications of clinical research conducted by the Boston team (Glass *et al.* 1989; Gunderson *et al. 1983;* Horwitz *et al.* 1996; Lotterman 1996; Robbins 1993) and, in particular, the study by Kanas (1996) on the application of group psychotherapy to schizophrenic patients. He delineated three approaches of present-day group therapy for schizophrenic patients:

educational, interactional, and psychodynamic. After conducting research that included a controlled study, he concluded that the psychodynamic approaches and the integrative approaches of all three categories are safe and effective. Thus the psychodynamic approach, when conducted by sensitive and skillful therapists, seems supported not only by clinical impression but also by scientific research as a safe and effective method that can help severely disturbed patients develop a capacity for psychological growth, which enables them to better use their internal and external resources, eventually resulting in a more meaningful life.

Application of object relations theory

Object relations group psychotherapy is psychodynamic par excellence. It is derived from Bion's theory (1961) on small group dynamics. When people interact within a group, two opposing tendencies develop: a mature tendency of collaboration to achieve the group goal in objective and scientific ways (the 'work culture'), or a regressed tendency to collectively experience developmentally primitive fantasies, affects, and defenses.

Here readers are referred to Segal's (1964) explanation of Melanie Klein's object relations theory (Klein *et al.* 1952). Still, additional explanation, although sketchy, is offered below.

Melanie Klein's theory concerns the earliest developmental 'relatedness' between the subject and an object in the mind. Until five months of age, the subject relates only to orally perceived parts of the mother that become split into good/bad maternal objects. This developmental position is called the paranoid-schizoid (P–S) position, because it is predominately paranoid anxiety with a splitting defense. At five months of age, the subject begins to relate to the object as a whole, seeing the good and the bad aspects together, and as a result, the subject's capacities for ambivalence and concern develop. This position is called the depressive (D) position. Both the P–S and the D positions continue to operate in varied proportions in the mind throughout life. The object relations approach allows sensitive observations and interpretations on shifts as tensions are created between the two positions (with psychotic-like anxieties (Ganzarain 1980) as well as primitive fantasies and defenses).

Types of group cultures

According to group dynamics, an unstructured group tends to regress and develop one of three kinds of group culture that Bion (1959) called 'basic assumption cultures': dependency, flight–fight, or pairing. In the dependency culture, members assume that either the leader or the group is omnipotently dependable, and thus they expect to be taken care of. In the flight–fight culture, members assume that the leader or the group is omnipotently dangerous, and thus they feel the need to fight against (or flee from) the leader or the group. In the pairing culture, members attempt to allay their anxieties about the group's despair by creating a pair that will, in fantasy, create a messiah or messianic product to save the group.

These three cultures are considered collective defenses against psychotic-like anxieties. Here again readers are referred elsewhere for a more sufficient study of the theory (Bion 1959; Grinberg *et al.* 1977; Rioch 1970). When patients regress within a group, these defenses develop. But sensitive analysis of them can help patients to experience containment and thus healing.

Although psychodynamic groups are criticized for not paying enough attention to the importance of members' interactions in the here-and-now (Kanas 1996), contemporary psychoanalysis, at least in the United States, recognizes a significant therapeutic role of the intersubjective transference–countertransference interaction between the psychoanalyst's and the analysand's minds. Likewise, in object relations group psychotherapy, the therapist regards the here-and-now experience as most important in effecting change and in recognizing, understanding, and working through the patient's transference to the group-as-a-whole, to the therapist and the therapist's countertransference, and to fellow patients.

Chronic, severely disturbed patients, including those who are psychotic or borderline, can readily regress in an analytic therapy group and can develop basic assumption groups (Bion 1959), part-object relations, fantasies, affects, and defenses. In these group cultures, where the dynamics of aggression predominate, some patients may withdraw or act crazily, hence reinforcing alienation or becoming retraumatized. This is how they have typically experienced their lives. Positive interpretation of negative behavior can mobilize a patient's inner resources for work group culture, which is more effective than basic assumption group culture, because patients may experience significant containment and hence find a new object in the therapist and the group, both capable of transforming the tenacious negative withdrawal or the traumatic experience. It is widely recognized by sensitive clinicians that a disturbed, often psychotic patient can serve as a barometer of group tension. Such a patient responds to tension either with complete withdrawal or with disruptive behavior. It is therefore quite relevant to interpret such behavior within the context of the group as a whole. Furthermore, focusing on the group as a whole as a positive transference object helps to diffuse the potential intensification of the transference experience (Horwitz 1994), negative or positive, such as in a regressed patient.

Unlike the above-mentioned common criticism that the psychodynamic approach pays too little attention to the here-and-now interaction, in our object relations group we interpreted the positive meanings of the negative behavior within the context of the here and now rather than just encouraging patients to learn more appropriate behavior. It is important to note, however, that such interpretations were not merely theoretical explanations, but rather representative of intuitive, empathic understanding.

A patient who is fixated in the P–S position will get creative tension restored between that and the D position and will work through the two positions, repairing the caring relationship he or she once damaged or split off in the mind. This work is crucial for personality growth. The following clinical vignettes from two inpatient psychotherapy groups illustrate this process.

CLINICAL EXAMPLE 1

In one session of an inpatient group consisting of three male patients (Bud, John, and Steve) and one female patient (Debbie), the patients returned to a previously discussed issue of the discrepancy between their internal experience and their exterior behavior. During an earlier session when their suicidality was being discussed, they had revealed that they regarded smiling as an expression of inner anxiety. Back to this session: Debbie was a borderline patient who recognized both her suicidal feelings and her guilt feelings when she was angry. Two other patients, John and Steve, noted that suicide was a violent expression of anger against oneself. Bud, who was schizoaffective, was apparently asleep, while John, a person with schizophrenia, stood up and walked around the room. As everyone remained silent, tension elevated in the group. Their anxiety was interpreted as being induced by the discussion of suicide. Some patients act out through self-isolation or disruptive behavior; group members show their own difficulty asking for, as well as initiating, help when it is needed. Bud opened his eyes and said that he had been silent because he could not relate at all to the issue of suicide. The therapist responded, 'So you joined the group with your action of leaving the group psychologically, like the rest of the group had tried to leave other people by suicide.' Then the therapist turned to John: 'By walking around, you tried hard to keep yourself in the group in spite of your anxiety.' This interaction resulted in Bud waking up and John sitting down. The group expressed concern about John who, in turn, talked about his lifelong feelings of alienation because of having been adopted and being Oriental; then about his anger and sadness at losing the Oriental therapist who was about to retire, just as John was going to be able to vent his anger at his loving yet powerful and controlling father.

The group's fixation on the P–S position was apparently shaken and their work on the D position had begun. Intuitive positive interpretation of their negative behavior apparently enabled this change.

The following example illustrates in more detail the shifts and working through of the P–S and D positions.

CLINICAL EXAMPLE 2

This group comprised four patients: Sahlim, a 38-year-old Arab man suffering from major depression with psychotic features; Brian, a 36-year-old American man with chronic paranoid schizophrenia who had spent 15 years going back and forth between state hospitals and the streets; Carolyn, a 27-year-old American Jewish woman who was suffering from borderline personality disorder; and Franco, a 34-year-old Spanish immigrant with a borderline personality disorder, including antisocial features. Carolyn and Franco had been behaving like adolescents in love with each other. While Franco was seen as a womanizer, Brian frequently complained loudly and bitterly that no woman on the unit liked him at all. When someone pointed out to him that he might alienate people because of his 'weird looks' (very long curly black hair and the lack of a front tooth), he yelled that he was being treated unfairly. Brian seemed to be particularly interested in Franco, trying to relate to him, but Franco would scornfully reject him.

In this particular session, a substitute therapist who had previously been a co-therapist of the group was covering for the regular therapists. A month prior during the session before the change in therapists, some members had devalued the group, worrying about its future. They felt hurt and abandoned by the therapist who was leaving.

All four patients were late to the session with the substitute therapist. After they settled in, their lateness was noted. They unanimously stated that the group was useless and that no staff member really cared about them. Carolyn brought up a good example: the previous evening she had felt desperate and was contemplating suicide; she needed a nursing staff member to talk to but no one was immediately available. When it was suggested that she examine what had contributed to her desperation with the group her explanation was vague. Franco (apparently irritated) gave a deep sigh, to which Carolyn reacted by screaming, 'Here is a good example that this group is useless!' Franco apologized, but tension had already developed between them and within the group. Then Brian looked at Franco with a provocative, eerie grin and said 'Muchacho,' a word no one else understood, and teasingly laughed. This further aggravated the situation.

Although taken aback for moment, Franco shrugged his shoulders and made a scornful face as if to say to the group, 'Brian is an impossible, crazy man.' The group appeared to be the epitome of the P–S position, where paranoid anxiety and the splitting defense prevailed. Contrary to the group's approach, the substitute therapist interpreted Brian's behavior differently because of previous group circumstances wherein Brian had erupted with silly or 'crazy' behavior. The therapist noted that, 'When tension develops in the group, Brian interrupts with comments that are out of tune and seem to lessen the tension. It is as if Brian, being very sensitive to tension in this group, were trying to keep the group from exploding from that tension.' Brian suddenly stopped grinning and looked serious, even nodding lightly in response to this interpretation. The group was also listening intently. Sahlim looked straight at Carolyn and asked her to explain more factually how her despair had developed the previous night. The group had thus shifted from the P–S to the D position. Recalling an intense argument with her parents, Carolyn claimed that they always sent double messages and that she reacted with *complex feelings* in response. Although not wanting to be affected by her parents, she could not deny her dependence on them. Brian and Sahlim joined with her in sharing their fears about losing their parents. Brian somberly stated, as if pushing out each word, 'My grandfather is dying from cancer,' and tears welled up in his eyes. Prompted by the therapist's encouragement to talk about his feelings, Brian tried to stifle his tears as he said, 'I worried him a lot. He might have become sick because of me.' Other patients reassured Brian that he had not caused his grandfather's illness.

The therapist recognized a relevant here-and-now issue, and pointed out that nothing had been mentioned about the absence of their regular therapists (the patients had not been aware of their plan to be absent). Sahlim resentfully stated that for therapists the group meant nothing. Somebody remembered that the therapists had previously announced their plan to be absent from this session. The patients also mentioned that they were glad to see their old therapist again. The substitute therapist pointed out that their negative feelings were enacted not only with the nursing staff but also with the absent therapists. The patients readily agreed. When asked how they felt about the change in therapists, and the temporary return now of their old therapist, the group became quiet. The therapist made an observation that everyone seemed to have *complex feelings.* (In terms of transference, refer back to Carolyn's and the group's feelings about their parents.) When Sahlim asked why the therapist had quit, the explanation was repeated that he had left to return to a former role as supervisor of all the psychotherapy groups. When asked if anyone had felt responsible for the therapist's departure. Sahlim admitted that he felt that way because he had talked too little in the group.

As part of the session's structure, a brief wrap-up review was conducted. The patients then agreed that the meeting had been a good one, because they had been able to talk about how they really felt. The substitute therapist added that the group addressed some difficult issues, shared experiences, and understood other people better, so therefore they had created a good session. They all observed how once-damaged relationships in the group were now restored. They were becoming more tolerant of their feelings of guilt and ambivalence, more accepting of the complexity of true mutuality, and more responsible for themselves without condemning others or themselves, or distorting reality. Thus this session marked the beginning of the group working through the D position.

But what prompted this shift, or therapeutic mutation, that was exemplified in Brian's sudden change from being 'crazy' and 'silly,' to being reflective and serious? The substitute therapist's interpretation apparently prompted the change. Brian's crazy behavior symbolized the P–S position in that he and the group became dangerous to each other and were split off. Were it not for the interpretation, Brian would most likely have been scapegoated as a destructive member, then reacted to and alienated from the group just as he had been in society at large. In other words, the P–S position provided the very opportunity for Brian to be retraumatized. The therapist's interpretation revealed an adaptive side of Brian's behavior, unnoticed by him or the group, that functioned to integrate instead of disrupt and split the group. Through the interpretation, the potentially retraumatizing experience turned into a focus instead on the reparative part of Brian's self, now seen by Brian himself and also by the others as constructive rather than destructive. This experience enabled Brian to reflect on, rather than to project onto others, his capacity either to harm others or to repair his relationships.

Our clinical experience with both inpatient and outpatient group psychotherapy with severely disturbed patients has revealed that such chronic patients can progress to the D position and can work through their depressive anxieties when helped to deal with their primitive defenses, including manic distraction. But they must first know that they are valued and respected members of their group. This is a crucial change in the patient's life experience (i.e. having an alive and constructive mental life as opposed to a mechanistic, ruthless P–S mental state). The therapist can observe how the very behavior that the patient ostensibly uses to disrupt the group may have an equally important function on uniting the group. Such observation helps the patient and the group to begin to look at events bilaterally, and it also encourages a tolerance of ambivalence that, in turn, modulates the affects of love and hate. Once individual patients are recognized as contributing to the life of the group and can also begin to see themselves as important group members, they need to experience a balance of the destructiveness of reaffirming themselves as disruptive and alienated, and its simultaneous alleviation in the active life of the group.

Special transferential circumstances under which the second clinical example took place were helpful in working through the patients' depressive anxieties. The substitute therapist who had once 'disappeared' had returned or been 'revived' in the group, which helped the group feel secure enough to face reality about the therapist's departure and reappearance, checking their fantasies and unresolved feelings about him. Here again, experiencing both the loss and the restoration of a loved object in the here-and-now fostered their exploratory work on their depressive anxieties.

One of us has emphasized elsewhere (Takahashi and Washington 1991) that with severely disturbed patients, a therapist's interpretations must be simple, clear, and more integrative than open-ended and exploratory. Chronic, severely disturbed patients seem to benefit from experiencing their capacity to make reparations before realizing and elaborating on their guilt, paranoid anxiety, and manic and splitting defenses. As they contribute to the life of the group this way, they are better able to tolerate the painful self-exploration that must follow.

As a follow-up, Brian, the most disturbed patient in the second clinical vignette, deserves a few words. He continued to improve along the same lines as those during this particular session, in which he began to work through P–S and D positions. This improvement is consistent with a recent research finding about borderline patients (Horwitz *et al.*, 1996). After several years, he was able to live within the community, to enjoy a few close friends, and to work part-time. He maintains fair personal hygiene and appearance.

Conclusion

This chapter contains the perspectives of three different group psychotherapists from different disciplines. In common, they worked toward using different group structures to facilitate patient participation. Whether in a music interaction group (group M), in a more supportive group (group A), or in a more expressive group (group B), patient involvement was facilitated through approaches that enabled engagement. Every patient, from the least communicative to the most expressive, was viewed as having his or her own experience of self and other to relay. When working with profoundly mentally ill patients, the therapists find that an understanding of Bion, Ogden, and Klein helps them to interpret the group-as-a-whole and the individual group members' movement toward relatedness. Whatever tool, technique, or method is used, both psychodynamic and object relations theory guide our interventions, helping us to target our treatment to the needs of our patients.

References

Alexandrowicz, D.R. (1962) 'The meaning of metaphor.' *Bulletin of the Menninger Clinic 26*, 92–101.
Arieti, S. (1967) *The Intrapsychic Self: Feeling, Cognition, and Creativity in Health and Mental Illness.* New York: Basic Books.
Arieti, S. (1976) *Creativity: The Magic Synthesis.* New York: Basic Books.
Benenzon, R.O. (1997) *Music Therapy Theory and Manual: Contributions to the Knowledge of Nonverbal Contexts,* 2nd edn. Springfield, IL: Charles C. Thomas.
Bion, W.R. (1957) 'Differentiation of the psychotic from the non-psychotic personalities.' *International Journal of Psycho-Analysis 38*, 266–275.
Bion, W.R. (1959) *Experiences in Groups.* London: Tavistock.
Bion, W.R. (1962) 'A theory of thinking.' *International Journal of Psycho-Analysis 43*, 306–310.
Bollas, C. (1987) *The Shadow of the Object.* London: Free Association Press.
Buckley, P. (ed) (1988) *Essential Papers on Psychosis.* New York: New York University Press.

Butler, J.S. (1887) *The Curability of Insanity and the Individualized Treatment of the Insane.* New York: G.P. Putnam's Sons.

Colson, D.B. (1979) 'Photography as an extension of the ego.' *International Review of Psycho-Analysis 6,* 273–282.

Durkin, H.E. (1981) 'Foundations of autonomous living structure.' In J.E. Durkin (ed) *Living Groups: Group Psychotherapy and General System Theory.* New York: Brunner/Mazel, 24–29.

Ganzarain, R. (1980) 'Psychotic-like anxieties and primitive defenses in group analytic psychotherapy.' In R. Ganzarain(1989) *Object Relations Group Psychotherapy: The Group as an Object, Tool, and a Training Base.* Madison, CT: International Universities Press.

Ganzarain, R. (1989) *Object Relations Group Psychotherapy: The Group as an Object, Tool, and a Training Base.* Madison, CT: International Universities Press.

Glass, L.L., Katz, H.M., Schnitzer, R.D., Knapp, P.H. *et al.* (1989) 'Psychotherapy of schizophrenia: an empirical investigation of the relationship of process to outcome.' *American Journal of Psychiatry 146,* 603–608.

Grinberg, L., Sor, D. and Tabak de Bianchedi, E. (1977) *Introduction to the Work of Bion: Groups, Knowledge, Psychosis, Thought, Transformations, Psychoanalytic Practice* (Tr. A. Hahn). New York: Jason Aronson.

Gunderson, J.G., Will, A., Jr and Mosher, L.R. (1983) *Principles and Practice of Milieu Therapy.* New York: Jason Aronson.

Hartocollis, P. (1972) 'Time as a dimension of affects.' *Journal of the American Psychoanalytic Association 20,* 92–108.

Horwitz, L. (1994) 'Depth of transference in groups.' *International Journal of Group Psychotherapy 44,* 3, 271–290.

Horwitz, L., Gabbard, G. O., Allen, J.G., Frieswyk, S., Colson, D.B., Newsom, G.E. and Coyne, L. (1996) *Borderline Personality Disorder: Tailoring the Psychotherapy to the Patient.* Washington, DC: American Psychiatric Press.

John, D. (1995) 'The therapeutic relationship in music therapy as a tool in the treatment of psychosis.' In T. Wigram, B. Saperston and R. West (eds) *The Art and Science of Music Therapy: A Handbook.* Langhorne, PA: Harwood Academic Publishers, 157–166.

Kanas, N. (1996) *Group Therapy for Schizophrenic Patients.* Washington, DC: American Psychiatric Press.

Katz, J.A. (1983) 'The non-interpretation of metaphors in psychiatric hospital groups.' *International Journal of Group Psychotherapy 33,* 53–67.

Kibel, H.D. (1993) 'Inpatient group psychotherapy.' In A. Alonso and H.I. Swiller (eds) *Group Therapy in Clinical Practice.* Washington, DC: American Psychiatric Press, 93–112.

Klein, M. (1952) 'Some theoretical conclusions regarding the emotional life of the infant.' In J. Riviere (ed) *Developments in Psychoanalysis.* London: Hogarth Press, 198–236.

Langer, S. (1957) *Philosophy in a New Key: A Study in the Symbolism of Reason, Rite, and Art.* Cambridge, MA: Harvard University.

Lipson, G. (1988) 'Rock and rage: music and internal experience.' Unpublished paper presented at the Menninger Clinic, Topeka, Kansas.

Lotterman, A. (1996) *Specific Techniques for the Psychotherapy of Schizophrenic Patients.* Madison, CT: International Universities Press.

Marsh, L.C. (1931) 'Group treatment of the psychoses by the psychological equivalent of the revival.' *Mental Hygiene 15,* 328–349.

Matte-Blanco, I. (1988) *Thinking, Feeling, and Being: Clinical Reflections on the Fundamental Antinomy of Human Beings and World.* New York: Routledge.

McGlashan, A.R. (1987) 'Music as a symbolic process.' *Journal of Analytic Psychology 32,* 327–344.

McIntosh, D., Stone, W.N. and Grace, M. (1991) 'The flexible boundaried group: format, techniques, and patients' perception.' *International Journal of Group Psychotherapy 41,* 49–64.

Ogden, T.H. (1986) *The Matrix of the Mind: Object Relations and the psychoanalytic Dialogue.* Northvale, NJ: Jason Aronson.

Ogden, T.H. (1989) *The Primitive Edge of Experience.* Northvale, NJ: Jason Aronson.

Pavlicevic, M. (1995) 'Interpersonal processes in clinical improvisation: towards a subjectively objective systematic definition.' In T. Wigram, B. Saperston and R. West (eds) *The Art and Science of Music Therapy: A Handbook.* Langhorne, PA: Harwood Academic Publishers, 167–178.

Pine, F. (1985) *Developmental Theory and Clinical Process.* New Haven, CT: Yale University Press.

Pruyser, P.W. (1983) *The Play of the Imagination.* New York: International Universities Press.

Rioch, M (1970) 'The work of W. Bion on groups.' *Psychiatry 33,* 55–66.

Robbins, M. (1993) *Experiences of Schizophrenia: An Integration of the Personal, Scientific and Therapeutic.* New York: Guilford.

Scheidlinger, S. (1989) Group Psychotherapy Workshop Sponsored by Kansas Group Psychotherapy Society and Menninger, Topeka, Kansas.

Segal, H. (1952) 'A psycho-analytical approach to aesthetics.' *International Journal of Psycho-Analysis 33,* 196–207.

Segal, H. (1964) *Introduction to the Work of Melanie Klein.* New York: Basic Books.

Steiner, J. (1979) 'Holistic group therapy with schizophrenic patients.' *International Journal of Group Psychotherapy 29,* 195–210.

Stewart, D. (1997) 'The sound link: psychodynamic group music therapy in a therapeutic community setting.' *Psychoanalytic Psychology 11,* 29–46.

Stone, W. (1996) *Group Psychotherapy for People with Chronic Mental Illness.* New York: Guilford.

Symington, N. (1986) *The Analytic Experience.* New York: St Martin's Press.

Takahashi, T. (1988) 'Boundary as guiding principle in inpatient treatment.' Unpublished manuscript.

Takahashi, T. (1995) 'Boundary changes in inpatient group psychotherapy – struggles to adjust.' Unpublished manuscript.

Takahashi, T. and Washington, P. (1991) 'A group-centered object relations approach to group psychotherapy with severely disturbed patients.' *International Journal of Group Psychotherapy 41,* 79–96.

Wells, L. (1985) 'The group as a whole perspective and its theoretical roots.' In A.D. Colman and M.H. Geller (eds) *Group Relations Reader.* Springfield, VA: Goetz Printing.

Winnicott, D.W. (1966) 'The location of cultural experience.' *International Journal of Psycho-Analysis 48,* 368–372.

Winnicott, D.W. (1971) *Playing and Reality.* London: Tavistock.

Yalom, I. (1983) *Inpatient Group Psychotherapy.* New York: Basic Books.

CHAPTER 10

Psychodynamic Group Psychotherapy with Chronically Mentally Ill Women

Lawrence L. Kennedy, Susan Bach, Shauna Corbin, Mary Ann Abbott and Bette Ferbrache

In this chapter we shall describe the treatment of chronically mentally ill women in a psychoanalytically oriented group psychotherapy with female therapists. The staff for this seven-year experience included one co-therapist who was with the group for six years and four other co-therapists who were with the group for one to two years. In addition to the benefits gained by the patients, the group had a profound impact on the therapists who gained a deep appreciation of the intense struggles experienced by mentally ill women, their ability to work in group therapy and their ability to assist one another.

Historical, clinical and sociocultural background

Over the past thirty years there have been major socio-political developments related to the devalued status of women in western culture. Simultaneously, progressive deinstitutionalization of the mentally ill has been taking place. As a result, interest in the plight of chronically mentally ill women and their special issues and concerns has grown.

Test and Berlin (1981) noted that mental patients have been 'faceless' and that therefore gender has been ignored. As they state, 'Very little research has been directed toward studies of sex differences among severely mentally ill individuals. Further, clinicians often do not respond to the chronically mentally ill as sex-differentiated persons' (Test and Berlin 1981, p.136). To illustrate the differences, they indicate that males are apt to be hospitalized at a much earlier age than females and have a poorer outcome than females. Females are more likely than males to experience a course of recurrent illness with full remission. Chronically mentally ill women are apt to marry at nearly the same rate as females in general whereas males are much less likely to marry. However, many of the women have marital problems and end up divorcing.

Test and Berlin also suggest that the needs of chronically mentally ill mothers have been neglected. Because chronically mentally ill women are able to assume instrumental roles such as traditional homemakers, they are apt to do better. But chronically mentally ill women's special needs have been ignored in such places as hospitals and community settings where, for example, the women are not provided with adequate supplies for personal hygiene. Also, the clothing given to these women has usually been very unattractive.

Chronically mentally ill women are very vulnerable to victimization: rape and other forms of sexual abuse are common. Bachrach and Nadelson (1988) indicate that, in the case of chronically mentally ill women, gender-determined considerations are superimposed on general problems related to providing services to the chronically mentally ill. Some women with chronic mental illness apparently do well but there are others who suffer greatly. For example, in one study (Lamb 1984) the homeless mentally ill women were found to exhibit more serious psychiatric problems than male patients (Lenehan et al. 1985; McGerigle and Lauriat 1983). With deinstitutionalization in the 1960s and 1970s, women did more poorly than men. They have often had insufficient community supports to aid them. For example, in programs which provide rehabilitative skill training, chronically mentally ill women were often viewed as unemployable or employable only in such roles as domestics housekeepers and babysitters. The tendency has been to view women as more helpless and more dependent in general and hence to treat mentally ill women as even more helpless.

Apfel and Handel (1993) have also spoken of unique problems with which chronically mentally ill women must struggle. They state, 'Treating women with long-term mental illness is a great challenge because these patients touch so many of our own deepest feelings and beliefs about gender and relationships. They also require knowledge about female biology, psychological development and social context.' These authors note that when women with schizophrenia are in acute psychotic states they tend to be much 'more overtly hostile, physically active and dominating, seductive, sexually delusional, louder, more emotional, and more visible than men' (Apfel and Handel 1993, p.327). At the same time, women who have been moved to community treatment were often successful because of their greater social sensitivity and response to supports. They note that women with long-term mental illness are concerned about their appearance and what other people think of them but that clinicians often seem to be unaware of this fact. Women are more apt to have suffered from some form of sexual abuse, therefore complicating their diagnoses when symptoms of post-traumatic stress are present. Drug abuse is as important a problem in mentally ill women as in men and is very likely to affect their ability to conceive and give birth to children. Women patients often have great concerns about their sexuality and clinicians may avoid enquiring into the nature of their sexual problems. These individuals may not get the same type of sex education or be as aware of contraceptive measures as other women. Psychotropic medications cause a whole array of complications for women's sexuality. The wish to have children may continue in women who are mentally ill and be a source of considerable frustration and disappointment to them.

A further and crucial problem has been to define which of women's mental health problems are caused by mental illness and which are caused by their being women with devalued roles in society. Broverman (1970) in a study on sexual stereotypes noted that 'clinicians are more likely to suggest that healthy women differ from healthy men by being more submissive, less independent, less adventurous, more easily influenced, less aggressive, less competitive, more excitable in minor crises, having their feelings more easily hurt, being more emotional, more concerned about their appearance, less objective, and disliking math and science' (Broverman 1970, pp.4–5). The tendency has been to define mental health in terms of male behavior and much of women's behavior in our culture has at times been viewed as less healthy. Broverman asserts that 'our predisposition to define women as disordered and to hold them accountable for their own problems and those of others no doubt influences their self-esteem, well-being, and functioning' (Broverman 1970, p.1).

Eating disorders, perhaps as much as any illness, are viewed as a 'women's disease' and appear to be very much intertwined with the view of women in our society. Women who suffer from schizophrenia may be able to function in our society because they may be dependent and low-functioning which makes them actually more 'desirable.' These writers have felt that schizophrenic women in psychotherapy may be excessively compliant and that these women may often not share their dissatisfactions and problems because of their tendency to be so deferential.

Anderson and Holder (1989) indicate that most research and treatment programs have failed to differentiate patients on the basis of gender and have often failed to recognize the special needs of women.

Group psychotherapy for the chronically mentally ill

Although, quite strikingly, we were unable to find any description in the literature of group psychotherapy especially designed for chronically mentally ill women, we did find many references to the treatment of chronically mentally ill patients in general in groups. Stone (1996) reviews the history of the use of group psychotherapy for treating chronically mentally ill patients (schizophrenia, personality disorders, depression, and serious substance abuse). Based on over twenty years of clinical experience, he presents a carefully thought through method for treating chronically mentally ill outpatients in group psychotherapy. Many of the techniques utilized in group psychotherapy for higher functioning patients can be modified appropriately to treat seriously mentally ill patients in groups. Dr. Stone's groups are long-term in nature in that the patients may choose to come to the same group over a period of years. Kanas (1996) has also written a text on the treatment of schizophrenic patients in group psychotherapy. He has developed group psychotherapy techniques for both inpatients and outpatients in short-term groups. Also, he documents his own research which demonstrates the efficacy of group treatment for this population.

Feminist groups

Group psychotherapy with women emerged in the 1960s with the advent of the women's movement in the United States. No attempt will be made to review all of this work but only to make reference to certain writings.

Feminist psychodynamic group psychotherapy has been utilized for women-only group psychotherapy with the belief that these groups have a particular advantage in helping women to define their identity separate from men. It has been noted that when women are treated in groups with men and women, the women tend to defer to the men in many arenas as is typical of their behavior in general society. Women have been trained by society to be unassertive and to contain their anger.

Consciousness-raising groups were popular in the early phases of the feminist movement (Lieberman, Solow, Bond and Reibstein 1979), and subsequently group psychotherapy for women in women's groups was introduced. Early on, a number of these groups were self-help and consciousness-raising groups which later served as a model for therapy groups with women (Brodsky, 1973; Brody 1987.) Bernardez (1996) believes that such groups provide opportunities for women to explore their transference reactions to the female therapist thus facilitating their relationships with their mothers and other female authority figures. Also, the groups are viewed as being particularly valuable to help women examine such issues as competition among women and expression of anger among women. Many such women's groups also focus on special women's issues and trauma such as incest, eating disorders, rape, and breast cancer.

In an interesting survey on issues in the lives of mentally ill women, Ritsher, Coursey and Farrell (1997) drew together groups of chronically mentally ill women from clubhouses, eight treatment settings, and other community facilities to discuss the special problems of their mental illness. Most of the women indicated that their severe mental illnesses were not the center of their identities. Even though most of them said that their illness had some adverse impact on them, many of them were satisfied with their lives. Many of the women stated that they did not have a mental illness. Many described having at least one abusive relationship. Most of them described having friends. Also, most of the women indicated that in the area of professional relationships and health care they felt that their relationships were good.

Surprisingly, the only reference we found having to do directly with group psychotherapy for chronically mentally ill women was a study done by Alyn and Beckar (1984). In this study, the women in a day hospital were exposed to feminist theory and ideas in weekly meetings of a group lasting two hours each for a period of up to 14 to 16 weeks. Some material was presented in a didactic fashion and other in a typical unstructured group psychotherapy. The authors were interested in the effect of greater awareness of women's issues. They noted that considerable improvement in self-esteem occurred for most of the women in the course of the treatment and also that they developed an increasing knowledge of sex and sex-related topics. The authors believe that their results supported the usefulness of an extension of feminist therapy to a more severely disturbed population.

The setting for the women's psychodynamic therapy group

The group to be described in this chapter had its beginnings as part of a large partial hospitalization service of a private non-profit psychiatric hospital. This service offers a full range of therapeutic group activities five days a week plus individual psychotherapy, pharmacotherapy, family therapy, and a wide array of psychoeducational programs. Treatment is intensive and the average length of stay is about five months in this level of care. More than half the patients continue in a step-down program which might be described as intensive outpatient treatment or aftercare treatment. Group psychotherapy, in the program, is twice-weekly, 50-minutes per session, and includes groups for lower- and higher-functioning patients.

The women's group was originally one of these partial hospital groups. The group evolved spontaneously into a group for chronically mentally ill women with a pair of co-therapists who were also women and who were interested in the special needs of chronically mentally ill women.

It soon became clear that the newly evolved small psychodynamic group offered a special opportunity to see how chronically mentally ill women might utilize an 'open-ended' group psychotherapy which could extend over a period of several years. The decision was made to limit the group size to eight, to add new members as members left, and to open the group up to additional referrals from the outpatient services.

The group as it evolved developed several unique qualities. Importantly, all the women had a history of hospitalization for serious psychiatric illnesses including schizophrenia, bipolar illness, major depression with psychosis, and dissociative conditions. All had been ill for at least three to four years before having come to this particular hospital for treatment. Following their most recent inpatient treatment, they had been discharged to the partial hospital program with plans to continue intensive treatment in order to establish themselves at the highest level of functioning possible.

One surprise to the staff, considering the severity of diagnoses, was that over half the women in the group were college educated. For example, one woman had a degree in education, another was a lawyer, and another was a minister. This proved to be a group of very bright and verbal women who were interested in receiving insight-oriented group psychotherapy. Also, they quickly developed a cohesive group in which they could discuss many very difficult issues, partly as a consequence of the fact that they had been functioning for at least six months with no admissions to and discharges from the group. The group members seemed to want to 'do more' in the group though it was originally believed by the staff that they were incapable of addressing deeper and more difficult layers of their problems.

All of the members had several other treaters during the time they were in group. This included individual, family and pharmacotherapy for all of them as well as, for some, structured day hospital treatment and utilization of a halfway house program or a similar supported living program. This substantial additional treatment made it possible for these women to use a more expressive form of group psychotherapy than would have been thought possible initially. The fact that all the patients were in some other form of treatment also necessitated communication with these other treaters on a regular basis. It was a standard practice for the group therapists in the partial hospital program to tell the patients in the group that they work as a team with the other treaters in the program and that they will be communicating freely about the patient's experiences in the group and be receiving information about the patients from the other treaters. This has some drawbacks in that the patients may feel they are not sufficiently in control of what is told one treater or the other, but it has been the practice in the program because it is felt to promote a collaborative effort by all the treaters and to discourage splitting. Also, the fact that the program is large with over a hundred patients makes it even more important that there is an active amount of communication between the various treaters. One problem that is encountered in this arrangement is that the patients may assume that the group therapists know things that they do not necessarily know. The group therapists make a practice not to bring information from the outside to the sessions and, instead, expect the patients to bring information to the group about themselves. Only occasionally have patients objected to the arrangement of treaters having open communication with one another. For the most part, they are reassured by this arrangement and see it as evidence that the various team members are interested in them.

There are times when the group therapist and the individual treaters have had to work together very closely to help a patient through a difficult time when she may want to quit the group or be too disorganized or too anxious to go to the sessions. Every effort is then made to keep the patient from missing too many sessions or totally dropping out. For example, at times some of the patients in these groups have required hospitalization due to crisis. Every effort has then been made to encourage the patient to attend the group sessions while they are hospitalized. The hope here is that the patient does not lose the significant attachment to the group and also that the group provides a safe place where the patients can process their reasons for being hospitalized. Group members can be very supportive at these times since crises are not unusual in such groups.

The group therapy format and process

The groups met for 50 minutes twice weekly. The orientation was psychoanalytic object relations group psychotherapy. All the group therapists had been in a two-year didactic training program and had regular weekly supervision of their groups. The therapists utilized a group-centered approach as developed by Horwitz (1977). In this approach, the therapist focuses on unconscious group themes as they emerge. Often such themes or 'common group tensions' are voiced by one member and followed by other members. At times, the groups were very supportive and required considerable activity on the therapist's part but *the major technique was the interpretation of the group process in a way that would facilitate the work of the patients.* In other words, the emphasis was on the patients' taking as active a role as possible in doing the group psychotherapy work themselves. The therapist's role was viewed as facilitative, that is, to help the patients deal with resistances or basic assumption behaviors which interfered with work group activity. The philosophy was that patients had a great deal to offer one another and, over time, as they had more and more experience in group therapy, they were able to provide considerable psychological help to one another. Patients were viewed as 'quasi-therapists' in their own right and it was felt that emphasizing patients' abilities to assist one another promoted self-esteem and growth. The groups were seen as a central part of the patient's treatment and were considered by them to be as useful as the individual therapy or the medication. This high value placed on the groups not only emphasized the importance to the patients, but also promoted staff growth through ongoing participation in group psychotherapy training of various kinds. The staff, hence, highly valued their role as group therapists.

Frequently in such groups the group process can become extremely intense due to the regressive pull generated where a number of the members may have poor ego strength and may have an increased tendency to utilize primitive defenses such as projective identification. The expectation was that the therapists would be able to determine these times and, by actively engaging in interpretive work, to help the patients work through and gain strength from such regressive experiences.

The patients

The group members ranged in age from 19 to 49. All were white and only one had been married. As mentioned earlier, most had been ill for three or more years, had a number of hospitalizations, and were in treatment in a partial hospital when they started in the group. Two patients entered the group from outpatient treatment. There were a total of 14 women treated in the group. At its inception the group had five members and at no time were there more than six members. Members stayed in the group from three months to seven years. Five members were in the group for four or more years. Diagnoses included three patients with borderline personality disorder with psychosis, two with major depression with psychotic features and eight with schizoaffective disorder. Two patients suffered from dissociative states and four had histories of substance abuse.

Criteria for membership

The group was designated officially as a group for women with chronic mental illness. We did not specify an age range, but as it worked out, we did not have members younger than 19. The age range was from the twenties through late fifties. Other treaters who had knowledge of the patients' individual treatment issues and believed this group would offer good opportunities for them referred most members.

Although it was not an absolute requirement, we recommended that members have an individual therapist as well as their group experience. We looked for women who would be able to participate in hearing other members' issues and were willing to discuss their own. We relied on the applicants themselves, as well as their other treaters, to assess their ability to focus and tolerate anxiety enough to participate in group process. Motivation was an important factor.

One constant dilemma was the issue of functionality and social presentation. Members could be exquisitely sensitive to someone who struggled with problems they themselves had overcome. They could also be easily threatened and put off by others who demonstrated the very problems they were addressing. How to help the members adequately manage this was an issue frequently discussed by the co-therapists and in supervision.

The two co-therapists met together with each candidate for three sessions prior to joining the group to provide them with information about the group and to discuss what they hoped to get from being a member of a group. Each potential member was asked to make a time commitment of at least six months to give the group sufficient opportunity to be effective.

The therapists

Early in the group's history, the therapists were all staff members or trainees in the partial hospital program. One therapist in particular, a staff nurse, was with the group from its inception to shortly before its demise. She had a series of student social workers and psychiatric residents working as co-therapists, each serving for a one-year period. To have students in such groups was not unusual for the setting but it was felt to be even more disruptive when the group stabilized and there were fewer shifts in membership. At that time, about three years after its inception, it was decided to have the co-therapist be a member of the institution's clinical staff and to omit trainee therapists. After that time two co-therapists were doctoral level clinical psychologists and one an experienced master's level social worker. The nurse and all the other staff co-therapists who were part of the group all had at least two years of training in group psychotherapy plus supervision. This included experiences in doing both inpatient and outpatient group psychotherapy.

Co-therapy issues

It was a frequent occurrence in this group for patients to be particularly attached to one therapist. Sometimes this was related to the fact that the patients had known one of the treaters in another role in the partial hospital. They tended to feel that this staff member was closer and more important to them than the other therapist who was viewed as an outsider. For example, there was one member who was frequently scapegoated. She had a hard time focusing, and she had difficulty containing her anxiety. Some of her behaviors were quite irritating to the other members. It was interesting that the individual therapist had more tolerance for these behaviors and worked valiantly with this member to improve her behavior so that she would be more accepted. The therapist from inside the system felt more aligned with the group members who had to 'put up with' these behaviors. In another instance, there was one member who enjoyed 'torturing' treaters with threats of self-destructive behaviors. The outside therapist had little tolerance for this, unlike the inside one who had worked with the individual for years and had been privileged to know another side of her.

One patient made telephone calls to a therapist's home as if trying to create a special relationship. She made it clear that she thought the other therapist was much less competent. This attempt to split the therapists into 'good' and 'bad' was apt to occur more often when one of the therapists was absent for several sessions.

Supervision

During group sessions, the therapists were under considerable pressure to comprehend what was going on and to offer meaningful interpretations. The therapists required support to do such work. This support was provided through regular supervision. The therapists met for one hour weekly supervision with the supervisor, who was a psychiatrist, psychoanalyst and a group psychotherapist with over 15 years' experience. The supervisor was a male, and this was not planned but a result of circumstances. Over a period of time, however, both the therapists and the supervisor recognized that there might be some value in having a male supervisor rather than a female one. They felt that the male supervisor helped them to see aspects of their behavior as women and of the patients as women that they might be 'blind' to simply because it was too close to their being women in the same culture. For example, the male therapist was repeatedly able to pick up situations in which he noted 'that must be more true with women than it is with men.' In other words, a female therapist felt that the male supervisor had a less 'prejudiced eye'. Of course, it could be said that the male therapist also saw things from a male perspective and missed many aspects of the women's behavior in the group. The supervisor also noted how much he felt he had learned about women that he had not known previously despite over 25 years experience in treating psychiatric patients. For instance, the supervisor became keenly aware of the extent to which chronically mentally ill women suffer from severe narcissistic devaluation of their bodies.

The supervisory sessions became a place where the therapists could receive the necessary support and understanding to enable them to withstand the pressures of such a group. Serious regressive behaviors in the group often made the therapists feel incompetent. At times in the group there were intense expressions of affect such as angry outbursts from one individual toward another. These outbursts needed to be tolerated by the therapist and handled in a respectful, cautious way so as not to disrupt the group process and at the same time to promote learning. At times all the intense affect came from one member of the group with the others silently sitting back and allowing this member to express all the anger for the group. The therapists needed to listen and to process these incidents and their reactions to them so as to be able to interpret any such group-as-a-whole behavior which they felt was taking place in the group. Frequently the therapists felt themselves to be extremely inadequate and deficient people and would state that they had never felt less able in any of their clinical professional work. It became clear that what were being experienced here were the projections of the patient's intense feelings of unworthiness and ineptness. The therapists seemed to have taken on all of these aspects of their patients and to feel intensely unable to help. Most of the time these feelings could be processed within the supervision, enabling the therapists to gain insight into what had occurred. They could then try to determine how to utilize their own feelings to interpret to the patients what they felt was occurring in the group. They recognized how overwhelmed and frightened they felt when they did not have a sense of what was going on. They could understand that this was multiplied several times over with the patients who did not have the cognitive data and knowledge to process what was occurring.

Frequently a parallel process occurred with the supervisor who would feel incompetent and begin to wonder if the therapy might not be harmful or inappropriate.

Early on in the supervision the two therapists, though very experienced clinicians, would sit and take notes of whatever the supervisor might say, as if his 'pearls of wisdom' would provide them with all the answers. When the supervisor asked them to think about why they were so rapidly taking notes they were initially put off and felt criticized. Then they began to examine their own feelings of incompetence and their need to view the supervisor as all-knowing which quite naturally paralleled the group members feeling incompetent and viewing the therapists as all-knowing. This understanding was a step toward the therapists being more comfortable in the group.

Such supervision was viewed as a central and vital part of the experience for the therapists. The therapists' discouragement and self-criticism would often change when they came to the supervision feeling delighted about a session in which they had understood the process and had been able to make effective interpretations. They would describe how the patients had come together in the session and were able to assist one another. These times produced feelings of considerable satisfaction in the therapist and the supervisor and a profound new respect for mentally ill female patients and what impressive work they could accomplish.

Major themes and issues

In the following sections, we present some of the major themes which occurred frequently in the group.

Transference and countertransference

The therapists were often seen as the parents who failed them, as the parents who could take away all their pain and suffering, but who would not do so – as the parents who knew everything, but chose not to share it. The therapists at times felt very withholding, totally incompetent, and often very sad about what they were not able to do in terms of 'rescuing' them from their pain.

One woman in the group had very controlling parents. One of her responses to this was to engage in a relationship with a man of whom her parents did not approve. They were devout Catholics; he was Jewish. Her attendance in the group became very erratic, most likely in part to avoid any perceived criticism about this relationship. Any effort on the part of the therapists to get her to look at her avoidance of the group was perceived as the parents trying to control her. Unfortunately, she had a treatment coordinator who was determined to be the 'good parent,' who would allow her to do as she pleased. She left the group without any sort of termination.

Additional transference and countertransference issues are discussed in the sections which follow, in the context of the recurrent group focal themes.

Helplessness and dependency

It was common in the group sessions to encounter strong dependency behaviors. One could say that the group operated almost entirely in a basic assumption dependency mode. This was not surprising since all of these women had been patients for some time and often felt very helpless in dealing with the problems of their illness and in negotiating various aspects of their lives. In the group they presented themselves as helpless and incompetent and conveyed to the therapists their tremendous sense of inadequacy and inability to problem-solve. Not only were they saying in their behavior that each of them needed help from the therapist but also, that they could offer no help to their peers. The therapists were frequently drawn into parental roles. Patients would attempt to get advice on any number of subjects including medication and health. These problems were often addressed to the nurse co-therapist who would try to avoid responding directly to them for two reasons. First, it was clear that they had other resources for such information. Further, since there was often great difficulty in redirecting patients to turn to each other, this was an opportunity to encourage them to take more active roles and to recognize their own expertise. As one might expect, advice-giving from member to member frequently occurred but was noted more particularly when a group was just beginning or when new members joined. Sometimes the advice-giving made sense and was useful to members, as when they discussed symptoms such as hallucinations or medication issues, matters about which they had considerable experience.

Most of the patients were dependent on their parents for their treatment costs as well as all living expenses. Some of the patients received social security disability incomes. Being dependent on their parents when most were in their thirties and older was a great source of shame. Being able to share this with the other members was quite useful.

Dependency issues would also manifest themselves in contacts with other treaters. Sometimes the patients would complain about the group to their treatment teams. These other treaters might go along with the patients and not talk with the group therapists about their concerns. There were times even when the other treaters pulled the patients out of the group saying the group was harmful to the patients. A particular treatment coordinator was appalled to learn that his patient had been involved in a verbal altercation during a group session. He thought the therapists were totally inept to allow such a process to occur. His patient had a rather 'nasty' streak and another member, who had great difficulty with any sort of confrontation, had had enough of it. There were no threats, no name-calling, just an intense argument, but this treater thought the therapists should not have permitted it. He encouraged her to quit the group which was most unfortunate. It was a lost opportunity for her to look at a part of herself which was offensive to others, and resulted in keeping her in a lonely place.

One young woman who was bent on rejecting her family's highly conditional offer of help – 'I want to make it on my own!' – was at the same time lonely and fearful, both determined and intimidated at the prospect of finding an affordable place to live and being alone and depressed. She was desperate for financial and psychological independence from her parents, but ran head-first into her own intense anxieties. Others were relatively non-plussed by the same issue; one stating 'My parents will probably be paying bills till the day they die.' Another, who was also directly challenged about being more independent became angry and pointed out that her reality was having to call her father to discuss plans and hope for his approval. A peer asked if this made her feel like a baby. While many of these women did have real financial problems, their economic concerns were very closely connected to their psychological problems and self-esteem.

Anger at parents for non-support was often displaced onto the hospital and its programs, especially as individual members confronted the discontinuing of public or family funds. The request to negotiate reduced fees within the group itself created much turmoil for all; at other times there were bitter complaints that the hospital only wanted their money ('they cut you off if you can't afford it!') and did not do enough to assist patients needing the transition out of treatment or to other forms of treatment.

The element of psychological dependency was a closely related issue. One young woman admitted that deciding even about the timing of her as-needed medications was a matter of self-confidence – 'I don't trust my own judgement.' This same woman was overwhelmed at the prospect of a part-time job at a shelter for women and children, in which 'taking care of babies and cooking would remind me too much of my own issues.' Though seeking company and solace, she had felt 'I shouldn't consume other people like food.' Others urged her to 'give (herself) a break,' however, affirming that it was all right to have needs. Such concerns also represented the larger issue of the capacity to take care of oneself, without heavy support from treaters. Peers in the group were often quite compassionate with each other in such situations, providing encouragement and practical suggestions, as if to reassure each other (and themselves) that their concerns were realistic and their goals legitimate and attainable. In this way, they demonstrated an ability to take care of each other. For one woman, the decision to leave the group was cast in terms of feeling 'ready to move on,' though it seemed more a flight from her own dependency longings.

Jobs and careers ('are we worth anything if we can't work?')

As stated earlier, many of these patients had college educations and some had careers and had actually functioned in professions before they developed symptoms of their mental illness which became so crippling that they could not return to these jobs. This was an enormous source of embarrassment to these bright women who could not use their intelligence and skills. Also, many were from families where achievements in education and professions were highly valued, and they were often the only family member who was mentally ill and unable to work. Many of the patients had to take jobs in much lower-level occupations. One woman, for example, worked as a janitress. This job seemed to match her low self-esteem more than her qualifications. In one group she wondered, in all seriousness, if she would be cleaning toilets in heaven!

For most of these women, having a job was a marker of success, independence and self-worth. Those who landed even part-time work were a model for others. One, who had held responsible jobs before her acute symptoms escalated, found a part-time job baking for a local restaurant, and described her growing repertoire of foods with some pride. Volunteer jobs, though a natural transitional step for many of these women, were viewed more ambivalently, as having less status ('where does it lead?'). One group member disclosed that her father had been disabled, as she was, although she said 'Lots of nervous people work'. Her embarrassment was such that she used to fabricate a story about him being an artist. She herself felt like 'a leech on social security.' The daughter of a wealthy family shared that neither of her parents ever worked and, though it was not exactly 'the Mafia,' there had been a prosecution for illegal activities. She herself struggled with feeling she could manage the stresses of virtually any job and feeling 'stuck' for ideas and threatened and overwhelmed at most things she considered. Even the successful 'baker' tearfully admitted that she couldn't have done the job if it had not offered flexible hours. She admired those who could work 9 to 5; 'they're the backbone of the country ... I can't do it.' Anxieties about being able to hold a job and the dilemma of working for the minimum wage *versus* relying on social security was a poignant topic, in that it was another dimension on which these women were always comparing themselves to others and coming up short.

Medications

All of the patients received some type of psychotropic medication. This included antipsychotics as well as antidepressants. Medication was a major source of conversation in the groups particularly early on since it was a 'safe' topic. Members shared their great difficulty in being compliant with medication when it caused serious and debilitating side effects. They could also be very supportive of one another in taking medication and reassuring each other that taking the medication was better than having another psychotic episode that required hospitalization. Patients shared their stories of the early days of their illnesses, their hospitalizations, their psychotic episodes. Often these were quite poignant stories. Members talked about medication problems related to menstrual and sexual functioning. This was very difficult material to share but it became clear that these side effects were often reasons for non-compliance. During the time the patients were in the group several members suffered from psychotic episodes requiring rehospitalization. Sometimes the members continued to attend the group while hospitalized. Occasionally members were noted to hallucinate in the group and to express delusional ideas. At times, they required therapists to intervene but at other times another member would be actively helpful.

Suicidal ideation and suicide attempts

It was not unusual for members to share details of previous suicide attempts which had occurred early on in their illnesses, and some of them recounted repeated episodes of being suicidal. This material was difficult for the therapists to hear. They would find themselves wishing the patients would change the subject. This may have been related to the therapists' resonating with several other members who also had difficulty listening to these stories. But, for some members, such recounting of histories was a way of coming together. Periodically, members would suffer from acute suicidal feelings which they would share in the group. The therapist then made every effort to clarify to what extent the members were suicidal and whether or not they should share this information with other treaters. Gradually the members with the most discomfort became more comfortable with such sharing and with that, the therapists also relaxed, realizing the feelings were daily concerns for many women with chronic mental illness. It was preferable for the patients to be able to talk about these feelings rather than keep them to themselves and remain fearful and at risk due to their own tendencies to self-harm.

Although the levels of functioning of these women was variable and diverse, all had had acute episodes of one kind or another and it was touching to see how much they could be of help to each other. Events and symptoms that would be daunting and secretive with less disturbed individuals were discussible, such as medication failures, auditory hallucinations, delusions, flashbacks, suicide attempts, sexual attractions, rageful feelings towards family members and fears of being unable to have loving relationships. These women shared, in a matter of fact way, their need for extra supports, hospitalizations and so on, and often showed considerable kindness and understanding towards each other.

Men and sex

The subject of relationships with men was, of course, a common theme, and many individuals talked about their boyfriends, husbands, and male relatives. One woman talked about her relationship with a man who was drug dependent and who encouraged her to smoke marijuana against her will. He was often abusive and demanding of her sexually. Though she recognized how harmful this man was to her well-being, she indicated that this was the only man she was able to attract, and sex, whenever he wanted it, was the only way she had to hold onto him. One member stated, on the contrary, 'to me, a boyfriend is just *work!* Why would you want it?' The group also contained a mix of sexual orientation, with at least two women acknowledging a homosexual preference. One, with great difficulty, finally expressed some sexual attraction to one of the therapists, who physically resembled someone else she had been attracted to. The other, while never citing an attraction to either therapist, spoke of another intimate friendship and was inclined frequently to telephone both therapists (as well as her female individual therapist) outside of treatment hours. Homosexuality and bisexuality were not topics these women easily discussed, however, and tended to be alluded to indirectly more often than cited clearly. To some extent, it appeared to be a version of the desire for closeness, intimacy and identification with admired figures or an ego-ideal. On occasion, however, it was possible to talk candidly about conflicts, aversion and spiritual dilemmas related to aspects of sexuality.

The attractive, younger members of the group also tended to elicit envy and unfavorable self-comparison by others, for whom appearance was tied to their feelings of self-worth. One woman, who was overweight and tended to 'hide' her appearance by never removing her coat during group meetings, about a year later (and well after the termination of one particularly beautiful young woman) began removing it and wearing clothes that were distinctly more feminine and colorful. The contrast was so striking, yet seemed so fragile, that the therapists chose not to mention the shift for fear of making the patient self-conscious again! This probably would have been a helpful observation further down the road, however.

Discussion about sex provoked dissociative episodes in one woman who had been sexually abused as a child. For her, the discussions were not helpful. When she was able to stay with the group and not dissociate, she found it exacted a toll on her. Eventually she decided that, although the group was beneficial in many respects, it was not worth the price. However, in many instances, such episodes were handled quite sensitively by the patients, who gently and supportively inquired of the dissociating individual about her mental state.

Issues related to men and sex often demonstrated a progression in individual members. When one woman, who was an avid reader of women's magazines, first joined the group, she took on the role of providing the group with helpful titbits gleaned from the magazines. For example, she informed the group that women who wear nylon hose and then rub their legs together at the level of the thighs while walking would make a noise which was a turn-on to men. She also admonished members not to spend too much time on the toilet because pressure from the toilet seat on the top of the thighs could eventually lead to varicose veins. But several years later, she was dealing with issues related to discipline problems in the children of a partner from a previous marriage. Recognizing that she was not the mother, but seeing some real problems, and wondering how she could intervene, was a sign that she had come a long way developmentally from the person who talked about how the sound of nylons attracted men.

Homicidal ideation

Homicidal rage was described by several members and one woman described her fury at an ex-husband for whom she had made sometimes outrageous sacrifices, who had once again gratuitously provoked her and whom she admitted she felt like shooting. Having expressed this anger, incipient psychotic thoughts were defused.

Low self-esteem

Low self-esteem was a major problem for all the members. This was primarily related to their serious and chronic mental illness but also to specific behaviors which occurred during the episodes of disturbance. This included the previously mentioned suicidal episodes and homicidal thoughts as well as severe guilt over sexual promiscuity, drug-taking and the inability to work with chronic dependency on their families. Over and over again members would tell of shameful and embarrassing experiences and their guilt over not being able to behave better or live differently. Often they presented themselves to the therapists as loathsome, disgusting creatures. The therapist had to take care to not overly sympathize with the patients. Instead they focused on defining the low self-esteem as a symptom and encouraged the members to interact with each other rather than to over-rely on the therapists.

Issues of worthlessness and devaluation were revived with each change in co-therapist, as patients often wondered why they were unable to keep a leader. One lower-functioning member attributed it to 'bad luck,' but several others felt that their treatment was devalued as a result of a string of co-therapists who had been in training or who had left for other jobs. Upon asking one of the incoming hospital therapists to tell something about her background, one member expressed relief and satisfaction that the therapist had been at the hospital for several years – 'Oh, good, so we're not at the bottom of the totem pole.'

The sense of being devalued surfaced occasionally as members themselves terminated and left the group. One woman left in favor of her other 'theme' group, stating more than once that 'you (peers) just weren't very helpful to me.' Another reacted with anger, saying she was offended; 'you can't be in a group that long and not get anything out of it!' Her anger disguised some sadness and anxiety, in that she had felt she was just getting to know her and it seemed she was 'jumping ship.' The impact of members leaving was always difficult, as the group both feared new members (being replaced 'for the sake of money') and shrinking into nothing. In the case of leaving for another group, however, the remaining members tended to feel like 'left-overs.' Being able to look at their anger and bruised sense of self had the paradoxical effect of increasing the group's cohesiveness, perhaps as both a negative bonding and an expression of a common identity.

Competition / envy / gifts

Competition in women's groups is often a very difficult issue to manage since many women have been raised to be non-competitive and to hide any feelings of competition. In the group competitive feelings manifested themselves around everything from education to boyfriends to clothing to school, to who was doing the best in treatment and who was doing the best in the group. Sometimes competition was about who was prettiest. For example, a young, attractive woman who was younger than all the other members in the group presented herself as very self-assured when she was admitted to the group. She questioned the group's worth and said the group had too many 'sick' members. One member had an intense reaction to her, viewing her as the young, pretty sorority girl that she remembered from her own college days and how inferior and ugly she always felt in relation to this other girl. She had an extremely difficult time after this new member arrived in the group and often put herself down or made derogatory remarks about herself. She also displayed a number of behaviors which made her look chronically mentally ill. She was forgetful, overly excitable and talked about some of her own 'crazy ideas'. This made the young pretty girl all the more uncomfortable and she began repeatedly to insist that this other member was far too sick to be in a group such as this. This became a difficult issue for the therapists since they felt they had to protect the sicker member who was becoming a scapegoat. It was as if she embodied all the mental illness of the members and the new person seemed to be saying, 'If she is out of this group, then we will have a group with no mental illness.' She actually said such things when that member was absent. It took a great effort to try to get her to look at her own fears about mental illness and her own concerns as to whether or not she was chronically mentally ill. For instance, she had not told the members about several episodes when she had made serious suicide attempts.

Competition arose also in relationship to the therapist as to who was the therapist's favorite, who was special, and so forth. For instance, some of the original members of the group seemed to resent new individuals coming in, as if they had to scramble to get enough from the therapists. Such rivalries could be very intense.

The silence of one of the more angry and withholding members of the group was a sort of competition, intended to draw attention to herself. This is the same woman who, feeling envious of a friend's new car, purchased the very same car – a sports model – though it was a highly indulgent use of her limited resources and she was uncertain whether support for her treatment would even be continued. It was also a very visible status symbol, which certainly impressed other members of the group and which probably drew the envy of others whom she herself had envied for other personal attributes. At the same time, she felt guilty about having something so nice, as if she didn't deserve it.

The gift of Christmas cookies by one of the women, which the therapists did not directly accept, elicited anger that what she had made was turned down and reinforced her complaints that the group was not as supportive (i.e. affirming and validating) as another 'theme' group to which she belonged. A peer challenged her that the other group sounded 'perfect' and that she herself would not like that kind of a group as it would seem 'phony' and untrustworthy. She was relieved to know that, in this group, there was no 'teacher's pet.' Another patient endorsed this, stating that she had learned a long time ago that, with respect to gifts to the therapist, that it was a professional relationship, 'not a debt, and you can't repay what you get from parents (i.e. therapists) and you don't have to!' She also admitted to feeling angry (and jealous), however, at the other member's gift of cookies, wondering how she could do it on the same disability budget she herself was on.

Envy manifested itself in the group mostly in terms of envy toward the therapist. The therapists were often idealized and viewed as women who 'made it.' The patients would wonder about the therapists' jobs, friends and families as if to say, 'you have it all and we have nothing.' This was often very difficult for the therapists to tolerate since they felt excessively idealized by some of the patients and would try to break out of the idealization by making a mistake or by making some self-deferential remark. Instead, the envy had to be interpreted.

The stigma of mental illness

One woman, feeling burdened by a friend who was in hospital, yet fearful of rejecting her because of the lack of other relationships, stated, 'I'm tired of just having patients for friends.' Forced to consider moving, she eschewed a halfway house – 'People in a halfway house are "mental patients",' an attitude challenged by another member who retorted, 'What's wrong with people in a halfway house? Those people are dealing with mental illness; there are lots of others out there who are sick and get no help.' Another member challenged, 'Just because they're on the outside doesn't mean they're healthy.' Yet another affirmed, 'People with mental illnesses have a certain strength they can call on.' In fact, one therapist felt well reminded about some of her own biases as she heard these women struggle with the biases of society.

Family relationships: at what price acceptance?

The families of most of these women generally lived at some geographical distance, yet the quality of relationship with them was often a focus of discussion. For one schizoaffective woman, her family's willingness to have her return to their home community was conditional upon avoiding contact with a homosexual relative, not joining a band (though she was intensely interested in music – 'it's my life!'), and having fewer boyfriends, to all of which she agreed for the sake of being able to return home. When another member indignantly challenged the parents' right to impose such conditions, the patient justified their position by acknowledging that she 'used to be pretty wild.' Another, formerly married woman and mother of two adult children who struggled with bipolar illness endorsed a seemingly common attitude among families, in that the only way for her to be accepted by her family was 'not to be ill' and to 'just get out there and do it!' In order to survive, she had to disengage and distance herself from her nuclear family members, none of whom admitted to their own mental disorders (father, like her, suffered from bipolar illness); as a result, she had not lived near her family for several decades. One attractive younger woman found it was the opposite for her – 'In my family, the only way to be accepted is to be sick.' Her wealthy parents refused her money for continuing treatment during the course of her participation in the group, asking her to leave treatment and live in her own apartment as a condition for financial support. Her brother typically turned to the parents for money when he needed help, but this young woman saw the cost of compliance as too high. The cost of refusal was also steep, in that she was both determined and terrified of finding a way to sustain herself separate from her parents. She pointed with sadness and outrage to the lack of feeling or 'soul' in parents who would deny her funds for continuing treatment, while moving into a luxury home and holidaying in luxury resorts. Quite touchingly, another member encouraged her to 'let go of the past,' that she could 'get to a place where you can decide you don't have to be ruined by your family.'

'The group-outside-of-group'

Several members of this group developed the habit of going out to eat together after the ending of group, citing the positive feelings of being with 'friends' and the growth in trust of the group. On occasion, one might join another at home to watch TV together. For some, money constrained the possibility of eating out, although this was not the only issue. One very attractive young woman who was an object of envy by others and who had struggled in the past with an eating disorder, objected vigorously to going out to eat, especially as others were trying to commiserate about her limited funds, stating 'I don't want to eat, I didn't sign up for this! I don't want to be in a group to eat.' She was, in fact, one of the few who thus defined the optimum attitude towards preserving the framework of the group, while others tended to seek a wider benefit of expanding social contacts. This dilemma also introduced the issue of whether there could be a minority opinion. Unspoken in the group was the issue of extra-group contacts (with each other or with therapists) as a vying or jockeying for position within the group.

Group as a reality-check

Either explicitly or implicitly, the women made use of the group as a reality check for their own perceptions and judgements, as well as guides in how to deal with specific problems. In fact, one schizoaffective woman whose capacity for insight was limited complained about the focus on 'group process' versus being able to bring problems, 'like what you do if you're mad at your mother – but all we do is talk about who's mad at whom (in here)!' Another group member, troubled by a friend who routinely took advantage of her, was helped to identify the substantive issues bearing on how mutual the relationship was and whether it was offering anything to her. A group member who had decided to terminate admitted that she was feeling frightened about leaving, afraid she might become increasingly isolated or paranoid without the group as an anchor point.

Food and nurturance

Food and eating seemed to be something of a metaphor for this group – the neediness of the members but also their ability to offer something to each other and the meanings of this. One member baked Halloween cookies for the group, another baked Christmas cookies, and all were attuned to whether or not the therapists accepted one. Another obtained a job at a restaurant, where her gradually increasing responsibilities, productivity and successfully selling baked goods were a source of pride for her and for the group on her behalf. She enthused, 'You've got to stop by and try my croissants!' One member, whose investment was in traditional female roles, admired this woman's competency and asked for recipes. The fact that the baker was also a relatively mature and even-tempered woman who had been married and had children seemed to cement her image for some as a maternal figure and, for some, a role model.

Anger

Patients struggled with accepting and expressing their own anger. These women tended to feel guilty about getting angry, such that full and genuine relationships were difficult for them. One group member felt that it should be okay to get angry in the group, while another asserted her fear and ambivalence by saying that 'Mental illness is not an excuse for acting out and getting rageful.'

This remark precipitated a dilemma for another patient who indeed struggled with borderline rage, and tearfully admitted to believing that she was damaging and destructive, afraid to get angry because it was not acceptable to let it go. Faced with this dilemma, she felt tortured and persecuted by the group, retreating into her usual victimized posture. Despite being reassured that the comments were not about her, she said, 'I feel that if I make one more mistake, the world will cave in!'

The search for a good object

Being able to talk openly with therapists about sexuality and sexual attractions to persons both inside and outside of the group was a liberating and reparative experience for these women, whose mothers had largely neglected or quashed their development of positive female sexuality. One shared her earlier anger and confusion about attractions to other women, never having been educated by her mother and believing, upon encountering her first menstrual period, that she was dying. Most of the women echoed the absence of feminine role models, receiving books or pamphlets as token efforts to inform them. The therapists, in their willingness to discuss sexuality openly and to acknowledge these attractions, became the 'good object' that these women were striving to internalize as they reflected on current and past experiences. One admitted giving up her virginity just to reassure herself that she was heterosexual; another – a devoutly religious woman – struggled with her attractions *vis-à-vis* the teachings of the Bible, but also admitted to having 'crushes.' She felt that a 'crush' is what happens when you're a young adolescent, surmising that she must be developmentally slow. 'They say you go through a normal stage in a family I had no male role models you have a kind of romance in the family with your father between three and six and then you get over it.' This was one instance of a woman with ambivalent and confusing feelings about women who were willing to give voice to difficult-to-discuss issues. At the end of this particular session, as the group was leaving, another member commented in a heartfelt way, 'I'm so glad you brought this up!'

The therapists often felt protective of these women, wanting to become the rescuers and good parents who could help to launch these women into independence in ways in which their own families had failed.

Case examples

In order to provide illustrations of how individual patients evolved within the group, case examples of three specific group members now follow.

Case example 1

C was a 45-year-old divorced mother of two young adult children who were out of the home when she was referred to this group. She had been discharged from a brief psychiatric hospitalization and was referred to this group because she had seemed to make good use of group treatment on the hospital unit. She had a history of childhood sexual abuse and had experienced episodes of dissociation throughout her adult life. She also became psychotic at times and unable to manage her job and her responsibilities at home. She had maintained employment for several years with the help of an understanding and supportive employer and a job description that allowed her to work quite independently within her workplace. She was involved in a dating relationship that had numerous ups and downs, but had been sustained over several years. This member had been in outpatient psychotherapy for several years. Emergence of memories of abuse, the loss of her outpatient therapy due to her therapist leaving, and the pending marriage of her daughter had precipitated the hospitalization just prior to referral to group. She described her reasons for joining the group as her wish to work on childhood issues related to abuse, and her need to receive support.

Initially this member was the only mother in the group and found herself at the center of intense interactions about mother–daughter relationships. She was able to acknowledge the fears, dilemmas, and uncertainties that she experienced as a mother, and by doing so, represented a maternal perspective that was very useful to other members. Her own confidence was enhanced by her recognition that she had something worthwhile to offer. Her open discussion of her mood fluctuation helped other members discuss their similar experiences and she often served as a catalyst for discussions about dealing with the stigma of mental illness. Dealing with conflict was very difficult for this woman and she found herself involved in a polarized position with another member on at least two separate occasions over the course of her four years in the group. Both times she was able to stay with the process long enough to appropriately express her position with the help and support of the group. It was clear that her own tendency was to simply avoid these discussions, but she allowed herself to respond to the group's encouragement to seek some kind of resolution. As time went by she developed the ability to represent herself in an assertive and appropriate manner to members who held an opinion different from her own. This woman used the group to explore questions of how to have a close relationship with another person and how much of oneself had to be given up in order to attempt that. The relationship with her boyfriend progressed to an engagement and eventually a marriage. She was able to discuss her experience of gradually developing enough trust in him to discuss her psychotic symptoms and finding that he continued to accept and care about her.

The group provided unavoidable opportunities to address her reaction to loss. After losing an individual therapist and two group co-therapists she addressed her sense of abandonment by treaters. She became the spokesperson for other members who had similar experiences and both provided and received support around this issue. The termination of other members from the group left her feeling rejected by them even though she could intellectually identify other reasons for their decisions to leave. She was often the member willing to initiate discussion of these topics and seemed surprised to learn how frequently others shared her experiences.

This member let the group know that she had memories of being abused as a child. She spoke in a limited way of how this has continued to influence her throughout her adult life. She indicated that she addressed this issue in her individual psychotherapy and frequently wondered if she should become involved in another group in the community, which was organized specifically for treatment of survivors of abuse. This member and others participated in viewing the community group as the one designated to deal with issues of sexual abuse. Efforts by the co-therapists to address the splitting involved in this designation were helpful in fostering discussions of trust in this group. Nevertheless, this member did not utilize this group as a place to work directly on her own abuse. She occasionally informed the group of her progress on these issues in her individual therapy.

This member decided to leave the group after some significant changes in her life. She married, and took a new job that resulted in scheduling conflicts with group sessions. She missed numerous sessions as she struggled with her ambivalence about what to do about membership in the group. She was clearly in the position of the senior member of the group by this time, and viewed by the other members as a success. Other members sought advice from her about how she managed so much progress and how she had learned to make use of the group. She spoke about the importance of allowing oneself to learn from shared experiences. She had difficulty accepting other members' statements about how important she had become to them and how much she was missed when she was absent.

Case example 2

B was a 30-year-old never-married participant in the partial hospitalization program when she began group psychotherapy. The group was part of her regular treatment program, but when it became an optional outpatient group, she chose to stay with it. She experienced delusional fears and psychotic episodes, and had difficulty maintaining social relationships. She was not involved in a dating relationship at the time, but had been in the past. Her parents lived in another state but maintained frequent contact with her and were involved in her treatment. She wanted their approval, but struggled with her ambivalence over her financial and emotional dependence on them.

This member was frequently the scapegoat and contributed to this process by exhibiting behaviors that provoked other members. She interrupted other members and redirected the discussion to her issues. She was preoccupied with delusional fears. Other members who had also experienced delusions attempted to reassure her or even to make links between her delusions and other events currently going on in her life. She was unable to make sense of the links and unable to sustain comfort from the reassurance. When she became uncomfortable with group discussion or interaction, her discomfort was demonstrated in very obvious ways. She would leave to go to the bathroom or frequently and pointedly look at the clock. When other members attempted to point out the social consequences of her behavior, or help her consider other options, she became quite defensive or simply announced that she could not change. The group's attempts to work with her ranged from very sensitive and gentle, to 'I've been there so I know what it's like,' to general frustration and anger.

There were times when this member demonstrated impressive strengths. When she could concentrate and follow discussions, she was able to comment on the group process with astute clarity and insight. On one occasion the group struggled to develop a plan of how they might confront an absent member in an appropriate manner. In the planning process, the others discounted this member's ability to be involved at all. When it was time to implement the plan, she was the one who initiated and led the process and did an excellent job. These examples were in contrast to her presentation most of the time, which was one of being so preoccupied with her own anxieties and delusions that is was difficult for her to follow a discussion.

In addition, this member seemed to become less able to function after a new member joined the group. The new member appeared to be socially skilled and articulate. She also struggled with some issues that were very similar to those of the senior members, although the outward manifestation looked quite different in each member's life. The new member was quite offended by and critical of the senior member's conduct, but her expression of this was not significantly different than that of other members. The senior member seemed to react more strongly to this new member. She indicated that she considered the new member to be very physically attractive and was intimidated by her.

This all occurred at a time when this member's treatment had to be cut back because of financial limitations. For various reasons, the decision was made that one of the elements of treatment to be discontinued would be her therapy group. She participated in a planned process of termination.

Case example 3

K joined this group at age 32 after a period of inpatient hospitalization followed by participation in the partial hospital program, which included living in a supervised halfway house. She attended individual psychotherapy on a regular basis. She had never married and had no children. She was socially withdrawn, often silent, and tended to mistrust the motivation of others who wanted to be her friend. This woman struggled with a pervasive sense of deprivation and anger. She was depressed, with mood-congruent psychosis. She had been employed in nursing prior to the onset of her depression. Her parents were divorced and she maintained contact with each of them, but they were geographically distant. She was emotionally distant from her siblings, who also lived in another state. Her treatment team initiated her referral to this group, and while she was skeptical, she was willing to make a commitment out of the hope that she could learn to improve her social relationships.

This woman experienced and expressed a wide range of emotions as anger rather than allowing herself to acknowledge the underlying affect. She was irritable and shared little personal information about herself. She was easily offended and became involved in conflicts with other members. Her anger became quite intense at times. The feedback she received from other members as a result of these interactions was painful for her to hear. She was invested in staying with the process and was gradually able to look at her own contributions to interactions with other individual members. She began to articulate her anger more appropriately, but moved into the position of spokesperson for the group's anger. Although this was addressed, the other members were generally willing to allow her to continue that role.

This member was frequently critical of the therapists for failing to be active and directive. She particularly felt the therapists should correct other members who demonstrated annoying behavior, missed sessions, or monopolized the time. As she gradually resigned herself to the realization that this would not happen, she started to call attention to these behaviors herself, usually in a very appropriate manner.

When it became clear that the financial support for her treatment would be terminated earlier than expected, this member began sharing more details about her life and on a few occasions became tearful and allowed herself to express the vulnerability she felt. She used the group very appropriately to consider her options and to discuss her fears. It was significant that she was able to express her feelings of loss related to leaving treatment in terms of sadness and vulnerability as well as anger and frustration.

Advantages of treating chronically mentally ill women in group psychotherapy

The group can be a safe place for members to discuss their shame about their illnesses and subsequent losses of hopes and dreams for the future which are unattainable due to the limitations brought about by their psychiatric difficulties. They may discuss openly their psychiatric symptoms, hospitalizations, and experience of bearing the stigma of mental illness.

Given the homogeneity of the group and the sense of long-standing struggles with self-esteem, identity, and a lack of a sense of belonging, members can help each other by empathically understanding each other, thus enhancing their own self-esteem. Women typically feel victimized by society, incomplete or defective because of their illness and inability to sustain intimate relationships and have children. The group can provide a comparative experience in a holding environment where other members share a similar plight. Group experience can help these women 'rise above' their psychiatric symptoms and express their womanhood. In a gender homogeneous group there is less need for woman to assume a passive, compliant position, *vis-à-vis* other group members, but, rather, take risks and opportunities in a safe situation to assert self-expression. The group provides the opportunity for members to explore their transference reactions to women therapists, which lead to insights about the relationship with their own mothers and friendships with women. The group members may use the therapist as a mentor and role model supporting their journey toward enhanced self-esteem and higher functioning. By the same token, for women therapists, groups provide opportunities to explore countertransference issues including beliefs about our own gender roles, dependency, expression of anger, and self-assertion.

The issues with which these chronically mentally ill patients struggle are universal to all women. Such issues include low self-esteem, femininity and sexuality, spirituality, appearance, competition and envy of other women, management of negative affect, gender role differences, the impact of their psychiatric illness on their sense of self, loss of hopes and dreams about their lives and futures, appearance, feelings of helplessness and dependency.

Given the heterogeneous nature of the group in terms of diagnosis, length and severity of illness, and level of functioning, these concerns and dilemmas can be explored in a variety of particularly meaningful ways.

Since at one time or another, each woman has negotiated her way from a more regressed level of functioning, the women who are better integrated and demonstrating higher ego-functioning can provide hope that a greater degree of well-being can be reached.

Thus, as noted in the introduction, these historically 'faceless, voiceless people' can begin to be heard.

Disadvantages of treating chronically mentally ill women in group psychotherapy

There is a caveat about the term 'disadvantages.' The traditional technique and strategies used in group psychotherapy for treating higher functioning patients can be modified by adding different parameters. Thus, disadvantages may in fact mean a challenge to find the appropriate modification that fits a particular group. This population requires greater tolerance and flexibility in order to participate in a group psychotherapy setting.

Since these women have been, in their experience, victimized and devalued in their relationships and by society, they understandably feel angry. At times expression of raw, primitive anger can be presented in verbally destructive ways in the absence of ego controls to help modulate the expression of anger that has accumulated and intensified over time. Left unchecked, this aggressive way of relating to the group can undermine group cohesiveness and the corrective emotional experience of the family. A group psychotherapy setting may be the first place and opportunity for a woman to express anger directly where it can become a learning experience. These attempts will initially be awkward since the containment of anger has long been a societal gender expectation. Therapist interventions are essential and critical to helping make this aspect of the group process a useful therapeutic experience.

The women may tend to be more action oriented and at times psychotic, which makes it difficult for them to sit through a group session. Pacing around the room, leaving the room for a time out from over-stimulation may be helpful to the individual but disruptive to the communication flow. However, group tolerance goes a long way in accepting these behaviors. Absenteeism may be greater with this population due to the more frequent need for crisis hospitalizations, however, encouraging attendance, even at times going to the hospital unit as a group is workable.

At times the therapist may underestimate group members' potential due to the long-term nature of their illness. Identification with their illness appears to be more a way to fulfill the yearning to belong and be part of a group. At times, however, there is a gradual identification process where they can experience themselves more as women willing to cope with problems we all face as human beings.

Periodically members would suffer from acute suicidal feelings which they would share in the group. The therapist then made every effort to clarify to what extent the members were suicidal and whether or not they should share this information with other treaters. Gradually the members with the discomfort became more comfortable with such sharing and with that, the therapists also relaxed, realizing the feelings were daily concerns for many women with chronic mental illness. It was preferable for the patients to be able to talk about these feelings rather than keep them to themselves and be fearful of their own tendencies to self-harm.

References

Alyn, J.H., and Becker, L.A. (1984) 'Feminist therapy with chronically and profoundly disturbed women.' *Journal of Counseling Psychology 31*, 2, 202–208.

Anderson, C. M., Holder, D. P. (1989) Women and serious mental disorders. In M. McGoldrick, C, Anderson, and F. Walsh. F. (eds) *Women in Families: A Framework for Family Therapy.* New York: Norton, Chapter 19.

Apfel, R., and Handel, M. (1993) 'Women with long-term mental illness: A different voice.' In S. Soreff *Handbook for the Treatment of the Seriously Mentally Ill.* Seattle: Hogrefe & Huber (1996).

Bachrach, L., and Nadelson, C.C. (1988). 'Chronically mentally ill women: An overview of service delivery issues.' In L.L. Bachrach and C.C. Nadelson (eds) *Treating Chronically Mentally Ill Women.* Washington DC: American Psychiatric Press, Inc.

Bernardez, T. (1996) 'Women's therapy groups as the treatment of choice.' In B. DeChant *Women and Group Psychotherapy.* New York: Guilford.

Brodsky, A.M. (1973) 'The Consciousness-raising group as a model for therapy with women.' *Psychotherapy: Theory, Research and Practice 10*, 1, 24–29.

Brody, C. M. (ed) 1987. *Women's Therapy Groups: Paradigms of Feminist Treatment.* New York: Springer.

Broverman (1970) 'Study on sexual stereotypes and clinical judgments in mental health.' *Journal of Consulting and Clinical Psychology 34*, 1, 1–7.

Campbell, A. (1989) 'Women's group therapy: a clinical experience. *Perspectives in Psychiatric Care 25*, 1, 10–14.

Eastwood, J., Spielvogel, A., and Wile, Joanne (1990) 'Countertransference risks when women treat women.' *Clinical Social Work Journal 18*, 3, 273–280.

Hauser, P., and Seeman, M.V. (1985) 'Schizophrenia in males vs. females.' *Medical Aspects of Human Sexuality 19*, 109–119.

Horwitz, L. (1977) 'A group-centered approach to group psychotherapy.' *International Journal of Group Psychotherapy 27*, 423–439.

Kanas, N. (1996) *Group Therapy for Schizophrenic Patients.* Washington, DC: American Psychiatric Press.

Lamb, H.R. (ed) (1984) *The Homeless Mentally Ill.* Washington, DC: American Psychiatric Association.

Lieberman, M.A., Solow, N., Bond, G.R., Riebstein, J. (1979) 'The psychotherapeutic impact of women's consciousness-raising groups.' *Archives of General Psychiatry 36*, 161–168.

Lenehan, G.P., McInnes, B.N., O'Donnell, D., et al. (1985) 'A nurses' clinic for the homeless.' *American Journal of Nursing*, 85, 11, 1237–1240.

McGerigle, P., Lauriat, A.S. (1983) *More than Shelter: A Community Response to Homeless.* Boston: United Planning Corporation and Massachusetts Association for Mental Health.

Ritsher, J.E., Coursey, R.D., Farrell, E.W. (1997) 'A survey on issues in the lives of women with severe mental illness.' *Psychiatric Services 48*, 10, 1273–1282.

Seeman, M.V. (1988) 'Toward mastery of psychotic symptoms: a group phenomenon.' *Canadian Journal of Psychiatry 33*, 702–704.

Stone, W. (1996) *Group Psychotherapy for People with Chronic Mental Illness.* New York: Guilford Press.

Test, M.A., and Berlin, S.B. (1981) 'Issues of special concern to chronically mentally ill women.' *Professional Psychology 12*, 1, 136–145.

CHAPTER 11

Clinical Interventions in Group Psychotherapy

Raman Kapur

Introduction

Clinical interventions in group psychotherapy[1] are primarily influenced by theoretical preference, clinical training, clinical experience, and the personality of the psychotherapist conducting the group. The group psychotherapist will bring together his own particular style of conducting the group depending on these factors. Individual and group psychotherapists demonstrate a dedication and a commitment to using their own personal subjective experiences to help their patients which is borne out of their own experience of being a patient in a group or in individual therapy along with their own supervision and clinical work. Theoretical preferences bring all of this together to help formulate treatment interventions. While this presents a strong argument to allow clinical psychotherapists to practice their own particular style of psychotherapy it does not incorporate the idea of selecting therapeutic interventions according to their empirically proven effectiveness. Potentially, this could create many situations where patients are receiving ineffective interventions because of the personal bias of the clinician.

The hermeneutic defence of psychoanalysis claims that any interference with complex intersubjective processes would damage therapeutic work (Strenger 1991). This argument, widely supported within analytic psychotherapy, claims to protect the complexity of the psychotherapy relationship from the 'Occam's razor' of empirical research (Elliott and Anderson 1994). Psychotherapists will often state that these processes cannot be measured or that any 'extra-therapeutic intervention' (e.g. collecting questionnaires, tape recording sessions) would

---

1   I will use the term group psychotherapy to include group analysis.

interfere with the therapeutic process. In the United Kingdom,[2] this argument is still very strong with most individual and group psychotherapy research occurring in the United States and Canada (Bergin and Garfield 1994; Miller *et al*. 1993; Roth and Fonagy 1996). However, in the United Kingdom, this approach is no longer proving acceptable. The drive towards evidence based medicine in health and social care now places demands on all clinicians to gather evidence to justify their interventions. In the public sector, psychotherapists are now actively considering different methodologies to measure process and outcome. This is a welcome move, although it seems forced more out of anxieties of survival rather than adopted from the empirical argument of trying to find out what interventions are most effective. Nevertheless, the trend towards outcome-guided interventions is now gathering momentum and is particularly relevant for working with psychotic patients in groups.

The research on investigating process and outcome in groups with psychotic patients is sparse compared to the individual and group psychotherapy research literature with neurotic patients (see for example Bergin and Garfield 1994). These groups are more difficult to conduct and often have a short therapeutic life span because of drop-outs. Also, psychotic patients are often more reluctant to complete questionnaires and allow recording of sessions than neurotic patients. Clinically, psychotic patients present greater difficulties than neurotic patients, whereby most interventions are aimed at containing and holding huge amounts of paranoid disturbance. All these factors lead to a paucity of clinical and research work in an area of psychiatry that is often in most need of group interventions to offer more comprehensive treatments to vulnerable and severely mentally ill patients.

What follows is an overview of the research that has taken place in groups with psychotic patients. In reviewing this literature, I have selected papers which give group therapists some guidance on their clinical interventions. This will meet the demand of many psychotherapists (Morrow-Bradley and Elliott 1986) that research should be clinically relevant rather than providing findings that are of little use outside a controlled experimental setting. To guide this review I will use Strupp's (1973) differentiation between specific and non-specific interventions. This will help the group therapist to intervene either with a specific focus or to attend to more general group processes (see Table 11.1).

2   Specifically, England, Wales, Scotland and Northern Ireland.

Table 11.1 Summary of findings from research studies on group psychotherapy with psychotic patients.

Specific interventions

Study findings

Karterud (1989): Positive effects of interpretations with severely mentally ill patients.

Kapur (1993): Poor response to transference interpretations.

Non-specific interventions

Kapur (1986/1988), Pappas *et al.* (1997): Therapeutic factor of Cohesiveness is most helpful.

Profita (1989): Continuity, stability and reliability are important.

Green and Cole (1991): Psychotic patients prefer task-focused groups; borderline patients prefer unstructured groups.

Opalic (1989): Existential variables indicate positive effects.

Opalic (1990): Describes a qualitative view of stages of group development.

Legevre (1994): Highlights countertransference reactions of group facilitators.

Specific interventions

Karterud (1989) explores the effect of therapeutic styles with patients suffering from mainly psychotic disorders in an inpatient setting. Karterud asks the question whether therapists contribute to a favourable or negative interpersonal environment in their work with small groups. He identifies the main therapeutic techniques as prompting interaction, clarification, confrontation, interpretation, giving advice and suggestions, technical neutrality and managing boundary issues. In reviewing these therapeutic interventions, he highlights the negative effects of aggressive confrontation with the patient (Leibermann, Yalom and Miles 1963). Karterud (1989) explored the effects of these therapeutic techniques across three different therapeutic community settings. Therapeutic Community Setting 1 was a traditional psychiatric ward which had a long tradition of therapeutic community work within the overall hospital setting. Overall, 46 per cent of these patients suffered from a psychotic disorder with the remaining percentage diagnosed as suffering from personality disorders, neurosis and alcohol abuse respectively. This group will be referred to as TC-1. Two other therapeutic communities existed outside of the traditional psychiatric setting.

Therapeutic Community Setting 2 (referred to as TC-2) had a lower percentage of psychotic patients in its unit (27%), with neurotic disorders comprising (45%). In contrast, the third Therapeutic Community Setting (TC-3) had the highest percentage of psychotic patients (58%) with the remaining percentage of patients suffering from personality disorders (42%).

Within TC-1, TC-2 and TC-3, all patients were randomly assigned to small therapy groups. Group attendance was compulsory unless seriously disturbed behaviour occurred due to florid psychosis. The small group meetings lasted for 45 minutes, with a frequency of 3–5 times a week. The group therapists conducting these groups were a mixture of neophyte and experienced group therapists.

Karterud (1989) used a group process instrument to explore interactions within these groups and their relationship to leadership style or technique. The Group Emotionality Rating Scale (GERS) originally devised by Thelan (1954) was refined by Karterud to apply this process measure to studying small therapy groups. The GERS is based on the theoretical framework of Wilfred Bion of dependency, fight/flight and pairing basic assumptions. Karterud (1988) developed a rating scale to measure these basic assumptions in groups. For this particular study, he reports an inter-rater agreement between two independent judges on 4,343 verbal statements as 0.77 (Pearsons Correlation Coefficient) on the basic assumption variable used in his research of fight/flight.

The results of applying the GERS instruments to the three therapeutic communities revealed that TC-2 exhibited less fight and flight behaviour (4.5%) than TC-1 (10.9%) and TC-3 (5.8%). These findings were confirmed by the clinical observations of Karterud where he describes therapists in the small groups in TC-2 adopting a calm, friendly, supportive and mildly interpretative stance. However, TC-1 is described as confrontational and focused on one or more therapists speaking directly and individually to group members; what Karterud calls 'turn-taking'. Similarly, TC-3 was characterized by 'turn-taking' through a milder confrontational approach.

Overall, the study found that the therapists who were in the fight/flight groups, particularly in TC-1 deviated significantly from the recommended therapeutic techniques of 'sticking to the primary task of a psychological exploration of the here-and-now, favouring patient interaction and taking a supportive, empathic and non-aggressive attitude' (Karterud, 1989, p. 14 in paper 5).

In particular, the small groups in TC-1 were especially confrontative in their approach with patients. The group therapists in TC-3 were less confrontative though also less skilful than the therapists in TC-1. Reviewing the findings of his study, Karterud suggests that perhaps the severe nature of the mental illness or psychopathology within TC-1 and TC-3 led to group therapists abandoning their usual, less confrontative techniques with these patients. Karterud seems to use the fight/flight variable as the main indicator of dysfunction and fails to take adequate account of the particular interventions of each group leader.

However the data for the other basic assumption phenomena of dependency and pairing also support his conclusion that the basic assumption functioning is less in TC-2 than the others though TC-3 has a similar pairing score to TC-2. Karterud (1989) does not explain why he chooses fight/flight as the main predictor variable of group dysfunctions. As noted above and as pointed out by Karterud, he made no attempt to systematically record and analyse the interventions made by the therapist; these were made through his own clinical observations of the video recording of the groups. Consequently, it is difficult to suggest any empirical link between negative therapeutic interventions and dysfunctional group processes as defined by Bion's (1961) concept of group functioning.

Despite the above reservations, there may be some evidence from this study to suggest that non-empathic, directive and less immediate group therapist interventions correlates with poor patient responsiveness. Unfortunately, Karterud does not operationally define his intervention specifically as either supportive or interpretative and thus the above elements of a therapeutic intervention may apply if the group therapist is being either supportive or interpretative. In conclusion, this single group psychoanalytic psychotherapy process research study in the literature reporting work with severely mentally ill patients, suggests that to elicit good patient responsiveness and/or group functioning with patients suffering from severe mental illness, the therapist should be empathic, immediate and supportive in his intervention.

In my own research looking at specific interventions, an investigation was made into the effects of group interpretations with severely mentally ill patients (Kapur 1993). Clinically, my interest focused on the anecdotal, but common experience reported by group psychotherapists that their best efforts to offer interpretations to severely mentally ill patients were often defeated. Here, I adopt a general definition of interpretation and refer to a verbal utterance from the therapist aimed at conveying the meaning of the communication to the group of patients by the therapists. This interpretative style focuses on the immediacy of the group relationship where the therapist is putting into words the affective atmosphere of the group.

This research reports findings from conducting inpatient psychotherapy groups in acute psychiatric settings. The theoretical orientation of the interpretative interventions relies on contemporary Kleinian and post-Kleinian psychoanalysis and particularly on the work of Wilfred Bion (1959, 1962). The concept of interpretation was subdivided into several elements which were derived from the clinical and research psychoanalytic literature and clinical experience. Hypotheses were then generated from these seven independent variables in their suggested effect on the dependent variable of patient responsiveness which was defined as the interest shown by the patient in exploring further the interpretation offered by the therapist. This definition was taken from the clinical observations of Wolman (1960), Battegay (1965), Alikakos (1965) and Resnik (1985) who all report negative responses from patients to the interpretations. The seven elements of interpretations are as follows:

- *Accuracy.* This refers to the agreement between the content of the material provided to the therapist and the meaning offered by the therapist.

- *Transference.* This reflects the degree to which the therapist makes links between what the patients have spoken about in the group and himself/herself.

- *Bridge-Making.* This reflects the extent to which a comment serves as a 'bridge' between the clinical material reported in the group and the meaning inferred.

- *Clarity.* This dimension refers to the clearness with which the interpretation has been offered.

- *Group focus.* This refers to the extent to which the interpretation addresses the 'group-as-a-whole'.

- *Immediacy.* This dimension refers to the degree to which the interpretation addresses the immediate affect of the group.

- *Empathic.* This refers to the extent to which interpretations understand the state of mind of the group or individual patient.

The hypotheses suggested that three of the seven elements of interpretation will elicit a negative response from the group, namely, accuracy, transference and immediacy. The therapist 'bridging', speaking clearly ('clarity') and speaking to the group-as-a-whole ('group focus') would elicit a good response. For the other element, empathy, the hypothesis predicted that the patient would respond moderately.

As stated earlier the research was collected in acute inpatient settings. The following intra-class correlations[3] were achieved for the above variables; accuracy 0.35, transference 0.67, bridge-making 0.37, clarity 0.72, group focus 0.75, immediacy 0.4, empathy 0.15 and patient responsiveness 0.48. A partial correlation analysis removing between group differences for the 13 studied

3   Intra-class correlations provide one of the most reliable indices of the degree of agreement between judges (Shrout and Fleiss 1979).

groups revealed that four of the independent variables were significantly correlated with patient responsiveness, namely, accuracy, transference, clarity and empathy. The low reliabilities achieved for empathy and accuracy lessens the strength of this associative relationship. Semi-partial or part-correlations between each of the independent variables and patient responsiveness with the influence of the other variables being removed from the one correlated, offering a correlated value of pure variance between each of the independent variables and dependent variables, revealed that only transference significantly predicted patient responsiveness with a semi-partial correlation of -0.167. In other words, high transference-orientated interpretations are slightly associated with low patient responsiveness, and vice versa.

Clinically, this may be an interesting finding for group therapists conducting groups with severely mentally ill patients. Put simply, when speaking about the transference relationships patients may respond poorly. This may indicate that this is not an appropriate intervention for such patients or, from a Kleinain theoretical perspective, it may indicate that the psychotic personality of the patient is opposed to exploring or developing any relationship with the group therapist. These links are proposed to be essential for mental and emotional growth (Bion 1967; Grinberg *et al.* 1975). While this research finding offers some data which supports the phenomenon of 'attacks on linking' (Bion 1959) it may be that this negative relationship may change over time.

Non-specific interventions

Profita *et al.* (1989) adopted a multimodal outpatient group therapy approach to their treatment of chronic psychotic patients. Medication was used to treat anxiety, depression or psychosis so that patients were more able to participate fully in the psychodynamic group. Profita *et al.* do not indicate the theoretical basis for their interventions which seem to combine structured and unstructured group sessions. They used the first and last 5–10 minutes of each session for announcement and opening and closing the group and then, 'each group session had a 10–15 minute free association period in which patients were encouraged to discuss any issues of concern or relevance' (p. 942) During this period, the therapists maintained relative silence. Themes and common concerns become evident through verbalizations, behaviour and non-behaviour and non-verbal cues. The themes and concerns served as topics for the therapists' intervention and interpretation and promoted additional group participation and group processing. It seems that they used a combination of interpretative and interpersonal styles of intervention for their psychodynamic groups.

The subjects in the study had been patients at the Veterans Administration Medical Centre for 5–15 years. These patients showed high rates of relapse and rehospitalization. The criteria for participation in the programme were:

motivation to attend the groups, the capacity to apply to the programmes rules and regulations and a formal contract to attend meetings every two weeks for a minimum of six months. Twelve patients were involved in the study with an age range of between 42 and 74 with an average age of 60 years; eleven patients were male. The patients suffered from a wide range of psychotic disorders from chronic schizophrenia to psychotic depression. All of the subjects had been severely ill just before their admission to the group.

Profita *et al.* assessed outcome through their own objective and subjective measures of change. Patterns of relapse and rehospitalization were clear objective measures of any changes that had taken place. Four of the 12 patients had no psychiatric hospitalizations during the five years before entering the group; the other 8 patients had required hospitalization at an average of 1 admission every 2–9 years prior to the group. All 12 patients did not require hospitalization while participating in the group therapy. A chi square analysis showed a significant difference in pre- and post-group hospitalisations for those 8 patients who had previously been in hospital. These group therapists made subjective judgements about each of these patients' level of functioning through the capacity to comply with treatment recommendations over an extended period and by the acquisition of independent living skills.

In evaluating the effectiveness of these groups, Profita *et al.* place considerable importance on the continuity of having the same group therapist conduct the sessions. They also place importance on adopting an interactive psychodynamic approach which was employed in conjunction with traditional pharmacological treatments. They ascribe the success of these groups to these three important variables, namely, continuity of the therapist, an interactive approach and appropriate interventions during therapy.

While Profita *et al.* describe a useful and effective group therapy approach to working with psychotic patients, they do not systematically explore the relationship between process and outcome; in other words they do not make any empirical analysis between the independent and dependent variables. This lack of empirical rigour makes it difficult to support their conclusions. For example, it may be that the main effect was drug therapy alone, rather than in combination with group therapy. While this is unlikely, the lack of control of any of the many independent variables prevents any confident conclusions. The study does provide some limited evidence that a group therapy intervention when combined with medication could have significant positive benefits for chronic psychotic patients in preventing hospitalization.

There has been considerable research into the presence of therapeutic factors in psychotherapy groups (see for example Bloch and Crouch 1985). Research carried out with inpatient groups working with severely mentally ill patients reveal some consistency in those factors that are perceived to be most helpful by

288 GROUP PSYCHOTHERAPY OF THE PSYCHOSES

patients. Klein, (1977), Waxer (1977), Cory and Page (1978), Budmann (1981), Betcher (1983), Marcovitz and Smith (1983), Yalom (1983), Leszcz *et al.* (1985), Brabender (1985), Pekala *et al.* (1985) along with my own research, Kapur *et al.* (1986), Kapur *et al.* (1988) and the recent research by Pappas *et al.* (1997) suggest that the therapeutic factors of cohesiveness, universality and learning from interpersonal actions are the most important therapeutic factors. I will briefly describe my own previous research in this area along with a description of the therapeutic factor that appears to be most favourably perceived by patients and thus would require specific interventions from group therapists.

The research presented by Kapur *et al.*, 1988, compared the therapeutic factors operative in inpatient and outpatient psychotherapy groups. inpatient subjects consisted of 22 patients who had an inpatient group experience who attended three or more group sessions. Most inpatients suffered from an affective disorder (64%) with a small percentage exhibiting a psychotic state (13.5%); other diagnostic categories were anorexia (4.4%), personality disorder (9%), and alcohol dependence (9%). In the final inpatient sample, 64 per cent were female and 36 per cent were male. The outpatient sample consisted of 25 patients who had been primarily referred for long-term group psychotherapy. Most of them suffered from either an anxiety state (20%) or an affective condition (56%). The male/female ratio was similar to that of the inpatient sample.

The inpatient groups followed closely the format of the higher-level inpatient group devised by Yalom (1985). This involved focusing on interpersonal feedback concerning here-and-now behaviour. A clinical description of this type of group is outlined in Kapur *et al.* (1986). The therapeutic work was discontinuous between sessions with the focus of activity being within the time frame of the setting. The outpatient group followed the model described by Yalom (1975) which highlights interpersonal processes and psychogenetic insight. Data were collected from three long-term psychotherapy groups which met once-weekly on average for two years.

The instrument to measure therapeutic factors was adopted from Yalom's therapeutic factor questionnaire. This contained 60 items, 5 describing each of the 12 items where patients were asked to rank each item from the most helpful to the least. The therapeutic factors are as follows:

1. *Altruism:* The patient feeling better through the help extended to others in the group.

2. *Cohesiveness:* A feeling of togetherness/acceptance with other group members.

3. *Universality:* The feeling of being in the 'same boat' as other group members.

4. *Interpersonal learning:* (input) Others sharing perceptions of each other.

5. *Interpersonal learning*: (output) An opportunity for 'interpersonal experimentation'.

6. *Guidance*: Imparting information or giving advice to others.

7. *Catharsis*: Ventilation, the release of strong feelings in the group.

8. *Identification*: Modelling oneself on others, including the group therapist.

9. *Family re-enactment*: The repeat of the original family experience in the group.

10. *Self-Understanding*: Psychogenetic insight, where the patient learns about the mechanisms underlying behaviour and its origin.

11. *Instillation of hope*: Perceives that others are improving, therefore optimistic.

12. *Existential*: Taking personal responsibility for actions.

A Mann-Whitney U test compared the differences in rankings between the two samples and found a statistically significant difference for seven of the 12 factors, namely, altruism, cohesiveness, interpersonal learning (output), guidance, family re-enactment, self-understanding and the existential factor, indicating potential differences in therapeutic processes between inpatient and outpatient groups.

For the inpatient groups, these patients valued cohesiveness, altruism, existential factors and interpersonal learning (output) highly. In other words, the feeling of being accepted, helping others, considering issues of personal responsibility and solitude while in a life crisis along with learning from the feedback of others were particularly valued. The first of these findings has recently been strongly supported by Pappas *et al.* (1997).

From all of the research into therapeutic factors in groups of severely mentally ill patients the factor of cohesiveness emerges most strongly as the one most valued by patients. Yalom (1975) has pointed to its positive correlation with successful outcome. It does seem that the feeling of being accepted and supported by others is an important factor when working with patients who have been significantly impaired by mental illness. In this state patients often report that 'their mind is in pieces', 'no one really cares' and 'they feel close to no one'. Through the therapist actively intervening to promote cohesiveness in the group the patient does seem to feel less isolated and marginalized and thus more accepted. This could be achieved by the group therapist actively involving all group members and ensuring they are included in the group process.

One of the most difficult and controversial issues facing the group therapist conducting a group of psychotic patients is whether to adopt a structured approach to minimize the psychotic anxieties of patient (Yalom 1983) or to allow such anxieties to emerge whereby patients can introject more positive experiences and so negate the primitive internal object relations which so quickly manifest with such disturbed states of mind (Kernberg 1976). There are many clinical arguments for and against unstructured and structured approaches. In a nutshell, the argument focuses on whether therapists are exposing patients to unnecessary frustration and pain by not directing events or whether the eruption of primitive anxieties within such groups has a detoxification (Bion 1962) and 'evaporation' effect whereby patients are relieved of the burden of carrying such intensive emotions. Greene and Cole (1991) explore this question by investigating the effects of structured and unstructured groups with groups of severely mentally ill patients. Using their own theoretical ideas (Greene 1982, 1983) along with the work of Kernberg (1976) they point to the powerful primitive affects which take over the state of mind of disturbed patients leading to a wish to fuse self–other boundaries. The central question addressed in this research centres on the clinically held belief by many therapists that greater structure is necessary with primitively regressed patients; this is neatly summarized as follows:

> One core notion shared by these diverse traditions is that of an inverse relationship between the degree of structuring of a group and its participants' regressive functioning. In essence, the less clearly differentiated the rational work roles in the group and the less explicit and detailed the values are for governing interactions, the more likely that the group process will manifest developmentally archaic phenomena in several interrelated domains: a shift in object relations from whole to part objects and a reemergence of need gratification as the primary basis for relationships, an intensification and primitivisation of drive and affect expression, a distilling in cognitive capacities, and a revision of projective and introjective mechanisms as primary defenses. (Greene and Cole 1991, p.500)

These researchers explored two specific hypotheses around the question of structured groups for more regressed patients. First, they suggested that patients with a borderline level of psychopathology would show favourable self-assessments in comparatively unstructured therapy groups while psychotic patients would respond more favourably in groups with a more explicit internal organization. Second, they posited that borderline patients would be more sensitive than psychotic patients to variations in social structure, given their greater contact with social reality.

There were 51 patients in this naturalistic study who were inpatient in an intermediate-term psychiatric ward of a Veterans Administration medical centre. The age range was from 22 to 69, most patients were female and all had extensive previous psychiatric treatment including an average of three prior hospitalizations. Classifications on the level and form of psychopathology was made independently by both authors in reviewing current clinical records in terms of psychotic vs borderline organization and anaclitic vs introjective, respectively. The psychotherapy groups were co-led by psychiatry residents along with psychology social work trainees and were conducted with a minimum of structure as suggested by Rice and Rutan (1987). In comparison, the task-orientated groups were conducted by pairs of occupational therapy students and were much more internally organized. These differences in the structure of group were validated by both authors throughout the period of the study.

To measure the effects of the different structure to these groups the authors constructed a semantic differential of six items (Osgood *et al.* 1957) which measured validated factors of evaluation ('good–bad', 'valuable–worthless'), potency ('strong–weak', 'heavy–light'), and activity ('active–passive', 'fast–slow'). These were used to assess patients' reactions to themselves as participants in each group, each group-as-a-whole and co-therapists of each group. The study used a repeated measures design where nine groupings of six to eight patients participated concurrently in group psychotherapy and task-orientated groups. These researchers carried out three way (level x form of pathology x group structure) repeated measures analyses of covariance on the patient's ratings of self-evaluation potency and activity. Further analyses of covariance were also applied to explore other relationships between the measured variables. Inter-rater reliabilites for level and form of pathology based on independent classifications revealed a Cohen's Kappa of 0.84.

The findings of their study broadly supported their clinical hypotheses. On the evaluation using the semantic differential patients evaluated themselves less favourably than their evaluation of the groups-as-a-whole. The devaluation of self was greater in the task groups. This would be consistent with clinical theory that points to narcissistic injuries and attacks on self-esteem as a feature of psychiatric patients (Kohut 1977). The evaluation data supported the hypotheses which predicted that psychotics tend to hold a more positive view of self than borderline patients in task groups while in psychotherapy groups borderlines had a higher self-regard. Borderline patients also showed greater differential reactions from both groups. Greene and Cole (1991) offer an explanation for this; they suggest that psychotic patients are so disconnected from reality that they would be insensitive to any variations in group structure, though they would welcome structuring of group sessions which would give some organisation to their internal chaos. They also suggest borderlines favour unstructured groups as it offers an opportunity to develop basic assumption primitive functioning (Karterud 1988) which are emotionally laden rather than the routinized, mundane task-orientated group which fail to produce these opportunities. These researchers note the effect of levels of psychopathology and the structuring of inpatient groups. They suggest that the nature of the pathology of the patient does have an interactive effect with the structure of the group though this interaction is not straightforward; other variables within the setting have an effect on how the patient reacts to the group eg. content of the groups. While overall trends are found in how borderlines and psychotics responded to different group structures, variations within each psychopathology (e.g. anaclitic borderlines) are also found.

In conclusion, this study confirmed the generally accepted clinical view that psychotic patients prefer structured groups with borderline patients expressing their preference for unstructured groups. The complexity of interaction with other variables such as the content of the groups and different types of pathology is noted. While Greene and Cole (1991) speculate on the theoretical constructs which explain these findings they do not consider the alternative hypotheses of psychotics exhibiting a negative therapeutic reaction to unstructured groups (Rosenfeld 1987) which, if they work through, could lead to the internalization of psychic structures from the therapist that can lead to positive change. Clinically, in inpatient settings it is appropriate to follow clinical wisdom and these research findings which suggest that structured group activity is the effective model of group intervention. However, in long-term group psychotherapy with psychotic patients the research question has still to be answered as to whether the containment of such psychic chaos could lead to a successful therapeutic outcome.

Opalic (1989) investigated the effects of group psychotherapy with neurotic and psychotic patients using instruments from general psychopathological and existential frameworks. He studied 100 patients who were divided equally into control and experimental groups. The experimental group were given small group therapy while the control group only had psychiatric checkups. Three main research instruments were used reflecting the above two theoretical frameworks. As with Green and Cole's (1991) research, Opalic (1989) adopted the semantic differential test to measure experimental changes along the dimensions of evaluation, activity and potency. Twenty concepts covered these three dimensions with the greatest number, twelve, measuring 'life in general' and others measuring general therapy categories. Opalic complemented this test with another existential measure which measured the total value or purpose in life: the Kotchen test consists of 30 questions which tap the existential qualities of uniqueness, responsibility, self-confirmation, courage, transcendence, trust, and outlook on the world. Finally, the MMPI was administered to measure any general psycho-pathological changes.

The results from the application of the above instruments to the experimental and control conditions revealed significant differences for the treatment group before and after the group therapy intervention on the variable of 'understanding among people'. Opalic suggests that this finding indicates that the patients' experience of being understood in his own world by others was conducive to understanding of them and himself for both neurotic and psychotic patients. Also, both groups comment on the favourable experience of membership of a psychotherapy group.

For the treatment group only, significant test-retest scores emerged for several existential factors for the psychotic group only. These referred to evaluations on categories of freedom, love, sex, 'my place in society' and medication therapy.

Psychotic patients seem to feel that group psychotherapy allowed them to speak more freely of their own views along with a value in verbalizing the entire range of the emotional and sensual life of group members which previously may have been inhibited. The positive rating of 'love' indicates that the group therapy setting seemed to allow patients an opportunity to express positive feelings to others. Group psychotherapy also had a statistically significant test/retest effect in helping psychotics to feel they had a place in society. Opalic suggests that this may represent the feelings of support and acceptance that psychotics receive in a group. The patients gave medication therapy an unexpectedly high rating which may indicate their perceived benefits of drug therapy.

The Kotchen test did not reveal any statistically significant findings for the psychotic patients. The MMPI did not find any significant changes in the reduction of psychotic symptoms for psychotic patients. Opalic argues, somewhat weakly, that changes in the psychopathy scale of the MMPI indicates that group therapy may prevent the appearance of psychopathic symptoms. His argument is based on the appearance of these behaviours in the control group, although this cannot provide enough evidence in itself for a causal connection. The main conclusions from this study point to the usefulness of using existential variables to measure and subsequently pick up the effects of group psychotherapy with psychotic patients. Several of these variables did change after the group intervention and revealed that patients seem to benefit from the opportunity of verbalizing feelings and thoughts relating to their existence in relation to themselves and the world around them. Unfortunately, no general psychopathology changes were found which limits any significant claims in the effectiveness of group psychotherapy with this patient population.

Opalic (1990) continues his research interest in using more qualitative approaches to psychotherapy groups for psychotic patients by investigating group processes via changes in the individual. This idiographic approach places importance on finding out about the internal world of the patient which may give indications of what external processes may be taking place. Opalic conducted this research in an inpatient setting with short-term group interventions. From his review of the group psychotherapy process literature and his own clinical experience, he suggests four main stages of therapy process. Firstly, there is the 'accepting of the group' as a medium of therapy. Here, the patient is uncertain as to whether the group is a place that can offer some help with the duration of this phase depending on several variables such as nature of the psychopathology, previous experience of group therapy, capacity for verbalization etc. The next stage is 'opening up before the group' where the patient is carefully encouraged by the group to share his or her experiences. The third stage is called 'confronting the fundamental psychic problems' whereby the patient addresses emotions by facing reality. Opalic reports that at this stage the patient frequently goes through unpleasant and painful experiences. Finally, the patient is seen to reach a stage whereby he or she is 'gaining support in recovery and socialization'. Here, patients experience feelings of cohesiveness and belongingness gained from early stages in the group membership.

Opalic then illustrates the presence of these stages through focus on a case study of a female 55-year-old unemployed art historian who suffered from a depressive illness. This patient attended 21 sessions some of which were post-hospitalization. Opalic then provides transcribed excerpts from the groups to illustrate the above stages. I will present some of the patient and therapist speech to highlight these stages (taken from Opalic 1990).

ACCEPTING OF THE GROUP

My resistances come down to building a barrier between myself and others. That's easiest for me. I protect myself, keep aloof. I construct a barrier and I permit no one to approach me. (patient)

OPENING UP BEFORE THE GROUP

That's right. I constructed the barriers. As the enemy? No! Doctor, I am not afraid of the enemy. Let them attack me, let them blacken me, let them do what they want to me. I will always construct a barrier, and that is a defense. And I can shout. (patient)

The barriers stand between enemies. (therapist)

CONFRONTING THE FUNDAMENTAL PSYCHIC PROBLEMS

Yes, I proposed this theme. I couldn't say exactly how I arrived at this conclusion, but 4 or 5 days ago, I understood that in effect I escaped into illness, that I was getting my own back at my husband. I don't know how true this is, and I can't explain my situation just now, but I used some avenue of thinking and arrived at the conclusion that I'm a coward, that I have opted for this method of torturing him and myself. Actually, I am a masochist and a sadist. What should I do now? Should I forgive him, should I forget everything, and thus stop torturing myself as well? I don't know whether I'm capable of it. (patient)

GAINING SUPPORT IN RECOVERY AND SOCIALIZATION

Yes (loneliness), that was my big problem even when I left this place. I used to let nobody come into the house and I went nowhere. That's still with me. But now I have started visiting my friends and relatives. It doesn't work as if you waved a magic wand, but it's gradual and getting better. (patient)

Opalic presents a non-quantitative analysis of the different stages of four group processes which he suggests psychotic patients experience in group therapy. This is consistent which some of his other observations (Opalic 1983, 1986) and also fits with general theories of group process behaviour (Bergin and Garfield 1994). His model is very helpful for group therapists conducting groups with psychotic patients in inpatient and outpatient settings through giving some cognitive parameters as to what may be taking place in these groups and thus aiding the therapist to make different interventions at different stages. As such it is a useful theoretical map for clinicians though as with all theoretical frameworks it may produce a bias in missing other events which may be no less important.

In the final paper to be reviewed in this chapter, Lefevre (1994) measured the power of countertransference in groups for the severely mentally ill. This study took place in a large mental hospital and consisted of small group therapy for 26 schizophrenic and 4 major affective-disorder patients. Each group consisted of 4 to 6 group members and met one hour per week with its own nurse-facilitator. The researcher used Heimann's (1960) definition of countertransference as covering all the feelings of the therapist towards the patient along with Gitelson's (1952) further subdivision of this concept into a reaction by the therapist of transference material only or a reaction to partial aspects of the patient such as his/her material or personality.

Countertransference processes were measured by asking the facilitators of the groups to record their feelings in terms of frequency, powerfulness and importance immediately after the groups. A list of the ten most common feelings was then drawn up which were rank ordered from 1–10 as follows: empathy, frustration, achievement, exhaustion, feeling shattered, anxiety, sadness, happiness, hopelessness and emptiness. Lefevre then suggested that phases within these groups for psychotic patients could be modelled on a bereavement reaction involving denial, rage, sadness, anxiety, and reality testing. Facilitators were then asked to record their countertransference reactions, with the help of the above ten categories and other verbal description. Countertransference reactions from the therapists are summarized as follows:

- *Denial*: shattered; apathy; frightening
- *Anger*: frustrated; shocked; upset
- *Sadness*: sad, weepy; listless; empathic; exhausted
- *Anxiety*: anxious
- *Reality testing*: relieved sense of achievement; optimistic

The strength of this paper is in being able to describe and highlight the disturbing reactions that psychotic patients evoke in therapists. Unfortunately its rudimentary methodology and lack of empirical data prevents any clear conclusions as to what universality there may be to such reactions. Her conclusion reinforces the need for professional support for psychotherapists undertaking this work, but the absence of quantitative data limits the strength of her work.

Conclusion

In conducting groups with psychotic patients, group psychotherapists want guidelines that will help them achieve positive outcomes. As stated earlier most of these guidelines have come from theoretical preference, clinical experience, personal therapy and clinical supervision, all of which will interact with the personality of the group psychotherapist. From the available research findings I can offer the following general guidance to maximize the effects of their interventions in group psychotherapy:

1. Speak empathically, supportively and at times about the affective emotional state of the group but expect considerable opposition from the group to accept this style of intervention. This opposition may change over time, so don't let the force of the negative response persuade you to adopt unnecessarily punitive or confrontational techniques. Psychotic patients will value your efforts to make them feel accepted along with your help to explore the effects of their mental illness on their existence as human beings.

2. These patients have lost their capacity for sex and love along with their role in life and want to talk about this to you. Be as constant and reliable as possible with these groups but be aware that you will feel under tremendous pressure to retaliate and/or collapse. You may find it helpful to offer a firm structure to these groups, though some patients may value a lack of structure to allow their psychotic anxieties to be released and so ease the burden on their mind.

The research findings support the idea that group psychotherapy can benefit psychotic patients along with the presence of other traditional interventions such as drug therapy. There is no clear evidence that group therapy alone is effective in reducing symptoms. Its interaction with drug therapy seems positive but has not been fully investigated. Psychotic patients do value these groups, though group psychotherapists should receive as much support as possible to conduct what is probably the most difficult type of group in psychotherapeutic psychiatry. This support can come from personal therapy, clinical supervision, clinical theory and being aware of the research findings of other colleague group psychotherapists.

References

Alikakos L.C (1965) 'Analytical group treatment of the post-hospital schizophrenic. *International Journal of Group Psychotherapy 15*, 492–504.

Battegay, R. (1965) 'Psychotherapy of schizophrenics in small groups.' *International Journal of Group Psychotherapy 15*, 3, 316–320.

Bergin, A.E. and Garfield, S.L. (1994) *Handbook of Psychotherapy and Behaviour Change.* New York: J Wiley and Sons.

Betcher, R.W. (1983) 'The treatment of depression in brief inpatient group psychotherapy.' *International Journal of Group Psychotherapy 33,* 365–85.

Bion, W.R. (1959) 'Attacks on linking.' *International Journal of Psychoanalysis 40,* 308–317; also in *Second Thoughts.* London: Maresfield (1967).

Bion, W.R. (1961) *Experiences in Groups and Other Papers.* London: Tavistock/Routledge.

Bion, W.R. (1962) *Second Thoughts.* London: Maresfield.

Bion, W.R. (1967) *Second Thoughts.* London: Maresfield.

Bloch, S. and Crouch.E. (1985) *Therapeutic Factors in Group Psychotherapy.* Oxford: Oxford University Press.

Brabender, V.M. (1985) 'Time-limited in-patient group theory: A developmental model.' *International Journal of Group Psychotherapy 35,* 373–390.

Budmann, S.H. (1981) 'Significant treatment factors in short-term group psychotherapy.' *Group 5, 4,* 25–31.

Cory, T.L., and Page, D. (1978) 'Group techniques for effecting change in the more disturbed patient.' *Group 2, 3,* 149–55.

Elliott, R. and Anderson, C. (1994) 'Simplicity and complexity in psychotherapy research.' In R.L. Russell (ed) *Reassessing Psychotherapy Research.* New York: Guilford Press, 65–113.

Garfield, S.L. and Bergin, A.E (1996) *Handbook of Psychotherapy and Behaviour Change.* London: John Wiley & Sons.

Gitelson, M. (1952) 'The emotional position of the analyst in the psychoanalytic situation.' *International Journal of Psychoanalysis 33,* 1, 1–10.

Greene, L.R. (1982) 'Personal boundary management and social structure.' In M. Pines and L. Rafaelson (eds) *The Individual and the Group: Boundaries and Interrelations in Theory and Practice.* London: Plenum Press, 279–293.

Greene, L.R. (1983), 'On fusion and individuation processes in small groups.' *International Journal of Group Psychotherapy 33,* 3–19.

Greene, L.R. and Cole, M. (1991) 'Level and form of psychopathology and the structure of group therapy.' *International Journal of Group Psychotherapy 41,* 4, 499–521.

Grinberg, L., Sor, D. and DeBianchedi, E.T. (1975) *Introduction to the Work of Bion.* Perthshire: Clinic Press.

Heimann, P. (1960) 'Countertransference.' *British Journal of Medical Psychology 33,* 9, 9–115.

Kapur, R. (1993) 'The effects of group interpretations with severely mentally ill patients.' *Group Analysis 26,* 4, 411–432.

Kapur, R., Miller, K. and Mitchell, G. (1988) 'Therapeutic factors within inpatient and outpatient psychotherapy groups.' *British Journal of Psychiatry 152,* 229–233.

Karterud, S. (1988) 'The valance theory of Bion and the significance of (DSM-III) diagnosis for inpatient group behaviour.' *Acta Psychiatrica Scandinavia 78,* 462–470.

Karterud, S. (1989) *Group Processes in Therapeutic Communities.* London: Artesian.

Klein, R.H. (1977) 'Inpatient group psychotherapy: practical considerations and special problems.' *International Journal of Group Psychotherapy 27,* 201–14.

Kernberg, O. (1976) *Object Relations Theory and Clinical Psychoanalysis.* New York: Jason Aronson.

Kohut, H. (1977) *The Restoration of the Self.* New York: International Universities Press.

Lefevre, D. (1994) 'The power of countertransference in groups for the severely mentally ill. Special section: group analysis and the psychoses.' *Group Analysis 27,* 441–447.

Leszcz, M., Yalom, I.D, and Norden, M. (1985) 'The value of inpatient group psychotherapy: patients perceptions.' *International Journal of Group Psychotherapy 35,* 411–33.

Lieberman, M., Yalom, M. and Miles, M. (1963) *Encounter Groups: First Facts.* New York: Basic Books.

Marcovitz, R.J, and Smith, J.E. (1983) 'Patients' perceptions of curative factors in short-term group psychotherapy.' *International Journal of Group Psychotherapy 33,* 21–39.

Miller, N.E., Doherty, J., Luborsky, L. (eds) (1993) *Psychodynamic Treatment Research. A Handbook for Clinical Practice.* New York: Basic Books.

Morrow-Bradley, C. and Elliott, R. (1986) 'Utilisation of psychotherapy research by practising psychotherapists.' *American Psychologist 41*, 2, 188–197.

Opalic, P. (1983). 'Proces lecenja pojedinaca u maloj u stacionarnim uslovima.' *Zbornik Filozofskog Fakulteta u Beogradu 13*, 2.

Opalic, P. (1986) *Mogucnosti grupne psihoterapije*. Belgrade: IIC SSO Srbije.

Opalic, P. (1989) 'Existential and psychopathological evaluation of group psychotherapy of neurotic and psychotic patients.' *International Journal of Group Psychotherapy 39*, 3 (special issue), 389–411.

Opalic, P. (1990) 'Group processes in short-term group therapy of psychotics. *Small Group Research 21*, 2, 168–189.

Osgood, C.E., Suci, G.J., and Tannenbaum, P.H.(1957) *The Measurement of Meaning*. Urbana, IL: University of Illinois Press.

Pappas, D., Yannitsi, S., and Liakos, A. (1997) 'Therapeutic communities: evaluation of inpatient groups in a general psychiatric unit.' *The International Journal for Therapeutic and Supportive Organisations 18*, 4, 285–296.

Pekala, R.J., Siegel, J.M. and Farrar, D.M. (1985) 'The problem-solving support group: Structured group therapy with psychiatric in-patients.' *International Journal of Group Psychotherapy 35*, 391–410.

Profita,J., Carrey, N. and Klein, F. (1989) 'Sustained, multimodal outpatient group therapy for chronic psychotic patients.' *Hospital and Community Psychiatry 40*, 9, 943–946.

Resnik, S. (1985) 'The space of madness.' In M. Pines (ed) *Bion and Group Psychotherapy*. London: Routledge, 220–246.

Rice, C.A. and Rutan, J.S. (1987) *Inpatient Group Psychotherapy*. New York: Macmillan.

Rosenfeld, H. (1987) *Impass and Interpretation: Therapeutic and Anti-Therapeutic Factors in Psychoanalytic Treatment of Psychotic, Borderline and Neurotic Patients*. London and New York: Routledge (New Library of Psychoanalysis).

Roth, A. and Fonagy, P. (1996) *What Works for Whom? A Critical Review of Psychotherapy Research*. New York, London: Guilford Press.

Shrout, P. and Fleiss, J. (1979) 'Interclass correlations: uses in assessing reliability.' *Psychological Bulletin 86*, 2, 420–428.

Strenger, C. (1991) *Between Hermeneutics and Science: An Essay on the Epistemology of Psychoanalysis*. Madison, CT: International Universities Press.

Strupp, H.H. (1973) *Psychotherapy: Clinical Research and Theoretical Issues*. New York: Jason Aronson.

Thelan, H. (1954) *Methods of Studying Work and Emotionality in Groups*. Chicago: University of Chicago.

Waxer, P.H. (1977) 'Short-term group psychotherapy: some principles and techniques.' *International Journal of Group Psychotherapy 27*, 33–42.

Wolman, H. (1960) 'Group psychotherapy with latent schizophrenics.' *International Journal of Group Psychotherapy 10*, 301–312.

Yalom, I.D. (1975/1985) *The Theory and Practice of Group Psychotherapy*, 2nd and 3rd edns. New York: Basic Books.

Yalom, I.D. (1983) *Inpatient Group Psychotherapy*. New York: Basic Books.

PART 3

Training, Supervision and Countertransference

Supervision of Group Psychotherapy with Chronic Psychotic Patients

Eugene Della Badia

Introduction

Group psychotherapy for psychotic patients is a task which evokes considerable anxiety and poses significant difficulties for the psychotherapist. Supervision of such groups is an essential step in the learning process, but it poses its own parallel concerns. In what follows, I will share some of the principles and concepts that I have found useful in supervising group psychotherapists working with a psychotic population.

It is important at the outset to note that the chronic psychoses encompass many diagnostic categories. In order to simplify my task, I will be referring to schizophrenic patients unless otherwise specified. Although schizophrenia itself can be seen as a group of disorders, there are certain similarities which allow for the development of generalized theoretical and treatment concepts. These concepts could also be transferred with some variation to other diagnostic categories such as the major affective disorders (bipolar disorder, schizoaffective disorder, psychotic depression) and organic mental disorders. Some of the differences derive from the fact that the premorbid personality of the schizophrenic is quite different from those of the other diagnostic categories.

Since the early days of my experience as a psychiatric resident on a chronic ward, I have worked with the psychoses in many different capacities, in the acute care hospital and in long-term residential centers, both conducting and supervising group psychotherapy with chronic psychiatric patients. For sixteen years, I directed group psychotherapy programs in acute hospital settings. At the present time, I teach group psychotherapy to psychiatric residents and psychology interns. I have always maintained a strong interest in chronic psychotic patients and their treatment in group psychotherapy.

GROUP PSYCHOTHERAPY OF THE PSYCHOSES

The relevance of my early experience as a psychiatric resident

My interest in group psychotherapy with psychotic patients began at the very beginning of my residency in psychiatry 28 years ago, where my first rotation was with a ward of chronic female patients. Most of these women had been in the hospital for a long duration and received little more than medication and occasional supportive psychotherapy. I became envious of my fellow residents for their work with bright, insightful patients on other services.

As we began training in group psychotherapy, I became frustrated, since the training didn't seem to apply to my population of mostly psychotic patients. I was told that socialization or educational groups were appropriate with this population, but that they could not benefit from other, more meaningful in-depth work. Since I possessed considerable empathy for these individuals, I found this very proposition difficult to accept and felt that more could be done to help them. When I discussed my views with the unit supervisor, he agreed to let me try a more traditional, psychodynamic group psychotherapy. In turn, I had to promise I would consult with a group supervisor. Little did I know that this would be a formidable task. Most of the supervisors who were familiar with group therapy did not work with psychotic patients. I settled for one who worked with psychotic patients but unfortunately had minimal group skills. He assured me we would learn together. We first tried to locate literature on the subject and found to our dismay that it was almost non-existent. I remember him pulling an old textbook of psychiatry off the shelf, blowing the dust off the cover, and telling me to read the chapter on group psychotherapy. It contained about three lines on psychotic patients, essentially stating that they were not good candidates for group.

Despite our concerns, we decided to start a small group of six women to meet every day for 90 minutes. This venture became an extremely frustrating experience. I began by attempting to set boundaries and noticed the patients ignored me. Patients would not stay in their seats, talked at the same time, and lit up cigarettes even though there was no smoking in the group. My supervisor and I began to confront the boundary issues by continually bringing them to the attention of the group until they would conform. However, as soon as we got one issue under control another came up. Whenever I was not active and engaged with the patients, regressive behavior would start. Patients would begin to talk to themselves, hallucinate, or stare into space. The group seemed to be avoiding any meaningful work.

I was just about to throw in the towel in desperation when my supervisor suggested I bring in the head nurse, who had worked on the ward for several years, as my co-therapist. After talking with her, I was pleasantly surprised. She had experience in group and knew the patients very well. She laughed at my insecurity and told me the nurses were taking bets to see how long I would last! She gently explained that the patients were trying to frustrate me. I began to recognize that psychotic patients put up a wall of very powerful defenses to avoid relatedness.

Since she clearly had a relationship with the patients that allowed for a sounder type of therapeutic milieu, the head nurse was a pleasure to work with as my co-therapist. We were able to contain the group and work on issues despite the fact that the avoidant defenses returned whenever the group's anxiety level increased. The patients became less withdrawn and seemed to relate to us and each other less defensively. Our gains were small compared to the high-functioning groups but everyone seemed to benefit, including, I must admit, myself. When I left the unit, the group continued with the head nurse as therapist.

From this experience, I developed a sense of the major factors that helped me to make the transition from a well-meaning, interested therapist to an experienced and skilled clinician:

- *First, you must have respect for the patient's illness.* The patient's behavior is not merely a random set of biologically induced responses. Their responses have a defensive purpose that protect a fragile self from re-experiencing emotional trauma. Understanding the meaning behind the symptoms is important if the therapist is to develop empathy and interest in the psychotic patient which will allow him to stay involved.

- *Second, the therapist needs to develop authentic relationships with the patients.* Relatedness is where most of the work needs to be done. The therapist's relationship with the patients in the group sets the tone for the group and models behavior for the patients.

- *Third, the context of group psychotherapy significantly affects the psychotic patient and when managed properly can be a valuable therapeutic tool.* Groups of psychotic patients differ developmentally from higher functioning groups. Knowing these differences will help the therapist maximize the gains of the group instead of becoming frustrated due to unrealistic expectations.

- *Fourth, supervision is crucial to learning how to do this work.* The supervisor must be familiar both with the nature and dynamics of group treatment and also with this type of patient.

- *Fifth, and perhaps most importantly, the supervisor must have a certain optimism that allows him to believe that these patients can improve.* This optimism makes the difficult work tolerable and allows the supervisor to help the supervisee develop interest and perseverance and overcome his ongoing frustration and disappointment about the slow, limited progress of these groups.

The significance of meaning

In my role as supervisor in several group psychotherapy programs, I have repeatedly noted the initially strong aversion and lack of interest shown when unseasoned group psychotherapists begin to work with chronic psychotic patients. Even the most skilled therapists tend to avoid them. A few therapists do turn out to have an interest, as I did, but unless this motivation is nurtured and developed, it soon diminishes due to the intense frustration of the work.

Much of this frustration and discouragement is due to the mythology that such patients are not treatable and do not improve. I learned early on that unless I could kindle the therapist's interest in the psychotic patient, I would never train anyone to deal with this population in group psychotherapy. I found *one of the major motivating factors in this type of work is searching for meaning and purpose in the behavior of the psychotic patient.*

In order to develop an appreciation for the psychotic patient, we must answer three basic questions: (1) do the symptoms have meaning? (2) Does this meaning conform to any workable theoretical construct? (3) Will utilizing such a construct in group psychotherapy lead to a meaningful interaction between the therapist and the patients? Students at first tend to see this area as a wasteland, devoid of meaning and any hope of deep-seated therapeutic interaction. A more comprehensive exposure is needed if the supervisees are to learn to look beyond the symptoms.

To address the first question about the meanings of the symptoms, we begin with the idea that patients can evoke severe symptoms such as delusions and hallucinations when confronted with a threat to their well-being. As we explore the meaning behind the symptoms, supervisees are better able to comprehend the tragic predicament of the psychotic patient. The students learn, for example, that many patients develop grandiose delusions after a narcissistic injury:

> Martin, a 26-year-old male, had his first psychotic breakdown following an intense argument with his father, who would not accept his son's limitations. His father ridiculed him for not being successful and for having few friends. Martin tended to be sensitive and withdrawn. He felt powerless to deal with his father and could not bear the pain of his father's attacks. He soon developed a delusion that he was on a secret mission to save mankind, and that the entire world would be thankful. Armed with this belief, Martin could manage the constant belittling by his father. The delusion allowed Martin to maintain the relationship with his father without being overwhelmed by his pain or facing the fear of separation by a loss of the relationship. The symptom thus was relevant to understanding the interpersonal source of Martin's difficulty.
>
> Another example is that of Richard, a 46-year-old schizophrenic male who lived at home with his mother. She treated him like a child and paradoxically parentified him by having him take care of her needs. Mother went through severe mood swings. When she became depressed she would yell at Richard

who would then become terrified. He developed auditory hallucinations which consisted of voices telling him to kill the demons that were affecting his mother. He also developed a delusion that he was charged by an angel to kill the demons. As long as Richard stayed focused on the demons his relationship with his mother and his fragile self-esteem were preserved.

These instances show that even though psychotic symptoms may have a biological basis, they are often invoked in a defensive manner to protect against narcissistic injury in a crucial interpersonal relationship. Miller *et al.* (1993) found that a majority of patients reported positive effects from hallucinations and concluded that this finding was consistent with the idea that psychological factors contribute to their expression.

As supervisees become proficient at understanding the conflicts of psychotic patients, their interest and ability to work with these patients in group psychotherapy increases. A further benefit of understanding the meaning behind the patient's symptoms is that the supervisee is in a position to develop a stronger sense of empathy for psychotic patients. From this position he is better able to help them with their conflicts.

I presented both of the above cases in group supervision to students who were beginning to work with psychotic patients. First, I described the symptoms and many students simply laughed at the bizarre behavior involved. However, when we discussed the symptoms in terms of the patients' internal conflicts and deficits, the students were very moved and attentive. Only when they could comprehend the meaning behind the symptoms could they experience real empathy for the patients. One must be able to identify with patients' pain and suffering, and many times the symptoms alone do not convey the true picture. The psychotic patient is more than a collection of symptoms.

The theoretical base for supervision

Teaching the relevance of meaning would not be complete without the appropriate theoretical and conceptual considerations. Supervisees need to incorporate a theoretical point of view in order to develop a technique for treatment.

My own theoretical base is consistent with object relations theory. In this view, human beings are motivated by the need to relate to others. Fairbairn's concept (1952), that libido is object-seeking and not pleasure-seeking, set the stage for the exploration of problems in early relationships. Beginning with the mother–child relationship, pathology can emerge which affects the individual's capacity for authentic relatedness. The normal child uses splitting and projective identification to maintain early object ties and as maturation occurs, the child is able to contain the split parts of the self and other. At this point primitive defenses are no longer needed. In the psychotic patient this maturation does not occur. Relatedness leads the individual to come in contact with conflicting images of himself which can lead to regression and resurrection of primitive defenses. When these defenses fail, safety is found only through withdrawal from relatedness.

Sullivan (1962) was one of the first to emphasize that the main dysfunction in schizophrenia was a disturbance in the capacity to relate to others. Gabbard (1994) in a review of the literature found that all psychodynamic theories of schizophrenia had three common threads. First, psychotic symptoms have meaning. Second, human relatedness is difficult and filled with terror for these patients. Third, schizophrenic patients improved significantly when involved in a dynamically oriented therapeutic relationship. Therefore working with relatedness is a primary consideration.

Group psychotherapy is an attempt to repair the damage resulting from faulty early relationships by the containment and detoxification of primitive defenses which leads to ultimate improvement in the ability to relate to others. The therapeutic process begins with the development of a holding environment which is established through the therapist modeling an empathetic relatedness that will allow the patient to bring his primitive defenses into the group. When these defenses are contained by interaction with the therapist and the group they can be modified. When primitive defenses are modified the patient's concept of self and other can change. Change at this level opens the way for the patient to relate to others and develop a healthier self-esteem.

The question of whether object relations and other key concepts lead to meaningful interactions between the therapist and the group of schizophrenics must be answered as the therapist becomes involved in the drama unfolding with each patient in the group. Kanas (1986), in an extensive review of the literature, has shown that studies indicate that group psychotherapy is useful for schizophrenics and that an interactive approach was more beneficial than an insight-oriented one. In my opinion, group therapy is effective for such patients when the therapist's ability to develop interest and empathy towards patients leads to an environment that is safe for the patients to engage in meaningful interactions with each other. This is a path filled with difficulty. Theoretical constructs can be helpful when we use them as a guide to follow psychotic patients along this path, instead of getting the patient to understand our formulations of his predicament.

One of the inhibiting factors is the tendency of the therapist's misuse of theory to distance himself from patients. Many students come to group supervision expecting they will learn the 'true religion' that will make the work with psychotic patients make sense. They are very surprised when I repeat what one of my mentors told me early on in my career: 'If you are thinking of theory while you are treating psychotic patients you will not be successful.' I had a lot of difficulty understanding this caveat and would often argue that patients could not be treated without a good theory. How would one know what interpretations to make? How would we understand the chaos? How would we stop from hurting patients? How would we know what they need?

However, as I continued my work, it became clear that what the mentor was suggesting was not that theory isn't useful but that the cornerstone in working with psychotic patients is forming an authentic relationship. In order to do this we must be present, available, and attentive. Thus, when the use of theory and insight becomes the primary goal, relatedness may suffer. In the beginning of supervision I try to take the emphasis off theoretical preoccupation and help the therapist to an understanding of the plight of the psychotic patient. This plight is as follows: the lack of trust, fear of engulfment and the wish for relatedness create a tenuous situation which sets the stage for personal relationships that continually cause pain, withdrawal and failure, occurring in a context of a thought disorder which may include delusions and hallucinations and the absence of appropriate affect, depression and anxiety. We can not think of curing the psychotic process through insight but more on making an impact on the particular symptom constellation by an ongoing group process, thus improving the psychotic patients' capacity for relatedness.

The crucial role of the therapeutic relationship

As we have seen, a key factor in working with chronic psychotic patients in groups is the therapist's ability to remain consistently related to the patients. Not all therapists can form a genuine relationship with this type of patient. In order to accomplish this goal, *the therapist must act as a container for the projections of the patient which would allow for modification of the patient's internal images through the therapeutic work.* Psychotic patients tend to project very primitive parts of themselves on to the therapist. These projections can evoke very strong responses in the therapist, and unless the therapist is comfortable dealing with these feelings he will not be able to remain related to the patients and continue the therapeutic work.

The therapist must join the patients in their primitive world and lead them on a journey through isolation and terror toward genuine relatedness. This path is made even more difficult by the fact that the psychotic patient does not trust the spoken word. The patient will be watching the actions of the therapist as the therapist tries to provide a holding environment where this kind of trust can develop. The chronic patient reproduces the infantile environment of early object relations and induces care-giving objects into duplicating dysfunctional interpersonal process (Frankel 1993). Through primitive projections, powerful countertransference responses are evoked that will cause a great deal of difficulty if not contained. Feelings of isolation, helplessness and hopelessness can ensue. These feelings can be experienced as anger, boredom or rejection, which, if acted out, can lead to a confirmation of the patient's internal world. Then, instead of the therapeutic relationship being a corrective emotional experience, it becomes a repetition of the trauma that is responsible for the patient's primitive functioning. Supervision is the safety net the therapist can use to help avoid this pitfall, as in the following illustration:

> A chronic psychotic female patient joined an ongoing group of very ill patients in a psychiatric hospital. The group had been meeting together five times a week for several weeks. The new patient was delusional, believed the therapist to be the devil and projected her sadistic anger and rage onto the therapist. She tried to convince the rest of the group that the therapist was evil and out to hurt them. The group began to accept her projections as valid. The psychotic patient began shouting and interrupting the therapist, who then became furious and angrily confronted the patient with reality. The patient became distraught, withdrew and would not speak. the therapist then angrily scolded the group for cooperating with the patients's acting out. The group empathized with the patient whom they knew was very ill. The major feeling in the group was unexpressed anger. The group became stuck and could not work. The therapist came for supervision furious at the patient for ruining her group. She felt the patient was too sick to be in group and wanted my permission to remove her. She was very surprised when I pointed out that she, rather than the patient, might be the problem. I worked with the therapist to help her understand the defenses of the patient and her own underlying conflict. I told her that the key factor in entering a genuine relationship with a psychotic patient is the ability to act as container for the patient's projections while remaining empathetic to her difficulties.
>
> In this case the therapist was initially unable to contain the patient's projections and was not able to generate any empathy. Instead she focused on what the patient was doing to her and the group and not on what it was like to be in the patient's predicament. We also worked on the meaning of the therapist's anger which was related to her insecurity in her ability to run the group. We then began to look at the patient's actions as a defensive measure to manage destructive rage. Once the therapist could understand these concepts and come to grips with her own uncertainty, she could begin to feel empathy for the patient and was able to attune herself to the patient's needs.
>
> When the therapist returned to the group, the patient again accused her of being the devil. This time, the therapist was able to connect with the patient and help her bring her fear and rage into the group. As the patient was able to explore her feelings, the therapist was able to find others in the group to join her to explore their emotions. The group began working again with the psychotic patient taking an active membership role.

The above example of empathetic failure can happen with any type of patient. However, with psychotic patients, empathetic failure is common due to the intensity and primitive nature of the patient's responses which in turn must be contained by the therapist:

Two co-therapists were running a group of very regressed patients in the hospital. They both became frightened when a psychotic patient, who had been very silent and passive, began to talk about his homicidal feelings. Other group members began to regress. The anxiety level in the group became extremely high. The members sensed that the therapists felt there was danger. As the patient raised his voice, one therapist left the room and came back with a security guard. The patient was told that if he acted out in the group he would be subdued immediately. The patient reverted to his silence, and the rest of the group also became silent. They remained silent for the entire session despite the therapists' interventions.

In supervision both therapists admitted that they were frightened of the patient and were responding to the need to protect themselves and the group instead of the patient's need for help in containing his feelings. In working with psychotic patients, powerful feelings will surface in the patient and the therapist's work is to try to contain them and feed them back to the patient in a more realistic context that the patient can accept and the group can manage. In supervision we worked on the overreaction of the therapists and their failure to intervene and work with a difficult patient. Both therapists were surprised by the intensity of the patient's feelings and were not able to collect data on the dangerousness of the patient. In spite of the fact that this patient had often threatened staff, he had never acted on his threats. In response to the patient's projections, intense affect and feelings of anger, fear and helplessness were generated in the therapists. These powerful feelings interfered with their reality testing and, in this case, the boundaries of the group were broken and the group was unnecessarily traumatized. As a last resort the patient could have been asked to leave the group. The therapists never attempted to work with the patient because of the primitive nature of his feelings. The therapist who brought in the security guard talked about how this psychotic patient reminded her of her abusive father who frightened her a great deal in her childhood. This catharsis gave her a great deal of relief and enabled her to separate that issue from the relationship with her patient in group.

After their supervision session, the therapists returned to the group and confronted the issue. They found that the group was no longer afraid of the patient and that the patient was making progress by bringing up his feelings. The group had been concerned about the therapist who they felt was frightened of them and began to feel guilt and shame over the incident. As the therapists continued to work in supervision they became less fearful and more confident. They came to understand more about the group reaction as well as that of the angry patient, and the patient was encouraged to bring his anger into the group. The therapists were then able to explore the reality of the situation and help the group deal with their feelings so that the atmosphere was again conducive to work.

This type of acting out is especially common with inexperienced therapists. It always amazes me that in most clinic or hospital situations the most inexperienced therapists are assigned to work with psychotic patients. The myth that these patients are not going to improve gives rise to this mentality. This is a recipe for failure.

Addressing countertransference in supervision

An important aspect of the supervision of therapists working with difficult patients is the management of countertransference feelings. There is considerable controversy in the field about how appropriate it is for a supervisor to work with countertransference. It is frequently held that such feelings should be brought back to individual therapy. The old adage that supervision is teaching and not therapy still holds sway. I question this statement. If the supervisor does not develop an awareness in the therapist that his feelings can have an effect on the patient, a valuable source of therapeutic information is lost. By working with those feelings in supervision the supervisor can provide an environment that promotes honesty and openness with little chance of traumatizing the therapist.

In my opinion, supervision is both educational and therapeutic. I have learned a great deal about myself in supervision over the years and appreciate my supervisors for their work with my countertransference. The above examples show how helping therapists understand and manage their own feelings leads to better understanding of the patient and enables the development of a holding environment where the patient can establish a genuine relationship with the therapist and the group. Here is a further illustration of the process:

> Two co-therapists and their supervisor came to me for a consultation. The therapists were running a group with chronic schizophrenic adolescents in a residential treatment center. One of the members of the group brought a wooden hammer to group and went after another group member. A therapist stopped him and took the hammer. The incident had gotten back to the administration who then questioned the merit of running this type of group therapy with this population. The two therapists were enraged at the patient for violating the boundary which now threatened the group's existence. The supervisor was furious with the therapists for persuading him to allow them to run a more dynamic group rather than the traditional educational group that had been customary at this institution in the past.

The therapists reported that the group had been going on for four months once a week. In that short time several of the six members had shown an improvement in their social functioning. The particular patient who acted out was usually a silent member of the group who was sometimes scapegoated for not being more verbal.

He had been neglected by his parents and abused by his older brother. He had chosen silence and isolation rather than deal with his feelings. His outburst in the group was the first expression of rage that was noticed. I met with the co-therapists and their supervisor for three sessions. As I did so, I began to notice that I was angry at this trio for their lack of concern about the patient. I also felt that I would like to get rid of this consultation and that perhaps these therapists should not be running this group. Importantly, I was able to get a perspective in which *I began to see the patient's influence on the group leaders was isomorphic with the effect they had on their supervisor and the effect the entire group was having on me.* Our anger, lack of concern, and neglect stemmed from a fear that things could not be managed if feelings were allowed to emerge. We were acting as neglectful parents and confirming the patients' constructed reality.

To undo this bind, I had to contain my own angry feelings and bring them into the supervising process. This helped the therapists and the supervisor to explore their own angry feelings. The supervisor began to deal with his fear of the group getting out of control and proving his incompetence. As this issue became conscious, he could become more available to the therapists who were dealing with their fear of the patients rage and the narcissistic hurt of possibly losing their group. The supervisor became available to the therapist and helped them understand the group was still workable. Then they could begin to empathize with the patient. In a follow-up consultation, I learned that the patient had brought his anger at his brother into the group and the group was working.

In this situation, the image of neglectful caretaker had been projected down the line and was not contained so it could not be worked with but only acted out. Such repetitions can cause harm to the patients and the group if not addressed. The example illustrates the importance of the supervisor as a container for the affective reactions of the therapist and the isomorphic parallel process that often includes many levels of staff.

The group-*qua*-group context

Helping therapists understand the importance of the group process is one of the tasks of a good supervisor. The group context (group system, group-as-a-whole) is a major influence on the course of therapy. Generally speaking, working with the dynamics of the group has a more powerful influence on the manifestations of personality in the group than working with individual dynamics (Della Badia, 1989). The group factors influencing this type of patient include the group's phase of development and the powerful phase-specific 'role suction' of selected members as the 'identified patient' and the 'scapegoat'.

For work with the psychotic patient, certain modifications of technique are useful depending upon the group's phase of development. For example, in the early phase of flight in a therapy group, social behaviors can be usefully understood and interpreted as resistance to the fear of the unknown. By contrast, for psychotic patients, social behaviors that enable communication between the group members are an important therapeutic step. At this stage, if a group member can interact on even a very superficial level with another member, such interaction should be encouraged and built upon. We must remember that the goal for the patient is not insight into his conflicts but to improve his ability to relate to others.

Mismanagement of the overt dependency manifestations of compliance and defiance can easily threaten to fixate a group. However, there is a therapeutic potential in their manifestations when the therapist focuses upon the constructive elements in such behaviors. For example, particularly with the psychotic patient, a compliant response enables the therapist to relate the patient to the group context and to other members as well as to the therapist's self. The defiant response introduces into the group an important self-affirmation that the therapist will do well to legitimize, support and help the patient and the group to contain. For example, the angry patient who frightened the therapists with his homicidal rage, in my previous example, voiced for the group important issues about anger and fear.

Every patient is always simultaneously a voice for himself and for the group (Agazarian and Peters 1981, p.83.) With higher-level patients, facilitating insight into the dual role of each member encourages patients to see themselves and experience context of the group. For the psychotic patient, however, the boundary between self and other is so fluid that reinforcing the development of personal boundaries is paramount, since it is less likely that the members will be able to follow the group process. It may be more advantageous for the therapist not to interpret the group-as-a-whole issue for the group but rather to help the member deal with his conflict within the group. In the example of the angry patient who frightened the therapists, pointing out that the patient was a voice for the group would have increased the patient's anxiety and caused more difficulty. In this case, the priority was to help the individual to get containment of his powerful affect and bring it into the group.

> A middle-aged schizophrenic patient entered an inpatient hospital group. Although his acute symptoms were under control with medication, the group objected to his participation. He was accused of inappropriateness and insensitivity. The group asked for him to be removed. The therapist came to supervision with this dilemma. The therapist was not uncomfortable with the patient but felt under some pressure from the group. I suggested to him that, before we made that decision, we should explore the dynamics of the group. The group was angry at the patient for little reason. In fact, the patient only became inappropriate and insensitive *after* he was confronted by them.

The therapist had been on vacation and returned a few days before this incident. The group had been together for about three weeks meeting on a daily basis, and the patients all had serious psychopathology (several had a diagnosis of schizophrenia). It became obvious that the group was angry at the therapist for abandoning them and had drafted the psychotic patient into the role of scapegoat. With their anger contained by one patient the group could 'safely' continue.

This group had not yet reached a level of development that would allow them to confront their anger at the leader. We know that these groups tend to become fixated in early developmental work that is relatively free of separation–individuation conflict. Kanas (1996) postulates that this is because the schizophrenic patient has an inability to tolerate anxiety and strong affect. Agazarian and Peters (1981) state that these patients do not reach the level of dealing with authority issues, and that a more realistic goal is to help them enter into a valid dialogue with others. In a higher-level group, the group-as-whole issue would be brought to the attention of the members who would take back their projections and work with their anger at the leader. However, in less sophisticated groups that intervention would not be successful. We decided to work by supporting the new member and helping the rest of the group to take back their projections by pointing out reality distortions the members were making about the new patient. Slowly the patient was accepted in the group and the scapegoating stopped. This group was not able to deal with their anger at the therapist but we were able to get to a point where people felt safe dealing with each other. Although this seems on the surface to be only a minimal gain, it facilitated the symptomatic improvement of each member of the group. This work became possible when the therapists gained new understanding of the group context.

The supervisory process

The main goals and objectives of the supervision process with chronic psychotic patients are: (1) to kindle interest in the patient while providing support for the therapist; (2) to provide help for the therapist to manage his countertransference and to form a working relationship with patients and group; (3) always to keep in mind the context of the group while teaching technical skills and theoretical concepts. In this section, I will discuss how the focus of supervision changes when dealing with chronic psychotic patients and some of the common problems brought by students to supervision. These issues include (1) the role of the supervisor; (2) supervising peer groups of therapists; (3) boundary issues; (4) the dangers of preconceived ideas; (5) patient selection; and (6) choosing among therapeutic approaches.

The role of the supervisor

The difficulty I described earlier, of finding someone to supervise my group of chronic psychotic patients, is not uncommon. Besides the obvious qualities of being knowledgeable about both group psychotherapy and treatment of psychosis, the supervisor must take an active role when dealing with this type of group. From studies on the supervisory process in psychotherapy, we know that a good supervisor is active, focuses on the case being presented, and is willing clearly to express definite opinions about the patient, the therapist and the transference (Kline *et al.* 1977). These factors are even more important in supervising groups of psychotic patients. The supervisor should role model and teach very active intervention with psychotic patients. A passive stance that encourages waiting, anonymity and interpretation by the therapist will make it difficult to reach psychotic patients, who are, as we know, unable to verbalize feelings and instead live out their difficulties in the group. If the therapist is not active the patient will remain withdrawn and at times act out with a multitude of primitive defenses. Empathetic recognition of the patients' conflict with a focus on the patients bringing that conflict into the group should be encouraged. These patients are usually responsive to a therapist who they feel has a sincere interest in them. They do not trust verbal interaction and their ability to develop trust depends on their interaction with the therapist. The atmosphere that is created in the group must be safe and foster the expectation that the patient will work to involve himself with the group.

John, a 25-year-old paranoid schizophrenic male who had been in an outpatient therapy group for several years, found himself saying very little and remaining a passive member. When confronted, he stated that his feelings were too strong to talk about and that if he brought them into the group he would be arrested (!). Therapists were frightened of him, and would usually allow him to be silent. John had a multitude of defenses to push people away. He would become sarcastic or insulting, projecting very negative images onto the therapist or other members of the group. It was common for him to say 'I know you want to hurt me' or 'I know you would like to kill me.' Such a response would usually be denied by the group, and John would become silent again. His therapists brought this case to supervision after John was hospitalized. After a short period of stabilization, John was placed back in group therapy. His therapists were frustrated with the same pattern of behavior he exhibited prior to his hospitalization.

In supervision, we worked actively to understand John's projections, but the therapists had first to resolve their identification with John's projections. He felt they were angry and wanted to hurt him, and also that they believed he was a hopeless case. Only when the therapists and the group could contain their own angry and negative feelings could they move out of this position and be helpful. The obstacle to bringing John into the group was centered in the therapists' avoidance of their own feelings. When the therapists could recognize the projective identification, they saw that John's powerful defenses held in place a constructed reality in which John made himself unlovable and hopeless, which relieved him of the burden of coming out of his shell, and which repeated his original trauma. He used splitting (seeing just the bad self and bad other) as well as projective identification to lock himself in a safe but painful world.

As the therapists pointed out these defenses, John's anger began to surface. He admitted he had been angry all his life and was never able to bring it into therapy because he feared there would be serious repercussions. Over the next few months, he was able to explore his anger and began to bring it into group. As the powerful feelings were contained and explored by the group, John became less fearful and offensive. His individual therapy began to evolve from a supportive psychotherapy with medication monitoring to a more explorative therapy. It was our feeling that John's group experience was a significant component of his overall treatment plan. John became more verbal and less withdrawn. This change happened by a gentle confrontation of primitive defenses in the context of a supportive, empathetic relationship with his therapists and the group. This process was initiated by the confrontation of the therapists' defenses in the supervision process. The supervisor must be active and monitor the interaction of the therapists with the group. He must challenge the therapists' feelings, behaviors or thoughts toward the patient and group when they are not helpful.

A note on supervising peer groups of therapists

In work with the psychoses, I frequently find it more rewarding to supervise therapists in groups than individually. Therapists need considerable support to conduct this demanding therapy and can easily feel isolated and overwhelmed when working alone. A co-therapist can be helpful in this respect. However, one can still become bewildered and frustrated. In group supervision, therapists receive the support not only of the supervisor but also of their peers. Because the supervisor's interventions can be processed by the group and each therapist is likely to find a subgroup to help him deal with his feelings, there is reduced likelihood that the therapist will be narcissistically hurt by the comments of the supervisor. The group situation thus facilitates dealing with countertransference issues.

A female co-therapist of a group of psychotic men reported to me in individual supervision that one of the men disturbed her and that she would become furious with him for no apparent reason. He was an elderly, withdrawn man who, when verbal, would become paranoid and blame others for his difficulties. The therapist thought of dropping the group because she could not tolerate her feelings. She interacted minimally with the patient and had little interest in his case. When I confronted her with the fact that something was blocking her from dealing with this patient and possibly the whole group, she replied, 'Isn't it OK not to like a patient?'

I encouraged her to explore the reasons for her dislike. She mentioned his unkempt appearance, his sadistic anger and the negative effect he was having on the group. At this point she realized that he reminded her of her alcoholic, abusive father with whom she was never able to get close. As she divulged this, the therapist was ashamed and became tearful. She was so ashamed that she now became sure she had to drop the group. I recommended she begin her own individual therapy to work on the issue. She refused this but did take my second recommendation to join my supervision group, where she received a great deal of support. As the therapists shared their experiences with patients they found difficult, she began to see that others had similar difficulties. She was able to understand why she was angered by this patient and wanted to leave the group. She also realized that she was at odds with her co-therapist, whom she felt could not understand her behavior. She decided to continue her work with the therapy group and in the supervision group. She reported positive changes: the patient became much more verbal and the group climate became more supportive. Countertransference interventions like this are common in supervision groups where I find that therapists receive more support and are able to work better with their own issues. In addition, the therapist has a forum for modeling leadership with these difficult issues. This therapist after her experience with the supervision group did go into individual therapy. She thanked the supervision group for helping her allay her prior fears of addressing her own personal issues.

BOUNDARY ISSUES

Another valuable tool of group supervision is the use of its own group process to understand what is going on in the therapy group and to demonstrate effective management. As Lesser and Godofsky (1983) have pointed out, issues arising in the supervision group often parallel the issues of the therapy group. I can usually tell what kind of difficulties the patient group is having by the difficulties and behavior of the therapists. The most common problem seen in the supervision group, and which parallels the difficulty in the therapy group, is the boundary issue. With this population one must be sure the therapists understand the importance of boundaries. Boundaries of space, time, and reality define the difference between inside and outside the group. Boundaries contain the energy of the system and make it possible to direct it towards a goal (Agazarian 1997). These patients lose sight of boundaries easily, and therapists tend to overlook the problem because of the severe psychopathology. Since these patients have a difficult time with boundaries, they must be clearly defined, otherwise the potent defenses of the patients will turn the group life into the same chaotic turmoil as their internal world.

In group supervision with therapists in an acute hospital setting I constantly get confronted with the issue that attendance at groups is sporadic and nothing can be done. Patients attend infrequently, are not on time or leave early. In exploring this issue in supervision, we usually find staff attend sporadically. Many hospitals and clinics believe boundaries do not apply to staff. This problem changes as the staff attend regularly and keep time boundaries. When therapists are late, miss sessions or leave early on a regular basis in the supervisory group, it is likely their therapy group will have boundary difficulties.

When the therapists are constantly bringing in the patients historical data the group is probably working in the past. This is not productive with the psychotic patient. When working with this population, it is important to stay in the here-and-now and focus on relatedness in the group. Keeping firm boundaries in the supervision group will help model this for the patient group. The reality–irreality boundary maintenance will help keep the patients grounded and stop splitting and projection from being accepted as valid communication (Agazarian 1997). These patients live in a world where fantasy, 'mind reads,' negative predictions and distortions are used as data. As the supervision group deals with its own reality this can be demonstrated.

> A therapist who was running a group in a psychiatric hospital was asked by his unit director to attend my supervision group because patients in his groups were complaining that the groups were chaotic and of little help. The therapist defensively told the unit director that the problems were due to the number of psychotic patients in the group. He was late for the first few sessions. When questioned about time boundaries he said that he was very busy and could not start his group on time. He often ended early due to his other duties. When he talked of his patients he defined them by their historical conflicts. He talked of the patient who was abandoned by his mother or abused by his father and how his attempts to focus on these traumas had met with little success. This therapist had a very poor sense of time boundaries. He was working in the past and many times accepting the patients' constructed reality. The supervision group confronted him with his time boundary problem. He began to attend the supervision group regularly on time. The supervision group began to work with his own constructed reality of being too busy to set time boundaries. As he was able to undo this his groups on the unit started and finished on time. He became more aware of the patients' constructed realities. The supervision group helped him to change his focus to the present where he could be more helpful to his patients.

Getting chronic psychotic patients to attend group can be a formidable task. As mentioned earlier, such patients manage their anxieties by withdrawal and distancing. Some authors have suggested 'flexible boundaries groups' (McIntosh *et al.* 1991) as a way of dealing with this issue. The boundaries of the group can be set up in a number of creative ways, however, the therapist must be aware that he must place an importance on the boundaries and model them for the patients. The supervisor must keep a close watch on this issue.

The dangers of pre-conceived ideas

A male and female co-therapist reported to their supervisor that they were having difficulty at the outset of an outpatient group of five schizophrenic men. The anxiety level was very high and the members were hesitant in talking. The therapists consulted the supervisor because they could not agree on their approach. The female therapist was very active and supportive of group members. The male therapist would remain silent, and as the patients' personal conflicts became clear he would interpret the dynamics of the individuals and the group. His interpretations were usually followed by silence and then regressive behavior on the part of the patients. The therapists were furious at each other, blaming one another for the difficulties of the group. As they began to discuss the differences it became clear that each therapist had preconceived constructions that were the source of the difficulty. The female therapist, while well versed in group dynamics, believed that schizophrenia was a biological illness which prevented patients from making any real personal growth. Therefore her therapy was limited to support and working on coping skills. She was avoiding any meaningful contact with the patients. The male therapist had an understanding of both individual and group dynamics and, unlike his co-therapist, believed he would be able to help these patients through insight into their internal conflicts and interpretation of group process. He was not able to use his knowledge in the context of real relatedness. He would break eye contact with the patients when making his interpretations. Both therapists were avoiding any meaningful contact with the patients. The approaches of the two therapists were not compatible.

Supervision focused on defining clear goals for the group. All agreed that improved interpersonal relationships and coping skills would be the group goals. Both therapists were able to discuss their fears of this population and how their preconceived positions kept them at a distance from their patients. As they were able to deal with their differences in the supervisory group their bickering stopped and they were available to help the group move forward.

There are three misleading and dangerous concepts that therapists are apt to misuse, consciously or unconsciously, in conducting a group of psychotic patients. The first is that psychotics cannot improve their situation. This belief becomes a self-fulfilling prophecy and is unfortunately quickly absorbed by the patients. The second recipe for failure is the belief that psychotic patients will respond to insight through the interpretation of conflict. Both of these positions fail to establish the necessary holding environment. The third is that the psychotic patient will improve if you (magically) meet their needs. A therapist who is overly nurturing and/or a 'rescuer' does not keep proper boundaries or set appropriate limits and is easily manipulated by the patients. This will cause severe stress on the therapist and potentiate acting out or regression.

A female therapist sought supervision for a group of inpatient schizophrenic patients whom she could not get to work as a group. The group had been in existence for several sessions with very poor boundaries. They met on the hospital ward and patients were allowed to go to their rooms if they could not sit through the session. The therapist was put in the position of rounding up patients and promising them a reward if they would come to group. Too often, she would allow patients leave unnecessarily for medication during group. She would go to excessive lengths to meet the patients' needs and required very little in return from them. This therapist had a very skewed idea of the corrective emotional experience. The patients saw her as weak, ineffective and unable to cope with their powerful defenses. They would manipulate for extra privileges and if they became frustrated they would leave the group. Little therapeutic work if any could be done.

In supervision, we began to work with the therapist's construction that psychotic patients needed nurturing to make up for failures in their development. She was trying to supply what she thought was missing for the patient and had little understanding that in order for these patients to improve they must make changes in their internal world. Without such inner change, the patient is doomed to distort reality and find relating to others impossible. Once the therapist could see that the priority was getting the patients to bring themselves into the group and not satisfying their regressed needs, she was able to begin to work effectively to develop a relationship with the patients which would in turn become a container for the patients to address their inner conflicts and reality distortions. With this shift in position, effective therapy was now possible.

The supervisor must recognize that most therapists begin this work with preconceived ideas and theories, and unless they are uncovered and addressed in supervision the therapist will flounder and feel emotionally drained by the experience.

Patient selection

A dilemma which is constantly brought to supervision is the question of patient selection. What type of chronic psychotic patients would benefit from group psychotherapy and which type of group would be appropriate? *I have always advocated the grouping of patients by ego strength instead of diagnosis.* There are two types of psychotic patient. The first has an ego which has become totally overwhelmed by the psychotic process. At this time, the patient has little ability to relate to others and is self-absorbed. This development usually occurs in the acute phase when the patient needs to be stabilized with antipsychotic medication. This process can continue into the chronic phase of the illness where the symptoms are so disruptive that the patient has little ability to work on interpersonal issues. When such a patient is evaluated there is no sense of a relationship to the interviewer.

The second type of patient has an ego that is partially intact. Such individuals do not appear totally overwhelmed and try to achieve some type of relatedness. Youcha (1976), in evaluating patients for inpatient groups, distinguished these two categories through allying himself with the observing ego of the patient. If the patient were able to get outside of his issues and look at himself objectively, it would indicate he was higher functioning than the patient who could not. This maneuver can also be the beginning of a working alliance.

To place patients in groups properly, ego strength must be evaluated and patients with similar strengths and weaknesses grouped together. I have been more successful working with psychoses in homogeneous groups than in heterogeneous groups, and higher goals can be set where there is more ego strength.

> While evaluating Jim for an outpatient group after hospitalization, I noticed that he continued to have auditory hallucinations and strong paranoid ideation. He had previously been diagnosed as schizoaffective and was hospitalized after his third suicide attempt. His schizophrenic wife had left the state with their newborn child. Although Jim related only superficially to his wife and child he still experienced a sense of loss. He was able to explore with me his lack of trust which kept him distant. He had a wish to change the way he related to others. I felt that there were some threads of ego strength that would make Jim a good candidate for group therapy.

> By contrast, Rich had been diagnosed as paranoid schizophrenic. He was hospitalized when he threatened to kill several people whom he thought were demons sent by the devil. After he was stabilized, he still heard voices and was fearful. Rich could not explore his anger or his fear with me. He was married and his wife was a prostitute who had taken all his money and left him. Every experience he had at relationships met with failure and victimization. He could not comprehend his predicament and wanted to be left alone. He wanted to join a group to stop the disruptions in his life. It was difficult to get any type of working alliance and his internal world was in constant turmoil.

> These two examples show different ego strengths for which group therapy should have different goals. For Jim, a group where he may explore his issues would be appropriate. Rich required a group where he could define his issues and learn about his illness in a very supportive climate. The goals for both patients would include improved interpersonal relatedness but the context would be different. The focus of the lower level group would be socialization and education and would be leader directed. While the higher functioning

group would be less leader directed, however, the leader would be active in use of group process to develop interpersonal relationships.

Choosing among therapeutic approaches

The question of therapy approaches for the psychoses has been controversial. Students continually ask which one is most beneficial. In the current era of managed care, shorter approaches are more efficient financially but probably less effective in the long run. In the psychiatric hospital, treatment becomes so shortened that every group may have different membership and the group may have a life as short as one session. At times we must be creative and design groups to fit the needs of the situation. However, there are certain principles that must be kept in mind to achieve effective group work with this population.

According to Kanas (1996), three models of group therapy for schizophrenic patients have evolved: educative, psychodynamic and interpersonal. Kanas advocated a synthesis of the three theoretical orientations in what he calls the 'integrative approach.' His research on outcomes is positive and impressive. I believe this is because Kanas' approach encompasses the major principles that make group psychotherapy effective for the chronic psychotic patient. These principles are:

1. The establishment of a holding environment by empathetic therapists.

2. The ability of the therapists to manage the powerful affects of the patients and to deal with their own countertransference.

3. The work is done primarily in the group's experience 'here and now' and not so much in terms of the past.

4. The therapist takes an active role in leading the group and carefully monitors the anxiety level of the group.

5. The therapist works to help the patients to improve their ego functioning by decreasing the effect of primitive defenses, thereby enhancing both reality testing and the ability to relate to others.

6. Patients are taught how to improve their interpersonal relationships and to better deal with their illness.

7. The therapist monitors group process to facilitate boundarying and group defense modification (scapegoating and role suction).

8. The therapist understands and accepts that these patients can only work through early phases of group development. Treatment goals must be those that these patients can attain.

The supervisor works with these principles and helps the therapist to modify his technique depending on the design. For example if he is running a one session group there would be an emphasis on patient education. However, if the student is cognizant of all the above principles, then further work can be done to help patients enter into meaningful dialogues with others even in the short time allotted to the group.

Conclusion

Nearly every psychiatric institution has its population of chronic psychotic patients. It is accepted clinical practice that group psychotherapy is a viable treatment for this population. However, it is disconcerting to see the limited amount of training and supervision given to therapists who deal with these patients in group psychotherapy. Furthermore, due to staff downsizing with managed care, many therapists are left to find supervisors on their own. Most teaching institutions are trying to recruit volunteer faculty to assume this role. This method has proved less than desirable. Traditionally this area of training has been sidelined and this neglect is further exacerbated by the fact that students themselves are initially hesitant to get involved because of the severity of the patients' pathology and the lack of support for the work.

For those brave souls who pursue their interest in this field, supervision is a necessity. Such therapists will thereby begin to understand and manage these neglected patients appropriately, which will in turn lead to considerable personal satisfaction. Through work with primitive patients therapists develop a better awareness of themselves and the confidence to handle difficult situations in group psychotherapy.

As I alluded to earlier, I often recall the frustration and anxiety of my early years and compare it to that of my students as they begin to contain and work with psychotic groups. I remember how years ago I felt cheated to have to work with this population. I take great satisfaction in the fact that this initial apprehension has not been validated, and indeed that taking the road less traveled has proved to be a very rewarding path, personally and professionally.

References

Agazarian, Y. and Peters, D. (1981) *The Visible and Invisible Group.* London: Routledge and Kegan Paul.

Agazarian, Y. (1997) *Systems-Centered Therapy for Groups.* New York: Guilford Press.

Della Badia, E. (1989) 'Group-as-a-whole concepts and the therapeutic milieu on the inpatient psychiatric unit.' *Group 13,* 165–172.

Fairbairn, W. (1952) *Psychoanalytic Studies of the Personality.* London: Tavistock/Routledge and Kegan Paul.

Frankel, B. (1993) 'Groups of chronic mental patients and the legacy of failure.' *International Journal of Group Psychotherapy 43,* 157–172.

Gabbard, G. (1994) *Psychodynamic Psychiatry in Clinical Practice: The DSM-IV Edition.* Washington, DC: American Psychiatric Press.

Kanas, N. (1986). 'Group therapy with schizophrenics: a review of controlled studies.' *International Journal of Group Psychotherapy 36,* 339–351.

Kanas, N. (1996) *Group Psychotherapy for Schizophrenic Patients.* Washington, DC: American Psychiatric Press.

Kline, F., Kraft Goin, M. and Zimmerman, W. 'You can be a better supervisor.' *The Journal of Psychiatric Education 1,* 1, (2).

Lesser, I. and Godofsky, I. (1983) 'Group treatment of chronic patients: educational and supervisory aspects.' *International Journal of Group Psychotherapy 33,* 535–546.

McIntosh, D., Stone, W. and Grace, M. (1991) 'The flexible boundaried group: format, techniques and patients' perceptions.' *International Journal of Group Psychotherapy 41,* 49–64.

Miller, L., O'Connor, E. and DiPasquale, T. (1993) 'Patients' attitudes toward hallucinations.' *American Journal of Psychiatry 150,* 584–594.

Sullivan, H.S. (1962) *Schizophrenia as a Human Process.* New York: WW Norton.

Youcha, I. (1976) 'The short-term inpatient group: formation and beginnings.' *Group Process 7,* 119–137.

CHAPTER 13

Psychotherapy Training for Nurses as Part of a Group Psychotherapy Project

The Pivotal Role of Countertransference

Dianne Campbell Lefevre

Introduction

A psychotherapy training for nurses in a large mental hospital was set up as part of the development of a psychoanalytically informed group psychotherapy project, named the Hawthorn project, for patients with chronic psychotic illnesses. The project consisted of a discrete group of rehabilitation wards within a large Victorian psychiatric hospital. The patients suffered from long-term mental illnesses, mainly schizophrenic and affective psychoses. A psychoanalytical understanding of and approach to treatment was at the centre of the integrated treatment approach which included social, pharmacological and educational treatments.

Originally part of the project, the one year training was extended later to all staff in the hospital and continued for a period of five years. Developing an understanding of countertransference responses through the consultant psychiatrist's sharing of her own countertransference experiences, helped to overcome the nurses' initial resistance to taking up the training.

In what follows, the story of the project is told; the role of countertransference responses, the psychotherapy training, its assessment and results are described.

The story

In the mid 1980s I started work as a consultant psychiatrist at a large, century-old mental hospital whose patients were drawn from poor areas of east London. I had trained at a postgraduate teaching hospital of the University of London, the Maudsley Hospital, and had never worked in a pejoratively called ' bin' before. I had under my care a ward for acute admissions, the 'acute ward' with 25 beds and several wards for patients with long-term psychiatric illnesses, 'continuing care' wards, as well as part of a day hospital situated miles away.

I had trained as a psychoanalytical psychotherapist, was politically on the left and filled with the idealistic notion of combining psychotherapy with acute psychiatry in an under-funded hospital that served a socially deprived area. In attempting this I was unaware of the challenges that would inevitably accompany a change of the pre-existing clinical and theoretical orientation and a readjustment in interdisciplinary relating. These difficulties were amplified by the destabilization that resulted from repeated and inadequately planned changes that were occurring in the British National Health Service at the time.

Taking ward rounds on the dismal barn-like continuing care wards with strange, half dressed people skulking in corners smoking and staff hiding in the staff room left me feeling depressed, demoralized, hopeless, despairing and sometimes enraged. Staff, doing what was expected of them, would straighten up and immediately become attentive and cheerful the moment they saw me and behave as if this ugly, cheerless, malodorous, Spartan environment and the people in it were entirely unremarkable. We would briskly get on with what amounted to the suppression and control of madness and deal with patients' problems in the most rudimentary way with little attention to the human aspects of individual patients or staff. I experienced feelings of loneliness and madness at such moments. Surprised and alarmed at the strength of my feelings, I noticed that I was doing everything I could to avoid the ward rounds, which I loathed. The staff felt hurt and rejected by my unexplained attitudes. Conversely I noticed that patients preferred to be invisible and were pleased to avoid me, mirroring my own feelings of recoil.

My training and experience as a psychoanalytical psychotherapist demanded a deeper understanding of patients and the staff–patient relationships from a psychoanalytical theoretical perspective. However, I confess to feeling the seductive pull to defensive institutional rigidity and drug manipulation with short, sharp, behavioural therapies such as token economy which had been tried from time to time, when a new wind in the form of a person or a new kind of despair blew through the unit.

My patients included some of the most disturbed patients outside of the special hospitals. The severity of their illnesses was represented in their intrapsychic self-destructiveness and this destructiveness was also acted out towards staff and other contacts.

For example, Edward, one of our patients with a schizophrenic illness, had been a pub fighter in the East End, an amateur boxer fighting illegally in one of the poorer inner city areas. Staff were always wary of him and his unpredictability. Acting on a delusional belief, he beat up Joseph, a fragile old man, who was left with severe injuries. When taken to task, he held out his knuckles which bore a few minor scratches which had been incurred when he punched Joseph, and said in an injured voice: 'Look what *he* did to me'.

Martin, who suffered from a chronic schizophrenic illness, believed delusionally that various famous people including royalty and staff members were his mother. Unfortunately he had almost killed his real mother in a physical assault. It was of great concern to us that he was inclined to search for the people he had incorrectly so identified and indeed once hit the headlines doing so. He not infrequently and without warning attacked staff members. On one occasion he accused a male staff member of sexually assaulting him in a series of bizarre ways. But for the fact that his descriptions were a physical impossibility, the nurse would have been immediately suspended pending investigation. This caused a lot of fear, anxiety, and unspoken dislike of the patient amongst staff, particularly those who were in charge of his care, sometimes alone, for long periods of time, on the sparsely staffed wards.

I worked with Frank Morrison who was later to become the project manager of the Hawthorn project (Lefevre and Morrison 1997). We were to work in a fruitful partnership for many years. He was generous and empathetic, had a unique ability to hold people psychologically in times of stress and a real concern for staff whose considerable talents had been underused for a long time. He was looking for something better for patients.

Frank conducted some research on staff–patient relationships using social networks as a tool. A 'social network' is the number of friends, relatives, acquaintances and staff members named by patients (Lefevre and Morrison 1997). He compared staff's views of social networks with patients' views on their own networks and found that staff who thought they knew patients well made remarkably inaccurate estimates. The differences between staff and patients views were statistically significant in the estimated number of contacts and highly significant in the identification of friends.

Independently, the recognition that my unwelcome feelings must have a great deal to do with countertransference was like a healing interpretation accompanied by a great sense of relief. In discussing this with Frank Morrison, we realized that the misreading of patients by perfectly competent and humane staff seemed likely to be connected to a countertransference communication in that the psychotic process eschews all experiences involving relating (Williams 1998). Staff were not meant to know about the secret lives of patients who needed to keep at a distance.

Frank and I had observed that outsiders coming on to wards to run groups, frequently encounter trouble and such groups rarely last long as they are destroyed by other staff members. This may be because of primal scene envy – 'What are they doing in there, all alone and in secret?' We felt that we needed to create a discrete unit using psychoanalytically informed psychotherapy as the central therapeutic core. This would require a special training for the nurses. The training would need to include theoretical seminars, the practice of running groups, supervision of groups, and staff support in the form of attendance at an experiential group.

To our advantage at that time was the management decision to close wards in response to the much publicized 'care in the community' policy. Patients would have to leave the hospital and needed to be helped to do so if they were not to rapidly relapse and require readmission.

In addition the hospital needed the approval of the Nurse Training Board to continue to train nurses. The innovative project we envisaged would improve the chances of gaining such approval. This proved to be a lever in persuading management to support it.

The Hawthorn project

These factors allowed for the conception and gestation of the Hawthorn project but persuading the nurses of the benefits of training was necessary for its birth. The idea of running groups frightened staff many of whom stated the fear that they might damage the patients, and attending seminars, supervision and being part of a staff group caused even greater anxiety. The fear of facing a total change in orientation and attitude reverberated like a discordant clash of symbols through the wards.

To placate staff anxieties, I spent the first part of every ward round discussing frankly my own countertransference feelings evoked by patients and by the institution, relating them to theoretical concepts and tying them in with the abundant 'clinical material'. The nurses realized how important it was for them to make sense of their feelings connected with their work and to allow patients to be people and not 'clinical material'. Gradually they became more able to look at their own feelings and when one nurse reported that she sometimes felt like knifing a particularly hostile patient, the feelings in all the staff present poured out and for a while these sessions extended into the time allocated for the ward round. Strong feelings are inevitable in people who spend large periods of time in close proximity. How much more so must this be the case on inadequately staffed psychiatric wards, where nurses work long shifts and are in close contact with patients who are profoundly disturbed.

I have been trying to work towards a psychotherapeutic way of thinking at another hospital where there are too few staff and many difficult and provocative patients. An intelligent, competent nurse complained about me to the consultant psychiatrist, saying with a sense of outrage: 'She asked me if I felt like hitting a patient, I have *never* hit a patient in all my life …'

Anxiety makes the boundary between fantasy and action blurred and then the fantasy of hitting a patient cannot be separated from the action. Getting this boundary firmly in place is essential for staff working with severely disturbed patients who are sometimes physically violent, quite often threatening and frequently provocative. The primitive defence mechanisms commonly used, such as splitting and projective identification, result in staff being recipients of the patients' strong and often bizarre feeling states which are often difficult to describe and are experienced as countertransference feelings. One could say that being 'inhabited' by the projected psychotic process led in the case above, to a confusion between fantasy and action in the staff member/container. Failure to recognize this process will lead to an involuntary acting out in an attempt to deal with these feelings in some way or another. And to begin to recognize and understand the process requires a willingness to undertake some kind of instruction.

While edging towards an acceptance of the need for training, what was evolving within the Hawthorn project was a qualitative difference in the hierarchical structure. The boundaries and roles of individuals remained clear. However with a leasing out of power in the interests of staff taking responsibility for facilitating their own groups, staff came to regard me as what they called a 'knowledgeable peer' and a person to whom they could entrust their feelings about patients and other staff.

Searles is one of the few psychoanalysts who has treated chronically psychotic patients using psychoanalytical psychotherapy. He has written frankly about his countertransference feelings, which included sexual and murderous feelings as well as the special non-human feelings that occur with the projection of part-objects into the analyst (Searles 1979).

Williams' (1998) theory of psychotic functioning draws a distinction between the non-psychotic personality present (but not always available in the transference) in all psychotic patients, and the object-repudiating impulses which underlie the patient's psychotic defences. The disorganized, severely regressed state which makes up the psychotic process comprises poorly or unsymbolized instinctual impulses which cathect split off, part objects (self-representations) and this confused instinct/object admixture is regularly, violently projected into the therapist due to the ego's incapacity to respond to the demands of (and need for) object relating.

For the therapist, the shock of encountering the psychotic process at the point that it totally overshadows the non-psychotic personality was likened by Frank Morrison to suddenly and forcefully realizing that one is talking to what feels like a television screen – a profoundly disturbing experience.

The negative consequences of not recognizing and dealing with the results of massive projections from distressed patients – resulting in countertransference reactions in staff – is in my view the most important message in Isabel Menzies Lyth's work with nursing staff in institutions (Menzies Lyth 1988). However, the organization and the defensive nature of the institution militates against individual staff members' acknowledging this. This leads to the acting out in the countertransference taking the form of countertherapeutic and even inhuman behaviours towards patients by staff.

I shall define later what I mean by countertransference and the problems that can arise from not identifying countertransference feelings and their application to the background of the project and the training.

Our story continues with the freeing up of the nurses' feelings on the 'continuing care wards' alongside the greater awareness of training advantages on the 'acute ward' leading to the birth of the project.

None of us predicted where the greatest interest and creativity would take place. It was rather like the birth of Gargantua whose mother Gargamelle, while carrying him, ate 'sixteen quarters, two bushels, and six pecks ' of tripe which set off the labour after an 11-month gestation. The baby Gargantua was so big that he could not get out via the prolapsed fundament, but slipped into a placental vein, to the inferior vena cava, climbed through the diaphragm and out via Gargamelle's left ear! (Rabelais 1963). Like the greedy Gargamelle, in my unseemly enthusiasm I got it wrong! Thus the Hawthorn project which we initially expected to involve predominantly patients with short term psychotic illnesses, ended up as a psychotherapy project with chronically ill, long-term patients and it led to the development of a formal training for nurses.

A pilot study was started on the 'acute ward'. A training with all the elements mentioned above commenced. The training was to last a year for each intake of nurses starting with the staff already within the project. Later staff from all over the hospital were invited to apply. The course continued for five years.

About 18 months into the training a new senior nurse who claimed, it turned out later inaccurately, to have had experience on a psychotherapeutically orientated unit, was appointed on the 'acute ward'. We had been running weekly groups and monitoring the effects of groups on patients who were ' revolving door admissions' – that is, patients who were repeatedly discharged and readmitted with a recurrence of their illness. The readmission decreased in those patients who had been placed in a group which they continued to attend after being discharged from hospital. Similarly there was a demonstrable reduction in the number and the severity of violent incidents nine months after the onset of group work with patients on the ward.

While I was on leave, the senior nurse just mentioned told the psychoanalytical psychotherapist that she was not wanted as facilitator of the staff group and discouraged the staff from attending supervision. The groups could therefore not continue. Senior non-clinical management, secretly delighted to find someone who was as hostile to doctors as they were, supported her until some years later, when the extent to which she was putting the institution and the management staff at risk became apparent.

The result was that the 'acute ward' dropped out of the project and the research projects in that area were discontinued. The Hawthorn project then consisted of the continuing care wards. The staff training and regular psychoanalytically informed group psychotherapy for as many patients as would attend, continued.

Social networks measurements were being done by an independent team on all the continuing care patients in the hospital. On our patients they were taken at the start of the group project and two years later and compared with measures of a comparison group at the same time. At the start of the project in 1986 the group psychotherapy patients had smaller numbers of contacts on all counts and in 1989 the networks were larger on all measures except, as expected, in the relatives category. The staff on the project also made significant gains that have been described elsewhere, not least in gaining the experience of the psychotherapy training, in the pleasure of using the extra therapeutic tools and in seeing the results in both ourselves and the patients (Lefevre and Morrison 1997).

The premature destruction in the early 1990s of the Hawthorn project on the continuing care wards, its relevance to countertransference reactions in project staff on an institutional level, details of social networks research, counter-transference responses and their putative effects on staff facilitating groups, have all been described elsewhere (Lefevre and Morrison 1997; Lefevre 1994).

The psychotherapy training and the staff

We needed more trained psychotherapist time in order to deliver the training and having taken advice from the relevant senior psychiatrist colleague about how to go about it, I went ahead and engaged a psychoanalytical psychotherapist for a few sessions a week. The department that traditionally ought to have been helpful had turned down our requests for help with the training and running of groups. Despite that, a senior member of that department complained vociferously to the equivalent of the hospital director about the way I had made the appointment as a means of putting a stop to it and thus to the proposed project. I was forced to make an apology at a formal meeting to the hospital director and the senior staff member.

This may demonstrate, at least in part, one of the effects of working in a hospital in which predominantly psychotic patients reside. Staff enact the splitting, envy and projections which are the stock in trade of primitive mental processes. The need for all staff to have some understanding if not training, in the workings of primitive mental mechanisms and their effects on staff, patients and the institution cannot be emphasized enough.

To enlist management support, Frank Morrison prepared a number of papers outlining the evidence for the benefits of psychoanalytical psychotherapy for psychotic patients and the benefits of training for nurses. Kanas' (1986) review paper on the outcome of inpatient groups was particularly useful.

To prepare nursing staff for the onset of the project, in addition to discussion of countertransference responses at the start of ward rounds, we had several 'brainstorming' meetings on the 'acute ward' and 'continuing care wards' during which discussion of fears, doubts and new ideas was welcomed. The staff were qualified as either State Enrolled Nurses (SEN) or Registered Mental Nurse (RMN). Those who were not attracted to the idea of working on a discrete, group orientated unit, were free to move to other wards within the hospital. Those who chose to work on the unit had worked in the hospital for between 6 and 25 years. None had any training in group psychotherapy or had ever run a group before. To replace those nurses who had left, new nurses were carefully selected, not for their knowledge of psychotherapy (which was virtually non existent) or for their dedication (since projected personal needs can pose as dedication to damaging effect) but for their capacity for empathy and their ability not to act out despite sometimes intolerable frustrations.

The pilot study started with weekly theoretical seminars and the experiential group. Nurses on the 'acute ward' started facilitating weekly groups for patients and attending weekly supervision at which all nurses were welcome. Staff on the 'continuing care wards' soon gained enough confidence to take on their own groups.

Within a few months all the elements of the pilot study were running and the course was set to last for one year. It was eventually extended to staff in the rest of the hospital and applicants were interviewed and offered a place if appropriate.

The course consisted of the following:

1. Weekly theoretical seminars on basic psychoanalytical theory. Course members were given papers on basic theoretical topics. We used a selection of papers by Sandler Dare and Holder, Freud, Klein, Winnicott, Josephs, H. Rosenfeld, Mahler, Searles, Ogden, Guntrip and others. The Sandler, Dare and Holder papers that we used have been gathered together and published (1993). Relevant papers were selected from Herbert Rosenfeld's books, *Impasse and Interpretation* and *Psychotic States*. Thomas Ogden's paper (1979), 'On projective identification', was particularly valuable as was Melanie Klein's *Envy and Gratitude and Other Works* and key papers on countertransference, particularly Paula Heimann's 'Countertransference' (1960). Candidates were expected to read the papers in their own time and to offer comment and criticism during the seminars.

Emphasis was placed on the understanding of basic psychoanalytic concepts such as transference, countertransference, resistance, therapeutic alliance and so on, as well as object relations theory and an understanding of defence mechanisms, especially primitive defence mechanisms likely to be operating in psychotic and severely borderline patients. These theoretical concepts were related to the clinical problems we encountered in our patients.

2. Candidates were expected to attend a closed experiential group. This was to afford support to staff during the upheavals in the hospital following the reforms, and to give nurses an experience of being a 'patient' in a group.

3. All candidates ran weekly patients' group therapy. It was surprising how much initial resistance there was to this, based, so it was reported, on fear of damaging the patients. This seemed to reflect the fears patients had of their destructiveness, projected into the staff.

    Patients were selected by the nurse facilitator and this was discussed with the supervisor and at the ward round. The groups were small closed groups with between six and eight patients. The interactions between patients and with the facilitator were recorded verbatim in as far as that was possible, as were the feelings of the facilitators evoked by the patients verbal and non-verbal responses during the group.

4. Candidates had to attend weekly supervision to discuss their groups during the year's training. In the Hawthorn project facilitators were expected to attend supervision for the whole life of the group, which may have been several years. Special attention was paid to countertransference feelings.

    It was noteworthy that nurses were willing to attend all these events even when not on duty in the hospital. As far as the Hawthorn project was concerned, it had been officially agreed with managers that the rigid 'shift' system would be abandoned and that nurses would be able to arrange their duties in a way that made running groups at the same place and time each week possible.

For the nurses within the Hawthorn project there were two further elements to the training.

5. At the ward round the medical model including discussions of formal symptoms and medication would be linked with an understanding of the psychological state of the patient. There would be emphasis on countertransference feelings as they manifested in staff working on wards or in rehabilitation houses with patients as well as in facilitation of the groups.

In addition, the idea of countertransference was broadened to help understand the reactions of other staff in the institution to people in the project and to management reactions to demands for rapid and repeated changes in policy. Attempts were made to understand some of the more traumatic attacks that the birth of this new baby, in the form of the Hawthorn project, occasioned from time to time.

6. Nurses in the Hawthorn project were expected to participate in various assessment procedures and research projects. One monitored the countertransference responses of nurses and correlated these responses with changes that took place in the groups (Lefevre 1994).

In an unpublished paper, Frank Morrison recorded how facilitating groups changed nurses perceptions of patients. Facilitators tended to relate to the whole patient including psychotic and non-psychotic aspects of the patient whereas some new staff tended to think of the patient as if he were the delusional character he claimed to be – not expressed in this concrete way but rather similarly to the way medical students refer to ' the liver fourth on the left from the end' – both examples demonstrating the need for a defensive dehumanization of the patient.

Assessment of the psychotherapy training course

In an unpublished 'Study of nurses constructs and comments' Frank Morrison devised a format using Kelly's repertory grid theory (Fransella and Bannister 1977) to look at how nurses construed the psychotherapy course. The overall aim was to see if the nurses doing the course valued it, and how the course compared with other ' post-basic' training courses that they had completed in the hospital. The psychotherapy course was one of 24 courses, only 4 of which took place over the period of a year. The other courses included Counselling, Holistic Nursing, Social Skills, Stress and Assertion and others. We were surprised that 100 per cent of the nurses rank ordered the psychotherapy course as the course that 'helped them and their patients most'! There were positive constructs relating to all the courses but those concerning psychotherapy were particularly positive. The following comments were selected as they represented common themes. They are all verbatim quotes:

1. 'Change of perception of myself and others, more aware.'

2. 'Allowed me to move outside the medical model, transcends into real life.'

3. 'Broader view of self, peers and patients.'

4. 'Profound effect on relationships between clients and myself.'

5. 'Major influence on me, made me aware of clients' behaviour as an attempt to communicate.'

6. 'Felt able to help people, able to understand behaviour and my responses better.'

7. 'Only decent course I've done in yonks.'

8. Based 'on the trusting patient–staff relationship, creates a climate of understanding.'

9. 'Greater understanding of not only others but also myself.'

Thus the individual comments centered on the trainee acquiring more self knowledge, an appreciation of the broadening of their theoretical and clinical understanding, a sense of personal growth, a feeling of increased autonomy, a sense of achievement and of pride in the work being done.

A common concern of ward managers is that sending nurses on courses may have no impact on their practice and carry no benefit for patients. This was not the case where nurses took on the task of facilitating a group and attending supervision for the year's duration of the course.

Some nurses who were doing the training from wards outside of the Hawthorn Project reported encountering all sorts of unnecessary difficulties – rooms made unavailable, patients taken out of a group to attend the ward round, nurses given 'urgent' tasks during their supervision time and so on. They had to be doggedly determined to complete the course. This demonstrates one of the difficulties in a training so organized that the trainees are set aside from the rest of the staff and one of the difficulties that may be particularly relevant to a training in psychotherapy in a predominantly non-psychotherapeutic environment. Being part of the Hawthorn Project was a protection against this.

Definition of countertransference and regression and fixation in the countertransference

I believe that the strength and nature of countertransference feelings evoked in nursing staff working with psychotic patients can be a deterrent to pursuing an interest in the psychotherapeutic treatment of psychosis. Since I believe that an understanding of this is crucial, I shall briefly give an account of what I mean by countertransference, and the difficulties that follow the failure to recognize it when it arises.

I have used Heimann's (1960) view that countertransference covers all feelings the analyst has towards the patient. Her paper applied to individual psychoanalysis but was helpful in thinking about the work we were doing in groups.

Kernberg (1980), using Racker's work, described two types of identification that take place in the countertransference. The first was concordant identification which is an identification of the analyst with the corresponding part of the patient's psychic apparatus. The second was complementary identification where the analyst identifies with the transference object of the patient.

In order to keep in touch with the patient, the therapist experiences regression which can be used to the patient's advantage or can lead to destructive acting out on the part of the therapist. Over time this can lead to chronic countertransference fixations and this is a particular danger in the treatment of severely disturbed patients, which would include patients suffering from borderline and psychotic disorders. Kernberg (1975) described three categories of chronic counter-transference fixations, all of which can be seen quite commonly in staff on busy wards.

In the first there is the emergence of pregenital aggression (oral and anal sadism) in the patient which prevents the patient from using the therapy and is reproduced in the therapist who may then cancel sessions or meetings unnecessarily, switch off or behave aggressively toward the patient. For example, there was at one time on one of our wards, an efficient, white coated nurse who got everybody up, dressed and shaved on time. He would give the Hitler salute and shout 'Heil Hitler!' or 'gehen sie aus – schnell!'. A patient who believed that he was Hitler said sadly to Frank Morrison: ' I knew him in Auschwitz, and the bastard hasn't changed since then.' This demonstrates an acting out of pregenital aggression by the staff member and the undesirable reinforcement of the patient's delusional system.

A further example of this type of countertransference fixation can be seen in the staff member who used to shout at mealtimes: 'Last to the table is a poofter!' The patient who had voices calling him a homosexual would become very agitated, could not eat and eventually attacked the nurse.

In the second category described by Kernberg, the experience of giving something good and getting bad in return can feed into the therapists excessive superego function, leading to the therapist developing paranoid fears or depressive guilt, the experience of phases of masochistic submission, and fears of criticism from third parties.

An example that stands out in my mind is that of a rather disturbed senior nurse on the 'acute ward'. Staff doing relatively short term work with very disturbed psychotic patients often feel that the enormous effort that goes into the therapeutic relationship yields poor returns both in the sense of clinical improvement and appreciation from the patient and may fail fully to understand this as part of the nature of the illness. This senior nurse told me, the consultant psychiatrist, that he/she would not tell me what transpired in sessions with a patient under my care, as the content was confidential! The managers did not act when informed of this until I wrote a formal letter pointing out the medico-legal consequences. By the time the matter was sorted out, the patient had been discharged (or discharged himself) and shortly afterwards committed suicide.

This secrecy for fear of criticism by a third party, was something that could not have been tolerated in nurses doing the training and indeed, to be selected they had to agree to attend weekly supervision of all their psychotherapeutic work, individual and group.

An example of the consequences of getting good for bad is as follows. A mute, immobile, psychotically depressed woman from abroad refused food and had to be fed, bathed dressed and cared for by nurses. As with all such depressives she was filled with rage directed against both herself and those around her. The nurses who were inhabited by 'toxic introjects', the results of her hatred projected into them, did not feel entitled to say how they found themselves loathing her since she was so ill. When I was on leave an inexperienced psychiatrist who was standing in for me, satisfied the staff by pronouncing her a malingerer. She became dehydrated and had to be admitted for intravenous rehydration and feeding to a general hospital where emergency ECT was given. One of the nurses on the ward who was from the same country, hit her. One can see here the acting out in the countertransference of the patient's sadism, which was never named or understood.

In the third category, Kernberg described the reappearance of neurotic traits within the therapist with the resultant arising of secondary defences. These may take two forms. The first leads to a narcissistic withdrawal or detachment from the patient, loss of empathy and the therapy being discontinued emotionally before unsuccessful termination.

I have many times been aware of wanting to 'switch off' myself, and seen it in supervisees. It is sad, although understandable in areas where there are very difficult and primitively disturbed, provocative patients, to see nurse therapists forcing themselves as they often do, into a blank, unfeeling stance while convincing themselves that it is 'better not to be involved'. The psychotherapy training made it possible to discuss the wish to withdraw with real understanding of the patient's and therapist's contribution, without fear of blame and criticism and with positive results for nurse therapist and patient.

The second form of defence described by Kernberg in this category, leads to narcissistic withdrawal from reality and an unrealistic certainty of being able to help a patient. The patient and therapist become an island with the therapist deflecting the patient's aggression to outside objects, rationalized as total dedication.

This was very much the case in the example above where the patient committed suicide. This particular nurse got into unhealthy, exclusive relationships with patients, and with managers, and as a result any attempt to look at the destructive nature of the relationships was impossible.

All these countertransference fixations operate, usually unrecognized and unnamed, in hospitals and institutions like the one in which these examples took place. I believe they are inevitable and can be helpfully recognized and dealt with to the advantage of the staff members and patients.

In Main 's (1957) words, 'Where the arousal of primitive feelings within can be detected by the therapist, he may, of course, put it to good use, and seek to find what it is about the patient that disturbs him in this way' (p.130). The problem is that excessive anxiety in staff about the presence of such feelings accentuated by the rigidity of institutional rules make it imperative that the therapist (nurse) does not even admit such feelings to himself. Our task was to reverse this defensive process.

On an institutional level the defences against anxiety aroused by working with patients suffering from severe short term and enduring mental illness took the form of the application of rigid institutional rules (Menzies Lyth 1988). Patients were summarily moved to different wards and staff were often moved without warning to themselves or to the patients. These practices together with regimentation, staff uniforms, lack of privacy and a rigid shift system for nurses prevented therapeutic relationships from being formed. In addition to causing considerable distress to both staff and patients, this practice hindered patients' recovery and the personal and intellectual development of nursing staff. It is not difficult to imagine that the hopelessness and despair felt by staff when failing again and again to elicit reasonable responses from the very disturbed patients in addition to the failure to receive support and empathy from more senior colleagues, would result in the withdrawal of empathy and the treatment of individuals and groups of individuals as objects. It is interesting that this phenomenon of the freezing of empathy was more evident amongst medical and management staff and it no doubt fuelled the development of the dehumanizing culture change and the ruthless practices that went with it, that has developed in the British National Health Service since the 1970s (Bruggen 1997). The nurses seemed better able to support each other and may have been more clinically in touch.

Results of establishing the psychotherapy training course

These are summarized in terms of the impact on staff, on patients and on the Institution.

The staff

The establishment of the psychotherapy training and the Hawthorn project were inextricably bound up and it is difficult to know where the positive and negative effects came from.

The establishment of the Hawthorn project involved changing the shift system, abandoning uniforms, creating mixed sex wards, allowing couples to cohabit, and withdrawing staff from some wards at night in order to save money to enable the project to survive. Simultaneously the nurses who worked on the project were expected to sign up for the psychotherapy training.

Along with both went a change in the usual hierarchical relationships. I, as the consultant psychiatrist and psychotherapist and Frank Morrison, the project manager, formed a united leadership that was able to resist splitting by staff. The fact that I had discussed openly and regularly my own countertransference feelings with staff helped them to risk being assessed on the course in supervision and seminars.

The project with the training as part of it had a remarkably positive influence on staff, in particular as regards the increase in morale reported by staff and observed in them. As far as staff in the Hawthorn project were concerned the record that was kept of staff sickness showed a decrease in the casual absenteeism that is so common in large, under-resourced hospitals.

Individual staff members achieved things that would not have previously attempted. For example, one member wrote a book, which has not been published and said that she would not have thought of doing so before. One completed a BSc. with group psychotherapy as the subject and has gone on to do a masters degree. Nurses read classical psychotherapy papers and willingly attended seminars and supervision outside of their working hours. The positive comments of nurses, including those who were not part of the Hawthorn project, have been documented above. They reflect the increased morale and confidence experienced by those who had completed the course.

Positive comments were received from two consultant psychiatrists who both remarked on the benefits to staff and to patients attending groups, particularly those patients with the sort of diagnoses that made decisions about their placement difficult.

The negative effects included the fact that some staff left early on in the project, one because of a sudden acute illness. This may have been related to the stresses of greater risk taking.

Later in the project, four of six group facilitators developed serious illnesses requiring weeks and in one case months off work. The possibility that this was related to the inevitable taking in of patients projections as 'toxic introjects' and the stress that that incurs with a possible deficient immune response as a result, has been discussed elsewhere (Lefevre and Morrison 1997; Lefevre 1994). Thus the support of staff in training in this setting, where there is a great deal of contact with patients with psychotic illnesses, seems important and desirable. Ideally such staff would benefit from being in intensive individual psychoanalytical psychotherapy in order to deal with the deep seated, primitive parts of the self which are revived with a vengeance by seriously disturbed patients. At the very least an experiential group ought to be available for such trainees as part of the training.

The patients

The results of the social networks research done alongside the Hawthorn project demonstrate the considerable positive benefits to patients of having nurses-in-training running groups (Lefevre and Morrison 1997).

Fifteen of the 30 Hawthorn patients moved out in 1989 and 1991. A further 5 moved out in 1994. None had been readmitted over a 4-year period. While the small numbers in our survey mean that the results have to be interpreted with care, this compares well with the 20 per cent readmission rates reported by the Team for the Assessment of Psychiatric services (TAPS) (Thornicroft 1991) for a similar population.

The institution

The immediate aim of regaining nurse training status for the hospital was fulfilled and with it came pride in the work place and increased morale.

Increasing numbers of trained nurses over a period of five years were able to take groups in a variety of settings such as rehabilitation houses and other wards outside of the project. Because many of these nurses no longer received direct supervision from the course supervisors, we have been unable to assess fully the impact this had on the working of the rest of the hospital. However we do know that the trained nurses made considerable impact in the areas of rehabilitation of the long-term patients and those who were labelled 'new long stay' patients.

Frank Morrison notes in his assessment of the psychotherapy course that the nurses never regarded themselves as psychotherapists, rather, as nurses using a psychotherapeutic approach under the supervision of a qualified psychoanalytical psychotherapist. Amidst the nurses comments on the course were expressed concerns about the possible loss of availability of supervision. Supervision incurs costs, although the financial benefits in terms of reduced readmission rates alone would seem, at the very least, to make up for such costs. However, managers on relatively short-term contracts with an obligation to save money have been known to bypass such considerations for immediate gain. This might change if we are able to give top priority to patients in carefully thought out, long-term plans for health services in the future.

Conclusion

The concept of integration as healthy and desirable is not a new one. Plotinus (c.203–270) wrote about parts coming together as one, and unity, from a mystical perspective. Almost 2000 years later, the King's Fund is advocating that a variety of therapeutic interventions be available to meet each patient's expressed need (King's Fund Organisational Audit 1997, p.299). Psychoanalytic theories which were developing at the turn of the century, regard unintegration and disintegration as pathological states and therapeutic intervention aims at integration. Trainee psychiatrists are encouraged to formulate patients' problems in psychological, biological and social terms in order to achieve a more complete understanding of the situation.

We do not however routinely offer a range of such psychological, biological and social treatments and neither psychiatric trainees nor nurses need have much experience of anything but the most time limited psychological treatments. In the case of trainee psychiatrists the recommendations made by the Royal College of Psychiatrists which, I understand, are mandatory, include amidst a long list of other experiences, one long-term case of individual psychotherapy and group therapy experience (Grant, Holmes and Watson 1993). Sadly these recommendations are not necessarily followed and are sometimes blatantly ignored. Thus those trainees who move up to consultant grade have not been encouraged to value psychodynamic understanding and treatments as an essential part of a whole treatment plan and indeed may know very little about such treatments. As a result some consultant psychiatrists feel threatened at the idea of co-working with a psychotherapist and feel that some degree of what they perceive to be their control, would be lost if this were to be the case. This is hardly encouraging for nurses wishing to expand and deepen their understanding of the problems in their patients.

In the Scandinavian countries and in Finland, group and individual psychotherapy of neurotic and psychotic patients has been thriving for one or two decades. Alanen in a comprehensive treatise on schizophrenia, describes 'need-adapted' treatment designed for individual patients. It includes social, psychological and biological approaches offered to patients with schizophrenia and allied psychoses and their families (Alanen 1997). Family therapy and psychodynamic individual therapy is offered according to the patients' needs and ability to use the treatments.

The Finnish project study demonstrates an impressive decrease, over a period of twenty years, of new and old long-term schizophrenic patients, psychiatric hospital patients and psychiatric hospital beds. This would hold out financial advantages if viewed as part of a long-term plan for mental health services quite apart from the obvious advantages to patients. Intelligent long-term planning in this country is something that has been sorely lacking in the last two decades. Alanen emphasizes the importance of adequate psychotherapy training for all disciplines as part of a deeper and richer approach to the psychoses.

Jackson and Williams (Jackson and Williams 1994), point out that nurse training in psychodynamic psychotherapy could revive interest in a creative career in psychiatric nursing and this seems ever more important as nursing as a career seems to have become increasingly unattractive.

In writing about the treatment of psychoses based on his experience of working on a psychotherapeutically orientated ward at a London teaching hospital, Williams in his Ph.D. thesis, (Williams 1985–1987) argues for the effectiveness of holding the core impact of the treatment in the transference which develops in psychoanalytical psychotherapy. He predicts that if this were to occur, there would be less need for institutional treatment and this has subsequently been borne out in the Finnish study (Alanen 1997).

Jackson and Cawley (1992) raise the difficulties of psychotherapeutic treatments in the community and the need for the integrated functioning of the multidisciplinary team in the community setting as well as in the ward setting. Along with that goes the need for better training in psychotherapy for psychiatrists as this would facilitate effective multidisciplinary working and encourage the work of nurse therapists within the multidisciplinary team.

If we are to provide an adequate service for the psychoses, social, psychological and biological treatments are all essential components. Williams makes the point that nurses are particularly good at engaging difficult patients in psychotherapeutic treatment (Williams 1985–1987). The shift system requires that relatively long periods are spent on the wards in close contact with disturbed patients. This affords nurses the sort of intensive experience of psychosis that no other discipline has. It must be very frustrating for a sensitive and creative nurse to be limited to rather wooden treatment approaches which do not include a deep understanding of the meaning of psychosis and a way of dealing with it.

I was made aware if this recently when an occupational therapist told me sadly how nurses running a crafts group would appropriate all the exciting pieces of work leaving the patients to do some simple colouring. The nurses' work was displayed on the walls and admired and the patients complained of being bored and wishing they could use the more exotic materials.

The nurses were using tasks as a defence against genuine emotional engagement with the patients and as an antidote to boredom and lack of creativity in the job. These nurses worked under an efficient but controlling ward manager. When a psychoanalyst who was consulted about a particular patient with an intractable depression demonstrated in an interview how angry the patient was, the ward manager concerned protested vigorously that, on the contrary, she could manage the patient who was 'a really nice man', as if being angry meant the reverse and implied that there was some nursing incompetence in terms of failure to suppress the anger and madness in the patient. Nobody took up the proffered supervision of a nurse who might be willing to see the patient psychotherapeutically. They would not have dared to do so.

The psychotherapy training of nurses as part of the Hawthorn project, which had at its centre psychoanalytically informed group psychotherapy with biological, social, educative and other psychological treatments clustering around it, transformed work which lacked depth, meaning and interest into something creative, inspiring and enriching.

It was a great advantage to have the course run from a background of intensive clinical work as theory and practice came together in a way that was complementary. The staff support group, as part of the training, served as a support and a learning experience and improved inter-ward working.

In the UK much has been written about the difficulties in recruiting doctors and nurses to fill shortages in extant posts. The shortages seem to be due not only to inadequate numbers of newly qualified staff, but also to early retirement (medical and from choice) and prompted by a variety of stresses at work (*BMA News Review* 1998). Bruggen (Bruggen 1997) in his shocking and moving book about the effects of NHS reforms highlights the fear and confusion infiltrating the organizations within the National Health Service. There is available a great deal of very helpful information about the psychodynamic understanding of organizations.

It is my view that if institutions in the NHS are to return to a state where we will be coping with the usual difficulties that occur in groups of people working together, if we are to restore reasonable morale to the workplace, a great deal of work in terms of the psychodynamic understanding of how we have arrived at where we are is required. Probably the largest workforce in the NHS is the nursing body. To have nurses trained in the psychodynamic understanding of the nature of relationships would be enormously helpful in the work needed to enable us to return to a healthier mode of functioning and in dispelling some of the extant confusion and fear.

In conclusion, there is increasing demand for a wider range of therapeutic interventions, including psychodynamic psychotherapy, to be available to patients suffering from severe and enduring mental illness including schizophrenia and related psychoses. Nurses spend the longest periods of time with such patients and are well suited to deliver the psychotherapy (Williams 1985–1987). There is a need to provide training for nurses and this can be done successfully 'on site' with advantages to patients, staff and the institution. Nurses' resistance to taking up such training can be seen as part of the defensive structure (Menzies Lyth 1988) that arises in hospitals and similar institutions, particularly at times when morale and staffing levels are low as has been increasingly the case with the rapidly changing health 'reforms' since the 1970s. Careful presentation of what countertransference means and how it is applicable to understanding patient–staff interactions, can break through the seal of defensive disinterest and liberate the capacity of nurses to put the extensive nursing experience into the deeper, more meaningful, framework of a psychoanalytical theoretical understanding and, in time and if desired, practice.

The training not only has to include a theoretical grounding, practical experience of providing group or individual psychotherapy and regular, ongoing supervision but also adequate staff support. This should take the form of a staff group run by an outside facilitator and if possible individual psychotherapy.

To have a supply of nurse therapists available to offer psychotherapy to carefully selected patients with schizophrenia and related psychoses would hold great advantages for patients, for staff, and in the long term, for those who finance the Health Service.

References

Alanen, Yrjo. O. (1997) *Schizophrenia: Its Origins and Need-Adapted Treatment.* London: Karnac Books.

BMA News Review (1998) February, 20–21.

Bruggen, P. (1997) *Who Cares? True Stories of the NHS Reforms.* The Spendlove Centre, Charlbury: Jon Carpenter Publishers.

Fransella, F. and Bannister, D. (1977) *A Manual for Repertory Grid Technique.* London: Academic Press.

Grant, S., Holmes, J. and Watson, J. (1993) 'Guidelines for psychotherapy training as a part of general professional psychiatric training.' *Psychiatric Bulletin 17,* 695– 698.

Heimann, P. (1960) 'Countertransference.' *British Journal of Medical Psychology 33,* 9, 9–15.

Jackson, M. and Cawley, R. (1992) 'Psychodynamics and psychotherapy on and acute psychiatric ward: the story of an experimental unit.' *British Journal of Psychiatry 160,* 41–50.

Jackson, M. and Williams, P. (1994) 'Integration.' In *Unimaginable Storms: A Search for Meaning in Psychosis.* London. Karnac Books, Chapter 8.

Kanas, N. (1986) 'Group therapy with schizophrenics – a review of controlled studies.' *International Journal of Group Psychotherapy 36,* 339–351.

Kernberg, O. (1980) 'Countertransference' and 'General Principles of Treatment.' In *Borderline Conditions and Pathological Narcissism.* New York: Jason Aronson, Chapters 2 and 3.

King's Fund Organisational Audit-Accreditation UK (1997) *Standard 46. Mental Health Treatment,* 299.

Lefevre, D. (1994) 'The power of countertransference in groups for the severely mentally ill.' *Group Analysis 27,* 441–447.

Lefevre, D. and Morrison, F. (1997) 'The Hawthorn project. A group psychotherapy project with chronically psychotic inpatients.' In C. Mace and F. Margison (eds) *Psychotherapy of Psychosis.* London: Gaskell Publishers.

Main, T.F. (1957) 'The ailment.' *British Journal of Medical Psychology 30,* 130.

Menzies-Lyth, I. (1988) 'The functioning of social systems as a defence against anxiety.' In *Containing Anxieties in Institutions.* London: Free Association Books.

Ogden, T. (1979) 'On projective identification.' *International Journal of Psycho-Analysis 60,* 357–372.

Rabelais, F. (1963) *The Histories of Gargantua and Pantagruel.* Great Britain: Penguin, Chapters 4 and 6.

Sandler, J. Dare, C. and Holder, A. (1993) *The Patient and the Analyst.* London: Karnac Books.

Searles, H. (1979) 'Countertransference and related subjects.' In *Selected Papers.* Madison: International Universities Press.

Thornicroft, S. (1991) Team for Assessment of Psychiatric Services (TAPS). Fifth Annual Conference.

Williams, P. (1985–1987). 'Aspects of a psychiatric therapeutic milieu.' Unpublished Ph.D. thesis.

Williams, P. (1998) 'Psychotic developments in a sexually abused borderline patient.' Symposium on Independent Psychoanalytic Thought, *Psychoanalytic Dialogues 8,* 4, 459–491.

PART 4

Adjunctive Treatment, Setting and Context

CHAPTER 14

The Role of Assessment and Pharmacotherapy in Group Psychotherapy for Psychosis

Alan M. Gruenberg and Reed D. Goldstein

Introduction

This chapter addresses the role of assessment and pharmacotherapy in individuals with psychosis who are referred to and treated in group psychotherapy. Since the movement toward moral treatments in psychiatry and the later advent of therapeutic communities for the mentally ill, group treatments have been offered to the individual with both psychotic and neurotic illnesses. Initially, the group treatments augmented individual psychotherapies, while biological interventions in psychosis were largely ineffective. With the development of more effective antipsychotic treatments, a shift occurred in the treatment of psychosis which highly emphasized biological interventions. However, the typical antipsychotic medications were often associated with unpleasant side effects which made participation in groups more problematic. In the 1990s, the development of newer atypical antipsychotic drugs and understanding of synergistic mechanisms of biological change and psychosocial support have reinvigorated interest in the role of combined pharmacotherapy and group psychotherapy. For the purposes of understanding the distinction between typical and atypical antipsychotic medications, we shall define typical antipsychotic drugs as having a preponderance of dopamine (D_2) antagonism, resulting in associated neurological side effects including dystonia, akathisia, parkinsonism, and tardive dyskinesia. These medications have been effective in treating positive psychotic symptomatology including delusions, hallucinations, and incoherence. An atypical antipsychotic is characterized by a relative predominance of serotonin $(5HT_2)$ antagonism over dopamine (D_2) antagonism, and associated dopamine $(D_1$ and $D_4)$ antagonism. The atypical antipsychotic has minimal extrapyramidal

347

(neurological) side-effects, does not raise serum prolactin levels, has minimal risk of causing tardive dyskinesia, and is effective in treating both positive and negative symptoms of psychosis, such as avolition, anhedonia, and poverty of content in speech.

In this chapter, we will address several issues which are critical to effective combined pharmacotherapy and group psychotherapy: (1) the assessment process for psychosis including severe depression with psychotic features, bipolar disorder with psychotic features, schizoaffective disorder, and schizophrenia; (2) strategic pharmacologic treatment to recovery in psychosis; (3) the referral process to group psychotherapy for the individual with psychosis; (4) the function of group psychotherapy in providing education, decreasing isolation, improving social support, encouraging insight and offering nurturance to the patient; (5) identification of symptom exacerbation which would require review and modification of pharmacotherapy; (6) clarification of the roles of pharmacotherapist and group psychotherapist.

Assessment

The patient with a psychotic disorder is assessed in a detailed fashion for the nature of the psychosis. Careful introduction of pharmacotherapy is recommended based upon systematic assessment. After symptomatic remission is achieved with pharmacotherapy, we evaluate all individuals for the most appropriate psychosocial intervention whether it be family therapy, individual therapy or group psychotherapy. The process of systematic assessment is discussed below.

It is important to clarify the longitudinal history of episodes of illness so that the patient and therapist have a shared understanding of the psychotic vulnerability. The genetic history of psychiatric disorder including a three generational pedigree is taken to increase the appreciation for constitutional factors in the genesis of the disorder. We require a general medical analysis including physical examination, laboratory screening assessing complete blood count and differential, biochemical profile, free thyroxine (T_4), and thyroid stimulating hormone (TSH). If indicated, studies of inflammatory or immunologic disease are completed. Many of our patients also have brain imaging (MRI) and electroencephalogram (EEG) to inform the patient, family, and doctor about ongoing neurological contributions to the disorders. In these neuropsychiatric studies, we are evaluating the presence or absence of cerebral dysrhythmia on EEG as a correlate of potential dyscontrol, irritability, or other emotional volatility. The assessment of brain parenchymal changes, ventricular enlargement, and cortical atrophy is accomplished in the MRI assessment, which may correlate with symptoms such as cognitive decline and incomplete response to pharmacotherapy. Following the clinical interview, family history, and medical evaluation, we find it useful for purposes of diagnostic differentiation and confirmation to administer structured diagnostic schedules, such as the Schedule for Affective Disorders and Schizophrenia (SADS) or the Structured Clinical Interview for DSM-IV Axis I Disorders (SCID). When patients are admitted to acute hospital settings, many of these procedures can be completed in the hospital as active treatment intervention is initiated and referral to outpatient group treatment is considered.

Treatment of psychotic illness must be informed by valid and reliably administered diagnostic procedures. Historically, there was poor agreement among clinicians regarding psychotic symptom presentation. In the United States, criteria sets for major psychiatric syndromes were posited by the Washington University Group in St Louis and further delineated in the Research Diagnostic Criteria (RDC 1972) and the Diagnostic and Statistical Manual III-R (1987) and IV (1994). Subsequently, distinctive criteria sets for syndromes, such as schizophrenia or depression, were specified with attention to the degree of certainty as well as the pattern and duration of symptoms. Moreover, the Schedule For Affective Disorders and Schizophrenia (SADS 1978), which is a clinician-administered structured diagnostic interview, enabled professionals to assess specific syndromes delineated in the RDC. The RDC and SADS preceded the development of DSM-III which represented a return to the prominence of descriptive psychiatry. Now, the clinician is asked to evaluate specified and observable symptom patterns according to diagnostic categories in DSM-IV. Clinician administered structured diagnostic interviews, such as the SCID (1995) yield a DSM-IV diagnosis. Informed by diagnosis, the clinician is able to designate classes of medication, such as antipsychotic, mood stabilizing, or antidepressant, as well as psychotherapeutic interventions such as cognitive behavioral, interpersonal, specialized group psychotherapy, or intensive psychoanalytic psychotherapy.

Our premise is that the diagnostic assessment will facilitate more appropriate pharmacologic intervention and will inform the referral to psychotherapy. With adequate symptom relief and greater understanding of the nature of the disorder, individuals with a history of psychosis can participate in group psychotherapy. Most important, the clinician and patient will understand whether the psychotic disorder is associated with schizophrenia, schizoaffective disorder, major depressive disorder with psychotic features, or bipolar disorder with psychotic features.

The DSM-IV defines symptoms associated with the major psychiatric syndromes. Briefly, DSM-IV stipulates that for schizophrenia, at least two active symptoms (e.g. delusions, hallucinations, disorganized speech or behavior) must be present to a significant degree during a 1-month period, with ongoing signs of the disturbance present for at least six months. The presence of negative symptoms (e.g. flattening of affect, avolition, alogia), which is defined as a distinct criterion in DSM-IV, is now emphasized as well. Prediction of an individual's capacity to tolerate a group psychotherapy experience is dependent upon the resolution of bizarre delusions, auditory hallucinations, alogia, and inattentiveness to personal hygiene. Antipsychotic medication is required when characteristic symptoms are present during an active phase of schizophrenia. Maintenance of antipsychotic treatment is essential in the ongoing course of schizophrenia. Clinicians working with individuals with schizophrenia in group psychotherapy as well as the patients themselves must be committed to ongoing maintenance treatment with pharmacotherapy. In addition, appreciating the nuances of schizophrenia allows the clinician to understand differences in symptom presentation, age of onset, course of illness, and prognosis.

In schizoaffective disorder, the individual must experience an uninterrupted period of illness lasting two weeks during which an episode of depression, mania, or a mixed state occurs in combination with criterion A for schizophrenia. Furthermore, either delusions or hallucinations must occur for at least two weeks in the absence of significant mood symptoms. Finally, symptoms which meet criteria for a mood episode are present to a substantial degree over the total duration of active and residual periods of the illness. Proper recognition of schizoaffective disorder and vigorous mood stabilizing and antipsychotic treatment may enable the individual to participate meaningfully in group psychotherapy.

Assessment of cross-sectional features (e.g. psychotic, catatonic, melancholic, atypical) in mood disorders is essential (Gruenberg and Goldstein 1997). Presence of delusions or hallucinations that occur in the context of a major depressive episode warrant treatment with antipsychotic medication in combination with antidepressant medication, or a course of electroconvulsive therapy to remission. This course of treatment is likely to differ from the standard pharmacological treatment of schizophrenia.

Identification of bipolar disorder and the emergence of psychosis during a specific episode of mood disturbance if manic or mixed, warrants distinctive pharmacological intervention with mood stabilizing and associated antipsychotic medication. Whereas the use of structured interview assessments will yield a diagnosis based upon DSM-IV criteria, the administration of traditional projective tests (e.g. Rorschach Inkblot Test; Thematic Apperception Test) will inform diagnosis as well as the individual's fantasies and conflicts, and assess capacity to tolerate stress and frustration. Clarification about the extent of thought disorder and one's customary pattern of defenses can be achieved through the use of projective tests. Historically, clinicians have administered a psychological test battery to an individual at the time of an acute exacerbation of symptomatology during an inpatient hospitalization in order to guide treatment and develop a dynamic formulation. In contrast, we have found it useful to recommend projective testing during symptom remission to guide decision making around recommendations for individual or group psychotherapy. Both the individual and group therapist may benefit from knowledge about the extent of thought disorder, the ability to integrate thought and feeling, and the capacity to tolerate frustration prior to the final decision about referral to a group psychotherapy experience. Capacity for success in treatment is essentially an issue that warrants longitudinal evaluation.

One important component of the assessment process involves evaluation of an individual's cognitive abilities and weaknesses. For example, determination of an individual's ability to attend and concentrate, learn and make use of memory, problem-solve, and maintain cognitive flexibility may help to guide treatment recommendations and tailor interventions in a group psychotherapy experience. Erickson (1989) provided illustrative case examples regarding similar neuro-psychological functions. He emphasized the assessment of cognitive functions in order to recognize and intervene in an appropriate manner for each group member. Determination about the degree of structure and the therapist's active and directive therapeutic stance may be informed by the amount or type of cognitive impairment manifested by each of the group members.

Strategic pharmacologic management

Careful assessment prepares the patient and clinician for the initiation of systematic pharmacotherapy in individuals with a psychotic vulnerability. The central question in differential diagnosis is whether the psychosis is occurring in the midst of a psychotic mood disorder or in the course of a longitudinal vulnerability to schizophrenia or schizoaffective disorder.

We have established well delineated treatment algorithms based upon specific diagnoses. A review of these pharmacotherapy protocols in the management of psychosis follows and may be helpful to the group psychotherapist.

If the disorder upon longitudinal assessment is most consistent with schizophrenia, specific antipsychotic pharmacotherapy will necessitate standard clinical trials of typical antipsychotic treatments for 8–12 weeks to assess remission of acute positive and negative symptomatology. A second trial may involve one of three available atypical antipsychotic treatments for 8–12 weeks including olanzapine (Zyprexa) 5–20 mg, quetiapine (Seroquel) 50–250 mg, or risperidone (Risperdal) 2–10 mg daily. In the absence of complete symptom remission, a course of clozapine (Clozaril) 200–600 mg is initiated. The treatment with clozapine requires ongoing medical monitoring of white blood cells to assure that agranulocytosis, a serious side effect, does not occur.

If the psychotic disorder has its onset in midlife or later, this syndrome is most consistent with major depressive disorder with psychotic features (i.e. delusional

Table 14.1 Available medications to treat schizophrenia in the United States: Typical and atypical anti-psychotic medication

Benefits: Relieves positive symptoms of psychosis including hallucinations, delusions, disorganized thoughts and behavior and may alleviate associated negative symptoms, such as social withdrawal and isolation. Modifies paranoia, hostility, irritability and aggression

Category	Trade Name	Compound	Equivalent Dose (mg)	Usual Therapeutic Daily Dose (mg)	Side Effects			
					Sedation	Hypotension (decreased blood pressure)	Anticholinergic (i.e. dry mouth, constipation)	Extra-pyramidal (i.e. tremor, rigidity, decreased mobility)
Typical Antipsychotics								
Aliphatic	Thorazine	Chlorpromazine	100	300–600	high	high	moderate	low
Piperidine	Mellaril	Thioridazine	100	300–600	high	high	high	low
	Serentil	Mesoridazine	50	75–300	moderate	moderate	moderate	moderate
Piperazine	Proxilin	Fluphenazine	2	6–20	low	low	low	high
	Stelazine	Trifluoperazine	5	8–20	moderate	low	low	high
	Trilafon	Perphenazine	8	12–48	low	low	low	moderate
Thioxanthene	Navane	Thiothixene	5	10–30	low	low	low	high
Dibenzodiazepine	Loxitane	Loxapine	10	30–60	moderate	moderate	moderate	high
Butyrophenone	Haldol	Haloperidol	2	6–20	low	low	low	high
	Inapsine (injection only)	Droperidol	1		low	low	low	high
Indolone	Moban	Molindone	10	40–80	moderate	low	moderate	moderate
Diphenylbutylpiperidine	Orap	Pimozide	1	2–10	low	low	low	high
Atypical Antipsychotics								
Dibenzodiazepine	Clozaril	Clozapine	100	150–600	high	moderate	moderate	none
Benzisoxazole	Risperdal	Risperidone	1.5	2–16	low	low	low	low
Thienobenzodiazepine	Zyprexa	Olanzapine	4	5–20	moderate	low	low	minimal
Dibenzothiazepine	Seroquel	Quetiapine	100	150–750	moderate	low	low	minimal

depression, unipolar mood disorder with psychosis). If severe depression with psychosis occurs in adolescence or young adulthood, we raise the differential question of bipolar vulnerability or schizoaffective disease. For delusional depression, patients will require adequate doses of typical antipsychotic treatments. These include perphenazine (Trilafon/Fentrazin) 8–24 mg, trifluoperazine (trifluoroperazine) (Stelazine) 5–20 mg, or butyrophenones such as haloperidol (Haldol) 2–10 mg. The typical antipsychotic treatments are combined with either standard tricyclic antidepressants such as nortriptyline (Pamelor/Motival) 50–150 mg to therapeutic doses or in more recent trials, newer antidepressant agents such as sertraline (Zoloft/Lustral) 50–250 mg, venlafaxine (Effexor) 75–450 mg, or mirtazapine (Remeron) 30–60 mg. If there is incomplete response in the severely depressed and psychotic middle age or elderly patient without longitudinal vulnerability to psychosis, then electroconvulsive therapy (ECT) is recommended.

If the disorder has late adolescent or young adult onset, a careful assessment of whether the psychosis has bipolar (manic-depressive) features is indicated. Standard clinical trials of mood stabilizing treatments such as lithium carbonate 600-900 mg daily to therapeutic serum levels of 0.6–1.0 meq/l are recommended. Alternative mood stabilizing treatments which are commonly used include divalproex sodium (Depakote) 500-2000 mg sufficient to achieve serum levels of 50–100 ng/ml or alternatively carbamazepine (Tegretol) 200–800 mg sufficient to achieve serum levels of 8–12 meq/l. Mood stabilizing efficacy of lamotrigine (Lamictal) 50–300 mg and gabapentin (Neurontin) 600–2400 mg is being investigated. The patients with ongoing bipolar disorder with psychotic features will often be prescribed adjunctive trials of typical antipsychotics as well. The introduction and availability of clozapine (Clozaril) for use in the USA as a treatment for refractory schizophrenia has also stimulated research in the use of atypical antipsychotic treatment in schizoaffective disorder and bipolar disorder. These new atypical antipsychotic medications such as olanzapine (Zyprexa), quetiapine (Seroquel), and risperidone (Risperdal) are being used extensively in individuals with bipolar disorder with psychotic features.

In the 1990s, the new developments in antipsychotic pharmacotherapy for schizophrenia have been based upon the putative therapeutic actions of clozapine (Clozaril). The pharmaceutical industry has discovered atypical antipsychotic compounds which do not carry the risk for agranulocytosis associated with clozapine. All of the atypical antipsychotic agents are designed to meet the standard of D1 and D4 receptor antagonism, limited or no extrapyramidal symptoms, no associated risk of tardive dyskinesia, no rise in serum prolactin levels, and efficacy in the treatment of negative symptoms. As of 1998, three atypical antipsychotic agents including olanzapine (Zyprexa), quetiapine

(Seroquel), and risperidone (Risperdal) have followed the introduction of clozapine in the USA. Both typical and atypical antipsychotic medications used in the treatment of psychosis are delineated in Table 14.1.

Symptom remission and referral to group

Remission of psychotic symptoms is the goal of pharmacotherapy including improved reality testing, coherence and organization of thought processes, amelioration of severe depression and anxiety, and capacity for self-observation. The determination regarding appropriateness for group psychotherapy follows the careful monitoring of symptomatic improvement. The patient and clinician then engage in a process of clarification of further goals. Consideration of group psychotherapy is warranted if those goals include increased social support, decreased isolation, and improved capacity for sharing one's experience of the disorder and its treatment.

The baseline cognitive and projective test results will inform the clinician as to the patient's capacity to participate in more structured or less structured group treatment. Knowledge of this assessment can also assist in the match between patient and therapist. If the group therapist is more directive and active, then the patient with greater cognitive impairment will be more likely to tolerate the group. If the group therapist is less directive and active, a patient with greater ego strength and capacity for anxiety tolerance may be referred. In our experience of group treatment for psychotic patients maintained on clozapine (Clozaril), the degree of organization following symptom remission has enabled patients to achieve greater insight and tolerate a more exploratory process. When patients have had less complete symptomatic remission from psychosis, the therapist has necessarily organized the group to be more structured and directly supportive. Response of patients to atypical antipsychotic treatments has included decreased negative symptomatology and diminished neurological side effects including akathisia, akinesia, and parkinsonism. This antipsychotic response with diminished side effects has broadened the patient population, which may be available for more intensive and longer-term group treatment.

Issues related to pharmacotherapy, symptom exacerbation and medication monitoring

All patients who are maintained on antipsychotic treatments require at least monthly monitoring of pharmacotherapy. For patients treated with clozapine (Clozaril), the requirements for dispensing in the United States include weekly white blood cell assay. Once the patient is stable on clozapine (Clozaril) therapy, then the dosage adjustment is minimal. Individuals with bipolar disorder with psychosis and schizoaffective disorder generally require lower clozapine (Clozaril) dosages in the range of 150–300 mg daily. Individuals with refractory schizophrenia have typically been treated with doses in the 300–600 mg range.

The other typical and atypical antipsychotic treatments are used adjunctively in individuals with bipolar disorder with psychotic features, and as primary treatments for schizoaffective disorder and schizophrenia. In general, the lowest effective dose is recommended. Individuals maintained on lithium carbonate, valproate (Depakote), or carbamazepine (Tegretol) will require regular monitoring of serum levels and appropriate assessment of renal, liver, and thyroid function depending on which mood stabilizer is used. In addition, adjunctive antidepressant treatment will often be prescribed and regular monitoring of response and side effects will be necessary.

Thus, the clinician working with individuals in group psychotherapy may encounter patients who are taking multiple psychotropic agents. Sophistication about side effects of medications and their interactions is required for proper management of individuals with psychosis in groups. Access to the pharmacotherapist is necessary for clinicians who are providing group psychotherapy for psychotic patients. The clinician must be comfortable with managing psychotic exacerbations in the context of the therapy as well as exacerbations of depression or hypomania. In the group treatment, the clinician must refer individuals rapidly for pharmacologic consultation if necessary. If a psychiatrist is the group therapist, the patient's pharmacotherapy may be reviewed immediately. The clinician, whether a group therapist or pharmacotherapist, must recognize the difference between transient symptom manifestation as a result of the group process as opposed to a recurrent episode of the psychotic illness. The baseline diagnostic assessment can assist in recognition of transient stress-related vulnerability as opposed to a recurrent full syndromal episode.

When group psychotherapy is led by nonpsychiatrists, a number of issues related to collaboration are relevant. The clinicians must have an open and easy channel of communication with psychiatrists so that symptom exacerbation can be addressed promptly. There is a need for clarification of roles such that the patients understand where and when to seek appropriate pharmacologic intervention. Adherence to maintenance pharmacologic treatment is essential in the ongoing collaboration. If a patient does not adhere to treatment recommendations from the psychiatrist or psychotherapist, this must be reviewed vigorously with the primary clinician responsible for the patient's care. The collaboration between group therapist and psychiatrist must be characterized by mutual respect and open review of ongoing treatment issues. When the group psychotherapist is a psychiatrist who receives patients referred by other psychiatric colleagues, issues of role confusion and competition may emerge. In the group treatment process, clarification of treatment boundaries must be addressed carefully because the patients may seek pharmacologic consultation from the group psychotherapist who is a psychiatrist.

Transference and countertransference

The management of acute exacerbation of psychotic symptoms as well as the maintenance of continuing treatment in general is best accomplished in the context of collaboration between clinician and patient. In such a collaboration, the treating clinician is responsible for the provision of a clear, empirically based rationale for the unfolding of treatment while the patient is asked to engage in an honest, inquisitive, and participatory fashion. Moreover, once established, an ongoing treatment collaboration provides a structure in which the patient's experience of threatening feelings, projections, fears around intimacy, as well as concerns regarding compliance can be monitored and addressed just as the clinician can observe the emergence of countertransference feelings. That is, transference and countertransference issues are best addressed in the context of an evolving treatment collaboration. It is especially useful to establish a sound treatment alliance as transference and countertransference issues may have an impact on the success of pharmacotherapy and group psychotherapy. Clear guidelines regarding the use of medication to treat symptomatic regressions can be delineated at the start of treatment in order to lessen the likelihood of overmedicating the 'difficult' patient. Continuing discussion between psychiatrist and group therapist is imperative as well as a straightforward, unclouded, and unified presentation of treatment rationale to the patient in order to lessen the emergence of treatment resistance. In that way, combined treatment might unfold in a steady fashion rather than either medication or group psychotherapy taking on a more important role relative to the other, with associated disagreement between clinicians about treatment priorities.

The group psychotherapist is called upon to recognize and understand transference and countertransference issues in order to sustain the patient's compliance with treatment.

Clinical example

A is a 29-year-old single white male with schizoaffective disorder who evolved a five-year history of progressive signs of psychosis, characterized by profound social isolation in his room and marked preoccupation with anagrams. His writing consisted of two- or three-word sentences which held great meaning for him. Prior clinical trials of typical antipsychotic pharmacotherapy including thioridazine (Mellaril), trifluoperazine (Stelazine), and perphenazine (Trilafon) did not interrupt the profound social withdrawal, reluctance to care for self, and incoherence. Following comprehensive diagnostic reassessment, testing, and the development of a treatment alliance, a trial of clozapine (Clozaril) was begun. Four weeks after initiating clozapine, the patient appeared somewhat more communicative in individual psychotherapy. Eight weeks later, at three months, the patient began participation in a low intensity social rehabilitation program, two days per week. Moderate depressive symptomatology was reported and a careful augmentation with venlafaxine (Effexor) was introduced. Continuation of clozapine (Clozaril) and venlafaxine (Effexor) led to more animated and integrated conversation and the beginning of more social contact. At eight months after initiation of clozapine (Clozaril), the patient was referred to group psychotherapy.

The group psychotherapy addressed the nature of the disease, the contribution of substance use to its exacerbation, and the isolation associated with the illness. Shared feelings and support from other young adults provided a setting of mutual comfort and intimacy for the members. A was viewed as contributing valuable insight and became a leader for the group. He described new opportunities which afforded him an independent living experience and initial exposure to college course work. The combined pharmacotherapy and group psychotherapy served to facilitate consolidation of symptomatic improvement and social functioning. A enrolled in a film program. He soon found himself taking courses and writing in response to course demands. The group setting addressed his anxiety about performance. His participation in the group terminated when he resumed full time college work, eighteen months after initiation of clozapine (Clozaril) and stabilization of symptoms. The nine months of supportive group psychotherapy along with consistent individual psychotherapy facilitated recovery from psychosis in a young man who had previously suffered for five years with predominantly negative symptoms of psychosis.

In summary, early careful diagnostic reassessment and comprehensive psychological testing confirmed a persistent negative symptom picture of psychosis and secondary depressive symptomatology. The sequential response to antipsychotic and antidepressant pharmacotherapy was carefully monitored. In this example, the individual therapist was supported by consultation with a pharmacotherapist who also provided the ongoing group psychotherapy. Because of the collaborative nature of the working relationship, the patient derived combined effects of consistent individual and group psychotherapy as well as careful medical monitoring.

Conclusion

This chapter has detailed a rational approach to the assessment, pharmacotherapy, and referral of individuals with psychosis to group psychotherapy. We have suggested that a careful assessment including longitudinal history of psychosis, genetic history, current clinical assessment, and more formal psychological evaluation should inform pharmacotherapy strategy. A cautious but vigorous approach to pharmacotherapy of psychosis will often lead to symptom resolution. Our thesis is that optimal benefit from group psychotherapy follows sustained symptom remission. The benefits of group psychotherapy include the opportunity for clarification of issues of identity consolidation, maturation, and social skills. In the context of group psychotherapy, ongoing monitoring of symptom change is possible and active collaboration between group psychotherapist and pharmacotherapist is critical. The use of combined pharmacotherapy and group psychotherapy, when offered in an integrated and collaborative fashion, offers the patient an opportunity to mature in a therapeutic environment, practice newly developed interpersonal strategies, and improve overall functioning. Ultimately, these goals serve to shape the pharmacologic and psychotherapeutic treatment process.

References

American Psychiatric Association (1980) *Diagnostic and Statistical Manual of Mental Disorders*, 3rd edn. Washington, DC: American Psychiatric Association.

American Psychiatric Association (1987) *Diagnostic and Statistical Manual of Mental Disorders*, 3rd edn, revised. Washington, DC: American Psychiatric Association.

American Psychiatric Association (1994) *Diagnostic and Statistical Manual of Mental Disorders*, 4th edn. Washington, DC: American Psychiatric Association.

Endicott, J., Spitzer, R.L. (1978) 'A diagnostic interview: the schedule for affective disorders and schizophrenia (SADS).' *Archives of General Psychiatry 35*, 837–844.

Erickson, R.C. (1989) 'Applications of cognitive testing to group therapies with the chronically mentally ill.' *International Journal of Group Psychotherapy 39*, 223–235.

Feighner, J.P., Robins, E., Guze, S.B., *et al.* (1972) 'Diagnostic criteria for use in psychiatric research.' *Archives of General Psychiatry 26*, 57–63.

First, M.B., Spitzer, R.L., Gibbon, M., *et al.* (1995) *Structured Clinical Interview for DSM-IV Axis I Disorders – Patient Edition (SCID-I/P)*. New York: Biometrics Research Department, New York State Psychiatric Institute.

Gruenberg, A.M., and Goldstein, R.D. (1997) 'Depressive disorders.' In A. Tasman, J. Kay, and F.A. Lieberman (eds) *Psychiatry*. Philadelphia: W.B. Saunders Company.

CHAPTER 15

The Therapeutic Community and Schizophrenia

Geoffrey Pullen

He expressed delusions of enlightenment

(Referral letter to the Eric Burden Community)

The therapeutic community was a wartime baby, its parents improbably brought together by overriding national needs. Its mother was the asylum, child herself of the Age of Enlightenment. Reformers such as Pinel (1806), Tuke (1813) and Conolly (1856) believed that the course of mental illnesses could be largely determined by the patient's environment. Asylums were built, therefore, to be pleasant, peaceful communities offering the opportunity to engage in purposeful activities.

> We require that the building should be on a healthy site freely admitting light and air, and drainage. Space should be allowed for summer and winter exercise, for various employment, and for all the purposes of domestic economy. Warmth must be provided for during the winter, light for the winter evenings, coolness and shade in the summer. Separate wards and bed-rooms, for the tranquil, for the sick, for the helpless, for the noisy, the unruly, or violent, and the dirty; a supply of water so copious, and a drainage so complete, that the baths, water-closets, and building in general, may always be kept perfectly clean and free from bad odours. There should be workshops and workrooms, and schoolrooms, separate from the wards, and cheerfully situated; a chapel, conveniently accessible from both sides of the asylum; as also a kitchen, a laundry, a bakehouse, a brewhouse, and rooms for stores, and all the requisites for gardening and farming; and also a surgery, and all that is necessary for the medical staff. All these are indispensable in every large public asylum. (Conolly 1847, p.8)

In the United States moral treatment became established in some institutions (Rothman 1971), but in 1848 the reformer Dorothea Lynde Dix submitted a 'memorial' to Congress which included:

more than 9,000 idiots, epileptics and insane in the United States, destitute of appropriate care and protection, … bound with galling chains, bowed beneath fetters and heavy iron balls attached to drag-chains, lacerated with ropes, scourged with rods and terrified beneath storm of execration and cruel blows; now subject to jibes and scorn and torturing tricks; now abandoned to the most outrageous violations. (Zilboorg 1941, pp.583–4)

That the experiment in 'moral management' (or psycho-social treatment as it might now be called) failed is well known. Partly this was due to the over-optimism of the reformers; not as many patients as hoped were cured. The population explosion and urbanization of the second half of the nineteenth century led to asylums becoming ever larger and more overcrowded. 'It is particularly necessary to observe, that almost every desirable quality, both in the construction and government of an asylum, becomes more difficult to be obtained or preserved when the size of the asylum is greater than is required for 360 or 400 patients' (Conolly 1847, p.10). The decline of asylums into nihilistic, custodial institutions was also encouraged by the idea that the mentally ill were the evolutionary unfit, 'Social Darwinism'. In Britain some asylums eventually housed over 2000 patients, in the United States, over 5000. Goffman vividly describes how such huge 'Total Institutions' became dysfunctional worlds of their own (Goffmann 1961).

Despite occasional 'whistle blowers' (e.g. Lomax 1921) most mental hospitals were still underfunded and demoralized at the outbreak of the World War II. Hollymoor Hospital in Northfield, Birmingham, built in 1905 for long stay psychiatric patients, was probably no better and no worse than any other at the time. In 1942, however, it was converted into a military psychiatric hospital, the largest in the United Kingdom. If the 1920s and 1930s contributed little more than depressing footnotes to the history of the treatment of the psychotic and chronically mentally ill, it was, paradoxically, a time of exciting developments in the understanding of the neuroses. But for the war, the analyst fathers of the therapeutic community, Bion, Foulkes, Main, and Rickman, would probably have never 'met' the asylum. They were drafted into the army, however, sent to Hollymoor, and led the two 'Northfield Experiments' (Bion and Rickman 1943; Foulkes 1948) which resulted in Main proposing the concept of the therapeutic community as

an attempt to use a hospital not as an organisation run by doctors in the interests of their own greater technical efficiency, but as a community with the immediate aim of full participation of all its members in its daily life and the eventual aim of resocialization of the neurotic individual for life in ordinary society. (Main 1946, p.67)

The two experiments were in many ways similar, differing 'from other contemporary practice because of the underlying concepts of responsibility to society, respect for patients'... use of groups and the hospital as therapeutic instruments, and an emphasis on process (rather than outcome)' (Harrison and Clarke 1992, pp.706–707). At another military psychiatric hospital, Mill Hill, Ezriel, Maxwell Jones (and Eysenck) were also experimenting with various forms of treatment (Bridger 1985). In 1947 the Industrial Neurosis Unit, Belmont Hospital, opened under the leadership of Jones (1952). It was at that unit, eventually renamed the Henderson Hospital, that many of the characteristic features of the therapeutic community developed, including the daily community meeting attended by all patients and staff. The emphasis was upon the therapeutic potential of all activities and interactions, summed up by Jones' phrase 'the living-learning situation'. He also coined the slogans 'blurring of role' and 'flattening of hierarchy' to stress the skills and therapeutic potential of all members of the community.

In 1958 an ex-alcoholic, Chuck Dederich, also called his Synanon Community in California a therapeutic community (Yablonsky 1965). This became a model for communities developed world-wide for ex-drug abusers. Concept-house 'hierarchical' therapeutic communities are very different from the 'democratic' therapeutic community of Main, although Kennard (1983) has argued that they have a number of features in common. The 'hierarchical' therapeutic community developed in the United States is not the subject of this chapter; it would seem highly inappropriate for psychotic patients.

Between 1953 and 1957 Rapoport, an anthropologist, and his team which included sociologists and psychologists, studied the Henderson Hospital, known at that time as the Social Rehabilitation Unit. By then the unit saw itself as 'treating working-class psychopaths' (Rapoport 1960). Four themes were seen to 'broadly encompass the distinctive elements of the Unit's ideology', namely: 'democratisation', 'permissiveness', 'communalism' and 'reality confrontation'. It has often been suggested that an adherence to these four 'principles' by a unit could be taken as being the defining feature of a therapeutic community (Morrice 1979; Pullen 1986).

These early experiments were not extended to patients suffering from psychoses, and immediately after the war their lot seems to have remained as bad as ever. A subgroup of these patients had earlier been distinguished from the general group 'functional psychoses' (i.e. psychoses with no obvious organic cause) by Kraepelin on the basis of their poor prognosis; he called the syndrome Dementia Praecox (Bleuler (1911) later coined the term schizophrenia). Kraepelin's own series of patients admitted to the Heidelberg Clinic suggested only 21 per cent made a good or even fairly good recovery (Kraepelin 1913). Mayer-Gross followed up 260 out of 294 patients admitted to the same clinic in 1912 and 1913, and 16 years later found 60 per cent had never left hospital (Mayer-Gross 1932). Some people, however, began to suspect (again) that many of the handicaps of chronic schizophrenia were in fact caused by the patients' environments. Russell Barton working in the large, and then almost new, Shenley Hospital suggested that many of his patients' symptoms were caused by an iatrogenic disorder he called 'institutional neurosis' (Barton 1959).

> Institutional neurosis is a clinical disease characterized by apathy, lack of initiative, loss of interest more marked in things and events not immediately personal or present, submissiveness, and sometimes no expression or feelings of resentment at harsh or unfair orders. There is also a lack of interest in the future and an apparent inability to make practical plans for it, a deterioration in personal habits, toilet and standards generally, a loss of individuality, and a resigned acceptance that things will go on as they are – unchangingly, inevitably and indefinitely.
>
> These signs vary in severity from the mute stuporose patient who sits in the same chair day after day, through the ward worker who has without protest surrendered the rest of her existence to the institution, to the active cheerful patient who enjoys the facilities available, often does some handicraft during the day, but shows no desire to leave the hospital, shows no interest in plans for a future in the world outside, and raises numerous difficulties and objections when anyone tries to help her to be discharged.
>
> Occasionally, the passive submissive cooperation of the patient is punctuated by aggressive episodes which are casually attributed to mental illness but which, if carefully investigated, often seem to be provoked by some unkindness from another patient, a hospital employee or visitors. At other times an apparently similar provocation may produce no such response.
>
> The patient often adopts a characteristic posture with the hands held across the body or tucked behind an apron, the shoulders drooped and the head held forward. The gait has a shuffling quality. (Barton 1959, pp.2–3)

He went on to define eight aetiological factors (pp. 6–7):

1. Loss of contact with the outside world.

2. Enforced idleness.

3. Brutality, browbeating and teasing.

4. Bossiness of staff.

5. Loss of personal friends, possessions and personal events.

6. Drugs.

7. Ward atmosphere.

8. Loss of prospects outside the institution.

Whilst World War II can be said to have directly brought about the birth of the therapeutic community it had a less direct, but still important, effect upon asylum psychiatry. The desire for a new and better society, valuing all its members, which led to the election of a Labour government in Britain, also seems to have inspired a significant number of the men who were appointed asylum medical superintendents after the war. Bell by 1949 had unlocked all the wards at Dingleton Hospital, Melrose, Scotland (Bell 1955), starting the 'open door campaign' of the next decade. The majority of asylums eventually unlocked most of their doors, sometimes cautiously, and sometimes (Mandelbrote 1958) in one grand gesture.

For a hundred years physician superintendents had been absolute rulers of their private domains. Some were enlightened despots, others petty tyrants, many it seems were as demoralized as their institutions. Finally, however, for about twenty years (c.1955–75) a group of energetic, far-seeing, British pioneers used their power and authority to transform psychiatry. A memorable event for many of them seems to have been a one month course for physician superintendents run in London by the King Edward's Fund Staff College in 1957. Its participants included Rudolf Freudenberg (Netherne), Duncan MacMillan (Mapperley), T.P. Rees (Warlingham), Russell Barton (Severalls), David Clark (Fulbourn), Bertram Mandelbrote (Littlemore), and Maxwell Jones. Both Clark and Mandelbrote single out Jones in their memoirs of that event, 'bubbling, irreverent, charismatic, fascinating' (Clark 1996, p.127), 'irrepressible … would continue discussions well into the early hours of the morning' (Mandelbrote 1996, p.151). Jones moved to the USA, and in 1960 took up the post of Director of Training at the State Hospital at Salem, Oregon. After three years, however 'the outraged establishment of Oregon fired him' (Clark 1991, p.121) and he took over as the Superintendent of Dingleton (Jones 1968; Jones 1982).

The participants at the King Edward's Fund Conference included most of those who created the speciality of psychiatric rehabilitation as they retrained and resettled their institutionalised longstay patients. David Clark described his approach as 'Social Therapy' (Clark 1974). He characterized social therapy as being summarized by: 'Activity,' 'Freedom', and 'Responsibility'. Freedom, of course, harked back both to the 'open doors' (Bell 1955), and the 'no restraint' (Conolly 1856), movements. Activity had its roots in the original nineteenth-century asylum movement. It proved perhaps the least controversial aspect of social therapy; workshops pose little threat to the status quo. A whole approach evolved around this work training model with its 'ladder of rehabilitation,' (see for example Morgan and Cheadle 1981). As Clark wrote, however

> The big organization tends to take away an individual's responsibility and make him passive, hostile and dependent. Doctors and nurses are highly skilled at removing an individual's responsibility. This is necessary for a person who is physically ill and in high fever; he needs to regress into dependence. But it is very crippling over the months and years – and often quite unnecessary. We should

always question any limitation of a person's responsibility – whether we are refusing to let a patient decide to go for a walk or refusing to allow a junior doctor to decide what drugs to prescribe. In general people are more ready for responsibility than doctors and nurses will credit. This requires reorientation for many nurses and doctors, who only too easily decide. It will be done better and quicker if I do it myself. It is painful and may be time-wasting to let someone make a muddle of a job – but it may be far more helpful to him to exercise his own responsibility, make his own mistakes, surmount his crisis and grow a little. (Clark 1974, p.68)

Allowing patients 'responsibility' was, and is, the real challenge and one that continues to be resisted by professionals. It is this aspect of social therapy that most closely links it to the therapeutic community approach. The challenge was taken up, however, at many hospitals where both patients and staff experienced the changes as exciting and liberating. The message was popularized by books such as those written by Clark, by Jones and by Denis Martin; (*Adventure in Psychiatry*, Martin 1962, who would now dare to use such a title?). Of course not everyone was happy with the overturning of the old order. Letemendia, Harris and Willems published a paper from Littlemore in which they claimed to show no benefits resulting from the reforms instituted at that hospital (1967), but the study was methodologically seriously flawed (Wing and Brown 1970).

In 1960 John Wing, Director of the Medical Research Council Social Psychiatry Research Unit, with a sociologist, George Brown, started a major study of the relationship between institutionalism and schizophrenia at three mental hospitals. The clinical condition of female longstay patients suffering from schizophrenia and aspects of their environments were measured over eight years. The first hospital studied was Netherne which under the leadership of Freudenberg had built up an excellent reputation for its rehabilitation programme. Little progress, however, had been made at Severalls until in 1960 its new physician superintendent, Russell Barton, was appointed. The third hospital, Mapperly, had under its superintendent, Macmillan, concentrated on other groups of patients' needs.

Social differences between hospitals in 1960 were evident both in matters of central importance in everyday life and in small details. For example, there was a 50 per cent difference between Netherne and Severalls hospitals in the proportion of the sample leaving the ward during the day, and a 60 per cent difference in the proportion of patients possessing a toothbrush. Severalls patients, on average, spent 5 hours 39 minutes of their waking time doing absolutely nothing, compared with 2 hours 48 minutes at Netherne. Mapperley Hospital, on the whole, approximated to Netherne Hospital, but also showed certain similarities to Severalls Hospital. In matters of obvious importance, such as the amount of time spent off the ward, the opportunities for constructive work, the provision of respectable personal clothing, the amount of locker space, etc., Mapperley Hospital was more or less equivalent to Netherne Hospital. But in more intimate, and perhaps less obvious, details, the patients at Mapperley were not so well off as those at Netherne. Fewer patients, for example, possessed scissors or a mirror, and fewer baths were 'screened' from onlookers. Patients went to bed on average nearly one hour before those at Netherne and leisure activities were more restricted. These differences were further reflected in the opinions of the nursing staff. Ward sisters thought, at Mapperley, that all patients should be helped to buy clothing and, at Netherne, that 91 per cent of patients should. On the other hand they thought, at Mapperley, that only 27 per cent of patients could be trusted with matches, while Netherne ward sisters said that 79 per cent of patients were trustworthy in this way. (Wing and Brown 1970, p.100)

The patients' clinical condition and attitudes to discharge were rated using a structured interview, whilst a ward behaviour scale was completed by their nurses. The samples were controlled for the usual conditions including medication. Data was also collected on patients' possessions, time budgets, nurses' opinions, patients' occupations and contact with the outside world, and ward restrictiveness. Attempting to summarize such a massive study (which includes 82 tables and figures) is difficult, but a clear correlation was demonstrated between the signs and symptoms of the patients' 'illnesses' and their social milieu. The importance of this finding cannot be over-estimated. The study went on to show that as the conditions at each hospital improved so did their patients' behaviour. Figure 15.1 illustrates these findings using three powerful markers: Social withdrawal, patients' occupation and nurses' attitudes. In 1960 all three measures showed Netherne 'good', Mapperley 'middling', and Severalls 'bad'. At the first follow up (1962 or 1964) all three measures for each hospital show an improvement.

The figure also shows, however, a subsequent collapse in progress at both Netherne and Mapperley. After testing for, and excluding, other possibilities Wing and Brown can only conclude,

> The... explanation is, in some ways, more disheartening; that the therapists (doctors, nurses, occupational therapists and supervisors) began to feel, at different turning-points in different hospitals, that they had done as much as they could; that expenditure of further time and energy would prejudice the chances of other patients, or simply that enough was enough. The fact that Dr. Macmillan retired in 1966, that Dr. Freudenberg was seconded to the Ministry of Health from 1961 to 1964, and that Dr. D.H. Bennett, who had done so much to build up the rehabilitation and resettlement services at Netherne, left in June 1962, must also be taken into account. (p.191)

Earlier they write,

> none of the three hospitals we studied claimed to be a 'therapeutic community' in the sense described by Jones (1968) or Clark (1964). Several of the wards at

Netherne did have regular patient–staff meetings, and patients were organised in small groups, each with its own nurse or occupational therapist. There was certainly an emphasis on communication between staff at different levels of the various hierarchies. On the other hand, the group organisation was not as thoroughgoing, the staff 'democratisation' was not as far-reaching, the communication links were not as ubiquitous, the work organisation was not as 'creative', the leadership pattern was not as ill defined and the staff routine not as 'spontaneous' as the requirements laid down would require, – nor, in any case, would these have been regarded as ideal, at Netherne. (p.187)

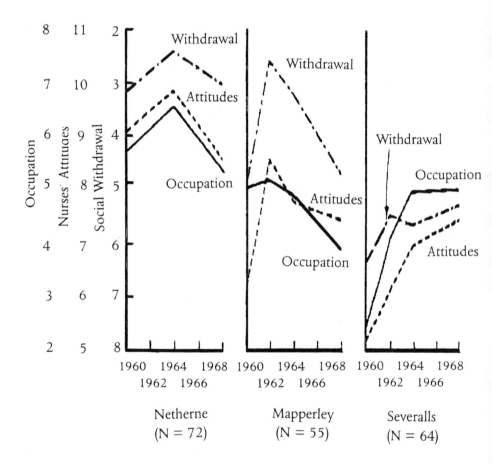

Figure 15.1 Three measures of clinical and social condition, 1960–1968 (three hospitals separately; N = 191). Adapted from Wing and Brown (1970).

It was unfortunate that a hospital like Fulbourn was not included in the study as it would have been interesting to see if an explicit therapeutic community approach led to a more sustained improvement. An eight year follow up of male patients at Fulbourn did not show the same pattern of reverses (Clark and Oram 1966). I will argue later that one of the main reasons for using the therapeutic community is that it maintains staff morale and enthusiasm. The serendipitous bringing together of the right people at the right place at the right time as described above meant that the post-war reforms in asylum care happened first in England and Scotland making possible Wing and Brown's monumental study. Reforms, of course, did also take place elsewhere, for example at the Boston Psychopathic Hospital (Greenblatt, York and Brown 1955; Greenblatt, Levinson and Williams 1957), but as Clark wrote after spending 1963 in California,

> The development of open doors in the United States has been slower and the same controversies are exercising American psychiatrists in the 1960s as concerned the English in the 1950s. They have greater difficulties; the hospitals are larger; there are probably more violent persons committed to state hospitals; public opinion is not so favourable. (Clark 1964, p.22)

Perhaps the most important contributions from the United States at that time were the observational studies made by a number of social scientists. Mention has already been made of Goffman; Dunham and Weinberg (1960) and Belknap (1956) also studied custodial institutions, whilst Caudill described a small neurosis unit first as a 'patient' and then as an observer (1958). Stanton and Schwartz (1954) published a well known study of Chestnut Lodge, a small private hospital offering daily psychoanalysis to psychotic inpatients at a cost (in 1950) of $850 per month. This body of work contributed to the theoretical foundations of social therapy (Clark 1964).

Any account of schizophrenia and the therapeutic community in the 1950s, 1960s and 1970s would not be complete without a discussion of the work of R.D. Laing. Although a few years younger than most of those mentioned so far, Laing was of the same generation; another bright young man thrown into the world of the asylum, in his case by National Service. In 1985 he wrote an autobiography of his early professional life, *Wisdom, Madness and Folly*. Although precociously interested in academic philosophy he reveals very clearly that his route to psychiatry was via neurology. As someone who shared with him the bizarre experience of starting a medical career as a neurosurgical houseman, his vivid account brought home powerful memories. 'Clinically, neurosurgeons are entitled to that sense of authority that comes from physical intimacy with the human brain and nervous system, steeped as they are – day in, day out, year in, year out – in observing correlations between brain damage and disease, and loss of function and partial or complete recovery of function' (Laing 1985, p.84).

His memoirs also reveal, even in the context of that era, that he was unusually heavily involved in physical treatments, for example insulin coma therapy at the British Army Psychiatric Unit at Netley. Perhaps the image of the reactionary 'organic' psychiatrist against whom he always so vigorously contrasted his own work, was that of his former self. In about 1954 he carried out a modest experiment in social therapy at Gartnavel Royal Mental Hospital in Glasgow. He took 11 'chronic patients' from the female refractory ward and allowed them to spend the day, nine to five, in 'A large, bright newly decorated, comfortably furnished room, in which were magazines, material for knitting and sewing, rug and blanket-making, drawing and other pastimes' (Laing 1985, p.115). Characteristically, in none of his accounts of this experiment does the widely read Laing give any hint that anyone had ever thought or tried anything similar before (Cameron, Laing and McGhie 1955; Laing 1976; Laing 1985). Laing's colleagues built upon this work (Freeman, Cameron and McGhie 1958) but in 1957 he himself moved to the Tavistock Clinic. In 1960 he published *The Divided Self*, followed by *Self and Others* (1961) a year later. In 1967 Cooper introduced the term 'anti-psychiatry', the same year as Laing's *The Politics of Experience*.

In this chapter I am more concerned with the anti-psychiatrists as clinicians than as philosophers and theoreticians, although they were, arguably, more significant as the latter. (Kotowicz 1997, provides a good summary of the evolution of Laing's ideas.) Nevertheless, when Cooper in 1962 opened Villa 21 at Shenley he was, as far as I know, the first to use milieu therapy explicitly for people suffering from active, acute schizophrenia. Shenley Hospital, ten miles into the countryside north of London, was one of the last and largest British asylums built. When it was opened in 1934 it was designed to have 2000 beds with 18 'block' wards, 24 villas and a chapel the size of a cathedral. In the first five years 1241 patients were transferred from Napsbury and Springfield, and in 1957 the population peaked at 2370. There were still 1782 beds in use when I arrived in 1972. The most distinctive feature of Shenley was the villas, spacious self-contained buildings dotted around the hundreds of acres of grounds tended by 31 gardeners. The hospital's design made it possible for the medical staff to pursue all sorts of enthusiasms and experiments in different villas. Cooper was, therefore, permitted to set up Villa 21 (ironically in the old 'Deep Insulin Unit').

By the time he wrote of Villa 21 Cooper was already disillusioned with his experiences and it has tended to be remembered, if at all, as a 'failed experiment' (Kennard 1983). The only results published were in a study carried out with Laing and Esterson (Cooper, Esterson and Laing 1965) which is not really focused on the Villa and were dismissed by Cooper himself as 'An ironic addendum' (1967). Tantam (1991) in a widely circulated history of British psychiatry states that Villa 21 closed when Cooper left in 1966. In fact it continued for another six years, if anything more 'anti-psychiatric' than ever (Conran 1970). When it opened the

Villa had nineteen beds to which were admitted men aged between fifteen and the late twenties, over two-thirds of whom had been independently diagnosed as suffering from schizophrenia. Cooper had a period of a year before the Unit opened in which to select suitable nursing staff. In addition to himself he had the help of two other doctors part time. There was also a full-time occupational therapist and social work input. (Cooper's reference to 'gross staff shortages' will cause wry amusement to many contemporary British psychiatrists.) Cooper described the original programme of the unit as 'not unlike that of the "classical" therapeutic community'. There was a daily thirty minute community meeting, formal therapeutic small groups, work groups and a significant number of staff group meetings. In addition Cooper draws attention to 'spontaneous' groups which would form at any time around some particular issue.

On re-reading Cooper's account of his time at Villa 21 I was struck by the apparent high quality of the work carried out in that unit and by the important lessons which were learnt, and then, alas, largely forgotten: the 'staying in bed problem'; the 'ludicrously trivial' nature of much hospital work; role blurring; and of course authorities' horror of 'disorder'. Cooper asks, 'a number of disturbing and apparently paradoxical questions; for example, can patients "treat" other patients, and can they even treat staff' (Cooper 1967), but he did not stay to answer them. It is not clear why Cooper felt he had to leave Villa 21, although he makes a great deal of the larger institution's hostility. He describes the hospital's negative response to the 'reality confrontation' experiment of making the patients experience the consequence of not washing up the pots and pans, namely no more food could be cooked! When I came to Shenley some six or seven years later, however, I was told the tale with some pride; I would say there still was then quite widespread tolerance and respect for Villa 21. What was going on in the Villa was of course provocative, devaluing by implication the 'life's work' of other staff and challenging all the defences they relied on to survive. In such circumstances envy, hostility, and, yes, persecution will be aroused. It is not easy to deal with these forces: Cooper quit. Villa 21, in my opinion finally 'committed social suicide' in 1973 by over indulging in the pleasures of provocation. A National Health Service Hospital Advisory Service Inspection Team was told to go and look in the Medical Records Department if they wanted to find out about the results of the treatment! Not surprisingly the inspectors angrily pointed out that none of the 17 inpatients were on any medication, (Cooper had used neuroleptics), 14 were completely unoccupied, that they seemed to alternate between marked phases of catatonic stupor and excitement, and so on.

Laing did not work in a hospital again after he left Gartnavel in 1957, but in 1965 he helped to found the Philadelphia Association which opened Kingsley Hall into which he moved for its first year. Kingsley Hall had been built in the East End of London for deprived children but had served a number of charitable functions, most famously as a residence for Gandhi. The project only lasted five years as the lease was not renewed. Ironically the refugees from the alienating institution found much intolerance and hostility from their working class neighbours. No entirely satisfactory account of the community's work has ever been published: fragments by Laing (1968) and Schatzman (1970); a novel (Sigal 1976); and most famously, Barnes and Berke (1971). The latter is an account by and of Mary Barnes who used her stay at Kingsley Hall for what was, for her, a therapeutic regressive experience; using generally agreed criteria, however, few would now diagnose her as suffering from schizophrenia (Wing 1978). The best account published is probably that by Clay (1996) who interviewed many of the participants for his biography of Laing. Kingsley Hall seems to have had more in common with the counterculture communes of the time rather than any therapeutic community, even Villa 21. A former resident told me that in reality there were only ever three or four people living there who were psychotic at any one time. Despite its fame and prestige not everyone was impressed. Sally Vincent, a journalist who lived with Laing for a time, told Clay (1996, p.96):

> I'd been initially fascinated by it and was very supportive. I thought it was just the thing to have, just the thing to do. I went but I didn't like what I saw, because what I saw was Laing behaving like a zombie and a collection of spectacularly physically hideous men, Californian shrinks. It was odd because apart from the beautiful Laing who was, I think, wearing white, all the patients were young beautiful girls. There was one young patient, a pretty young thing, sitting on one of these shrink's laps and his hands were all over her. I was screaming at Laing, 'What's going on here, what did he imagine he was doing?' and Laing said something pious like 'Helping her down from the cross.'

I never visited Kingsley Hall and on my later visits in the early 1980s to the Philadelphia Association's Ascot Farm in Oxfordshire I was impressed by its warm, supportive and responsible regime. However, I have had other experiences when I did see vulnerable people being abused as described by Vincent. My membership of some Gestalt groups for trainee therapists, for example, convinced me both of the power of the techniques and of the dangers of my fellow group members using them (or me – power corrupts). Perls (who visited Kingsley Hall) in his autobiography is quite open about the sexual pleasures of his guru status (Perls 1969).

After Kingsley Hall, the Philadelphia Association and the Arbours Association (the latter founded by Joseph Berke and Morton Schatzman) developed a number of small communities. Kotowicz (who trained with the Philadelphia Association) writes:

> Probably the best way of describing the changes would be to point out the increased importance of the psychoanalytical ethos of the communities. This is understandable as both The Philadelphia Association and the Arbours

Association have become part of the psychoanalytically oriented psychotherapy mainstream. This is reflected in the way the community therapists engage – they tend to work to strictly arranged and strictly timed meetings. In some houses of The Philadelphia Association these meetings are, with the exception of some serious crises, the sole therapeutic involvement. In such cases one could perhaps speak of community-analysis, a modified form of group-analysis. The Arbours, unlike The Philadelphia Association, still emphasise the role of the therapist as a full living-in member of the community – their psychotherapy training programme requires all trainees to live for six months in the community. (p.111–112)

In San Francisco Loren Mosher set up Soteria House, a staffed, domestic scale setting with six places for 'young first-admission schizophrenics' (Mosher, Menn and Matthews 1975). Although neither the anti-psychiatric nor therapeutic community movements are explicitly acknowledged by the authors, elements from both seem to have been present. The 'essential characteristics' were (Mosher and Burti 1994, p.129):

1. Small (6 clients), temporary, family-like social organization.

2. Ideologically uncommitted non-professional staff.

3. Peer/fraternal relationship orientation.

4. Preservation of personal power valued.

5. Open social system (easy access, departure and informal contacts).

6. Clients actively involved in planning and carrying our necessary house functions.

7. Minimal staff role differentiation.

8. Minimal hierarchy.

9. Use of community resources encouraged.

10. No formal in-house 'therapy'.

Carefully conducted trials appeared to show the value, at least in the short term, of this approach (Mosher, Vallone and Menn 1995), but nevertheless Soteria House was closed in 1983. An attempt at a controlled trial was carried out at 'Soteria Berne' which opened in Switzerland in 1984. Unfortunately, as usually happens, biases from admission decisions occurred. Nevertheless, the results were again encouraging (Ciompi *et al.* 1992).

In 1961 Franco Basaglia, another charismatic young psychiatrist, was appointed medical director to a backward 500-bedded asylum in Gorizia on the Italian–Yugoslav border. He visited both Maxwell Jones at Dingleton, which he criticized for not being 'political' (Jones and Poletti 1985), and Laing at Kingsley

Hall (Clay 1996). Basaglia and his colleagues' radical attempts to transform Gorizia were described in *L'Istituzione Negata* (Basaglia 1968). In 1971 Basaglia moved on to San Giovanni Hospital in Trieste, and in 1974 he founded Psichiatria Democratica, a movement which led the passing of Law 180 by the Italian Parliament in 1978. The law's provisions included the banning of any new patients being admitted to mental hospitals and the setting up of small 'Diagnosis and Cure' units in general hospitals. Jones and Poletti studied the resultant services throughout Italy and summarized their conclusions in their paper (1985). Pedriali's (1997) explanations for the subsequent decline in Italian therapeutic communities for psychotic patients include 'the extreme idealisation of those experiences' (p.3) and the charismatic notions of their leadership. Nevertheless, there remain vigorous Italian therapeutic communities, such as the Maieusis Community (Caltagirone and Smargiassi 1997) mainly, however, in the private sector.

All the experiments in the use of the therapeutic community described so far have been with patients whose schizophrenic illnesses have tended to be either 'burnt out' or of relatively recent onset. In 1963, however, Clark decided to try the therapeutic community approach with the most severely disturbed patients in Fulbourn Hospital (Clark 1996). In 1966 the male and female 'disturbed wards' were merged to form Hereward House.

> Nowhere in Britain had anyone attempted to gather in one open-door, mixed-sex therapeutic community all the most disturbed patients from an ordinary mental hospital; reporters, film makers and professional colleagues came to see what we were doing. For many of the patients, long trapped in rigidly controlled back wards, it was greatly liberating to be in charge of their own lives and to be able to participate in making decisions about the running of their wards. For many staff, too, challenging charge nurses, doctors and consultants and helping to decide policy was very exciting. Rumours ran round the rest of Fulbourn telling of filth, disorganization, violence, subversion and sexual orgies going on in Hereward House. The forbearance of the nursing officers and the administrators was sorely tried. However, the administrators, who had lived and worked long years in the hospital, saw patients whom they had known as crazy troublemakers change and become pleasant, co-operative and cheerful people. They could see the method was working. (Clark 1996, p.200)

Myers carried out a study of Hereward House male patients, comparing them with a control group who had been transferred into the disturbed ward of another nearby hospital (Myers and Clark 1972). The Hereward group showed significantly greater improvements both in their mental state and spontaneity of interactions. Many more patients were able to be discharged into the community.

I started my psychiatric career at Shenley Hospital in 1972, based in a 50-bedded acute admission ward, Villa 10. Inspired by Laing's writing, prior to taking up my appointment I had resolved not to read any psychiatric text for the first six months so that I would be able to make my own observations and draw my own conclusions concerning 'madness'. Several like-minded young staff also joined the unit round about the same time. Our conclusions were unremarkable and predictable, but they were our own. We felt we could understand our 'mad' patients and that given their circumstances, what they said generally made sense. The fact that they were 'patients' did not seem to mean that they did not have views worth listening to. Like most people they were best treated with trust, and were amenable to honest confrontation.

> When I started work on the ward the prevailing feeling was of aimless waiting. I remember making the observation that it was like a station to which the train never came. The patients sat around listlessly, watched over by puzzled nurses. My friends and I intuitively felt that if the patients and the staff could live, work and interact as a group it would be a 'good thing'. We therefore started exploring the use of group activities, initiated a thirty minute ward meeting three times a week, and so on. (Pullen 1985b, pp.165–166)

In other words we re-discovered for ourselves the therapeutic community. At the same time I explored the antipsychiatry movement and some of the alternative therapies such as Gestalt. I have already mentioned my worries at what seemed to me the abusive style of some of my fellow 'therapists'. I also grew disillusioned with those who believed that by leaving the National Health Service they freed themselves from external constraints. The places I visited certainly had not done so, being severely constrained by a system related to the power of money. I felt there was something deeply wrong about importing the offspring of rich Californians to houses set up in deprived inner London areas. My worst disillusionment in retrospect really only came about because of my own naivety. I had persuaded a small antipsychiatry commune, with whom I had become friendly, to admit a young man who was under my care at Shenley. One day, to my horror, I discovered that he had been admitted the night before to the local 'bin' following disturbed behaviour which would have been easily contained on Villa 10. I then realized that, despite all the rhetoric to the contrary, if I wanted to continue working with the most seriously disturbed and deprived I had to do so 'within the system'.

In 1975 I had the good fortune to be appointed a Senior Registrar at Fulbourn, at the time probably the most exciting and dynamic hospital in Britain. For the next four years I divided my time between outpatient psychotherapy and managing Street, an acute admission ward, with the benign support of its Senior Consultant Oliver Hodgson. Before 1975 few acute admission units had attempted to run as therapeutic communities, the patients being seen as too ill and their length of stay too short for any effective therapy to occur. Wilmer, who had worked with Maxwell Jones, ran a 34-bed Navy admitting ward in Oakland,

California which had acute admissions for up to ten days. He set up a daily community meeting and observed a fall in the use of sedation and seclusion (Wilmer 1958). Another successful ward was the Phoenix Unit at Littlemore Hospital, Oxford (Sugarman 1968). This had been opened as a male rehabilitation unit by Bertram Mandelbrote in 1961 (Mandelbrote 1965) but quickly evolved into a more comprehensive service including acute admission. It always retained a core of 'longstay' day patients in order to ensure continuity of the therapeutic culture. This well respected unit functioned as a therapeutic community until Mandelbrote retired in 1988.

In sharp contrast was the brief life of the Shrodells Psychiatric Unit, Watford, which opened in 1973. 'Some of us made a considerable effort to involve the Assistant Administration Officer in the unit processes. When this was unsuccessful, my efforts to get him replaced were the cause of friction with other unit leaders, as they suggested a policy of appeasement' (Haddon 1979, p.38). Hardly 'working within the system'! Another early experiment involved Malcolm Pines' heroic efforts at the Atkinson Morley Hospital in London: 'The setting for this challenging work was an inpatient unit of some forty beds under three consultants, each of whom had special research interests ranging from metabolic aspects of psychiatric disturbances to a specialized research programme in psycho-surgery. The unit admitted a very wide range of psychiatric disorders: acute and chronic psychosis, organic disorders, patients for psycho-surgery, neurotic and personality disorders, alcoholism and drug dependency problems' (Pines 1979, p.27). Clark had also run an acute admission ward, Friends, as a therapeutic community from 1971 until 1976 when Martin Roth was appointed as Cambridge's first Professor of Psychiatry and took over the ward. 'Sir Martin found much that he disliked about psychiatry in Cambridge – and made his distaste apparent. He found the culture of open discussion which we had developed at Fulbourn quite unacceptable. The fact that junior doctors, social workers and nurses argued and challenged the view and instructions of consultants – and even *his* opinions – appalled him. He could see no value in the therapeutic community approach' (Clark 1996, p.232).

Street Ward 1975–1979 is probably still the most sustained and intensive British attempt that has been made to run an orthodox acute admission ward as a therapeutic community; most of its patients were in an acute phase of a psychotic illness, either schizophrenia or depression. Its 35 beds were the only psychiatric inpatient service for the adult, non-dementing population of its sector of about 150,000. Although many patients received compulsory treatment under the Mental Health Act, there was no access to 'intensive care' or other secure facilities. The mixed sex open ward was in a pleasant airy modern building on two floors, with the upstairs areas being used mainly for dormitories and offices (Pullen 1982). Street was unusual in the 1970s in claiming to be a therapeutic community whilst using both drugs and electroconvulsive therapy (ECT). Physical medical treatments were usually regarded as anathema by the anti-psychiatrists (although, as already mentioned, Cooper used neuroleptics), and claims that they were only agents of social control, or worse, came from both the left and the right (see for example Hill 1983; Szasz 1970). These attitudes influenced many working in the therapeutic community movement (see for example, Baron (1987) on the Paddington Day Centre). At the very least, using medication was seen as second best. When I started psychiatry I had 'wanted' schizophrenia to be caused by 'schizophrenogenic' mothers and drugs to be useless. However, what if the evidence points the other way? Stewart, a geneticist writing in the *Radical Science Journal* (1979), describes how he dealt with some work on schizophrenia he was given. 'My unconscious guilt successfully sabotaged the way I constructed the genetic models, so that none of them worked and I could make it look as though *non*-genetic models explained the data better' (p.122). Eventually he had to acknowledge what he was doing. 'If true, this model has quite nasty implications; perhaps the worst being that the way is wide open for a complete "medicalisation" of schizophrenia based on "objective" classifications made at birth' (p.122). Some twenty years later, I believe one now has to accept that there must be a biological factor involved in at least some of the schizophrenias, and that neuroleptic drugs are not simply pharmacological 'coshes' but do have a specific, and sometimes therapeutic, effect. This is not to argue that psychiatry is never used abusively, nor medication, nor, of course, psychological treatments.

Street delivered medical treatments, so why bother with a therapeutic community? If any group is forced to live together, especially under conditions of stress, powerful forces quickly come into play. Hospital wards are a classic example; this was still more the case in the days when even minor surgery led to a couple of weeks living in such a 'total institution' (Goffman 1961). This was recognized even in popular culture as seen, for example, in the comic British film *Carry on Nurse*. An archetypal figure was always the tyrannical ward sister who embodies both the need and the fear of dependence. Ken Kesey's (1962) Nurse Ratched is a particularly terrifying example, 'Big Nurse'. The development of communal dynamics, therefore, is unavoidable, but they are not necessarily therapeutic. The sister of a psychiatric ward once informed me that she ensured the patients never talked to each other about their problems. She knew she could rely on me to talk to them about such matters at least once a week. Not surprisingly the patients on the ward resorted to dramatic and destructive acting out, often in collusion! A minimum desirable outcome, therefore, was to create a group living experience on Street that was not anti-therapeutic and did not interfere with other treatments. Even though the average length of admission was only 17 days there was often a powerful sense of community and shared purpose. Reality confrontation was usually vigorous and an emphasis was placed upon democratization and permissiveness. Residents were encouraged to share in each others' treatment as much as possible, even the use of sedation (Pullen 1980).

The keystone of the ward's life was the daily 'Community Meeting' which lasted 45 minutes (9.30–10.15 a.m.), and was attended by everyone present in the unit at that time. Street's Community Meeting developed its own style. There was no chairperson or agenda, little formal business was transacted, and votes rarely taken. Naturally, with a constantly changing population, meetings varied a great deal, but usually they were free-floating, often emotional and confrontational, large groups drawing upon the happenings of the previous day. An anthropologist, Malcolm Ruel, while studying large groups, attended Community Meetings on Street. His general descriptions of large group processes, both 'individual bound' and 'interactive', concisely encapsulate much of the life of this particular meeting. His identification of the 'Commentator', for example, clarifies why staff who make interpretations during Community Meetings are usually (and in my opinion correctly) greeted with little enthusiasm. Ruel writes that in the large group the 'Commentator' is

> often an intelligent, perceptive person who contributes to discussion but always in terms of secondary comments on what others have done and said. People's dissatisfaction with this will vary with the degree of detachment and intellectualism shown. It is a difficult split to negotiate since the commentator's perceptions are usually relevant and often helpful, but his position is brittle and when personally challenged he may have little to defend himself with. (Ruel 1980, pp.106–107)

Ruel also proposes a general schema for all groups: small or large; structured, counterstructured or structurally destructured. A structured group is one with a form and a purpose of its own, a committee for example, while counterstructured groups

> are the constituted groups whose members are drawn from previously existing organisations or institutions and who thus carry with them, at least implicitly, something of the roles and interest of the formal organisation ... what were informal personal relations operating within a formal organisation (cliques on a shop floor) become now the very substance of the group's existence and interest, while the formal relations (the hierarchies of the organisation) are suppressed to a secondary, implicit place in the group's discussions. In this light a therapeutic community is Goffman's 'underlife' given space, air and legitimacy. (pp.103–104)

Structurally destructured groups have a structure primarily concerned with boundary maintenance so that within that boundary is created a 'structurally empty space', such as is found in the group analytic small group. Ruel firmly places the Community Meeting within his category 'large counterstructural group.' I have argued, however, (Pullen 1985a) that one way of trying to understand the complexity of a Community Meeting is to see it as a large group which can change its 'mode' from structured (e.g. when making ward business decisions) to counterstructured to structurally destructured. Turquet vividly described the power, and threat, of the structurally destructured large group (1975).

While within the Community Meeting there was strong emphasis upon the common role of community member, the staff always met immediately afterwards for a 30 minute private review. This seemed to me one of the most important meetings on Street, in many ways functioning as a daily 'sensitivity' encounter. All patients attended one of two small groups held twice a week and there were also weekly sociodrama and art therapy sessions. Staff were encouraged to attend the last two in the role of community member rather than as therapist. It was recognized that the staff also had legitimate therapeutic needs and I have suggested that Street could be seen as two parallel and interrelating therapeutic communities, that is the short-stay patient community and the longer-stay staff community. Certainly it was demonstrated over a period of two years that nurse sickness rates were only three-quarters those of the hospital's other acute admission wards (Pullen 1982). In purely medical and administrative terms Street was highly successful. I compared admission and re-admission rates, together with length of stay, for the three acute admission wards of Fulbourn, all of which served similar mixed rural and city sectors. Friends Ward by then under the leadership of Roth was positively hostile to the therapeutic community, whilst Adrian was a more typical 'eclectic' ward of the time (see Table 15.1).

Table 15.1: Admission and re-admission rates, Fulbourn Hospital			
	Street	*Friends*	*Adrian*
a) Number of admissions from 1.10.78–30.9.79	300	277	232
b) Average length of stay (in days) for (a)	16.8	34.9	38.1
c) Number of admissions 1.7.78–30.9.78	77	73	65
d) Number of patients involved in (c)	69	63	58
e) Number of patients from (c) re-admitted during following 12 months. (1.10.78–30.9.79)	16	15	22

Source: Pullen (1982), p.124

Nieminen, Isohanni and Winblad (1994) reporting 14 years' experience from a 'closed therapeutic community acute ward' in Oulu, Finland, suggest, however, that patients with lengths of stays of between 20 and 80 days were best able to use their programmes. Staff's opinion on immediate treatment outcome was most positive for patients staying between 40 and 60 days. However Hansen and Slevin (1996) claim to demonstrate positive therapeutic benefits on an inner-city acute admission ward where the average length of stay was only 8.4 days. Another ward within the hospital which did not implement therapeutic community principles was used as a control.

It was much harder to measure the extent to which the residents of Street gained deeper psychological insights during their brief stays. My impression was that some did, particularly perhaps the more psychologically naive who really seemed to learn something new about themselves. In any case, I remained convinced that schizophrenia was not a contra-indication for group and therapeutic community therapy. In 1980, therefore, I accepted the post of Consultant Psychiatrist with Special Interest in Rehabilitation at Littlemore Hospital, Oxford. Under Bertram Mandelbrote's leadership nearly all of that hospital's 'old longstay patients' had been rehabilitated, and my 'inheritance' included Ward B5 which:

> had been 'male disturbed' until becoming a mixed sex 'medium dependency' ward in the late 1970s. In the summer of 1980 it was home to a rather ill-assorted group of 23 men and women whose ages ran from 23 to 81 years. Most suffered from a severe, chronic psychotic illness and many were actively disturbed. The hospital wing they occupied was designed by the same architects as Oxford Prison, to which it bears a close resemblance ... On the first floor it has a 137 foot long day room, ineffectually divided into three by glass partitions, with a similar space on the second floor divided into two shabby open dormitories. The windows are high and inadequate, and the only direct access to the outside is down a fire escape. (Pullen 1986, p.192)

Nevertheless as my colleague Heather Hull wrote

> My first involvement with the ward was at Christmas, 1979. At this time a group of nurses on B5 had begun to question the system, and to challenge the basic concept that the ward's inmates were a bunch of 'no-hopers'. There were attempts to change the basic running of the place: small groups of patients were encouraged to cook for themselves at weekends; staff tried to step-back a little and allow patients to join in on a few decisions; a Community Meeting was started. The changes were small in some ways but revolutionary in that they were the first heralds of what was to be a total turn around in our attitudes and practices in caring for very damaged, chronically psychotic individuals. (Hull and Pullen 1988, pp.109–110)

I introduced the staff to some of the ideas of the therapeutic community, trying to facilitate as far as possible them making their own discoveries (Pullen 1985b;

Pullen 1986), hopefully a 'living-learning experience'. The patients too embraced the changes and asserted their right to rename the ward after their recently deceased fellow, Eric Burden. Eric was a long-term patient who, when he developed an oral carcinoma, was nursed and died in his 'home', the ward. He suffered from a chronic schizophrenic illness and had a long history of delinquent and disturbed behaviour but he faced his final illness, with bravery and dignity. Although at the time I had wanted to give the ward a more 'political' and upbeat name, I now believe the community was right, and that Eric's life was a powerful and appropriate symbol for our new endeavour, the Eric Burden Community (EBC).

At that time there was increasing awareness of the problem of the so-called 'new longstay' (Mann and Cree 1976). We developed, therefore, a service for the 'young adult chronically mentally ill', the Young Adult Unit (YAU). Referrals are accepted from local Consultant Psychiatrists of patients who meet the following criteria:

1. Aged between 18 and 35.

2. Diagnosed as suffering from a functional psychosis (usually schizophrenia) or a borderline personality disorder.

3. Normal intelligence (i.e. IQ of 70 or above).

4. a) No or partial response to conventional medical treatments (i.e. medication).

   b) *and* breakdown of social network (usually family support).

5. Compliance with transfer to the YAU.

These criteria were chosen to identify the young men and women who had the worst prognoses (Kolakowska *et al.* 1985) and who were at greatest risk of becoming the 'new longstay'. Early referral is encouraged, hopefully before the institutionalizing effects of traditional care have taken hold, and there is no requirement regarding length of previous admission. In our experience normal intelligence is needed to be able to use our therapeutic community programme. Many of our patients are compulsorily treated under the terms of the 1983 Mental Health Act, but we still feel we can require the patient's agreement to the transfer of their care to our unit. The YAU also accepts referrals from the Special Hospitals (that is maximum security hospitals such as Broadmoor); for these patients we are more flexible, especially with regard to age and diagnosis (see also Pullen 1998a). Drug use, offending behaviour, or a history of violence are not criteria but in reality most patients referred have one or more of these problems. (The therapeutic community itself was used to confront the problem of abuse of prescribed drugs, the anticholinergics (Pullen, Best and Maguire 1984; Poller and D'Arcy 1990).)

The approach of the Young Adult Unit is based upon three fundamental concepts: social therapy (Clark 1974); continuity of care; and social disablement. Continuity of care is symbolized by the YAU case register. Once a person is accepted after referral they are first admitted to the 20 bedded mixed sex Eric Burden Community for a period lasting from a few days to up to two years. The goals are, as far as possible, to assess and meet the residents' psychiatric needs and, most importantly, to form a 'therapeutic alliance'. Most patients are then transferred to a nine-bedded hospital hostel, Thorncliffe House, in a suburb of Oxford. Although Thorncliffe House has a small number of nurses who work mainly at the hostel they, like their colleagues based at the EBC, are considered as part of the wider YAU team.[1] Medical, occupational therapy and social work input is provided by people who work for the whole YAU. The same team also provides community support when the patient is discharged from Thorncliffe House usually after six months to a year, to either independent or sheltered housing such as a Group Home. There are at any one time about 25 members of the YAU community living outside the hospital or Thorncliffe House. Their support includes six of the beds of the EBC which are reserved for them for 'acute admissions'. Anyone whose name is on the YAU Case Register has the *right* to request readmission. Part of the work of the initial admission to the EBC is to help the resident recognize, and admit to themselves, when they need the help and support of the ward. This extended partnership between hospital staff and patient is unusual, but I believe very valuable (Pullen 1987; Pullen 1988). By the time patients reach the age of about 45 most have settled in the wider community and can be discharged from the YAU. A few people need a supporting or containing environment for longer, and Littlemore Hospital has three continuing care wards, one a hospital hostel, 18 Morrell Crescent is associated with the YAU. The others are a low secure and a medium secure ward.

Social disability is a term coined by John Wing:

> 'Social disablement' is the state of an individual who is unable to perform socially up to the standards expected by himself or herself, by people important to him or her, or by society in general. Both medical and social components of disablement, often in intimate combination, must be recognized; exclusively medical or social 'models' are inadequate to describe, explain, or help psychiatric disabilities. Three main types of cause must be considered:
>
> 1. Psychiatric impairments or dysfunctions (often described as 'symptoms').
>
> 2. Social disadvantages.

---

[1]   Unfortunately Thorncliffe House was closed in 1998 as one of the measures to meet overspending elsewhere in the hospital.

3. Personal reactions to impairment or disadvantage, or to a combination of both. (Wing and Morris 1981, p.4)

The YAU team tries to work with the patient to achieve optimum control of their illness. Medication is only used to attempt to help with symptoms to the extent that the patient finds them distressing, or of course, to reduce any risks posed to the lives of the patient or others. It is not the staff's role to eliminate 'delusions'. Many patients associate their experience of schizophrenia with positive feelings of vigour and creativity, and some 'titrate' these against more distressing consequences by their own management of their medication. We have a very limited ability to rectify the social disadvantages of the mentally ill, but we do have social workers as integral members of the staff team. The most important work of the EBC relates to the third factor of 'social disablement'. Bloch and Crouch, building on the work of Yalom (1985, see also Chapter 11 in this volume), identified ten therapeutic factors in group psychotherapy:

1. *Acceptance* – the patient feels a sense of belonging and being valued (cohesiveness).

2. *Universality* – the patient discovers that he is not unique with his problems (universalization).

3. *Altruism* – the patient learns with satisfaction that he can be helpful to others in the group.

4. *Instillation of hope* – the patient gains a sense of optimism about his potential to benefit from treatment.

5. *Guidance* – the patient receive useful information in the form of advice, suggestions, explanation, and instruction.

6. *Vicarious learning* – the patient benefits by observing the therapeutic experience of fellow group members (spectator learning, identification).

7. *Self-understanding* – the patient learns something important about himself, usually through feedback or interpretation (insight, intellectualization).

8. *Learning from interpersonal action* – the patient learns from his attempts to relate constructively and adaptively within the group (interpersonal learning, interaction).

9. *Self-disclosure* – the patient reveals highly personal information to the group and thus 'gets it off his chest'.

10. *Catharsis* – the patient releases intense feelings which brings him a sense of relief (ventilation). (Bloch and Crouch 1985 p.246)

Whiteley and Collis (1987) demonstrated the relevance of these factors at the Henderson Hospital. I can find no better summary of the therapeutic forces operating in the EBC. I do not believe I can 'cure' schizophrenia, but I do know that the residents are existential beings with a need to feel they understand their own experiences and emotions.

The EBC in many ways is a 'pure' form of the therapeutic community with the community life being the primary therapeutic agent – the 'living–learning' experience. Some 'psychotherapeutic communities' have in my opinion become inpatient group therapy units, ('community analysis': Kotowicz 1997). The EBC undoubtedly values 'communalism', with a strong culture of mutual responsibilities and opportunities for altruism. The formal expression of communalism is the daily 30 minutes community meeting. Attendance for residents is publicly valued but not compulsory. Occasionally when the numbers attending have dropped, suggestions have been made to reduce the meetings' frequency. Every time, however, this has been vigorously vetoed by the residents. It seems important to know that the meeting reliably exists and is available, whilst having the freedom not always to attend. As in Street, the meeting is followed by a compulsory 30 minute staff feedback meeting. A verbal 'process recording' is there made jointly by the staff members who then attempt to analyse the group's dynamics. The six 'themes' described by Clark and Myers (1970) from Hereward House often seem relevant:

1. rejection

2. violence

3. sexuality

4. staff divisions

5. dependence–independence

6. relationships with outside bodies.

'Democratization', 'permissiveness' and 'reality confrontation' underpin the practice and philosophy of the community, although of course the reality of who we are and where we are cannot be denied (see discussion in Pullen 1986).

Interestingly, small groups have never thrived on EBC, although at any one time a few residents are in individual dynamic psychotherapy or interpretative art therapy. Most of the therapeutic work is done in the informal interactions between members of the community. The move into a newer two storey building, *with a garden*, made this easier for both staff and residents. There are few structured activities but every day the community shops for, cooks and eats its meals together. In many ways I believe we have achieved what Cooper set out to do in Villa 21. Some years ago in an attempt to portray the life of the EBC a number of colleagues and myself used music, pictures, and poems as well as prose in a presentation we called 'The Eric Burden Community and the Kama Sutra'. A transcript was later published as 'Stultitiae Laus' (Evans *et al.* 1990). We tried to convey the rollercoaster experience of the community as it swung between horror and humour, silliness and seriousness, 'our paper has been an attempt to explain the value of ways of being that are neither the delivery of therapy nor the giving of nurturance ... but the "Third Way" ' (p.176).

In the era of 'evidence based medicine' this chapter should finish with a summary of the results of the YAU using the therapeutic community in the treatment of schizophrenia. The first problem that would have to be solved, however, would be the identification of a control group. To the best of my knowledge the YAU is the only British service targeted on 'poor prognosis' schizophrenia in young people. The next problem would be to agree desirable outcome measures for a group of people who have not developed the stereotyped handicaps of institutionalization. There would then be the task of identifying which factors in the treatment package are therapeutic. Unfortunately I have not attempted this massive project (comparable to that of Wing and Brown 1970) and I do not know who would ever pay for it, certainly not the pharmaceutical companies. There is some positive anecdotal evidence: for example, over 18 years only two patients have committed suicide and no member of the public has been injured. In fact the EBC, being 19 years old, apparently thriving, and never having difficulties in recruiting or retaining staff is perhaps the most strikingly favourable result. Staff working on the EBC not only have to spend their time with people who are usually seen as aggressive, demanding, unattractive and incurable, but are required to abandon their usual defences, in particular the projection of all of their 'madness' into the patients so that they can feel omnipotently 'sane'. Many patients of course are equally ready to project away their 'saneness' in return for the comforts of dependence. Both groups, however, are depleted and diminished, and end up being persecuted by what they tried to 'give away'. We do however, offer, staff the right to use the therapeutic community to meet some of their own legitimate therapeutic needs (see Pullen 1985b; Pullen 1986; Hull and Pullen 1988; Evans et al. 1990; Pullen 1998b). I believe, therefore, that at the very least the therapeutic community is a good method for ensuring the sustained delivery of a service for the severely mentally ill.

It cannot be denied that over the centuries madmen have been abused, sometimes cruelly and grotesquely (Szasz 1970). I hope this chapter has illustrated that when their lot has improved it has been not only because of the development of new treatment technologies but also because fear and revulsion have been overcome to recognize shared common humanity. There is the famous story of Pinel freeing the shackled guardsman Chevigné at the Bicêtre and offering his hand saying 'You are a reasonable man'. Whenever liberal and democratic values have been allowed to flourish in psychiatry so has the care of the mentally ill. The therapeutic community is the latest manifestation of that fact.

References

Barnes, M. and Berke, J.H. (1971) *Two Accounts of a Journey Through Madness.* London: MacGibbon & Kee.

Baron, C. (1987) *Asylum to Anarchy.* London: Free Association Books.

Barton, R. (1959) *Institutional Neurosis.* Bristol: John Wright and Sons.

Basaglia, F. (ed) (1968) *L'Instituzione Negata.* Torino: Einaudi.

Belknap, I. (1956) *Human Problems of a State Mental Hospital.* New York: McGraw-Hill.

Bell, G.M. (1955) 'A mental hospital with open doors'. *International Journal of Social Psychiatry 1,* 42.

Bion, W.R. and Rickman, J. (1943) 'Intra-group tensions in therapy: their study as a task of the group.' *Lancet 2,* 678–681.

Bleuler, E.P. (1911) *Dementia Praecox or the Group of Schizophrenias.* Leipzig: Deuticke [trans. Zinkin, J. (1950) New York: International Universities Press.]

Bloch, S. and Crouch, E. (1985) *Therapeutic Factors in Group Psychotherapy.* Oxford: Oxford University Press.

Bridger, H. (1985) 'Northfield revisited'. In M. Pines (ed) *Bion and Group Psychotherapy.* London: Routledge & Kegan Paul.

Caltagirone, I. and Smargiassi, M.M. (1997) 'Therapeutic and non-therapeutic communities.' *Therapeutic Communities 18,* 167–181.

Cameron, J.L., Laing, R.D. and McGhie, A. (1955) 'Patient and Nurse.' *Lancet ii,* 1284–1286.

Caudill, W.A. (1958) *The Psychiatric Hospital as a Small Society.* Cambridge, MA: Harvard University Press.

Ciompi, L., Dauwalder, H-P., Maier, C., Aebi, E., Trütsch, K., Kupper Z. and Rutishauser, C. (1992). 'The pilot project "Soteria Berne" clinical experiences and results'. *British Journal of Psychiatry 161* (suppl. 18), 145–153.

Clark, D.H. (1964) *Administrative Therapy.* London: Tavistock.

Clark, D.H. (1974) *Social Therapy in Psychiatry.* Harmondsworth: Penguin Books.

Clark, D.H. (1991) 'Maxwell Jones and the mental hospitals.' *International Journal of Therapeutic Communities 12,* 117–123.

Clark, D.H. (1996) *The Story of a Mental Hospital: Fulbourn 1858–1983.* London: Process Press.

Clark, D.H. and Myers, K. (1970) 'Themes in a Therapeutic Community.' *British Journal of Psychiatry 117,* 389–395.

Clark, D.H. and Oram, E.G. (1966) 'Reform in the Mental Hospital: an eight year follow-up.' *International Journal of Social Psychiatry 12,* 98–108.

Clay, J. (1996) *R.D. Laing, A Divided Self.* London: Hodder and Stoughton.

Conolly, J. (1847) *The Construction and Government of Lunatic Asylums.* London: John Churchill.

Conolly, J. (1856) *The Treatment of the Insane without Mechanical Restraints.* London: Smith, Elder and Co.

Conran, M.B. (1970) 'The family as a model, in an application of psychoanalysis to the care and treatment of young male schizophrenics.' Unpublished MD thesis, University of London.

Cooper, D. (1967) *Psychiatry and Anti-Psychiatry.* London: Tavistock.

Cooper, D., Esterson, A., and Laing, R.D. (1965) 'Results of family-orientated therapy with hospitalized schizophrenics.' *British Medical Journal ii,* 1462–1465.

Dunham, W., and Weinberg, S.K. (1960) *The Culture of the State Mental Hospital.* Detroit: Wayne State University Press.

Evans, V.M., Huk, M., Hull, H. and Pullen, G.P. (1990) 'Stultitiae Laus.' *International Journal of Therapeutic Communities 11,* 157–177.

Foulkes, S.H. (1948) *Introduction to Group-Analytic Psychotherapy.* London: William Heinemann Medical Books.

Freeman, T., Cameron, J.L. and McGhie, A. (1958) *Chronic Schizophrenia.* London: Tavistock.

Goffman, E. (1961) *Asylums.* New York: Doubleday.

Greenblatt, M., Levinson, D.J., and Williams, R.N. (1957) *The Patient and the Mental Hospital.* Glencoe, IL: The Free Press.

Greenblatt, M., York, R.H., and Brown, E.L. (1955) *From Custodial to Therapeutic Patient Care in Mental Hospitals.* New York: Russell Sage Foundation.

Haddon, B. (1979) 'Political implications of therapeutic communities.' In R.D. Hinshelwood and N.P. Manning (eds) *Therapeutic Communities: Reflections and Progress.* London: Routledge and Kegan Paul.

Hansen, J.T. and Slevin, C. (1996) 'The implementation of Therapeutic Community principles in acute care psychiatric hospital settings: an empirical analysis and recommendations to clinicians.' *Journal of Clinical Psychology 52,* 673–678.

Harrison, T. and Clarke, D. (1992) 'The Northfield experiments.' *British Journal of Psychiatry 160,* 698–708.

Hill, D. (1983) *The Politics of Schizophrenia. Psychiatric Oppression in the United States.* New York: University Press of America.

Hull, H. and Pullen, G.P. (1988) 'The EBC-madness and community.' *International Journal of Therapeutic Communities 9,* 109–114.

Jones, K. and Poletti, A. (1985) 'Understanding the Italian Experience.' *British Journal of Psychiatry 146,* 341–347.

Jones, M. (1952) *Social Psychiatry.* London: Tavistock.

Jones, M. (1968) *Beyond the Therapeutic Community.* New Haven: Yale University Press.

Jones, M. (1982) *The Process of Change.* London: Routledge & Kegan Paul.

Kennard, D. (1983) *An Introduction to Therapeutic Communities.* London: Routledge & Kegan Paul.

Kennard, D. (1998) *An Introduction to Therapeutic Communities, 2nd Edition.* London: Jessica Kingsley Publishers.

Kesey, K. (1962) *One Flew over the Cuckoo's Nest.* New York: Viking Press.

Kraepelin, E. (1913) *Lectures on Clinical Psychiatry,* 8th edition. London: Baillière, Tindall and Cox.

Kolakowska, T., Williams, A.D., Arden, M., Reveley, M.A., Jambor, K., Gelder, M.G. and Mandlebrote, B.M. (1985) 'Schizophrenia with good and poor. Outcome: 1 – early clinical features, responses to neuroleptics and signs of organic dysfunction.' *British Journal of Psychiatry 146,* 229–239.

Kotowicz, Z. (1997) *R.D. Laing and the Paths of Anti-Psychiatry.* London: Routledge.

Laing, R.D. (1960) *The Divided Self.* London: Tavistock.

Laing, R.D. (1961) *Self and Others.* London: Tavistock.

Laing, R.D. (1967) *The Politics of Experience.* Harmondsworth: Penguin.

Laing, R.D. (1968) 'Metanoia: some experiences at Kingsley Hall.' Paris: Recherches. Reprinted in H.W. Ruitenbeek (ed) *Going Crazy.* New York: Bantam (1972).

Laing, R.D. (1976) *The Facts of Life.* London: Allen Lane.

Laing, R.D. (1985) *Wisdom, Madness and Folly.* London: Macmillan.

Letemendia, F.J.J., Harris, A.D. and Willems, P.J.A. (1967) 'The clinical effects on a population of chronic schizophrenic patients of administrative changes in hospital.' *British Journal of Psychiatry 113,* 959–971.

Lomax, M. (1921) *The Experiences of an Asylum Doctor.* London: George Allen and Unwin.

Main, T.F. (1946) 'The hospital as a therapeutic institution.' *Bulletin of the Menninger Clinic 10,* 66–70.

Mandelbrote, B.M. (1958) 'An experiment in the rapid conversion of a closed mental hospital into an open-door hospital.' *Mental Hygiene 42,* 3–16.

Mandelbrote, B.M. (1965) 'The use of psychodynamic and sociodynamic principles in the treatment of psychotics. A change from ward unit concepts to grouped communities.' *Comprehensive Psychiatry 6,* 381–387.

Mandelbrote, B.M. (1996) 'The Northfield experiment: its contribution to developments in psychiatry.' *Therapeutic Communities 17,* 149–153.

Mann, S.A. and Cree, W. (1976) 'New long-stay psychiatric patients: a national sample survey of fifteen mental hospitals in England and Wales 1972–3.' *Psychological Medicine 6,* 603–616.

Martin, D.V. (1962) *Adventure in Psychiatry.* Oxford: Bruno Cassirer.

Mayer-Gross, W. (1932) 'Die Schizophrenie.' In O. Bumke (ed) *Handbuch der Geisteskrankheiten,* Vol. 9. Berlin: Springer.

Morgan, R., and Cheadle, J. (1981) *Psychiatric Rehabilitation*. Surbiton: National Schizophrenia Fellowship.

Morrice, J.K.W. (1979) 'Basic concepts: A critical review.' In R.D. Hinshelwood and N.P. Manning (eds) *Therapeutic Communities: Reflections and Progress*. London: Routledge & Kegan Paul.

Mosher, L.R. and Burti, L. (1994) *Community Mental Health: A. Practical Guide*. New York: Norton.

Mosher, L.R., Menn, A. and Matthews S.M. (1975) 'Soteria: Evaluation of a home-based treatment for schizophrenia.' *American Journal of Orthopsychiatry 45*, 455–467.

Mosher L.R., Vallone R. and Menn, A. (1995) 'The treatment of acute psychosis without neuroleptics: six week psychopathology outcome data from the Soteria Project.' *International Journal of Social Psychiatry 41*, 157–173.

Myers, K. and Clark, D.H. (1972) 'Results in a Therapeutic Community.' *British Journal of Psychiatry 120*, 51–58.

Nieminen, P., Isohanni, M. and Winblad, I. (1994) 'Length of hospitalization in an acute patients' therapeutic community ward.' *Acta Psychiatrica Scandinavica 90*, 466–472.

Pedriali, E. (1997) 'Italian therapeutic communities: from historical analysis to hypotheses for change.' *Therapeutic Communities 18*, 3–13.

Perls, F.S. (1969) *In and Out the Garbage Pail*. Moab, UT: Real People Press.

Pines, M. (1979) 'Therapeutic communities in teaching hospitals.' In R.D. Hinshelwood and N.P. Manning (eds) *Therapeutic Communities: Reflections and Progress*. London: Routledge & Kegan Paul.

Pinel, P. (1806) *A Treatise on Insanity*. London: Cadell and Davies.

Pullen, G.P. (1980) 'Communal Medication.' *International Journal of Therapeutic Communities 1*, 125–127.

Pullen, G.P. (1982) 'Street: the seventeen day community.' *International Journal of Therapeutic Communities 2*, 115–126.

Pullen, G.P. (1985a) 'Supervision of the therapeutic large group.' *British Journal of Psychotherapy 2*, 114–118.

Pullen, G.P. (1985b) 'Conflicts in Starting Therapeutic Communities.' *International Journal of Therapeutic Communities 6*, 165–169.

Pullen, G.P. (1986) 'The Eric Burden Community.' *International Journal of Therapeutic Communities 7*, 191–200.

Pullen, G.P. (1987) 'The Oxford service for the young adult chronically mentally ill: Part 1.' *Bulletin of the Royal College of Psychiatrists 11*, 377–379.

Pullen, G.P. (1988) 'The Oxford service for the young adult chronically mentally ill: Part 2.' *Bulletin of the Royal College of Psychiatrists 12*, 64.

Pullen, G.P. (1998) 'Special Hospital transfers'. *Journal of Forensic Psychiatry 9*, 241–244.

Rapoport, R.N. (1960) *Community as Doctor*. London: Tavistock.

Rothman, D. (1971) *The Discovery of the Asylum*. Boston: Little, Brown.

Ruel, M. (1980) 'Process without structure: some anthropological observations on the large group'. *Group Analysis 13*, 99–109.

Schatzman, M. (1970) 'Madness and Morals.' In J.H. Berke (ed) *Counter-Culture: The Creation of an Alternative Society*. London: Peter Owen.

Sigal, C. (1976) *Zone of the Interior*. New York: Thomas Y. Crowell.

Stanton, A., and Schwartz, M. (1954) *The Mental Hospital*. New York: Basic Books.

Stewart, J. (1979) 'Scientific findings that look awkward for socialists: how are we to respond?' *Radical Science Journal 8*, 121–123.

Sugarman, B. (1968) 'The Phoenix Unit: alliance against illness.' *New Society 11*, 830–833.

Szasz, T.S. (1970) *The Manufacture of Madness: a Comparative Study of the Inquisition and the Mental Health Movement*. New York: Harper and Row.

Tantam, D. (1991) 'The anti-psychiatry movement.' In G.E. Berrios and H. Freeman (eds) *150 Years of British Psychiatry 1841–1991*. London: Gaskell.

Tuke, S. (1813) *Description of the Retreat*. York: W. Alexander.

Turquet, P. (1975) 'Threats to Identify in the Large Group.' In L. Kreeger (ed) *The Large Group: Dynamics and Therapy*. London: Constable.

Whiteley, J.S. and Collis, M. (1987) 'The Therapeutic Factors in Group Psychotherapy Applied to the Therapeutic Community.' *International Journal of Therapeutic Communities 8*, 21–32.

Wilmer, H.A. (1958) *Social Psychiatry in Action.* Springfield, IL: C.C. Thomas.

Wing, J.K. and Brown, G.W (1970) *Institutionalism and Schizophrenia: a Comparative study of Three Mental Hospitals, 1960–1968.* Cambridge: Cambridge, University Press.

Wing, J.K. and Morris, B. (1981) *Handbook of Psychiatric Rehabilitation Practice.* Oxford: Oxford University Press.

Yablonsky, L. (1965) *Synanon: The Tunnel Back.* New York: Macmillan.

Yalom, I.D. (1985) *The Theory and Practice of Group Psychotherapy*, 3rd edition. New York: Basic Books.

Zilboorg, G. (1941) *A History of Medical Psychology.* New York: W.W. Norton.

CHAPTER 16

Confusions in a Therapeutic Milieu

Joseph H. Berke

Confusional states in both residents and staff are among the most frequent, disturbing and disruptive group processes that can occur in a therapeutic community. These are states of mind, but also social relations, whereby patients as well as therapists find it hard, sometimes impossible, to distinguish who is who and what is what. Surprisingly, there has been little specifically written about such states in the professional literature.

I have become increasingly aware of the prevalence of personal and interpersonal confusion among residents and therapists while working at the Arbours Crisis Centre in north London. The centre is a small, specialized therapeutic community where many of the residents inhabit the border between sanity and madness, and clearly manifest psychotic episodes while living there. These episodes inevitably give rise to serious mixups between inner and outer reality, self and others, past and present, adult and child, as well as between animate and inanimate experiences. In this chapter I shall provide several examples of confusional phenomena, discuss the psychological and social dynamics involved and consider how the therapists have struggled to resolve confusional crises.

To begin, I would briefly like to describe the Arbours Centre, which is a unique psychotherapeutic facility that was established in 1973. Six residents stay together in a large Edwardian house with three live-in therapists. These, in turn, are supported by at least 12 'visiting' therapists and trainees who do not live at the residence. The exceptionally good patient/staff ratio is enabled by the devotion and interest of the staff and by a financial structure in which the centre is supported in an individual client/guest basis by social services, area health authorities, medical health insurance, private payments, and by the therapists themselves. They work there at very reduced fees in order to be able to practise in a unique way. The centre has also received charitable grants for capital projects, notably from PETT (Planned Environment Therapy Trust).

At the centre there are three separate but interrelated and interrelating therapeutic systems. These are the team, the group and the milieu. The team consists of a resident therapist (that is, one of the therapists who live at the centre, hereafter called the RTs), team leader (the TL, often a visiting psychotherapist), the guest (Arbours refers to the residential patients in a non-pathologizing way as 'guests'), and perhaps an Arbours trainee. It meets three to five times a week.

The house group consists of everyone who lives at the house, resident therapists and guests, and encompasses four formal house meeting per week.

The milieu is the centre as an active therapeutic environment, perhaps active interpersonal environment is more correct, since the milieu can also be non-therapeutic or even antitherapeutic, depending on, as we shall see, who is at the centre and what is going on. It includes three resident therapists, six guests, nine team leaders and everyone else directly involved with the centre. The therapists and helpers frequently meet, in various combinations and settings, in order to help recognize, experience and tolerate the powerful emotional currents that flow through the house. In other words, we emphasize the role of the countertransference in coping with guests who are often verbally inarticulate. I have previously provided more detailed information about the structure and functioning of the centre in several papers and book chapters (1981, 1982, 1987, 1990).

Over the years, we have become increasingly aware of the power that confusional muddles, whether originating in a guest, or, as sometimes happens, in a therapist, can exert on the house group. I refer both to individual and collective functioning, or should I say, misfunctioning. We first began to realize the importance of confusional issues during the early years of the crisis centre, when we were located in a small, rented house in West London. A young woman, whom I shall call Samantha, had just become a guest at the centre. She was in the throes of a psychotic breakdown and had eluded all attempts by her parents and other psychiatrists to help her. I thought it would be difficult to make contact with her, as she maintained a detached, unreal look about herself and when greeted tended to exclaim, 'It's been a pretty spacey day.'

However, it transpired that Samantha could be quite reflective and articulate about herself. When not lost in a spacey haze, she would explain that she was basically a sad child, who tended to lose herself in people, because her feelings were all over the place, especially when she was 'down'.

It was evident that Samantha avoided her feelings by evacuating them into people and things. Then she barely knew who she was or where she was. With others she said she felt trapped inside a crowd, muddled, lost, like being with people with whom one can never strike the right chord.

After some team meetings, the RT and myself would emerge as if in a fog. When the fog seemed to be inside ourselves, we could not recall that was said in the meeting, whether by Samantha or ourselves. At other times, the fog seemed to lie between ourselves. Then, no matter how hard we tried, we could not get through to each other. All this should have rung warning bells in my head. But my observations were muted because Samantha seemed to be getting better as her stay progressed. She became less withdrawn, more sociable and generally engaged with the activities of the centre.

Then the time came for Samantha to begin the process of leaving. Even though she could still be quite chaotic in her thinking and feelings, she seemed to be positive about the forthcoming separation. She talked about going back to work, but also about joining an Arbours longstay community, for she realized the need for additional support.[1] The RTs tried to help by arranging a meeting at Argyll Lodge (the predecessor of our Brondesbury house) or Crouch End. But try as they might, something went wrong with every appointment. Either she didn't show up, or the community changed the time, or the RT got the day wrong. There seemed to be great confusion about who was doing what or responsible for what. Concurrently, we all became furious and blamed each other for the mixups, which were never resolved. I remember trying to overcome my own sense of disarray by browbeating the RTs to work harder to arrange appointments at the communities. And when their efforts weren't successful, I felt very anxious and angry.

Meanwhile Samantha began to fall apart. She couldn't concentrate on tasks around the house and alternated silliness with tears. She withdrew from friendships she had made, and more than once was returned to the house by the police after wandering around the neighbourhood aimlessly. In the end, Samantha never did get to a community. She just returned to her parents who proceeded to hospitalize her.

Subsequently, I have seen this pattern repeat itself in other interventions. A combination of regression and confusion tends to occur in borderline guests, in particular, who have initially responded well to being at the centre. Then, when the time comes to leave, they display all the chaos at their command. The regressive features of this group process have been noted, in a diversity of group therapies, by Malcolm Pines and Victor Schermer, who have observed: 'primitive regression is an increasing impinging and insistent aspect of the ongoing context within which all group therapy is conducted' (Schermer and Pines 1994). They essentially conclude that therapists who ignore such regressive phenomena are whistling in the dark.

After coping with many regressive crises at the centre, we could see that the leaving was a catastrophe for guests who experienced intimacy as potentially catastrophic, but that all guests whether psychotic or not, passed through a

---

1   In addition to the Crisis Centre, the Arbours supports three long stay therapeutic communities, one in
      Brondesbury, one in Crouch End and the other in Muswell Hill.

leaving crisis that was intrinsic to their stay at the centre. I have described this process in my paper on 'stages of stay' (1987). However, it took many more years of confused and confusing attempts to place guests at Arbours communities, or simply arranging for their return home, to appreciate that our seeming inability to accomplish this, and consequent angry recriminations, were related to confusional states in the guests when they were about to leave.

On at least one such occasion, I was painfully privileged to experience the direct passing of anxiety, confusion and anger from a guest, who had a long-standing reputation for autism and schizophrenia, to myself and a colleague. Ingrid was a 'gift' from a Norwegian social service whose hospitals had not been able to cope with her. She was a huge woman and very aggressive. If she had lived a thousand years previously, she could easily have been a Viking raping and pillaging the North of England. In fact this referral was so unusual, that we wondered whether the main point was to get her out of Norway.

Anyway, Ingrid had been at the centre for several months, but wanted to leave in order to live in a place of her own. No one thought this was possible. Late one afternoon, I was called to the centre by a nearly incoherent RT, who shouted: 'Ingrid has thrown a chair at me for the last time! Either she goes or I go!' In fact, Ingrid had been upset by someone's leaving. Unable to tolerate sadness or depression, she responded in the one way she knew that would destroy the feeling, with violence. What she did was not much different from her previous episodes, and I thought that once I came over and spoke with people, it would blow over. But it didn't. The RT was adamant. Either Ingrid went, or he did. In desperation I called my colleague Morton Schatzman, a cofounder of the Arbours, to come over and help me out. He too argued with the RT, while Ingrid was stomping around in the garden, declaiming a chaotic mish mash of grunts and threats.

Several hours had passed, but the atmosphere remained explosive. Morty and I realized that neither gentle persuasion nor harsh facts would work. So we told the RT to stay and said we would take Ingrid to the Royal Free Hospital Emergency room for some Largactil (phenothiazine), and hopefully a bed for the night. We didn't know what else to do. By then, we were tired and desperate and Ingrid was still storming. Off we went to the Royal Free. By the time we arrived, Ingrid had begun to calm down, but we had become extremely anxious, so much so that I was prepared to do something I rarely do, revert to tranquillizers and hospitalization.

By now it was one in the morning. We had to wait for a couple of hours. Ingrid insisted that I buy her endless cups of coffee and cigarettes. 'Anything to shut her up,' I thought. 'This whole thing is crazy.' Finally the duty psychiatrist, Dr D came out for Ingrid. I pounced on her, practically yelling a potted history and insisting on what I wanted her to do. She looked up calmly and reminded me that she was the doctor in charge and wouldn't decide anything until she had seen the patient.

Morty and I felt our agitation level rise to new heights. Then the doctor came out. I was just beginning to feel relieved that we could go home when I heard the hideous news. 'This person can go home. She doesn't need any medication.'

'What!' I yelled. 'You can't do that. Look how upset and violent she is.'

While all this was going on Ingrid came out and sat on a chair smoking a cigarette. Dr D pointed out that Ingrid was perfectly calm and didn't need treatment. I was dumbfounded. Suddenly a smile crossed my lips. The duty psychiatrist and I had exchanged roles. I had called her a dangerous schizophrenic. Dr D saw her as a tired if slightly confused young woman. I was arguing for drugs, she was arguing against drugs. I wanted hospitalization. She said it wasn't necessary. Moreover, not only had I changed roles with the doctor, I had exchanged roles with Ingrid. She was calm and quiet. I was raging like a maniac. The irony was not lost on Morty or myself. With that we began to calm down. Morty said, 'Listen, it's 2.30 in the morning. I'll take Ingrid back to my house for the night. A good night's sleep will do us all good.' I readily concurred and that's how the crisis ended. Ingrid never did go back to the centre. She stayed as Morty's guest for a few days and then we found her a small flat of her own in North London. She had never lived in her own flat before.

I have just been describing the passage of an angry, confused state of being from a very disturbed guest at the centre to myself. But there is a further way to consider these situations, whether with regard to the guests or therapists. I refer to the clouding of ego functions, or as Bob Hinshelwood more specifically puts it, the deterioration of reflective space, a term he defines as 'that aspect of the group in which members link emotionally and from which personalities emerge' (Hinshelwood, 1994) .

Hinshelwood also notes that others have referred to the same phenomenon. It is possible to show, with minimal extrapolation, that the converse, the deterioration of reflective space, can be described as the nullification of free floating discussion (Foulkes), the interference with dialogue (De Mare), attacks on linking (Bion) and the reduction of experience to meaninglessness (Meltzer). All of these conceptualizations help to make sense of confusional conundrums at the Arbours Centre, and by extension, other large groups, whereby the therapists, as well as the clients, are the ones who regress and give rise to an antitherapeutic milieu.

I focused on such an occasion in a paper entitled 'Psychotic interventions' (1995). The title was deliberately vague, as befitting a study of a confused and confusing circle of therapists. Thus the title could and did refer to an intervention done on behalf of someone who was psychotic. But it also referred to an intervention that had itself become psychotic or crazy, once the therapeutic container, that is, the RTs and part of their support network, had collapsed under the weight of intolerable pain, confusion and anger.

The story concerns Hamid, a large man in his early twenties, whose family originally came from the Middle East. Hamid had a good intellect and did well at school. But as he approached university age, he began to bully his parents and younger sister and to make crude sexual overtures to women both inside and outside his home. He was first admitted to hospital in his late teens because of severe aggressive outbursts. He seemed to seek out women who were weak and vulnerable and terrorized them. He was referred to the Arbours Centre because, after several bouts of hospitalization, he remained an incorrigible human being.

At first Hamid repeated his repertoire of wildly abusive and erratic behaviour. Yet, as his stay progressed he gradually calmed down and became more sociable. He surprised everyone with a keen sense of humour and a capacity for clear thinking. People began to see him as a 'bad boy', rather than a 'mad boy'.

Towards the end of his stay, Hamid showed long periods of sadness and could also be intellectually impressive, engaging people in longish discussion about politics or philosophy. But all this changed for the worse as his leaving date approached. He reverted to being unreflective, chaotic and unbearable. Both the resident therapists and other guests were replete with outrage and despair. Obviously his 'leaving crisis' had begun.

Soon afterwards the physical environment, the house itself, seemed to respond in kind. The kitchen sink suddenly blocked up with a black, foul smelling liquid, on the same morning that we had our semi-annual medical inspection. There was a frantic rush to get the sink unblocked, a feat that was barely accomplished just before the inspector, a pleasant, elderly doctor arrived. She had been to the centre many times before and always enjoyed a quite relaxed visit. As she had entered the kitchen for a cup of tea, Hamid suddenly brushed past her, screaming 'Get out of the way, you fucking old bag!' Everyone was appalled and one of the guests, Katie started to cry. Remarkably, the doctor was not the least upset. While even the RTs were shaking, she calmly commented, 'You know, it sure is exciting to have a taste of real life!'

The inspection being over, the RTs began to prepare for a reception in the evening. Several months a year, the Arbours sponsors a public lecture. Afterwards, the lecturer and invited guests and therapists return to the centre for refreshments and further discussion. So, having set out the food and drink in the front room, they specifically asked Hamid not to touch the stuff. Well, this was like a red rag to a bull. Upon getting back to the centre after the lecture they found that he had not only eaten a lot of the food, but been bullying the other guests as well!

Hamid saw the RTs and tried to be jolly: 'George, George did you have a nice evening?' But the RTs were furious. For them, gobbling the food was the straw that broke the camel's back. Once again Hamid had broken all boundaries, and they were left in complete chaos, rage and despair. All they wanted was for *him* to go, immediately.

They called his team leader and told him what had happened, that Hamid had been warned and had to go. They feared that if they backed down and he didn't leave, they would lose face and appear like his father, waffling and indecisive. The team leader concurred and suggested they call the family to come and collect him.

While they were about to do this, they saw that I had just come back from the lecture and was about to sit down and talk with people. Before I could do so, they literally pounced on me and insisted that I retreat with them to the rear consulting room to discuss him. So I excused myself and joined a group of very angry RTs. At this point I myself felt quite menaced. I could see that they would not take no for an answer:

'Hamid has been on the rampage. He's eaten the food, hit another guest. He's been warned several times. He has to go!'

Nervously, I replied, 'I can see that you have tried and sentenced him. It seems that I'm to act as your executioner.'

In the meantime, I realized no one was able to think, and there was no space for discussion or dialogue. The situation was crazy. The RTs had collectively reverted to concrete or what Bion called 'beta functioning'. Hamid had become a dreaded object. Their sanity, or at least peace of mind, depended on my getting rid of him.

However, I did not intend to be the knight in shining armour, the omnipotent father who galloped from afar to rescue his regressed children with omniscient solutions. But the RTs had given me no choice. They were determined that I assume the position of the impotent father who had to do their bidding. This was their sadistic revenge for my having inflicted him on them in the first place, and for having caused them so much psychic pain.

Angrily, they said, 'Well, what are you going to do? We can't spend another night with Hamid in the state he's in.'

'Well,' I said, hanging my head a bit for effect, 'I don't know. I really don't know what to do.' In fact I had some ideas about how to enable the group to reconstitute itself. But before I describe how the situation was resolved, I would like to review the three examples I have outlined in order to consider the personal and interpersonal dynamics of confusion.

The confusional pressures at the centre are strongest at a time of leaving and separation, with its consequent sadness and depression. Each guest tends to protect him or herself from being overwhelmed by these emotions by regressing to a chaotic state reminiscent of the time when he or she entered the centre. A second line of defence, often deployed by borderline or psychotic individuals when faced with the possibility of depression, is to flood significant others (here the RTs, and other therapists and guests), with bits and pieces of their anxiety and spaceyness. This produces mind-threatening emotional currents in the therapists who are unable to maintain their role as containers of the guests' feelings. Often the RTs, for example, report that they are on the edge of collapsing or falling apart. These feelings are countertransferential, in as much as the RTs have been invaded with and subsequently introjected the bits and pieces of the guests' mental state. But they were also transferential in as much as the guests' 'bad vibes' tugged the strings of their own undigested and undigestible terrors (catastrophic loss, suicidal depression, fragmentation, implosion, etc). Consequently there is a mutual passing back and forth of upsetting experiences and destructive behaviour. The experiences include confusion, spaceyness (lost in space), timelessness (lost in time), selflessness (loss of self), mental paralysis, and intense anxiety.

The behaviour of the therapists, including myself, has been striking because it has tended to parallel the actions of the guests who often, as we have seen, become extremely aggressive when faced with depressive anxiety. Guests have attacked the house (break furniture and windows as Ingrid), assault other persons (verbal and occasional physical assaults as Hamid) and injure themselves (self-mutilation and suicidal thoughts and actions as Samantha). Then the RTs and TLs have felt under pressure to respond in kind, although their confusion and aggression tends to be disguised. Thus, they have become overly intrusive or emotionally withdrawn, have made too many, too few, wrong or inexact interpretive interventions, or have become exasperated and lost their capacity to think. Even worse, they have returned verbal violence with verbal violence and outright rejection.

These reactions included angry attempts to blame the guests, as well as each other, for what was happening, or, in the case of Samantha, what was not happening. In consequence, containment has broken down. The guests, threatened with confusion, and the therapists, similarly threatened (whether originating in the guests or from themselves), essentially have reverted to what Louis Zinkin (1983) has termed 'malignant mirroring'.

Morris Nitsun, in his book, *The AntiGroup*, extended Zinkin's analysis by pointing out that in the creation of an antitherapeutic group, other destructive processes are at work, not just mirroring. As Nitsun (1996) puts it: 'projective identification is a crucial medium in the formation of the antigroup'. He especially cites projective identification of a most intense, cruel, omnipotent kind, such as that delineated by Herbert Rosenfeld (1971) in his seminal paper on the aggressive aspects of narcissism. This defensive structuring, which gives rise to the gang mentality, serves to deny need, dependency, intimacy, envy and other intolerable aspects of reality. Interestingly, some years before, Rosenfeld (1950) had pointed out that confusional defences can serve the same purpose in his paper: 'Notes on the psychopathology of confusion states in chronic schizophrenias' which was republished in his book *Psychotic States* (1965, pp.52–62). Rosenfeld's continues to be the most important statement on the psychopathology of confusion. So it is worthwhile to review what he said.

According to Rosenfeld, confusional states arise during periods of improvement or deterioration, or, as Salomon Resnik has so eloquently put it, at times of catastrophic deglaciation. (1994, p.286). So we can consider that when our borderline or psychotic guests begin to improve, or achieve some integration in their lives, that a confusional state may be a recurrent danger. Why? Rosenfeld explains: the confusional state is an attempt to overcome the inner situation that occurs when aggressive impulses begin to predominate and the person feels that his or her self is in acute danger of fragmenting or being destroyed.

But why should aggressive impulses suddenly predominate? Rosenfeld goes on to say that when the person begins to reconstitute himself, there is a decrease in splitting processes. Or to put it another way, when the person begins to form attachments and his symptoms diminish, the person begins to establish a more direct relationship with his good and bad impulses and to perceive connections between them. Therefore, splitting mechanisms diminish. More succinctly, we can see that as guests begin to improve, and touch depressive issues, there is a decrease in splitting. This results in an upsurge of aggression.

Rosenfeld points out that there are two reasons for this. First, splitting, as a mechanism of defence, soaks up aggressive energy. In other words, aggressive energies fuel splitting and are stored up in the process. When splitting diminishes, a lot of this aggressive energy is released.

Second, when splitting diminishes libidinal energy is also released and seeks immediate gratification. If inhibited, the person feels intense frustration, and, this frustration, in turn leads to an upsurge in aggression.

With people who harbour a very fragile personality, these reasons succinctly account for the operative mechanisms in confusional conditions. Recovery of self leads to a temporary upsurge of aggressive forces. In less wounded persons, these forces can be contained by strong egoic and libidinal ties which modify and control the damage done, and which make reparation and keep the ego intact. In more wounded persons, this task is not so easily accomplished. They may try to preserve themselves from aggression and ward off the catastrophe of inner disintegration by muddling up their feelings. Intrapsychically, we are dealing here with a highly dynamic interplay of emotions. Harold Searles has also tackled the mechanism of confusion in his paper, 'Concerning a Psychodynamic Function of Perplexity, Confusion, Suspicion, and Related Mental States', which was published in 1952, soon after Rosenfeld's work. Searles concludes that confusion is essentially a defence against repressed emotions. But this analysis is more limited than that of Rosenfeld.

Indeed, if Rosenfeld's model is correct, it should be readily applicable to a wide variety of situations including the problems we have encountered with confused and confusing guests at the centre, and we have found this to be the case. In recent years there have been a spate of interventions that have broken down just after therapists at the centre thought that they had achieved an excellent therapeutic result. I would now like to consider the events generated over the 1991 Christmas period by two additional guests, Amanda and Adam, who were enveloped by confusional processes. Their episodes appear to have closely followed the path that Rosenfeld set out.

Amanda was an orphan who had suffered years of abusive foster care. Having been sent to a children's home as an adolescent, she was sexually assaulted by various members of staff. Subsequently she was revolved through many hospitals. Yet, she could be helpful, charming and maintained a warm relationship with one set of foster parents. Adam, also in his early twenties, lived with his parents, but suffered a number of angry paranoid outbursts which led him to be hospitalized on several occasions. Both Amanda and Adam initially responded very well at the centre. They settled down, got engaged with their team and formed relationships, often warm and close, with their fellow guests and RTs. Essentially, they calmed down and began the laborious process of thinking about themselves.

During the first six weeks of her stay, Amanda was quiet, helpful, pleasant and accommodating. But, as the Christmas period approached, she needed to meet with her social worker to renew her stay for a further three months. Under pressure to confirm her attachment to us, she began to get increasingly agitated. She would disappear for days on end, then pop in at the centre like a cat in from the cold. After a few hours of relative quiet, Amanda would become very demanding, especially for attention by George, her RT. Like a woman who was still a child, Amanda could not tolerate frustration, and often threatened to mutilate or kill herself or George, if she didn't immediately get what she wanted.

Likewise, Adam aroused goodwill and sympathy during the first part of his stay. But rapid oscillation between compliance and aggression, self-destruction and attacks on others soon became evident. All this was intimately related to an upsurge of sexual urges, for Adam had developed the charming custom of waking the female RTs in the middle of the night by entering their rooms without permission. This kind of coming alive was something the RTs found very hard to take and led to angry exchanges.

Tremendous confusion characterized the centre's approach to Amanda and Adam after Christmas. It seemed that the TLs and RTs couldn't decide what was happening. There was a great divergence of opinion and a paralysis of effort.

Perhaps worse, there was a spiral of confusion from the therapists to the guests and back. This was connected with the fact that Amanda and Adam not only mixed up their feelings in themselves, but also projected them all over the house. In retrospect, it is clear that the therapists could not cope with the intensity of these projections. As a result, the RTs and TLs became frustrated, furious and despairing, and relationships all around began to simmer with resentment and blame. Such an outcome is closely related to the countertransferential hatred and confusion which Rosenfeld describes in his later work, *Impasse and Interpretation* (1987).

Both Rosenfeld and Searles correctly demonstrate the importance of attending to the mental and emotional states of the therapists when they are working with confused patients, whether individually or in small or large group situations like a therapeutic community. Essentially they are asking us to consider the subjective realities that impinge on the warm, but firm and reflective interventions which should be the ideal response when working with groups of confused and damaged persons. As they demonstrate, there is a constant transferential and countertransferential pressure not to understand and not to respond appropriately. Put simply, it is all too easy for the therapists to get caught up in despair and sadism, that is, the mirror image of their clients' experience.

Although we have found that guests invariably improve during the early and main body of their stay with psychotic and borderline individuals, this improvement may be lost when the time comes to leave the centre and guests enter their leaving crisis. Then signs of their underlying frailties begin to re-emerge, with all the attendant splitting processes, agitation and anger. Not infrequently, they may become confused and uncertain about wanting to remain at the centre, or not. Moreover, they may begin to get befuddled about their identity and that of others, and about time, place and personal boundaries.

Concomitantly the RTs and TLs (first, members of their team, subsequently, other RTs and TLs) become confused and uncertain about what to do. Their role relations begin to crumble and their capacity to think becomes clouded or paralysed. In part, this situation arises because the therapists who are members of a particular team have a strong tendency to identify with the guest involved. Indeed, in the best of circumstances, one might say that the therapists rely on introjection in the manner of a shaman, who, as Mircea Eliade (1964, p.508–511) has detailed, takes in the disturbance of another in order to heal him. In more modern terms, Hanna Segal has shown how a mother may introject the anxious cries of her infant child, modify the anxiety by having contained it, and then allow the modified, calmer state of mind to return to the infant (1981).

The pressure of confusional spirals, however, puts containment at risk, because of an escalating buildup of tension and turmoil. This spiral can often be countered by the process of benign identification I have just mentioned. But at a certain intensity, even this breaks down and people plunge into chaos, a transformational process which cannot be explained on the basis of excessive identification. Rather, I refer to an antitherapeutic dynamic brought about by the inability of the team to cope with the intensity of projections, initially from the guest, and subsequently, from the therapists themselves.

The power of destructive projections is Rosenfeld's second major contribution towards understanding the incapacity to contain confusional states. In *Impasse and*

Interpretation, having initially focused on intrapsychic transactions, he emphasizes interpersonal transactions. Specifically Rosenfeld relates the failure of the therapist to bear and to hold a tumultuous barrage because it is too intense and powerful, and because it is too close to the bone, that is, the projections arouse too much psychic pain in the therapist. This is the moment where, as Nitsun, points out, the antigroup is likely to form. But as I have previously mentioned, we are not only dealing with countertransferential pressure, but transferential conflicts which borderline clients are exquisitely skilled in setting off. In this respect Searles complemented Rosenfeld's work by emphasizing the transferential aspect of the transference–countertransference relationship. Searles (1952) held that disturbances which emanate from the therapist (not reflections nor uncontained emotional currents) are major factors in confusional muddles that cloud individual and group relations. Of course, this applies both at the centre, and other facilities and therapy groups.

There is, however, a unique feature of the centre which other therapeutic milieus do not share. I refer to the therapists who actually live at the centre full time, the RTs. One might well ask, isn't it inherently confusing for the guests to live with their therapists? Don't different levels of role and non-role relations get all mixed up, when people are eating, sleeping, playing, as well as having or giving therapy, all under one roof? The answer is yes and no. The centre, as a large group, specializes in creative ambiguity. Much of our therapeutic success has to do with overcoming role expectations, such as with chronic patients, who have been hospitalized so often, that they can act as patient, nurse or psychiatrist with equal aplomb. We have found that even the most disturbed guest can distinguish between persons who are therapists and those who are guests, and what is appropriate to one or another setting and situation. Thus he or she can depart that kitchen after having lunch with his RT, go to a team meeting, engage in a productive therapeutic exchange and later remerge for a coffee or tea in the kitchen when his or her RT is free.

The structure of the centre can be confusing at the beginning of a stay before people know the ropes. But this is true for the new RTs too. Mostly the confusional muddles arise from the internal dynamics of the guests and, as bounced off, aroused in and triggered off inside the therapists. Certainly, once this happened, as with Samantha, the RTs could not carry out their roles and the therapy began to fall apart. On the other hand, the very structure of the house has allowed the centre to contain equally disturbing episodes, once the basic dynamics of the confusional relationship were understood.

Remarkably, many guests who have been actively psychotic while at the centre, have been able to utilize their confusional crises in a positive way. By this I mean that the guest has completed the whole stay, and has held on to sad, depressed feelings when leaving, while usually going on for further therapy. Such a constructive outcome also includes the RTs. A good intervention is one in which the RTs discover that they are able to emerge from a befuddled state with their reflective capacity strengthened, their interpersonal awareness heightened and their aggression under better control. Not surprisingly, a positive experience for an RT is necessary for a positive experience for a guest, and *vice versa.*

Nonetheless, we have developed specific strategies for borderline and psychotic guests who have precipitated confusional crises. Perhaps the basic strategy, as Bob Hinshelwood (1994) has elucidated, is to repair and maintain the reflective space. The structure of the centre is conducive to doing so because there are a multiple levels of meetings and supervision sessions going on during the week. This means that even when an RT is taken over by a confusional state (as sometimes has to happen), the TL can help sort things out. Even when the team (RT, TL and guest) has been taken over, the centre as whole can serve as the reflective or auxiliary ego which can help the team see through the muddle. And so forth. The concurrent principle is that there has to be a provision for therapists who are outside the team or RT group, to have an input into what is happening. My intervention with Ingrid provides a good example of this process. I was called in when the centre could not deal with the crisis. In turn I called a colleague. And when we were both overtaken by the currents involved, a further person, the hospital psychiatrist, had to function as our ego, until we could stop the role reversal.

In many ways our strategy for dealing with confusional states is similar to the strategies we have developed for dealing with guests who come to the centre while psychotic, or develop a psychosis while at the centre. Although chaos may overflow the house, we seek to create a time and place, within the overall stay, which is highly organized. Thus, the team itself maintains a strict delineation of roles whereby it functions on a differentiated basis, rather than a shared basis. As I have previously explained, this means, that one member of the team, usually the TL, takes an active role and focuses the transference through interpretive comments, while the others involved remain as silent witnesses during the team meetings (Berke 1990).

Second, with certain guests the team can anticipate confusional states and prepare for them at the beginning of a stay. For example, the team can make a provision for other TLs to provide supervision for itself. So a non-team therapist may have to act for the team, as the TL acts for the RT.

Related to the need to anticipate confusional issues, the therapists need to allow for regression in thought (reversion to the concrete), feeling (aggression) and action (withdrawal, self-destructiveness) of the guests and themselves during the course of the stay. These events are not necessarily the components of a negative reaction. On the contrary, they may be a part of the unfolding of the intervention, and must be seen that way.

Needless to say, special care may be essential during crisis periods. This can include extra team meetings and extra supervision meetings (whether during the week or weekends). In addition, the tone of the meetings may have to change, from an exchange which is client centred and directly interpretive, to one which is more silent and reflective. Sometimes the RTs will use these occasions to talk about their own muddle and upset. Borderline individuals in particular, need to see that their confusion, aggression, despair and, of course, love can be felt by and contained in others, the RTs and TLs, before, or even without, being given back to them.

Where all else fails, we can and do use the whole house, including guests, RTs, TLs, other therapists, trainees and visitors, as an active agent in the intervention. Then this large group acts as an auxiliary therapist and can be a remarkably effective one as occurs when the RT group stops being a container and acts more like a flusher-outer.

With Hamid, this was my big idea. To use the whole house, including all the visitors who had come to the reception after the lecture, as a container for both Hamid's and the RTs' confusion and craziness. In fact, while I was being barraged by RT hostility, I recalled my friend Ross Speck. He used to work with large family groups. When they threatened to fragment and expel a member, he acted to expand the group with people who were able to think, and thereby ameliorate destructive actions (Speck and Attneave 1973).

With only a little dissent the RTs agreed. Frankly I didn't know what to expect. I wanted to buy time in the hope that something positive might emerge. Indeed, it did. The visitors included a Dr T, the guest lecturer, who took upon himself the task of listening carefully to a lot of complaints from the RTs and other guests. Then he interjected, 'You say you want him to leave. This is an unusual problem. Usually we try to get patients to stay, not to leave.'

He was quickly accosted by Katie, a thin young woman who liked to cut her arms and face to reduce the tensions in herself. 'How can you say that? Don't you know what I've been through?' Another resident interjected that she hadn't been able to sleep for days because of Hamid, and the RTs still angry, joined in.

The lecturer commented. 'You know, we could all leave. Leave *him* in the house. But then, where would the RTs go?'

An animated discussion ensued. After a while, I encouraged Dr T to expand his earlier remarks. He brought up questions of diagnosis and drugs and managed the useful task of shifting the group's hostility from Hamid to himself. By then the whole mood of the house changed. People volunteered to bring milk to Hamid, who by then had retreated to his room.

In his talk, Dr T had also spoken about guilt and forgiveness. I said I hoped that the anger and guilt that previously had pervaded the house might be replaced by a mellowing of mood and feeling of forgiveness. Almost magically, people wanted to talk about Hamid and his problems, not get rid of him. Not long afterwards, Hamid, who was very sensitive to moods in the house, rejoined the meeting. To my astonishment everyone hugged him.

It had been a good night. The group had reconstituted itself. The psychotic anxieties, and thoughts, or rather lack of thinking, and the crazy behaviour of Hamid as well as the therapists and other guests had subsided. Meanwhile, a creative free floating dialogue among all the residents had resumed. They rediscovered the links between each other as well as the meaningfulness of their experiences. The result was a strictly limited breakdown, contained by the willingness of the therapists involved to suffer, and by their capacity to ask for help and regain their thinking processes, and especially by their discovering and rediscovering their own humanity.

I would like to conclude by sharing one further thought; that is, in working with and within groups that are permeated by confusion and other psychotic processes, it is very important to remain patient and avoid omnipotent solutions. It is difficult, but not impossible to remain humane in the face of provocation, and to allow for reparative forces to unfold. In this regard, it helps to keep in mind that the cycle of confusion may be time limited, but that the overall pattern may have to be repeated several times, before it begins to shift. My hope is that a deeper understanding of this sequence of events may mean that the psychotic and near-psychotic persons who attend the centre will do well for longer and more sustained periods. And my further intention is to confirm the practicality and desirability of a psychodynamic approach in working with severely disturbed individuals.

References

Berke, J. (1981) 'The case of Susan and Peter: the psychotherapeutic treatment of an acute psychotic episode at the Arbours Crisis Centre.' *Journal of Contemporary Psychotherapy 12*, 2, 75–87.

Berke, J. (1982) 'An alternative sanctuary: The Arbours Crisis Centre.' In U. Rueveni, R. Speck and J. Speck, *Therapeutic Intervention: Healing Strategies for Human Systems.* New York: Human Sciences Press.

Berke, J. (1987) 'Arriving, settling in, settling down, leaving and following up: stages of stay at the Arbours Centre.' *British Journal of Medical Psychology 60*, 181–188.

Berke, J. (1990) 'Conjoint therapy within a therapeutic milieu: the crisis team.' *International Journal of Therapeutic Communities 11*, 4, 237–248.

Berke, J. (1995) 'Psychotic interventions.' In J. Berke, C. Masoliver and T. Ryan (eds) *Sanctuary: The Arbours Experience of Alternative Community Care.* London: Process Press.

Eliade, M. (1964) *Shamanism: Archaic Techniques of Ecstasy.* London: Routledge & Kegan Paul.

Hinshelwood, R.D. (1994) 'Attacks on the reflective space: containing primitive emotional states.' In M. Pines and V.L. Schermer (eds) *Ring of Fire.* London: Routledge.

Nitsun, M. (1996) 'Determinants of the antigroup: regression, survival anxiety, failures of communication, projective identification, envy.' In L. Nitsun *The AntiGroup: Destructive Forces in the Group and their Creative Potential.* London: Routledge.

Resnik, S. (1994) 'Glacial times in psychotic regression.' In M. Pines and V.L. Schermer (eds) *Ring of Fire.* London: Routledge.

Rosenfeld, H. (1950) 'Notes on the psychopathology of confusional states in chronic schizophrenias.' On *Psychotic States: A Psycho-Analytical Approach.* London: Hogarth Press (1965).

Rosenfeld, H. (1971) 'A clinical approach to the psychoanalytical theory of the life and death instincts: an investigation into the aggressive aspects of narcissism.' *International Journal of Psycho-Analysis 52,* 169–178.

Rosenfeld, H. (1987) *Impasse and Interpretation.* London, Tavistock Publications.

Schermer, V. and Pines, M. (1994) 'An Editorial Introduction, Silence = Death.' In M. Pines and V.L. Schermer (eds) *Ring of Fire.* London: Routledge.

Searles, H. (1952) 'Concerning a psychodynamic function of perplexity, confusion, suspicion, and related mental states. In *Collected Papers on Schizophrenia and Related Subjects.* London: The Hogarth Press (1965).

Segal, H. (1981) 'A psychoanalytic approach to the treatment of psychosis.' In *The Work of Hanna Segal: A Kleinian Approach to Clinical Practice.* New York: Jason Aronson.

Speck, R. and Attneave, C. (1973) *Family Networks.* New York: Pantheon Books.

Zinkin, L. (1983) 'Malignant Mirroring.' Reprinted in H. Zinkin *et al.* (1998) *Dialogue in the Analytic Setting.* London: Jessica Kingsley Publishers.

CHAPTER 17

Voluntary Work in the Area of Mental Health

The Voluntary Worker's Role in a Therapeutic Centre in Florence

Gianni DiNorscia and Walter Romeo

What is voluntary work? The range of meanings which fit this term is extremely wide. According to a statutory regulation issued in Italy in 1991, voluntary work is that which is spontaneously and freely undertaken by a given person within a given organization without intention to earn a profit. According to the same regulation, an organization has the right to call itself voluntary if it has been created in order to carry out voluntary work by the sole or predominant use of its members' services and if it is totally not for profit and exclusively motivated by a sense of human solidarity. In Italy, voluntary work is present in nearly all areas of social life and represents an invaluable resource upon which the state itself relies. Voluntary work is a term which covers the most varied kind of activities from the most spontaneous to the most highly organized, pursuing different objectives and following different models. Voluntary organizations are to be found in both religious and non-religious contexts.

The training of voluntary workers

In Italy, voluntary work often replaces, either temporarily or long-term, non-existing or defective social services. This situation, which renders the need for voluntary workers' training imperative, must be taken into account at the earliest planning stages. Such training, which until very recently typically involved one voluntary worker passing on his/her skills to another in a one-to-one informal manner, is now moving towards a more professional, more impersonal style. In fact lately there has been a tendency to apply a more managerial type of system both to the training of voluntary workers and to the running of voluntary organizations in an effort to pursue the efficiency of non-voluntary organizations, an endeavor which may or may not suit the nature of voluntary work.

This raises the problem of how to set up training which is both professional and in tune with the nature and objectives of voluntary work. Any serious form of training needs to foster the development of emotional self-knowledge especially in relation to one's motivations, alongside the acquisition of theoretical knowledge and the development of skills such as how to work with groups and their dynamics. On a more practical level, one needs to improve one's organizational and planning skills and to be aware of what laws are pertinent to one's work.

Some writers make a distinction between initial and ongoing training. In the initial training what needs to be underlined and validated is the particular nature of voluntary work, its motivations and its aims, in other words its uniqueness.

By fostering an awareness of what makes voluntary work so special one re-affirms its identity and protects it from being trivialized. Ongoing training on the other hand is complementary to the initial training as it provides support for the voluntary worker in his/her day-to-day work activities as they develop and undergo changes. Ongoing training allows one to keep abreast of new theories and techniques and to fill the gaps which were present in one's initial training (Barbagli 1995).

A satisfactory type of training should encourage its trainees to learn how to define needs and how best to plan in order to try and meet those needs within a particular historical context. Such training should draw its foundations from the social sciences so as to accommodate the emotional and intellectual levels of human experience together with the external levels of reality. A good training should also look at how best to foster in its trainees a spirit of co-operation in relation to non-voluntary workers (Antonucci 1995; Palmonari 1995).

A great variety of volunteer training exists in Europe, ranging from self-instruction to guidance by experienced voluntary workers to education by professionals.

What motivates voluntary work?

One needs to pay attention to what may motivate voluntary work, and indeed a good deal has been written on this subject (see for example Bertini 1996). Among the motivational components which have been widely acknowledged are a wish to express solidarity and a need in the individual to relate to society in a way which might diminish his or her insecurities and thus foster individual development (Milanesi 1995).

Another cluster of motivational factors derives from a tendency to perform parental roles, a trait which usually stems from one's personal history and leads to a certain pattern of relating to others. Such a tendency often leads to a need to take care of others which is characteristic not only of voluntary workers, but also of 'helping professionals': doctors, nurses, therapists and teachers among others (Guerra 1992).

Much has been written on the motivations to be found behind altruistic or 'proto-social' behaviour, and different theories have been formulated, for example, the 'social exchange theory' (according to which one gives in order to get something back) and the 'social norms theory'. According to another theory, altruistic behaviour would originate from a genetic component linked to the survival of the species. This would explain why many animals also exhibit this type of behaviour, at times to a very marked degree. However as far as humans are concerned it seems likely that early learning experiences relating to the baby's need for the mother for its survival are fundamental to any altruistic type of behaviour. Such experiences open the way to a life-long effort to balance dependence and independence which can lead to such opposites being creatively channeled into 'mutuality' (Bertini 1996).

It is important to remember that many young people are drawn to voluntary work because of a sense of inner discomfort that can be the first step to depression and apathy and in extreme cases even mental illness and suicide. Some youngsters cope with such discomfort by relying on their families or by committing themselves to their academic or professional careers. Others choose voluntary work (Milanesi 1995).

Voluntary work in psychiatry

In Italy, a great deal of voluntary work is being carried out in the field of psychiatry. Such a variety of situations is involved that reaching an overall perspective is far from easy. Equally difficult is to assess the quality and the effectiveness of different kinds of experiences. Nevertheless the overall feeling is that voluntary work in psychiatry is dedicated to analysing social needs and to finding innovative ways to deal with problems. One must add that voluntary workers also have a very important role to play in those situations where the professionals move to a background position.

Some patients find it easier to relate to voluntary workers when the professionals are absent. For example, L, a patient from our centre 'Il Villino', on one particular occasion, told a voluntary worker that she felt better because the official carer was absent.

On the other hand we agree with voluntary workers that they have a wider function than to replace the absent professionals. A more appropriate understanding of voluntary workers sees them as equipped with their own particular skills which are different from and complementary to the skills of the professional workers.

One could also say that voluntary work provides an area which is in-between the patient who has been expelled by society, the social group which has carried out the expulsion and the professional group which has been entrusted by society with the emergency care of the patient (Iannuzzi 1997).

The method

It is important to stress that when working with psychotic patients, voluntary workers find themselves in contact with patients whose self appears fragmented, barren and severely damaged. These patients need to find themselves surrounded by an emotional climate within which they can begin to experience a different quality of themselves. These ideas have been explored among others by Neri (1995) and Correale (1991). A feeling of belonging opens up for these patients the possibility of a better integrated self. On the other hand if such patients find themselves in a context which favours the acquisition of skills *and where such acquisition is seen as a condition for the patient's acceptance*, then there is a risk that rather than becoming better integrated, the patient will be encouraged to develop a 'false self'. It is also worth remembering that some patients are not suitable for a skill-oriented treatment which they are likely to find too frightening and too demanding. Such patients can only benefit from being immersed in an emotionally nourishing environment where they feel that they belong and where they have the chance to experience a less conflictual, more empathic kind of relating than the one to which they have been subjected by their families and by society at large. This in itself constitutes a very honourable therapeutic aim for the kind of intermediate structure in which we operate. In order to achieve such an objective, it is essential that voluntary workers as well as professionals be given all possible support so they can maintain a genuinely empathic stance rather than become rigidly defensive when they are in daily contact with such damaged patients. One of the most important forms of support is supervision for their group work.

It is well known how the dangers of working with psychotic patients can lead not only to rigid defenses in the individual, but also to severe paralysis in institutional dynamics. Voluntary workers on the other hand, because of the temporary and unofficial nature of their contract, are less likely to be caught up in such dynamics and therefore can provide for both patients and staff an impartial reference point, mediating the maintenance of an empathic atmosphere within the unit and in relation to the outside world. They can also be ideally placed to mediate between the patient and his/her family and society.

It is not easy to introduce voluntary workers for the first time into a unit or system which has been run exclusively by professional workers. The arrival of voluntary workers can create misunderstandings, ambivalent feelings and conflicts and requires a great deal of attention and careful handling in both planning and day-to-day management stages (Iannuzzi 1997) What does seem essential to enable voluntary workers to function effectively is the presence of professional leaders who are convinced of the usefulness of voluntary work and are favourable towards introducing it into their system. In particular it is essential that the consultant in charge can make himself/herself available. If the context is conducive, then the presence of voluntary workers becomes part of a wider strategy which involves all sorts of networks from the medical to the administrative to the social and sees them united in trying to achieve better communication (Correale 1991).

Our experience in Florence

'Il Villino' has been operating in Florence since 1991. It was initiated by a group of mental health professionals who were dealing with psychotic patients and felt the need to have a place for them. 'Il Villino' is an intermediate type of structure, a partly residential therapeutic centre which is affiliated with and coordinates treatment with the local psychiatric services.

There are about thirty patients, mostly quite young, but usually with a history of inpatient treatment. About twenty of these patients have psychotic disturbances with schizophrenia high on the list. At present there are also four borderline patients, four with learning disabilities and three with eating disorders associated with severe personality disorders.

The small group is the most important instrument being used within the centre both for the understanding of group dynamics and for treatment. The therapeutic aim is to help the patient to change his/her inner world by working in groups, although some individual work is also available.

The day and the activities of the centre are structured around small groups of different kinds: the cultural group, the art group. the music group, the theatre group, the yoga group, the work group, and so forth.

We will now describe one of the therapy groups in greater detail.

The group meets weekly for an hour and a half and consists of twelve patients, six of whom have psychotic illnesses, two are borderline, three have learning disabilities and one has an eating disorder associated with a personality disorder.

There are eight patients who attend quite regularly and four others who are much less consistent. During the group session there is a great deal of acting out especially in the form of people leaving the room to go to the lavatory. This acting out makes it essential for the therapist to be able to be firm enough on boundaries to contain the group while being flexible enough not to become punitive. Often the therapists structure their group by putting forward a topic, a theme for discussion. At times this works well and each patient uses the theme according to his/her needs while contributing to the group creation of an interaction on a theme; at other times the discussion escalates into an aggressive confrontation which the therapist has to diffuse. It is important and difficult to balance spontaneity with containment.

In our opinion, it is critical for our patients to be able to rely on the consistency of the setting and the quality of the interaction within that setting.

The care of the centre is entrusted to a team made up of psychiatrists, nursing staff, psychologists and educationalists. Trainees and voluntary workers are involved in some of the centre activities.

Within this centre voluntary workers have always been regarded as very important both as a source of vital therapeutic resources and as a bridge with society. Our openness towards voluntary work and society has been greatly helped by the geographical position the centre occupies in the city. 'Il Villino' is situated in the lively Rifredi area, next door to some remarkable voluntary organizations like 'La Misericordia', and 'La Madonnina del Grappa' which is one of the most important Catholic organizations for voluntary work in Italy.

The voluntary workers involved in our centre are representative of the different levels of society present in the area. We have among others secondary schools and university students, teachers, clerical workers, professional people and pensioners. Some of them have previous experience of voluntary work, but the majority are at their first experience and they come to the centre as private citizens operating independently and not attached to any organisation. This frees them from some of the potential complications that arise from being part of an organisation. This is why we encourage the presence of independent voluntary workers.

Before any individual can work on a voluntary basis with us, he/she has to attend an internal training course. The course lasts six months and includes weekly meetings with mental health 'experts' (psychiatrists, psychologists. sociologists, public administrators etc.). The themes discussed are all related to the analysis of acute mental illness and how to deal with patients suffering from different types of symptoms and pathology and their families.

Another important component of the training involves taking part in an experiential group made up of trainee voluntary workers and relatives of the patients. The group discusses the problems encountered by patients and their families and this allows the trainee to understand and be part of the emotional climate of the centre.

After completing their training, voluntary workers start taking part in the cultural group where they are helped into becoming part of the group structure by the wide range of participants and the richness of the discussions. Voluntary workers with specific skills or interests may join other groups like the music or theatre groups which are led by other, more experienced voluntary workers.

The musical group benefits from the presence among its members of a pianist from the orchestra of the *'teatro comunale'* and his wife who is a classical dancer. In the theatre group, there are some professional theatre directors who have come to give a hand as voluntary workers. In the art and craft group, one of the members is the owner of a terracotta vase factory from Siena who offered his factory and supervision for the benefit of patients wanting to have a go at working with terracotta.

Voluntary workers with a long experience in our centre have been responsible for the setting up of important initiatives like the one allowing patients to go and live for a time with other patients' families or with the families of voluntary workers themselves.

In some cases such experience has proved very therapeutic as it was for L, a 20-year-old patient who suffered from eating disorders and had a symbiotic type of relationship with her own family. She was given the opportunity to live for several months with M, a 55-year-old teacher and her family. L was able to establish with the host family a less pathological relationship than the one she had with her own family. In the course of time she improved in every sense, including a healthier eating pattern.

However, as we have already highlighted, the arrival of voluntary workers in a psychiatric service like ours can give rise to problems. One of the first difficulties may well be linked to the preconceived image that voluntary workers have in relation to psychotic patients. They may think that all psychotic patients are aggressive and dangerous in line with widespread popular opinion.

More frequently observed, however, is the voluntary worker's difficulty in understanding and respecting the therapeutic and management plan set up for each patient. It frequently happens that a voluntary worker finds a particular patient's situation very distressing and may want to intervene or to push the rest of the staff to intervene in ways which clash with the therapeutic plan.

Another danger is related to a situation where the administrators, because of a lack of professional mental health workers, rely excessively on voluntary workers, upsetting an important balance and weakening the solidity of the whole structure.

Both professional and voluntary workers agree that it is vital to be able to thoroughly discuss thoroughly their respective roles and to agree upon a programme of activities and their different tasks within that programme. In our experience this open discussion is facilitated by a work atmosphere inspired by group-analytic principles. The definition of tasks is carefully reached following an open discussion and some basic considerations. It seems logical that the professional staff will be responsible for the protection of the setting, since they can offer a guarantee of consistency and solidity. Voluntary workers, given the nature of their work, seem better suited to join in various activities and projects where their input helps enrich and balance what the patients themselves contribute.

The presence of voluntary workers in our service has been extremely positive for the patients and this has encouraged us to try to describe our ongoing experience and to continue to promote an integration between the work of professional teams and that of voluntary workers.

References

Antonucci, S. (1995) 'Esperienze di Formazione del Volontariato in Alcuni Paesi Europei.' In *Per Una Nuova Solidarieta*. Firenze: Istituto Andrea Devoto.

Baracani, N. (1995) 'Formazione nel Volontariato: con cautela'. In *Il Seme e L'Albero 6*, August. Firenze: Istituto Andrea Devoto.

Barbagli, G.(1995) 'La Formazione e L'Aggiornamento per Il Volontariato.' In *Il Seme e L'Albero. 6*, August. Firenze: Istituto Andrea Devoto.

Bertini, M.(1996) '"Per Se" e Per Gli Altri. Le Radici Psicologiche dell'"Impegno Volontario".' In *Rivista del Volontariato* December.

Correale, A. (1991) *Il Campo Istituzionale*. Roma: Borla.

Guerra, G.(1992) *Psicosociologia dell'Ospedale: Analisi Organizzativa e Processi di Cambiamento*. Firenze: Nuova Italia Editrice.

Iannuzzi, G.(1997) '"Volontariato tra Societa" Civile ed Istituzione Psichiatrica.' In *Lavorare nelle Strurrure Intermedie*. Roma: Borla.

Milanesi, G.(1995) '"I Giovani per Una Solidarieta" Diversa.' In *Per Una Nuova Solidarieta*. Firenze: Istituto Andrea Devoto.

Neri, C. (1995) *Gruppo*. Roma: Borla.

Palmonari, A.(1995) 'I Processi Formativi per La Qualificazione dei Volontari e Contribuire a Una nuova Cultura delle Istituzioni.' In *Per Una Nuova Solidarieta*. Firenze: Istituto Andrea Devoto.

Note

Editors' note: Both within and outside the doors of mental health facilities, significant persons other than professional therapists serve crucial roles in the care of psychotic patients. Whether it is a storekeeper or employer who shows unusual compassion for a schizophrenic individual, a residential counsellor, a student doing a field placement, or a volunteer in a clinic or mental hospital, such persons may have a positive and lasting impact on patients who otherwise feel misunderstood and rejected by society-at-large. Non-professional and social networks play an essential, often unacknowledged, part in mental health care. (The Philadelphia Child Guidance Center has had specific training programs for members of the community such as hairdressers, bartenders, police, and others who may interact with the mentally ill in the course of their work.) In Italy, according to DiNorscia and Romeo, volunteers play a major role in the mental health system. The education and training of non-professional caregivers and the role of the professional community are of increasing importance there. In this chapter, DiNorscia and Romeo provide a discussion of the role relationships, systems impact, training, and therapeutic aspects of the volunteer working with psychotic and character disordered patients.

The Contributors

Mary Ann Abbott, Psy.D., is a clinical psychologist in private practice in Topeka, Kansas. She specializes in the treatment of trauma survivors, eating disorders and women's issues. She is on the adjunct faculty of the Karl Menninger School of Psychiatry where she teaches Group Dynamics and Group Psychotherapy. She is currently co-founder of the program for women at New Beginnings Health Care, Topeka.

Susan Bach, MSN, ARNP, is a Nurse Practitioner at Community Psychiatric Clinic, Seattle, Washington. She was formerly a Nurse Manager of Partial Hospitalization Services at the Menninger Clinic.

Joseph H. Berke, MD, is an individual and family psychoanalytic psychotherapist. He is the co-founder and Director of the Arbours Association and the Arbours Crisis Centre, London. Previously, he has lived and worked at the Kingsley Hall Community, London. He is a lecturer and teacher. Dr Berke is the author of many articles and books on psychological, social, political, and religious themes. His latest work (co-edited) is *Even Paranoids Have Enemies: New Perspectives on Paranoia and Persecution* (London: Routledge, 1998).

Nicolas Caparros, MD, is a psychoanalyst and group analyst in private practice in Madrid, Spain. He is the author of several books, including *Psicopatologia Analitico Vincular,* Quipu Ediciones, Madrid, 1992; and *Tiempo, Temporalidad y Psicoanalisis,* Quipu Ediciones, Madrid, 1994.

Rachael Chazan, MBBS, DPM, MA, is a psychiatrist, psychotherapist and group analyst, educated at London University. Since 1967 she has worked in Jerusalem and is Supervisor at the Faculty of Psychotherapy, Tel Aviv Medical School. She also studied philosophy at the Hebrew University and her MA thesis is on 'Mental health and moral integrity'. She has written numerous papers and is working on *The Group as Therapist.*

Lane Chazdon, MME, is a music therapist at the Menninger Clinic, Topeka, Kansas, USA, where he is attached to the psychotic disorders unit (HOPE). He earned his masters degree in music therapy from the University of Kansas, Lawrence, Kansas. A board-certified music therapist, Mr. Chazdon has given several presentations for both the American Music Therapy Association and the National Therapeutic Recreation Society, as well as taught at Washburn University, Topeka, Kansas. Mr Chazdon is a frequent performer of jazz guitar and a guitar instructor in the Topeka community.

Shauna Corbin, Ph.D., is a Senior Psychologist at the Southdown Institute, Aurora, Ontario, Canada. She has been project coordinator for the California Children of Divorce Follow-Up Studies and was formerly Section Pscyhologist for the Crisis Admissions and Specal Evaluation Unit at the Menninger Clinic in Topeka, Kansas.

Eugene Della Badia, DO, FAGPA, CGP, is in the private practice of individual and group psychotherapy in Philadelphia, PA. He is Attending Psychiatrist at the Horsham Clinic and the Pennsylvania Hospital, Clinical Assistant Professor of Psychiatry at the Philadelphia College of Osteopathic Medicine, Assistant Dean of the Philadelphia Academy of Psychoanalysis, and Distinguished Fellow in the American Osteopathic College of Neurology and Psychiatry. He is a Fellow of the American Group Psychotherapy Association and a Certified Group Psychotherapist.

Gianni DiNorscia is Chief Psychiatrist of the North-Western Section of Psychiatry in Florence, and initiator of 'Il Villino' therapeutic community.

Bette Ferbrache, LSCSW, is a clinical social worker with the Professionals In Crisis Program at the Menninger Clinic in Topeka, Kansas. She is on the faculty of the Karl Menninger School of Psychiatry. She works with couples, families, and is an individual and group psychotherapist.

Reed D. Goldstein, Ph.D., is Research Associate, Dave Garroway Laboratory for the Study of Depression, Pennsylvania Hospital, Philadelphia, Pennsylvania and Clinical Associate, Department of Psychiatry, University of Pennsylvania School of Medicine, Philadelphia, Pennsylvania.

Alan M. Gruenberg, MD, is Professor, Department of Psychiatry and Human Behavior Jefferson Medical College, Philadelphia, PA, and President, Gruenberg and Summers, PC.

Nick Kanas, MD, is Professor and Director of the Group Therapy Training Program in the Department of Psychiatry at the University of California, San Francisco. He also is Associate Chief of the Mental Health Service at the Department of Veterans Affairs Medical Center, San Francisco. Dr Kanas is a Fellow of both the American Psychiatric Association and the American Group Psychotherapy Association. He is the Principal Investigator of two NASA-funded studies involving crewmember interactions in space. Dr Kanas has written more than 90 papers, books, and book chapters on group therapy and small group behavior, including a book entitled: *Group Therapy for Schizophrenic Patients.*

Raman Kapur, M.Phil., is a Consultant Clinical Psychologist working in mental health and social care in Northern Ireland. He is an Honorary Lecturer with the Queen's University of Belfast and is currently Assistant Director (Clinical) with Threshold (Richmond Fellowship, Northern Ireland), a mental health charity providing therapeutic communities for severely mentally ill patients and psychotherapeutic services for children and young people. He has published clinical and research papers in individual and group psychotherapy and is joint Course Director for the Queen's University of Belfast/Threshold training course providing psychotherapeutic training for mental health and social care professionals in Northern Ireland.

Lawrence L. Kennedy, MD, is Director of Partial Hospitalization Services at Menninger Clinic in Topeka, Kansas, a training and supervising analyst in the Topeka Institute for Psychoanalysis, and a teacher and supervisor of group psychotherapy in the Karl Menninger School of Psychiatry. He is a Fellow of the American Group Psychotherapy Association and a former board member of that organization. He is editor of the journal *Continuum: Developments in Ambulatory Mental Health Care.*

Dianne Campbell Lefevre MB, Ch.B., MRCP, FRCPsych., is a BAP-trained Psychoanalytical Psychotherapist. Her original specialization was as a physician, later training in psychiatry and psychoanalytical psychotherapy. She worked for 14 years as a consultant in general adult psychiatry, attempting to combine psychoanalytical and biological models with both non-psychotic and short- and long- term psychotic disorders and has written and lectured on psychoanalytical group and individual treatment of psychoses. Since December 1995 she has worked as a consultant psychotherapist at a National Health Service Hospital, Basildon Hospital in Essex, UK, runs a psychosis workshop and is in the process of setting up a masters degree course in the psychoanalytical psychotherapy of schizophrenia and related psychoses with Anglia Polytechnic University.

Glenn S. Lipson, Ph.D., ABPP, is a clinical and forensic psychologist in private practice in Rancho Santa Fe, California. He is on the adjunctive faculty of the California School of Professional Psychology, San Diego. He is a member of the American Group Psychotherapy Association and listed in the National Register of Group Psychotherapists.

Malcolm Pines, MB, FRCP, FRCPsych., is a founding member of the Group-Analytic Institute and former consultant at the Tavistock Institute. Author of numerous books and articles in the fields of group psychotherapy and psychoanalysis, he has served as President of the International Association of Group Psychotherapy. His collected papers have recently been published (1997) by Jessica Kingsley under the title *Circular Reflections.* He is Series Editor of the *International Library of Group Analysis,* Jessica Kingsley Publishers.

Geoffrey Pullen, MRCPsych., is a consultant psychiatrist based at Littlemore Hospital, Oxford, where he has combined his interests in both schizophrenia and the therapeutic community. Dr Pullen has published papers on these subjects as well as on the large group and the dynamics of institutions.

Salomon Resnik, a training analyst of the Psychoanalytical Society of Argentina, became a member of the International Psychoanalytical Association in 1956, after specializing in work with autistic children and young schizophrenic patients. He then studied anthropology and philosophy in Paris with Maurice Merleau-Ponty, Claude Lévi-Strauss and Roger Bastide. He worked with Melanie Klein and her training group and underwent analysis with Herbert Rosenfeld, from which he gained a new insight into dream interpretation and the psychotic transference. He has also worked with some of the pioneers of group analysis, including S.H. Foulkes, Malcolm Pines, P.B. de Maré, and Robin Skinner. He is now a practising psychoanalyst in Paris and Venice, and a consultant psychiatrist working with groups and institutional dynamics in Verona (Italy).

Walter Romeo is a specialist in clinical psychology and psychotherapy (University of Florence) and a collaborator in 'Il Villino' therapeutic community.

Victor L. Schermer, MA, CAC, is a psychologist in private practice and clinic settings in Philadelphia, PA. He is co-author with Charles Ashbach of *Object Relations, the Self, and the Group* (Routledge, 1987, 1994), co-editor with Malcolm Pines of *Ring of Fire* (Routledge, 1994), and author of journal articles and book chapters on psychology and psychotherapy, including the chapter on 'The therapist's role from a self psychological perspective' in Klein, Singer, and Bernard (eds) *The Handbook of Contemporary Group Psychotherapy* (International Universities Press, 1992). A frequent presenter and organizer of conferences and workshops, he is a full clinical member of the American Group Psychotherapy Association, Executive Director of the Psychoanalytic Study Group and Director of the Institute for the Study of Human Conflict.

Stanley Schneider, Ph.D., is a psychoanalyst and group analyst. He is Professor and Chairman of the Program for Advanced Studies in Integrative Psychotherapy at the Hebrew University in Jerusalem, Professor and Coordinator of Graduate Studies at Michlalah Jerusalem College, and Adjunct Professor at the Wurzweiler School of Social Work in New York City.

Marvin R. Skolnick, MD, is a psychiatrist in private practice in Alexandria, Virginia. He is a Clinical Professor of Psychiatry at George Washington University Medical School in Washington DC, senior faculty member of the Washington School of Psychiatry, former Dean of the Washington School Group Psychotherapy Training Program at the Washington School of Psychiatry, and Fellow of the A.K. Rice Institute. He is a frequent director of conferences of the A.K. Rice Institute and the Washington School National Group Psychotherapy Institute, lecturer, and contributor to literature on group psychotherapy and psychosis. He was clinical director of an intensive day therapeutic community for psychotic patients for 25 years.

Tetsuro Takahashi, MD, is a graduate psychoanalyst of the Topeka Institute for Psychoanalysis, a fellow of the American Group Psychotherapy Association, and former director of the psychotic disorders program (HOPE) at Menninger Clinic, Topeka,

Kansas. He is currently in private practice in Osaka, Japan, and teaches at a few universities.

Ivan Urlic, MD, Ph.D., is a neuropsychiatrist, psychotherapist and group analyst. He is Head of the Department for Acute Psychoses at the Psychiatric Clinic of the Clinical Hospital, Split. He is associate professor of medical psychology and psychiatry at the School of Medicine, University of Split, and teaches postgraduate studies in Split, Rijeka, Zagreb, and Bologna, Italy. He was co-ordinator for the World Health Organization of education on PTSD in Croatia and in Mostar, BiH. He trained at the Institute for Group Analysis (IGA), London, and is organizing education in group analysis throughout Croatia, with a special interest in the application of this approach to the psychotherapy of the psychoses. He is the author of many articles and book chapters on a variety of topics in psychiatry and psychotherapy.

Subject Index

accuracy, interpretations 285
acting-out 183–4
activities, therapeutic 236–9
activity, social therapy 363–4
adaptation
    theory of 20
    through group therapy
        64–5
adaptive context 34
adaptive response 214
administration, group
        analysis 208–9
aetiology, of neuroses 101
affective contact 116
aggression
    projective identification 55,
        56
    recovery of self 396
    transference situations 171
altruism
    therapeutic factor 288
    voluntary work 406
amputation 84–7
analyzing 191
anatomo-clinical approach
    101–2
anger
    countertransference 295
    psychodynamic therapy
        group 271–2
angor pectoris 102
angst 102
angstanfall 102, 104
angstneurose 102
annihilation anxiety 26
antipsychiatry movement
    373
antipsychotic medications
    37–8
    clinical trials 351
    hallucinated voices 69
    interpersonal relationships
        23
    major depressive disorder
        351–2

regressive manifestations
    30–1
schizophrenia 49–50, 132,
    135, 151, 350, 353
antitherapeutic groups 395
anxiety
    blurring of fantasy and
        action 328
    concerning change 186
    countertransference 295
    distinction between
        neurotics and
        psychotics 102
    institutional rules 337
    structured approaches
        289–92
Arbours Association 370–1
Arbours Centre 388–402
archaic defence mechanisms
    170–1
archaic metaphors 26
as-if attachment 94
assertiveness 237
assessments 16–20, 348–51
asylums 360, 362–3
Atkinson Morley Hospital
    374
attachment 84, 86–7, 89, 94
atypical medication *see*
    antipsychotic
    medications
Aulagnier, Piera 121
authoritative therapists 160
authority, conflicts over 161
autism, infantile 117
autistic level, communication
    156–7
autistic-contiguous
    experience 227
autistic-contiguous
    metaphors 230

Bakhtin, Mikhail 54–5
barometric event 29
Basaglia, Franco 371–2
basic anxiety 108
basic assumption cultures
    243
basic assumption dramas
    66–7

basic assumption groups
    58–9
basic depression 111, 118
belief systems 59
Berke, Joseph 120
bi-logic, theory of 56–7, 85,
    224
biases, concerning psychoses
    21
bifocal theory 58–9
Binet, Alfred 100
biological theory
    lack of evidence for 47–50
    of psychoses 20–1, 44–6
    schizophrenia 16
Bion, W.R. 119, 123–4
bipolar disorder
    assessment 350
    diagnosis 19
    group therapy 138–45
    interpersonal relations 22
black hole experience 26
blind spots, groups 122
blocked groups 182
blurring of role 361
borderline patients 200–19
boundaries
    advent of 88
    development of personal
        312
    fantasy and action 328
    group therapy 235–6
    supervision groups 316–18
brain imaging 45, 348
brain pathology,
    schizophrenia 48
breakdown centre 125
Breuer, J. 98–100, 104
Bria, Dr Pietro 120
bridge-making,
    interpretations 285
Burden, Eric 379
Burq 101
butyrophenones 352

carbamazepine 353, 354
Carry on Nurse 375
Cartesian dualism 44, 46
castration anxiety 118
catastrophic deglaciation 396
catharsis 289

cathexis 121
change, group analysis
    217–18
Charcot, J.M. 100, 101, 121
Chaslin 121
chemical imbalance,
    schizophrenia 49–50
Chestnut Lodge 367
children, projective
    identification 55, 56
Christ, as mystic 61
chronic countertransference
    fixations 335–7
chronic mental illness
    music interaction group
        222–31
    talk groups 231–48
chronic paranoia, case of
    103–7
chronic psychotic patients,
    supervision, group
        therapy 301–22
chronic schizophrenia 22, 57
chronically mentally ill
    diagnosis of 19
    psychodynamic therapy
        group 251–79
clarity, interpretations 285
clinical illustrations
    basic assumption groups
        244–8
    bipolar group therapy
        143–4
    empathy and interpretation
        194–6
    hospital based therapy
        162–5
    outpatient group therapy
        165–8, 170–3
    pharmacotherapy 356–7
    schizophrenic group
        therapy 136–7
clinical interventions 280–96
clinical issues
    bipolar group therapy
        140–3
    schizophrenic groups
        134–6

clinicians, collaboration with
    patients 355
clozapine 353, 354, 356
clozaril 37
co-therapy
    bipolar group therapy
        142–3
    psychodynamic therapy
        group 259
    schizophrenic group
        therapy 135–6, 138
cocaine episode 97
code of silence 33
cognitive assessments 351,
    354
cohesiveness 288, 289
Coller, Karl 97
commensal relationships 60
communalism 381–2
communication
    holding group 233–4
    levels of 156–7
    psychotic patient groups
        123
Community Meetings, Street
    Ward 376–7
competition, psychodynamic
    therapy group 268–9
complementarity, importance
    of 214
complimentary identification
    335
concordant identification
    334–5
condenser phenomenon 30
conductors
    group analysis 29
    types of 177
    vs leaders 173–6
confusional states 388–402
consciousness-raising groups
    254
containing function
    of mothers 56
    of therapists 70
context
    identification of 214
    importance of 33–4

continuum theory 20, 21
contradictions 83–96
Cotard 121
counter-identification 32–3
counter-resistance 32–3
countertransference 32–3
    definition, regression and
        fixation 334–7
    and empathy 189
    group analysis 207
    impact on
        pharmacotherapy
            355–6
    interpretations 193
    maternal fantasies 94
    nursing staff 329
    power of 295–6
    psychodynamic therapy
        group 261–2
    in supervision 310–11
creativity, musical
    improvisation 224
cross-sectional features,
    mood disorders 350
curiosity, in therapists 36

Daumezon, G. 120, 121,
    123
De Clérambault 121
death instinct 184
Dederich, Chuck 361
defence mechanisms
    archaic 170–1
    effect on nurses 328
    institutional rules 337
delusional convictions 119
delusional transference 99,
    108–13, 116
delusions 46, 107
DeMare, Patrick 123
Dementia Praecox 361
democratic group cultures 29
denial
    bipolar patients 140
    countertransference 295
dependency
    bipolar disorder 139
    group culture 59, 243, 284

manifestations, therapeutic
    potential 312
needs 207
psychodynamic therapy
    group 262–3
depressive position 242
metaphors 231
desymmetrization, law of
    56–7
detachment, schizophrenic
    22
diagnosis 16–20
diagnostic schedules 349
*Diagnostic and Statistical
    Manual of Mental
    Disorders see DSM–IV*
dialectic
    musical improvisation
        224–7
    object relations, modes of
        experience 227–8
    paranoid-schizoid and
        depressive positions
        56–7
Diatkine, R. 121
differentiation of self 54–5
disavowal 83–96
discontinuity theory 20, 21
discontinuous self 50–3
dissociation 121
distancing procedures,
    institutions 53
distortions, hallucinated
    voices 105
divalproex sodium 353
Dix, Dorothea Lynde
    359–60
dopamine hypothesis 49
Dostoevsky, F. 55, 61
double bind 26, 62, 69
double blind studies 45–6,
    49
double conscience 100
DSM-IV 17, 18t, 45,
    349–50
dynamic matrix 156

economic perspective,
    schizophrenia 51

educative approach
    group therapy 25
    schizophrenic groups 133
effectiveness
    bipolar group therapy
        144–5
    group therapy 24–32
    schizophrenic group
        therapy 137–8
ego strength, evaluation of
    320
ego-supportive
    interpretations 25
eigenbeziehungen 103
ejaculating words 115
Elisabeth, Fräulein 100, 101
Emmy, Frau 100, 101, 121
emotional knowing 187
empathy 186–91
    interpretations 193, 285
    process, disruption of 33
endoceptual awareness 224
envy
    manifestation of 92
    negative therapeutic
        reaction 185
    projective identification 55,
        56
    psychodynamic therapy
        group 268–9
equality, group analysis
    213–14
Eric Burden Community
    379–83
etiological diagnoses, lack of
    51
evidence based medicine 281
existential factor, therapy
    289
expressive psychodynamic
    approach 241–2
Ey, Henry 121

families
    creation of psychosis 62–3,
        111, 186
    psychodynamic therapy
        group 270

family groups, changes in
    patients 201–3
family re-enactment 289
fantasies 35, 91, 93, 154
Federn, Paul 116, 117
feminist groups,
    psychodynamic group
        therapy 254–5
Ferenczi, Sandor 106
fight–flight culture 59, 243,
    283–4
Finland, psychotherapy 340
fixation, in
    countertransference
        335–7
flattening of hierarchy 361
Fleischl-Marxow, Ernst von
    97
flexible boundaries groups
    317–18
Florence, voluntary work
    408–11
focal therapy 161
folie hystérique 98, 102
folie-à-deux 19
food, psychodynamic therapy
    group 271
forclosure 115
Foulkes, S.H. 123
foundation matrix 156
Frank, J.D. 122
free association 238
free floating discussions
    155–6, 392
freedom, social therapy 363
Freud, Anna O. 98–100
Freud, S. 97–107
friends, in suffering 212–13
Fromm-Reichmann, Freida
    117, 122
Fulbourn Hospital 367, 372,
    373
functional psychoses 129

gabapentin 353
Garma, Angel 117
Gartnavel Royal Mental
    Hospital 368
Gellé 101

gender, mentally ill 251–3
genetic factors, schizophrenia 45, 48
Germany, holocaust 59
gifts, psychodynamic therapy group 268–9
Glover, Edward 99
good object, search for 272
Gosling, R.H. 124
Green 121
Griesinger, W. 107, 111, 118
group analysis 28–31
  benefits 209–18
  difficulties 205–9
  hospital conditions 151–7
group culture 69–70
  clinical illustrations 244–8
  democratic 29
  types of 243–4
group dialogue
  content of 218–19
  learning to take part 211–12
Group Emotionality Rating Scale (GERS) 283
group of feelings 121
group focus, interpretations 285
group of ideas 121
group matrix 28
group minds 122
group nature of being 57–63
group revolt 29
group therapy 15–16
  adaptation 64–5
  approaches and effectiveness 24–32
  bipolar disorder 138–45
  challenges of 14–15
  clinical illustrations 72–7
  clinical interventions 280–96
  psychotic and borderline personalities 200–19
  schizophrenia 131–8
  splitting and disavowal 83–96

therapist's role 148–78
  transformation of the psychotic 65–72
  ways of using 63–4
  see also psychodynamic group therapy; supportive expressive group psychotherapy
group-as-a-whole 30–1, 157
group-outside-of-group 270–1
groups
  consequence of splitting 90–3
  instrument of therapy 215
  psychologies in 160
guidance, therapeutic factor 289
guidelines, for group psychotherapists 296
guilt 184

hallucinated voices
  group psychotherapy 68–9
  repression of thoughts 105–6
  transference to external containers 106–7
hallucinations 46, 99
halopiderol 352
Hawthorn project 327–30
  assessment of training 333–4
  countertransference 334–7
  psychotherapy training and staff 330–3
  results 337–9
helplessness, psychodynamic therapy group 262–3
Henderson Hospital 361
Henri, long–distance projection 113
here-and-now 26, 29, 133, 154, 234
heredity 101
Hereward House 372
heterogenous groups 130–1
hierarchical systems model, schizophrenia 61–2

hierarchical therapeutic communities 361
historical perspective, schizophrenia 51
historicity 231
holding environment 25, 30, 71, 306
holding group, supportive expressive therapy 231–41
holocaust, group process 59
homicidal ideation 267
homicide, psychosis as alternative to 65
homogenous psychotic groups 130–1
hope, installation of 289
hospitals, group analysis 152–7, 161
  clinical illustration 162–5, 169–70
hypochondriasis 102
hysteria 21, 100
iatrogenic effects, institutionalization 52–3
ICD-10 17, 45
identification
  concept of 122
  in countertransference 334–5
  therapeutic factor 289
identity, in therapy 174
Il Villino 408–11
immediacy, interpretations 285
improvisation see musical improvisation
individual analysis 97–107
individuals, relationships between 60–1
Industrial Neurosis Unit, Belmont 361
infantile autism 117
inner reality, musical improvisation 226
inpatients
  clinical illustrations 162–5, 169–70

group work 200–3
supportive–expressive
    therapy 232–5
institutional neurosis 362
institutional psychiatry,
    group madness 59
institutionalism, and
    schizophrenia 364–6
institutions
    iatrogenic effects 52–3
    impact on treatment 38
    rules and anxiety 337
integrative approach 31–2,
    152, 153
    bipolar group therapy 141
    schizophrenic group
        therapy 134–5
inter-relatedness, move
    towards 240–1
interactive group therapy
    26–7
internal projections 101
internalization, of languages
    54–5
International Classification of
    Diseases see ICD–10
interpersonal approach
    group therapy 26–7
    schizophrenic groups 133
interpersonal issues, bipolar
    patients 140
interpersonal language,
    translating symptoms
    209–11
interpersonal learning 288–9
interpersonal relations see
    object relations
interpretations 191–4
    by groups 215
    elements of 284–5
    group therapy 93
intersubjective perspective 26
interventions
    clinical 280–96
    psychosocial 47, 359–60
    psychotic 392–3
intragroup dialogue 36
intrapsychic conflicts 91

introjection 106, 398
introjective identification
    basic assumption dramas
        66–7
    by groups 63
intuitive empathy 189
Italy
    therapeutic community
        371–2
    voluntary work 406–7,
        408–11

Janet, Pierre 100, 121

Kelly's repertory grid theory
    333
Kestembergs, the 121
King Edward's Fund
    Conference 363
Kingsley Hall 370
Klein, Melanie 113, 117
Knight, R.P. 118
Kotchen test 292, 293

Lacan, Jacques 114–15, 121
Laing, R.D. 120, 367–8,
    369–70
lamotrigine 353
languages, internalization of
    54–5
large group psychotherapy
    77–9
leadership
    dilemma 173–6
    role 159–62
Lear, King 43–4
learning, group analysis 214
Leonardo, hallucinated
    objects 106–7
Liberman, David 118
libidinal drives 171
lithium carbonate 354
living-learning situation 361
logic, of unconscious and
    conscious 56–7
logical positivism medical
    model 45
logos spermatikos 113
long-distance projections
    113, 115

Löwenfeld 102

madness 43–4, 50–1
magnetic resonance imaging
    45, 348
Mahler, Margaret 118–19
major depressive disorder
    351–2
Mâle, Pierre 121
malignant mirroring 395
manic-depressive disorder see
    bipolar disorder
Mann-Whitney U test 289
Mapperly 364–6
masses, concept of 122
maternal function 88, 93
maternal reverie 56, 119
Maxwell-Jones 123
meaning, psychotic
    symptoms 304–5
media, function of 239–40
medical model 16–17, 207
medicalization, casualties of
    social change 51–2
medication
    bipolar patients 142
    monitoring 354–5
    psychodynamic
        psychotherapy group
        264–5
    see also antipsychotic
        medications
memories, objects as retrieval
    stimuli 237
men, psychodynamic therapy
    group 266–7
me(ness) 59
Menninger Self-Administered
    Test Packet 238
mental hospitals 360
mental illness, stigma of
    269–70
Mesmer tradition, magnetism
    104
metallotherapy 101
metaphoric displacement
    237
metaphors
    archaic 26

musical 229–31
use of 216–17
milieu therapy 368
Mill Hill 361
mind–body split 44, 46
mirroring 92
mirtazapine 352
misunderstandings,
    unconscious 119–20
Money-Kyrle, R. 111, 119,
    120
mood disorders 350
mood stabilizers 46–7, 353
moral masochism 184
Morgan, Dr John 122
Morrison, Frank 326–7
Mosher, Loren 371
motivation, voluntary work
    405–6
multimodal treatment 33–4
multiple selves 55
music, therapeutic function
    223–4
music interaction group 222,
    228–31
musical improvisation 224–7
musical metaphors 229–31
mutative psychotherapy
    groups 65–72
mutual mirroring 29
Myenert, Th. 98
mystics 60, 61

narcissism 55
narcissistic depression 111
narcissistic injuries 33
narcissistic withdrawal 336
need–fear dilemma 71, 174
negative attention 35
negative capability 69–70
negative hallucination 99
negative symptoms 49
negative therapeutic reaction
    184–6
negative transference
    116–17, 125
Netherne 364–6
neuroleptics 46–7, 49
neuropsychiatric studies 348

neurosis, heredity and
    aetiology 101–2
neurotic patient groups
    intrapsychic conflicts 91
    psychotics in 71–2
new longstay 379
nonrationality, groups and
    individuals 60
normal autism 158
Northfield Experiments
    360–1
nortriptyline 352
Nunberg, Herman 116–17
nurses, training project
    324–43
nurturance, psychodynamic
    therapy group 271

object, as trauma or recipient
    of instincts 87–9
object relations
    application of theory 242
    deficit or dilemma in 22–3
    dialectic, modes of
        experience 227–8
    intersubjective perspective
        26
    nature of psychoses 20, 21
    supervision 305–6
    supportive-expressive
        therapy groups 222
objects, in projective
    techniques 239–40
olanzapine 353
ontogenetic splitting 86
open door campaign 363,
    367
organisations, impact on
    treatment 38
original loss 86
Oury, Jean 121
outer reality, musical
    improvisation 227
outpatients
    group therapy
        characteristics 153
    clinical illustration
        165–8, 170–3
    role and goals 155

supportive function 24
post-psychotic patients
    203–5

pairing culture 59, 243, 284
paranoia somatica 116
paranoid-schizoid metaphors
    230–1
paranoid-schizoid position
    55, 56, 93, 242
parasitic relationship 60, 61
part-object relations 92–3,
    94
partial deegoization 175
paternal reverie 119
pathoneurosis 102
patients
    collaboration with
        clinicians 355
    Hawthorn project 338
    psychodynamic therapy
        group 258
    selection of 319–21
perception, of self and others
    214
perphenazine 352
persecuting object 91
personality split, transference
    experience 158
PET scan studies,
    schizophrenia 45, 48
PETT (Planned Environment
    Therapy Trust) 388
pharmacotherapy 150–1,
    161
    clinical illustration 356–7
    management of psychosis
        351–3
    symptom exacerbation and
        medication monitoring
        354–5
    symptom remission and
        group referrals 353–4
    transference and
        countertransference
        355–6
Philadelphia Association
    369, 370–1

Phoenix Unit, Littlemore 374
photographs, memory retrieval 237–8
physician superintendents 363
Pichon-Rivière, Enrique 117, 118, 121
Pines, Malcolm 123
play, in psychotherapy groups 67
play therapy 55
pleasure–unpleasure boundaries 88
positive expressions 185
positive interpretation 25
positive symptoms, neuroleptics 49
post-psychotic patients 203–5
Powdermaker, Florence 122, 125
Powell, J.W. 122
pre-conceived ideas, supervision groups 318–19
preconscious falsification 190
pregenital aggression 335
primal rage 65–6
primary envy 90
primary process
  acceptance of 233
  creativity and 224
primitive fantasies 91, 93, 154
primitive regression 390
primitive splitting 85–6, 89
Prince, Morton 98
privileged regressive setting 153
problem-solving, group therapy 25
projections
  destructive 399
  repression of self-reproach 105–6
projective identification

antigroups 395
basic assumption dramas 66–7
by groups 63
countertransference 32–3
envy and aggression 55, 56
patient's constructive use of 70
power of 35
psychotics 94–6
relational disturbances 14–15
projective tasks, holding group 236–9
projective techniques
  holding group 222, 231–2
  objects used in 239–40
  theoretical background 232–5
projective testing 350, 351, 354
providers, therapists as 177
pseudo-mutuality, families 62
Psichiatria Democratica 372
psychiatry 45, 51
psychoanalytic approach 46
  individual analysis 97–107
  psychotic patient groups 121–5
psychodynamic group therapy 27–8
  chronically mentally ill women 253–4
  advantages 277
  case examples 272–6
  co-therapy issues 259
  criteria for membership 258
  disadvantages 278–9
  feminist groups 254–5
  format and process 257–8
  patients 258
  setting for 255–7
  supervision 259–61
  themes and issues 261–72
  therapists 259

schizophrenics 133
psychological testing, holding group 233
psychologies, in groups 160
psychopathology 20, 91–2
psychopharmacotherapy see pharmacotherapy
psychosis
  biography of 97–125
  changes in understanding of 15–16
  deviations, categories 90–1
  diagnosis and assessment 16–20
  group perspective 43–79
  underlying nature of 20–1
psychosocial interventions 47, 359–60
psychosomatics 102
psychotic conditions 129
psychotic re-introjection 106
psychotics
  group therapy 200–19, 293
  in neurotic patient groups 71–2
  non-psychotics, link with 54–6
  relationships
    between group and 91–2
    with therapist 14, 157–9, 307–10
  selection of patients 153
  as vulnerable mystics 61

quetiapine 353

Racamier 121
realistic level, communication 157
reality
  conflict over 14
  differentiation 154
  psychotics 54
reality check, psychodynamic therapy group 271
reality testing 152
  countertransference 295
reductive biology 46
reflective space

deterioration of 392
group psychotherapy 14
repairing of 400
regression 335, 390
relatedness
  importance of 27
  withdrawal from 306
relational disturbances,
    projective identification
    14–15
relational group therapy
  26–7
relationships
  between individuals 60–1
  patient–therapist 14,
    157–9, 307–10
  psychotic patients and
    groups 91–2
repression, of thoughts
  105–6
rescue fantasies 35
research studies 282–96
resistance 181–3, 184–6
  tolerance of 234
responsibility
  group analysis 213–14
  social therapy 364
return of the repressed 106
risperdal 37, 353
Rosen, John, N. 118
Rosenfeld, Herbert 113, 117
rubber fence phenomena 62
rules, in group therapy 67

sadness, countertransference
  295
Schilder, Paul 122
schizoaffective disorder 19,
  350
schizophrenia
  biological disease 16, 45–6
  brain pathology 48
  as chemical imbalance
    49–50
  diagnosis and assessment
    16, 17, 19, 148–9
  families 62–3
  genetic factors 48
  group therapy 131–8

hierarchical systems model
  61–2
interpersonal relations
  22–3
pharmacotherapy 151,
  350, 353
preconscious falsification
  190–1
relatedness 306
social environmental
  factors 51–2
therapeutic community
  359–83
Schreber, Daniel Paul
  108–13
Searles, Harold 118
security, group
  psychotherapy 67–8
Séglas 121
self, differentiation of 54–5
self-analysis, therapists 70
self-esteem, low 267–8
self-psychology 20, 26
self-reproach, paranoia
  105–6
self-transitional objects
  239–40
self-understanding 289
semipermeable boundaries
  235–6
sensory-based exercises
  238–9
separation, from wholeness
  to 84–7
separation anxiety 117–18
  bipolar disorder 139
separation-individuation 88
sertraline (lustral) 352
Severalls 364–5
sex
  aetiology of neuroses 101
  psychodynamic therapy
    group 266–7, 272
Shenley Hospital 368,
  372–3
Shrodells Psychiatric Unit
  374
signifiers 115

Skolnick, Marvin 125
social disability 380–1
social environment,
  schizophrenia 48, 51–3
social exchange theory 406
social norms theory 406
social psychological barriers,
  institutions 52
social psychological
  perspective 63
social therapy 363–4, 367
Soteria House 371
splitting
  and aggression 396
  Anna O. Freud case 99
  group therapy 83–96
  patient–therapist
    relationships 158
staff, Hawthorn project
  337–8
stereoscopic projection 106
stigma, of mental illness
  269–70
stimmung 102–3
Stone, A. 122
Street Ward 374–8
structured approach,
  anxieties 289–92
subjectivity, emergence of 86
suicide
  ideation and attempts 265
  psychosis as alternative to
    65
Sullivan, Herbert Stack 117,
  122
supervision 34–6
  countertransference
    310–11
  experience as psychiatric
    resident 302–3
  group-qua-group context
    311–13
  meaning, significance of
    304–5
  psychodynamic therapy
    group 259–61
  supervisory process
    313–22

theoretical base for 305–7
therapeutic relationship
    307–10
supervisors, role of 314–15
supportive approach, group
    therapy 24–5
supportive-expressive group
    psychotherapy 221–48
Sutherland, Dr Jock 120,
    124
symbiotic relationships 60–1
symbolic equation 56
symbolic function, music
    223–4
symbolic registers 54
symbolism 231
symmetric mirroring 86
symmetrization, law of 56–7
symptoms
    diagnostic criteria 349
    exacerbation 354–5
    meaning of 304–5
    remission 353–4
    transformation of 209–11
Synanon Community 361

talismans 237
talk groups 231–48
Tausk, Victor 116
temporal contiguity 230
theory, misuse by therapists
    306
therapeutic community
    38–40
    schizophrenia 359–83
Therapeutic Community
    Settings 282–4
therapeutic factors
    group psychotherapy 381
    research 287–9
therapeutic milieu,
    confusional states
    388–402
therapists
    basic assumption dramas
    67
    countertransference
    reactions 295–6
    curiosity in 36

functions
    group analysis 171–2,
    176–7
    semipermeable
    boundaries 235–6
group culture 69–70
introjection 398
leader vs conductor 173–6
leadership role 159–62
misuse of theory 306
narcissistic injuries 33
pre-conceived ideas
    318–19
psychodynamic therapy
    group 259
relationship with patients
    14, 157–9, 307–10
skilled and experienced
    303
supervising peer groups
    315–16
therapy
    choosing 321–2
    stages of 293–5
Thorncliffe House 380
thought transference 191
thoughts, repression of
    105–6
topics
    bipolar group therapy 143
    schizophrenic group
    therapy 135–6
Tosquelles, François 121
training
    group psychotherapy 34–6
    nurses 324–43
    voluntary workers 404–5
transference
    aggressive and libidinal
    themes 171
    bipolar patients 142
    discovery of 100–1
    establishing relationships
    158
    group analysis 207
    impact on
    pharmacotherapy
    355–6

interpretations 285
psychodynamic therapy
    group 261–2
transference level,
    communication 156
transitional phenomena 119,
    239
trauma 21, 87–9
tricyclic antidepressants 352
trifluoperazine 352
Turckey, Dr 124

unalphabetized beta elements
    60
unconscious, internalisation
    of languages 54–5
unconscious
    misunderstandings
    119–20
uncontained 60
United States, therapeutic
    community 367
universality 212, 288
Usandivaras, Dr Raul J. 122

valproate 354
venlafaxine 352, 356
verbal communication 155–6
Veterans Administration
    Medical Centre 286–7
Villa 21 368–9
voluntary work, mental
    health 404–11

Wernicke, Karl 102, 103
wholeness, from separation
    to 84–7
Winnicott, Donald 119
wish-fulfilment 107
Wolf-man 113–16
women see chronically
    mentally ill women

Young Adult Unit 379–83

zoon politikon 150
zyprexa 37, 353

Author Index

Ablon, S.L., Davenport, Y.B., Gershon, E.S. and Adland, M.L. 140, 144
Abraham, K. 20, 190
Adler, D.B., Astrachan, B.M. and Levinson, D.J. 150
Agazarian, Y. 30, 316, 317
Agazarian, Y. and Peters, D. 312, 313
Alanen, Yrjo.O. 340, 341
Albert, H. D. 190
Alexandrowicz, D.R. 237
Alikakos, L.C. 285
Alyn, J.H. and Becker, L.A. 255
American Psychiatric Association 17, 130, 131, 138, 139, 349
Anderson, C.M. and Holder, D.P. 253
Antonucci, S. 405
Anzieu, D. 192
Apfel, R. and Handel, M. 252
Arieti, S. 224
Asbach, C. and Schermer, V.L. 29
Azima, F.J. Cramer 188

Bachrach, L. and Nadelson 252
Barbagli, G. 405
Barham, P. 51
Barnes, M. and Berke, J.H. 370
Baron, C. 375
Barton, R. 362
Basaglia, F. 372
Bateson, G. 62, 214
Bateson, G., Jackson, D., Haley, J. and Weakland, J. 26
Battegay, R. 285
Baumeyer, F. 111
Belknap, I. 367
Bell, G.M. 363
Benedetti, G. 172

Benenzon, R.O. 223, 230
Bennis, W.G. and Shepard, H.A. 29
Berger, D.M. 190
Bergin and Garfield 281
Berke, J. 400
Berke, J. and Barnes, M. 39, 120
Bernauer, J. 50
Bernardez, T. 254
Bertini, M. 405, 406
Betcher, R.W. 288
Bion, W.R. 20, 27, 30, 46, 56, 57, 58, 60, 64, 68, 69, 106, 122, 124, 190, 223, 224, 242, 243, 284, 286, 290
Bion, W.R. and Rickman, J. 360
Blanck, G. and Blanck, R. 20, 25
Bleuler, M. 48, 121
Bloch, S. and Crouch, E. 287, 381
BMA News Review 342
Bollas, C. 222, 223, 229
Bowlby, J. 26
Boyle, M. 149
Brabender, V.M. 288
Brazelton, T.B. and Cramer, B.G. 35
Breggin, P. 48, 49, 50
Bridger, H. 361
Brodsky, A.M. 254
Brody, C.M. 254
Broverman 253
Brown, D. and Pedder, J. 156
Bruggen, P. 337, 342
Buckley, P. 242
Budmann, S.H. 287
Burnham, D., Gibson, R. and Gladstone, A. 22, 71
Butler, J.S. 241

Caltagirone, I. and Smargiassi, M.M. 372
Cameron, J.L., Laing, R.D. and McGhie, A. 368
Cannon, T.D. and Mednick, S.A. 149
Caparrós, N. 13, 85

Carpenter, W.T., Bartko, L.J. and Strauss, J.S. 49
Carpenter, W.T. and Buchanan, R. 45
Caudil, W. 52, 367
Cerbone, M.J.A., Mayo, J.A., Cuthbertson, B.A. and O'Connell, R.A. 140, 143, 144
Charcot, J.M. 101
Chazan, R. 201, 209
Ciompi, L. 48
Ciompi, L., Dauwalder, H.P., Maier, C., Aebi, E., Trütsch, K., Kupper, Z. and Rutishauser, C. 371
Cividini-Stranic, E. 156, 157, 161
Clark, D.H. 363, 364, 365, 367, 372, 374, 379
Clark, D.H. and Myers, K. 382
Clark, D.H. and Oram, E.G. 367
Clay, J. 370, 372
Cohen, David 48, 49
Cohen, M.B., Baker, G., Cohen, R.A., Fromm-Reichmann, F. and Weigert, E.V. 139, 142
Cohn, B.R. 182
Colson, D.B. 237
Conolly, J. 359, 360, 363
Conran, M.B. 368
Cooper, D. 368, 369
Cooper, D., Esterson, A. and Laing, R.D. 368
Correale 407, 408
Cory, T.L. and Page, D. 287

Davenport, Y.B., Ebert, M.H., Adland, M.L. and Goodwin, F.K. 144
Day, M. and Semrad, E.V. 194
Debanne, E.G., Carufel, F.L. de, Bienvenu, J.P. and Piper, W.E. 193
Della Badia, E. 311
DeMare, P.B. 28, 30, 123

Deutsch, H. 189
Dickinson, E. 13
Drake, R.E. and Sederer, L.I. 131, 133
Druck, A. 20
Dunham, W. and Weinberg, S.K. 367
Durkin, H. 26
Durkin, J.D. 182

Eigen, M. 56
Eissler, K. 28
Eliade, M. 398
Elliot, R. and Anderson, C. 280
Emerson, C. 36
Endicott, J. and Spitzer, R.L. 349
Erickson, R.C. 130, 351
Etchegoyen, R.H. 14, 32, 192
Evans, V.M., Huk, M., Hull, H. and Pullen, G.P. 382, 383
Ezriel, H. 123

Fairbairn, W. 305
Federn, P. 116, 190
Feighner, J.P., Robins, E., Guze, S.B. et al. 349
Ferenczi, S. 102, 106
First, M.B., Spitzer, R.L., Gibbon, M. et al. 349
Fisher, S. and Greenberg, R. 49
Foster, J. 37
Foucault, M. 50
Foulkes, S.H. 29, 57, 156, 173, 182, 189, 190, 205, 209, 215, 216, 360
Foulkes, S.H. and Anthony, E.J. 159, 183
Frankel, B. 307
Fransella, F. and Bannister, D. 333
Freeman, T., Cameron, J.L. and McGhie, A. 368
Freud, S. 46, 84, 99, 100, 101, 106, 108, 111, 113, 181, 182, 183, 184, 186, 187, 190, 191
Fromm-Reichmann, F. 15, 22, 46, 150, 194

Gabbard, G. 306
Ganzarain, R. 183, 234, 242
Garfield, S.L. and Bergin, A.E. 295
Geczy, B. and Sultenfuss, J. 131, 133
Gibson, R.W. 139
Gibson, R.W., Cohen, M.B. and Cohen, R.A. 139
Gill, M.M. 191
Gitelson, M. 295
Glass, J.M. 59
Glass, L.L., Katz, H.M., Schnitzer, R.D., Knapp, P.H. et al. 242
Goffman, E. 360, 375
Goffman, I. 52
Goldhagen, D. 59
Gordon, J. 27
Grant, S., Holmes, J. and Watson, J. 340
Greenblatt, M., Levinson, D.J. and Williams, R.N. 367
Greenblatt, M., York, R.H. and Brown, E.L. 367
Greene, L.R. 290
Greene, L.R. and Cole, M. 290, 291, 292
Greenson, R.R. 187, 191
Greenspan, S. 63
Griesinger, W. 107
Grinberg, L. Sor, D. and Tabak de Bianchedi, E. 243, 286
Grotstein, J.S. 26, 46
Gruenberg, A.M. and Goldstein, R.D. 350
Guerra, G. 406
Gunderson, J.G., Will, A. Jr and Mosher, L.R. 221, 242

Haddon, B. 374

Hallensleben, A. 142, 143, 144
Hamburg, P. 193
Hansen, J.T. and Slevin, C. 378
Harrison, T. and Clarke, D. 361
Hartmann, H. 20
Hartocollis, P. 234
Haugsjerd, S. 15
Haynal, A. and Pasini, M. 153
Heimann, P. 94, 295, 331, 334
Hinshelwood, R. 14, 33, 67
Hinshelwood, R.D. 88, 185, 392, 400
Hollingshead, A. and Redlich, F. 48
Hopper, E. 34
Horwitz, L. 244, 257
Horwitz, L., Gabbard, G.O., Allen, J.G., Frieswyk, S., Colson, D.B., Newsom, G.E. and Coyne, L. 242, 248
Howells, J.G. and Guirguis, W.R. 149
Hull, J. and Pullen, G.P. 378, 383
Hummelen, J.W. 151, 152

Iannuzzi, G. 407, 408

Jackson, R. and Cawley, M. 341
Jackson, M. and Williams, P. 340
Jacobson, E. 190
Jacques, E. 56
James, D.C. 57
Janowsky, D.S., El-Yousef, M.K. and Davis, J.M. 140
Janowsky, D.S., Leff, M. and Epstein, R.S. 140
John, D. 223
Jones, K. and Poletti, A. 371
Jones, M. 361, 363, 365
Jung, C.G. 55

Kadis, A.L., Krasner, J.D., Weiner, M.F., Winick, C. and Foulkes, S.H. 182

Kafka, J.S. 69

Kanas, N. 64, 132, 137, 138, 140, 142, 144, 149, 151, 152, 176, 193, 208, 242, 243, 254, 306, 313, 321, 331

Kanas, N. and Barr, M.A. 137, 138

Kanas, N., Barr, M.A. and Dossick, S. 137

Kanas, N. and Cox, P. 141, 144, 145

Kanas, N., Deri, J., Ketter, T. and Fein, G. 137, 138

Kanas, N., DiLella, V.J. and Jones, J. 137, 138

Kanas, N., Rogers, M., Kreth, E., Patterson, L. and Campbell, R. 131, 133

Kanas, N. and Smith, A.J. 137, 138

Kanas, N., Stewart, P., Deri, J., Ketter, T. and Haney, K. 137

Kanas, N., Stewart, P. and Haney, K. 137, 138

Kaplan, H. and Sadock, B. 16, 20

Kaplan, H.I. and Sadock, B.J. 139

Kapur, R. 133, 284

Kapur, R., Miller, K. and Mitchell, G. 288

Kapur, R., Ramage, J. and Walker, K. 288

Karon, B. and Vandenbas, G. 46

Karterud, S. 282, 283, 284, 291

Katz, J.A. 237

Kennard, D. 361, 368

Kernberg, O. 28, 290, 334, 335

Kesey, K. 375

Kibel, H.D. 229

King's Fund Organisational Audit-Accreditation UK 339

Klain, E. 157

Klein, E. 55, 78

Klein, M. 20, 95, 117, 185, 331

Klein, M. et al. 235, 242

Klein, R.H. 287

Klein, R.H. and Schermer, V.L. 33

Kline, F. et al. 314

Kohut, H. 55, 187, 188, 291

Kolakowska, T., Williams, A.D., Arden, M., Reveley, M.A., Jambor, K., Gelder, M.G. and Mandlebrote, B.M. 379

Kotowicz, Z. 368, 381

Kraepelin, E. 361

Kreeger, L. 39, 205

Kripke, D.F. and Robinson, D. 144

Kuipers, L. 64

Lacan, J. 54, 114, 115

Laing, R.D. 26, 214, 367, 368, 370

Lamb, H.R. 252

Lane, R.C. 185

Langer, S. 223

Langs, R.L. 34

Laplanche, J. and Pontalis, J.B. 182

Laseque, C. and Falret, J. 19

Lawrence, W.G., Bain, A. and Gould, L. 59

Lazell, E.W. 132

Lefevre, D. 295, 330, 333, 338

Lefevre, D. and Morrison, F. 326, 330, 338, 339

Lenehan, G.P., McInnes, B.N., O'Donnell, D. et al. 252

Leopold, H.S. 130

Lesser, I. and Godofsky, I. 316

Leszcz, M., Yalom, M. and Norden, M. 288

Levine, M.S. 151

Liberman, R. 47

Lidz, T. and Blatt, S. 48

Lidz, T., Fleck, S. and Cornelius, A. 62

Lieberman, M., Yalom, M. and Miles, M. 282

Lieberman, M.A., Solow, N., Bond, G.R., Riebstein, J. 254

Lipson, G. 237

Little, M.I. 27

Loewald, H.W. 35, 184

Lofgren, L. 78

Lomax, M. 360

Lotterman, A. 242

MacDonald, W.S., Blochberger, C.W. and Maynard, H.M. 131, 133

McGerigle, P. and Lauriat, A.S. 252

McGlashan, A.R. 223

McIntosh, D., Stone, W.N. and Grace, M. 317

Main, T.F. 34, 52, 78, 337, 360

Maldonado, J.L. 184

Mandelbrote, B.M. 363, 374

Mann, S.A. and Cree, W. 379

Maratos, J. 89

Marcovitz, R.J. and Smith, J.E. 288

Marsh, L.C. 241

Martin, D.V. 364

Matte-Blanco, I. 56, 85, 224

May, P.R.A. 46, 49

Mayer-Gross, W. 361

Mender, D. 44, 45, 46, 48

Menzies, E. 52

Menzies Lyth, I. 329, 337, 342

Milanesi, G. 405, 406

Milders, C.F.A. 151

Miller, E.J. 59

Miller, E.J. and Gyne, G.V. 52

Miller, E.J. and Rice, A.K. 71
Miller, L., O'Connor, E. and DiPasquale, T. 305
Miller, N.E., Doherty, J., Luborsky, L. 281
Mitchell, S.A. 26, 36
Money-Kyrle, R. 119
Morgan, R. and Cheadle, J. 363
Moro, L. 157, 162
Morrice, J.K.W. 361
Morrow-Bradley, C. and Elliott, R. 281
Mosher, L.R. and Burti, L. 371
Mosher, L.R., Menn, A. and Mathews, S.M. 371
Mosher, L.R., Vallone, R. and Menn, A. 371
Muacevic, V. 152, 161
Muller, J. 54
Myers, K. and Clark, D.H. 372

Neri, C. 407
Nieminen, P., Isohanni, M. and Winblad, I. 378
Nitsun, M. 162, 395
Nunberg, H. 116

Ogden, T. 36, 56, 227
Ogden, T.H. 190, 224, 231, 237, 331
Opalic, P. 292, 293, 294, 295
Osgood, C.E., Suci, G.J. and Tannenbaum, P.H. 291

Palmonari, A. 405
Pao, P.N. 190, 191
Pappas, D., Yannitsi, S. and Liakos, A. 288, 289
Pattison, E.M., Brissenden, E. and Wohl, T. 131, 133
Pedriali, E. 372
Pekala, R.J. et al. 288
Perls, F.S. 370
Pichon-Rivière, E. 117
Pine, F. 234
Pinel, P. 359

Pines, M. 39, 58, 92, 156, 157, 374
Plante, T.G., Pinder, S.L. and Howe, D.M.S.W. 151
Pollack, L. 142, 144
Pope, K. and Johnson, P. 59
Popovic, M. 161
Powdermaker, F. 125
Profita, J., Carrey, N. and Klein, F. 286, 287
Pruyser, P.W. 230
Pullen, G.P. 361, 373, 374, 376, 377, 378, 380, 383

Rabelais, F. 329
Racker, H. 32, 207
Rapoport, R.N. 361
Rayner, E. and Wooster 56
Reich, A. 189
Resnik, S. 30, 46, 67, 101, 115, 123, 124, 285, 396
Reyes, A., Reyes, P. and Skelton, R. 56
Rice, C.A. and Rutan, J.S. 291
Rioch, M. 243
Ritsher, J.E., Coursey, R.D., Farrell, E.W. 254
Robbins, M. 48, 61, 62, 64, 65, 242
Rogers, C.W., Gendlin, E.G., Kiesler, D.J. and Truax, C.B. 190
Rose, N.D.B. 149
Rosen, John N. 118
Rosenfeld, H. 20, 46, 292, 331, 395, 396, 398
Roth, A. and Fonagy, P. 281
Rothman, D. 359
Ruel, M. 376
Ruesch, J. and Bateson, G. 210

Sandison, R. 151, 194
Sandler, J., Dare, C. and Holder, A. 331
Sass, L. 57
Schatzman, M. 370

Scheidlinger, S. 151, 176, 192, 239
Schermer, V.L. 152
Schermer, V.L. and Klein, R.H. 33
Schermer, V.L. and Pines, M. 390
Schlachet, P.J. 151
Schneider, S. 183
Schwaber, E.A. 193
Searles, H. 20, 35, 36, 46, 62, 78, 328, 399
Searles, H.F. 185, 186, 189, 194
Sechehaye, M.A. 118
Segal, H. 56, 223, 231, 237, 242, 398
Shakespeare, W. 43, 148
Shakir, S.A., Volkmar, F.R., Bacon, S. and Pfefferbaum, A. 144
Shapiro, R. 63
Shrout, P. and Fleiss, J. 285
Sigal, C. 370
Simitis, I.G. 85
Simmel, E. 186
Singer, D.L., Astrachan, B.M., Gould, L.J. and Klein, E.B. 71
Skolnick, M.R. 17, 30, 72, 78, 150
Slater, P. 29
Slavson, S.R. 160, 175
Speck, R.V. and Attneave, C.L. 30, 39, 401
Spotnitz, H. 182
Stanton, A. and Schwartz, M. 52, 367
Steiner, J. 56, 241
Stern, D. 35
Stewart, D. 223, 224, 229
Stewart, J. 375
Stolorow, R.D., Atwood, G.E. and Brandchaft, B. 26, 36
Stone, W. 241, 253
Strassberg, D.S., Roback, H.B., Anchor, K.N. and

Abramowitz, S.I. 131, 133
Strenger, C. 280
Strupp, H.H. 281
Sugarman, A. and Jaffe, L.S. 155
Sugarman, B. 374
Sullivan, H.S. 26, 46, 62, 194, 306
Swensden, J., Hammen, C., Heller, T. and Gitlin, M. 141
Symington, N. 223
Szasz, T.S. 16, 375, 383

Takahashi, T. 235
Takahashi, T. and Washington, P. 232, 239, 241, 248
Tansey, M.J. and Burke, W.F. 193
Tantam, D. 368
Tausk, V. 116
Test, M.A. and Berlin, S.B. 251
Thelan, H. 252, 283
Thomas, P. 45, 46, 48, 49, 54
Thornicroft, S. 339
Tienari, P. 48
Tucker, G. 51
Tuke, S. 359
Turquet, P. 78, 377

Urlic, I. 149, 154
Urlic, I. and Caktas, J. 149
Urlic, I. and Krstulovic, M. 166

Volkmar, F.R., Bacon, S., Shakir, S.A. and Pfefferbaum, A. 140, 144

Walker, E. and Levine, R. 61
Waxer, P.H. 287
Weiner, M.F. 131, 133
Whiteley, J.S. and Collis, M. 381
Williams, P. 328, 340, 341, 342

Wilmer, H.A. 374
Wing, J.K. and Brown, G.W. 364, 365
Wing, J.K. and Morris, B. 380
Winnicott, D.W. 25, 57, 187, 222, 227, 229, 239
Winther, G. 139, 142
Wolf, A. and Schwartz, E.K. 160, 175
Wolf, E.S. 26
Wolman, H. 285
Wordnet 13
World Health Organization 130
Wulsin, L., Bachop, M. and Hoffman, D. 144
Wynne, L., Ryckoff, M.I., Day, J. and Hirsh, S. 62

Yablonsky, L. 361
Yalom, I.D. 131, 139, 143, 152, 154, 160, 175, 212, 232, 288, 289, 381
Yalom, I.D. and Lieberman, M. 177
Youcha, I. 320

Zaslav, M.R. and Kalb, R.D. 142
Zilboorg, G. 360
Zinkin, L. 395